Strategies for Business Sustainability in a Collaborative Economy

Ramona-Diana Leon
National School of Political and Administrative Studies, Romania

IGI Global
PUBLISHER of TIMELY KNOWLEDGE

A volume in the Practice, Progress, and
Proficiency in Sustainability (PPPS) Book Series

Published in the United States of America by
IGI Global
Business Science Reference (an imprint of IGI Global)
701 E. Chocolate Avenue
Hershey PA, USA 17033
Tel: 717-533-8845
Fax: 717-533-8661
E-mail: cust@igi-global.com
Web site: http://www.igi-global.com

Library of Congress Cataloging-in-Publication Data

Names: Leon, Ramona Diana, 1986- editor.
Title: Strategies for business sustainability in a collaborative economy / Ramona Diana Leon, editor.
Description: Hershey : Business Science Reference, 2020. | Includes bibliographical references and index. | Summary: "This book focuses on organizational tools and practices that may foster a company's success in the new economic context, which is defined by the faster pace of technological progress and the entrance of Generation Z on the labor market"-- Provided by publisher.
Identifiers: LCCN 2019060054 (print) | LCCN 2019060055 (ebook) | ISBN 9781799845430 (hardcover) | ISBN 9781799852131 (paperback) | ISBN 9781799845447 (ebook)
Subjects: LCSH: Industrial management. | Industrial management--Environmental aspects. | Knowledge management. | Personnel management.
Classification: LCC HD31.2 .S87 2020 (print) | LCC HD31.2 (ebook) | DDC 658.4/012--dc23
LC record available at https://lccn.loc.gov/2019060054
LC ebook record available at https://lccn.loc.gov/2019060055

This book is published in the IGI Global book series Practice, Progress, and Proficiency in Sustainability (PPPS) (ISSN: 2330-3271; eISSN: 2330-328X)

British Cataloguing in Publication Data
A Cataloguing in Publication record for this book is available from the British Library.

Practice, Progress, and Proficiency in Sustainability (PPPS) Book Series

Ayman Batisha
International Sustainability Institute, Egypt

ISSN:2330-3271
EISSN:2330-328X

Mission

In a world where traditional business practices are reconsidered and economic activity is performed in a global context, new areas of economic developments are recognized as the key enablers of wealth and income production. This knowledge of information technologies provides infrastructures, systems, and services towards sustainable development.

The **Practices, Progress, and Proficiency in Sustainability (PPPS) Book Series** focuses on the local and global challenges, business opportunities, and societal needs surrounding international collaboration and sustainable development of technology. This series brings together academics, researchers, entrepreneurs, policy makers and government officers aiming to contribute to the progress and proficiency in sustainability.

Coverage

- Eco-Innovation
- Outsourcing
- Global Content and Knowledge Repositories
- Strategic Management of IT
- Innovation Networks
- Environmental informatics
- Technological learning
- Sustainable Development
- E-Development
- Socio-Economic

The Practice, Progress, and Proficiency in Sustainability (PPPS) Book Series (ISSN 2330-3271) is published by IGI Global, 701 E. Chocolate Avenue, Hershey, PA 17033-1240, USA, www.igi-global.com. This series is composed of titles available for purchase individually; each title is edited to be contextually exclusive from any other title within the series. For pricing and ordering information please visit http://www.igi-global.com/book-series/practice-progress-proficiency-sustainability/73810. Postmaster: Send all address changes to above address.

Titles in this Series

For a list of additional titles in this series, please visit: http://www.igi-global.com/book-series/practice-progress-proficiency-sustainability/73810

Sustainability in the Entrepreneurial Ecosystem Operating Mechanisms and EnterpriseGrowth
Yang Gao (Dalian University of Technology, China) Sang-Bing Tsai (Regional Green Economy Development Research Center, Wuyi University, China & Research Center for Environment and Sustainable Development of the China Civil Aviation, Civil Aviation University of China, China) Xiaomin Du (Yingkou Institute of Technology, China) and Chunlin Xin (Beijing University of Chemical Technology, China)
Business Science Reference • © 2020 • 342pp • H/C (ISBN: 9781799834953) • US $215.00

Digital Solutions and the Case for Africa's Sustainable Development
Albert Ong'uti Maake (UNIVERSITY OF LAY ADVENTIST OF KIGALI, Rwanda) Benard Magara Maake (Kisii University, Kenya) and Fredrick Mzee Awuor (Kisii University, Kenya)
Information Science Reference • © 2020 • 300pp • H/C (ISBN: 9781799829676) • US $195.00

Developing Sustainable Food Systems, Policies, and Securities
Abiodun Elijah Obayelu (Federal University of Agriculture, Abeokuta, Nigeria) and Oluwakemi Adeola Obayelu (Unversity of Ibadan, Nigeria)
Engineering Science Reference • © 2020 • 300pp • H/C (ISBN: 9781799825999) • US $195.00

Building an Entrepreneurial and Sustainable Society
Brizeida R. Hernández-Sánchez (University of Salamanca, Spain) José C. Sánchez-García (University of Salamanca, Spain) and Antonio Carrizo Moreira (University of Aveiro, Portugal)
Business Science Reference • © 2020 • 369pp • H/C (ISBN: 9781799827047) • US $235.00

Toward Sustainability Through Digital Technologies and Practices in the Eurasian Region
Gainiya Tazhina (University of International Business, Kazakhstan) and Judith Parker (Teachers College, Columbia University, USA)
Information Science Reference • © 2020 • 294pp • H/C (ISBN: 9781799825517) • US $195.00

Examining the Environmental Impacts of Materials and Buildings
Blaine Erickson Brownell (University of Minnesota, USA)
Engineering Science Reference • © 2020 • 358pp • H/C (ISBN: 9781799824268) • US $245.00

Cross-Border Cooperation (CBC) Strategies for Sustainable Development
Rui Alexandre Castanho (University of Dą browa Górnicza, Portugal)
Engineering Science Reference • © 2020 • 348pp • H/C (ISBN: 9781799825135) • US $225.00

IGI Global
PUBLISHER of TIMELY KNOWLEDGE

701 East Chocolate Avenue, Hershey, PA 17033, USA
Tel: 717-533-8845 x100 • Fax: 717-533-8661
E-Mail: cust@igi-global.com • www.igi-global.com

Editorial Advisory Board

Table of Contents

Detailed Table of Contents

Many studies deal with the determinants of countries' culture or efficiency of microfinance institutions (MFIs). This chapter aims to fill the gap in the literature by analyzing the connection between national cultural features and indicators of countries' MFIs. The summary of analyses made regarding MFIs is followed by the national cultural dimensions, and how knowledge strategy could serve poverty reduction. Forty-five countries represent the subject of the research. Their statistics are available for both MFIs and national culture. Rank correlation and investigation of TOP5 countries show that the MFIs are successful in countries characterized by high levels of power distance, collectivistic, long-term-oriented and restraint culture. Based on these results, the chapter lists countries where MFIs could be successfully introduced based on their national cultural features and recommends certain knowledge strategies for effective operation. Finally, research directions as a continuation of this study are also presented.

The globally competitive environment of higher education is exemplified by many UK universities, private education institutions, and public colleges entering into collaborative agreements with partner organisations. No more is this movement seen than with private higher education institutions (HEIs) entering into collaborative arrangements with many stakeholders, including new partners once seen as competitors. Those entrepreneurial-minded executives leading and governing HEIs have thus seen partnerships as strategies for business sustainability in a collaborative economy, giving them competitive advantage and enhancing their strategic intent. This chapter provides a critical and useful review of HEI knowledge management (KM) factors that enable successful stages of collaboration. Within this chapter, sustainability practices in higher education partnerships are reviewed through examination of KM factors and discussions of a private HEI using case study examples from their sustainability journey.

The collaborative economy (CE) involves an intensification of direct or intermediated peer-to-peer trade, underpinned by robust digital infrastructures and processes, hence an increased use of new technologies and a redefinition of business activities. As an inherently connected economy, the CE is, therefore, prone to integrating the most recent technological advances including artificial intelligence, big data analysis, augmented reality, the smart grid, and blockchain technology. As an innovative payment and finance technology, the blockchain and cryptocurrencies could have potential implications for the CE. This chapter consists of a conceptual review analyzing how the CE connects with the blockchain technology. The chapter presents subsequently the organizational and managerial implications related to the use of blockchain technology in terms of governance, transaction costs, and user confidence. An illustrative case further examines the role of a prominent social media in the CE-blockchain nexus.

By leveraging knowledge of subconsciousness seducing technique combined with building algorithms capable of analyzing internet users' needs as well as providing relevant information, disruptive ads that appear abruptly (in terms of the timing, placement, and method of ending/closing the content) in web pages and mobile applications are accepted as a quality effective means of consumer persuasion. This present study proposed uncertainty avoidance, perceived usefulness, and openness personality trait as the predictors of attitude towards online disruptive advertising. Participants of this study were 137 Indonesian internet users (75 males, 62 females, Mage = 23.02 years old, SDage = 3.367 years). Multiple linear regression analysis showed that only perceived usefulness and openness personality trait are able to predict the attitude (i.e., in positive directions). The uncertainty-certainty paradoxes contained in disruptive advertising are discussed to understand the psychological dynamics involved in a facet of the attitude ambiguity.

The aim of this chapter is to investigate the firm-related factors that moderate the effect size of corporate scandals that brands are faced with at times. The issue is analyzed from consumer market and capital market perspectives. An extensive literature review is presented to reveal the existing viewpoints and applications in this aspect. Among the firm-specific factors discussed are brand equity, firm size and industry, corporate reputation, social responsibility, CEO traits, source, and timing of disclosure. It is concluded that although brand scandals are hard to control, depending on various conditions related to both the firm and industry, their effect size can at least be managed with a proactive approach, which is handled at the strategic level.

Sustainable tourism refers to those tourism activities that respect the natural, cultural, and social environment and the values of a community, which allows it to enjoy a positive exchange of experiences between residents and visitors, where the relationship between the tourist and the community is fair and the benefits of the activity are evenly distributed, and where visitors have a truly participatory attitude in their travel experience. One of the main keys to sustainable tourism is the involvement of the visitors and the host and local community.

the reliability of a managerial early warning system, based on an artificial neural network. The analysis focuses on seven Romanian sustainable knowledge-based organizations and brings forward that managers tend to influence the results provided by a managerial early warning system based on artificial neural network, voluntarily and involuntarily. On the one hand, they are the ones who consciously decide which departments and persons are involved in establishing the structure of the managerial early warning system. On the other hand, they unconsciously influence the structure of the managerial early warning system through the authority they exercise during the managerial debate.

Borsa Istanbul Sustainability Index (XUSRD) was launched on November 4, 2014. Initially, there were 15 firms in the index. This number grew to 56 as of December 2019. This study aims to investigate whether the firms' inclusion in or exclusion from XUSRD affect their trading volume. Both the effects of the announcement days and the effective days of the index changes were considered, and six index events that occurred between Nov 2014 and Dec 2019 were studied. On the effective days and their subsequent days, there were no significant trading volume changes for both included and excluded firms. On the announcement days, the trading volume increased for the included firms and decreased for the excluded firms, though only the experience of the deleted firms was statistically significant. Therefore, there was an asymmetric response to additions and deletions. In addition, the index effect on the included and excluded firms was temporary, which supports the price pressure hypothesis.

Online innovation contests represent one of the most interesting new ways of utilizing creative skills in the new collaborative economy, but we still know very little about what motivates the problem solvers. Previous studies suggest that the economic reward is not the only motivational factor, but there are many other motives too. The aim of this research study is to identify the core motivational dimensions based on the experiences of top solvers in three different types of online innovation contests. The empirical findings are used to construct a motivational typology for creative problem solving that can guide future research.

This chapter deals with the performance measurement systems (PMS) for healthcare organisations topic. PMS have been proved to be a widely used management tool to control, monitor, and manage performance and, extensively, organisations. However, most of the developed works have focused on industrial organisations, being the application of this topic to health organisations not fully exploited.

This chapter brings, based on scientific literature, some sound reviews that could be the starting point for researching activities in this topic. Then, it shows an overview of performance measurement elements applied to healthcare organisations from different optics such as efficacy, quality, adequateness, use of ICT and sustainability at both intra- and inter-organisational contexts.

The research aims to perform an intergenerational analysis regarding the impact of counterproductive behavior and contextual performance on employees' task performance. The analysis is performed on a convenience sample of 165 employees from three different generations who work in the banking system. The results show that (1) 33.50% of task performance variance is determined by the variance of contextual individual performance and counterproductive behavior, (2) 13% of the variance of contextual individual performance can be explained by the variance in counterproductive behavior, (3) 33.70% of the variance of contextual organizational performance can be explained by the variance of task performance and counterproductive behavior. In addition, significant differences appear regarding the influence of (1) the counterproductive behavior on the contextual performance (Generation X vs. Y), (2) the contextual individual performance on task performance (Generation X vs. Z), and (3) the counterproductive behavior on the contextual individual performance (Generation Y vs. Z).

The increasingly complex and turbulent 21st century work environment poses challenges for businesses that can threaten their long-term sustainability. Given the rapid developments in technology, increasing rates of employee turnover, skills shortages, and changing expectations from Generation Z, the youngest generation now entering the workforce, organizations are recognizing the importance of developing a career resilient workforce. Individual employees' career resilience frames their capacity to respond when faced with career challenges, allowing them to continue functioning effectively, adapt in a flexible manner, and to successfully deliver work outcomes. To sustain a resilient workforce, managers must actively plan, develop, and deploy human resource management initiatives aimed at instilling career resilience in the youngest workplace entrants. By strategically designing generationally-appropriate management practices to maximize Generation Z talent, organizations can bolster their business sustainability to remain competitive in the changing economy.

Preface

It is the long history of humankind (and animal kind too) that those who learned to collaborate and improvise most effectively have prevailed.

Charles Darwin

The concept of "collaborative economy" is frequently used for describing the characteristics of the current economy but so far, a common definition of it or of its synonyms, namely sharing economy (Sundararajan, 2016), peer-to-peer economy (Frenken, Meelen, Arets, & van de Glind, 2015), collaborative consumption (Belk, 2014), gig economy (Ravenelle, 2017), and access-based consumption (Bardhi & Eckhardt, 2012), is still missing. Some scholars (Botsman & Rogers, 2011; Frenken et al., 2015) adopt a general perspective and state that the collaborative economy is either the one in which consumers are "granting each other temporary access to their underutilized physical assets, possibly for money" (Frenken et al., 2015) or a socio-economic phenomenon characterized by non-ownership, temporary access, and redistribution of material goods or service (Botsman & Rogers, 2011). On the other hand, Laurell and Sandström (2017) and Schlagwein, Schoder, and Spindeldreher (2019) adopt a technological approach and label it as a technology-based economy; thus, the former defines it as "ICT-enabled platforms for exchanges of goods and services drawing on nonmarket logics such as sharing, lending, gifting and swapping as well as market logics such as renting and selling" (Laurell & Sandström, 2017, p.63) while the latter describes it as "an IT-facilitated peer-to-peer model for commercial or noncommercial sharing of underutilized goods and service capacity through an intermediary without a transfer of ownership" (Schlagwein et al., 2019, p.2).

But the true collaboration is driven by social and environmental concerns, not by technological issues; the latter is just the mean to a purpose. As Li, Ding, Cui, Lei, and Mou (2019, p.2) state "sharing is always thought to be eco-friendly and less resource-intensive and to provide stronger social ties". Thus, the accent is on the rational exploitation of resources and bringing closer customers and providers.

Up until today, the development of the collaborative economy influenced various economic activities from the services area, such as accommodation (Airbnb, HomeAway, Couchsurfing), car/ride sharing (Uber, Bolt, Taxify, Blablacar), and services provided by plumbers and electricians (TaskRabbit). However, it expends rapidly to the other economic sectors from the service and production area due to its impact on sustainability, the way it challenges the traditional business models, and also the emphasis it puts on intellectual capital and intangible resources.

Against the backdrop, the purpose of this book is to emphasize the business tools and strategies that may facilitate the development of sustainable organizations in the current collaborative economy. It aims to highlight how corporate tools and strategies can improve the company's sustainability at the economic, social and environmental level while benefiting from the technological advancements.

The reminder of the book is organized around two sections that shed light on how business sustainability is perceived from both external and internal stakeholders' perspectives. Thus, the first section of this book, entitled *Business Sustainability from the External Stakeholders' Perspective*, brings forward the changes that appeared or may appear in the general external environment. In other words, it concentrates on the legal, socio-cultural, and technological factors that foster the development of the collaborative economy and influence the company's sustainability. Last but not least, it emphasizes how corporate social responsibility serves as a bridge between the firm and its external stakeholders, getting it closer not only to the customers but also to the community.

Chapter 1, entitled *Changes in Regulatory Laws Over the Sharing Economy Business on the Example of Brazil: A Crucial Point for Its Feasibility*, highlights the challenges that occur in the legal environment due to the advancement of the collaborative economy. The author analyzes the Brazilian economy and legal framework and shows how the state regulation can act as an inhibitor for innovation and the development of new business models.

Chapter 2, called *The Role of the State in Optimizing Communication Between Generation Z and Migrants in the Human Resources Management*, concentrates on another pressing issue of the current environment, namely migration. This is either caused by hostilities or poverty and it influences the political, social and economic development of the host countries. taking these into account, the authors develop a game-theoretical model in order to identify the best process for harmonizing the state's and migrants' interests and prove that training can be a satisfying solution.

Chapter 3, titled *How Does National Culture Influence Microfinance Institutions? Evidence Based on Investigating 45 Countries*, focuses also on poverty reduction only this time the cultural framework and the efficiency of the microfinance institutions are taken into consideration. Thus, based on Hofstede's cultural dimensions, the authors prove that the microfinance institutions are successful in the countries characterized by high levels of power distance, collectivistic, long term oriented and restraint culture, and recommend several knowledge strategies that could increase their efficiency.

Chapter 4, entitled *Factors Affecting Sustainable Higher Educational Partnerships*, maintains the attention on the socio-cultural environment, only this time the higher education institutions represent the cornerstone. If the sharing economy aims to bring closer customers and sellers and to foster the rational exploitation of resources based on collaboration, the current chapter emphasizes the need for collaboration among the academic partners. Within this framework, it unveils the knowledge management factors that could enable collaboration among the higher education institutions and it examines the sustainability practices involved in higher education partnerships.

Chapter 5, called *When Giants Meet: Collaborative Economy, Blockchain Technology, and Social Media*, concentrates on the classical technological approach of the sharing economy and it deals with the development of blockchain technology and cryptocurrencies. Nevertheless, it examines the role of social media in the collaborative economy – blockchain nexus.

Chapter 6, titled *Predictive Factors of Attitude Towards Online Disruptive Advertising*, emphasizes the link established among the socio-cultural factors, technology, and customers by analyzing the influence of the uncertainty avoidance, perceived usefulness, and openness personality trait on the attitude towards online disruptive advertising. Using multiple linear regression analysis, the authors prove that the perceived usefulness and openness personality traits are able to predict customers' attitudes to online disruptive advertising.

Chapter 7, called *Firm-Specific Moderators in Recovery from Brand Scandals: Insight Into Consumer Markets and Capital Markets*, remains to concentrate on customers' perspective and deals with the issue of corporate scandals. Thus, it brings forward the impact of several factors, such as brand equity, firm size, and industry, corporate reputation, social responsibility, CEO traits, source and timing of disclosure, on the effect size of the corporate scandals with which brands are faced with.

Chapter 8, entitled *The Corporate Social Responsibility (CSR) and the 2030 Agenda in the Framework of New Trends in Tourism and Hotel Companies' Performance*, switches the perspective from customers to community and brings to light concepts like eco-efficiency, ecological crisis, triple bottom line, and sustainable tourism. It goes back to the main goal of the sharing economy – fostering the rational exploitation of resources – and it emphasizes the need for companies from the hospitality industry to adapt progressively to the structural changes, taking into account customers', environment's and community's influence. Thus, the authors highlight several practices that could enhance the sustainable development of the Spanish tourism industry.

Chapter 9, titled *Corporate Social Responsibility as a Part of the Strategies for Business Sustainability Based on the Innovative Activity Development*, takes a step further and presents corporate social responsibility (CSR) as an innovative activity for modern businesses which is influenced by individuals' socio-demographic characteristics. Therefore, it proves that there is a strong relationship between stakeholders' education and their CSR knowledge while job title has no influence on CSR awareness. Starting from these, several recommendations are made on how to improve innovation through CSR.

Section 2 is entitled *Business Sustainability From the Internal Stakeholders' Perspective* and it approaches sustainability form managers' and employees' points of view. Thus, it deals with the changes that occur at the business models and tools level (especially, thus related to strategic management, human resource management, performance management) and it also emphasizes the challenges generated by the new generations of employees (Generation Z and Generation Y). Last but not least, this section is closed by presenting talent management as an enhancement of sustainable human resource management.

Chapter 10, called *Addressing Sustainability and Industry 4.0 to Business Model*, highlights the business opportunities brought by the technological advancements and the increased interest in ensuring social, environmental and economic sustainability, generally labeled as the triple bottom line. Based on these, the authors emphasize the need for adapting the business models by taking into account the sustainability and Industry 4.0 drivers.

Chapter 11, titled *Developing Strategies in the Sharing Economy: Human Influence on Artificial Neural Networks*, combines the classical technological approach of the sharing economy with the human approach of strategic management. Given the fact that the business strategies are developed and implemented by and with humans, this chapter aims to examine how managers influence, voluntarily or involuntarily, the reliability of a managerial early warning system, based on an artificial neural network.

Chapter 12, entitled *The Response of Trading Volume to Borsa Istanbul Sustainability Index Inclusions and Exclusions*, concentrates on the Turkish stock market and brings forward managers' and shareholders' perspectives on business sustainability. Thus, it analyzes whether the firms' inclusion in or exclusion from the Borsa Istanbul Sustainability Index affects their trading volume.

Chapter 13, called *Creative Problem Solving in Online Innovation Contests: What Motivates Top Solvers to Participate in the New Collaborative Economy?* brings back the topic of innovation only this time it is approached from an internal perspective and not from an external one. The focus is on the motivational aspects of creative problem-solving. In other words, the author aims to identify the core motivational dimensions based on the experiences of top solvers in three different types of online innovation contests.

Chapter 14, titled *Performance Measurement Systems for Healthcare Organisations*, addresses the challenges raised by the sharing economy at the performance management level. Thus, it deals with the influence of several issues, such as efficacy, quality, adequateness, use of ICT and sustainability, on the performance management systems developed for the healthcare organizations.

Chapter 15, entitled *Predicting Employees Performance: An Intergenerational Approach*, remains focused on performance management but the perspective switches from the organizational level to the employee level. An intergenerational analysis is performed regarding the impact of counterproductive behavior and contextual performance on employees' task performance. The authors prove that significant differences appear regarding the influence of (i) the counterproductive behavior on the contextual performance (Generation X vs. Y); (ii) the contextual individual performance on task performance (Generation X vs. Z); and (iii) the counterproductive behavior on the contextual individual performance (Generation Y vs. Z).

Chapter 16, called *Strategies for Business Sustainability in a Collaborative Economy: Building the Career Resilience of Generation Z*, maintains the focus on the generations of employees that are active on the labor market and it deals with another stringent human resource issue, namely career resilience. Thus, it discusses concepts like agile management, intrapreneurship, career shocks, and stressors, counseling and mentoring from the perspective of Generation Z.

Chapter 17, titled *3W1H Approach to Understand Millennial Generation*, examines the characteristics of the Generation Y by providing an answer to the following questions: Who? Why? What? and How?

Chapter 18, entitled *Talent Management as a Part of Sustainable Human Resources Management*, closes the book by emphasizing how talent management is used as part of the sustainable human resource management in the Slovakian industrial sector.

Hence, against the backdrop of globalization, digitalization, the development of the aging society, and the entrance of the Generation Z on the labor market, the economic environment started to be more dynamic, complex and uncertain than ever. Therefore, the purpose of this book is to emphasize the business tools and strategies that may foster the company's sustainability in the current collaborative economy.

Ramona-Diana Leon
National School of Political and Administrative Studies, Romania

REFERENCES

Bardhi, F., & Eckhardt, G. M. (2012). Access-based consumption: The case of car sharing. *The Journal of Consumer Research*, *39*(4), 881–898. doi:10.1086/666376

Belk, R. (2014). You are what you can access: Sharing and collaborative consumption online. *Journal of Business Research*, *67*(8), 1595–1600. doi:10.1016/j.jbusres.2013.10.001

Botsman, R., & Rogers, R. (2011). *What's mine is yours: How collaborative consumption is changing the way we live*. Collins.

Frenken, K., Meelen, T., Arets, M., & van de Glind, P. (2015). Smarter Regulation for the SE. *The Guardian*, 20.

Laurell, C., & Sandström, C. (2017). The Sharing Economy in Social Media: Analyzing Tensions between Market and Non-Market Logics. *Technological Forecasting and Social Change*, *125*, 58–65. doi:10.1016/j.techfore.2017.05.038

Li, Y., Ding, R., Cui, L., Lei, Z., & Mou, J. (2019). The impact of sharing economy practices on sustainability performance in the Chinese construction industry. *Resources, Conservation and Recycling*, *150*, 104409. doi:10.1016/j.resconrec.2019.104409

Ravenelle, A. J. (2017). Sharing economy workers: Selling, not sharing. *Cambridge Journal of Regions, Economy and Society*, *10*(2), 281–295. doi:10.1093/cjres/rsw043

Schlagwein, D., Schoder, D., & Spindeldreher, K. (2019). Consolidated, systemic conceptualization, and definition of the "sharing economy". *Journal of the Association for Information Science and Technology*, asi.24300. Advance online publication. doi:10.1002/asi.24300

Sundararajan, A. (2016). *The sharing economy*. MIT Press.

Section 1

Business Sustainability From the External Stakeholder Perspective

Chapter 1
Changes in Regulatory Laws Over the Sharing Economy Business on the Example of Brazil:
A Crucial Point for Its Feasibility

Luiz Guedes da Luz Neto
https://orcid.org/0000-0003-1245-4344
Universidade Federal da Paraíba, Brazil

ABSTRACT

The shared economy gained importance in the early 21st century, gaining scale through the internet. With this, various business models were created, offering innovative products and services to people. Many of the businesses in the sharing economy, because of their innovative character, challenge state regulation, which still does not know how to fit them, because, as disruptive, these businesses no longer seem to fit into traditional legal categories. And this difficulty in the legal framework can create burdens on innovative companies that can negatively impact results, as well as maintaining these companies in the market in a competitive manner. The search for state regulation that can adequately frame new businesses born in the sharing economy is a major challenge for the state regulator, which must seek regulation that protects users without impeding the development of new business. The regulation of new businesses in the sharing economy is a great challenge in Brazil because this regulation creates a lot of problems to the companies born in the sharing economy.

DOI: 10.4018/978-1-7998-4543-0.ch001

INTRODUCTION

The sharing economy has been taking center stage this early 21st century, increasing its scale through the Internet, which is available anytime and anywhere through mobile devices. New business models have been created offering services and products in innovative ways to thousands of people and have impacted traditional trading, which initially did not know how to handle the competition.

Because of its innovative features, much business encompassed into the sharing economy has challenged the state regulation, which is not able to frame them. Since they are disruptive, such businesses seem not to match traditional legal categories.

This legal difficulty in framing the new activities of the sharing economy ambiance might create legal onus to innovative companies such that it will take a negative impact on their results and even compromise their presence as competitive businesses as well.

Considering this huge challenge for companies of the sharing economy, the following research question emerges: has the impact caused by state regulation directly affected the feasibility of sharing economy businesses, or is it a secondary and reflexive outcome?

As an answer for the above problem, here is the hypothesis: being drawn upon compelling laws in which the obedience is binding to anyone submitted to the authority of the state upon a particular territory, the economic state regulation has direct impact on the feasibility of activities in the sharing economy and depending on its shaping, it may even crucially compromise some modalities.

As a first step, a descriptive methodology is applied to analyze the regulation ambiance of the sharing economy in Brazil. Then a prescriptive approach is adopted through the design of a legal framework proposal aimed to generate conditions of feasibility for the business models of the collaborative economy. The analyzed experience is mostly that of Brazil due to the importance of that country in South America. Brazil has the capacity to influence neighboring countries with its legislative policy.

This work aims to verify how economic regulation over the sharing economy can directly impact the viability of its business models. The specific objectives are as follows:

- Conceptual delimitations will be defined on the main categories employed in the study for the economic regulation of the sharing economy;
- An analysis will be undertaken about the interaction between technology and the collaborative economy as a means for disruptive innovations;
- The first reactions of the state regulator with regards to the sharing economy will be verified;
- The need for a regulatory disruption to face reality created by the sharing economy will be ascertained;
- The state legal regulation as an impact factor on business feasibility will be analyzed.

This theme matters a lot today. Although national legal frames are different requiring case studies, this world phenomenon seems to have practical and real outcomes over the dynamics of the national economies anywhere, since the regulatory challenge would have similar effects. This reasoning justifies the analysis of those businesses' impact on regulatory economics. Therefore, regulation shaping might be a decisive dimension for business feasibility. Considering such a dimension on a large scale, it will generate whether a positive or negative impact on the nation's wealth.

METHODOLOGY

As stated above, a descriptive methodology is applied to analyze the regulation ambiance of the sharing economy in Brazil. Then a prescriptive approach is adopted through the design of a legal framework proposal aimed to generate conditions of feasibility for the business models of the collaborative economy that can be applied to Brazil and other countries because challenges are similar.

OF THE CONCEPTUAL LIMITS OF THE CATEGORIES HERE APPLIED

In this article, the concepts of "sharing economy" and "collaborative economy" are understood as synonyms being used to describe "an economic model based on the swap of assets, what may or not be remunerated" (Guedes da Luz Neto, 2017a). The sharing economy reached a range of uses because of information technology, which has erased physical barriers and decreased transactional operation costs as well.

This study takes the term digital platform as "a business model that uses technology to connect people and drive interactions. Or, in trade language, platforms aim to maximize the encounter between demand and supply." (Rockcontent, 2018).

Regulatory economics shall mean "an institute that would encompass any way of the state agency that may intervene in private choices, being such a role traditionally undertaken through state intervention." (Saddy, 2014).

In this article, the term feasibility means the quality of what is feasible due to the existence of a normative ambiance capable of generating both predictability and business security. For the entrepreneur, norms applied to his business mustn't be amended to the will of the ruler of the moment, but as well from whom is about to take the task of interpreting the law for administrative and judicial purposes.

Another relevant term here taken is the regulatory frame. This expression describes the set of legal devices such as *leis, portarias, decretos*, etc. They are the regulatory statute itself establishing the limits within which all the agents (rulers, referees or judges, and economic agents) must play their roles, whether in or over the market.

For all the other terms here applied, the reader should consider the traditional terminology of legal sciences. Therefore, they do not deserve a particular explanation about their meaning, since they are all part of the legal knowledge for whoever is managing any expertise in Law.

TECHNOLOGY IN CONJUNCTION WITH THE SHARING ECONOMY AS THE BASIS FOR DISRUPTIVE INNOVATIONS

The most valuable asset of the sharing economy is creativity. Creativity is how new services show up while old services would gain a reshaping to be placed on the market. The use of information technology has provided a scale gain; therefore, a reduction in the transaction cost of the sharing economy business. This way, the use of information technology combined with creativity has triggered disruptive products and services which have broken the usual logic until now employed in commerce and business.

The World Wide Web has made it possible to expand the range of business models designed and developed according to the logic of the sharing economy. In times before the Internet, such businesses had a very limited outreach with operation within the radius of the boroughs and cities where they were located.

Following the advent of the popularization of the Internet, there virtually is no geographic limits for new businesses. Besides, technological development allowed the invention of mobile devices connecting users anywhere, any time through Internet access what has considerably amplified possibilities in business.

It is relevant to remember that the sharing economy is not recent, not a twenty-first-century phenomenon, having existed for many years. It is important to recall the sharing of goods among acquaintances when neighbors used to share goods for the mutual benefit of all involved, for instance, in case one would have needed a tool to perform a service. Performing like that, this person did not invest his or her financial capital in acquiring a tool that would be used just once. However, in its traditional shaping, the sharing economy was not reproduced in scale, then companies were not attracted by it.

This traditional behavioral logic has changed with technological evolution in society. These changes have made available devices on a massive scale due to internet access with low cost and satisfactory quality connection to the Web. This possibility of increasing scale combined with low transaction costs has pushed companies and entrepreneurs to create services and products within the logic of the sharing economy.

Concerning the reduction of the transaction cost of the sharing economy business, the spreading of information technology is valuable to portable equipment, as found in a report issued by the Getúlio Vargas Foundation (2016): "Before the spread of information technology for portable equipment, the transaction cost for this type of service was so high that it was not feasible to have a lasting service. It meant that the amount of information to keep people involved in supply and demand was extremely high.".

Technology allowed the emergence of new economic players giving room for small and medium-sized companies to enter the market in conditions of effective competition with large ones already consolidated. Most interestingly, many of these technology-intensive start-ups have taken off large companies their market slice.

An interesting example is fintech, financial start-ups that have entered a highly regulated market to win customers from traditional financial institutions. Using artificial intelligence, they offered lower-cost financial products and services to their customers with more efficiency.

According to the Central Bank of Brazil (2019), fintechs are "companies that bring innovations to the financial markets by the intensive use of technology, with the potential to create new business models. They operate via online platforms offering industry-leading innovative digital services."

Technology-intensive companies have created disruptive services and products that break the traditional mindset of the market, pushing well-established companies to adjust to real challenges newly brought up. Otherwise, they would have become obsolete and consequently gone bankrupt.

Across the globe, thousands of cases demonstrate that companies, whether startups or those already in the market, have intensively used technology to deliver disruptive products and services. They have changed the economic mindset. And this paradigm shift came about with the fruitful conjunction of technology and the sharing economy.

The disruption, as mentioned earlier, has consequences not solely in Economics but at Law studies. This assessment undermines state regulators since a paradigmatic change will push the government to rethink the old shape of regulatory economics. It might be the greatest challenge for law in the twenty-first century.

FIRST REACTIONS FROM THE STATE REGULATOR TO THE SHARING ECONOMY

The sharing economy has modified the paradigm of business models while it uses technology in a change that was not limited to economy and business. They have effects on national legal frames. State regulators are facing new challenges for which they do not have appropriate answers.

Before the first impact of new models of business, regulators reacted trying to ban them. It did not occur just in Brazil but also in the United States of America and Portugal.

An example of a negative reaction from the state regulator occurred in the case of the Uber ride-hailing service. In the city of João Pessoa, Paraiba state, in northeastern Brazil, the starting reaction was the law enactment number 13.105/2015 by the municipal chamber of representatives (City Council of João Pessoa, 2015). It made unlawful all ways of alternate taxi developed by app or by any digital means in the city of João Pessoa. In Portugal, such a service had a similar reaction from lawmakers discouraging transportation by private vehicles that were not regular taxis. According to Guedes da Luz Neto (2017b) "The Draft Law nº. 50 / XIII at the Council of Ministers recognizes that no law in the legislation encompasses currently the reality created by online platforms of individual transportation. This proposal features a model of regulation through the establishment of a legal regime for the activity of remunerated transportation of individuals in non-chartered vehicles, except for the sharing of non-profit vehicles, and rentals of short-term driverless vehicles with sharing.".

Looking at that law bill, it finds that Portugal, as much as Brazil, follows the trend of making it difficult to provide paid private transportation services offered through apps. It required compliance to many demands including a mandatory presentation of a special driving certificate going against the business logic of the sharing economy since it would create a burden on the business. It will likely make it less competitive and more expensive as well for the user. The bound advantage to the innovative service over taxis might disappear.

Later on, the regulator switched to a more appropriate posture changing from the legal ban to allowing the deployment of the ride-hailing services, in spite of some restrictions.

An example that may illustrate this change occurred when the representatives of the municipal chamber of João Pessoa repealed the law enacted in 2015 to issue a new act, the law nº 1.866/2017. In the beginning, they felt squeezed by lobby groups formed by taxi drivers and bus companies. The representatives realized over time that the collaborative economy was about to overcome the balance of power of the agents involved. Now they felt under attack, this time by a countermove from users of the ride-hailing service who wanted them to keep the service on working. Today, the municipal jurisdiction of João Pessoa remains without legal regulation over the service performed through apps.

Given the tension between taxi drivers and app ride-hailing service providers, the federal legislative branch acted proposing a regulation through a bill at the House of Representatives within the parameters of a legal authorization of the service but imposing some limitations. The House of Representatives introduced Bill 5.587-A/2016, which regulated private transportation through apps or any other digital platform. Bill No. 5,587-A/2016 (Chamber of Deputies, 2016) amended article 4th of Law No. 12.587/2012 to state as follows:

Art. 4th [...]

X – Private remunerated transportation of individual passengers: remunerated service for transportation of passengers, not open to the public, utilizing rental vehicles, for individual or sharing rides exclusively **ordered by users previously registered in an app or other communication platforms into a network.** *(my emphasis).*

Bill 5587-A /2016 provided for the additions of arts. 11-A and 11-B to article 3 of Law no. 12,587 of January 3, 2012 (Câmara dos Deputatos, 2016):

Article 11-A. It is for exclusive responsibility of the Municipalities and the Federal District [Brasília] to regulate and oversee the individual private paid passenger transportation service as established at item X of art. 4th of this Law within their territories.

Single paragraph. In the regulation and inspection of the private individual passenger transport service, the Municipalities and the Federal District shall observe the following guidelines, given efficiency, efficacy, safety, and effectiveness in providing the service:

I - an effective collection of municipal taxes due to the provision of the service;

II - Requirement to contract Passenger Personal Accident insurance (Acidentes Pessoais a Passageiros, APP) and Compulsory Personal Injury Insurance caused by Motorway Land Vehicles (Danos Pessoais causados por Veículos Automotores de Vias Terrestres, DPVAT);

III - the requirement of registration of the driver as an individual contributor of the National Institute of Social Security (Instituto Nacional do Seguro Social, INSS), under the terms of point h of item V of art. 11 of Law No. 8,213 of July 24, 1991.

Art. 11-B. Municipalities that choose to regulate the private paid passenger service provided for in item X of article 4th of this Law, it will only be allowed for drivers who meet the following conditions:

I - have a National Driver's License in category B or higher that contains the information that he or she performs the remunerated activity;

II - drive a vehicle that meets the maximum age of use of the vehicle and characteristics required by the traffic authority, and the municipal government, and the Federal District;

III - have and carry specific authorization issued by the municipal government or the Federal District of the place where the authorized service is provided;

IV - issue and keep the Vehicle Registration and Licensing Certificate (Certificado de Registro e Licenciamento de Veículo, CRLV) in the Municipality of the provision of the service, mandatorily in its name, as owner, beneficiary or leaseholder, with vehicle registration and license plate of the vehicle in the rental category.

Single paragraph. The exploitation of remunerated services of private individual passenger transport without the fulfillment of the requirements foreseen in this Law and the regulation of the municipal public power and of the Federal District will typify illegal passenger transportation.

Bill 5.587/2016 imposes limits on item IV, article 3rd of the Law 12.587/2012, without blocking the transportation work via apps. However, it makes it difficult for some variations for the use of the ride-hailing service, as shown in another publication of this author (Guedes da Luz Neto, 2017a). The amendment would make it impossible for the driver to rent a vehicle for a short period to provide the service since the driver must have his or her name on the CRLV, as read on the item IV mentioned earlier.

The technological disruption experienced in these new businesses directly impacts the law, especially the state entities responsible for regulatory economics. Thus, "the emergence of this new market has generated several difficulties, which are more than known. In particular, it has created a difficulty for regulation by the government. It is unclear to some government actors even what would be the correct instance for such regulation" (Fundação Getúlio Vargas, 2016).

The doubt about the correct governmental body or agency for regulation is a minor difficulty, which will be overcome by interpreting constitutional norms. The real difficulty lies in the format of regulation over the sector. While providing security for users, a good design would match stability, foreseeability for those offering products and services, at the same time, it would be adaptable to new technologies as they arise. Thus, from a total ban on business activities of the new sector, it moved to a phase of imposing boundaries. Depending on the type and intensity, these limitations have virtually made it impossible for such new business models to compete in the market, which is detrimental to the nation's wealth.

The common thread between the starting reaction of the regulators and the current one in Brazil is the difficulty of finding a legal frame for the new business. This way, they tried to frame it within the traditional concepts prevailing so far. The sharing economy has spawned regulatory disruption through disruptive innovation. According to Nathan Cortez (2014), technological innovation "disrupt existing regulatory schemes". It means that the disruptive innovation presented by technology imposes disruption in the regulatory mindset. This reality is already experienced by countries, which are facing the configuration in which these challenges are present. They must rethink how to regulate these phenomena created by the intensive use of technologies, which have economic and legal repercussions.

REGULATORY DISRUPTION AS AN OUTCOME OF THE SHARING ECONOMY

State regulators must accept the following fact: The technology-intensive use in the sharing economy is a lasting reality and there is no way of returning to the same conditions that prevailed in the twentieth century. That model of business and consumption that shaped western culture, and the law included in it, underwent major transformations from the late twentieth century more intensively in the first decade in the twenty-first century through the creative force embedded in the collaborative economy.

It is no longer necessary to buy a particular consumer good to use it today. For example, in the dominant market mindset over the past century, if a consumer wanted to drive a luxury car, he or she should have been able to buy it. With models generated through the sharing economy, renting a vehicle from whoever is the proprietor or in possession of it is simply sufficient with no rental agreement signed between the consumer and a particular company. The agreement can be signed between the user and whoever is the owner.

With the sharing economy developed through apps, there was the rapprochement between natural and legal persons, whoever owns the consumer good and that who wants to use it. A platform is a tool to connect people. The business of the company that developed the platform is not renting, but to develop the electronic environment, a platform that allows those interested in sharing. It changes the traditional logic of consumption wholly, with relevant impacts on the law and the way of thinking about legal regulation.

The sharing economy businesses use digital platforms through which they can make the connection between the user or consumer and whoever intends to offer the product or service. And these platforms often operate in legal gray zones, in zones of blurring, due to the innovation brought about by the sharing economy, as well stated by Katz (2015), "sharing platforms often operate in legal gray areas, and the regulatory vacuum surrounding these services has raised complex legal questions. Sharing companies erode the distinction between commercial and personal, public and private, and the definition of goods and services".

The sharing economy has annihilated the traditional and sharp distinction in the legal culture between commercial and personal use, between the private and public realms, generating legal uncertainties that have direct repercussions on state legal regulation.

While thinking about regulation along the lines existed so far, the regulator will not be able to present effective and efficient regulatory formats for the new business models that have been developed. It generates negative externalities in legal regulation, which can prevent or hinder the implementation of new services and the supply of new products.

In a seminar held in conjunction with the Municipal Chamber of São Paulo and the Getúlio Vargas Foundation (2016), the participants presented the options regarding the sharing economy that the state regulator has and stated that "There is a pressing issue in this debate: the state - here represented by the São Paulo City Hall and the Municipal Chamber - is required to decide on the legality of ride-hailing online platforms. Possible decisions can be made on a linear spectrum: the government can totally ban these platforms, regulate them or release them entirely".

The options that the government has in the face of the reality created by the sharing economy are very clear. On the one hand, the government may opt for a total ban on these platforms. It was precisely the first reaction adopted by the state regulator, as happened in the municipality of João Pessoa, with Law nº 13.105/2015, which prohibited ride-hailing services offered through an app or any digital platform within the municipal jurisdiction. On the other hand, there was the repeal of the law mentioned above. Today, João Pessoa has no law about regulatory economics concerning this type of transportation.

Thus at the other extreme, no law means a total liberation. It is the option of not regulating the businesses of the collaborative economy, letting the market regulate itself. Private stakeholders create their rules. At first sight, it may seem like the best option in terms of free trade, as there will be no regulatory strings attached to the creation and implementation of new products or services. However, it is difficult to predict whether there will be effective and free competition between competitors. Some players might form cartels to dominate the market, preventing other competitors from entering and participating through pricing or other instruments that may be used for the same purpose.

Between total prohibition through regulation and the absence of regulation, there is the intermediate option of regulating. Finding a regulatory format that does not block the feasibility of the sharing economy business while providing certainty and predictability for both users and consumers, as well as those offering products and services in the marketplace, is a major challenge.

It seems that the answer will not come from the regulator (e.g., regulatory agencies, the executive or legislative branch). The cases in Brazil have shown highly limiting regulations. Regulators have no incentive for paradigm-shifting, so it is easier to keep making laws and doing administrative acts traditionally. In addition to not taking the regulators out of their comfort zone, this still meets the demands of certain lobby groups that usually contribute to the election campaigns for the executive and legislative powers.

Proposal for new regulatory models seems to come from scholars, through studies, research, and qualified debates to analyze the ideological-free economic phenomenon that will give society plausible and feasible solutions that can contribute to the construction of more improved regulation. These reflections can lead to disruption in regulation, as it is already clear that traditional models of regulation have become obsolete. They no longer generate effective outcomes to create a regulatory environment for allowing the development of new businesses as well as the broadening of the economy to embrace the needs of the business models of the fourth industrial revolution.

According to a lesson taught by Khun (1997), from time to time, the paradigms of the scientific world change, requiring a new perception from the scholars about their environment. Scholars must primarily learn to figure out a new form in situations with which they are already familiar. Law is experiencing a new period of crisis, which "is a necessary precondition for the emergence of new theories" (Khun, 1997). The regulatory impasse is today one aspect of this crisis of law.

The university has begun to prize the issue of disruptive innovation, as stated by Cortez (2014), when he writes that "legal scholars have examined disruptive innovation in various disciplines, such as civil procedure, environmental law, and intellectual property". However, the study of disruption theory is still in its beginning, needing further investigations and use in the respective areas of knowledge. According to Cortez (2014), "no one has yet applied disruption theory to the field in which it should be most useful—administrative law. Administrative law scholarship contains a rich, sprawling discourse on how agencies should regulate new markets. These questions, incidentally, can be particularly vexing with categorically novel technologies and business practices". Cortez (2014) understands that Administrative Law is a useful field for the application of the theory of regulatory disruption, an area with enormous possibilities of contribution to regulating new markets and even comments that Administrative Law is the discipline that can benefit most from the application of the theory mentioned above.

Cortez (2014) made the point in saying that the theory of regulatory disruption will be most useful to administrative law. This branch of law is the most averse to change, remaining practically in the nineteenth century, sometimes maintaining almost all the dogmas of a bureaucratic public administration inspired by Weberian lines. Not only is Administrative Law the most reluctant to thinking revolutions, but also other branches of public law, such as Constitutional Law, and Economic Law. It seems that they share the same mindset as Administrative Law, and are therefore more difficult to incorporate change.

The theory of regulatory disruption may be the beginning of the response to the new regulatory challenge posed by the sharing economy. It may not be sufficient, as also recognized by Cortez (2014). The object of the present article is not the analysis of the regulatory disruption theory, however. The mention of this theory is used to reinforce the specific objectives analyzed in this study based on the idea that the regulatory response is necessary for the current horizon of technological innovations because it demands the paradigm shift. It seems that the change needs to be intense, radical, since disruptive innovations are requiring disruption of regulation, given that the traditional model accepted hitherto no longer satisfies.

If factual reality has considerably changed in the field of sharing economics through the use of technologies, the regulatory framework needs to be redesigned as an adaptation to this new reality. Otherwise, instead of creating a regulatory environment conducive to the development, deployment, and provision of new services and products, the law will act as a deterrent to business evolution, generating huge losses for the entire economy.

There is no point in tinkering the existing regulation as it was designed based on past business models. These reforms will not work in the pursuit of optimal regulation that seeks the best results for market players, as it will be replicating insufficient modified models of a past regulatory culture that can no longer legally approach new businesses.

In this way, a real regulatory disruption needs to be met, capable of facing not only the present challenges, which are already huge but also the future ones. A satisfactory regulatory response today should embrace the challenges that will come with the evolution of technology that will increasingly be employed in the sharing economy.

LEGAL REGULATION AS AN IMPACT FACTOR ON BUSINESS SUSTAINABILITY

The State has a monopoly on the use of violence, being the sole legal entity that has the monopoly on physical power, the legitimate violence, i.e., legitimated by law with constitutional competence to issue abstract and effective *erga omnis* legal norms. Thus, the legal rule issued by the State has the dimension of enforcement, and one may be asked to comply by force with what is predicted in law under the state authority. Therefore, due to coercibility, state regulation is the most used, although there are examples of self-regulation.

Through regulation, state intervention has the power to alter market forces. It can encourage competition between economic actors or might guarantee monopolies to certain groups depending on how the government manages its policy on the sector. It is an instrument with a wide capacity to change the economic balance, whether or not promoting free competition. By interfering with economic dynamics, the State can choose who remains in the market or who is unable to participate in it, whether or not it encourages competition, establishing artificial monopolies, among other negative externalities.

Due to these features above described, the interest groups of the already consolidated economic sectors in the market have called for state regulation as a barrier to the entry of new competitors, especially those that bring innovations to the market. They are against business models that are disrupting the industry in the market.

Considering the direct influence of state legal regulation over the balance among economic agents, it plays an important role in the feasibility of the business because of the competition between players in the market. Offering to the market a minimum of feasible conditions means a state regulation worded to be stable, clear, and able to absorb the concept of new technologies, new products, and services designed in the sharing economy within its legal framework.

It is impossible to elaborate and undertake a business model when there is no stability in the rules that compose the state regulatory acquis. Regulation must not be changed at all times by the state, creating an environment in which it is impossible to make a certain degree of predictability for the future. In a scenario without legal certainty, it is not possible to produce medium and long-term productive investments that are so important for the socio-economic development of a country. Hence it is important to assert that stability is a positive outcome of the rules enacted by lawmakers and enforced by the administrative public sector.

In addition to being stable, the regulation needs to be clear, avoiding doubts for the interpreter of the norm. Clear rules tend to generate certainty[1] regarding its normative content, which contributes to lasting effects as it removes the lack of certainty and foreseeability found in an imprecise and obscurely worded norm.

Added to this is the possibility of legal regulation to adapt to technological progress. It is valuable for the society that the regulatory norm may absorb in its frame the concept of new technologies, new products, and services conceived in the sharing economy. This dimension is of fundamental importance since technological advance occurs at a speed that is not compatible with the normative change operated by the State, tending to become outdated in a short time given the faster advance of technology.

An important feature is the possibility of the legal regulation to adapt to technological advances for the sector in question. There is a delay that causes the rule to become outdated in a short time, given the faster pace of technological improvements. The regulatory norm must absorb within its framework the concept of new technologies, new products, and services designed in the sharing economy. It is crucial because technological advance occurs at a different speed that is not the same as the state-operated normative change.

This last dimension is the greatest challenge of regulation in the 21st century, in an era in which society will increasingly use technologies. These technologies are reproducible, generating new ones, new products, new services, in a unique evolutionary cycle of its use to respond to the new needs of society and the productive sector. In addition to the emergence of new demands, other ones will be invented to put in market new products and services that did not exist before.

As mentioned above, disruptive technological innovations defy the law, especially those formulated by the governments at different nations and levels into the national state, which still drafts the legislation looking for the most appropriate solution ways. They exercise their regulatory power remaining in the shape of the legal culture of the past without adapting to current challenges. This tension configuration is given to future problems created by new technologies that break with a resistant mindset. Such disruptive technological movement has generated the need into the Law community of scholars of making the same shift as well. If the law is to provide effective answers to the challenges created and imposed by disruptive technologies, it must also make its disruptive evolution. Otherwise, it seems that it will be more a generator of negative externalities than an instrument that can be used to promote the development and socioeconomic sustainability of a nation.

The entire regulatory environment generated from stable, clear assumptions that can adapt to technological developments is a necessary condition for the feasibility of the sharing economy business.

The term feasibility is used here as the quality of what is viable due to the existence of a normative ambiance capable of generating legal certainty but also safety for businesses. The business owner must be assured that the rules that regulate his or her business have a reasonable length of time, that it meets the requirements of an entire generation of trend market development instead of being made to please reluctant groups tied to the values of the past. It must not be altered according to the wishes of the ruler of the moment, as well as there must be certainty regarding law enforcement by administrative agents and judicial interpreters. It requires some consistency according to the jurisprudence on the regulated subject.

Last year some companies gave up on the scooter sharing business in Brazil because of state regulation. One of them was 99 (Exame, 2019), a Brazilian company that is the direct concurrent of Uber in Brazil. The other one was the Lime Company, that closed its activities in Brazil. This is a multinational company that will also close operations in Bogotá, Buenos Aires, Montevideo, Lima and Puerto Vallarta (Estadão, 2020). The reason is the same. The problematic state regulation of the sharing economy.

The current reality of state legal regulation of the sharing economy is not business-friendly as it is not capable of generating lasting viability for business as it creates huge risks that can result in its total unfeasibility given the way it is designed.

Regulation of the sharing economy is a big challenge to every State. In this chapter is proposed a way of improving the state regulation of the collaborative economy. The sharing economy, due to the innovation of the services offered on the market, causes emulsification to emerge among the concepts of traditional legal institutes, demanding that a new concept be created, or that the previous concepts be modified, to adapt to the new reality.

The intersection area must contain an **open concept** that can adapt to the evolution of information technology, allowing the monitoring of technological innovation through regulation and, thus, in addition to maintaining effective regulation over time, it does not impede technological innovation and its implementation in the economy. Thus, the need for change is found in the adaptation of the legal regulation of the area of intersection of traditional concepts of law. It seems the best way to regulate the sharing economy: to adopt an open concept that can adapt to the evolution of the technology.

CONCLUSION

The research problem addressed in this study was as follows: does the economic regulation undertaken by the government have direct impacts on the feasibility of the sharing economy business, or is the impact secondary as a reflective reaction of little relevance?

The impact of the regulatory environment on the feasibility of business in the collaborative economy was analyzed taking into account the Paraiba state in correlation to the House of Representatives of the Federal Republic of Brazil. This relevant topic today has a direct impact on the economy. State legal regulation can be the differential for the consolidation of a viable sharing economy with wealth generation for the country. Otherwise, it can be the state and lobbying instrument that will stifle initiatives from the sharing economy, alienating the nation from the opportunity of creating innovative products. These products meet the needs of their users and thus generate wealth for the whole society, and bring the benefit of increased tax collection to the public coffers.

It was found that the disruption in the traditional mindset of consumption throughout the twentieth century occurred because of the following changes, the technological innovation, the popularization of the use of the Internet along with the emergence of mass use of computing devices, especially mobile equipment. It allowed people and businesses to be connected anytime and anywhere at a lower cost, thereby lowering the transaction cost and enabling the creation of new business formats that previously would not have been possible due to the high cost of the transaction. Technological innovation, therefore, has opened previously unimaginable possibilities in the business world. The insertion of innovative companies intensified, such as startups in some markets previously dominated by large corporations, such as fintechs in the financial market.

The analysis undertaken confirmed the hypothesis here presented. State economic regulation is a compelling law whose obedience is mandatory to whoever is subject to state authority in a given territory. It has a direct impact on the feasibility of businesses in the sharing economy and, depending on their formatting, may even hinder the development of any business model in the sector.

This research confirmed the hypothesis and was carried out according to the following main objective: verifying how the economic regulation of the sharing economy has directly impacted the feasibility of its business models.

As for the specific objectives, the following were proposed. First off, it established the conceptual delimitation of the main categories employed in the study on the economic regulation of the sharing economy. It analyzed the interaction between technology and the collaborative economy as a substrate for disruptive innovations. It verified the first reactions of the governmental regulator concerning the sector. It asked about the need for a regulatory disruption to face the challenging reality of the sharing economy. The article also analyzed state legal regulation as an impact factor on business feasibility.

From the analyses carried out throughout here, it gives as lines of a conclusion that all the normative and empirical evidence studied point up to the fact that state legal regulation is a crucial assumption for the feasibility of the business inserted in the sector of this new branch of online services. Indeed, the format of regulation will determine whether the success or failure of the business in the ambiance of the sharing economy.

The efforts of the sectorial entrepreneurs to develop and market new products and services designed for the sharing economy will not succeed if the regulatory environment is highly hostile. This failure will occur under some precise circumstances like if:

- State regulation is designed to create market reserves for certain traditional economic groups;
- There are stipulations of highly restrictive conditions that hinder or even prevent new players from entering the market;
- Criteria are created that burden new business to such an extent that competitive advantage is taken over traditional and established business.

The above conclusions are further enhanced by the need for regulation to be designed and implemented in a stable, clear, and capable way to absorb in its frame the concept of new technologies. It means new products and new services conceived in the ambiance of the sharing economy. Feasibility presupposes stability of the rules and their interpretation over time by the administrative agents involved and the Judiciary, as well as clarity of content, so as not to create hermeneutic problems that affect the legal certainty that the market needs to attract and maintain investments.

Thus said above, the sharing economy, due to the innovation of the services offered on the market, causes emulsification to emerge among the concepts of traditional legal institutes, demanding that a new concept be created, or that the previous concepts be modified, to adapt to the new reality.

The intersection area must contain an **open concept** that can adapt to the evolution of information technology, allowing the monitoring of technological innovation through regulation and, thus, in addition to maintaining effective regulation over time, it does not impede technological innovation and its implementation in the economy. Thus, the need for change is found in the adaptation of the legal regulation of the area of intersection of traditional concepts of law. It seems the best way to regulate the sharing economy: to adopt an open concept that can adapt to the evolution of the technology.

The great challenge for any national regulatory law is to draw up a regulation that could be synchronized with the evolvement of technological disruptions. For this, a regulatory disruption is essential, as traditional legal categories no longer provide satisfactory answers to the challenges introduced by the sharing economy.

To this end, the legal professional must understand the dynamics of disruptive business, which can accurately typify new products and services, especially given the difficulty of classification resulting from the emulsification of private and commercial uses in the sharing economy.

Only after the proper classification of products and services will it be possible to think of a regulatory framework that encourages the business environment of the sharing economy, generating the potential of continuous investment in new businesses. This reality will provide a viable long-term environment for businesses. Regarding companies, it is positive for the society that regulation does not hinder the entry of companies of all sizes, from a small startup to a large company.

As for the aspect of the effectiveness of the sharing economy regulation over time, the regulatory model must be able to keep up with technological changes. Given the high capacity for innovation inherent in this model of the economy that intensively uses new technologies, it must not lose effectiveness with technological development.

This design is the regulatory challenge that nations need. They must deal with the crisis with careful and well-designed laws and rules. It is necessary to find the appropriate regulatory format that allows the socio-economic development of society because the sharing economy plays an important role in the economy of the country. In addition to bringing innovative products and services to the market that are user-friendly, it can help with other contemporary issues. It can reduce emissions of polluting gases, help in the improvement of traffic in big cities by removing cars from the streets, such as in the case of the car-sharing, among other varied possibilities of the inventions from the human mind.

The worst posture of the public power is to prohibit, through regulation, the businesses of the sharing economy. This initial conduct has been adopted not solely in Brazil but in various parts of the planet and continues to be in others. The absence of state regulation is only better than prohibitive regulation. Still, experience has shown that the market is not as efficient in promoting self-regulation accompanied by the minimization of negative externalities. The alternative that best fits with regulatory feasibility is the establishment of state regulation along the lines set out above, i.e., stable, clear, and capable of absorbing in its frame the concept of new technologies, new products, and services conceived in the sharing economy as a whole over time.

It was found that public authorities, solely by their own motivation, seem to have no incentive to change their regulatory mindset. This inertia occurs especially through the dynamics of lobby groups that represent the interests of opposing firms and economic sectors already established in the market. This latter sees the sharing economy as a threat. Thus, in a democratic rule of law, it is imperative that people and companies in the sharing economy also adopt the lobbying strategy to press the lawmakers and governmental sectors in favor of interests politically connected to the majority. Society should seek to influence the elaboration of regulation so that it is thought and elaborated to foster the business of the sharing economy.

The more room for the development of the technology-intensive sharing economy is present in the society, the better for the economy of the country and people. There will be more income generation options as it will boost new business to provide the flowing dynamics of economic and social interactions. The construction of a friendly regulatory framework is crucially important for the feasibility of the business inserted in the sharing economy.

REFERENCES

Banco Central do Brasil. (2019). *Fintechs*. Retrieved on November 25, 2019, from https://www.bcb.gov.br/estabilidadefinanceira/fintechs

Chamber of Deputies. (2018). *Ley Project no. n°5.587-A/2016* [Projeto de Lei n°5.587-A de 2016]. Retrieved on November 13, 2019, from http://www.camara.gov.br/proposicoesWeb/fichadetramitacao?idProposicao=2088280

City Council of João Pessoa. (2015). *Ordinary Law no. 13.105 of November 30, 2015* [Lei ordinária nº 13.105, de 30 de novembro de 2015]. Retrieved on November 13, 2019, from http://177.200.32.195:9673/sapl/sapl_documentos/norma_juridica/16865_texto_integral

Cortez, N. (2014). Regulating Disruptive Innovation. *Berkeley Technology Law Journal*, *29*(1), 177–179. doi:10.15779/Z38NM5G

Estadão. (2020). *Scooter giant, Lime closes operation in Brazil after six months* [Gigante dos patinetes, Lime encerra operação no Brasil após seis meses]. Retrieved on January 15, 2020, from https://link.estadao.com.br/noticias/inovacao,lime-encerra-operacao-no-brasil-apos-seis-meses,70003150714

Exame. (2019). *99 gives up bikes and scooters in Brazil* [99 desiste de empreitada de bikes e patinetes no Brasil]. Retrieved on January 15, 2020, from https://exame.abril.com.br/blog/primeiro-lugar/99-desiste-de-empreitada-de-bikes-e-patinetes-no-brasil/

Fundação Getúlio Vargas. (2016). *Sharing and intensive use of urban roads in São Paulo. Follow-up report of the seminar held jointly with the São Paulo City Council* [Compartilhamento e uso intensivo do viário urbano em São Paulo. Relatório de acompanhamento do seminário realizado em conjunto com a Câmara Municipal de São Paulo]. São Paulo: Centro de Estudos de Política e Economia do Setor Público da Fundação Getúlio Vargas. Retrieved on November 23, 2019, from https://bibliotecadigital.fgv.br/dspace/handle/10438/19431

Guedes da Luz Neto, L. (2017a). The Shared Economy and its Challenges in Brazil [A Economia Compartilhada e seus Desafios no Brasil]. In M. R. Gonçalves, F. S. Veiga, & M. M. Magalhães (Eds.), *Derecho, gobernanza e innnovación: Dilemas jurídicos de la contemporaneidad em perspectiva trans-disciplinar* (pp. 420–427). Universidade Portucalense.

Guedes da Luz Neto, L. (2017b). Shared Economy: Regulatory Approaches between Brazil and Portugal [Economia Compartilhada: Aproximações Regulatórias entre Brasil e Portugal]. In M. R. Gonçalves & F. S. Veiga (Eds.), *O Direito Actual e as Novas Fronteiras Jurídicas no Limiar de uma Nova Era* (pp. 972–978). Universidade Católica Editora.

Katz, V. (2015). Regulation the sharing economy. *Berkeley Technology Law Journal*, *30*(4), 1067–1126. doi:10.15779/Z38HG45

Khun, T. S. (1997). *The Structure of Scientific Revolutions* [A estrutura das revoluções científicas] (5th ed.). Editora Perspectiva S.A.

Legisweb. (2017). *Law no. 1866 / 09.03.2017* [Lei nº 1866 de 09/03/2017]. Retrieved on November 13, 2019, from https://www.legisweb.com.br/legislacao/?id=350888

Rockcontent. (2018). *Digital platforms: what they are and how do the big companies in the world use them?* [Plataformas digitais: o que é e como as grandes empresas do mundo utilizam?]. Retrieved on November 23, 2019, from https://inteligencia.rockcontent.com/plataformas-digitais/

Saddy, A. (2014). *Regulation of Direct Delivery of Public Services: Divergences Arising from the Regulatory Framework for Basic Sanitation* [Regulação da Prestação Direta de Serviços Públicos: Divergências Decorrentes do Marco Regulatório para o Saneamento Básico]. Retrieved on November 25, 2019, from http://www.cedipre.fd.uc.pt

ENDNOTE

1 Absolute legal certainty will never be achieved for every norm must be interpreted and the process of interpretation depends on the interpreter. Therefore the interpretive result tends to vary to some degree according to the interpreter. However, as much as the rule is clear, less substantial variation in the content of the norm is found, therefor it increases the degree of security.

Chapter 2
The Role of the State in Optimizing Communication Between Generation Z and Migrants in the Human Resources Management

Anatolii Shyian
https://orcid.org/0000-0002-5418-1498
Vinnitsia National Technical University, Ukraine

Liliia Nikiforova
Vinnitsia National Technical University, Ukraine

ABSTRACT

The aim of this work is to develop methods of government migration policy in order to motivate migrants to joint economic activities, especially with generation Z. The goals of a developed state are to include migrants in social, political, and economic institutions to increase the welfare of their citizens, as in the short-term, so in the long run. Migrants who are not suitable for the realization of the interests of indigenous peoples should be repatriated (deported). Migrants can run away from hostilities; they can run away from poverty. The game-theoretic model built in the article made it possible to identify the fundamental features of the process of harmonizing the interests of the state (government) and migrants. To implement the motivation of migrants, the chapter offers an example of consistent general trainings that migrants must successfully develop for successful joint activities with Generation Z.

DOI: 10.4018/978-1-7998-4543-0.ch002

INTRODUCTION

Generation Z is growing under conditions that differ from previous generations. The main condition is that they actively use electronic devices to receive, process and present information. Their entry into economic and social relations in society will lead to a certain dissonance with the now actively functioning generations. In the field of the functioning of sustainable organizations, this discord will be most noticeable.

However, the appearance of Generation Z on the economic and social scene is not the only feature in the current period. Today, migratory flows are rapidly growing on the planet. People migrate domestically mainly for economic reasons (although there are other reasons as well: the example of Ukraine is indicative). Today there is a large flow of migrants between countries. For example, people with high intelligence and professional skills migrate (the so-called brain drain, which is carried out mainly from developing countries).

Moreover, most migrants are people with disabilities, skills and professional experience. These people came from undeveloped countries, and they need specific help from a developed country to adapt to new conditions for them. They do not adapt well to living conditions and culture in a developed community. However, adaptation methods for migrants, as a rule, are still under development.

The emergence of a sufficiently large number of migrants for whom in a developed country economic, social, political and cultural norms of behavior are unacceptable, sooner or later will lead to confrontation with the indigenous (domestic) population. Migrants will seek to form local territorial settlements and organize business with the involvement of main migrants. The economic activities of firms with immigration personnel will differ from firms consisting of indigenous (domestic) peoples. As a result, difficulties will arise in managing the economic development of this developed country.

In addition, as a rule, migrants have more children than the indigenous (domestic) population. Therefore, the relative part of migrants in the population of a developed country will increase.

Generation Z is quite different from previous generations. However, their difference from migrants from undeveloped countries is much stronger. A migrant will not be able to overcome such an abyss on his own. Therefore, state assistance is necessary for a migrant.

Unfortunately, migrants from undeveloped countries are left "on their own" when they themselves are forced to try to narrow the gap in knowledge, skills, and abilities between themselves and the population of a developed country. However, migrants, as a rule, are not accustomed to efficiently absorb huge amounts of new information, which is common for generation Z – see, for example, (Westerman, & Yamamura, 2007). Therefore, they can fall into conditions of strong cognitive dissonance. And this can already lead to the rejection of all that is unusual for them.

Thus, the problem of adaptation of migrants from an undeveloped country and their communication with the indigenous (domestic) population of a developed country is still relevant. The relevance of research in this area with the advent of generation Z only increases.

BACKGROUND

Scientific studies of the impact of migrants on indigenous peoples' life are usually carried out within the framework of economics, sociology, education, comparative psychology, marketing, communication, law, and education. For example, Kivisto and La Vecchia-Mikkola (2015) discusses the perception of the safety of Iraqi migrants in Helsinki and Rome. In Peri, Romiti, and Rossi (2015), the problems of the influence of migrants on the elderly care market are explored. Jacquemet (2015) is devoted to the study of communication problems of migrants who have little command of the native language of the indigenous population while Jerrima, Chmielewski, and Parker (2015) show that the low-income stratum of people cannot count obtained on higher education. However, migrants can be attributed to just such people. Finally, Hallowell and Yugar-Arias (2016) found that there is an increased level of injury among migrants.

Zmigrod, Rentfrow, and Robbins (2020, p.407) found that: "In a sample of over 700 U.S. citizens, partisan extremity was related to lower levels of cognitive flexibility, regardless of political orientation ... These findings suggest that the rigidity with which individuals process and respond to nonpolitical information may be related to the extremity of their partisan identities."

Thus, the influence of cultural characteristics that manifest themselves in ideology is associated with their cognitive flexibility.

The results of this work show that the most plastic in the cognitive sense migrants will have a higher level of adaptation to the conditions of a new country and will more successfully integrate into the new world. Therefore, the use of tests to identify cognitive flexibility can be used as a criterion for identifying promising migrants for the country.

Migrants with low cognitive flexibility who are more focused on adhering to their country's cultural traditions will protest against a new culture in a developing country. Therefore, they can be considered natural candidates for repatriation.

Zmigrod, Rentfrow, and Robbins (2019, p.1) wrote that "present original evidence that objectively assessed cognitive inñexibility predicts extremist attitudes, including a willingness to harm others, and sacriðce one's life for the group". It was also found that "cognitive inñexibility was related to greater conðdence in the decision to sacriðce one's life in an in-group trolley problem scenario. Analysis of participants 'performance on the cognitive tasks revealed that cognitive rigidity - distinctly from other aspects of cognition - was speciðcally implicated as a cognitive antecedent of extremist attitudes" (Zmigrod et al., 2019, p.1).

As a result, today there are powerful tools for reliably identifying the signs of migrants, which indicate both the successful integration of migrants in the social and economic life of the new society and their commitment to extremist manifestations.

The methods described above for identifying both migrants with limited adaptive abilities and extremist-minded people can be used within the tools proposed in this article to identify migrants most needed for the country.

Thus, it becomes necessary to identify the part of migrants who can adapt to the conditions of a developed state. However, this is not enough today, as migrants must adapt to joint activities with generation Z. This fact leads to new challenges that need to be addressed at the level of state migration policy.

Artero and Chiodell (2019) draw attention to the fact that the spatial localization of migrants can be caused by their religious preferences. The authors emphasize the need for further research in this area, especially with a view to avoiding the emergence of possible critical problems related to residential concentration, especially in the long term (e.g., further stigmatization on a territorial basis).

Pérez and Salgado (2019) examined the use of mobile phones by adolescent migrants in everyday life. They found that migrant teens are actively involved in the youth subculture, both locally and globally. It is noted that "they are able to access different social networks that allow them to play out the personas they wish to adopt." Thus, migrant adolescents are actively involved in the life of Generation

Z. However, this involvement must be manageable. First of all, in the direction, that migrant adolescents must assimilate both a developed country culture and the Z generation culture.

Ramirez, Liebig, Thoreau, and Veneri (2018) indicate that migrants prefer to settle in separate local territorial entities, and in them, they adhere to their home culture and behavior. However, these cultures and behavior are in many ways not acceptable for the indigenous population of a developed country (and especially for Generation Z). Moreover, the young generation of migrants, who are outside the cultural environment and norms of behavior of a developed country, is at a disadvantage compared to generation Z from the indigenous population of a developed country.

Thus, a significant progressive difference arises between migrants from undeveloped countries and generation Z from the indigenous population.

The aim of the work is to develop methods for government migration policy in order to motivate migrants to joint economic activities, especially with Generation Z.

The work is structured in this way.

Section 3 describes the methodology of the chapter. Section 4 describes the goals of both a developed country and migrants. Section 5 builds a game-theoretic model to coordinate the interests of the government and migrants. Section 6 provides an example of sequential general training that migrants must successfully complete for successful collaboration with Generation Z. Section 7 discusses the results. Section 8 is a conclusion.

METHODOLOGY

As a research methodology, this way is used. First, the interests (goals) of the government of a developed state and migrants were identified. Here, attention is drawn to the need for the continuous growth of welfare for all residents. Based on personal research, the goals of migrants are identified. Sustainable development of the state requires the optimization of communication between the government and migrants. An appropriate game-theoretic model is constructed for its description. The requirement to fulfill the goals of the government was chosen as a concept for solving this game-theoretic model.

Implementation of the results of the game-theoretic model is carried out taking into account the fact that the most effective adaptation of migrants to the conditions of a developed country requires their communication with generation Z. This generation is today a very dynamic driver for the development of a developed state. It is proposed to use a consistent set of general training for migrants as an improvement in the effectiveness of adaptation. The requirements for migrants take into account both the need for their socialization and the need for their participation in highly skilled labor in a developed country. Also, the identification of extremist-minded people was proposed in the process of passing these pieces of training.

The use of such a research methodology allows identifying areas for improving the state management of migration processes in developed countries.

INTERESTS (GOALS) OF THE DEVELOPED COUNTRY AND MIGRANTS

The purposes of a developed country when receiving migrants are as follows.

1. A developed country accepts migrants in order to increase the welfare of its citizens, both in the short and long term.
2. A developed country has the goal of supporting (and developing) existing cultural, economic and social institutions.
3. A developed country accepts migrants who are suitable for the realization of indigenous society interests, for which country allocates some resources. The remaining migrants must be repatriated (deported).

Resources allocated by a developed country should be spent on the following directions:

- on the identification of migrants who possess the features necessary for a developed country;
- for training and adaptation of migrants with the necessary traits with a view to the subsequent integration of them and their families in a developed society;
- to repatriate (deport) migrants who do not have the necessary traits to their home country.

Among the interests of migrants are the following can be distinguished.

1. Migrants who run away from hostilities. As a rule, these migrants are forced to leave their country. For the most part, they are not inclined to integrate into the new society. Many of them have psychological injuries and deformations, often quite serious. Their goal is to first "wait" and then return to their homeland. However, after some time in a developed country, the goal of many of them may change. Migrants intend to stay in a developed country. But at the same time, they will persistently strive to keep the cultural, economic and social institutions of their home country unchanged. That is those institutions from whose activities they fled. These institutions are often quite contrary to the institutions that exist in a developed country.
2. Migrants who "run away from poverty". This is a rather heterogeneous group of migrants.

The first group of migrants intends to settle in a developed country.

Some of them immediately bring their family. Thus, the signal that they are ready to consciously cut off all the paths to return to themselves. These families require a lot of help from the state, as they almost always have several young children. The salary of parents in the conditions of a new country is almost always insufficient. As a result, conditions are created for such a family to fall into the trap of poverty (Costas & Stachurski, 2005). However, such "family" migrants, under certain conditions, will make every effort to integrate into a developed country's economy and society. Integration into the economy of a developed country will give them an increase in the standard of living of the family. Integration into the society of a developed country will give them confidence in the future of their children.

Another part of the migrants is planned to transport the family only after they themselves adapt to the conditions of a developed country. These migrants, in fact, leave themselves the opportunity to return to their homeland. They strive not to lose touch with the home country; therefore they shy away from full integration both in the economy of a developed country and in its social and public life. These migrants also strive not to lose touch with the community of migrants from their country (for example, with the aim of transferring money to their home country for the family). As a result of this, it is more advantageous for them to settle compactly, that is, to form local territories where mainly migrants from this country live. Of course, such conditions sharply reduce the ability of migrants to adapt to the economy and social life of a developed country. For example, due to the fact that a migrant has to exist in "two different worlds": both in a developed country and the developing world of his native country. As a result, discontent may develop among this stratum of migrants, which can serve as a breeding ground for extremism.

The second group of migrants intends to earn a certain amount of money in a developed country and return to their homeland (for example, in order to open their own business). These migrants are usually men who intend to adhere to the social, economic and political institutions of their homeland. They also strictly observe the cultural and religious rules of their country. They are prepared for the risk of engaging in "slightly illegal" operations in a developed country in the event that it can bring them financial benefits. In the event of a conflict of interests between the requirements of the developed and their home country, they will usually choose the interests of their homeland.

Finally, the third group of migrants arrives in a developed country with the intention of "living on social benefits." They do not initially intend to integrate into the social, economic and political institutions of a developed country. They will preserve the cultural, religious and institutional habits of their homeland. They will also seek to raise children in the "traditions of their homeland." Such migrants are a danger to the national security of a developed country. Indeed, they are the inclusion of a foreign culture, adhere to moral and ethical values alien to a developed country. In addition, they feel in constant danger from the indigenous people of a developed country. Such migrants are forced to very aggressively resist teaching their children the lifestyle of the inhabitants of a developed country. They will strive to significantly limit the training of their young generation. In fact, migrants of this group are oriented towards a certain "robbery" of the gross domestic product of a developed country. They only intend to consume without producing anything in return. It is among such migrants that there will be many dissatisfied with the fact that they were "given insufficient finances": naturally, their standard of living will be lower than the standard of living of citizens of a developed country. All attempts by the administration of a developed country to adapt to this group of migrants will be met very aggressively.

These interest groups were highlighted by personal observation, as well as focus groups and surveys of migrants from Ukraine to developed countries. How widespread interest groups are found among migrants from other countries requires a separate study. However, in the game-theoretic model, consideration of migrant interest groups will be needed already at the stage of consideration of specific financing of the sequential general training proposed below.

In conclusion, we emphasize that migrants from the second and, especially the third group are often a breeding ground for extremists of different directions.

Thus, the main problem of the modern state is the identification of migrants who want to adapt to the existing culture, political, social and economic institutions. This identification method should be cost-effective. It is also necessary that this method involves migrants themselves in the identification process.

GAME-THEORY MODEL FOR AGREEMENT OF THE INTERESTS OF THE GOVERNMENT AND MIGRANTS

We are building a model of game theory to coordinate interests between two players: a developed state (more precisely, power and power structures) and migrants.

There are such basic goals for players.

The government aims to integrate migrants into existing cultural, social and economic institutions.

Migrants aim to provide themselves with a standard of living and security at least equal to that previously enjoyed in their home country.

As you can see, the goals of the players do not coincide, and therefore it is necessary to develop a model to harmonize them. The implementation of this model in real life falls on the shoulders of the state and government, as migrants do not have the necessary resources. Migrants can only agree or disagree with participating in inappropriate activities.

The game-theory model for harmonization of the interests of the developed state and migrants are shown in Figure 1.

Figure 1. A dynamic game of harmonization between the government and migrants

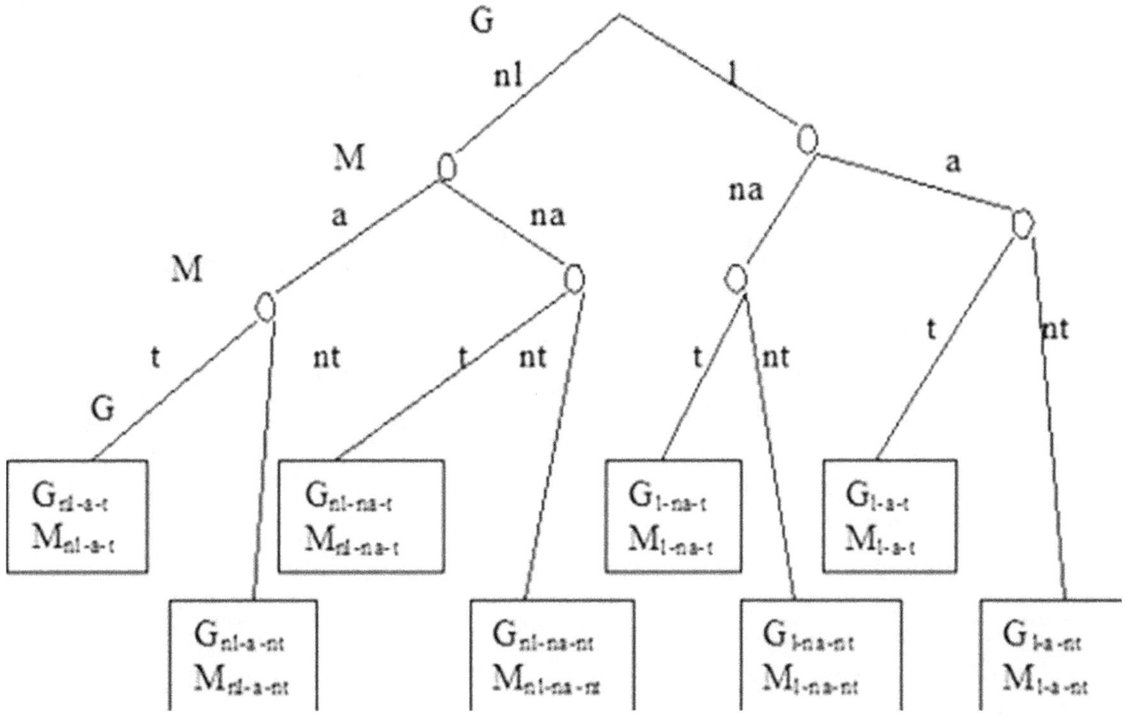

Let introduce the following notation.

Capital letters show *G* – the government (state), *M* – migrants. State (top) and migrant (bottom) winnings are shown in the rectangles below the end of the respective path of the game tree.

The timing of the game's deployment is as follows.

Step 1: The move is done by the government. It selects either the "*nl*" strategy, that is, the non-localized allocation of migrants between the indigenous people of the country, or the "*l*" strategy, i.e. the localized allocation of migrants by compact groups (creating a kind of Chinatown).

Note that these may also be, for example, detention camps for migrants. At these camps, migrants will be expected to turn to participate in certain state programs. It should be noted that such an organization of work with migrants is not rational, as migrants will be expected to receive information mainly from other migrants. This information will necessarily be distorted. Therefore, the government will have to make additional efforts to convince migrants that they have received inaccurate information from other migrants.

It should be noted that migrant recruitment to extremist organizations can begin in camps.

Step 2: Migrants make the move. They can choose the first strategy "*a*", that is, adapt to the conditions of the developed country. They can also choose a second "*na*" strategy, that is, not adapt to the conditions of the developed country and live by the rules of the country where they came from.

The interests of major migrant groups were described above. Therefore, the state should create conditions for migrants to choose their own strategy voluntarily and this will allow the state to get information about the migrants' goals. It is recommended to interview migrants so that they have the opportunity to choose one of the above strategies themselves before they interact with previous generations of migrants.

Note. Migrant adaptation also refers to the fulfillment of the rules and regulations of formal and informal social and economic institutions that make up the society, state, and culture of the indigenous population.

Step 3: The government creates the conditions for migrants to acquire a suitable profession. For example, it could be training, encouraging entrepreneurs to hire and train migrants and more.

At this stage, the special structures of government identify those personal traits that allow migrants to participate in the economic, social, cultural and political life of a developed country. This will be discussed in more detail below.

Migrants make the move. They can choose the first strategy "*t*", that is, study the proposed profession. Migrants can also choose the "*nt*" strategy, that is, not to acquire a profession. Thus, the state provides migrants with a list of possible professions for them, and migrants make a choice. It should be noted that the state can offer migrants a rating of the necessary professions for a developed country. State needs for the territorial localization of migrants can also be offered.

Step 4: The move is done by the government. It either decides to grant the migrant a long-term work visa (maybe, with subsequent citizenship) or decides to send the migrant to the home country. This aspect will be discussed in more detail below.

Let's justify the players' winnings. First of all, it is important to note that in the theory of games, not only the magnitudes of winnings are important, but their ordering for each player (Gibbons, 1992). Therefore, specific numerical values will not play a role.

We also emphasize that for a dynamic game, only those wins that come from one vertex are compared.

State's (government's) winnings: The state (government) will receive the greatest benefit if the migrant is successfully integrated into society, receives training and becomes actively involved in the economic growth of the country. This will be the case for "*nl®a®t*" strategies.

The smallest benefit of the government will be if the strategy "*nl®a®nt*" is chosen. Under this strategy, the state will lose an already adapted migrant, to whom it has invested large enough funds (for example, by providing housing and finances for living and learning).

When implementing the "*nl®na®t*" strategy, the state will receive a trained migrant who is not adapted to the conditions of life and activity in society. This is a good option, but the state will receive less from such a migrant than possible.

The "*nl®na®nt*" strategy will cause losses, but these losses will be less than in the case of the "*nl®a®nt*" strategy due to the lower possible "return" from the migrant.

The "*l®a®t*" strategy is beneficial to the state, but it has the "spoon of tar" benefit: the migrant has little involvement in public life. Therefore, in some cases, it may place the interests of its community above the interests of indigenous peoples.

The "*l®a®nt*" strategy requires relatively little expenditure from the state (in fact, only housing and migrant adaptation).

The "l®na®t" strategy offers the smallest benefits for state from a trained migrant, which, however, is not adapted to society and able to live only in the migrant enclave.

The "l®na®nt" strategy requires the smallest contribution of resources from the state but gives nothing for the economy.

It should be noted that the state's expenses when a migrant lives in the migrant's enclave are less than when the migrant lives surrounded by the indigenous population.

Migrant winnings: The greatest benefit will be provided to the migrant if he/she successfully integrates into society, undergoes training and is actively involved in the economic growth of the country.

This will be the case for "*nl®a®t*" strategies.

The smallest winning for a migrant will be if the strategy "*nl®a®nt*" is chosen, as the migrant will spend efforts to adapt to life in this society, which will be in vain when he returns to his country.

In implementing the "*nl®na®t*" strategy, the migrant will successfully participate in economic life, but he/she will not be adapted to the conditions of life and activity in society. It's a good option, but not the best for a migrant.

The "*nl®na®nt*" strategy will result in small losses for the migrant. In fact, he only loses time and learns skills that are superfluous in his country (where he/she will be repatriated).

The "*l®a®t*" strategy is advantageous to the migrant, but this benefit has the "spoon of tar": the migrant has little involvement in public life, his adaptive capacity will be less significant than in the case of "*nl®a®t*" strategies.

The "l®a®nt" strategy requires the migrant to adapt to the enclave of similar migrants. But he will not need these skills in his own country (where he/she will be repatriated).

The "l®na®t" strategy provides the least benefits for a migrant who remains to live and work in the country.

The "l®na®nt" strategy requires the least cost to the migrant.

Please note that if a migrant chooses the "*nt*" strategy, he/she will be repatriated from a developed country, which was taken into account in his / her winnings.

Solution the dynamic game: For a dynamic game, the Nash equilibrium is rational (Gibbons, 1992). This equilibrium is found by the reverse induction method, starting from the bottom-up motion (i.e. from the last stage to the first) (Gibbons, 1992).

Since the last move is made by the government, we firstly compare the winnings of the state and carry them to the corresponded top.

The government compares the winnings "$G_{nl\text{-}a\text{-}t}$" and "$G_{nl\text{-}a\text{-}nt}$" each other: With the «$G_{nl\text{-}a\text{-}t}$» winning, the state receives a migrant who is already able to exist independently in the cultural and social environment of a developed country. This is due to the fact that the migrant is forced to live in an environment of a new culture (choice of strategy "*nl*"). In addition, the migrant is making efforts to actively adapt to the new cultural, social, economic and political environment (choice of strategy "*a*"). Finally, the migrant has made to master a profession that is able to provide him with a sufficient standard of living (choosing a "*t*" strategy).

With the "$G_{nl\text{-}a\text{-}nt}$" is chooses, the state receives a migrant who is similar to the previous. The only difference is that this migrant does not have a profession that can provide him with a sufficient standard of living (he chose the "*nt*" strategy). This means that the state must spend additional resources to provide this migrant with a sufficient standard of living. As a result, the winning to the migrant who has chosen the "*nl-a-nt*" strategy will be smaller than the winning to the migrant to the "*nl-a-t*" strategy.

Thus, the government chooses the "*nl-a-t*" strategy and the corresponding payment to the state.

The state compares the winnings "$G_{nl\text{-}na\text{-}t}$" and "$G_{nl\text{-}na\text{-}nt}$" each other: With the «$G_{nl\text{-}na\text{-}t}$» winning, the state receives a migrant who is already able to exist independently in the cultural and social environment of a developed country. This is due to the fact that the migrant is forced to live in an environment of a new culture (choice of strategy "*nl*"). However, this migrant made no effort to fully adapt to the conditions of the developed country (choosing a "*na*" strategy). The migrant has made to master a profession that is able to provide him with a sufficient standard of living (choosing a "*t*" strategy).

With the "$G_{nl\text{-}na\text{-}nt}$" winning, the state receives a migrant who is similar to the previous. The only difference is that this migrant does not have a profession that can provide him with a sufficient standard of living (he chose the "*nt*" strategy). This means that the state must spend additional resources to provide this migrant with a sufficient standard of living. As a result, the cost for the state for a migrant with "*nl-na-nt*" strategy will be higher than that for a migrant with "*nl-na-t*" strategy.

Thus, the government chooses the "*nl-na-t*" strategy and the corresponding payment to the state.

The state compares the winnings "$G_{l\text{-}na\text{-}t}$" and "$G_{l\text{-}na\text{-}nt}$" each other: With the "$G_{l\text{-}na\text{-}t}$" winning, the state receives a migrant who is unable to exist independently in the cultural and social environment of a developed country. He/she remains the carrier of extractive economic, social, cultural and political institutions. He/she is familiar with life in a developed country very fragmentarily. This is due to the fact that the migrant is forced to live in an environment of a home culture (choice of strategy «*l*). In addition, this migrant made no efforts to fully adapt to the conditions of the developed country (choice of "*na*" strategy). The migrant has made every effort only to master a profession that is able to provide him with a sufficient standard of living (choosing a "*t*" strategy). However, this migrant requires additional resources from the state to control it. It is also necessary to protect both this migrant from the society of the developed country and to protect indigenous peoples from certain manifestations of the migrant's activity (for example, which engages in behavior that is unacceptable to indigenous peoples of the developed state).

With the "$G_{l\text{-}na\text{-}nt}$" winning, the state receives a migrant who is similar to the previous. The only difference is that this migrant does not have a profession that can provide him with a sufficient standard of living (he chose the "*nt*" strategy). This means that the state must spend additional resources to provide this migrant with a sufficient standard of living. As a result, the cost for the state for a migrant with "*l-na-nt*" strategy will be higher than that for a migrant with "*l-na-t*" strategy.

Thus, the government chooses the "*l-na-t*" strategy and the corresponding payment to the state.

The state compares the winnings "$G_{l\text{-}a\text{-}t}$" and "$G_{l\text{-}a\text{-}nt}$" each other: With the "$G_{l\text{-}a\text{-}t}$" winning, the state receives a migrant who is unable to exist independently in the cultural and social environment of a developed country. He/she remains the carrier of extractive economic, social, cultural and political institutions. He/she is familiar with life in a developed country very fragmentarily. This is due to the fact that the migrant is forced to live in an environment of a home culture (choice of strategy "*l*"). However, this migrant has made some efforts to adapt to the conditions of the developed country (choice of strategy "*a*"). The migrant has also made efforts only to master a profession that is able to provide him with a sufficient standard of living (choosing a "*t*" strategy). However, this migrant requires additional resources from the state to control it (however, these efforts will be smaller compared to the consideration of the state's "$G_{l\text{-}na\text{-}t}$" and "$G_{l\text{-}na\text{-}nt}$" gains). It is also necessary to protect both this migrant from the society of the developed country and to protect indigenous peoples from certain manifestations of the migrant's activity (for example, which engages in behavior that is unacceptable to indigenous peoples of the developed state).

With the "$G_{l\text{-}a\text{-}nt}$" winning, the state receives a migrant who is similar to the previous. The only difference is that this migrant does not have a profession that can provide him with a sufficient standard of living (he chose the "*nt*" strategy). This means that the state must spend additional resources to provide this migrant with a sufficient standard of living. As a result, the cost for the state for a migrant with "*l-a-nt*" strategy will be higher than that for a migrant with "*l-a-t*" strategy.

Thus, the government chooses the strategy "*l-a-t*" and the corresponding payoff for the state.

As one can see, the government always chooses the strategy "*t*". Thus, we obtain the graph shown in Figure 2.

Figure 2. Dynamic game after government choice

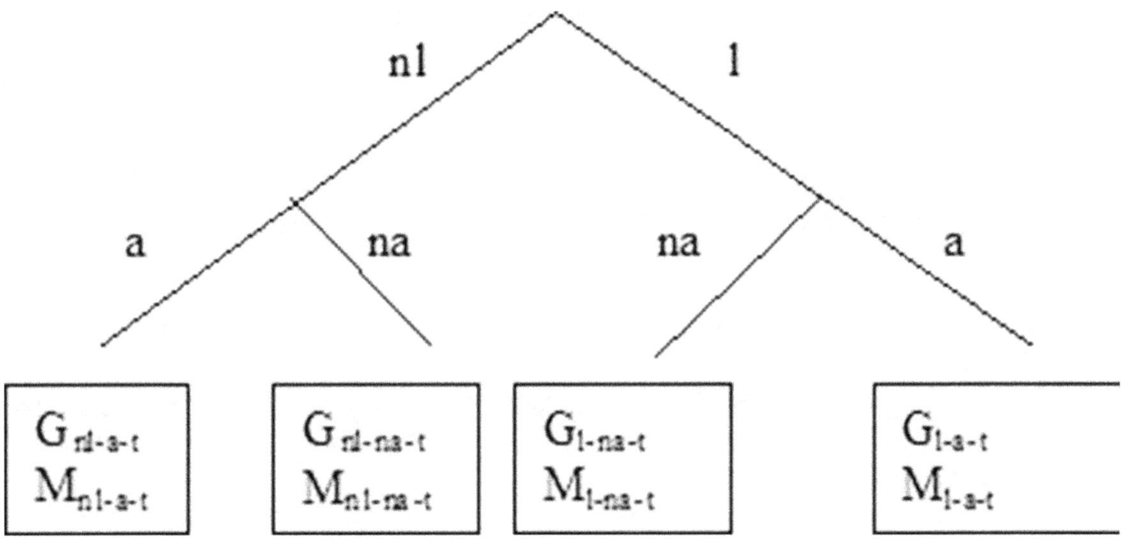

Migrants must now make the choice.

In this case, there may be several options for decision-making concepts for migrants.

The first conception: Migrants use a short-sighted strategy. That is, they focus solely on the current situation, trying to minimize their costs and efforts. Then they will choose at this stage a "*na*" strategy, that is, not adapt to the living conditions in a developed country.

It should be noted that the same strategy will be chosen by migrants in case they do not have complete information on what the developed country will look at in the future. That is when migrants have incomplete or incorrect information about a given dynamic game.

The second conception: Migrants use a long-term strategy. Then they will be guided by the further choice of the state and therefore will choose the strategy "*a*".

Migrants' choice of a strategy, that is, to adapt to the conditions of life in a developed country, will also be made if migrants are provided with complete and reliable information about the conditions of play. At the same time, migrants should be clearly aware of the interests of a developed migrant-receiving state.

The result of a rational choice of migrants of strategy "*a*" is shown in Figure 3.

Figure 3. Dynamic game after the choice of migrants

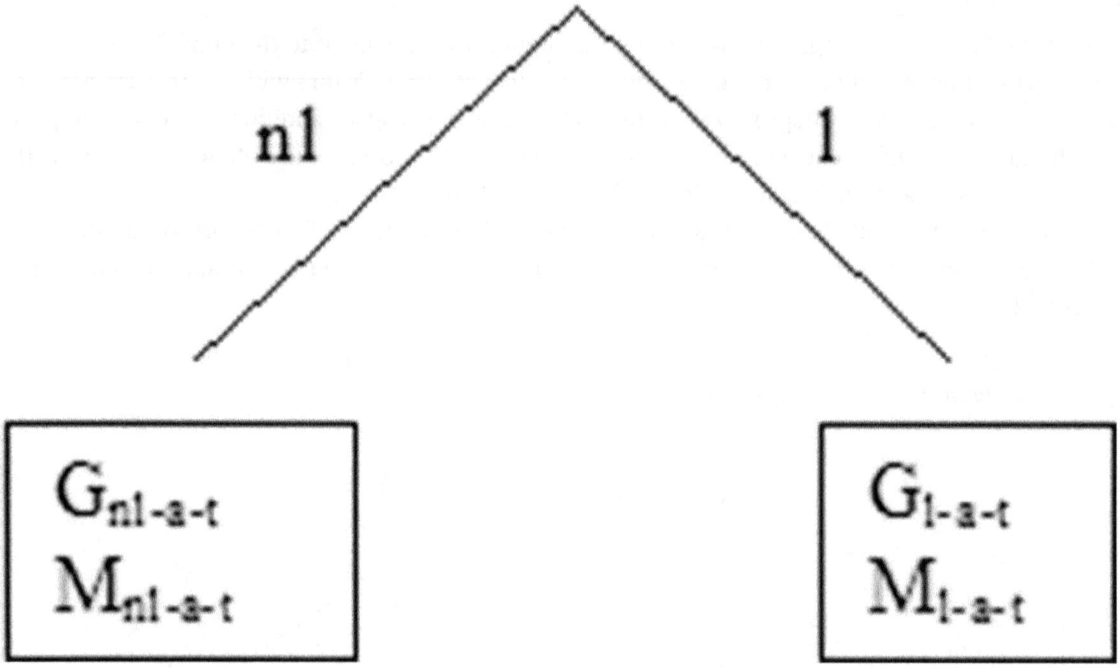

Choosing a strategy for migrants in the first stage of the dynamic game, shown in Fig. 3 may also be different. It repeats the two different concepts described above - short-sighted and long-term.

Similar to the above argument, the short-sighted choice of migrants will be an "*l*" strategy, i.e. localized residence surrounded by the same migrants (preferably not only from the same country but also from the same locality of their homeland).

The long-term choice will be the "*nl*" strategy, that is, the residence of migrants surrounded by indigenous peoples of a developed country.

Thus, the Nash equilibrium for this dynamic game will depend on the communication organization of the developed country and migrants from underdeveloped countries.

We would like to emphasize that the case when the Nash equilibrium is "*nl®a®t*" strategy will be optimal for a developed country.

AN EXAMPLE OF CONSEQUENTIAL GENERAL TRAINING WHICH SHOULD SUCCESSFULLY DEVELOP MIGRANTS FOR SUCCESSFUL JOINT ACTIVITIES WITH THE GENERATION Z

So, consideration of the game-theoretic model of interaction between a developed country and migrants from undeveloped countries revealed the need for a developed country to conduct special events. Among such measures should be both the creation of conditions for the identification of migrants necessary for a developed country, and the presence of a sufficiently large number of general and special training.

The following is an example of a possible set of such tools that should accompany the inclusion of migrants in the life of a developed country. Features arising from the need for migrants to communicate with Generation Z in a developed country are examined in detail.

It is most convenient to use the results of education and training as tools to determine the level of inclusion of migrants in the life of a developed country. Each training or educational program must be accompanied by exams. This allows us to use them as a signaling process both about the true intentions of migrants and about their capabilities (Spence, 1973).

Let's define the training requirements for migrants.

Generation Z uses the country's domestic language. The new language words, the new generation Z slang uses as well. Generation Z relies on its communication on certain linguistic structures, which are a kind of markers of "friend – foe". In addition, regardless of the language of their country, generation Z uses the English language quite well (of course, also with the presence of slang). Migrants, at best, know the language of a developed country. Sometimes they also fragmentary know quite English. At the same time, the linguistic forms that migrants use are either archaic enough (gleaned from old school literature) or slang-oriented for specific groups of the population (with which migrants spoke in their homeland). Thus, the state needs to teach migrants of 1) the language of a given developed country, 2) the slang of generation Z of a developed country, and 3) the English language with the slang features of generation Z (which is used in this developed country).

Generation Z is quite well oriented in the lifestyle, culture, and traditions of their country. However, Generation Z has also formed its own distinct lifestyle, subculture, and traditions. Migrants know neither the first nor the second. Moreover, migrants are carriers of the lifestyle, culture, and traditions of their homeland. Therefore, they can quite aggressively perceive the lifestyle, culture, and traditions of a developed country, as well as the features inherent in generation Z. In some cases, there may even be an aggressive rejection of this. Thus, the state should organize rather specific training for migrants in the way of life, culture, and traditions, both traditional for a developed country and inherent in the Z generation.

The main danger for a developed country is that the vast majority of migrant habits lie in the field of extract (exclusive) institutions. While in a developed country, migrants must abandon a number of familiar behaviors in their former way of life and traditions. They must adopt a new lifestyle, culture, and traditions.

Finally, migrants must learn to obey the laws of a developed country. Moreover, a sufficiently large number of laws will contradict their usual behavior. The social signals given to them by the indigenous people will also often contradict the signals to which migrants are accustomed.

All this requires the implementation of sequential multi-stage training for migrants. Each of the stages is general training in the sense of Becker (1962, 1964).

Another important circumstance is that after each such training a part of migrants should be repatriated. That is, migrants who did not cope with the assimilation of lifestyle, culture, and traditions should be returned to their homeland. The state should not integrate migrants who will not be able to support their own existence. Also, the state should not integrate migrants who will destroy the social, social, economic and political institutions that make the country developed.

Probably one of the most effective may be such a sequence of actions of a developed state.

First stage: During this stage, migrants will learn the language of a developed country. The term of study should be limited by the time sufficient for training "from scratch". This training is provided that the migrant makes efforts that exceed the level established by the state. This can be determined on the basis of specially conducted experiments. Moreover, partly these data can be found from the results of existing courses in the study of foreign languages.

Example 1. An engineer from Ukraine migrated to Israel. Since Israel has a fairly large number of citizens who use the Russian language, he did not learn Hebrew. He had to work without knowledge of the official language in the working professionals, that is, his labor productivity for more than 20 years was lower than that of the indigenous population.

Example 2. A migrant family moved their country with English to a country with German. The youngest child began to attend kindergarten in a new country and began to communicate in German for six months. The oldest child went to elementary school. In order to adapt, he was seated for six months next to a child who knew his native language. This child translated teacher requirements for a migrant. The oldest child had significant problems understanding German. And only when he was transplanted to a student who spoke only German, the eldest child mastered German in a few months. This example of one family clearly shows the necessity and importance of placing a migrant in the environment of the indigenous population of a developed country. In the case of non-localized allocation of migrants, a developed country spends significantly fewer resources (time, finances, qualified teachers and trainers, etc.) than with localized allocation of migrants.

All migrants who do not pass the language proficiency test must be repatriated.

Note. What to do in case of separation is a separate consideration. However, it seems to the authors that the smallest unit for deciding on repatriation will be the family (wife, husband, and children who are not independent of school-age).

Second stage: It consists in the fact that migrants study the legislation and culture of a developed country (including a kind of "unwritten laws" of behavior in a developed country). Such training should also be given as general training. Law training should probably be carried out separately from cultural training. As part of the study of culture, the study of the "unwritten laws" of a developed country should also be singled out as a separate unit.

The results of such general training will show how ready a migrant is to live and work independently in a developed country. Testing should consist in the analysis of fairly standard situations of a legislative and cultural nature.

Farashah and Blomquist (2019) found that "For managers, migrants' commitment to the host country way of life is more important than their job skills, educational level, and language proficiency." Thus, knowledge of legislation and culture of a developed country (including a kind of "unwritten laws" of behavior in a developed country) gives migrants access to more skilled work (and, therefore, higher-paid). They will more effectively integrate into a developed society. As a result, such migrants will quickly return to society the resources spent on their training.

At this stage, a minimum limit should also be set for the points scored. Migrants who have not reached the minimum order must be repatriated.

Note. Here it will be interesting to find the correlation between the points scored in the first and second stages.

Third stage: During this stage general training provides on digital literacy. (At this point, general learning provides digital literacy.) Migrants will be trained in the use of digital technologies not only in their personal and public life but also in business. They will also teach communication between people (and between people and organizations) both over the Internet and using various gadgets and applications. Tests to determine the level of assimilation of information technology today are widespread and widely used.

It is at this stage that migrants will be trained in the rules and methods of communication with generation Z. Training migrants in the slang of generation Z at this stage will also be useful.

Those migrants whose test results are below a certain limit should be repatriated.

Fourth stage: Both general and special training in mastering given professional skills should be at this stage. The migrant has already learned the general rules of behavior in a developed society and therefore can focus on gaining professional skills. Here it is necessary to take into account the results of the first three stages. We can say that the professions offered to the migrant are the result of his tests on language skills, legislation, the culture of a developed country and digital literacy. A migrant should be offered a choice of the profession from about one level of difficulty from a finite list of professions.

The results of the final test should also have a minimum boundary. Migrants who have not reached the border must be repatriated. There should also be a collective responsibility at the family level. For example, their level of control over the level of motivation of children can be identified.

At this stage, the successes of children in kindergarten or school should also be taken into account. This allows us to assess the level of family education of migrants. For example, the level of their management of the motivation for children to live and work in a developed society must be taken into account.

The training provides opportunities for identifying extremists-minded people using psychological tests on the level of cognitive flexibility. These tests can be used at each stage, which will create a temporary profile for each migrant.

DISCUSSION AND OUTLOOK

Obtained results can serve as the basis for further economic modeling of various strategies of state migration policy. For example, the further development of the game-theoretic model will make it possible to evaluate both the state's costs for the adaptation of migrants and the state's income from their work. The state can implement different strategies for managing migration flows. The state can also use different policies for managing migrants in different regions of the country, as well as in different areas of business. Finally, the state can also make a forecast of long-term income from the next generations of migrants who will be studying already in a developed country. Moreover, within the framework of the developed model, technologies can be used to identify those migrants who may be dangerous for the indigenous population.

Important for the practical implementation of migration policy is that the work draws attention to the institutional differences between migrants and the indigenous population of a developed country. It seems to us that insufficient attention has been paid to this issue before. So, Artero and Chiodell (2019, p.19) concludes that "a certain level of ethnic and religious residential concentration could have positive effects in favoring the insertion of migrants in Italian cities and the self-organized fulðllment of certain needs that public authorities are not willing to satisfy (e.g., the increasing need for places of worship), in particular within the framework of the current, growing hostility and social tensions connected to religious diversity in Italy."

However, the question of the conformity of the developed country's institutions with those social, economic and political institutions that are characteristic of the migrants 'country of residence is usually not considered. At the same time, the institutions of undeveloped countries may be unacceptable to the indigenous inhabitants of developed countries. The study of such institutional discrepancies began relatively recently. Acemoglu and Robinson (2012) give a large number of examples when the mismatch of political and / or economic institutions significantly affected the level of development of the country. If there is such a difference in institutions within one country, and especially if it is localized on social groups that have linguistic and / or cultural differences, then in such a country there may be a tragic confrontation between two (or more) different groups population. For a developed country, this can be extremely negative.

The article does not address migrants from developed countries and migrants from undeveloped countries who are invited to study or teach at universities and doctoral programs. These people undergo special control before they start their studies or work. In addition, as a rule, they win the competition with indigenous peoples for this work. Illegal migrants who violate the law of a developed country are also not considered.

The results relate primarily to migrants from undeveloped countries. These migrants may be refugees fleeing war. They can also flee from poverty or natural disaster.

The key in the dynamic model is that the government gets rid of those migrants who do not want to participate in its economic life (work), that is, to increase the country's GDP. If such migrants are left in the country, they will not contribute to the GDP, and the country will spend it on providing the migrants with the necessary resources for life. This will lead to destabilization of the social state of society due to the growing level of dissatisfaction of the indigenous population.

As a rule, today Europe (for foreign migrants) and Ukraine (for internal migrants) do not have the effective mechanisms by which official migrants can be returned to the countries (or regions) from which they came.

The developed game-theoretic model allows us to solve the problem. Its implementation requires wide dissemination of information, both for migrants and the general public, about their proposals.

For example, from the outset, migrants should be made aware that they must make an effort, first, to adapt to life in a given society and, second, to learn those professions that are necessary for them to participate in the social and economic life of the developed country. The developed country should also inform migrants that it provides them with the opportunity to live in indigenous populations. It is also mandatory to inform migrants that they must comply with institutional requirements that are specific to indigenous people. At the same time, migrants should be informed that they must fulfill the requirements in the developed country both in legal and cultural spheres.

The localized residence of migrants leads to their isolation from indigenous society and, as a result, to the onset of conflict with indigenous habitats. Now, this is not between people (these conflicts are regulated by law), but between separate groups of people.

As a result, such conflicts turn into conflicts between cultures, and this type of conflict is the least tolerant and the most irreconcilable.

Examples of this are the constant riots and acts of mass disobedience of the law, which are becoming increasingly commonplace in developed countries. Most of these social outbreaks take place just where migrants are concentrated in areas of compact living. In fact, this is what leads to the geographical stratification of cultures.

The dynamic model developed above allows us to solve the problem of not only motivating migrants to participate in the economic life of the country but also to participate in public life in the conditions adopted in a developed society.

The latter is due to the fact that dispersed (localized) migration of migrants is more economically viable and stimulated by the state and society. For example, a career for dispersed migrants will be more successful.

Ramirez et al. (2018, p.5) provide extensive data on the characteristics of migrant integration, especially in developed countries. In particular, it was found that "migrants are, on average, more spatially concentrated than natives, especially in most metropolitan and capital-city regions... Regions with initially high levels of development and with larger communities of foreign-born seem to be more attractive for new migrants to settle... Migrants tend to live in regions where the regional unemployment rate is lower than the national average. At the same time, unemployed migrants are more spatially concentrated than their native-born peers... Migrants, and especially in EU countries, are more likely to be employed in most metropolitan regions than in other types of regions, but their gap in employment rates relative to the native-born population is higher in such regions".

As follows from the results of Ramirez et al. (2018), today in developed countries, migrants implement the "*l-na-nt*" strategy. As follows from the above analysis, this strategy can be called "go with the flow" for both the government of a developed country and migrants. Note that this strategy is the worst option for a developed country.

So, migrants are concentrated more in the metropolitan regions and their environs. However, in this region predominantly highly skilled workers are required, but migrants from undeveloped countries, as a rule, do not possess highly skill. As a result, predominantly jobs are available for them that require unskilled labor. And, accordingly, migrants receive low salaries (compared to most residents of the capital regions). Therefore, their standard of living contrasts quite sharply with the standard of living of the indigenous population. This is confirmed by the results of Ramirez et al. (2018, p.5): "Across all types of regions, migrants in Europe tend to be more likely to live in overcrowded dwellings and deprived housing conditions than natives". As a result, the level of dissatisfaction with life among migrants (especially among young people and children) will constantly increase. This is a breeding ground for manifestations of extremism and recruitment to terrorist organizations.

A developed state receives a fairly small contribution from migrants to GDP, since they are predominantly employed in low-productive, unskilled labor. Thus, the developed countries are increasingly faced with the task of changing the methods of working with migrants. A number of European countries, for example, increase quotas on the number of migrants from Ukraine (for example, in Poland, and in the Czech Republic), since these migrants are close in culture to European countries.

However, so far these are all half measures, as the number of migrants to developed countries from Asian and African countries is growing. These migrants are extremely different in their religious, cultural, legal and social norms from the inhabitants of developed countries. Given this, the forms of tolerance and political correctness inherent in developed countries are likely to be substantially revised. This is necessary to preserve the identity of the indigenous population of developed countries. It is also necessary to preserve inclusive institutions, the presence of which is crucial for every developed country.

Obtained results allow outlining possible approaches to the work of the government of developed countries with migrants.

Example. In recent years, governments of developed countries have begun to actively manage migration processes. Examples of the United States (especially illegal migration from Mexico) or the United Kingdom (influence on Brexit) are quite revealing. Of the latter: new migration incentives that allow the government to deny visas to women who intend to come to the US for childbirth. This indicates that in developed countries there is a growing understanding of the need to implement an active migration policy. Therefore, the results of this chapter can help governments develop new migration rules with predictable consequences.

CONCLUSION

The emergence in the economy of developed countries of an ever-growing number of migrants is a feature of the modern period. At the same time, Generation Z also comes into the economy, that is, young people whose childhood and youth have largely passed in the digital world. The latter circumstance requires new methods of organizing both communication and joint activities of representatives of generation Z and migrants.

The aim of this work is to develop methods of government migration policy in order to motivate migrants to joint economic activities, especially with Generation Z.

The goals of a developed state are to include migrants in social, political and economic institutions to increase the welfare of its citizens, both in the short and long term. Migrants who are not suitable for the realization of the interests of indigenous peoples should be repatriated (deported).

Migrants can run away from hostilities, they can run away from poverty.

The game-theoretic model built in the article made it possible to identify such fundamental features of the process of reconciling the interests of the state (government) and migrants.

First, the state (government) will receive the greatest benefit if the migrant is successfully integrated into society, receives training and becomes actively involved in the economic growth of the country. This will be the case for "*nl®a®t*" strategies when the state accepts a migrant who is already able to independently exist in the cultural and social environment of a developed country. This is due to the fact that the migrant is forced to live in a new culture (the choice of the "*nl*" strategy). In addition, the migrant makes efforts to actively adapt to new cultural, social, economic and political conditions (choice of strategy "*a*"). Finally, the migrant has mastered a profession that can provide him with an adequate standard of living (by choosing the "*t*" strategy).

Secondly, the state (government) should at all stages of decision-making by migrants to motivate them to choose those decisions that are necessary for the state.

To implement the motivation of migrants, the article offers an example of consistent general training that migrants must successfully develop for successful joint activities with Generation Z.

Unfortunately, extensive data on the characteristics of migrant integration, especially in developed countries, indicate that today migrants choose the most harmful strategy for the state, "*l®na®nt*". The state accepts a migrant who cannot independently exist in the cultural and social environment of a developed country. He/she remains a carrier of extractive economic, social, cultural and political institutions.

He/she is very fragmented in life in a developed country. This is due to the fact that the migrant is forced to live in an environment of home culture (choice of strategy "*l*"). In addition, this migrant did not make efforts to fully adapt to the conditions of a developed country (choosing the "*na*" strategy). The migrant does not have a profession that can provide him with an adequate standard of living (he chose the "*nt*" strategy).

As a result, the level of dissatisfaction with life among migrants (especially among young people and children) will constantly grow. This is a breeding ground for extremism and the recruitment of terrorist organizations. These migrants, as a rule, are extremely different in their religious, cultural, legal and social norms from the inhabitants of developed countries. Given this, the forms of tolerance and political correctness inherent in developed countries are likely to be substantially revised. This is necessary to preserve the identity of the indigenous population of developed countries. It is also necessary to preserve inclusive institutions, the presence of which is crucial for every developed country.

ACKNOWLEDGMENT

We thank Anatoliy Fisenko for improving our English. This research received no specific grant from any funding agency in the public, commercial, or not-for-profit sectors.

REFERENCES

Acemoglu, D., & Robinson, J. A. (2012). *Why Nations Fail: The Origins of Power, Prosperity, and Poverty*. Crown Publishers.

Artero, M., & Chiodell, F. (2019). Migration, Religion, and Residential Segregation at the Urban Level: The Case of Muslim Migrants in Rome and Milan. *Sociological Inquiry*, 1–24. doi:10.1111oin.12322

Becker, G. S. (1962). Investment in Human Capital: A Theoretical Analysis. *Journal of Political Economy*, *70*(5), 9–49. doi:10.1086/258724

Becker, G. S. (1964). *Human Capital: A Theoretical and Empirical Analysis*. Columbia University Press.

Farashah, A. D., & Blomquist, T. (2019). *Exploring employer attitude towards migrant workers. Evidence from managers across Europe*. Evidence-based HRM. doi:10.1108/EBHRM-04-2019-0040

Gibbons, R. (1992). *Game Theory for Applied Economists*. Princeton University Press.

Hallowell, M. R., & Yugar-Arias, I. F. (2016). Exploring fundamental causes of safety challenges faced by Hispanic construction workers in the US using photovoice. *Safety Science*, *82*, 199–211. doi:10.1016/j.ssci.2015.09.010

Jacquemet, M. (2015). Asylum and superdiversity: The search for denotational accuracy during asylum hearings. *Language & Communication*, *44*, 72–81. doi:10.1016/j.langcom.2014.10.016

Jerrima, J., Chmielewskib, A. K., & Parker, Ph. (2015). Socioeconomic inequality in access to high-status colleges: A cross-country comparison. *Research in Social Stratification and Mobility*, *42*, 20–32. doi:10.1016/j.rssm.2015.06.003

Kivisto, P., & La Vecchia-Mikkola, V. (2015). The integration of Iraqis in two European cities: Emotions and identity work. *Emotion, Space and Society*, *16*, 90–98. doi:10.1016/j.emospa.2015.01.002

Pérez, K. M., & Salgado, M. M. (2019). Mobility and the mobile: A study of adolescent migrants and their use of the mobile phone. *Mobile Media & Communication*, *8*(1), 104–123. doi:10.1177/2050157918824626

Peri, G., Romiti, A., & Rossi, M. (2015). Immigrants, Domestic Labor and Women's Retirement decisions. *Labour Economics*, *36*, 18–34. doi:10.1016/j.labeco.2015.07.004

Ramirez, M. D., Liebig, Th., Thoreau, C., & Veneri, P. (2018). *The Integration of Migrants in OECD Regions: A First Assessment.* OECD Regional Development Working Papers 2018/01. doi:10.1787/fb089d9a-en

Spence, M. (1973). Job Market Signaling. *The Quarterly Journal of Economics*, *87*(3), 355–374. doi:10.2307/1882010

Westerman, J. W., & Yamamura, J. H. (2007). Generational preferences for work environment fit: Effects on employee outcomes. *Career Development International*, *12*(2), 150–161. doi:10.1108/13620430710733631

Zmigrod, L., Rentfrow, P. J., & Robbins, T. W. (2019). Cognitive Inñexibility Predicts Extremist Attitudes. *Frontiers in Psychology*, *10*, 989. doi:10.3389/fpsyg.2019.00989 PMID:31133930

Zmigrod, L., Rentfrow, P. J., & Robbins, T. W. (2020). The Partisan Mind: Is Extreme Political Partisanship Related to Cognitive Inflexibility? *Journal of Experimental Psychology. General*, *149*(3), 407–418. doi:10.1037/xge0000661 PMID:31380695

KEY TERMS AND DEFINITIONS

Adaptation: Active actions of a person, which are aimed at reducing the differences in his behavior from that adopted in this social community (social layer, society, etc.).

General Training: The development of such knowledge, skills, and abilities of a person that can be applied in different conditions of his life.

Generation Z: The people born from the mid-late 1990s to 2012. They have virtually unlimited access to any information that interests them, live in a world where face-to-face communication between people is quite limited. They are able to perceive and process huge amounts of information of various kinds (visual, sound, text).

Indigenous Peoples: People who live in a developed country, are usually its citizens and are carriers of certain norms of behavior, culture, habits, knowledge, skills of social, economic, political life, characteristics of a developed country.

Localized Allocation: The conditions under which circle of contacts for migrants (at work, training or leisure) is predominantly also migrants. These may be living and working in territorial enclaves, social networks (when migrants are also neighbors), companies (where the personnel are mainly migrants), etc.

Migrants: People who are citizens of other countries who come to live and/or work (permanently or temporarily) in another country.

Non-Localized Allocation: Conditions when migrants live and work, when their circle of contacts (at work, training, or leisure) are mainly indigenous citizens of a developed country.

Socialization: The process of including a person as an integral part of a certain social community, which, as a rule, differs from a migrant in a number of characteristics (behavior, language, habits, attitude to law, etc.).

Chapter 3
How Does National Culture Influence Microfinance Institutions?
Evidence Based on Investigating 45 Countries

Zsuzsanna Banász
https://orcid.org/0000-0003-4609-9504
University of Pannonia, Hungary

Anikó Csepregi
https://orcid.org/0000-0002-0100-659X
University of Pannonia, Hungary

ABSTRACT

Many studies deal with the determinants of countries' culture or efficiency of microfinance institutions (MFIs). This chapter aims to fill the gap in the literature by analyzing the connection between national cultural features and indicators of countries' MFIs. The summary of analyses made regarding MFIs is followed by the national cultural dimensions, and how knowledge strategy could serve poverty reduction. Forty-five countries represent the subject of the research. Their statistics are available for both MFIs and national culture. Rank correlation and investigation of TOP5 countries show that the MFIs are successful in countries characterized by high levels of power distance, collectivistic, long-term-oriented and restraint culture. Based on these results, the chapter lists countries where MFIs could be successfully introduced based on their national cultural features and recommends certain knowledge strategies for effective operation. Finally, research directions as a continuation of this study are also presented.

DOI: 10.4018/978-1-7998-4543-0.ch003

INTRODUCTION

One of the segments of the collaborative economy is open knowledge (Palos-Sanchez & Correia, 2018) and the twenty-first centuries itself can be considered undoubtedly the century of knowledge (Jelenic, 2011). The connection the management of knowledge and national culture appeared to be a dividing question for a while for certain researchers (Ang & Massingham, 2007). However, the relevance of national culture itself and cultural differences have become more crucial nowadays especially for organizations operating in several countries, international markets or even having employees from different cultures. The idea of cultural differences being associated with differences in management cannot be considered new. It can be traced back to the 1950s, e.g. to the work of Morris (1956) who developed his analysis of dimensional human values to give a scientific basis to previous philosophical elaboration of human values. On the other hand, from another point of view, it is suggested that every culture distinguishes itself from others by the specific solutions it chooses to certain problems that reveal themselves as dilemmas (Trompenaars & Hampden-Turner, 2000). For most countries reducing poverty is a key strategic goal, and the methods of applied to this could depend on national culture and cultural differences as well. To help the operation and spread of microfinance institutions (MFIs) and the establishment of good conditions to manage knowledge, it is important to be aware of the roots and reasons for cultural differences.

The idea of founding MFI comes from Professor Muhammad Yunus. MFIs lend very small sums of money to extremely poor clients (billions of unbanked adults, who are unable to access traditional banking services) in order to provide financial assistance for starting their small-sized enterprises. He established the first MFI named The Grameen Bank in Bangladesh (India) in 1979. The vision of this bank type does not focus on achieving more and more profit instead it fights against poverty, as an altruistic mission (Balogh et al., 2013). Muhammad Yunus and the Grameen Bank won the Nobel Peace Prize in 2006 for their efforts to create economic and social development from below.

The World Bank classifies countries based on income into the following four categories: low-income economies, low-middle-income economies, upper-middle-income economies, and high-income economies. As a result, the classification of some countries has changed each year. Sumner (2012) argued that most poor no longer live in the low-income economies, but the middle-income countries. The basis income levels of this classification are modified by World Bank each year. World Bank's Poverty and Equity Database can serve as a quick snapshot of the severity of poverty affecting the world. This database contains 64 series (plus population data) about 169 countries and 16 aggregates (e.g. Europe & Central Asia, Sub-Saharan Africa) covering 45 years from 1974 to 2018 (World Bank, 2019). Appendix 1 (Table 6) shows the average annual change of the number of people and the percentage of the population, living on less than $1.90 or $3.20 a day in 2011 purchasing power parity (PPP). Years were observed from 2000 to 2018 and 2017 was the last year from which data was available. Appendix 1 contains only those countries for which data for both years (2000, 2017) were available. That means only 15 countries. For example, Hungary has not provided data on the examined poverty indicators since year 2016. Appendix 1 shows that the number and the percentage of population living on less than $1.90 or $3.20 follows decreasing trend in the examined 15 countries.

The objective of this chapter is to identify the national cultural types in which MFIs widespread. Based on this knowledge those countries could be listed which do not have MFIs yet, but where introducing it would be worth and this might need some kind of knowledge strategy.

The chapter can provide useful information on the one hand to practicing managers of MFIs concerning the potential countries where the expansion of their activity could be a success, or evaluate their managerial strategies applied previously. On the other hand, this study can help all debutant managers of small business because MFI promotes small business, so these institutions can be considered as one of the elements which support small business strategies' sustainability. Furthermore this chapter serves helpful insights for individuals, entrepreneurs and policymakers from countries with limited availability of financial resources and big share of poor population.

The chapter is structured as follows. First, the Background section summarizes the analyses made regarding MFIs, presents different models of national culture and national cultural dimensions of Hofstede, and demonstrates what knowledge strategy is and how it could serve poverty reduction. After presenting the research question the databases used for the examination are presented which is followed by the hypotheses the study aimed to examine. Not only descriptive statistics are introduced, but the methods and their results are also presented in the paper. Based on these results the paper contains recommendations and shows research directions to be followed in the future as a continuation of this study.

BACKGROUND

This section starts with previous studies on microfinance institutions (MFIs) that are aimed to reduce poverty. The next part is about national cultural peculiarities which can determine the efficiency of MFIs. This section ends with the importance of knowledge strategy that can help the operation of MFIs.

This paper aims to fill in the gap in the literature, i.e. analyzing the connection between MFIs and national cultural features.

Previous Analyzes on MFIs

The microfinance industry is considered complex and highly innovative, having the potential to expand the financial frontier to the poor in a sustainable manner (Kalyango, 2009; Littlefield et al., 2003). The thought behind MFIs is in line with social sustainability, but in the long term it is hard to provide microfinance institutions' financial sustainability because of the low profit they can achieve. (Hermes & Lensink, 2011). This problem can be reduced by the client's social networks (Wydick et al., 2011).

The main criticism of microfinance institutions highlights that over time these institutions also become profit-driven banks (Bruck, 2006). However, many studies confirm that this mission drift is not true (Rhyne, 1998; Christen & Drake, 2002; Mersland & Strom, 2010).

The efficiency and sustainability of microfinance institutions represent the focus of most research (Annim, 2010; Haq et al., 2010; Gutierrez-Neito et al, 2009; Nghiem, 2006; Robinson, 2001). These papers examine the impacts of microfinance institutions on reducing the number of poor. Typically considered variables related to microfinance institutions (e.g. their size, age, average loan size, profit, cost, assets) and microfinance institutions' clients (e.g. women/men, rural/urban, individual/group borrowers) have been collected by previous and recent analyzes. The conclusions of previous research results are mixed, e.g. related to gender issues a study result has shown that those MFIs are more efficient and more sustainable which have fewer women borrowers (Hermes et al., 2011), while another study revealed that higher number of women clients meant higher repayment for microfinance institutions (D'Espallier et al., 2011).

The previous researches dealing with MFIs could be grouped into two parts according to the number of studied countries. There are studies whose object is just one country, for example Latvia (Baldi & Sipilova, 2014; Baldi et al., 2014), India (Imai et. al, 2010); and there are studies which explore more countries, for example 39 MFIs across Africa, Asia and the Latin America (Haq et al., 2010), 350 MFIs of 70 countries (D'Espallier et al., 2011), 435 MFIs of the World (Hermes et al., 2011).

National Culture

The understanding and overcoming of the potential barriers and difficulties related to MFIs' operation that may appear due to the different backgrounds, approaches and national particularities are of high importance. In order to help the operation and spread of MFIs and the establishment of good conditions to manage knowledge, it is important to be aware of the roots and reasons for cultural differences. National cultural dimensions can have a significant effect on the organization itself, furthermore on knowledge sharing within organizations and outside the organization (Heidrich, 2002; Gaál et al., 2009).

In Table 1 six models of national cultures widely cited and utilized in management literature are presented. The Table includes the models proposed by Kluckhohn and Strodtbeck (1951, 1961), Hall (1977, 1981), Hofstede (1980, 2010), Adler (1991) and Trompenaars and Hampden-Turner (2002). Each of them can be useful in understanding some aspects of culture and highlight different aspects of societal beliefs, norms, and values. These models of national cultures can also be grouped into three categories defined by Morden (1999) being single dimension models, multiple dimension models, and historical-social models.

The authors selected Hofstede's dimensions to investigate the similarities and differences of the national culture of the examined countries in order to understand the different preferences related to the usage of MFIs in them. The reason why Hofstede's classification will be applied to the following research is that only his qualifications have accessible quantitative results, which can be the base of our calculation. Hofstede's work (1980), having been widely cited (Tung & Verbeke, 2010), represents a real milestone for the following several reasons (Pauluzzo & Cagnina, 2016):

- the empirical value of the initial study was unprecedented in its discipline, due to the use of the large dataset collected in the IBM branches of 40 countries.
- attention was switched from individual responses to ecological analysis, where participants were aggregated as societal units at the level of the country
- emphasis was put on the examination and application of differences in cultural values at the workplace.

Nonetheless, the approach has also received important critiques as it offers a rather simplistic and stereotypical interpretation of the values nourished by any culture (among others, Bird & Fang, 2009; Chevrier, 2009; Fang, 2003; Fang, 2005; Fang, 2006; Fang, 2012; Holden, 2002; McSweeney, 2015; Osland & Bird, 2000).

Hofstede (1980) set up a database by using a standardized questionnaire in order to describe culture at national, organizational and individual levels. Since 1985 the Hofstede Centre has collected more than 60000 questionnaires from 52 countries. Hofstede et al. (2010, p. 25) define culture as "the collective programming of the mind distinguishing the members of one group or category of people from others". Based on the database analysis six dimensions of national culture have been differentiated (Hofstede & Hofstede, 2001):

Table 1. The Feature of National Culture Models (based on Morden 1999 and Szabó et al., 2010)

Author(s)	Discipline	Models	National cultural dimensions
Kluckhohn (1951) Kluckhohn & Strodtbeck (1951, 1961)	anthropology	multiple dimension	relationship with nature relationship with people relationship with time human activities human nature
Hall (1977, 1981)	anthropology	single dimension	context (low vs. high) space (center of power vs. community) time (monochronic vs. polychronic) relationship (deal vs. relationship-focused)
Hofstede (1980) Hofstede et al. (2010)	organization science	multiple dimension	power distance (low vs. high) individualism vs. collectivism masculinity vs. femininity uncertainty avoidance (low vs. high) long-term orientation indulgence vs. restraint
Adler (1991)	organization science	multiple dimension	human nature relationship with nature individualist vs. collectivist human activity (being vs. doing) space (private vs. public) time (past vs. present vs. future)
House et al. (2001)	organization science	multiple dimension	uncertainty avoidance collectivism I: societal collectivism collectivism II: in-group collectivism gender egalitarianism assertiveness future orientation performance orientation humane orientation
Trompenaars & Hampden-Turner (2002)	organization science	multiple dimension	universalism vs. particularism individualism vs. communitarianism affective vs. neutral specific vs. diffuse achievement vs. ascription time orientation internal vs. external control

- Power distance expresses "the degree to which the less powerful members of a society accept and expect that power is distributed unequally" (Hofstede & Hofstede, 2001, p. 79). In countries of high-level power distance people accept a hierarchical order, in low level of power distance people except an equal distribution of power.
- Individualism refers to one's preference for such a social framework in which one is expected to take care of only oneself and one's immediate families. However, in collectivistic culture in exchange for unquestioning loyalty, one could expect the relatives or certain groups to look after them. This dimension expresses whether we live in an "I"- or a "We"-centered culture.
- Masculinity describes the most important values of a society. In high masculine culture achievement, heroism, assertiveness or material rewards for success have a preference. Its opposite, femininity stands for a preference for cooperation, modesty, caring for the weak and quality of life.

- Uncertainty avoidance dimension represents the degree to which the society members do not feel comfortable with uncertainty and ambiguity. This dimension shows whether or not society tries to control the future. Countries with high-level uncertainty avoidance have rigid rules and regulations for the society, and with low-level uncertainty avoidance relaxed attitude and practice over principles are preferred.
- Long term orientation refers to the time-orientation of society. Societies with low scores maintain their tradition and view significant societal changes with suspicion. High score cultures have a pragmatic approach by preparing for the future.
- Indulgence stands for a society allowing "relatively free gratification of basic and natural human drives related to enjoying life and having fun", while restraint societies suppress gratification of needs which are regulated by means of strict social norms. (Hofstede et al., 2010, p. 281).

Hofstede's (1980) initial work was followed by several replications, follow-up studies, and related research projects were also conducted, expanding the target populations and the number of countries investigated as well (Pauluzzo & Cagnina, 2016).

Knowledge Strategies

This section deals with the importance of knowledge strategy that can help the operation of MFIs in countries with different national cultural features. During the development and formulation of strategic goals, the determination of operational plans, and the development of the control system, the achievement of goals and objectives defined in the vision and mission need to be taken into consideration (Szabó & Csepregi, 2016). However, as it was mentioned earlier, the vision of MFIs does not focus on profit, instead, it has an altruistically aim. Thus the strategies of MFI do not necessarily respond to the regularities of typical business strategies. Strategic decision making is of high importance and crucial due to the characteristics of strategic decisions and the involvement of fundamental decisions shaping the course of an organization (Eisenhardt & Zbaracki, 1992; Papadakis & Barwise, 1998; Papadakis, 2006). Furthermore, at European and American organizations the contribution of strategic decision making to higher performance depends upon the way best practice adaptation relates to not only products and services, but also to processes and management operations (Bogan & English, 1994; Boxwell, 1994; Iacobucci & Nordhielm, 2000).

In the era of the knowledge-driven economy, the strategic management of knowledge has become a key factor in enabling organizations to reach sustainable competitive advantage (Winch & Schneider, 1993). Competitive advantage for organizations can be provided by relating knowledge management to the organizational strategies and objectives, and the learning experience of organizations should be used to build on their knowledge positions (Davenport et al., 1998; Zack, 1999). Successful knowledge management implementation requires the selection of a favorable knowledge strategy, which is a strategic issue (Bratianu & Orzea, 2013) for MFIs as well. However, no absolute consensus exists on what a knowledge strategy is (Denford & Chan, 2011; Donate & Canales, 2012) as the following descriptions of knowledge strategy demonstrate. According to von Krogh et al. (2001, p. 426) knowledge strategy is "the employment of knowledge processes to an existing or new knowledge domain in order to achieve strategic goals". On the other hand, Ibidunni et al. (2017, p. 3) consider it as "the engagement of strategic dimensions that develop from possible interactions of a firm's knowledge-based resources and capabilities in relation to its organizational strategy as a means of achieving and sustaining competitiveness."

However, knowledge strategy can also be described as the ability that secures a distinct perception apart from its competitors in the hearts of a company's customers (Abdollahi et al., 2008). By analyzing several notions, Bolisani and Bratianu (2018, pp. 3-4) have collected some core keywords representing the possible concept of knowledge strategy, which are:

- its objects are the knowledge or cognitive resources of a company,
- it relates to guidelines and to the practical application of processes,
- its ultimate goal is to achieve a strategic or competitive advantage,
- it develops adequate capabilities to process information and knowledge.

De Toni et al. (2011), based on their literature review, identified three primary knowledge strategies that are (1) knowledge development (internal vs. external), (2) knowledge sharing (codification vs. personalization) and (3) knowledge exploitation (internal vs. external).

Knowledge development focuses on the internal and external development (exploration) of knowledge which is related to the organization's primary sources of knowledge. Based on this, Zack (1999) divided organizations into provincial firms exploring internal knowledge resources, cosmopolitan firms exploring external knowledge resources and boundless firms that do not consider the boundaries of the firm when acquiring knowledge.

On the one hand, concerning knowledge sharing strategy related to codification strategy, knowledge is stored in databases and can be accessed and used by any organizational employees. On the other hand, personalization strategy knowledge is considered to be closely tied to the knowledge developed by employees and is shared through person-to-person interactions (Hansen et al., 1999). In order to use knowledge effectively, Hansen et al. (1999) propose an 80/20 knowledge strategy mix of codification and personalization strategy. In addition, by combining personalization strategy with internal knowledge development and codification strategy with external knowledge development greater business performance can be achieved by organizations (Choi et al, 2008).

Knowledge exploitation, based on the ways an organization can profit from knowledge, can be characterized by internal and external exploitation of knowledge (Beckett et al., 2000). During internal exploitation knowledge is developed and codified within the organization, while during external exploitation knowledge is sold outside the organization. The joint adaptation of external exploitation with internal exploitation is suggested by Lichtenthaler (2007), and concerning exploiting existing knowledge, McKenzie and Van Winkelen (2004) stress that it can bring short-term returns by efficiency improvement and cost reduction. Finally, comparing exploitation and exploration (development) March (1991) argued that exploitation contributes to short-term profit maximization, while exploration (development) can result in long-term success of organizations.

THE EXAMINATION OF MICROFINANCING AND NATIONAL CULTURE

Research Question, Database, Hypotheses

The study's goal is to find an answer to the following research question (Q): Does any dimension of Hofstede's national culture have an impact on any indicator related to the countries' microfinance institutions? This chapter does not focus on indicators used so far for the analysis in field of the microfinance institution but examines a new variable. It aims to fill in the gap of investigating microfinance institutions in selected countries regarding their similarities and differences in terms of their national cultural features.

Our data was collected from two online sources. The data about MFIs (MIX, 2019) cover five variables that are easily accessible on the website of a global organization named MIX: the number of financial service providers, their gross loan portfolio (USD), number of active borrowers, deposits (USD), number of depositors. Among them, the sum of the gross loan portfolio and the number of active borrowers can be a more important indicator than others. More specifically, the most relevant variable can be their rate, because larger countries can borrow more. For this reason a further indicator is calculated by the authors: the sum of gross loans divided by the number of active borrowers. Their database contains 99 countries (which do not contain data with the value of zero). The data related to the countries' national cultural dimensions derive from 'the Hofstede centre', where 103 countries' national cultural dimension scores can be found.

The authors have conducted on filtering taking into consideration both databases. 52 countries can be found in both statistics. Furthermore, those countries have been ignored where 'number of active borrowers' data as one of the most relevant variables was zero. As a result, 45 countries have been included in the sample for further analyses. These countries are the following (from six regions): Eastern Europe and Central Asia (Albania, Russia, Serbia, Turkey), East Asia and The Pacific (China, Fiji, Indonesia, Philippines, Vietnam), Africa (Angola, Burkina Faso, Ethiopia, Ghana, Kenya, Malawi, Mozambique, Nigeria, Senegal, Sierra Leone, South Africa, Tanzania, Zambia), Middle East and North Africa (Egyp, Iraq, Jordan, Lebanon, Morocco, Syria), Latin America and The Caribbean (Argentina, Brazil, Chile, Colombia, Costa Rica, Dominican Republic, Ecuador, El Salvador, Guatemala, Honduras, Mexico, Peru), South Asia (Bangladesh, India, Nepal, Pakistan, Sri Lanka). Table 2 lists the TOP5 countries in the case of each MFI indicator.

Table 2. TOP5 countries based on MFI indicators

	TOP				
	1	2	3	4	5
1. No. of MFIs	India	Mexico	Ecuador	Peru	Pakistan
	126.00	73.00	55.00	46.00	44.00
2. Gross Loan Portfolio (USD) bn	India	Peru	Bangladesh	Vietnam	Ecuador
	30.36	13.34	8.82	8.75	6.95
3. No. of Active Borrowers m	India	Bangladesh	Vietnam	Mexico	Pakistan
	37.75	21.25	7.50	7.40	7.11
4. Gross Loan Portfolio per No. of Active Borrowers (bn USD / m capita)	Russia	Kenya	Ecuador	China	El Salvador
	107.00	6.60	4.76	4.03	3.92
5. Deposits (USD) bn	Peru	India	Ecuador	Bangladesh	Colombia
	11.25	9.61	5.61	5.39	4.70
6. No. of Depositors m	Pakistan	Bangladesh	Vietnam	Colombia	Peru
	33.89	28.60	9.56	8.47	8.45

Out hypotheses concern the relationship between the success of MFIs and the dimensions of Hofstede's model of national culture. The success of MFIs are measured by the values of MFI data: the higher the value is the more successful MFIs are (higher number of MFIs, higher amount of their gross loan portfolio (USD), higher number of active borrowers, larger rate of the sum of loans per active borrowers, higher amount of deposits (USD) and higher number of depositors).

Hofstede's dimensions are measured with a scale of 0 to 100 (less than 50 score means relatively low value, greater than 50 score means relatively high value). The two categories within each national cultural dimension is divided based on the scores being under or above 50 as follows: power distance (low, high), individualism (collectivism, individualism), masculinity (feminity, masculinity), uncertainty avoidance (low, high), long term orientation (short term orientation, long term orientation), indulgence (restraint, indulgence).

Our hypotheses are the following:

- **H1:** The MFIs are successful in countries where Hofstede's power distance dimension is higher.
- **H2:** The MFIs are successful in countries where Hofstede's individualism dimension is lower (in the countries with collectivist culture).
- **H3:** The MFIs are successful in countries where Hofstede's masculinity dimension is lower (in feminine countries).
- **H4:** The MFIs are successful in countries where Hofstede's uncertainty avoidance dimension is higher.
- **H5:** The MFIs are successful in countries where Hofstede's long term orientation dimension is higher.
- **H6:** The MFIs are successful in countries where Hofstede's indulgence dimension is lower (in countries with restraint culture).

Hypotheses formulate our assumptions that MFIs are successful in developing countries where most of the population is poor. These underdeveloped countries can be described by strict hierarchical order (H1), rigid rules and regulations for the society (H4), even human rights are limited (H6). The H2 based on the fact, that loans provided by MFIs are given not only to individuals but more often to groups whose members take responsibility for each other. The reason why H3 does not contain masculine culture is that in feminine countries caring for each other, the weak and the poor is more important. According to H5 MFIs spread more in countries in which the population prepares for the future.

The next section summarizes the descriptive statistics on applied data then applied analyzes will be disclosed.

Descriptive Statistics, Relationship Analyzes

Table 3 shows some descriptive statistics of all (45) selected countries. (Table 7 in Appendix 2 contains MFIs' indicators by regions. The most country belongs to the region 'Africa' (13 countries), then 'Latin America and The Caribbean' (12 countries). Due to the low number of countries within a region, analyzes not interpreted in regions.) There are countries with only one MFI, but there is a country (India) where 126 MFIs can be found. Most of the active borrowers are also in India (37.75 million people). India has the largest gross loan portfolio (30.36 billion USD). Peru has the largest amount of deposits

(11.25 billion USD). The highest number of depositors is in Pakistan (33.89 million people). Russia has the largest value regarding the variable 'sum of loans per borrowers'.

The scores (1-100) of Hofstede's dimension were divided into two groups. One containing the number of countries having scores under 50, the other over the score of 50. The data shows that the sample contains countries characterized by rather high power distance, collectivism, femininity, low uncertainty avoidance, low long term orientation, and low indulgence (10 countries have no data about indulgence).

Table 3. Descriptive statistics of all (45) countries

MFIs' indicators (variables no. 1-6)				
	Min.	**Max.**	**Mean**	**Standard Deviation**
1. No. of MFIs	1.00	126.00 (India)	16.84	22.97
2. Gross Loan Portfolio (USD) bn	0.00	30.36 (India)	2.28	5.16
3. No. of Active Borrowers m	0.01	37.75 (India)	2.49	6.49
4. Gross Loan Portfolio per No. of Active Borrowers (bn USD / m capita)	0.00	11.25 (Russia)	1.45	2.62
5. Deposits (USD) bn	0.00	33.89 (Peru)	2.82	6.89
6. No. of Depositors m	0.00	107.00 (Pakistan)	3.73	15.80
Hofstede's dimensions (variables no. 7-12)				
	Number of countries with score			
	≤ 50		**> 50**	
7. Power Distance	3		42	
8. Individualism	44		1	
9. Masculinity	27		18	
10. Uncertainty Avoidance	27		18	
11. Long Term Orientation	18		27	
12. Indulgence	28		7	

The more relevant questions are the correlation between MFIs' indicators and Hofstede's dimensions. Because the latter can be measured ordinal scale at most, Table 4 shows the non-parametric bivariate correlations coefficients (Spearman's Rho values) and their significance. These rank correlations were based on the 45 countries named before.

Table 4. Correlation matrix (N = 45) – Spearman's Rho

			indicators of MFIs MFIs' indicators					
			1. No. of MFIs	2. Gross Loan Portfolio (USD) bn	3. No. of Active Borrowers m	4. Gross Loan per Active Borrowers	5. Deposits (USD) bn	6. No. of Depositors m
Hofstede's dimensions	7. Power Distance	Rho	.003	.008	-.106	.059	.061	.020
		Sig.	.983	.959	.486	.699	.700	.900
	8. Individualism	Rho	-.183	-.064	-.053	-.108	-.167	-.326*
		Sig.	.228	.674	.727	.478	.291	.033
	9. Masculinity	Rho	.095	.181	.244	-.017	.175	.101
		Sig.	.534	.234	.106	.914	.269	.520
	10. Uncertainty Avoidance	Rho	.095	.181	.244	-.017	.175	.101
		Sig.	.534	.234	.106	.914	.269	.520
	11. Long Term Orientation	Rho	.027	-.003	-.172	.288	-.232	-.274
		Sig.	.859	.985	.257	.055	.139	.076
	12. Indulgence	Rho	.054	.141	.046	.033	.185	.047
		Sig.	.760	.420	.791	.853	.302	.791

* Correlation is significant at the 0.05 level.

Table 4 marks only one significant rank correlations at the 0.05 level. It is tied to Hofstede's individualism dimension and the number of depositors. In relation to the causality, we assume that indicators of MFIs can't influence national culture, but the culture could affect MFIs. Based on this, the following statement can be made:

- Countries with higher (lower) individualism score, i.e. the more individualistic (collectivistic) the culture, less (more) number of depositors have a country's MFIs. Thus these negative relationships confirm the H2 hypothesis.

Other methods have been used to examine the remaining hypotheses. Therefore, further analysis has been refined by dividing Hofstede's 1-100 scores into two intervals as follows: 1-50: low, 51-100: high. On the other hand, the analysis focuses on only those countries which are the most successful considering their MFI values. Any of TOP5 economies of Table 2 can serve as good example to those countries that do not have MFI yet. That is the reason why these TOP5 countries - which cover overall 14 countries listed in Table 5 - are the objective of the following investigations. According to the frequency of these countries in Table 2 Bangladesh, Ecuador, India, and Peru can be qualified as the most successful country, because each of them appeared 4 times in Table 2. Table 5 marks the low or high nature of these 12 countries based on Hofstede's dimensions.

Table 5. The characteristics of TOP5 countries by low/high nature of Hofstede's dimensions

	Frequency in Table 2	Hofstede's dimensions: low or high											
		Power Distance		Individualism		Masculinity		Uncertainty Avoidance		Long Term Orientation		Indulgence	
		≤ 50	50 <	≤ 50	50 <	≤ 50	50 <	≤ 50	50 <	≤ 50	50 <	≤ 50	50 <
Bangladesh	4		x	x			x		x		x	x	
China	1		x	x			x		x	x			x
Colombia	2		x	x			x		x		x	x	
Ecuador	4		x	x			x		x		x		
El Salvador	1		x	x		x		x			x	x	
India	4		x	x			x		x	x			x
Kenya	1		x	x			x		x	x			
Mexico	2		x	x			x		x		x	x	
Pakistan	3		x	x		x		x	x		x	x	
Peru	4		x	x		x		x			x	x	
Russia	1		x	x		x		x			x		x
Vietnam	3		x	x		x		x		x			x
Σ	30	0	12	12	0	5	7	5	8	4	8	6	4
Mode	-	50 <		≤ 50		50 <		50 <		50 <		≤ 50	

Table 5 confirms the results of the previous rank correlation analysis regarding the individualism dimension. All of the 12 most successful countries have low individualism scores, i.e. overwhelmingly collectivist countries. This reinforces H2 hypothesis.

The theses below can be formulated related to the hypotheses:

- **T1:** The MFIs are successful in countries where Hofstede's power distance dimension is higher. (H1 is accepted.)

This statement is true in all 12 countries belonging to any TOP5 countries by MFI indicators (see Table 5), and 42 countries represent this in the 345 examined countries (see Table 3). (Only Costa Rica, South Africa, and Argentina are exceptions.)

- **T2:** The MFIs are successful in countries where Hofstede's individualism dimension is lower (in the countries with collectivist culture). (H2 is accepted.)

Based on the Spearman's Rho values of the rank correlation, this statement is valid for one MFI variable, for the number of depositors a country has (see Table 4). Moreover, all of the 12 TOP5 countries (see Table 5) and 44 out of the 45 researched countries (see Table 3) are characterized by collectivist culture. Only South Africa has an individualistic culture.

- **T3:** The success of MFIs is influenced by Hofstede's masculinity dimension, i.e. the masculine or feminine cultural feature of a country determines the success of MFIs. (H1 is accepted for 45 countries.)

Considering all 45 countries, there are more countries (27) with feminine culture, than masculine (18) (see Table 3). However, among the 12 TOP5 countries there are more (7) countries with masculine characteristics, than feminine (5) (see Table 5).

- **T4:** The MFIs are successful in countries where Hofstede's uncertainty avoidance dimension is higher. (H4 is accepted for 12 TOP5 countries.)

Considering all 45 countries, there are more countries (27) with lower uncertainty avoidance, than higher (18) (see Table 3). However, among the 12 TOP5 countries there are more (8) countries with higher uncertainty avoidance, than lower (5) (see Table 5).

- **T5:** The MFIs are successful in countries where Hofstede's long term orientation dimension is higher. (H5 is accepted.)

In all 45 countries there were more long term oriented culture (27) than short term oriented (18) ones (see Table 3), their frequencies among the 12TOP5 countries: 4 short term and 8 long term oriented culture (see Table 5).

- **T6:** The MFIs are successful in countries where Hofstede's indulgence dimension is lower (in countries with restraint culture). (H6 is accepted.)

There were 28 countries with restraint culture and 7 with indulgence culture (10 countries have no data about indulgence) in the 45 examined countries (see Table 3). Their frequencies among the 12 TOP5 countries: 6 restraint and 4 indulgence culture (see Table 5).

In summary, the Hofstede's dimensions that are typical in both 45 countries and in the TOP5: lower individualism and indulgence, higher power distance and long term orientation.

RECOMMENDATIONS

This section deals with the recommendation based on the results of the study. On the one hand, those countries are listed which were not investigated in the present study but where the authors believe MFIs could operate successfully in the future. On the other hand, the authors also recommend certain knowledge strategies that can be applied by MFIs having given national cultural peculiarities to be more effective.

Being aware of the study results the authors would recommend certain countries where the institutions of MFIs could be introduced and could operate successfully based on the following features: the country cannot be found among the 45 countries investigated in this chapter; the country can be characterized by Hofstede's 6 national cultural dimensions. Thus these countries could show similarities and match to the theses stated concerning the study.

According to theses 1, 2, 5 and 6 MFIs are successful in countries characterized by high power distance, collectivistic culture, having high level of long term orientation and having restraint culture. The countries fitting these features but not having any MFI data yet are Croatia, Hong Kong, Japan, Singapore, South Korea, and Taiwan. Thus the authors would recommend these countries to consider the introduction and operation of MFIs since based on their national cultural peculiarities these institutions could operate successfully.

In this section of the chapter, the authors recommend certain knowledge strategies being more effective in the cultural clusters the research revealed. The primary knowledge strategies considered in this case were identified by De Toni et al. (2011) based on literature review, and are (a) knowledge development (internal vs. external), (b) knowledge sharing (codification vs. personalization) and (c) knowledge exploitation (internal vs. external).

In cultures having a high level of uncertainty avoidance, when the organizations (as MFIs) use knowledge from outside the organization by following an external development knowledge strategy the relevant knowledge for operating MFIs can be collected. In organizations having collectivistic culture and following this knowledge strategy, this can result in fresh thinking and benchmarking knowledge for the organizational members (Szabó & Csepregi, 2016). On the other hand because of the restraint culture and high power distance the organizations expect from its employees to collect and use knowledge from outside the organization from clients, competitors, etc. in form of best practices for example.

Furthermore, in countries with collectivistic culture members of organizations rather relying on informal discussions and networking to store their insights, and share those (Desouza & Evaristo, 2003). Thus personalization knowledge strategy could be applied by MFIs to share their knowledge within the organization with each other. Thus MFI employees can work together better and work out better ways to reach their present and possible future clients with their services. However the rigid rules of the society, because of being characterized by a high level of uncertainty avoidance, power distance, and restraint culture, can also influence the way knowledge should be shared in MFIs. In this case by ordering the storage of knowledge (client information, best practices, etc.) in databases, codification strategy could be applied to avoid uncertainty of losing it.

Finally in a collectivistic culture where the group work is stressed the culture enables working in teams and also group learning fostering the application of internal exploitation knowledge strategy where knowledge is developed within the organization (Szabó & Csepregi, 2016). Furthermore, depending on the regulations determined related to high level of uncertainty avoidance, high power distance and restraint culture, knowledge could be also codified within the organization.

MFI's knowledge strategies might show similarities and differences regarding their connection to their clients compared to the knowledge strategies applied only within the organization.

Because of having a collectivistic culture, being characterized by high level of uncertainty avoidance MFIs need knowledge from their clients outside the organization to be able to provide the best service fitting their clients and to maintain and improve their operation. Thus an external development knowledge strategy might be advised for MFIs. In addition, the leaders of MFIs expect their employees keeping in touch with the clients to gather the required knowledge from their clients as well.

Having a collectivistic culture can result in sharing knowledge much openly with clients and to avoid uncertainty. This kind of informal discussion can favor the application of a personalization knowledge strategy. On the other hand, high level of power distance and the restraint feature of the culture can result in the application of codification knowledge strategy in certain situations, since this way the knowledge controlled could be shared with clients.

Finally, external exploitation knowledge strategy could also be used by MFIs towards their clients in countries with a high level of uncertainty avoidance, high power distance, collectivistic and restraint culture. Based on this strategy they can propagate their knowledge outside the organization and they could extend their client base.

FUTURE RESEARCH DIRECTIONS

As a continuation of this study, several possible future research directions could be mentioned that are presented in this section.

This chapter only contains a filtered database (45 countries) however in the continuation of this study the countries missing from this study, because of the filtering used, could also be taken into consideration. Thus in the future, the whole database containing 99 countries could be investigated. This would allow the usage of other quantitative methods and not only those presented in this chapter. These methods could be one-way ANOVA, regression analysis, dimension reduction methods like cluster analysis, principal component analysis, and factor analysis.

A research model of the influencing factors affecting the success and successful operation of MFIs and their knowledge strategies could also be depicted. This multivariate model could contain not only national culture as an influencing factor but also other factors related to knowledge management and business strategy. The relevant variables of national cultural dimensions could be built into the existing models which measure the efficiency and/or sustainability of MFIs. Furthermore, the relationship of MFIs, knowledge strategies and collaborative economy could also appear on the model and be investigated. The countries could also be grouped based on various categorization (regionally, having similarities concerning national cultural features, etc.), and these country groups could be modeled and analyzed further.

A way of the study augmentation could be the cross-studying of MFI development within other countries' classification. This can be useful to specify the mechanisms and how cultural factors can influence MFI development.

In addition, instead of analyzing several countries together, countries individually could be chosen and investigated separately. This would provide the possibility to find country-specific results and focusing more on the MFIs operating in the given country. In this case, other variables could also be taken into consideration and thus a model could be created containing those influencing factors that affect the success and successful operation of MFIs and the knowledge strategies used by them.

Besides quantitative methods, qualitative methods could also be used (e.g. case studies, interviews, with MFI managers, employees, making a survey to find out the knowledge of current and potential MFI clients about MFIs). The successful application of knowledge strategy in practice for managing microfinancing depending on peculiarities of national culture could be explored only through case studies.

Regarding the application of knowledge strategies in MFIs company-specific investigation could also be used by focusing only on one company. As a result of this investigation, interviews could be conducted, case studies could be written, and best practices of MFI operation, their business strategies, knowledge strategies, their relationship and communication within the organization, outside the organization with clients could be collected. These could provide information and knowledge for researchers and practitioners investigating or working in these kinds of companies.

Based on these future research directions the following research questions could be answered by future research studies:

- How can the development, efficiency, successful operation or sustainability of MFIs be described and measured better and in more detail than current models?
- Which mechanisms can specify the development of MFIs?
- Which factors can influence the operation of MFIs besides national cultural dimensions?
- How are MFIs and their knowledge strategies connected to the collaborative economy and is there any multidirectional relationship between them?
- Which factors can affect the knowledge strategies of MFIs, the relationship between MFIs, the communication with the organization and outside the organizations?
- Is there any difference regarding the success and successful operation of MFIs from the viewpoint of MFI managers, MFI employees, and MFI clients?

These research questions could help the work of researchers investigating this topic in the future.

CONCLUSION

Reducing poverty is one of the biggest problems nowadays causes one of the biggest headaches for many economists and sociologists. MFIs aim at resolving or at least mitigating this very complex current social and economic problem. The mission of these institutions does not contain profit-oriented approach, instead universal and humanitarian aspects are validated.

Models exist to analyze the efficiency and sustainability of MFIs. Furthermore, the typically considered variables of these models are related to microfinance institutions (e.g. their size, age, average loan size, profit, cost, assets) and microfinance institutions' clients (e.g. women/men, rural/urban, individual/group borrowers). On the other hand, these models do not deal with national cultural-specific factors. However, to help the operation and spread of MFIs and to foster good conditions to manage knowledge and establish a successful knowledge strategy, being aware of the roots and reasons of cultural differences is of high importance. The purpose of the authors was to fill in this gap in the literature.

The authors selected Hofstede's (2001) dimensions of national culture to investigate their similarities and differences in order to understand the different preferences related to the usage of MFIs in them. Taking into consideration the various national cultural features of MFIs in different countries, three primary knowledge strategies identified by de Toni et al. (2011) were chosen and examined to help the operation of MFIs.

The study's goal presented here in this chapter was to find the answer to the following question: Does any dimension of Hofstede's national culture have an impact on any indicator related to the countries' microfinance institutions? Thus 45 countries the data of which were available for both MFIs and national culture were examined. Rank correlation and the investigation of 12 TOP5 MFI countries showed that the MFIs are successful in countries characterized by high level of power distance and long term orientation, and low level of individualism and indulgence. Accordingly, the chapter suggests the application of certain knowledge strategies being more effective in these cultural clusters. Furthermore, 6 countries have been identified that do not have MFIs (their data are missing in MIX database) yet, but it could be successful (i.e. these countries have higher power distance and long term orientation beside lower individualism and indulgence): Croatia, Hong Kong, Japan, Singapore, South Korea and Taiwan. Thus the authors would recommend these countries to consider the introduction of MFIs in the future.

Finally, as a continuation of this study several possible future research directions were also introduced at the end of the chapter.

REFERENCES

Abdollahi, A., Rezaeian, A., & Mohseni, M. (2008). Knowledge strategy: Linking knowledge resources to competitive strategy. *World Applied Sciences Journal*, *4*, 8–11.

Adler, N. J. (1991). *International Dimensions of Organizational Behavior* (2nd ed.). PWS-Kent Publishing Co.

Ang, Z., & Massingham, P. (2007). National culture and the standardization versus adaptation of knowledge management. *Journal of Knowledge Management*, *11*(2), 5–21. doi:10.1108/13673270710738889

Annim, S. K. (2010). *Microfinance efficiency trade-offs and complementarities.* BWPI Working Paper 127. Brooks World Poverty Institute, University of Manchester.

Baldi, G., Sadovskis, V., & Šipilova, V. (2014). Economic and Employment Effects of Microloans in a Transition Country. *Folia Pomeranae Universitatis Technologiae Stetinensis, seria Oeconomica*, *2014*(4), 5–26.

Baldi, G., & Šipilova, V. (2014). How big are the employment effects of microloans? Evidence from a case study in Latvia. *Theoretical and Practical Research in Economic Field*, *5*(1), 17–31.

Balogh, L., Gál, V., Parádi-Dolgos, A., & Sipiczki, Z. (2013). Kulcs egy alternatív mikrofinanszírozási modell sikeréhez. *Acta Scientiarum Socialium*, *16*(38), 153–161.

Beckett, A. J., Wainwright, C. E. R., & Bance, D. (2000). Knowledge management: Strategy or software? *Management Decision*, *38*(9), 601–606. doi:10.1108/00251740010357221

Bird, A., & Fang, T. (2009). Cross cultural management in the age of globalization. *International Journal of Cross Cultural Management*, *9*(2), 139–143. doi:10.1177/1470595809335713

Bogan, C. E., & English, M. J. (1994). *Benchmarking for Best Practices: Winning Through Innovative Adaptation*. McGraw-Hill.

Bolisani, E., & Bratianu, C. (2018). Knowledge strategies. In E. Bolisani & C. Bratianu (Eds.), *Emergent knowledge strategies: Strategic thinking in knowledge management* (pp. 97–116). Springer International Publishing. doi:10.1007/978-3-319-60657-6_5

Boxwell, R. J. (1994). *Benchmarking for Competitive Advantage*. McGraw-Hill.

Bratianu, C., & Orzea, I. (2013). Knowledge strategies in using social networks. *Management Dynamics in the Knowledge Economy*, *1*(1), 25–38.

Bruck, C. (2006). Millions for millions. *The New Yorker*. Retrieved June 12, 2016, from https://www.newyorker.com/magazine/2006/10/30/millions-for-millions

Chevrier, S. (2009). Is national culture still relevant to management in a global context? The case of Switzerland. *International Journal of Cross Cultural Management*, *9*(2), 169–184. doi:10.1177/1470595809335723

Choi, B., Poon, S. K., & Davis, J. G. (2008). Effects of knowledge management strategy on organizational performance: A complementarity theory-based approach. *Omega: The International Journal of Management Science*, *36*(2), 235–251. doi:10.1016/j.omega.2006.06.007

Christen, R., & Drake, D. (2002). Commercialization. The new reality of microfinance. In D. Drake, & E. Rhyne (Eds.), The commercialization of microfinance balancing business and development (pp. 2-22). Bloomfield: Kumarian Press.

D'Espallier, B., Guérin, I., & Mersland, R. (2011). Women and Repayment in Microfinance: A Global Analysis. *World Development*, *39*(5), 758–772. doi:10.1016/j.worlddev.2010.10.008

Davenport, T. H., & Prusak, L. (1998). *Working Knowledge: How Organizations Manage What They Know*. Harvard Business School Press.

De Toni, A. F., Nonino, F., & Pivetta, M. (2011). A model for assessing the coherence of companies' knowledge strategy. *Knowledge Management Research and Practice*, *9*(4), 327–341. doi:10.1057/kmrp.2011.36

Denford, J. S., & Chan, Y. E. (2011). Knowledge strategy typologies: Defining dimensions and relationships. *Knowledge Management Research and Practice*, *9*(2), 102–119. doi:10.1057/kmrp.2011.7

Desouza, K., & Evaristo, R. (2003). Global Knowledge Management Strategies. *European Management Journal*, *21*(1), 62–67. doi:10.1016/S0263-2373(02)00152-4

Donate, M. J., & Canales, J. I. (2012). A new approach to the concept of knowledge strategy. *Journal of Knowledge Management*, *16*(1), 22–44. doi:10.1108/13673271211198927

Eisenhardt, K. M., & Zbaracki, M. J. (1992). Strategic decision making. *Strategic Management Journal*, *13*(S2), 17–37. doi:10.1002mj.4250130904

Fang, T. (2003). A critique of Hofstede's fifth national culture dimension. *International Journal of Cross Cultural Management*, *3*(3), 347–368. doi:10.1177/1470595803003003006

Fang, T. (2005). From 'onion' to 'ocean': Paradox and change in national cultures. *International Studies of Management & Organization*, *35*(4), 71–90. doi:10.1080/00208825.2005.11043743

Fang, T. (2006). Negotiation: The Chinese style. *Journal of Business and Industrial Marketing*, *21*(1), 50–60. doi:10.1108/08858620610643175

Fang, T. (2012). Yin Yang: A new perspective on culture. *Management and Organization Review*, *8*(1), 1–26. doi:10.1111/j.1740-8784.2011.00221.x

Gaál, Z., Szabó, L., Kovács, Z., Obermayer-Kovács, N., & Csepregi, A. (2009). Consequence of Cultural Capital in Connection with Competitiveness. *International Journal of Knowledge. Culture and Change Management*, *8*(10), 79–90.

Gutierrez-Neito, B., Serrano-Cinca, C., & Mar Molinero, C. (2007). Microfinance institutions and efficiency. *International Journal of Management Sciences*, *35*(2), 131–142.

Hall, E. T. (1977). *Beyond Culture*. Doubleday. Anchor Press.

Hall, E. T. (1981). *The Silent Language*. Anchor Press.

Hansen, M. T., Nohria, N., & Tierney, T. (1999). What's your strategy for managing knowledge? *Harvard Business Review*, *77*(2), 106–116. PMID:10387767

Haq, M., Skully, M., & Pathan, S. (2010). Efficiency of microfinance institutions: A data envelopment analysis. *Asia-Pacific Financial Markets*, *17*(1), 63–97. doi:10.100710690-009-9103-7

Heidrich, B. (2002). Business as Unusual the Role of National Cultural Back-ground in Corporate Life. *European Integration Studies*, *1*(2), 25–36.

Hermes, N., & Lensink, R. (2011). Microfinance: Its Impact, Outreach, and Sustainability. *World Development*, *39*(6), 875–881. doi:10.1016/j.worlddev.2009.10.021

Hermes, N., Lensink, R., & Meesters, A. (2011). Outreach and Efficiency of Microfinance Institutions. *World Development*, *39*(6), 938–948. doi:10.1016/j.worlddev.2009.10.018

Hofstede, G. (1980). *Cultures's consequences: International differences in work-related values*. Sage.

Hofstede, G., Hosfstede, G. J., & Minkov, M. (2010). *Cultures and Organizations: Software of the Mind*. McGraw-Hill.

Hofstede, G. H., & Hofstede, G. (2001). *Culture's Consequences: Comparing Values, Behaviors, Institutions, and Organizations Across Nations* (2nd ed.). Sage Publications.

Holden, N. J. (2002). *Cross-cultural management: a knowledge management perspective*. Harlow, UK: Financial Times/Prentice Hall.

Iacobucci, D., & Nordhielm, C. (2000). Creative Benchmarking. *Harvard Business Review*, (November-December), 24–25.

Ibidunni, A. S., Ogunnaike, O. O., & Abiodun, A. J. (2017). Extending the knowledge strategy concept: Linking organizational knowledge with strategic orientations. *Academy of Strategic Management Journal, 16*(3), 1-11.

Imai, K. S., Arun, T., & Annim, S. K. (2010). Microfinance and Household Poverty Reduction: New Evidence from India. *World Development*, *38*(12), 1760–1774. doi:10.1016/j.worlddev.2010.04.006

Jelenic, D. (2011). The importance of knowledge management in Organizations - With emphasis on the balanced scorecard learning and growth Perspective. *Proceedings of the Management, Knowledge and Learning International Conference, 2011*, 33–43.

Kalyango, D. L. (2009, December). *Uganda's experience with tiered banking regulation*. Paper presented at the Tiered Banking Workshop, Kampala, Uganda. Retrieved June 12, 2016, from http://www.finmark.org.za/sites//wp-content/uploads/pubs/Paper_Kalyango_tiered_04.pdf

Kluckhohn, C. K. (1951). Values and Value Orientations in the Theory of Action. In T. Parsons & E. A. Shils (Eds.), *Toward a General Theory of Action* (pp. 388–433). Harvard University Press. doi:10.4159/harvard.9780674863507.c8

Kluckhohn, F. R., & Strodtbeck, F. L. (1961). *Variations in Value Orientations*. HarperCollins.

Lichtenthaler, U. (2007). Hierarchical strategy and strategic fit in the keep-or-sell decision. *Management Decision*, *45*(3), 340–359. doi:10.1108/00251740710744990

Littlefield, E., Morduch, J., & Hashemi, S. (2003). Is microfinance an effective strategy to reach the millennium development goals? *Focus Note*. Retrieved June 12, 2016, from https://www.cgap.org/sites/default/files/CGAP-Focus-Note-Is-Microfinance-an-Effective-Strategy-to-Reach-the-Millennium-Development-Goals-Jan-2003.pdf

March, J. G. (1991). Exploration and exploitation in organizational learning. *Organization Science*, *2*(1), 71–87. doi:10.1287/orsc.2.1.71

McKenzie, J., & Van Winkelen, C. (2004). *Understanding the knowledgeable organization: Nurturing knowledge competence*. Thomson.

McSweeney, B. (2015). Hall, Hofstede, Huntington, Trompenaars, GLOBE: Common foundations, common flaws. In Y. Sánchez & C. F. Brühwiler (Eds.), *Transculturalism and Business in the BRIC States: A Handbook* (pp. 13–58). Gower Punlishing.

Mersland, R., & Storm, R. O. (2010). Microfinance Mission Drift? *World Development*, *38*(1), 28–36. doi:10.1016/j.worlddev.2009.05.006

MIX. (2019). *Countries & Regions Database*. Retrieved November 05, 2019 from https://www.themix.org/mixmarket/countries-regions

Morden, T. (1999). Models of national culture: A management review. *Cross Cultural Management*, *6*(1), 19–44. doi:10.1108/13527609910796915

Morris, C. (1956). *Varieties of Human Value*. University of Chicago Press. doi:10.1037/10819-000

Nghiem, H., Coelli, T., & Rao, D. S. P. (2006). The efficiency of microfinance in Vietnam: Evidence from NGO schemes in the north and the central regions. *International Journal of Environmental, Cultural, Economic and Social Sustainability*, *2*(5), 71–78. doi:10.18848/1832-2077/CGP/v02i05/54258

Osland, J. S., & Bird, A. (2000). Beyond sophisticated stereotyping: Cross-cultural sensemaking in context. *The Academy of Management Executive*, *14*(1), 1–12. doi:10.5465/ame.2000.2909840

Palos-Sanchez, P. R., & Correia, M. B. (2018). The collaborative economy based analysis of demand: Study of airbnb case in Spain and Portugal. *Journal of Theoretical and Applied Electronic Commerce Research*, *13*(3), 85–98. doi:10.4067/S0718-18762018000300105

Papadakis, V. (2006). Do CEOs shape the process of making strategic decisions? Evidence from Greece. *Management Decision*, *44*(3), 367–394. doi:10.1108/00251740610656269

Papadakis, V., & Barwise, P. (1998). *Strategic Decisions*. Kluwer Academic Publishers. doi:10.1007/978-1-4615-6195-8

Pauluzzo, R., & Cagnina, M. R. (2016). Cultural dynamics and their impact on knowledge and organizational strategies of multinational corporations. In *Proceedings 11th International Forum on Knowledge Asset Dynamics - Towards a New Architecture of Knowledge: Big Data, Culture and Creativity.* (pp. 1297-1309). Dresden University of Technology.

Rhyne, E. (1998). The Yin and Yang of microfinance. Reaching the poor and sustainability. *MicroBanking Bulletin*, *2*(1), 6–9.

Robinson, M. S. (2001). *The Microfinance Revolution. Sustainable Finance for the Poor*. World Bank., doi:10.1596/0-8213-4524-9

Sumner, A. (2012). Where do the poor live? *World Development*, *40*(5), 865–877. doi:10.1016/j.worlddev.2011.09.007

Szabó, L., & Csepregi, A. (2016). Strategic management tools and techniques: the cultural influence. In *Proceedings 11th International Forum on Knowledge Asset Dynamics - Towards a New Architecture of Knowledge: Big Data, Culture and Creativity*. (pp. 178-193) Dresden University of Technology.

Trompenaars, F., & Hampden-Turner, C. (2002). *Riding the waves of culture: Understanding diversity in global business*. Nicholas Brealey Publishing.

Tung, R. L., & Verbeke, A. (2010). Beyond Hofstede and GLOBE: Improving the quality of cross-national research. *Journal of International Business Studies*, *41*(8), 1259–1274. doi:10.1057/jibs.2010.41

Von Krogh, G., Nonaka, I., & Aben, M. (2001). Making the most of your company's knowledge: A strategic framework. *Long Range Planning*, *4*(4), 421–439. doi:10.1016/S0024-6301(01)00059-0

Winch, G., & Schneider, E. (1993). Managing the knowledge-based organization: The case of architectural practice. *Journal of Management Studies*, *30*(6), 923–937. doi:10.1111/j.1467-6486.1993.tb00472.x

World Bank. (2019). *Poverty and Equity Database*. Retrieved November 05, 2019, from http://databank.worldbank.org/data/reports.aspx?source=poverty-and-equity-database#

Wydick, B., Karp, H., & Hilliker, S. (2011). Social networks, neighborhood effects and credit access. *World Development*, *39*(6), 974–982. doi:10.1016/j.worlddev.2009.10.015

Zack, M. H. (1999). Developing a knowledge strategy. *California Management Review*, *41*(3), 125–145. doi:10.2307/41166000

KEY TERMS AND DEFINITIONS

Cultural Dimensions: The number of cultural peculiarities characterizing the population of a nation.

Knowledge Strategy: Knowledge applied to the achievement of strategic goals.

Microfinance Institutions: Institutions lending very small sums of money to extremely poor clients being unbanked adults, who are unable to access traditional banking services.

National Culture: Norms, behaviors, and beliefs followed by the maturity of the population of a given nation.

Poverty: Population living on less than a certain budget a day.

Success of MFIs: The values of MFI data measured. The higher the value is, the more successful MFIs are.

TOP5 Countries: 14 countries belonging to the 5 most successful countries by any of the six examined MFI indicators.

APPENDIX 1

Table 6. Average annual change of some poverty indicator on countries for which data are available both 2000 and 2017 (Based on Data source: World Bank, 2019)

	Number of the people in million	Percentage of the population	Number of the people in million	Percentage of the population
	living on less than			
	$1.90		$3.20	
	a day at 2011 PPP			
Indonesia	-3.994	-1.976	-3.094	-5.712
Colombia	-0.276	-0.735	-1.171	-0.418
Ecuador	-0.182	-1.471	-2.424	-0.288
Peru	-0.182	-0.759	-1.218	-0.282
Kyrgyz Republic	-0.118	-2.388	-3.412	-0.153
Bolivia	-0.106	-1.341	-1.741	-0.129
Argentina	-0.100	-0.306	-0.600	-0.188
Thailand	-0.094	-0.147	-1.065	-0.671
Moldova	-0.076	-2.094	-3.959	-0.147
Belarus	-0.041	-0.418	-1.600	-0.159
Georgia	-0.041	-0.847	-1.676	-0.082
Chile	-0.035	-0.218	-0.624	-0.094
El Salvador	-0.035	-0.606	-0.912	-0.053
Panama	-0.018	-0.582	-0.818	-0.018
Costa Rica	-0.018	-0.324	-0.647	-0.024

APPENDIX 2

Table 7. Descriptive statistics of MFIs' indicators (variables no. 1-6) (Based on Data source: MIX, 2019)

	Regio	N	Min.	Max.	Mean	Std.Dev.
1. No. of MFIs	all	45	1.00	126.00	16.84	22.97
	AFRICA	13	1.00	27.00	8.23	7.52
	EAST ASIA AND THE PACIFIC	5	1.00	30.00	15.20	13.37
	EASTERN EUROPE AND CENTRAL ASIA	4	1.00	22.00	6.75	10.18
	LATIN AMERICA AND THE CARIBBEAN	12	3.00	73.00	25.42	21.46
	MIDDLE EAST AND NORTH AFRICA	6	1.00	6.00	3.67	1.97
	SOUTH ASIA	5	4.00	126.00	44.20	48.44
2. Gross Loan Portfolio (USD) bn	all	45	0.00	30.36	2.28	5.16
	AFRICA	13	0.01	3.10	0.58	1.09
	EAST ASIA AND THE PACIFIC	5	0.00	8.75	2.34	3.64
	EASTERN EUROPE AND CENTRAL ASIA	4	0.02	1.07	0.32	0.50
	LATIN AMERICA AND THE CARIBBEAN	12	0.03	13.34	3.23	4.01
	MIDDLE EAST AND NORTH AFRICA	6	0.02	0.63	0.21	0.22
	SOUTH ASIA	5	0.47	30.36	8.44	12.72
3. No. of Active Borrowers m	all	45	0.01	37.75	2.49	6.49
	AFRICA	13	0.02	1.96	0.30	0.52
	EAST ASIA AND THE PACIFIC	5	0.01	7.50	3.06	3.24
	EASTERN EUROPE AND CENTRAL ASIA	4	0.01	0.07	0.04	0.03
	LATIN AMERICA AND THE CARIBBEAN	12	0.03	7.40	1.91	2.41
	MIDDLE EAST AND NORTH AFRICA	6	0.06	1.05	0.33	0.39
	SOUTH ASIA	5	0.32	37.75	13.55	15.90
4. Gross Loan Portfolio per No. of Active Borrowers (bn USD / m capita)	all	42	0.00	11.25	1.45	2.62
	AFRICA	13	0.20	6.60	1.34	1.72
	EAST ASIA AND THE PACIFIC	5	0.00	4.03	1.12	1.69
	EASTERN EUROPE AND CENTRAL ASIA	4	0.40	107.00	27.73	52.85
	LATIN AMERICA AND THE CARIBBEAN	12	0.66	4.76	2.05	1.31
	MIDDLE EAST AND NORTH AFRICA	6	0.18	2.00	0.96	0.69
	SOUTH ASIA	5	0.27	1.47	0.69	0.48
5. Deposits (USD) bn	all	43	0.00	33.89	2.82	6.89
	AFRICA	11	0.00	4.52	1.08	1.60
	EAST ASIA AND THE PACIFIC	5	0.00	4.37	1.08	1.88
	EASTERN EUROPE AND CENTRAL ASIA	3	0.00	0.93	0.34	0.52
	LATIN AMERICA AND THE CARIBBEAN	12	0.00	11.25	2.11	3.49
	MIDDLE EAST AND NORTH AFRICA	6	0.00	0.02	0.00	0.01
	SOUTH ASIA	5	0.35	9.61	3.48	4.00
6. No. of Depositors m	all	45	0.00	107.00	3.73	15.80
	AFRICA	12	0.00	6.56	1.10	1.81
	EAST ASIA AND THE PACIFIC	5	0.00	9.56	3.61	4.51
	EASTERN EUROPE AND CENTRAL ASIA	3	0.01	0.06	0.03	0.03
	LATIN AMERICA AND THE CARIBBEAN	12	0.00	8.47	2.05	3.22
	MIDDLE EAST AND NORTH AFRICA	6	0.00	0.06	0.01	0.02
	SOUTH ASIA	5	0.08	33.89	13.05	16.73

Abbreviations in the column header: Min: Minimum, Max: Maximum, Std.Dev.: Standard Deviation

Chapter 4
Factors Affecting Sustainable Higher Educational Partnerships

Christopher John Bamber
https://orcid.org/0000-0001-8555-0690
Organisational Learning Centre (Europe) Ltd, UK

Enis Elezi
https://orcid.org/0000-0001-5031-6415
Teesside University Business School, UK

ABSTRACT

The globally competitive environment of higher education is exemplified by many UK universities, private education institutions, and public colleges entering into collaborative agreements with partner organisations. No more is this movement seen than with private higher education institutions (HEIs) entering into collaborative arrangements with many stakeholders, including new partners once seen as competitors. Those entrepreneurial-minded executives leading and governing HEIs have thus seen partnerships as strategies for business sustainability in a collaborative economy, giving them competitive advantage and enhancing their strategic intent. This chapter provides a critical and useful review of HEI knowledge management (KM) factors that enable successful stages of collaboration. Within this chapter, sustainability practices in higher education partnerships are reviewed through examination of KM factors and discussions of a private HEI using case study examples from their sustainability journey.

INTRODUCTION

This chapter provides the reader with a deep understanding of the factors that are affecting successful collaborations within the Higher Education sector. Moreover, the chapter focuses on how those factors contribute to sustainable higher education partnerships operating in a global economy. On completion of reading this chapter the following objectives shall be achieved:

- An understanding of the global context of Higher Education (HE)

DOI: 10.4018/978-1-7998-4543-0.ch004

- An appreciation of the need for HE partnerships
- A familiarization with the stages of partnership development
- Understanding of Knowledge Management factors (KM) for Sustainable HEI Collaborations
- The ability to assess a HE collaborative project using Knowledge Management Factors (KM) for Sustainable HEI Collaborations as a framework of analysis
- Recognizing the Socio-Economic impact of HEIs and its relationship with Social Capital

Thus, this chapter provides knowledge and understanding of the factors affecting successful collaborations within the HE sector and aims to plug the research gap that exists between theories of collaboration and the realities of practice in the context of the HE global domain. In this respect, a successful collaboration is one that promotes sustainability practices to the partners, through adoption and appreciation of KM factors, for sustainable HEI collaborations as shown through the case study examples included in this chapter.

THE GROWING NEED FOR SUSTAINABLE HIGHER EDUCATION PARTNERSHIPS

The population of the world is growing fast and knowledge transfer through education is key to global development. Likewise, Chatlani (2018) makes reference to the UNESCO Institute of Statistics when highlighting that by 2030 it is expected to have an increase of around 120 million students attending higher education programs. This growth in the student population presents significant opportunities and challenges for the executives of HEIs. Significantly, Altbach, Reisberg, and Rumbley (2019), Durnin (2019), and Atack (2019) explain that the increasing demand in the HE sector, student mobility and immigration policies, and the rise of non-traditional students, together with the technological developments, encourage HEIs to reconsider their business models. Moreover, in order to remain competitive and maintain business continuity and sustainability, research undertaken by Ilieva, Killingley, Tsiligiris, and Usher (2019), Shattock (2019), and Hunt and Boliver (2019) argue that HEIs need to become more resilient and focus on enhancing the ability of their organizations to learn and thus reinvent their strategies. Additionally, due to the scarcity of resources, lack of market knowledge and difficulties in budget availability necessary to operate an HEI, many HE executives have considered collaborative projects as alternatives to overcome such challenges (Stewart, Witte, & Witte, 2019).

The development of partnerships between HEIs presents opportunities to add value to the existing HE services by exchanging institutional knowledge. The exchange and management of institutional knowledge are of paramount importance when it comes to facilitating, and later on, consolidating, the collaboration between HEIs. Hence, elements of Knowledge Management (KM) take prominence in being able to understand how HEIs could work collaboratively in a knowledge economy with the purpose of developing and implementing sustainable HEI strategies.

Similar to other sectors, educational partnerships within the HE sector seek to add value to the existing operations and allow an HEI to attain outcomes that would not be feasible if operating alone (Li, 2020; Shattock, 2019). Literature in HE collaborations (Elliott, 2017; Li, 2020; Maringe & de Wit, 2016) highlights several examples of different types of partnerships in the HE sector that have allowed institutions to enhance the quality of research and teaching practices, student experience, and reduce costs. Furthermore, through collaborations, HEIs have been able to generate a wider range of academic programs that best respond to the diverse needs of the local economies and strengthening the quality and integrity of their degrees (Maringe & de Wit 2016; Stewart et al., 2019). Although according to DeWit (2017), Elezi and Bamber (2018a), and Stewart et al. (2019) collaborations may not be the ultimate answer of overcoming the sector challenges, referring to current political dynamics, socio-cultural and economic developments. However, joint cross-institutional efforts are seen as vitally important in developing and implementing sustainable strategies.

It is argued (Elezi & Bamber, 2018b; Iqbal, Latif, Marimon, Sahibzada, & Hussain, 2019) that KM elements serve the purpose of structuring, using and generating new knowledge which is essential for the betterment of society. In the context of the HE sector, KM plays a significant role in an HEI when working collaboratively in encouraging innovation and strengthening market competitiveness. Nevertheless, the application of KM elements in HE collaborations, where HEIs still remain competitors, does not come without challenges. It is important to highlight that identifying the developmental stages of a partnership and using KM elements, may help HE executives assess the suitability of their institutional strategies and adjust accordingly in attempting to respond to an ever-changing HE landscape.

THE GLOBAL CONTEXT OF HIGHER EDUCATION INSTITUTIONS

Operating in a knowledge economy is increasingly making the role of Higher Education Institutions (HEIs') more important in preparing the future workforce with the appropriate level of behavioral skills and expertise required from different industries. HEIs play a significant role in the economic progress and competitiveness of a country through the development of human capital, research, and innovation.

The landscape of the HE sector is explained by Atack (2019) and Bothwell (2017) as continuously changing and responding to market needs because of emerging challenges from issues related to market accessibility, student recruitment, allocation of resources and appropriate teaching and researching infrastructure. Therefore, HEIs are continuously seeking alternatives to working collaboratively in order to ensure their mission to the development of societies is delivered sustainably. Collaborations in HEIs are explained by Elliott (2017) as having developed dual and joint degrees, franchising, validation, branch campuses, and online programs. According to Maringe and de Wit (2016), Elliott (2017), UUK (2018a), and Li (2020), those dual and joint degrees take place mainly between US, UK, Germany, China, and India while, franchising and validation are more apparent in Latin America, Asia, and Africa. Importantly, there is an increase in student mobility where according to British Council (2012) by 2020 the largest student outbound comes from China (585k), India (296k), South Korea (134k), and Germany (100k).

A report prepared by British Council (2012) also highlights that by 2020 countries such as India, Nigeria, Malaysia, Nepal, and Pakistan will have the fastest-growing rate of outbound mobile student and USA, UK, Australia, Canada and Germany will be the top five countries that will experience the highest inbound mobile students. This British Council prediction has been somewhat been agreed with the publishing of the UK Universities report (UUK, 2018a) that provides similar figures. Maringe and de Wit (2016) and Elliott (2017) argue that with the predicted increase in global student mobility rates expected it is vitally important for HEIs to channel their resources and efforts when working collaboratively. Therefore, HEIs are facing a challenge from the dynamics of economic global change and require to develop new strategies for sustainability.

THE SOCIO-ECONOMIC IMPACT OF UK HIGHER EDUCATION INSTITUTIONS

According to the UUK (2018a) report "Patterns and Trends in UK Higher Education 2018", the income across all the UK HEIs counted for £35.7 billion reflecting growth of £1 billion from the preceding year. The report also highlights that almost half of the income comes from teaching, around £17.7 billion, and around 22.1%, £7.9 billion, is generated from research activities. Bothwell (2017) pointed out that HEIs contribute a significant figure of around £95 billion to the UK economy and support more than 940,000 jobs thus playing a crucial role in the UK economy.

The contribution to the UK economy from HEI activities, because of global economic changes and local government regulatory changes, is currently in flux. Accordingly, UUK (2018a, 2018b) and Shattock (2019) reflect views that HEIs contribution to the UK economy may change due to institutions facing numerous challenges in terms of global competition, the uncertainty of student funding and changes in the political landscape (i.e. Brexit). Highman (2018) argues that the economic impact of HEIs in the UK is also extended to the upskilling of the British workforce allowing the UK companies to remain competitive in the international arena. According to "Solving future skills challenges" (UUK, 2018b), there were 440,000 new professional jobs created however only 316,690 first-degree holders in the UK, with a gap of 123,310 jobs requiring qualified staff. Moreover, Marini, Locke, and Whitchurch (2019) explain that such circumstances may have negative socio-economic implications long term. "Solving future skills challenges" report (UUK, 2018b) also highlights that by 2030, the UK is projected to experience a talent deficit of anywhere between 600,000 to 1.2 million qualified workers. Accordingly, Ilieva et al. (2019) and Hunt and Boliver (2019) clarify that operating in a knowledge economy requires UK organizations to, not only be recruiting highly skilled employees but also to, apply up-skilling and re-skilling programs to the existing workforce. With the number of opportunities and challenges in the HE sector, Bothwell (2017), Hunt and Boliver (2019) and Shattock (2019) all argue that exploring collaborative working opportunities may result in positive outcomes for institutions themselves, and importantly, for the British society and economy.

The socio-economic impact of the UK HEIs sector, for those reasons, poses a significant strategic dilemma for institutional governance and leadership, when enduring their short term existence and creating long term strategic intent. Thus immediate collaborative opportunities can bring short and medium-term results while valuable long term partnerships can bring sustainable practices and future income.

THE SIGNIFICANCE OF COLLABORATIONS FOR DEVELOPING SUSTAINABLE HIGHER EDUCATION INSTITUTIONS

Collaborations are acknowledged for the level of complexity and hence pose numerous challenges to leaders and managers in their attempt to develop sustainable operations (Aleixo, Leal, & Azeiteiro, 2018; Alshahrani, Dadich, & Klikauer, 2016; Boliver, 2019). While there is a common agreement (Huang & Chiu, 2018; Kourti, 2017; Verdecho, Alfaro, & Rodriguez-Rodriguez, 2009) the success of collaborations depends on the performance of institutional and inter-institutional actions, there are different views on the nature of factors impacting the inter-organizational performance. For instance, a study was undertaken by Kourti (2017) discussed the performance management of inter-organizational collaborations highlighting that there are four collaborative patterns that may enhance collaborative performance such as confrontation, trust, adaptation, and resistance.

Furthermore, research presented by Huang and Chiu (2018) elaborates on the importance of the relationship between governance mechanisms and collaborative performance. According to Huang and Chiu (2018), the relationship between governance mechanisms and collaborative performance is dynamic and changes through the life-cycle stages of collaboration, thus making it a challenging process to assess performance in inter-organizational collaborations. Verdecho et al. (2009) argue the importance of performance management systems which have been advocated as tools that could assist with the management of collaborations, however, lack of understanding of the structure and dynamics of collaboration may lead to its failure. Therefore, the implication of current experts on collaborative factors and research findings suggest that there is a need for HEIs to adopt these concepts but adapt collaborative theories to the context of the global HEI sector with the purpose of reflecting sustainable development.

The need for HE sector sustainability is increasingly becoming a more prominent subject with an increasing level of competition, uncertainty in funding schemes, changes in legislation and policies and technological developments noted. Internationalization strategies, diversification of income streams, and quality assurance frameworks for academic services have been subject to numerous studies discussing sustainable HEIs. The research, undertaken by UUK (2018a, 2018b) and Hunt and Boliver (2019), evidence that HEI governance and leadership need to reconsider their business models and minimize bureaucracy by encouraging collaborations. Likewise, Hunt and Boliver (2019) and UUK (2016) explain that working collaboratively with other HEI establishments, or HE providers, encourages innovation and contributes to developing sustainable strategies fit for a knowledge economy. For example, Hunt and Boliver (2019) highlight that collaborating with HE providers encourages competition, stimulates innovation and enhances the quality of academic products and services which are likely to be offered at a lower cost.

In the 2016 UK Government White Paper "Success as a Knowledge Economy" communicated the plans for increasing the number of private HEIs that could award their own degrees. The White Paper also highlighting that private institutions are more responsive to labour market changes and skills required from graduate employers (Hunt & Boliver, 2019). Additionally, there is evidence that collaboration between HEIs, including private HE providers, promote innovation in the delivery of academic programs and accelerated courses (Hunt & Boliver, 2019). Collaborations between HEIs at departmental or institutional levels should be considered as opportunities to not only attain short term projects (to ride through Brexit, political dynamics and current government policies) and midterms financial objectives but as an instrument that allows partners to establish a clear sense of purpose and vision for operating sustainably. With the student removal cap in the UK, there is now no restriction on the number of students public HEIs can recruit (Azmat, Murphy, Valero, & Wyness, 2018; Johnes, 2016). Hunt and Boliver (2019) argue that such a move is expected to set pressure on some student recruitment campaigns and financial projections, thus raising issues about the sustainability of HEIs strategies. Sustainability is, vital but also, a complex issue that requires HEI executives to tackle issues of bureaucracy, be more market-driven and improve the efficiency of their institutional resources while working collaboratively with their competitors.

KNOWLEDGE MANAGEMENT IN PRIVATE HIGHER EDUCATION INSTITUTION COLLABORATIONS

In explaining HEI collaborations, Tan (2016) and Feiz, Dehghani Soltani, and Farsizadeh (2019) argue that the extent to which collaboration may yield positive results relies on the ability to exchange, applying and evaluating institutional knowledge. Therefore, it is vitally important for HEIs to take into account elements of KM in order to design and implement collaborative strategies that facilitate the achievement of concerted objectives. Managing knowledge is seen as an ongoing process that allows institutions and individuals to learn and unlearn through knowledge sharing (KS) and knowledge transferring (KT) techniques while seeking to develop an institutional relationship. Nevertheless, having two or more HEIs working collaboratively presents strategic as well as operational challenges particularly when one of the HEI partners is a private institution and that is where other aspects of KM are required. For instance, knowledge accessibility and absorption followed by the HEIs' ability to integrate new or updated knowledge (Iqbal et al., 2019) are aspects that collaborators need to manage. Other important KM aspects to assist the development of collaborative work between HEIs are linked with knowledge application and knowledge evaluation practices and procedures to ensure that synchronization of tasks and actions reflects partners' expectations.

Private HEIs are smaller in size, provide fewer academic programs and courses when compared with pubic HEIs and experience a much fiercer competition. Furthermore, private institutions may not necessarily attain the appropriate institutional infrastructure and could be experiencing a shortage of resources. However, as discussed by Hunt and Boliver (2019) private HEIs are more responsive to market changes which are possibly attributed to the size of the business as well as the financial pressure that public HEIs may not experience. According to Hunt and Boliver (2019), 64 percent of the private HEIs in the UK offer courses in one subject area only thus making such institutions very specialized in a particular area of study. Such limitation of academic programs allows private HEIs to establish an in-depth understanding of the market challenges and trends and ability to respond to frequent or short term projects quicker than a large HEI that operates in a more bureaucratic setting. Public and private HEIs could use KM aspects to assist each other in enhancing institutional skills and expertise, quality systems, designing and validating new programs and courses and improving student services.

THE ISSUES IMPACTING ON COLLABORATIVE SUSTAINABILITY

All organizations progress through a lifecycle of creation, development, and decline while collaborations are a combination of more than one organization working together, they to progress through a similar lifecycle. Moreover, alliance-based issues impacting sustainable collaborations are discussed by Reid, Bussiere, and Greenaway (2001) when describing collaborative partnerships and consequently they explain that partnerships have a life cycle consisting of three stages of pre-formation, formation, and evaluation. As shown in Figure 1, the pre-formation stage considers the motivation of institutions entering into collaboration as an issue impacting on the sustainability of partnerships. While, the formation stage indicates that collaborating institutions consider three different categories of issues which relate to partner characteristics, operating structure and norms and structural choices. Accordingly, the Reid et al. (2001) model of sustainable partnerships does not indicate the end of the collaboration lifecycle, rather it evaluates the effectiveness of partnership's collaboration in creating new knowledge to enhance sustainable practice.

Figure 1. Stages of Collaboration
Source: Elezi and Bamber (2018a); Reid et al. (2001)

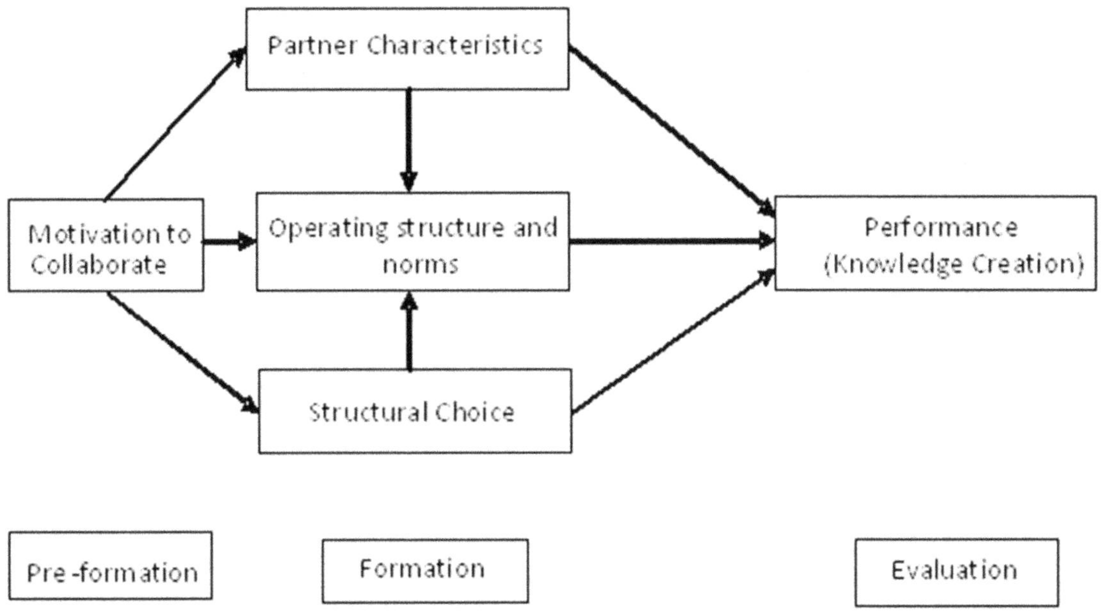

The lifecycle model, Figure 1 presents collaborations as a continuum leading to knowledge creation for the benefit of the partners and the partnership. This acceptance that there is a lifecycle can lead to sustainable practices being embedded into the individual organizations of the partnership or new developments of the partnership itself. Within the Reid et al. (2001) discussions, there is an acknowledgment that effective knowledge management is essential for collaborations and that a knowledge-based enterprise will have a competitive advantage over other organizational paradigms.

KNOWLEDGE MANAGEMENT FACTORS FOR SUSTAINABLE HIGHER EDUCATION INSTITUTION COLLABORATIONS

Previous case study research by Elezi and Bamber (2018a) into a particular educational partnership has shown that the Reid et al. (2001) construct of partnership development can be used as a framework to categorize identified knowledge management (KM) factors relevant to the specific context of Higher Education. Moreover, within the dynamic and competitive UK Higher Education private sector, Elezi and Bamber (2018a) identified KM factors within the stages of the lifecycle of collaboration. Likewise, Figure 2 has been developed from including the KM factors, found present during Elezi and Bamber (2018a) case study research, into the Reid et al. (2001) model shown in Figure 2.

Furthermore, Elezi and Bamber (2018a) model facilitates the sustainability of Higher Educational Partnerships by providing a framework of assessment or benchmarking for HEI business analysts to compare their collaborative practices. Accordingly, adoption of the Elezi and Bamber (2018a) model would improve the triple bottom line as described by Castka, Bamber, and Sharp (2004): Economic, Environmental and Social Impact for all partners in a collaborative project. Likewise, Jackson, Boswell, and Davis (2004) have discussed the triple bottom line as a strategy for sustainability.

Figure 2. Knowledge Management Factors for Sustainable HEI Collaborations
Source: adapted from Elezi and Bamber (2018a)

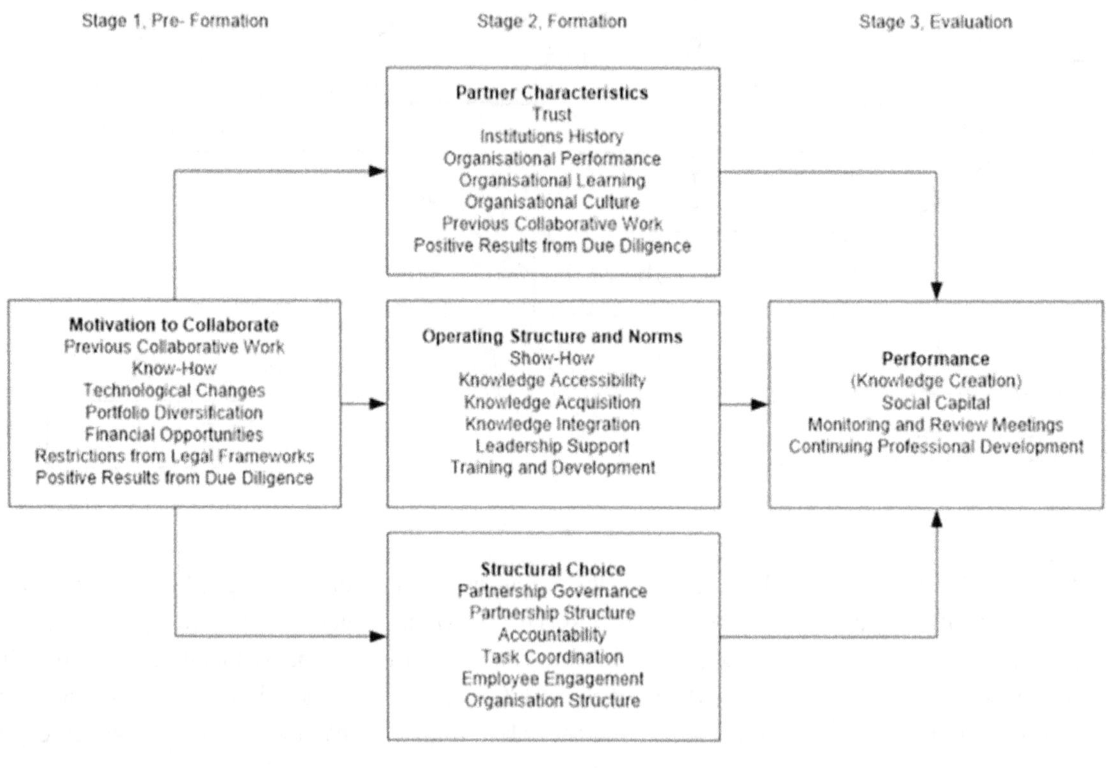

This revised model now shown in Figure 2, provides an indication of the KM factors required for collaborative success in the HEI sector. Furthermore, this model can be used to provide the factors affecting the sustainability of HEI partnerships. Likewise, Elezi and Bamber (2018a) suggest the KM factors shown in the stages of partnership development in Figure 2 could guide educational partnerships, but the authors do not suggest that this is the only set of factors because as described earlier every partnership and hence collaboration would be different.

Moreover, this model shown in Figure 2, which identified the KM factors present in HEI collaborations could be used for examination of other educational partnerships and according to Elezi and Bamber (2018a) is not expected to be used as a complete holistic model, moreover as one tool in helping identifying factors of sustainable collaborative practices. The researchers suggested that other educational institutions could use the model (Figure 2) for continuous improvement purposes and investigate KM factors in either potential or future HEI partnerships. Hence, the following sections describe a critical analysis of the case example of OLC (Europe) Ltd, using Figure 2, as a framework of the examination of their collaborative sustainability. The case study analysis will demonstrate that the model in Figure 2 can be used for evaluation of sustainable practices within HEI collaborations and also to validate the efficacy of the model presented and therefore validate the original ideas of partnership lifecycle factors presented by Reid et al. (2001).

EXPLORING FACTORS FOR HIGHER EDUCATION INSTITUTION SUCCESSFUL COLLABORATION AND SUSTAINABILITY

The competitive nature of the Higher Education sector is exemplified within the UK where more and more Universities, private education institutions and Public Colleges are searching for a competitive edge through partnership development (Ilieva et al., 2019; Marini et al., 2019). Hence, Knowledge Management (KM) factors are being explored to enable competitive sustainable practices, more predominantly than in previous years (Alshahrani et al., 2016; Elezi & Bamber, 2018a; Feiz et al., 2019; Iqbal et al., 2019). As such, the KM factors model presented in figure 2 can be used to illustrate the relationship and interconnection of knowledge management practices when striving for competitive advantage. Thus the following sections describe in more detail those knowledge management factors that support sustainability in the HE sector through collaborative practices. Moreover, the following sections include descriptions of each factor which are supported with case examples from the real world journey of a private HEI operating within the educational frameworks and governances of the UK HE sector.

The private (independent from government or public support) HEI described in this section is OLC (Europe) Ltd which has been operating since 1998 in the UK. Since, its conception and creation, OLC has been the lead organization or been a key member of collaborative programs within the UK education sector and across global training environments. Ensuring continued teaching and learning success has been one of the many credits of OLC, which is demonstrated and assessed annually for Quality Assurance by the UKs appointed Quality Assurance Association (see, QAA 2019) and has further government and non-government accreditations to operate as an HEI. The UK HE sector has been reported many times as being ever-changing and demanding (Shattock, 2019), hence OLC has had to adapt and maneuver its strategic direction to ensure sustainability and longevity, in a sector where many of its competitors have disappeared (Hunt & Boliver, 2019). The following sections of this chapter describe each of the knowledge management factors that affect sustainable HEI collaborations. Each of the descriptions is supported by case examples drawn from discussions with the OLC (Europe) Ltd Senior Management Team and thus represents a snapshot and indication of sustainable practices.

MOTIVATION TO COLLABORATE

Collaborations are designed with the purpose of adding value to current products or services of an organization with the purpose of enhancing financial performance through an exchange of experience, expertise, and resources and HEIs are not an exception. The motivation to collaborate may vary depending on the overall economic conditions at macro levels, governmental legislation, frameworks and policies, availability of financial and physical resources, and the important role of regulatory bodies within the HE sector. O'Reilly, Robbins, and Scanlan (2019) and Uslu, Calikoglu, Seggie, and Seggie

(2019) argue that portfolio diversification is one of the main motives of HEIs to explore collaborative projects. Diversification of portfolio may include the opening of new schools in a different geographical location, design, prepare and deliver new academic programs in class and online, or it may be the case of validating an academic program or course to mention a few, see Table 1 for a discussion of practice.

Table 1. Motivation to Collaborate Discussed using Case Study Experience

Stage of the Partnership	Key Issue	The Identified KM Factors related to Motivation to Collaborate and discussion within the case study experience
Pre-Formation	**Motivation to Collaborate**	· Previous collaborative work · Know-How · Technological Changes · Portfolio Diversification · Financial Opportunities · Restrictions from Legal Frameworks · Positive results from due diligence checks **Case Study Discussion** OLC (Europe) Ltd has been operating in Higher Education collaborative arrangements since 1998 and has, therefore, a plethora of partnership experience. They have, therefore, the knowledge and experience of working across differing management information systems and across multiple sites. OLC has developed a hugely diverse product range, as a result, of many different partnerships, expanding over a vast period of time, which has led to constant portfolio flux but does provide sustainability, in a changing market. Consequently, each new partnership has brought diversification in income streams and resilience against changing legal frameworks that adversely affected others in the same markets. Having worked in multiple partnerships and learned new methods of operations, potential partners have noted OLC to be providing quality HE provision across all their academic programs. Respect is gained from successful previous partnerships and positive referral references gained.

Another motive for collaboration could consist of the know-how, in other words, the expertise that one of the partners may have in an academic or commercial context and that is seen as an opportunity to combine efforts toward a common collaborative goal. The know-how could be essential in overcoming any restrictions posed by the legal frameworks or technological changes thus allowing HEIs to explore financial opportunities that contribute to the sustainability of their institutions. However, challenges may be experienced in aligning a mutual sense of motivation across HE partners due to previous experiences and due diligence process. The outcome of the previous experiences and due diligence processes, as well as the reputation of the institution, may have a significant impact on passing the pre-formation stage of the partnership development as explained by Reid et al. (2001) and establish a clear understanding of the motives of the collaboration.

PARTNERS CHARACTERISTICS

While going through the formation stage of the partnership research (Elezi & Bamber; 2018a) shows that trust is one of the main characteristics that partners seek to assess and develop as an exchange of information and knowledge takes place. While the contractual agreements are an indication of institutional trust, HE executives and practitioners develop a higher level of trust upon the delivery of results through working collaboratively in a partnership. OLC case study described in Table 2 provides further discussion and indicates team development as an element of partner characteristics should be encouraged. Nevertheless, as argued by Elezi and Bamber (2018a) it is important to design and apply collaborative activities across institutions with organizational learning elements in mind. As there is a plethora of knowledge found within HEIs that need to be transferred and processed between institutions would be highly beneficial to use organizational learning concepts to facilitate the exchange of institutional knowledge.

Table 2. Partners Characteristics Discussed using Case Study Experience

Stage of the Partnership	Key Issue	The Identified KM Factors within the case study experience
Formation	Partners Characteristics	· Trust · Institutions History · Organizational Performance · Organisational Learning · Organisational Culture · Positive results from due diligence checks · Previous collaborative work **Case Study Discussion** Whether a partnering organization is new to collaborative working or not, fundamental to success for OLC has been the building of team relationships across partners. Team development is enhanced through honest personal communications that are meaningful to the fulfillment of contract requirements. The OLC Senior Management Team has recognized that, building a common culture during the early periods of Partnership Formation, from which both collaborating organizations can work two, is essential for developing trust. This build-in trust between collaborators has often been developed when organizational performance measures are explicitly driving activities complimentarily to Service Level Agreements.

The literature on organizational learning and knowledge management argues that the ability of institutions to work collaboratively, exchange and absorb the necessary information and knowledge to manage and lead academic teams, departments and institutions will depend on the organizational culture. Yadav, Choudhary, and Jain (2019) explain that at the start of the partnership there is a significant amount of knowledge sharing and absorbing, as partners seek to align their actions and is of a paramount importance that leadership identify the accountable HE staff and provide the necessary guidance and support to facilitate the collaborative working.

OPERATING STRUCTURE AND NORMS

Another stage of the partnership formation is concerned with the operating structure and norms of the partnership (Elezi & Bamber, 2018a; Reid et al., 2001), where partners discuss and agree on a set of operational norms needed to facilitate the transferability of institutional knowledge. The focus lies in designing and applying timely and appropriate institutional systems that support knowledge accessibility and knowledge acquisition. While in the pre-formation stage of the partnership, when discussing the motivation aspects of collaborative work, "*know-how*" was considered as one of the main motives of bringing partners together, operating structure and norms are concerned with the "*show-how*" needed to be exchanged between partners. "*Show-how*" may include standardization meetings, as discussed in Table 3, involving academic and non-academic teams from different partner institutions, delivery of workshops in sharing best practices and training and development programs necessary to deliver partnership's expectations.

Table 3. Operating Structure and Norms Discussed using Case Study Experience

Stage of the Partnership	Key Issue	The Identified KM Factors within the case study experience
Formation	Operating structure and norms	· Knowledge Accessibility · Knowledge Acquisition · Show-How/Standardisation meetings · Knowledge Integration · Leadership Support · Training and Development **Case Study Discussion** Higher Education partnerships for OLC have focused on providing degree level courses across multiple sites that bring new geography reach for partner activities. Consequently, the primary data management requirement is always related to the student learning journey. A student journey starts from the advertisement, of course, offers to receipt of a student application, through to accepting the student on the course and then successfully teaching and assessments, eventually graduating the student into the alumni. OLC Management Information Systems (MIS) must therefore be student journey focused. The more aligned to the partners MIS systems the better and easier knowledge transfer accessibility, acquisition and integration. Supporting data transfer in an education collaborative environment is the need for training and development which is focused on standardisation meetings and understanding of the data relating to the student learning journey. What OLC have commonly noted is that collaborator's MIS are often not compatible and translators are needed to develop common communication methods. As such, file synchronisation across partner files has been at time troublesome and difficult and shared files in cloud based solutions is becoming more commonplace. The important drivers would be regular student attendance figures, regular assessment of student progress, student attainment of qualifications and any risk factors relating to impedance of the student learner journey (such as Mitigating Circumstances, limiting students ability to complete assessments at any learning stage.

While discussing the operating structure and norms, it is worth noting that leadership support is essential and at this stage is expected to demonstrate more of a "hands-on" approach and oversee the knowledge exchange processes. Yadav et al. (2019) argue that depending on leadership style, HE executives have the tendency to micromanage or unnecessarily centralize the decision making thus compromising the quality and robustness of institutional communication channels.

STRUCTURAL CHOICE

It is of paramount importance that partners work on defining and agreeing with a structural choice that best fits the operating structure and norms, fully reflects partnership characteristics and responds to the motives that instigated the partnership, see Table 4 for further discussion of methods of partnering. When forming collaborations, therefore, the partnership structural choice must take into consideration the purpose of coming together. Collaborative work between institutions is expected to have an impact on the organizational structure and functions. Therefore the structure and functions of collaborations are expected to clarify managerial issues related to task coordination and accountability. Another important element for discussion with respect to structural choice in the formation of a partnership stage would relate to the development of Communities of Practice (CoP) which should accordingly help with accountability issues.

Table 4. Partners Characteristics Discussed using Case Study Experience

Stage of the Partnership	Key Issue	The Identified KM Factors within the case study experience
Formation	Structural Choice	· Partnership Government Structure · Accountability · Task Coordination · Communities of Practice · Employee Engagement · Organization structure and partnership accountability **Case Study Discussion** Within Higher Education collaborations there are many forms of legal entity and methods of partnering. OLC predominantly have franchised course programs with UK Universities, franchised the OLC courses to overseas Universities, or gained course validation from UK HEIs. These partnership entities have allowed OLC to use their own premises throughout the UK for delivery of other HEI's UK accredited programs in regions that the OLC partners do not operate. While partnering with overseas Universities, OLC have enabled their own courses to be delivered in countries where OLC would not operate on their own. Accordingly, partner collaboration agreements would be individually customised for different projects and partnership arrangements. The challenges of collaboration across global, regional and widespread operations has led OLC to commonly use internet and cloud platform communication software such as *Zoom* or *Skype* for both staff conference meetings and student tutorials. Equally, knowledge and data transfer requirements has been enabled using Learning Management Systems (LMS) such as *Moodle*, where students and collaborators can access and interact with learning materials too. Technological communication solutions have not yet completely eliminated face to face meetings, in particular exam boards and module assessment boards are commonly attended in physical meeting places and only occasionally virtually.

As discussed by Robinson, Carrillo, Anumba, and Patel (2009) and Urzelai and Puig (2019), the CoP, accountability, and coordination of tasks within complex organizations, as it is the case of Universities, support the flow of knowledge sharing and knowledge transfer at inter- and intra- institutional levels. Additionally, when adopting CoPs, the KM practices, or systems, due to knowledge being decentralized and providing opportunities for regenerating knowledge may lead to the betterment of academic services, development of new products or exploring new business ideas. Agreeing on a structural choice also leads to a better level of understanding the purpose of the collaboration thus, helping with employee engagement (Yadav et al., 2019) and strengthening the commitment of staff included in the processes of exchanging and applying knowledge.

EVALUATION OF PARTNERSHIP

The performance stage of a partnership is strongly related to the initial step of the motivation of entering into collaborative projects. Moreover, in collaborative undertakings, it is vitally important to assess whether a partnership has delivered and achieved the expectations of the stakeholders identified at the start of the partnership. Assessing the performance of HEI collaborations reflects the ability of institutions to create new knowledge, which is one of the most fundamental themes of Knowledge Management within the HEI sector. Accordingly, Appleton-Dyer, Clinton, Carswell, and McNeill (2012) and Robinson et al. (2009) argue assessment of performance is usually discussed in the context of financial gains while Stern (2004), Metaxiotis and Ergazakis (2008), and Milagres and Burcharth (2019) highlight that it is important to consider the implications of a partnership in a wider scope. For instance, it may be the case that due to external factors (e.g. changes in legal frameworks) upon which HEIs have limited or no control over, the partnership may have had to adjust its activities and amend some of the expectations. The main purpose of a HEI is to transfer knowledge and skills to their learners, contributing to a more knowledgeable society that will assist with development of local and national economies, see Table 5 for further discussion.

Table 5. Performance (Knowledge Creation) Discussed using Case Study Experience

Stage of the Partnership	Key Issue	The Identified KM Factors within the case study experience
Evaluation	Performance (Knowledge Creation)	· Social Capital · Monitoring and review meetings · Continuing professional development of staff **Case Study Discussion** Monitoring and review meetings are commonplace when HEI collaborators are evaluating the student learner journey. They include meetings assessing Module statistics, Programme success dimensions and student progression information. OLC has become aware that monitoring must be more frequent than when working alone, because there is much implicit knowledge within an organization, while across organizational structures implicit knowledge is less common. While OLC contracts with partners and their relevant service level agreements mainly focus on both the management of the student journey and financial arrangements, OLC staff clearly recognizes the impact collaborations have on Social Capital. Improving the lives of staff, students and their colleagues and family members is paramount to OLC activities and ways of improving this social impact are a focus of their continuing professional development planning. OLC has established methods of evaluation against stakeholder assessment criteria that explicitly include mention of their impact on Society, Social Capital and partner Learning.

It is thus fundamental to the remit of the education sector that they provide a positive contribution to society through impacting on behavior, attitudes, and skills of their learners. Therefore, not fully meeting the expectations agreed at the pre-formation stage does not necessarily indicate a lack of performance, as during the collaboration HEIs may have successfully developed social capital. Thus, assessing the performance of a partnership should take into account the ability of an institution to create, absorb, disseminate, and apply knowledge for the purpose of ensuring a more sustainable approach to the commercialization of knowledge.

FUTURE RESEARCH DIRECTIONS

The global trend in increasing student movement and numbers will lead to more importance placed on HEI partnerships. Likewise, the chapter has demonstrated that HEIs can assess their organizations' partnership performance and shown the viability of collaboration in the global changing economy. Moreover, the chapter indicated, that entrepreneurially-minded executives, leading and governing HEIs, have seen partnerships as *Strategies for Business Sustainability in a Collaborative Economy*, consequently their direction has given them a competitive advantage and enhanced their business continuity. On the other hand, it may be argued that failing HEIs, whether public or private, may not have taken partnerships seriously and thus not reaped the benefits of the collaborative economy.

This chapter, therefore, encourages governors, executives and senior managers of HEIs to analyze their collaborative activities using the Knowledge Management Factors for Sustainable HEI Collaborations presented in Figure 2. Such an analysis can be carried out in the manner presented, in the tables shown in this chapter, which have provided discussions of the practices of the case study organization, OLC (Europe) Ltd.

This chapter suggests HEI researchers and HEI business analysts should consider both the soft issues of organizations and also the technological issues when assessing collaborative structures. Expert analysts and case study researchers could use the methods shown in this chapter but should look in much more detail than this chapter has been able to provide. For instance, more detailed process analysis, in-depth interviewing techniques, data analysis and reviews of MIS synchronicity focused along the student learner journey would reveal more than presented here.

The chapter has also indicated that both 'Impact on Society' and the creation of 'Social Capital' should be a major pursuit of HEIs. Consequently, measuring the performance of HEI partnership success should include both those criteria. Likewise, a future direction of sustainability in organizational studies is likely to include both the criteria of 'Impact on Society' and the creation of 'Social Capital' and not just be restricted to the realm of HEIs.

CHAPTER CONCLUSION

In this chapter changes in the global economy, the emergence of new markets and an increase in population presented not only a need for improvements in education systems worldwide but also presented an opportunity for HEIs to develop business continuity through adopting a collaborative mindset. Collaborations are not new between HEIs, moreover, they are more prevalent as a means for reaching new markets and introducing new course programs in their highly competitive and regulated environment.

This chapter presented KM factors affecting sustainability within an educational case study organization that has shown extensive experience in Higher Education Partnerships. The framework for investigations within the chapter was a model of the stages of partnership development, first presented by Reid et al. (2001) and further developed for HEI collaborators by Elezi and Bamber (2018a). The three stages of partnership development; (i) pre-formation; (ii) formation and; (iii) evaluation have provided five categories of Factors Affecting Sustainable Higher Educational Partnerships. That multiplicity of factors has been elaborated upon using a discussion of the case study activities and experiences of practitioners spanning many collaborative projects over 20 years.

The chapter has shown that the identified KM factors are considered important to the case study organization and that both soft organizational issues and technological structure issues affect collaborative performance. It should also, be clear from the content of this chapter that HEIs has a remit to provide Social Capital and as such any collaborative performance system must include an evaluation of their impact on society. It is, therefore, a fundamental argument presented within this chapter that Strategies for Business Sustainability in a Collaborative Economy, for HEI Partnerships that is, must include providing a positive impact on society mainly through improvements in the creation of Social Capital.

REFERENCES

Aleixo, A. M., Leal, S., & Azeiteiro, U. M. (2018). Conceptualization of sustainable higher education institutions, roles, barriers, and challenges for sustainability: An exploratory study in Portugal. *Journal of Cleaner Production*, *172*, 1664–1673. doi:10.1016/j.jclepro.2016.11.010

Alshahrani, A., Dadich, A., & Klikauer, T. (2016). Critical success factors of knowledge management in higher education. *The 30th Australian and New Zealand Academy of Management Conference (ANZAM 2016).* Retrieved on December 19, 2019, from https://www.anzam.org/wp-content/uploads/pdf-manager/2833_ANZAM-2016-357-FILE001.PDF

Altbach, P. G., Reisberg, L., & Rumbley, L. E. (2019). *Trends in global higher education: Tracking an academic revolution.* Brill.

Appleton-Dyer, S., Clinton, J., Carswell, P., & McNeill, R. (2012). Understanding evaluation influence within public sector partnerships: A conceptual model. *The American Journal of Evaluation*, *33*(4), 532–546. doi:10.1177/1098214012447672

Atack, P. (2019). *Global HE market "hugely competitive" – British Council report*. Retrieved on December 28, 2019, from https://thepienews.com/news/global-he-market-hugely-competitive-british-council-report/

Azmat, G., Murphy, R., Valero, A., & Wyness, G. (2018). *Universities and industrial strategy in the UK* (No. 539). Retrieved on December 18, 2019, from http://cep.lse.ac.uk/pubs/download/is06.pdf

Bothwell, E. (2017). *Universities 'generate £95 billion for UK economy.* Retrieved on January 02, 2020, from https://www.timeshighereducation.com/news/universities-generate-ps95-billion-uk-economy

British Council. (2012). *The shape of things to come: higher education global trends and emerging opportunities to 2020.* Retrieved on January 02, 2020, from https://www.britishcouncil.org/sites/default/files/the_shape_of_things_to_come_-_higher_education_global_trends_and_emerging_opportunities_to_2020.pdf

Castka, P., Bamber, C., & Sharp, J. M. (2004). *Implementing effective corporate social responsibility and corporate governance.* British Standards Institution.

Chatlani, S. (2018). 8 global trends impacting higher education. *EducationDive.* Retrieved on January 09, 2020, from https://www.educationdive.com/news/8-global-trends-impacting-higher-ed/515272/

De Wit, H. (2017). Global: Internationalization of Higher Education: Nine Misconceptions: International Higher Education, Summer 2011, Number 64. In *Understanding higher education internationalization* (pp. 9–12). Brill Sense. doi:10.1007/978-94-6351-161-2_2

Durnin, M. (2019). *Global student recruitment outlook: June 2019 update*. Retrieved on December 28, 2019, from https://education-services.britishcouncil.org/insights-blog/global-student-recruitment-outlook-june-2019-update

Elezi, E., & Bamber, C. (2018a). Knowledge management factors affecting educational partnerships within the British HE/FE sector. *International Journal of Knowledge Management Studies*, *9*(3), 243–259. doi:10.1504/IJKMS.2018.094213

Elezi, E., & Bamber, C. (2018b). Understanding the Role of Knowledge Management in Higher Education Partnerships through Experts. In E. Bolisani, E. Di Maria, & E. Scarso (Eds.). *19th European Conference on Knowledge Management* (pp. 225-234). Reading, UK: ACPI.

Elliott, G. (2017). Challenging assumptions about values, interests and power in further and higher education partnerships. *Journal of Further and Higher Education*, *41*(2), 143–154. doi:10.1080/0309877X.2015.1070397

Feiz, D., Dehghani Soltani, M., & Farsizadeh, H. (2019). The effect of knowledge sharing on the psychological empowerment in higher education mediated by organizational memory. *Studies in Higher Education*, *44*(1), 3–19. doi:10.1080/03075079.2017.1328595

Highman, K. (2018). *The Brexit White Paper: what does it mean for higher education and research.* Retrieved on January 02, 2020, https://www.researchcghe.org/perch/resources/publications/pb9.pdf

Huang, M. C., & Chiu, Y. P. (2018). Relationship governance mechanisms and collaborative performance: A relational life-cycle perspective. *Journal of Purchasing and Supply Management*, *24*(3), 260–273. doi:10.1016/j.pursup.2017.12.002

Hunt, S., & Boliver, V. (2019). *Private providers of higher education in the UK: mapping the terrain.* Retrieved on January 01, 2020, from https://www.researchcghe.org/perch/resources/publications/to-publishwp47.pdf

Ilieva, J., Killingley, P., Tsiligiris, V., & Usher, A. (2019). *The shape of global higher education: international comparisons with Europe, British Council, UK*. Retrieved on January 08, 2020, from https://www.britishcouncil.org/sites/default/files/k006_02_the_shape_of_global_higher_education_in_europe_final_v5_web.pdf

Iqbal, A., Latif, F., Marimon, F., Sahibzada, U. F., & Hussain, S. (2019). From knowledge management to organizational performance: Modelling the mediating role of innovation and intellectual capital in higher education. *Journal of Enterprise Information Management*, *32*(1), 36–59. doi:10.1108/JEIM-04-2018-0083

Jackson, A., Boswell, K., & Davis, D. (2011). Sustainability and Triple Bottom Line Reporting – What is it all about? *International Journal of Business. Human Technology*, *1*(3), 55–59.

Johnes, J. (2016). Why UK universities are returning to the public debt markets. *The Conversation*. Retrieved on December 18, 2019, from http://eprints.hud.ac.uk/id/eprint/27831/1/Why%20UK%20universities%20are%20returning%20to%20the%20public%20debt%20markets.pdf

Kourti, I. (2017). Effective performance management of inter-organisational collaborations through the construction of multiple identities. *International Journal of Business Performance Management*, *18*(2), 236–251. doi:10.1504/IJBPM.2017.083077

Li, J. (2020). Examining the Literature on Comprehensive Global Competence for Individual in Contemporary China. In J. Li (Ed.), *Comprehensive Global Competence for World-Class Universities in China* (pp. 89–100). Springer. doi:10.1007/978-981-15-1640-5_6

Lovett, C. M. (2013). The global contexts of higher education. *Change: The Magazine of Higher Learning*, *45*(1), 73–78. doi:10.1080/00091383.2013.749169

Maringe, F., & de Wit, H. (2016). Global higher education partnerships: Equity and epistemic concerns with distribution and flows of intellectual capital. In J. E. Cote & A. Furlong (Eds.), *Routledge handbook of the sociology of higher education* (pp. 299–314). Routledge. doi:10.4324/9781315772233-27

Marini, G., Locke, W., & Whitchurch, C. (2019). *The future higher education workforce in locally and globally engaged higher education institutions: a review of literature on the topic of 'the academic workforce'*. Retrieved on January 02, 2020, from https://www.researchcghe.org/perch/resources/publications/wp43.pdf

Metaxiotis, K., & Ergazakis, K. (2008). Exploring stakeholder knowledge partnerships in a knowledge city: A conceptual model. *Journal of Knowledge Management*, *12*(5), 137–150. doi:10.1108/13673270810902993

Milagres, R., & Burcharth, A. (2019). Knowledge transfer in interorganizational partnerships: What do we know? *Business Process Management Journal*, *25*(1), 27–68. doi:10.1108/BPMJ-06-2017-0175

O'Reilly, N. M., Robbins, P., & Scanlan, J. (2019). Dynamic capabilities and the entrepreneurial university: A perspective on the knowledge transfer capabilities of universities. *Journal of Small Business and Entrepreneurship*, *31*(3), 243–263. doi:10.1080/08276331.2018.1490510

QAA. (2019). *Review for Educational Oversight: OLC (Europe) Ltd trading as Organisational Learning Centre, monitoring visit report, July 2019*. Retrieved on January 02, 2020, from https://www.qaa.ac.uk/reviewing-higher-education/quality-assurance-reports/provider?UKPRN=10021609#

Reid, D., Bussiere, D., & Greenaway, K. (2001). Alliance formation issues for knowledge-based enterprises. *International Journal of Management Reviews*, *3*(1), 79–100. doi:10.1111/1468-2370.00055

Robinson, H., Carrillo, P., Anumba, C. J., & Patel, M. (2009). *Governance and knowledge management for public-private partnerships*. John Wiley & Sons.

Shattock, M. (2019). *University governance and academic work: the 'business model' and its impact on innovation and creativity*. Retrieved on January 05, 2020, from https://www.researchcghe.org/perch/resources/publications/to-publish-wp48.pdf

Stern, E. (2004). Evaluating partnerships. In O. N. Feinstein (Ed.), *Evaluation & Development: The Partnership Dimension* (pp. 29–41). Routledge.

Stewart, S. C., Witte, J. E., & Witte, M. M. (2019). Workforce Development and Higher Education Partnerships: Transdisciplinarity in Practice. In V. X. Wang (Ed.), *Handbook of Research on Transdisciplinary Knowledge Generation* (pp. 369–382). IGI Global. doi:10.4018/978-1-5225-9531-1.ch025

Urzelai, B., & Puig, F. (2019). Developing international social capital: The role of communities of practice and clustering. *International Business Review*, *28*(2), 209–221. doi:10.1016/j.ibusrev.2018.08.008

Uslu, B., Calikoglu, A., Seggie, F. N., & Seggie, S. H. (2019). The entrepreneurial university and academic discourses: The meta-synthesis of Higher Education articles. *Higher Education Quarterly*, *73*(3), 285–311. doi:10.1111/hequ.12198

UUK. (2016). *Working in partnership: enabling social mobility in higher education. The final report of the Social Mobility Advisory Group, London*. Retrieved on January 10, 2020, from https://dera.ioe.ac.uk/27586/1/working-in-partnership-final.pdf

UUK. (2018a). *Patterns and trends in UK higher education 2018, London*. Retrieved on January 01, 2020, from https://www.universitiesuk.ac.uk/facts-and-stats/data-and-analysis/Documents/patterns-and-trends-in-uk-higher-education-2018.pdf

UUK. (2018b). *Solving future skills challenges, London*. Retrieved on December 23, 2019 from https://www.universitiesuk.ac.uk/policy-and-analysis/reports/Documents/2018/solving-future-skills-challenges.pdf

UUK. (2019). *Higher education in Facts and figures, London*. Retrieved on January 03, 2020, from https://www.universitiesuk.ac.uk/facts-and-stats/data-and-analysis/Documents/higher-education-facts-and-figures-2019.pdf

Verdecho, M. J., Alfaro, J. J., & Rodriguez-Rodriguez, R. (2009). Foundations for collaborative performance measurement. *Production Planning and Control*, *20*(3), 193–205. doi:10.1080/09537280902721001

Yadav, M., Choudhary, S., & Jain, S. (2019). Transformational leadership and knowledge sharing behavior in freelancers: A moderated mediation model with employee engagement and social support. *Journal of Global Operations and Strategic Sourcing*, *12*(2), 202–224. doi:10.1108/JGOSS-08-2017-0030

KEY TERMS AND DEFINITIONS

Higher Education Institution: This is a tertiary education establishment providing academic programs leading to an academic degree. It could be a public or private institution and be either not for profit or a profit-based entity.

Social Capital: The collective value of human networks in a society, group or partnership that is connected with a common goal, demographic or geographic sense.

Student Learner Journey: The journey that students progress through from responding to a course advertisement with an inquiry to the award of qualification and becoming a member of the institutions' alumni. This journey would typically include processing of course applications, enrolment on course, payment of fees, attending classes, completing assignments and sitting exams, non-attendance during illness or accidents, or failure to achieve through other mitigating circumstances, progressing from year to year, graduating with an award and continuing to support via the alumni.

Chapter 5
When Giants Meet:
Collaborative Economy, Blockchain Technology, and Social Media

Myriam Ertz
https://orcid.org/0000-0001-9959-2779
LaboNFC, Université du Québec à Chicoutimi, Canada

Émilie Boily
https://orcid.org/0000-0002-2132-9142
LaboNFC, Université du Québec à Chicoutimi, Canada

ABSTRACT

The collaborative economy (CE) involves an intensification of direct or intermediated peer-to-peer trade, underpinned by robust digital infrastructures and processes, hence an increased use of new technologies and a redefinition of business activities. As an inherently connected economy, the CE is, therefore, prone to integrating the most recent technological advances including artificial intelligence, big data analysis, augmented reality, the smart grid, and blockchain technology. As an innovative payment and finance technology, the blockchain and cryptocurrencies could have potential implications for the CE. This chapter consists of a conceptual review analyzing how the CE connects with the blockchain technology. The chapter presents subsequently the organizational and managerial implications related to the use of blockchain technology in terms of governance, transaction costs, and user confidence. An illustrative case further examines the role of a prominent social media in the CE-blockchain nexus.

INTRODUCTION

Several confluences of technological, economic and sociocultural phenomena, are currently shifting conventional forms of commercial exchanges (Ertz et al., 2019a). This article discusses an exemplification of this supposed reconfiguration of commercial exchange. The study explores how the two societal phenomena of the collaborative economy (CE) and the blockchain technology (BT), both resulting markedly from technological advances and economic disturbances, intersect to reorganize and rearrange

DOI: 10.4018/978-1-7998-4543-0.ch005

commercial exchanges. Although having almost become a vernacular concept, the CE is an economic model that has taken on an unprecedented scale and scope through technological advances (Roos and Hahn, 2019). It has resulted in demultiplying peer-to-peer (P2P), peer-to-organization (P2O) and organization-to-peer (O2P) exchanges (Ertz et al., 2016). Other major developments in computer sciences and in mathematics have led to the emergence of the blockchain technology (Ghilal and Nach, 2019). This technology has led to an intensification of more genuine P2P exchanges with limited intermediation. Despite connections between both blockchain technology and the CE, in terms of technological advances and facilitation of peer-to-peer exchanges, few studies have examined the intertwining of both phenomena. Since the literature on this subject remains sparse, the objective of this article is to examine current information on the subject in order to understand the role played by blockchain technology in the development of collaborative practices.

This study adopts an exploratory descriptive design for its ability to provide a preliminary understanding of new and poorly documented phenomena. In addition, this design provides a frame for the formulation of new ideas and hypotheses. Since studies conducted on the topic of the CE and the blockchain technology are relatively recent, this article also aims at gathering state of the art research on the use of blockchain technology in order to understand its potential implication within collaborative practices. This technology may have the potential to act as a catalyst of the development of the CE by further decentralizing transactions and exchanges. Blockchain technology may therefore spur impacts on the diffusion of this new socioeconomic model known as the CE while also giving rise to a reconfiguration of existing actors, systems and roles. Since the impacts of blockchain technology on the development of the CE remains largely unexplored, the present study seeks to fill this theoretically and practically relevant gap by setting the following two objectives:

1) Define and conceptualize blockchain technology in the collaborative economy sphere;
2) Explore the potential implications of blockchain technology for the collaborative economy.

The contributions of this exploratory study are twofold. First, the paper provides a literature review that encapsulates the concepts of cryptocurrencies, blockchain technology and the CE. Second, the study results in the development of a theory-based research agenda to spur future research on the subject.

METHODOLOGY

We used Scopus, Web of Science, Business Source Complete and ABI/Inform databases to retrieve the articles containing the search terms "collaborative economy", "sharing economy", "blockchain", and "cryptocurrency". We then used the search strings "collaborative economy AND blockchain", "collaborative economy AND cryptocurrency" as well as "sharing economy AND blockchain", "sharing economy AND cryptocurrency" in order to retrieve relevant articles for the purpose of our study. We refined the search outcomes by retaining only publications in English, dating from 2010 onwards, as well as specific publication formats such as journal articles, books, conference proceedings, professional journal articles, and research reports.

CONCEPTUAL BACKGROUND

Defining Cryptocurrency

The notion of cryptocurrency has been explored in a variety of areas and contexts, including economics, sociology, political sciences and humanities (Swan, 2015; Huckle and White, 2016). In order to define this concept, the European Parliament has recently produced a document classifying the definitions provided by various organization, including the European Central Bank (ECB), the International Monetary Fund (IMF), the Committee on Payments and Market Infrastructures (CPIM), a component of the Bank for International Settlements (BIS), the European Banking Authority (EBA) and the World Bank (WB). The main conclusion of these different institutional viewpoints is that there is no generally accepted and regulated definition of cryptocurrency. Nevertheless, the majority of these jurisdictions view cryptocurrency as a subset, or a form of virtual currencies, also called digital currencies (Houben and Snyers, 2018).

At the most basic level cryptocurrency—digital currency or virtual currency—is a medium of exchange that functions like money (in that it can be exchanged for goods and services) but, unlike traditional currency, is untethered to, and independent from, national borders, central banks, sovereigns, or fiats (Maese et al., 2016, p. 468).

Cryptocurrencies exist fully in the digital world. For this reason, "digital currency" is generally preferred over "virtual currency" because of the more neutral connotations associated with the notion of digital currency. In fact, "virtuality" denotes negativity since "virtual' signals something that is "seemingly real" but not exactly "real" when referring to a currency that is stored in a "digital" or electronic register" (Lee, 2015, p. 6). In accordance with the above aspects, cryptocurrencies are used to integrate and exchange digital information through a process made possible by the principles of cryptography enabling secure and verifiable transactions (Maese et al., 2016). Cryptocurrencies are traded on global platforms (e.g., Coinbase) and are based on the principle of peer-to-peer exchange. While some cryptocurrencies may be used as a form of payment or as a means of exchange, they are not legal tender and are not issued by a government or central bank (AMF, 2019). The most well-known cryptocurrency is Bitcoin. It still dominates the digital currency market since it is the most highly priced digital currency available up to this date. Typically, this form of digital currency is exchanged when a party enters a transaction or generates a node in a software called the distributed ledger or blockchain (Ghilal and Nach, 2019). Therefore, no financial institution is involved in the transaction.

Bitcoin's major objective is to provide a global network of transactions and exchanges by allowing two willing parties to negotiate directly with each other without resorting to an expensive intermediary (Ghilal and Nach, 2019). This electronic payment system based on cryptographic evidence was introduced in a White Paper published in October 2008 by "Satoshi Nakamoto", to address the weaknesses of commerce as characterized by the intermediation of financial institutions, including: the costs of the mediation for the payment of a third party, the fact that transactions can be unilaterally rescinded, the existence of a minimum size for transactions and the possibility of fraud (Nakamoto, 2008). Also, except payment in person, there was no mechanism for making payments remotely through a communication channel without a trusted third party. The invention of Bitcoin has sparked the creation of many other alternative cryptocurrencies offering new features based on different algorithmic foundations (Ghilal and

Nach, 2019). On the other hand, the rapid increase in the number of digital currencies has led to higher price volatility. This volatility is determined by investors' feelings and not by a change in economic factors (Baker and Wurgler, 2007; Lee et al., 2018). It might however be noted that cryptocurrencies movements on Coinbase or similar platforms tend to follow conventional stock markets but by being negatively related to them. For example, if the stock markets increase (decrease), cryptocurrencies' value tends to stumble (increase), except for those pegged on fiat currencies such as the US dollar (e.g., Dai).

Defining Blockchain Technology (or Blockchains)

With the rapid growth of cryptocurrencies, an underlying technology has also gathered attention: blockchain. Primarily known for its use with digital currency, this technology has various applications that extend way beyond the financial and economic realm, including supply chain management, trade, health and government services (Ghilal and Nach, 2019). In fact, due to its emphasis on trust and security, the demand for blockchain's application is increasing in a variety of business sectors (Lee, 2019). The blockchain is therefore expected to create a new economic system by revolutionizing communication over the Internet, improving information security and transparency through the sharing of encrypted data on peer-to-peer networks (Lee, 2019).

Technically, blockchain is a decentralized and secure database of transactions based on decentralized nodes (i.e., miners) (Glaser, 2017). The blockchain is characterized by decentralization, persistency, anonymity, and auditability. Decentralization means that each transaction needs to be validated but the validation process does not occur through a central trusted agency (e.g., a central bank), but rather through a consensus algorithm in order to maintain data consistency in a distributed network (Zheng et al., 2017). Persistency means that it is impossible to delete or rollback any transaction once it is included in the blockchain. However, invalid transactions can be discovered immediately so that the persistency characteristic is not thought to be too much of a drawback overall. Anonymity, means that each user can interact with the blockchain in a generated address without revealing his/her real identify (Kosba et al., 2016). Finally, auditability means that any transaction has to refer to a previous unspent transaction (Nakamoto, 2008). Transactions can therefore be easily verified and tracked.

As shown in Table 1, there are four types of blockchain types according to characteristics such as "public or private" and "with or without permission". In a "permissionless" (without permission) blockchain (e.g., Bitcoin), anyone can operate a node and participate through spending CPU cycles (i.e., the time required for the execution of one simple machine instruction such as an addition or a subtraction [Encyclopedia, 2019]) and demonstrating "proof-of-work" (Cachin, 2016). Proof of work (PoW) is a consensus strategy or algorithm used in hashes' or blocks' validation processes (Nakamoto, 2008). Since in a decentralized network, such as the blockchain, someone has to be selected to record the transactions, there are multiple strategies for selecting that person, who is typically a miner. The easiest way, also used in PoW is random selection. However, this selection is vulnerable to attacks and requires a lot of energy due to the higher computing power needed to compute and recompute a hash value that cannot be attacked (Zheng et al., 2017). There are other consensus algorithms such as "proof-of-stake" (PoS) in which miners have to prove the ownership of the amount of currency. Although tending to favor the users with the most cryptocurrencies, PoS is a more energy-saving and efficient alternative to PoW, and many blockchains adopt PoW first before moving to PoS (Zheng et al., 2017). On the other hand, blockchains in the "permissioned" (with permission) model verify who participates in the validation and in the protocol (Swanson, 2015). Besides, an important second characteristic of blockchain architecture relates to the property regime.

A blockchain might have either a public or a private regime. In a public blockchain, each node (i.e., miner) could take part in the consensus process. As for private chain, it is fully controlled by one organization and the organization could determine the final consensus (Zheng et al., 2017). It logically follows that since only one organization is responsible for consensus determination in private blockchain, the process is centralized and can only be permissioned.

Table 1. Blockchain types

Types of blockchain	With permission	Without permission
Public	No restriction on network data reading; Predefined list of participants whose identity is known for adding transactions; e.g., *Ethereum*	Distributed network based on proof of work (PoW); Involves consensus among participants; e.g., *Bitcoin*
Private	Predefined list of participants for reading network data and adding transactions; e.g., *Ripple*	Network data reading and adding transactions are assigned to all participants; *Unlikely to occur*

Source: (Ghilal and Nach, 2019)

As an open and distributed registry, blockchain is used to record and track transaction data. Due to the principles of cryptography, these transactions are secure and verifiable. This registry solves the double-spending problem as well as the risk for digital files to be copied and shared infinitely. Thus, just like money in its physical form, a cryptocurrency cannot be spent twice (Nakamoto, 2008). With the peer-to-peer network (P2P), it is possible to set up a secure transaction register recording the transactions. These transactions are validated by the consensus mechanism based on the Proof of Work (PoW) held by miners who can accept or refuse all transactions within the system (Nakamoto, 2008). For doing that, different steps must be taken in order to guarantee operations as shown in Table 2.

Table 2. Steps for Building a Consensus-Based Blockchain Network

	Necessary steps to create a consensus-based blockchain network
1	Transaction data disseminated to all participants (nodes)
2	Each node collects new transactions in a block
3	Each node seeks to find Proof of Work (*PoW*) difficult to produce for its block
4	When a node finds Proof of Work, it disseminates the result of its calculus to all nodes
5	Nodes accept blocking if all transactions in it are valid and not spent
6	Nodes express their acceptance of the block by working on the creation of the next block of the chain, using the hash of the accepted block as previous

Source: (Nakamoto, 2008)

Supported by a community of anonymous miners, blockchain configuration has evolved to allow several types of transactions. For this purpose, Godebarge and Rossat (2016) denote commercial or stock exchange transactions, contracts, agreements and basic information entry or consultation operations. In addition, the use of blockchain exceeds the limits of cryptocurrency by benefiting to businesses and governments. While it is not possible to predict the future of blockchain, at this point it is widely assumed that it is destined to become a highly important technology. Some researchers describe it as being as important as the Internet, due to its potential attendant impacts on business and society (e.g., Beck, 2018). Research suggests that blockchain has the capacity to reduce uncertainty, insecurity, and ambiguity in transactions by providing full transactional disclosure and by producing a single truth for all network participants (Beck et al., 2018, p. 1021).

Recent studies highlight the positive effects and potentially transformational nature of blockchain, including the reconfiguration of market exchange (e.g., Pazaitis et al., 2017; Beck et al., 2018; Ghilal and Nach, 2019). For example, blockchain technology can enable the creation of "a new system of value that will better support the dynamics of social sharing" (Pazaitis et al., 2017, p. 105) or transform the organizations in a "new form of organizational design—decentralized autonomous organizations (DAO)—which are organizations with governance rules specified in the blockchain" (Beck et al., 2018, p. 1020). Implementation of the blockchain technology in combination with Internet of Things is also expected to achieve logistical and transportation objectives such as supply chain traceability, business process optimization, and financial savings (Merkaš, Perkov, and Bonin, 2020). Even standalone, the blockchain technology might improve supply chain adaptability, agility and alignment to sport competitive advantage and firm performance (Sheel and Nath, 2019).

Some studies also pinpoint negative aspects related to the that technology. For example, as feared by the financial press and the Securities and Exchange Commission (SEC), Investors are thus deceived by firms mentioning unwarrantedly the blockchain as a buzzword to generate a surge in stock price (Cheng, de Franco, Jiang, and Lin, 2019. In fact, investors tend to overreact to a firm's disclosure of a potential foray into Blockchain technology and this overreaction is function of the Bitcoin price bubble. Investors are thus deceived by firms mentioning unwarrantedly the blockchain as a buzzword to generate a stock price spike (Cheng, de Franco, Jiang, and Lin, 2019).

Defining the Collaborative Economy and Digital Platforms

This section introduces the collaborative economy and its digital component in the form of collaborative economy platforms.

Collaborative Economy

The collaborative economy (CE) is generally associated with concepts such as sharing economy, collaborative consumption, on-demand economy, on-demand services, group economy, independent economy, peer economy, digital economy, gig economy, and platform economy (Botsman, 2015; Rinne, 2017). For this study, the term "collaborative economy" is used as it is best suited to the idea of a new socio-economic model (Tussyadiah and Pesonen, 2018). It is also used because of its ability to include both redistribution and mutualization (Ertz et al., 2019b). While redistribution refers to exchanges involving transfer of ownership, mutualisation refers to access to resources without transfer of ownership (Acquier et al., 2017). Ertz et al. (2019b) argue that the CE allows for mutualization through new traffic systems that involve the presence of peers and that essentially imply the use of the Internet. While the CE transforms the respective role of consumers by moving them from buyers to suppliers or service providers, it also changes the nature of market exchanges. In fact, CE involves a redistribution of goods, not only through monetized exchanges, but also through resale, exchange or donation (Botsman and Roger, 2010). Ertz et al. (2016) synthesize these two aspects by defining the collaborative consumption taking place within the CE as: ''The set of resource circulation systems which enable consumers to both obtain and provide, temporarily or permanently, valuable resources or services through direct interaction with other consumers or through a mediator" (p. 6). The mediator in question might have varying degrees of mediation from facilitating exchanges to complete control over all aspects governing these exchanges. These activities are done mainly through organizations, offline channels or multi-channel systems.

Components of a Collaborative Economy

The CE is thus primarily a peer-to-peer economic model (Belk, 2014; Ertz et al., 2019b; Botsman and Rogers, 2010). Regarding new forms of consumption, the emergence of the collaborative economy has significantly disrupted the retail and consumer services landscape. This is noticeable in various areas such as food, accommodation, transportation as well as access to goods and services (Correa et al., 2019; Yeo et al., 2017). In fact, the CE is transforming the way people produce, consume, finance and learn, using networks of connected individuals and communities rather than centralized institutions. The CE consists of four major subdivisions: collaborative production, collaborative education, collaborative finance and collaborative consumption (Botsman, 2013). To others, the CE includes practices such as trading, renting, pooling or sharing, instead of traditional trade (Ertz et al., 2016).

Collaborative Economy Platforms

To some authors, the CE refers to the use of digital platforms such as Uber or Airbnb, as well as to participation in in-person exchange meetings or in a local exchange system (Arsel and Dobscha, 2011; Albinsson and Perera, 2012; Ertz et al., 2019b). In other words, they contend that the CE occurs both online and offline. Yet, the online segment of the CE is the one that has attracted the most attention in academia and in which the most innovative business models have emerged so far. In fact, the fast development of the CE relies heavily on digital technology (Acquier et al., 2017). Currently, there are various forms of digital platforms. Technically, they can be defined as extensible databases. More broadly, they correspond to a ''sociotechnical assemblage'' (de Reuver et al., 2018). The system is based on software that provides the basic functionality shared by the modules that interact with it (Tiwana et al., 2010; Tilson et al., 2012; Ghazawneh and Henfridsson, 2015; de Reuver et al., 2018). Essentially, the emergence of digital platforms (for example, Uber and Airbnb) has led to an intensification of collaborative practices.

IMPLICATIONS OF BLOCKCHAIN AND CRYPTOCURRENCY TECHNOLOGIES ON the COLLABORATIVE ECONOMY

This section introduces the various implications of the blockchain and cryptocurrency technologies on the CE. We propose that these technologies will further accelerate the diffusion and adoption of collaborative practices. It is also expected that such blockchain and cryptocurrency technologies will reconfigure the conventional model of intermediation within the CE. Finally, we also evoke some key managerial implications in terms of governance, costs, user trust, as well as links with social networks.

Emergence of Collaborative Consumption

The growth of collaborative platforms has made it possible for individuals to interact on a large scale. Hawlitschek et al. (2018) thus identify the existence of three parties involved in these transactions:

- **Suppliers (for example, hosts on Airbnb, car owners and drivers on Turo and Uber, respectively):** offering a private service, usually underutilized or unused and holding the resource for sale, donation, swapping, rental or co-use;
- **Users:** seeking to use, rent or obtain the proposed products or services through various means (for example, tenants or passengers);
- **Collaborative platforms:** acting as an infrastructure for the mutualization or redistribution of goods or services between users, as well as the establishment and maintenance of trust for the realization of exchanges.

The next sections emphasize how blockchain and cryptocurrency technologies modify the relationship and the dynamics of exchange between these parties.

Collaborative Economy Platforms

Technological development seems to be at the heart of increasingly more diffuse collaborative practices by facilitating peer-to-peer exchanges. Although collaborative practices and peer-to-peer exchange activities existed before the emergence of digital platforms (Ertz et al., 2019b), the main factors influencing the development of the CE are due to technological progresses, which have acted as catalysts (Dervojeda et al., 2013; Demailly and Novel, 2014; Daunorienė et al., 2015; Hamari et al., 2016; Selloni, 2017). For example, social networking sites, and Web 2.0 in general, but also geo-referencing, or online payment systems all constitute technological progresses that contributed to the development of the CE. Currently, similarly to the information and communication technologies mentioned before, blockchain could pave the way for major, and currently largely unknown, innovations in the CE. For this purpose, Baller and al. (2016) emphasize blockchain's ability to facilitate the creation of distributed and shared economy applications that enable individuals to create value by monetizing their resources securely.

With the recent interest in the Internet of Things and blockchain, the opportunity exists to create a myriad of sharing applications, e.g. peer-to-peer automatic payment mechanisms, foreign exchange platforms, digital rights management and cultural heritage to name but a few (Huckle et al., 2016, p. 461).

Therefore, IoT and blockchain technology would contribute to promote the diffusion of collaborative practices.

Reconfiguration of Collaborative Exchange Intermediation

According to Scott (2016), blockchain allows for non-hierarchical self-organization and peer-to-peer collaboration. In addition, the technology fosters a "cooperative consensus" that may be useful for the governance of large-scale projects (Nakamoto, 2008; Scott 2016). To this end, some authors have examined the presence of elements specific to ideological socialism within these structured collaborative networks (Swan, 2015; Huckle and White, 2016; Wright and De Filippi, 2015; Van Valkenburgh, et al., 2015) notably on democratization, decentralization of organisations, promotion of participation and the importance of the collective interest. Thus, blockchain technology plays a potentially vital role in the development of collaborative practices, but also in the implementation – by individuals themselves – of more egalitarian principles of production and distribution by facilitating peer-to-peer interventions that advance community interests.

To Huckle et al. (2016), the intersection of Internet of Things (IoT) and blockchain technology benefits to CE by offering opportunities such as creating secure automatic payment between counterparts or creating exchange mechanisms and platforms. In fact, blockchain technology has the potential to redefine governance and trade by decentralizing market practices. Thus, it evolves in parallel with the models of platforms (for example, Airbnb or Uber) operating through an intermediary that ensures the processing of transactions. In this context, blockchain technology would facilitate value exchange without intermediary (De Filippi, 2017, in Hawlitschek et al., 2018) and without affecting user confidence (Botsman and Rogers, 2010). Indeed, by transforming how trust builds between users, blockchain technology has "the potential to create a 2.0 sharing economy" (Lundy, 2016, in Hawlitschek et al., 2018, p. 51) with the capacity to disrupt traditional business models (Nowiński and Kozma, 2017).

In terms of innovation, the various strategies aimed at improving efficiency and organizational effectiveness enable businesses to gain a competitive advantage and create value (Moreira et al., 2012; Chuwiruch et al., 2015). This implies that when an organizational activity or function no longer creates any value, it disappears or is replaced for the sake of productivity (Prokopenko, 1990). This principle of efficiency raises the hypothesis of replacing traditional intermediaries by blockchain technology and the need for these platforms to adapt (Waelbroeck, 2017).

Organizational and Managerial Implications

Essentially, technological development and the increased use of digital platforms have led to an intensification of peer-to-peer exchanges such as online product reselling, web-mediated car-sharing or co-lodging. With the use of blockchain technology, collaborative platforms are subject to transformations in terms of governance, transaction costs and user confidence. The following section presents the organizational and managerial impacts of integrating this technology into collaborative activities.

Transferring Governance From Collaborative Platforms to Blockchain

Currently, the CE is made up of platforms whose owners receive remuneration through transaction fees. Criticism has been levelled against these practices, including the possible transformation of these supposedly sharing economy platforms into quasi-monopolistic organizations (The Economist, 2014, in Beck and al., 2018) acting predatorily by creating "neoliberalism on steroids" (Morozov, 2013, in Murillo et al., 2017) or a "nightmarish form of neoliberal capitalism" (Martin, 2016). In 2017, a group of engineers working on blockchain development based on Ethereum founded Swarm City (initiated from the decentralized carpooling service called Arcade City), a decentralized peer-to-peer platform giving access to a global community of consumers and service providers (Beck et al., 2018). Swarm City offers the opportunity for anyone to create their own brand at home without any third party intervention . The objective of this platform is to provide blockchain-based infrastructure to facilitate the creation of decentralized collaborative economy applications (Beck et al., 2018). Users have the option to determine prices themselves, without the involvement of a third party.

With Swarm City, the engineering group wants to eliminate intermediaries - owners of traditional platforms such as Airbnb or Uber - by transferring transactions and governance to the blockchain. Due to blockchain, many areas can benefit from a transparent infrastructure and reduce the power of intermediaries. The main purpose of Bitcoin is to enable a global network of transaction and exchange by allowing two consenting parties to negotiate directly without resorting to an expensive intermediary (Ghilal and Nach, 2019). Therefore, by allowing users to negotiate directly with each other when buying, selling or exchanging services, this technology can have a direct impact on the CE.

However, the transfer of transactions and governance from traditional actors of the CE to the blockchain, as innovative and positive it may seem, remains debatable in many regards. In fact, if some individuals will certainly rejoice over the potential disappearance of an Uber or an Airbnb, what assurance do we have that the blockchain will remain the impartial, objective, nonpolitical, stateless, disintermediated, and decentralized "Eldorado" it is today (if it has ever been as such)? The blockchain could become the new inescapable, central, monopolistic intermediary, and its army of miners, engineers and programmers could become the new elite of a technocratic ruling class.

This ambiguity associated with the notion of blockchain governance has already been largely discussed by forward-looking authors (e.g., Campbell-Verduyn, 2018). It seems to get even worse with the diversification of new forms of governance associated with a variety of cryptocurrencies (Arsenault and Ertz, 2019). In Campbell-Verduyn's (2018) collective book, there are three forms of internal governance associated with cryptocurrencies and that could possibly create new power nodes within the blockchain itself: miners' governance, the governance by the programs operating behind the applications and the governance of the exchange market. Therefore, blockchain "governance" does not belong to intermediaries, as is the case with traditional CE platforms, but to new anonymous bodies of governance, unknown to the general public and to the users themselves. Besides, the blockchain goes beyond the financial framework and permeates in the management of political, legal and judicial spheres, which raises numerous questions regarding the presence of a centralised technology within diverse governments and organizations (Arsenault and Ertz, 2019).

Reducing Transaction and Coordination Costs

Currently, various merchants around the world accept payments in Bitcoin (for example, Target, Dell and Home Depot). Also, online buying and selling platforms between users such as Amazon, eBay or Craigslist allow this method of payment. Recently, Bitrefill, a gift card provider, has offered US residents the option of booking on Airbnb through five different cryptocurrencies (Mowers, 2019). By moving transactions and governance from collaborative platforms to blockchain, it is possible to reduce costs and redistribute to users the share of value currently held by intermediaries (e.g., Amazon, eBay, Uber or Airbnb). In general, these savings are supported by the arrival of intelligent contracts relying on computing codes. These codes are executed when precise conditions are met (Deloitte Development LLC, 2017) whereas a third-party intervention is unnecessary.

Despite the relative immaturity of blockchain technology, recent research has estimated the reduction in costs resulting from its professional use for organizations (Huckle and White, 2016; White, 2017; Di Gregorio and Nustad, 2017). These include savings in labour, documentation, automation and as well as efficiency benefits. In terms of the CE, these cost reductions can benefit many areas such as sharing computer services, renting apartments and workspaces, carpooling services, decentralized market trading platforms or distributed social networks (Sun et al., 2016; De Filippi, 2017; Dobrovnik et al., 2018). For intermediary platforms without advertising revenues, the integration of technology could nonetheless mean the weakening or the disappearance of such business models.

Maintaining User Confidence and Safety

Trust has always been and remains a central aspect of digital intermediary exchanges in general, and in the CE in particular (Botsman and Rogers, 2011). Since the release of the Ethereum decentralized exchange protocol in 2015 (Christodoulou et al., 2018), the blockchain has evolved beyond Bitcoin. Currently, smart contracts based on this technology facilitate the transfer of an asset or currency. "Smart contracts are essentially lines of executable code accompanied by conditions; the latter are checked automatically and, if certain conditions are met, the code is executed and recorded on the blockchain" (Christodoulou et al., 2018, p. 185). A bug in a smart contract creates some unique issues though. Since transactions cannot be undone on a blockchain, contracts will need to be upgraded instead (Orcutt, 2019). This means deploying additional smart contracts to interact with them. Another possibility is to stop all activity once a hack is detected or to create a fork to a new blockchain and have everyone on the network agree to use the new network (Orcutt, 2019).

Cryptography ensures blockchain security by rendering transactions verifiable. Through blockchain technology, transactions are fully disclosed, reducing uncertainty, insecurity and ambiguity (Beck et al., 2016; Nærland et al., 2017), without disclosing users' personal information. In addition, the speed of transactions protects users from the insolvency of any participant since there is no time delay between the actual contract date and its execution (Mangano, 2018). Thus, transactions are instantaneous and irrevocable. While blockchain technology facilitates both producer-consumer and peer-to-peer exchanges, the fact remains that cryptocurrencies incur risks due to their high level of volatility.

In CE, the development of peer-to-peer activities leads to changes in the labour market (e.g., the increase in freelance activities or the reduction in the number of workers employed full-time by organizations). Changes may affect the stability of individual incomes or social protection, such as insurance or workers' pensions (Baller et al., 2016). In addition, the potential for change associated with the blockchain and users' trust in the blockchain remains dependent on its adaptation to the environment in which the technology is implemented. Consequently, its integration must be based on a peer-to-peer network and must be adapted to the political, economic, legal, social and cultural environment.

ILLUSTRATIVE CASE: SOCIAL NETWORKS, COLLABORATIVE ECONOMY AND BLOCKCHAIN TECHNOLOGY

Equipped with a deeper understanding of the implications of a technology such as the blockchain, some CE intermediaries have tried to act proactively by integrating the technology within their own operations. For example, Facebook is a social commerce platform and also a collaborative player through its ever-increasing Facebook Marketplace. In fact, consumers can be either obtainers or providers of products or services which makes the Facebook Marketplace platform an original collaborative exchange scheme (Ertz et al., 2019b). The social network Facebook announced the creation of its own cryptocurrency Libra, a global currency powered by its own blockchain technology. The latter is expected to be officially launched in 2020 and its value is expected to remain largely stable due to its attachment to another stable asset (e.g., gold) (Athena Information Solutions Pvt. Ltd, 2019). In fact, Libra will be backed by a reserve of real assets, such as bank deposits and government bonds, reducing the risk of inflation (Lu, 2019). Once launched, users will be able to purchase this currency and add it to their digital wallet (Lu, 2019). Yet, all of these developments remain uncertain given the pressure put by governments and central banks on Facebook to curb its Libra project (Mizrahi, 2019). Some also fear that if a Silicon Valley giant such as Facebook is in control of over what people can and cannot do with their money, the is a risk of shifting to a "total surveillance coin" that may become a dystopia if controlled by Facebook or the government.

In a study on product lifetime extension practices, Ertz et al. (2018a) argue that social networks can potentially weaken the role of platforms for the exchange of goods and services between individuals by combining interactions between relatives (for example, friends or family members) and foreigners. In fact, social networks amplify word of mouth by connecting people to each other (John, 2012). In particular, the authors raise the major impact of the creation of Facebook Marketplace on peer-to-peer exchanges, indicating that this space reduces the role of traditional intermediaries such as Kijiji, LesPAC, Leboncoin in France, or Craigslist, by allowing two consenting parties to negotiate directly with each other. Some Facebook apps allow consumers to exchange goods without meeting each other, such as on eBay or Amazon. With the creation of Libra, the social network will offer consumers the opportunity to exchange on the Marketplace or on their wall all types of goods and services without having recourse to an intermediary. As a result, by integrating blockchain technology and cryptocurrency payment, Facebook could weaken the role of traditional collaborative economic platforms that do not integrate the combination of interactions with close social circles, on the one hand, and foreigners, on the other. Nevertheless, this exchange model could make users more vulnerable with regards to the protection of their personal data.

THEORETICAL IMPLICATIONS

The CE has been criticized by many authors, observers and analysts (see Murillo et al., 2017 for a review). Past literature emphasized conflicts between traditional industry players and collaborative exchange schemes, such as hotel chains and Airbnb (Zervas et al., 2017); as well as disputes between Uber and local authorities or taxi drivers (Ertz et al., 2018b), to name but a few of these contentions. The most intense disputes however have involved seemingly "predatory" platforms (Murillo et al., 2017) yet not all of them are of that nature. Some platforms operate around genuine sharing and altruistic principles such as Peerby or Freecycle (Arsel and Dobscha, 2011). Yet, they do not attract as much financier or media attention for their lower return on investment and smaller propensity for scandal or subversion. In this paper, we contribute to the literature by providing a conceptual analysis of the influence of the blockchain technology on this state of affairs.

We submit that the blockchain and cryptocurrency will reduce the role, need and importance for intermediaries, that will appear redundant and parasitic. However, the intrinsic characteristics of auditability and decentralization that are inherent to the blockchain technology (Zheng et al., 2017), may contribute to create economic ecosystems in which intermediaries sharing similar characteristics of auditability and decentralization will be more likely to thrive. Genuine sharing platforms through their greater emphasis on prosocial behavior and open governance systems are more likely to display these features and as such, to thrive under blockchain technology operating under the "public mode without permission"

(Ghilal and Nach, 2019). A greater capability of traceability offered by the blockchain technology may further the rewarding of prosocial behaviors through tax deduction, or other incentives, due to enhanced capabilities for tracing prosocial behavior on such platforms and apps. Tremendous applications to foster the greater good thus exist, but remain contingent upon the type of blockchain technology underpinning operations, its governance, as well as complementary government regulation.

MANAGERIAL IMPLICATIONS

From a managerial viewpoint the abovementioned theoretical implications mean that, genuinely sharing platforms like Peerby or Freecycle could tremendously benefit from the blockchain technology by rendering their exchange schemes more effective through enhanced auditability and the creation of smaller exchange systems through decentralization. The impact of the blockchain technology is likely to be more positive for not for profit or social and solidarity economy schemes rather than for for profit intermediaries. As mentioned before, the larger, for-profit (and more controversial) platforms will be perceived as providing less to no added-value, putting into question their own existence. In sum, smaller-scale, local and socially-oriented (not for profits) organizations may derive larger benefits form the generalization of blockchain and cryptocurrency technology provided that these technologies retain the characteristics of decentralization and auditability of transactions.

CRITICAL DISCUSSION AND FUTURE RESEARCH AVENUES

The hypothesis that this technology has major impacts on the development of collaborative practices and on the entire ecosystem underlying these practices, seems to be confirmed in several ways. Blockchain technology allows digital platform users to negotiate directly with each other and create value without the intervention of a costly intermediary. In addition to ensuring the security of transactions and the solvency of the parties, the blockchain addresses fears associated with the development of quasi-monopolistic and predatory organizations and potentially having the ability to change the governance of collaborative platforms.

This study suggests potentially interesting avenues for future research. One of these avenues is the relative immaturity of the concepts of cryptocurrencies, blockchain technology, and CE. This makes it difficult to provide a generally accepted definition of these terms. Another avenue refers to the potential of integrating the blockchain technology by CE actors themselves. As for the integration of Libra by Facebook, it could be interesting to study how CE platforms could integrate some aspects of the blockchain technology in order to counter the potential negative impacts of the technology on their organization.

Additional studies are also needed with regards to the notions of governance, trust and protection of privacy of users realizing operations on a CE platform integrating blockchain technology in the likes of Facebook and its own cryptocurrency Libra.

The scattered nature of the literature on the intersection of the concepts studied in this paper, which makes it difficult to fully understand the phenomenon. Since blockchain is evolving alongside platforms such as Uber or Airbnb by decentralizing commercial activities, it might be interesting to study how these platforms can develop their own technology to counter the possible negative impacts on their organization (for example, the removal of intermediaries).

Finally, with regards to organizations, blockchain technology has the potential to improve management decision-making by increasing the amount of customer data (Ghilal and Nach, 2019). Network security also seems to reduce the risk of fraud, while reducing legal needs through the creation of smart contracts. It would then be appropriate to examine the impact of these improvements on the internal governance of companies, as well as on the management of collaborative platforms. The present study does not claim to have covered all of the potential avenues of analysis in the field of collaborative practices and the use of blockchain technology. However, hypotheses and ideas for future research as well as new managerial questions were presented. The objective of this study was therefore to inform research and academia on the impacts of blockchain technology on the CE.

ACKNOWLEDGMENT

The authors thank Jeanne Simard for her continuous support and for her approval to publish this study in English.

This research received no specific grant from any funding agency in the public, commercial, or not-for-profit sectors.

REFERENCES

Acquier, A., Daudigeos, T., & Pinkse, J. (2017). Promises and paradoxes of the sharing economy: An organizing framework. *Technological Forecasting and Social Change*, *125*, 1–10. doi:10.1016/j.techfore.2017.07.006

Albinsson, P. A., & Yasanthi Perera, B. (2012). Alternative marketplaces in the 21st century: Building community through sharing events. *Journal of Consumer Behaviour*, *11*(4), 303–315. doi:10.1002/cb.1389

Arsel, Z., & Dobscha, S. (2011). Hybrid pro-social exchange systems: The case of Freecycle. *ACR North American Advances*, *39*, 66–67.

Arsenault, J., & Ertz, M. (2019). *Towards a technocratic governance system?* International Journal of Innovation Studies. doi:10.1522/revueot.v27n2.877

Athena Information Solutions Pvt. Ltd. (2019). All you need to know about Facebook's cryptocurrency announcement. *Media Nama*. Retrieved from https://link.gale.com/apps/doc/A589567097/CDB?u=crepuq_uqac&sid=CDB&xid=61938bb8

Autorité des marchés financiers. (2019). *Bitcoin et autres cryptomonnaies*. Retrieved from https://lautorite.qc.ca/grand-public/investissements/bitcoin-et-autres-cryptomonnaies/

Baker, M., & Wurgler, J. (2007). Investor Sentiment in the Stock Market. *The Journal of Economic Perspectives*, *21*(2), 129–151. doi:10.1257/jep.21.2.129

Baller, S., Dutta, S., & Lanvin, B. (2016). *Global information technology report 2016*. Ouranos.

Beck, R., Czepluch, J. S., Lollike, N., & Malone, S. O. (2016). Blockchain—the gateway to trust-free cryptographic transactions. *Proceedings of the 24th European conference on information systems, (ECIS).* Retrieved from https://pdfs.semanticscholar.org/ee1e/fd77e8b6287438d312b244177bb143f7a072.pdf

Beck, R., Müller-Bloch, C., & King, J. L. (2018). Governance in the blockchain economy: A framework and research agenda. *Journal of the Association for Information Systems, 19*(10), 1020–1034. doi:10.17705/1jais.00518

Belk, R. (2014). You are what you can access: Sharing and collaborative consumption online. *Journal of Business Research, 67*(8), 1595–1600. doi:10.1016/j.jbusres.2013.10.001

Botsman, R. (2013). The Sharing Economy Lacks A Shared Definition. *Fast Company*. Retrieved from https://www.fastcoexist.com/3022028/the-sharing-economy-lacksa-shared-definition

Botsman, R. (2015). *Defining the sharing economy: what is collaborative consumption-and what isn't.* Repéré à https://www.fastcompany.com/3046119/defining-the-sharing-economy-what-is-collaborative-consumption-and-what-isnt

Botsman, R., & Rogers, R. (2010). *What's mine is yours*. Penguin Press.

Botsman, R., & Rogers, R. (2011). *What's mine is yours: how collaborative consumption is changing the way we live* (Vol. 5). Collins.

Cachin, C. (2016). Architecture of the hyperledger blockchain fabric. In *Workshop on distributed cryptocurrencies and consensus ledgers* (*Vol. 310*, p. 4). Academic Press.

Campbell-Verduyn, M. (Ed.). (2018). Bitcoin and beyond: Cryptocurrencies block chains, and global governance. Abingdon, UK: Routledge.

Cheng, S. F., De Franco, G., Jiang, H. B., & Lin, P. K. (2019). Riding the Blockchain Mania: Public Firms' Speculative 8-K Disclosures. *Management Science, 65*(12), 5901–5913. doi:10.1287/mnsc.2019.3357

Christodoulou, P., Christodoulou, K., & Andreou, A. (2018). A decentralized application for logistics: Using blockchain in real-world applications. *The Cyprus Review, 30*(2), 181–18. http://cyprusreview.org/index.php/cr/article/view/577

Chuwiruch, N., Jhundra-Indra, P., & Boonlua, S. (2015). Marketing Innovation Strategy and Marketing Performance: A Conceptual Framework. *Allied Academies International Conference. Academy of Marketing Studies. Proceedings, 20*(2), 82–93. http://sbiproxy.uqac.ca/login?url=https://search.proquest.com/docview/1764885744?accountid=14722

Correa, J. C., Garzón, W., Brooker, P., Sakarkar, G., Carranza, S. A., Yunado, L., & Rincón, A. (2019). Evaluation of collaborative consumption of food delivery services through web mining techniques. *Journal of Retailing and Consumer Services, 46*, 45–50. doi:10.1016/j.jretconser.2018.05.002

Daunorienė, A., Drakšaitė, A., Snieška, V., & Valodkienė, G. (2015). Evaluating Sustainability of Sharing Economy Business Models. *Procedia: Social and Behavioral Sciences, 213*, 836–841. doi:10.1016/j.sbspro.2015.11.486

De Reuver, M., Sørensen, C., & Basole, R. C. (2018). The digital platform: A research agenda. *Journal of Information Technology*, *33*(2), 124–135. doi:10.105741265-016-0033-3

Deloitte Development LLC. (2017). *La technologie de la chaîne de blocs et son incidence potentielle sur la profession d'auditeur et de certificateur*. Retrieved from URL://01529-RG-chaine-de-blocs-profession-auditeur-certificateur.pdf

Demailly, D., & Novel, A.-S. (2014). *The sharing economy: make it sustainable, Studies N03/14*. IDDRI.

Dervojeda, K. (2013). The sharing economy. Accessibility based business models for Peer to Peer markets. *European Union*.

Di Gregorio, R., & Nustad, S. S. (2017). *Blockchain Adoption in the Shipping Industry* (Master's Thesis). Copenhagen Business School, Copenhagen, Denmark.

Dobrovnik, M., Herold, D. M., Fürst, E., & Kummer, S. (2018). Blockchain for and in logistics: What to adopt and where to start. *Logistics, 2*(3), 1-18. Retrieved from https://www.mdpi.com/2305-6290/2/3/18

Encyclopedia. (2019). *CPU cycle*. Available at: https://www.encyclopedia.com/computing/dictionaries-thesauruses-pictures-and-press-releases/cpu-cycle

Ertz, M., Durif, F., & Arcand, M. (2016). Collaborative Consumption: Conceptual Snapshot at a Buzzword. *Journal of Entrepreneurship Education*, *19*(2), 1–23. doi:10.2139srn.2799884

Ertz, M., Durif, F., & Arcand, M. (2018a). Towards Multilife Marketing: How Goods Multiple Lives Practices Create Value for Consumers. *Journal of Promotion Management*, *24*(6), 863–894. doi:10.1080/10496491.2017.1408527

Ertz, M., Durif, F., & Arcand, M. (2019b). A conceptual perspective on collaborative consumption. *Academy of Marketing Science Review*, *9*, 27–41. doi:10.100713162-018-0121-3

Ertz, M., Hallegatte, D., & Bousquet, J. (2019a). *La reconfiguration de l'échange marchand. Tour d'horizon, enjeux et perspectives*. Les Presses de l'Université du Québec.

Ertz, M., Lecompte, A., & Durif, F. (2018b). "It's not my fault, I am in the right!" Exploration of neutralization in the justification of the support and use of a controversial technological collaborative consumption service. *Technological Forecasting and Social Change*, *134*, 254–264. doi:10.1016/j.techfore.2018.06.032

Ghazawneh, A., & Henfridsson, O. (2015). A Paradigmatic Analysis of Digital Application Marketplaces. *Journal of Information Technology*, *30*(3), 198–208. doi:10.1057/jit.2015.16

Ghilal, A., & Nach, H. (2019). La technologie de la chaîne de blocs: fondements et applications. In *La reconfiguration de l'échange marchand. Tour d'horizon, enjeux et perspectives* (pp. 113–131). Les Presses de l'Université du Québec. doi:10.2307/j.ctv10qqx4s.12

Glaser, F. (2017). Pervasive Decentralisation of Digital Infrastructures : A Framework for Blockchain enabled System and Use Case Analysis. *Proceedings of the 50th Hawaii International Conference on System Sciences (HICSS-50)*. Retrieved from https://ssrn.com/abstract=3052165

Godebarge, F., & Rossat, R. (2016). Principes clés d'une application Blockchain. *EMLyon Business School*. Retrieved from https://www.coursehero.com/file/29197828/GODEBARGE-ROSSAT-Blockchain-version-finalepdf/

Grybaitė, V., & Stankeviciene, J. (2018). An empirical analysis of factors affecting sharing economy growth. *Oeconomia Copernicana*, *9*(4), 635–654. doi:10.24136/oc.2018.031

Hamari, J., Sjöklint, M., & Ukkonen, A. (2016). The sharing economy: Why people participate in collaborative consumption. *Journal of the Association for Information Science and Technology*, *67*(9), 2047–2059. doi:10.1002/asi.23552

Hawlitschek, F., Notheisen, B., & Teubner, T. (2018). The limits of trust-free systems: A literature review on blockchain technology and trust in the sharing economy. *Electronic Commerce Research and Applications*, *29*, 50–63. doi:10.1016/j.elerap.2018.03.005

Hawlitschek, F., Teubner, T., & Gimpel, H. (2016). Understanding the Sharing Economy—Drivers and Impediments for Participation in Peer-to-Peer Rental. *Conference: Hawaii International Conference on System Sciences*. doi: 10.1109/HICSS.2016.593

Houben, R., & Snyers, A. (2018). *Cryptocurrencies and blockchain: legal context and implications for financial crime, money laundering and tax evasion*. European Parliament study: PE 619.024. Repéré à https://publications.europa.eu/en/publication-detail/-/publication/631f847c-b4aa-11e8-99ee-01aa75ed71a1

Huckle, S., Bhattacharya, R., White, M., & Beloff, N. (2016). Internet of Things, Blockchain and Shared Economy Applications. *Procedia Computer Science*, *98*, 461–466. doi:10.1016/j.procs.2016.09.074

Huckle, S., & White, M. (2016). Socialism and the Blockchain. *Future Internet, 8*(4), 49. Retrieved from https://www.mdpi.com/1999-5903/8/4/49

Kosba, A., Miller, A., Shi, E., Wen, Z., & Papamanthou, C. (2016, May). Hawk: The blockchain model of cryptography and privacy-preserving smart contracts. In *2016 IEEE symposium on security and privacy (SP)* (pp. 839-858). IEEE.

Lee, D. (2015). *Handbook of Digital Currency*. Elsevier.

Lee, D. K. C., Guo, L., & Wang, Y. (2018). Cryptocurrency: A new investment opportunity? *Journal of Alternative Investments*, *20*(3), 16–40. doi:10.3905/jai.2018.20.3.016

Lee, J. Y. (2019). A decentralized token economy: How blockchain and cryptocurrency can revolutionize business. *Business Horizons*, *62*(6), 773–784. doi:10.1016/j.bushor.2019.08.003

Lu, D. (2019). Facebook launches a digital currency. *New Scientist*, *242*(3236), 11. doi:10.1016/S0262-4079(19)31157-1

Maese, V. A., Avery, A. W., Naftalis, B. A., Wink, S. P., & Valdez, Y. D. (2016). Cryptocurrency: A primer. *The Banking Law Journal, 133*(8), 468-471. Retrieved from https://www.lw.com/thoughtLeadership/cryptocurrency-a-primer

Mangano, R. (2018). Blockchain Securities, Insolvency Law and the Sandbox Approach. *European Business Organization Law Review*, *19*(4), 715–735. Advance online publication. doi:10.100740804-018-0123-5

Martin, C. J. (2016). The sharing economy: A pathway to sustainability or a nightmarish form of neoliberal capitalism? *Ecological Economics*, *121*, 149–159. doi:10.1016/j.ecolecon.2015.11.027

Merkaš, Z., Perkov, D., & Bonin, V. (2020). The Significance of Blockchain Technology in Digital Transformation of Logistics and Transportation. *International Journal of E-Services and Mobile Applications*, *12*(1), 1–20. doi:10.4018/IJESMA.2020010101

Mizrahi, A. (2019). *Total surveillance coin will be a dystopia if controlled by Facebook or government.* Available at: https://news.bitcoin.com/total-surveillance-coin-will-be-a-dystopia-if-controlled-by-facebook-or-government/

Moreira, J., Silva, M., Simoes, J., & Sousa, G. (2012). Marketing Innovation: Study of Determinants of Innovation in the Design and Packaging of Goods and Services—Application to Portuguese Firms. *Contemporary Management Research*, *8*(2). Advance online publication. doi:10.7903/cmr.11047

Mowers, S. (2019). *#CryptoCorner: Brexit could benefit bitcoin according to recent research, facebook (NASDAQ: $FB) hiring more blockchain positions.* Retrieved from https://www.spreaker.com/show/crypto-corner-podcast

Murillo, D., Buckland, H., & Val, E. (2017). When the sharing economy becomes neoliberalism on steroids: Unravelling the controversies. *Technological Forecasting and Social Change*, *125*, 66–76. doi:10.1016/j.techfore.2017.05.024

Nærland, K., Müller-Bloch, C., Beck, R., & Palmund, S. (2017). *Blockchain to Rule the Waves – Nascent Design Principles for Reducing Risk and Uncertainty in Decentralized Environments.* Retrieved from https://www.researchgate.net/publication/319990622_Blockchain_to_Rule_the_Waves_-_Nascent_Design_Principles_for_Reducing_Risk_and_Uncertainty_in_Decentralized_Environments

Nakamoto, S. (2008). *Bitcoin: A Peer-to-Peer Electronic Cash System.* Retrieved from https://bitcoin.org/bitcoin.pdf

Nowiński, W., & Kozma, M. (2017). How Can Blockchain Technology Disrupt the Existing Business Models? *Entrepreneurial Business and Economics Review*, *5*(3), 173–188. Advance online publication. doi:10.15678/EBER.2017.050309

Orcutt, M. (2019). Once hailed as unhackable, blockchains are now getting hacked. *Technology Review.* Available at: https://www.technologyreview.com/s/612974/once-hailed-as-unhackable-blockchains-are-now-getting-hacked/

Pazaitis, A., De Filippi, P., & Kostakis, V. (2017). Blockchain and value systems in the sharing economy: The illustrative case of backfeed. *Technological Forecasting and Social Change*, *125*, 105–115. doi:10.1016/j.techfore.2017.05.025

Prokopenko, J., & Bureau international du travail. (1990). *Gérer la productivité. Bureau International du Travail.* Genève, Suisse: Bureau international du travail.

Roos, D., & Hahn, R. (2019). Understanding Collaborative Consumption: An Extension of the Theory of Planned Behavior with Value-Based Personal Norms. *Journal of Business Ethics*, *158*(3), 679–697. Advance online publication. doi:10.100710551-017-3675-3

Scott, B. (2016). *How Can Cryptocurrency and Blockchain Technology Play a Role in Building Social and Solidarity Finance*. United Nations Research Institute for Social Development.

Selloni, D. (2017). *New Forms of Economies: Sharing Economy*. Collaborative Consumption, Peer-to-Peer Economy. doi:10.1007/978-3-319-53243-1_2

Sheel, A., & Nath, V. (2019). Effect of blockchain technology adoption on supply chain adaptability, agility, alignment and performance. *Management Research Review*, *42*(12), 1353–1374. doi:10.1108/MRR-12-2018-0490

Sun, J., Yan, J., & Zhang, K. Z. K. (2016). Blockchain-based sharing services: What blockchain technology can contribute to smart cities. *Financial Innovation, 2*(1), 26. Retrieved from https://jfin-swufe.springeropen.com/track/pdf/10.1186/s40854-016-0040-y

Swan, M. (2015). *Blockchain: Blueprint for a New Economy*. O'Reilly Media.

Swanson, T. (2005). *Consensus-as-a-service: A brief report on the emergence of permissioned, distributed ledger systems*. Report. Available at: https://www.ofnumbers.com/

Tiwana, A., Konsynski, B., & Bush, A. (2010). Research commentary — Platform evolution: Coevolution of platform architecture, governance, and environmental dynamics. *Information Systems Research*, *21*(4), 675–687. doi:10.1287/isre.1100.0323

Van Valkenburgh, P., Dietz, J., De Filippi, P., Shadab, H., Xethalise, G., & Bollier, D. (2015). *Distributed collaborative organisations: Distributed networks and regulator frameworks*. Harvard Working Paper.

Waelbroeck, P. (2017). Les enjeux économiques de la blockchain. *Annales des Mines - Réalités industrielles, 2017*(3), 10-19. Retrieved from https://www.cairn.info/revue-realites-industrielles-2017-3-page-10.htm

White, G. R. T. (2017). Future applications of blockchain in business and management: A Delphi study. *Strategic Change*, *26*(5), 439–451. doi:10.1002/jsc.2144

Wright, A., & De Filippi, P. (2015). *Decentralized blockchain technology and the rise of lex cryptographia, SSRN Scholarly Paper, no 2580664*. Social Science Research Network Rochester., doi:10.2139srn.2580664

Yeo, V. C. S., Goh, S.-K., & Rezaei, S. (2017). Consumer experiences, attitude and behavioral intention toward online food delivery (OFD) services. *Journal of Retailing and Consumer Services*, *35*, 150–162. doi:10.1016/j.jretconser.2016.12.013

Zervas, G., Proserpio, D., & Byers, J. W. (2017). The rise of the sharing economy: Estimating the impact of Airbnb on the hotel industry. *JMR, Journal of Marketing Research*, *54*(5), 687–705. doi:10.1509/jmr.15.0204

Zheng, Z., Xie, S., Dai, H., Chen, X., & Wang, H. (2017, June). An overview of blockchain technology: Architecture, consensus, and future trends. In *2017 IEEE International Congress on Big Data (BigData Congress)* (pp. 557-564). IEEE.

ADDITIONAL READING

Boysen, N., Briskorn, D., & Schwerdfeger, S. (2019). Matching supply and demand in a sharing economy: Classification, computational complexity, and application. *European Journal of Operational Research*, *278*(2), 578–595. doi:10.1016/j.ejor.2019.04.032

Dabbous, A., & Tarhini, A. (2019). Assessing the impact of knowledge and perceived economic benefits on sustainable consumption through the sharing economy: A sociotechnical approach. *Technological Forecasting and Social Change*, *149*, 119775. doi:10.1016/j.techfore.2019.119775

Davlembayeva, D., Papagiannidis, S., & Alamanos, E. (2019). Mapping the economics, social and technological attributes of the sharing economy. *Information Technology & People*, ITP-02-2018-0085. Advance online publication. doi:10.1108/ITP-02-2018-0085

Ertz, M., & Arsenault, J. (2019). Towards a technocratic governance system? *International Journal of Innovation Studies*, *3*(3), 71–72. doi:10.1016/j.ijis.2019.11.001

Frey, A., Trenz, M., & Veit, D. (2019). A service-dominant logic perspective on the roles of technology in service innovation: Uncovering four archetypes in the sharing economy. *Journal of Business Economics*, *89*(8-9), 1149–1189. doi:10.100711573-019-00948-z

Guillemot, S., & Privat, H. (2019). The role of technology in collaborative consumer communities. *Journal of Services Marketing*, *33*(7), 837–850. doi:10.1108/JSM-12-2018-0361

Laurenti, R., & Acuña, F. M. B. (2020). Exploring antecedents of behavioural intention and preferences in online peer-to-peer resource sharing: A Swedish university setting. *Sustainable Production and Consumption*, *21*, 47–56. doi:10.1016/j.spc.2019.10.002

Oskam, J. (2019). Smart cities, 'sharing' and platform impact. In *Smart Cities in the Post-algorithmic Era*. Edward Elgar Publishing. doi:10.4337/9781789907056.00021

Sutherland, W., & Jarrahi, M. H. (2017). The gig economy and information infrastructure: the case of the digital nomad community. *Proceedings of the ACM on Human-Computer Interaction*, 1(CSCW), 97. 10.1145/3134732

Sutherland, W., & Jarrahi, M. H. (2018). The sharing economy and digital platforms: A review and research agenda. *International Journal of Information Management*, *43*, 328–341. doi:10.1016/j.ijinfomgt.2018.07.004

KEY TERMS AND DEFINITIONS

Blockchain Technology: A decentralized and secure database of transactions based on decentralized nodes typically miners.

Collaborative Economy: A set of resource circulation systems which enable consumers to both obtain and provide, temporarily or permanently, valuable resources or services through direct interaction with other consumers or through a mediator.

Collaborative Platforms: An infrastructure for the mutualization or redistribution of goods or services between users, as well as the establishment and maintenance of trust for the realization of exchanges.

Cryptocurreny: A medium of exchange that functions like money (in that it can be exchanged for goods and services) but, unlike traditional currency, is untethered to, and independent from, national borders, central banks, sovereigns, or fiats.

Proof of Stake (PoS): A consensus strategy or algorithm in which miners have to prove the ownership of the amount of currency on the blockchain.

Proof of Work (PoW): A consensus strategy or algorithm used in hashes' or blocks' validation processes on the blockchain.

Social Network: A social structure made up of a set of social actors sets of dyadic ties, and other social interactions between actors.

Suppliers: Individuals offering a private resource, usually underutilized or unused and holding the resource for provision (e.g., sale, donation, swapping, rental, or co-use).

Users: Individuals seeking to obtain (e.g., second-hand purchase, reception of donations, swapping, renting, or co-use).

Chapter 6
Predictive Factors of Attitude Towards Online Disruptive Advertising

Juneman Abraham
https://orcid.org/0000-0003-0232-2735
Psychology Department, Faculty of Humanities, Bina Nusantara University, Jakarta, Indonesia

Dean Lauda Septian
Psychology Department, Faculty of Humanities, Bina Nusantara University, Jakarta, Indonesia, Indonesia

Tommy Prayoga
Content Collision, Indonesia

Yustinus Suhardi Ruman
Psychology Department, Faculty of Humanities, Bina Nusantara University, Jakarta, Indonesia, Indonesia

ABSTRACT

By leveraging knowledge of subconsciousness seducing technique combined with building algorithms capable of analyzing internet users' needs as well as providing relevant information, disruptive ads that appear abruptly (in terms of the timing, placement, and method of ending/closing the content) in web pages and mobile applications are accepted as a quality effective means of consumer persuasion. This present study proposed uncertainty avoidance, perceived usefulness, and openness personality trait as the predictors of attitude towards online disruptive advertising. Participants of this study were 137 Indonesian internet users (75 males, 62 females, Mage = 23.02 years old, SDage = 3.367 years). Multiple linear regression analysis showed that only perceived usefulness and openness personality trait are able to predict the attitude (i.e., in positive directions). The uncertainty-certainty paradoxes contained in disruptive advertising are discussed to understand the psychological dynamics involved in a facet of the attitude ambiguity.

DOI: 10.4018/978-1-7998-4543-0.ch006

INTRODUCTION

The rapid development of advertising technology is changing the way brands and consumers interact. The increasingly collaborative economy happens not only in the service and the commerce industry but also in the marketing industry. Over the course of the years, the marketing and advertising industry has become more and more data-driven, and less reliant on static demographic information (Forbes Insights, 2017). Perhaps the impact sharing economy has on the advertising industry can be seen in the rise of data co-op practices (Swant, 2016). It is a practice where brand and business owners aggregate and compare non-transparent data across verticals to reveal cross-industry behaviors and trends, providing marketers with insight to map and formulate marketing objectives (Ismail, 2015). Some of the major examples of these verticals are marketplace such as e-commerce and service aggregators, as well as a content platform such as news publication (Everstring, 2020). These verticals register behavior in response to a content (often in one form of advertising or the other) in real-time. The data is then compiled by a third party co-op provider to be shared between business owners.

This data-sharing practice is a double-edged sword. On one side, consumers' needs based on their psychographics and demographics dimensions are increasingly recognized, mapped, and analyzed as tech firms take more and more interest in our digital footprints and identities. People's activities, profiles, interests, and even location are most probably logged in on *Google*, while their connections, preferences, and personal data are harvested by *Facebook* and its networks through a '*pixel*'—a code that tracks visitor's conversion from *Facebook Ads* network (Newberry, 2017). On the other, while innovative and disruptive, the acquisition and the management of consumer data within the framework of these technologies can be done in unethical ways that might violate users' privacy (Porter, 2018). One of the biggest concerns in practicing data co-op is the integrity (Ismail, 2015) and carefulness of the provider and practitioners in handling the data to prevent breaches, something which even giant tech firms like *Facebook* failed to do (Blumberg, 2020).

Some authors identified a number of changing trends brought by disruptive technology in advertising (Cox, 2016; Rezvani, 2017); they are (1) Jobs that manage and draw insights from big data (e.g. programmatic advertisers, digital marketers, data scientist), will be prioritized and increasingly utilized by brands and businesses, (2) Conversation becomes material for digital advertising, and the ability for "open engagement" and "social listening" online are essentials in producing effective digital ads, (3) Rejection of potential customers against disruptive ads (for example by installing *AdBlocker* on internet browsers) stems from consumer awareness not wanting to experience the "alienated self" when they are being the "object of manipulation" by digital advertisers, (4) Human interpretations and creativity are required in processing the information generated by bot algorithms to produce effective targeted advertising, and (5) The digital marketing field is decentralized, because today—unlike the advertising world of the past—anyone with minimum knowledge of programming, can adopt, build, customize open source, open access, and "plug-and-play" program that puts up ads on the web. Small institutions are increasingly savvy in utilizing native advertising. Bloggers and micro-influencers (rather than an influencer with a tremendous amount of follower base) become increasingly popular for brands to be partners with (Wissman, 2018). The fifth characteristic is closely related to the basic principle of disruptive innovation which states that "a process whereby a small company with fewer resources is able to succeed" (Christensen, Raynor, & McDonald, 2015, para. 6). Finally, the advancement in sharing economy has made marketing: (1) more effective due because of the data accuracy; (2) scalable because multiple marketing campaigns can be executed and tested at the same time across the globe; and (3) cost-effective and time-efficient (Ismail, 2015).

Those traits show the nature of innovation in the advertising industry is ever-changing, and it's changing fast. Perhaps one of the biggest revolutions in the year 2018 comes from *Google*, who in February announced that its proprietary browser, *Chrome*, will block any advertisement that its user deemed disrupting (Lennihan, 2018). Note that, these ads are the 'bad' kind of disruption. Unlike innovative viral marketing campaigns by big brands, they are not as "game-changing" as they are intrusive. These disruptive ads are any kind of advertisement that is affecting a user's experience and activity online. They are perceived as confusing, deceptive, annoying, and considered as an unwelcomed interruption in consumers' activities (Le & Vo, 2017).

This kind of advertising can be found in several forms: starting from pop-up ads that cover most of your device's screen, automatically-played video in the middle of an article or video, or a background skin poster that will only disappear if you scroll past it. Data sharing and co-op practices may have made positive impacts on marketing and advertisement practices, but the audience and users still play a major role in determining its effectiveness in bringing those impacts as the consumer of the contents or the ads. One of those roles is to exercise their right in selecting how an ad is presented to them. Disruptive ads may present product and brand information to promote awareness. They are highly targeted based on the user's behavioral algorithms. However, aside from clicking the ads, the audience can opt to block it or report it. These actions send feedback to the advertisers and business owners that their audience is not interested in this particular advertising.

Disruptive advertising, like any other form of disruption, has led to tiered socioeconomic changes in many aspects of society from research and development units, firms, industries, authorities, and ultimately consumers themselves (Kilkki, Mäntylä, Karhu, Hämmäinen, & Ailisto, 2018). Especially in the eye of customers, whose online journey is accompanied by the act of blocking or avoiding ads. In early 2017, there are about 615 million devices that use adblockers globally (Cortland, 2017). Around 31% of Americans use adblockers and 58% of Indonesian use mobile adblockers (Stewart, 2018).

Mainstream media in Indonesia has also reported user's irritation about this kind of advertising, and even provide tips on how to avoid them (Putri, 2019; Kinapti, 2019; CNBC Indonesia, 2019). The audience's reaction reflects their attitude towards this type of advertising delivery or channels, and in turn, may affect their perception towards the brand. A series of A/B testing via digital marketing tools and channels might need to be conducted to determine why audience block or report specific ads. However, how adblocking programs are used to block disruptive advertisements and no other forms like native advertisement suggests that the form of delivery or channels plays an important influence on the audience's behavior. This makes studying the audience's evaluation of disruptive advertising important for the sake of gathering accurate data to be shared and maintaining true brand loyalty and positive perception.

The results of the study of 5,213 adults aged 19 and older in 5 major ad markets (US, UK, France, China, and Brazil) confirmed the effects of disruptive ads (Kantar, 2017), e.g. (1) The dominant attitude to advertising are positive or neutral; only a few "dislike" advertising, (2) Negative attitude toward digital ads derived from the excessive repetitions of and less intuition of these ads in targeting, (3) Positive attitude comes from personalization and relevance (in accordance with the best interest of consumers, based on web cookies tracking) of digital ads content. The findings (Kantar, 2017, p. 37) states that the negative attitude "has less to do with any intrinsic dislike of advertising (47% of blockers even states that they are either tolerant or like ads) and more to do with the effect that ads have on consumers' online experiences." This is understandable because disruptive ads increasingly use techniques that interfere with people's sub-consciousness through subliminal messages. These techniques do not make people feel persuaded by the message of the advertisement despite seeing the ads (Apprich, 2017); whereas many human decisions are guided by subconsciousness rather than a conscious state of mind. The findings have implications for the advertising industries, such as changing the orientation to customer-centric based on contextual data-driven processing, as well as building an impartial and valid measurement system to appreciate the performance of workers in this field.

However, despite a big portion of internet users block ads, think it's intrusive, and trends are leaning towards native and partnership ads, it does not mean that disruptive advertising are all bad news. A recent study shows that disruptive advertising may have a positive effect on consumers (R. Bell & Buchner, 2018): it increases their fluency and affective preferences towards the brand, even though consumer perceptions tend to be negative towards the display. This can be attributed to the prevalence of these ads: because slots for these ads can be found almost everywhere, brands whose names appear on these ads are more likely to be remembered. On the other hand, they do also recognize that the benefits of disruptive ads obtained by companies or advertisers may be short-term, and in the long run may result in "unwanted and negative side effects" (R. Bell & Buchner, 2018, p. 13). Their finding suggests that our understanding of disruptive ads might be incomplete. Thoughts about abandoning disruptive ads usage might then be worth to be reconsidered by advertisers. Instead, they should focus on coming up with a better strategy in optimizing them. This makes the understanding of attitude towards disruptive ads an essential part of building that strategy, as attitude towards and ads generally reflects and can be used to predict consumer's online behavior, such as purchasing decision, e.g. (Kodjamanis & Angelopoulos, 2013; Srivastava, Srivastava, & Rai, 2014), social media sharing (J. Lee, Kim, & Ham, 2016), and even their addiction towards the internet, e.g. (Rudolph, Klemz, & Asquith, 2013). This makes a lot of sense, because "Developers are getting better at getting their users to watch, ads, or that's rewarded with a power-up in a game, a surge of dopamine from an achievement, or a deluge of adorable dog content" (West, 2018, para. 3).

Previously, it was indicated that there is the effect of non-cognitive disruptive advertising, which influences consumer judgment on the credibility of media that contains disruptive ads (Zha & Wu, 2014). It appears that empirical studies have so far favored advertising companies. There are still rare studies that explore further the psychological dynamics experienced by consumers. For example, existing studies still pay very little attention to the relationship between social media advertising and consumers' mental health. A recent study investigating, among others, the online predictors of anxiety and depression (Glaser, Liu, Hakim, Vilar, & Zhang, 2018), for example, did not relate itself with the conceptual network of "*advertising, ads, disruptive ads*" at all. Meanwhile, people sustainably engage with ubiquitous disruptive ads while doing online social networking (Voorveld, van Noort, Muntinga, & Bronner, 2018). In addition, theoretical models that are built on the intention to accept advertising' e.g. (Jafari, Jandaghi, & Taghavi, 2016) have not integrated personality, attitude, and cultural orientation factors in one model—all-important psycho-socio-cultural determinants of consumer behaviors. This study seeks to address this gap by investigating these factors. This study aimed at examining predictors of consumer's **attitude towards disruptive advertising**. The authors propose **three predictors**; they are uncertainty avoidance (cultural orientation), perceived usefulness (beliefs), and openness trait (personality factor).

BACKGROUND

An individual's attitude towards advertising certainly reflects their evaluation towards an ad based on their value, but at the same time also the brand the ad represents (Kamalul Ariffin, Ismail, & Mohammad Shah, 2016). This means that individuals will less likely evaluate an ad negatively if they have a positive attitude towards the brand and vice versa. This process ultimately helps them determine their purchasing decision. The reason is that people with higher positive evaluations usually pay more attention to the ads (Ting, Run, & Thurasamy, 2015). In the context of the video-type ad, individuals that posit a positive attitude might even share it online to their social circle (Huang, Su, Zhou, & Liu, 2013).

Attitude is a complex, multi-dimensional construct that explains our evaluation towards a thought or action. It has 10 explaining dimensions (Krosnick, Boninger, Chuang, Berent, & et al, 1993): (1) *Extremity* reflects individual's favorability; (2) *Intensity* refers to the magnitude of emotional reaction provoked ; (3) *Certainty* is individual's confidence in their attitude; (4) *Importance* reflects how much individual care and invested about his attitude; (5) *Interest* in gathering relevant information; (6) *Knowledge* is the amount of information the attitude is based on; (7) *Accessibility* refers to individual's proximity towards the object evaluated in the memory; (8) *Direct experience* shows that the frequency of interaction between individuals and the object; (9) *Latitude of rejection and non-commitment* reflect individual's acceptability towards notions regarding his or her attitude; (10) *Affective-cognitive consistency* reflects individual's affect and cognitive alignment over time. It can be said that if a person has a positive attitude towards an object, the person will be more favorable towards the object, experience positive emotions from it, confident with his evaluation towards it, perceives the objects to be important, has a suitable amount of knowledge about it and showed motivation to gather more, able to recall and describe the object based on previous experience, will be more likely to reject contradictive statements against his attitude, all reflected across his cognitive and affective domain over time. This conceptualization suggests that here are many aspects to be paid attention to in terms of attitude. Moreover, it emphasizes the object at hand, meaning to be pragmatic, one must always consider the nature of the object (e.g. disruptive advertisement) and its implication towards the human. It also suggests that attitude is highly dependent on many things—its many domains reflects an almost endless possibility of predictors. However, they could be deducted based on the context of the object evaluated. For example, an individual's attitude towards advertisement may vary according to their experience and knowledge with many kinds of advertisements they encounter. For example, attitude towards native advertising (J. Lee et al., 2016) that blends well with the content format people consume will certainly be different from disruptive advertising. By specifying to the individuals that the object to be evaluated is disruptive, one can get a general idea of where individual lean on these dimensions.

One of the biggest challenges in measuring attitude towards the advertising of any type is the abundant amounts of ads in reference. Individuals will have to encounter many ads during their lifetime. Although the type is specified (in this case disruptive), the experience will also differ from person to person. Thus, the objective of this chapter is to raise the predictive factors of attitude towards disruptive advertising based on the subjectivity of the evaluation – hoped to be communication materials for the advertisers.

Culture and value are two of the most discussed predictors of attitude towards advertising. Some researchers pick a diverse sample to incorporate as many cultural representations as possible (Kodjamanis & Angelopoulos, 2013), other suggest that culture and value are individual's evaluation basis towards an ad (Ting et al., 2015). These examples show the importance of including the factor in predicting attitude towards any kind of advertising, as an individual's values and its embodiment guide them on how to think and react. Some values may be related to the message and the brand; some may be related to the delivery or channels. In the context of disruptive advertising, this present study is focusing on the relationship between cultural value and the ads nature of delivery.

In predicting consumers' attitudes and acceptance towards advertisement, it is also suggested that researchers pay more attention to cultural factors, especially in terms of mobile advertising (Khan, Mahmood, & Jalees, 2017). It is known from Khan et al.'s report that the national culture of uncertainty avoidance (UA) is negatively correlated with innovation, as innovations are often associated with new changes and the unknown. The more a group feels that they are uncomfortable with innovations, they will choose to avoid it.

Uncertainty avoidance is a construct that reflects one's cultural value orientation. It can be defined as the extent to which an individual feels unease in the presence of change or new situations and is motivated to avoid it (Zhang & Zhou, 2014). It helps individual reasons and determines whether they want to perform certain actions in the face of new situations (Slawinski, Pinkse, Busch, & Banerjee, 2017). Individuals with a high level of uncertainty avoidance will be more determined to escape or block out the situations, whether its counterpart will be more likely to stay calm and face it. They will prefer stable, predictable situations, traditional way, and are less likely to seek a new way to deal with things (Prayoga & Abraham, 2016)—traits that can be found in the native advertisement that is more familiar and non-intrusive. People's positive attitude towards native advertising is influenced by the nature of its non-intrusiveness (J. Lee et al., 2016). This is understandable, as the lack of information in uncertainty situations makes it hard to make a decision and form an evaluation. People with higher uncertainty avoidance will be less impulsive when it comes to purchasing online (Dameyasani & Abraham, 2013). It is possible for individuals with high and low uncertainty avoidance to still for a positive attitude towards an advertisement, as long as the uncertainty is positive and there is room for speculation and imagination about the benefit of advertised products (Ketelaar, van't Riet, Thorbjornsen, & Buijzen, 2018). In the case of disruptive ads, this is unlikely because consumers often can not predict their arrival and the messages are often very short (relying heavy on visuals) to cram as much information as possible before individuals skip or click away.

UA is positively correlated with barriers of aspects of innovation resistance, particularly negative image (e.g. lower perceived ease of use of new technology) and perceived risk (i.e. physical, social, psychological, financial risk) (Laukkanen, 2015). Meanwhile, innovation is the essence of disruption. New things are bound to happen especially in the industry of advertising every short period of time. The new changes, such as implementing a new strategy of disruptive ads should cater to the emotional reaction of the audience. Emotion inherent in UA is anxiety based on perceived threat caused by unclear, unpredictable mechanisms, procedure and environmental situations (Czaika & Valerdi, 2009). Disruptive advertising in its essence is often surprising—the placement is in unusual places, the timing is sudden, and there are varying ways to close it. Some advertiser makes users wait, some 'hid' the close button in a transparent color, sometimes it's on the top, sometimes it's bottom, and some advertisers also redirect you immediately even after you clicked on the close button. It can be assumed that people with a higher degree of UAs will be more disturbed and feel uncomfortable with disruptive advertising characteristics and will have more negative affections towards them. Thus this research hypothesizes:

H1: The higher the uncertainty avoidance, the more negative the attitude towards online disruptive advertising will be.

Negative attitudes to disruptive ads are also shown in the form of deliberate ignorance towards the ads especially in people who have privacy concerns and distrust of the ads (John, Kim, & Barasz, 2018; Patel,

2018). It shows that people are less open to this kind of experience created by the disruptive advertisement—it's intrusive towards their privacy and it disrupts their online activities. Openness to experience was found to positively correlates with privacy concerns (I. A. Junglas, Johnson, & Spitzmüller, 2008). The reason is that the higher the openness, the higher the exploration, curiosity, and empathy will be. Those three characteristics contribute to the "deeper sense of awareness" (I. A. Junglas et al., 2008, p. 393) towards the surrounding of the experience. This awareness, according to the Protection Motivation Theory (PMT) increases the sensitivity to potential losses and threats. This explains why individuals choose to opt-out from the experience of disruptive ads through ad blockers—it is not that they are not open, but rather selective of the experience they are open to.

The concept of openness in this study refers to one of the five constructs of the Big Five personality traits (Stajkovic, Bandura, Locke, Lee, & Sergent, 2018). Openness or *openness to experience* in this sense can be referred to as the extent to which an individual prefers to have a wide versus a narrow range of perceptual, cognitive, and affective experiences (Soto & John, 2017). Individuals who prefer a larger range of these experiences are more open, welcoming, and unhesitant in facing them. They are more ready and interested to learn about new information (Ramdhani, 2012). Individuals with a higher degree of openness are able to imagine themselves in new situations without having to personally encounter them at the moment (Stajkovic et al., 2018). More importantly, they are also more willing to enjoy the new experience (Myers, Sen, & Alexandrov, 2010). In terms of advertising, the higher the degree of openness, the more likely an individual will form a positive attitude towards an ad. However, this is truer in transformational (focus on experience) ads rather than informational (focus on information of the products) ads (Myers et al., 2010). In the context of sponsored stories (native advertising), people with a higher degree of openness tend to share ads with their friends (Clark & Çallı, 2014). However, it is found that individuals with a lower degree of openness may have a better attitude towards advertisement in general, under the conditions that the advertisement is no longer 'fresh' (J. K. Lee, Lee, & Hansen, 2017). This means that given the chance, even individuals with lower openness degree can and will evaluate and form positive attitude towards advertisement.

However, although individuals can be selective in their experience, in general, a higher degree of openness often equals a higher degree of trust (Azam, Qiang, & Sharif, 2013). It was found that openness to experience negatively correlates with privacy concerns (I. Junglas & Spitzmüller, 2006). The reason is that people with high openness to experience have desires to experience new things, so they are more relaxed with issues related to privacies especially in the first time of encounter. Only when the experience is deemed negative, they will start to be more selective towards new ads as time goes on. People with higher openness are more liberal, more open-minded, and do not mind accepting new ideas, so theoretically should be more accepting towards new digital stimulus provided by brands and the internet. Furthermore, it was found that openness to experience (positively associated with imagination and creativity) positively affects the experience of transformational ads (i.e., ads associated with strong affection, which appreciate one's historicity – similar to the feature of disruptive ads – as well as offering transformative pleasure) (Myers et al., 2010). Based on the understanding of these findings, this research hypothesizes that:

H2: The higher the openness to experience personality trait, the more positive the attitude towards online disruptive advertising will be.

Advertisements are created with the intention to help the user makes decisions to purchase; especially in the digital ads, which are specifically targeted to match users' needs and goals. If a purchase is not their goal, then the ads will come across as useless (and disruptive). So, aside from relevant, ads are also useful in the sense that it can be used to help a person achieve their goal (purchase). If in the user's mind an innovation offers gains, improvement, and convenience, the user will perceive it as useful (Gironda & Korgaonkar, 2018). Usefulness is not the same as to benefit, as a benefit can be any positive values, like entertainment, unlike usefulness that relates to an individual's goal (Assegaff, Hussin, & Dahlan, 2011).

Perceived usefulness in this study is derived from the study formulating a theoretical model (Technology Acceptance Model/TAM) that explains individual's intention to use technology is shaped by their beliefs, such as perceived usefulness (Davis, 1989). Individual's perceived usefulness reflects their belief towards systems or technology's capability to help them achieve their designated goals (Schnall, Higgins, Brown, Carballo-Dieguez, & Bakken, 2015). However, usefulness needs to be distinguished with benefits. Benefits are related to the positive value one feel or get. Benefits can be passively obtained or felt without having to act upon a situation. While usefulness, on the other hand, requires an individual's interactions with a certain object. An ad might benefit an individual in many ways, but not necessarily useful (Assegaff et al., 2011). It will only be helpful if the users choose to engage with it to make a decision. As the individual finds it more helpful, they will also be more likely to find it more favorable (Gironda & Korgaonkar, 2018)

Perceived usefulness is an individual's belief in this value, which eventually shapes their attitude (Shi, 2018). This kind of belief has the power to shape an individual's attitude towards the object in context. In this sense, an individual's attitude towards disruptive advertising can be predicted by their perceived usefulness. Thus, an individual's degree of perceived usefulness towards disruptive ads will correlate with their attitude towards it. This research hypothesizes:

H3: The higher the perceived usefulness, the more positive the attitude towards online disruptive advertising will be.

HOW THE EMPIRICAL DATA WERE OBTAINED

Participants and Design

The participants of this study were 137 college students (75 males, 62 females; M_{age} = 23.02 years old, SD_{age} = 3.367 years) in Greater Jakarta, Indonesia, recruited via convenience sampling technique. The design of this study was correlational-predictive, with predictors (independent variables) and criteria (dependent variable). The independent variables are uncertainty avoidance, openness to experience, and perceived usefulness of disruptive advertising. Moreover, the dependent variable is the attitude towards disruptive advertising.

Materials and Procedure

The measuring tool used in this research is a questionnaire – in the form of *Google Form* – consisting of four psychological scales in Indonesian, disseminated via *WhatsApp* and face-to-face with the participants, with a cover letter that describes informed consent and brief explanation about disruptive advertising in the form of sentence (i.e. "*Disruptive advertisements are ads with characteristics of annoying, appearing not in the proper place-not usual, not predictable-, and tending to take up space on the screen of your digital device or gadget*") and three pictures of disruptive ads modes, as showed in http://bit.ly/disruptiveadvertising.

Attitude towards online disruptive advertising measurement was done by constructing a scale based on behavioral dimensions with 39 initial items (Krosnick et al., 1993). Examples of the items were (1) Disruptive advertising is smart, (2) I can be a source of information about the benefits of disruptive advertising, (3) There is no conflict between my mind and my heart about the goodness of disruptive advertising, (4) I once disseminated information about the positive impact of disruptive advertising, (5) Disruptive advertising is acceptable, (6) I hate people who do not support disruptive advertising (unfavorable item), and (7) I am sad when disruptive ads are blocked (unfavorable items). The response options were from "Strongly Disagree" (score of 1) to "Strongly Agree" (score of 6). The validity and reliability test results showed Cronbach's $\alpha = 0.948$ reliability index with corrected item-total correlations ranging from 0.366 to 0.696, after eliminating 3 items (final items number = 36), indicating that the scale has a good reliability (Cronbach's $\alpha > 0.6$), and good item validities (corrected item-total correlations > 0.250).

The measurement of the **cultural value orientation of Uncertainty Avoidance (UA)** at the individual level was done by adopting the Scale of Individual Cultural Values (CVSCALE) (Yoo, Donthu, & Lenartowicz, 2011) which had been adapted into Indonesian consisting of 8 items (Dameyasani & Abraham, 2013). The examples of the items were: (1) It is important to closely follow instructions and procedures, (2) Standardized work procedures are helpful. The response options were from "Strongly Disagree" (score of 1) to "Strongly Agree" (score of 6). The validity and reliability test results show Cronbach's $\alpha = 0.784$ reliability index with corrected item-total correlations ranging from 0.461 to 0.637.

The measurement of **perceived usefulness** was performed by adapting the perceived usefulness scale of the *Technology Acceptance Model* (TAM) (Davis, 1989). This scale consisted of 22 initial items divided into four dimensions. The first dimension was the feelings about the benefits of disruptive advertising, with sample items: (1) Utilizing disruptive advertising speeds up my search for objects that maybe my needs, and (2) Disruptive ads slow down my work (unfavorable items, reversely scored). The second was the feelings of increasing performance when consuming disruptive advertising, with sample items: (1) Disruptive ads make me more able to empower the objects that become my preferences through certain feature information, and (2) The appearance of disruptive ads surprised/disturbed me. The third was the efficiency of doing maintenance tasks, with sample items: (1) Disruptive ads use up my internet quota (unfavorable item) and (2) Opening disruptive ads makes it easy for me to get information about a product I need. The fourth was the perception of a significant improvement in a quality of life affected by the technology, with sample items: (1) Reading / listening to disruptive advertisements opens new perceptions on trending features, and (2) I often feel negative emotions when disruptive ads appear. The response options were from "Strongly Disagree" (score of 1) to "Strongly Agree" (score of 6). The validity and reliability test results showed Cronbach's $\alpha = 0.928$ reliability index with corrected item-total correlations ranging from 0.371 to 0.765, after eliminating 2 items (final items number = 20).

The measurement of the **trait of openness to experience** was done by adopting the *Big Five Inventory* (BFI) which has been adapted into Indonesian consisting of 10 items (Ramdhani, 2012). The examples of items were: (1) is original, comes up with new ideas, (2) is ingenious, a deep thinker, (3) value artistic, aesthetic experiences, (4) like to reflect, play with ideas (Ramdhani, 2012, p. 200). The response options were from "Strongly Disagree" (score of 1) to "Strongly Agree" (score of 6). The validity and reliability test result showed Cronbach's reliability index $\alpha = 0.869$ with corrected item-total correlations ranging from 0.366 to 0.696 without eliminating items (final items number = 10).

The data obtained from the variables were analyzed using multiple linear regression analysis technique, done with *IBM SPSS Statistics version 22 for Windows.*

SOLUTIONS AND RECOMMENDATIONS

The result of the study is presented in the tables below. Table 1 presents the descriptive statistics and bivariate correlations between variables. Table 2 presents the result of a linear regression analysis of the hypothesis.

Table 1. Descriptive and correlational statistics between variables (n = 137)

No	Variable	*M*	*SD*	1	2	3	4
1	Uncertainty avoidance	29.74	2.74	1			
2	Openness to experience	45.01	6.12	0.28**	1		
3	Perceived usefulness	74.91	15.50	-0.124	0.10	1	
4	Attitude towards online disruptive advertising	122.20	23.70	0.121	0.43**	0.70**	1

* $p < 0.05$ ** $p < 0.01$

Table 2. Multiple linear regression analysis predicting the attitude towards disruptive advertising (n = 137)

Variable	*B*	*SE B*	*β*	*t*	*p*
Uncertainty avoidance	0.515	0.484	0.060	1.065	0.289
Openness to experience	1.296	0.217	0.338	5.973	0.000
Perceived usefulness	1.075	0.087	0.668	12.343	0.000

Correlation analysis result shows that attitude towards online disruptive advertising is positively correlated with openness to experience ($r = 0.043, p > 0.01$) and perceived usefulness ($r = 0.070, p > 0.01$). Uncertainty avoidance is also found to correlate with openness to experience ($\beta = 0.028, p > 0.01$). No other correlations were found.

Multiple linear regression analysis results show a similar relationship result. The regression model fits empirical with the data (F (3, 136) = 72.140, $p = 0.000$, $R^2 = 0.619$). Uncertainty avoidance ($\beta = 0.060, p > 0.05$) is unable to predict attitude towards online disruptive advertising.Openness to experience ($\beta = 0.338, p < 0.01$) and perceived usefulness ($\beta = 0.668, p < 0.01$) were found able to predict attitude towards online disruptive advertising. Thus, H1 is not supported by the empirical data, but H2 and H3 are supported.

This present study does not find the role of Uncertainty Avoidance/UA (at the individual level) in predicting the attitude toward online disruptive ads. Therefore, Hypothesis 1 (H1) was not supported by empirical data. There are two possible explanations regarding the lack of empirical results to support H1. The first one is related to the emotion of readers. The uncertainty (timing, placement, etc.) nature of the ads causes emotional distress (e.g. shocked or annoyed), as discussed in the *Introduction* section. However, disruptive ads use "FUD" (Fear, Uncertainty, and Doubt) tactics (Deswal, 2015). In their unexpected appearance, disruptive ads initially do provide a feeling of uncertainty by showing the deficiencies or weaknesses of the readers of the ad. They are designed to communicate the FUD in the most effective and concise manner. This makes disruptive ads readers feel "missed" and "outdated" in terms of performance, appearance, and so on. However, disruptive ads somehow give a "sense of *certainty*" through ads contents in an immediate (within seconds) way of offering alternative products or services which reinforce the readers' self-esteem or self-confidence by just a click away.

The feature of disruptive ads, namely "ads [that] are shown to the people most likely to care about the content", is even further enhanced by Machine Learning (Olmedilla, 2016). Such ads increasingly have "integrity", in the sense of improving their quality continuously. The designers of disruptive ads have also created various techniques for overcoming banner blindness, or ignorance of ads, such as by creating banners that provoke interaction (not monologues) and using retargeting disruptive ads at a certain level (which does not end up with rejection). They are not being avoided due to their nature of uncertainty because people are already familiar with their nature. Unless they come in a new form that is more surprising then what we already experienced, it will be less likely to be deliberately avoided. Examples of disruptive ads could be found at the *Mobile Ads* web page (MobileAds Com, 2018). The ads have been around for so long, it gives people time to evaluate and prepare a strategy to cope with them (Ketelaar et al., 2018). Individuals most probably know what kind of actions will trigger these ads, and upon encountering them, they can click away, use ad blocks, or just scroll past it. The process is very prearranged. This is an application of the concept of "predictable disruption" (Accenture, 2016). Ecosystem of disruption always finds equilibrium; in addition to its technical sophistication, disruption seeks to stay connected to customer needs by optimizing "tailored marketing message to users" (Zha & Wu, 2014, p. 17). Those uncertainty-certainty paradoxes of disruptive ads make UA unable to predict the attitude.

This study finds that the **personality trait of openness to experience is able to predict the attitude towards online disruptive ads in a positive direction**. Therefore, Hypothesis 2 (H2) was supported by empirical data. The results of this study confirm the positive direction of the prediction. Openness was negatively correlated to change resistance, tradition attachment, but positively correlated with novelty-seeking and innovation (Clark & Çallı, 2014). However, the limitation of this finding needs to be watched out for. Openness was moderated by the experience of participants who found it difficult to interpret ads contents, especially the vague and indirect ones, as well as the ones which did not provide meaning guidance (Ketelaar, Van Gisbergen, Bosman, & Beentjes, 2010). Ads of this type display their contents (not timing) and are not like advertising, even though they actually are; this is referred to as "open ads". Therefore, the generalization of the results of this present study on the positive correlation between openness and attitude towards disruptive ads is limited in the context of disruptive ads that have clear messages, meanings, and objectives to the consumers only.

Openness correlates with "intellectual curiosity, aesthetic sensitivity, unconventionality, and thrill-seeking" (Chamorro-Premuzic, 2017, para. 10). Meanwhile, "With their features and the exaggerated way of their presentation, the 'ugly models' in the advertisements embody this disruption of the beauty ideal in advertising" (Buller, 2014, p. 49). This shows that unconventionality and aesthetic sensitivity can even make someone understand ugliness, an analogy to the disruption of an individual's beauty expectation (S. Bell, 2018), as a part that composes aesthetic systems and sees them as interesting. Thus, people with higher openness will be increasingly receptive to disruptive ads. Furthermore, thrilling and thrill-seeking are two qualities of important trends of disruption that makes people want to engage themselves with disruptive products (Barnett, 2017). The thrill-seeking phase occurs as part of the learning process in which the curve could be visualized in the form of an 'S' (Johnson, 2016). In a section entitled "Psychology of Disruption", it is explained that "Disruption can feel a bit scary, but the payoff of career growth and personal achievement makes overcoming the fear factor well worth it" (Johnson, 2016, p. xxvii). Using the analogy of personal disruption, this is the psychological dynamics that occur in people with high openness when addressing the surrounding disruption, including disruptive ads, as people with higher openness are able to see opportunities and usefulness potential in disruptive ads.

This study finds that **perceived usefulness is able to predict attitude toward online disruptive ads in a positive direction**. Therefore, Hypothesis 3 (H3) was supported by empirical data. Science data used algorithms (e.g. embedded in social media) that were capable of understanding the personalities and behavioral trends of social media users (e.g. pixels) (Sumpter, 2018). Algorithms then offer (through ads) news, products or services which "correlates" with the personality or trend. Both political and economic messages can be targeted to individuals based on the correlation analysis. This targeting can meet the needs of consumers or "create" ("manipulate") their needs so that they feel that their needs are noticed through ads. They can then execute their goal in a better manner based on the suggestion, such as purchasing certain products within certain periods or with a certain way to gain more benefits. With such intelligent disruptive ads appearing, individuals can feel facilitated in making better decisions and keep informed about issues, products, services that are relevant, important, even urgent to them. It is not surprising that perceived usefulness from the users' sides supports a positive attitude towards disruptive advertising.

The perceived usefulness of advertising cannot be separated from the social context. Social norms, the "behavioral standards that basically share ideas regarding the way that a member of a group should behave in certain kinds of situations" (Jafari et al., 2016, p. 58), affect the perception (Abraham & Trimutiasari, 2015). The algorithm of current disruptive ads accommodates social norms elements. This reinforces the explanation for why perceived usefulness can predict attitude toward disruptive ads. A study experimentally communicated openly the algorithmic process of ads; in other words, it improved "the opacity of algorithmic ad tailoring" (Eslami, Krishna Kumaran, Sandvig, & Karahalios, 2018, p. 1). They found that the increase was able to raise positive affective responses to the ads algorithm. A consumer can have a higher perception of control and trustworthiness for ads that are able to explain that the contents of it come from clear social information. Disruptive ads can be an analogy of social robots (Carlucci, Nardi, Iocchi, & Nardi, 2015), which have algorithms that are able to capture explicit social representation and integrate it with the intelligence of ads so that it can interact with humans effectively. What is meant by social norms in this context is the real data (Keller, 2015). The word *reality* should be placed in quotes because it could be a false consensus created by the ads (Jafari et al., 2016).

The high level of perceived usefulness and openness traits detected in certain groups of people could be optimized by the online marketers to bring to the groups experiences of two or more different brands combined in online disruptive advertising, such as exposure of, simultaneously, "*Diet Coke* and *Dunkin 'Donuts*; ... *Kraft Mac and Cheese* and *Levi's*" (Mullen, 2015, para. 6).

CONCLUSION AND LIMITATION

This study is designed to measure factors influencing the audience's attitude towards online disruptive advertising. This study incorporates some of the most theoretically relevant aspects of cultural values (uncertainty avoidance), personality traits (openness to new experience), and perception of technologies (perceived usefulness) in the analysis. This study found that openness to experience and perceived usefulness is able to predict the attitude towards online disruptive advertising, but uncertainty avoidance was not. These findings provide an understanding of how the audience's openness to new experience influences their attitude towards advertising that might disrupt their online activities, as new experience is what marketers and advertisers want to provide to their audience. To avoid being blocked by their audience, keeping the content of the ad informative and creative becomes the key. Keeping content fresh and focusing on how to keep the audience open-minded is important. This is supported in the second finding, as the audience will evaluate an ad positively if it provides useful information that might benefit them. This study suggests that brands refrain from creating ad content that only shows buzzwords with a call to action to engage in their product. Instead, meaningful and insightful content should be prioritized. Information on discounts, features, and how the advertised objects solve problems should be communicated in the ads (such as the practice of native advertising) to counter-balance negative feelings that might come from the experience-disrupting deliveries. These findings can serve as the base of formulating digital marketing campaigns in the future for marketers and advertisers.

This study also presents a set of limitations. First, the study has not incorporated other aspects of cultural values and personality traits in this study. Other variables such as collectivism or agreeableness might also influence an individual's attitude towards advertising. Secondly, because the participants of this study came from the Indonesian population (South-Eastern Asian society), especially college students, the generalization of the results of this study might be limited to this specific demographic group, i.e. Generation Z. Subsequent research can be done on alternative populations, namely baby boomers, generation X, and generation Y, in Western or other parts of Eastern societies. Thirdly, this study only measures the attitude towards the disruptive ads, but have not measures actions taken after being presented the ads (intention to engage) or the brand image perception as a whole. Last but not least, this study measures online disruptive advertising in general. Different formats of advertising might induce different reactions and evaluations, making A/B testing an important task to obtain accurate data to be shared and processed across platforms.

FUTURE RESEARCH DIRECTIONS

The contribution of this study is to make the relatively permanent self aspects (openness to experience) and less permanent (vulnerable to manipulation, such as perceived usefulness) as psychological predictors of attitude – which are important to be understood in the world of marketing and trade and the new economic world – largely intervened by algorithms. Marketers can be more empowered to use this psychological information to support their quality activities. Considering the finding in this study in setting up the data-collecting algorithm and ad content delivery may help in gathering more qualitatively accurate data and maintain the same level of perception among the audience by spending wisely and choosing the right channel or way of delivery. A study by Forbes Insights (2017) has shown that over 60% of marketers across various industries have used data to shape their marketing campaigns, and over 90% have felt little to significant improvement in their marketing campaign by accurately spending their marketing budget on the right communication channels.

The uncertainty-certainty paradox inspires marketers to further disseminate algorithms capable of rapidly arousing consumers' anxiety about their self aspects that are "overlooked, but supporting their performance" all along, but which at the same time answer the anxiety through online ads contents, certainly with methods that can still be accounted for ethically. Future researchers could use those findings to build more comprehensive models of the attitude towards disruptive advertising, perhaps by analyzing a real set of data shared across data co-op platforms.

ACKNOWLEDGMENT

This research received no specific grant from any funding agency in the public, commercial, or not-for-profit sectors.

REFERENCES

Abraham, J., & Trimutiasari, M. (2015). Sociopsychotechnological predictors of individual's social loafing in virtual team. *International Journal of Electrical and Computer Engineering*, *5*(6), 1500–1510. doi:10.11591/ijece.v5i6.pp1500-1510

Accenture. (2016). *People first: The primacy of people in a digital age - redictable disruption: Looking to digital ecosystems for the next waves of change*. Retrieved from https://www.accenture.com/_acnmedia/PDF-36/Accenture-Tech-Vision-Malaysian-Perspective.pdf#zoom=50

Apprich, F. (2017). Disruption is the core of everything. *European Scientific Journal, ESJ*, *13*(3), 23–36.

Assegaff, S., Hussin, A. R. C., & Dahlan, H. M. (2011). Perceived benefit of knowledge sharing: Adapting TAM model. *2011 International Conference on Research and Innovation in Information Systems*, 1–6. 10.1109/ICRIIS.2011.6125744

Azam, A., Qiang, F., & Sharif, S. M. (2013). Personality based psychological antecedents of consumers' trust in ecommerce. *Journal of WEI Business and Economics*, *2*(1), 31–40.

Barnett, M. (2017). *4 trends disrupting events – CEIR Blog*. Retrieved May 1, 2019, from https://ceirblog.wordpress.com/2017/05/07/4-trends-disrupting-events/

Bell, R., & Buchner, A. (2018). Positive effects of disruptive advertising on consumer preferences. *Journal of Interactive Marketing*, *41*, 1–13. doi:10.1016/j.intmar.2017.09.002

Bell, S. (2018). The ugly gaze. In S. Rodrigues & E. Przybylo (Eds.), *On the politics of ugliness* (pp. 411–426). Palgrave Macmillan. doi:10.1007/978-3-319-76783-3_19

Blumberg, P. (2020, February 8). *Facebook vows to improve security after hack of 29 million users*. Retrieved from https://www.bloomberg.com/news/articles/2020-02-08/facebook-vows-to-improve-security-after-hack-of-29-million-users

Buller, M. (2014). *Attraction, aesthetics and advertising: An interdisciplinary look at the presentation of "Ugly Models"*. Department of Arts and Cultural Sciences, Lund University. Retrieved from https://lup.lub.lu.se/student-papers/search/publication/4450299

Carlucci, F. M., Nardi, L., Iocchi, L., & Nardi, D. (2015). Explicit representation of social norms for social robots. *2015 IEEE/RSJ International Conference on Intelligent Robots and Systems (IROS)*, 4191–4196. 10.1109/IROS.2015.7353970

Chamorro-Premuzic, T. (2017). *A psychologist finally explains why you hate teamwork so much*. Retrieved from https://www.fastcompany.com/3068194/a-psychologist-finally-explains-why-you-hate-teamwork-so-much

Christensen, C. M., Raynor, M., & McDonald, R. (2015). What is disruptive innovation? *Harvard Business Review*. Retrieved on May 1, 2019, from https://hbr.org/2015/12/what-is-disruptive-innovation

Clark, L., & Çallı, L. (2014). Personality types and Facebook advertising: An exploratory study. *Journal of Direct, Data and Digital Marketing Practice*, *15*(4), 327–336. doi:10.1057/dddmp.2014.25

CNBC Indonesia. (2019, December 6). *Cara menghilangkan iklan di Chrome pada HP Android*. Retrieved from https://www.cnbcindonesia.com/tech/20191206193838-37-121109/cara-menghilangkan-iklan-di-chrome-pada-hp-android

Cortland, M. (2017). 2017 Adblock report. *PageFair*. Retrieved from https://pagefair.com/blog/2017/adblockreport/

Cox, L. (2016). *Disrupting the advertising industry*. Retrieved from https://disruptionhub.com/technology-disrupting-ad-industry/

Czaika, E., & Valerdi, R. (2009). *The culture of innovation styles: Are our corporate cultures tuned for innovation? Motivation for study and study context*. Retrieved from https://dspace.mit.edu/bitstream/handle/1721.1/84551/cp_090719_czaika,valerdi_incose.pdf;sequence=1

Dameyasani, A. W., & Abraham, J. (2013). Impulsive buying, cultural values dimensions, and symbolic meaning of money: A study on college students in Indonesia's capital city and its surrounding. *International Journal of Research Studies in Psychology*, *2*(4), 35–52. doi:10.5861/ijrsp.2013.374

Davis, F. D. (1989). Perceived usefulness, perceived ease of use, and user acceptance of information technology. *Management Information Systems Quarterly*, *13*(3), 319. doi:10.2307/249008

Deswal, S. (2015). *How fear, uncertainty, doubt are used positively for more readership*. Retrieved from https://www.adpushup.com/blog/increase-readership-using-fud-psychology/

Eslami, M., Krishna Kumaran, S. R., Sandvig, C., & Karahalios, K. (2018). Communicating Algorithmic Process in Online Behavioral Advertising. In *Proceedings of the 2018 CHI Conference on Human Factors in Computing Systems - CHI '18* (pp. 1–13). New York, NY: Association for Computing Machinery. 10.1145/3173574.3174006

Everstring. (2020). *What is intent data and how can i use it?* Retrieved from https://www.everstring.com/what-is-intent-data/

Forbes Insights. (2017). *Data-driven marketing: Push forward or fall behind*. Retrieved from http://www.oracle.com/us/products/applications/wp-forbes-data-driven-marketing-3847636.pdf

Gironda, J. T., & Korgaonkar, P. K. (2018). iSpy? Tailored versus invasive ads and consumers' perceptions of personalized advertising. *Electronic Commerce Research and Applications*, *29*, 64–77. doi:10.1016/j.elerap.2018.03.007

Glaser, P., Liu, J. H., Hakim, M. A., Vilar, R., & Zhang, R. (2018). Is social media use for networking positive or negative? Offline social capital and internet addiction as mediators for the relationship between social media use and mental health. *New Zealand Journal of Psychology*, *47*(3), 11–17.

Huang, J., Su, S., Zhou, L., & Liu, X. (2013). Attitude toward the viral ad: Expanding traditional advertising models to interactive advertising. *Journal of Interactive Marketing*, *27*(1), 36–46. doi:10.1016/j.intmar.2012.06.001

Ismail, A. (2015, January 18). *How the sharing economy will impact marketing*. Retrieved from https://techcrunch.com/2015/01/17/how-the-sharing-economy-will-impact-marketing/

Jafari, S. M., Jandaghi, G., & Taghavi, H. (2016). Factors influencing the intention to accept advertising in mobile social networks. *Marketing and Management of Innovations*, *1*, 57–72.

John, L. K., Kim, T., & Barasz, K. (2018). *Ads that don't overstep*. Retrieved from https://hbr.org/2018/01/ads-that-dont-overstep

Johnson, W. (2016). *Disrupt yourself: Putting the power of disruptive innovation to work*. Retrieved from http://www.thegoblegroup.com/wp-content/uploads/2016/01/Disrupt_Yourself.pdf

Junglas, I., & Spitzmüller, C. (2006). Personality traits and privacy perceptions: An empirical study in the context of location-based services. In S. Ceballos (Ed.), *Proceedings of the International Conference on Mobile Business* (pp. 36–46). Los Alamitos, CA: IEEE Computer Society. 10.1109/ICMB.2006.40

Junglas, I. A., Johnson, N. A., & Spitzmüller, C. (2008). Personality traits and concern for privacy: An empirical study in the context of location-based services. *European Journal of Information Systems*, *17*(4), 387–402. doi:10.1057/ejis.2008.29

Kamalul Ariffin, S., Ismail, I., & Mohammad Shah, K. A. (2016). Religiosity moderates the relationship between ego-defensive function and attitude towards advertising. *Journal of Islamic Marketing*, *7*(1), 15–36. doi:10.1108/JIMA-11-2014-0074

Kantar. (2017). *DIMENSION: Communication planning in a disrupted world | Kantar Media*. Retrieved from https://www.kantarmedia.com/us/thinking-and-resources/reports/dimension-communication-planning-in-a-disrupted-world

Keller, A. (2015). *Social norms in commercial ads – welcome to the National Social Norms Center*. Retrieved from http://socialnorms.org/social-norms-in-commercial-ads/

Ketelaar, P. E., Van Gisbergen, M. S., Bosman, J. A. M., & Beentjes, J. (2010). The effects of openness on attitude toward the ad, attitude toward the brand, and brand beliefs in Dutch Magazine Ads. *Journal of Current Issues and Research in Advertising*, *32*(2), 71–85. doi:10.1080/10641734.2010.10505286

Ketelaar, P. E., van't Riet, J., Thorbjornsen, H., & Buijzen, M. (2018). Positive uncertainty: The benefit of the doubt in advertising. *International Journal of Advertising*, *37*(2), 256–269. doi:10.1080/02650487.2016.1231163

Khan, M. M., Mahmood, N., & Jalees, T. (2017). Perceived usefulness of mobile and mobile advertising: Understanding relationship through structural approach. *Global Management Journal for Academic & Corporate Studies*, *7*(2), 111–120.

Kilkki, K., Mäntylä, M., Karhu, K., Hämmäinen, H., & Ailisto, H. (2018). A disruption framework. *Technological Forecasting and Social Change*, *129*, 275–284. doi:10.1016/j.techfore.2017.09.034

Kinapti, T. T. (2019, January 28). *Cara menghilangkan iklan di HP Android tanpa root, aman dan cepat*. Retrieved from https://www.liputan6.com/tekno/read/3881293/cara-menghilangkan-iklan-di-hp-android-tanpa-root-aman-dan-cepat

Kodjamanis, A., & Angelopoulos, S. (2013). Consumer perception and attitude towards advertising on social networking sites: The case of Facebook. In *Proceedings of International Conference on Communication* (pp. 53–58). Media, Technology and Design. Retrieved from http://www.cmdconf.net/2013/makale/PDF/11.pdf

Krosnick, J. A., Boninger, D. S., Chuang, Y. C., Berent, M. K., & Carnot, C. G. (1993). Attitude strength: One construct or many related constructs? *Journal of Personality and Social Psychology*, *65*(6), 1132–1151. doi:10.1037/0022-3514.65.6.1132

Laukkanen, T. (2015). How Uncertainty avoidance affects innovation resistance in mobile banking: The moderating role of age and gender. In *Proceedings of the 48th Hawaii International Conference on System Sciences* (pp. 3601–3610). Washington, DC: IEEE Computer Society. 10.1109/HICSS.2015.433

Le, T. D., & Vo, H. (2017). Consumer attitude towards website advertising formats: A comparative study of banner, pop-up and in-line display advertisements. *International Journal of Internet Marketing and Advertising*, *11*(3), 202–217. doi:10.1504/IJIMA.2017.085654

Lee, J., Kim, S., & Ham, C.-D. (2016). A double-edged sword? Predicting consumers' attitudes toward and sharing intention of native advertising on social media. *The American Behavioral Scientist*, *60*(12), 1425–1441. doi:10.1177/0002764216660137

Lee, J. K., Lee, S.-Y., & Hansen, S. S. (2017). Source credibility in consumer-generated advertising in youtube: The moderating role of personality. *Current Psychology (New Brunswick, N.J.)*, *36*(4), 849–860. doi:10.100712144-016-9474-7

Lennihan, M. (2018). *Google's Chrome browser starts blocking 'disruptive' ads*. Retrieved from https://www.cbc.ca/news/technology/ad-blocking-chrome-1.3713568

MobileAds Com. (2018). *Best mobile ad formats for display advertising campaigns*. Retrieved from https://www.mobileads.com/blog/best-mobile-ad-formats-sizes-display-ad-campaigns

Myers, S. D., Sen, S., & Alexandrov, A. (2010). The moderating effect of personality traits on attitudes toward advertisements: A contingency framework. *Management & Marketing*, *5*(3), 3–20.

Newberry, C. (2017). *The Facebook pixel: What it is and how to use it*. Retrieved from https://blog.hootsuite.com/facebook-pixel/

Olmedilla, D. (2016). Applying machine learning to ads integrity at Facebook. In *Proceedings of the 8th ACM Conference on Web Science - WebSci '16* (pp. 4–4). New York, NY: Association for Computing Machinery. 10.1145/2908131.2908134

Patel, N. (2018). *Your ads are getting ignored: 5 smart strategies to overcome banner blindness*. Retrieved from https://neilpatel.com/blog/your-ads-are-getting-ignored-5-smart-strategies-to-overcome-banner-blindness/

Porter, J. (2018). *Google accused of GDPR privacy violations by seven countries*. Retrieved from https://www.theverge.com/2018/11/27/18114111/google-location-tracking-gdpr-challenge-european-deceptive

Prayoga, T., & Abraham, J. (2016). Behavioral intention to use IoT health device: The role of perceived usefulness, facilitated appropriation, big five personality traits, and cultural value orientations. *International Journal of Electrical and Computer Engineering*, *6*(4), 1751–1765. doi:10.11591/ijece.v6i4.pp1751-1765

Putri, V. M. (2019, July 17). *3 cara menghilangkan iklan di smartphone Android*. Retrieved from https://inet.detik.com/tips-dan-trik/d-4627910/3-cara-menghilangkan-iklan-di-smartphone-android

Ramdhani, N. (2012). Adaptasi bahasa dan budaya dari skala kepribadian Big Five. *Jurnal Psikologi*, *39*(2), 189–205. doi:10.22146/JPSI.6986

Rezvani, J. (2017). *3 ways technology will continue to disrupt digital marketing in 2018*. Retrieved from https://medium.com/the-mission/3-ways-technology-will-continue-to-disrupt-digital-marketing-in-2018-60a3ee0a1fa7

Rudolph, R. L., Klemz, B. R., & Asquith, J. A. (2013). Young female users of social media and Internet addiction. *Journal of Mass Communication & Journalism*, *4*(2), 1–4. doi:10.4172/2165-7912.1000177

Schnall, R., Higgins, T., Brown, W., Carballo-Dieguez, A., & Bakken, S. (2015). Trust, perceived risk, perceived ease of use and perceived usefulness as factors related to mHealth technology use. *Studies in Health Technology and Informatics*, *216*, 467–471. PMID:26262094

Shi, Y. (2018). The impact of consumer innovativeness on the intention of clicking on SNS advertising. *Modern Economy*, *9*(2), 278–285. doi:10.4236/me.2018.92018

Slawinski, N., Pinkse, J., Busch, T., & Banerjee, S. B. (2017). The role of short-termism and uncertainty avoidance in organizational inaction on climate change. *Business & Society*, *56*(2), 253–282. doi:10.1177/0007650315576136

Soto, C. J., & John, O. P. (2017). The next Big Five Inventory (BFI-2): Developing and assessing a hierarchical model with 15 facets to enhance bandwidth, fidelity, and predictive power. *Journal of Personality and Social Psychology*, *113*(1), 117–143. doi:10.1037/pspp0000096 PMID:27055049

Srivastava, N., Srivastava, S., & Rai, A. K. (2014). Attitude and perception towards online advertising among students and young professionals: A study. *International Journal of Management*, *5*(5), 33–39.

Stajkovic, A. D., Bandura, A., Locke, E. A., Lee, D., & Sergent, K. (2018). Test of three conceptual models of influence of the big five personality traits and self-efficacy on academic performance: A meta-analytic path-analysis. *Personality and Individual Differences*, *120*, 238–245. doi:10.1016/j.paid.2017.08.014

Stewart, D. (2018). *Are consumers 'adlergic'? A look at ad-blocking habits*. Retrieved from https://deloitte.wsj.com/cmo/2018/04/03/are-consumers-adlergic-a-look-at-ad-blocking-habits/

Sumpter, D. J. T. (2018). *Outnumbered: From Facebook and Google to fake news and filter-bubbles -- The algorithms that control our lives*. Retrieved from https://www.bloomsbury.com/us/outnumbered-9781472947420/

Swant, M. (2016, March 22). *Adobe is creating a data co-op to compete with Google and Facebook*. Retrieved from https://www.adweek.com/digital/adobe-creating-data-co-op-compete-google-and-facebook-170347/

Ting, H., Run, E. C., & Thurasamy, R. (2015). Young adults' attitude towards advertising: A multi-group analysis by ethnicity. *Review of Business Management*, *17*(54), 769–787. doi:10.7819/rbgn.v17i54.1777

Voorveld, H. A. M., van Noort, G., Muntinga, D. G., & Bronner, F. (2018). Engagement with social media and social media advertising: The differentiating role of platform type. *Journal of Advertising*, *47*(1), 38–54. doi:10.1080/00913367.2017.1405754

West, H. (2018). *The attention economy to the addiction economy*. Retrieved from https://blog.mozilla.org/internetcitizen/2018/07/27/attention-addiction/

Wissman, B. (2018). *Micro-influencers: The marketing force of the future?* Retrieved from http://www.forbes.com/sites/barrettwissman/2018/03/02/micro-influencers-the-marketing-force-of-the-future/#3ab3827f6707

Yoo, B., Donthu, N., & Lenartowicz, T. (2011). Measuring Hofstede's five dimensions of cultural values at the individual level.pdf. *International Consumer Marketing*, *23*(3–4), 193–210. doi:10.1080/08961530.2011.578059

Zha, W., & Wu, H. D. (2014). The impact of online disruptive ads on users' comprehension, evaluation of site credibility, and sentiment of intrusiveness. *American Communication Journal*, *16*(2), 15–28.

Zhang, X., & Zhou, J. (2014). Empowering leadership, uncertainty avoidance, trust, and employee creativity: Interaction effects and a mediating mechanism. *Organizational Behavior and Human Decision Processes*, *124*(2), 150–164. doi:10.1016/j.obhdp.2014.02.002

ADDITIONAL READING

Altmeyer, M., Lessel, P., Dernbecher, K., Hnatovskiy, V., Schubhan, M., & Krüger, A. (2019). Eating ads with a monster: Introducing a gamified ad blocker. In *CHI'19 Extended Abstracts*, May 4–9, 2019, Glasgow, Scotland UK. Retrieved from https://umtl.cs.uni-saarland.de/paper_preprints/altmeyer_paper_Eating_Ads_With_a_Monster.pdf

Bisaria, R. (2016, December). Native advertising: Less intrusion, more meaningful connections. Retrieved from https://cmo.adobe.com/articles/2016/12/native-advertising-less-intrusion-more-meaningful-connections.html#gs.rukhe9

Lessard, K. (2018, August 25). What is native advertising? The 6 universal types & how to use them. Retrieved from https://business.linkedin.com/marketing-solutions/blog/linkedin-b2b-marketing/2018/What-Is-Native-Advertising

Raza, S. H., Abu Bakar, H., & Mohamad, B. (2019). The effects of advertising appeals on consumers' behavioural intention towards global brands: The mediating role of attitude and the moderating role of uncertainty avoidance. *Journal of Islamic Marketing, 11*(2), 440–460. Advance online publication. doi:10.1108/JIMA-11-2017-0134

Razzaque, M. A. (2019). Changes in attitudes towards advertising: 2007-2018 Evidence from the new generation Bangladeshi consumers. *European Journal of Soil Science, 2*(2), 7–17.

Rizk, W., Miriam, R. I. Z. K., & Englander, S. (2019). Systems and methods for providing non-disruptive in-game advertising and identifying target knowledge. *U.S. Patent Application No. 15/659,266.*

Tudoran, A. A. (2019). Why do internet consumers block ads? New evidence from consumer opinion mining and sentiment analysis. *Internet Research, 29*(1), 144–166. doi:10.1108/IntR-06-2017-0221

Wojdynski, B. W. (2016). Native advertising: Engagement, deception, and implications for theory. In R. Brown, V. K. Jones, & B. M. Wang (Eds.), *The new advertising: Branding, content and consumer relationships in a data-driven social media era* (pp. 203–236). Praeger/ABC-CLIO.

KEY TERMS AND DEFINITIONS

Attitude Towards Online Disruptive Advertising: Individual's evaluation regarding online advertisement practices that appears in the midst of their online activities.

Big Five Personality Traits: Theory of personality that explains every individual's personality can be analyzed by looking at five main universal traits: Openness, Conscientiousness, Extraversion, Agreeableness, and Neuroticism.

Disruptive Advertisement: Advertisements that disrupt the audience's online activities, usually by appearing suddenly in-between contents or as pop-ups.

Openness to New Experience: One of the Big Five Personality Traits indicating individual's degree of willingness to accept and engage in a new experience.

Perceived Usefulness: Individual's perception of the degree a technology or tool is able to help them achieve their goal.

Technology Acceptance Model: Theoretical model that explains factors predicting an individual's acceptance towards new technology or tools, consists of behavioral intention, attitude, perceived usefulness, and perceived ease of use as the theoretical foundation.

Uncertainty Avoidance: Individual's tendency to avoid elements of uncertainty, usually measured as a part of their cultural values.

Chapter 7

Firm-Specific Moderators in Recovery From Brand Scandals:

Insight Into Consumer Markets and Capital Markets

Betül Çal
https://orcid.org/0000-0002-5020-9430
Alanya Alaaddin Keykubat University, Turkey

ABSTRACT

The aim of this chapter is to investigate the firm-related factors that moderate the effect size of corporate scandals that brands are faced with at times. The issue is analyzed from consumer market and capital market perspectives. An extensive literature review is presented to reveal the existing viewpoints and applications in this aspect. Among the firm-specific factors discussed are brand equity, firm size and industry, corporate reputation, social responsibility, CEO traits, source, and timing of disclosure. It is concluded that although brand scandals are hard to control, depending on various conditions related to both the firm and industry, their effect size can at least be managed with a proactive approach, which is handled at the strategic level.

INTRODUCTION

More challenging than achieving growth is sustaining it for a long time in today's highly demanding economic environment. The real challenge does not lie in having a wide and profitable customer base anymore. It is more related to building an effective relationship based on collaboration with your customers, involve them in the production process and co-create with them. What is of critical importance in doing all these is accountability on the firm side. It would be hard to trace sustainable development in an environment where the corruption of the public officials, poor management of resources, leadership challenges and resulting lack of accountability prevail (Gberevbie, Joshua, Excellence-Oluye, & Oyeyemi, 2017). In a similar vein, sustainable development would be a challenge in an informal organizational

DOI: 10.4018/978-1-7998-4543-0.ch007

structure, which lacks the ethical cultural dimension of supportability for employees experiencing trust and respect to adopt certain ethical norms and rules (Zaal, Jeurissen, & Groenland, 2019). For this reason, it is considered to be a must to question the unethical behaviors in which firms may get involved from time to time in order to have an idea of the business sustainability in a collaborative economy today.

The aim of this paper is to investigate the differential effects of brand scandals that firms face in consumer markets and capital markets, as well as locating the firm-specific variables framing these effects on both markets. To this end, an extensive literature review regarding the impacts of brand scandals on these two market types is presented. The firm-specific factors, such as firm size and industry, brand equity, corporate reputation, and CEO traits, are further investigated as to their effects on the extent of these scandals. The study is concluded with the discussion of the conceptual viewpoints presented.

CONCEPTUAL BACKGROUND

What is a Brand Scandal?

The circumstances which lead to public controversy and threaten the corporate identity of the brand can be referred to by different names in the literature. Some examples include product-harm crisis (Dawar & Pillutla, 2000; Klein & Dawar, 2004); brand failure (Cheng, White, & Chaplin, 2012); brand crisis (Custance, Walley, & Jiang, 2012; Pace, Balboni, & Gistri, 2014); brand scandal (Roehm & Tybout, 2006) or corporate scandal (Jory, Ngo, Wang, & Saha, 2015; Kuhn & Ashcraft, 2003; Lee & Fan, 2014). Also, it is not uncommon for within-firm cases that draw negative public reaction to be called as bad news in general (Mendenhall & Nichols, 1989; Skinner, 1994). Regardless of the different terminology used in reference to the root of the public event, they are agreeably found to make an adverse effect on the corporate brand, and the efforts to rescue the brand are handled at the corporate level (Greyser, 2009, p.591). In this regard, the examples of brand scandals include Pan Pharmaceuticals' withdrawing a large portfolio of its medicines, Toyota's recall crisis, Enron's financial misdeeds, Coca Coca's contamination scandal in 1990s, Tyco International's fraudulent CEOs, WorldCom's accounting scandal and eventually Volkswagen's emission scandal out breaking in September 2015.

"A corporate scandal is broadly defined as an act knowingly committed by a company with the intent to deceive stakeholders, regulatory agencies and/or the public" (Tanimura & Okamoto, 2013, p.39). By another definition, it is "a scandal involving allegations of unethical behavior by people acting within or on behalf of a corporation" (Sivakumar, 2011, p.154). Brand scandals vary in the nature of the element or person subject to the controversy. Greyser (2009, p.591) in his research defines 9 main types of corporate brand crisis; product failure, social responsibility gap, corporate misbehavior, executive misbehavior, poor business results, spokesperson misbehavior and controversy, death of symbol of the company, loss of public support and controversial ownership. Although differing according to the causes related, the common ground making these crisis types life-threatening is "'the essence of the brand', i.e. the distinctive attribute/characteristic most closely associated with the brand's meaning and success" (Greyser, 2009, p.592).

As equally important as the basic causes of brand scandals are their implications in different market types. Karpoff, Lee, and Martin (2008, p.601) find in their study on the penalties that the firms are confined to pay following a brand scandal that those deriving from the market itself is 7.5. times higher than those from the legal system. When the scandal breaks out, the firm loses each dollar that it inflates its market value, together with an additional 3.08 dollar, 0.36 of which comes from the legal penalties; and 2.71 of which comes from the lost reputation. Thus, the main addressee of any brand scandal can be said to be the market with different customer portfolios. It is anticipated in this study that brand scandals will differ in character in consumer markets and capital markets, together with their life span, financial outcomes, managerial responsibilities to be needed and necessary precautions to be taken to alleviate their negative effects.

Theoretical Perspectives for Brand Scandals

In their study on brand scandals involving CEOs, Jory et al. (2015) mention two basic theoretical explanations to justify such misdeeds. According to transaction cost economics, agents, i.e. employees, who are characterized as self-centered, greedy, etc. will commit corporate crimes in their attempt to maximize their own utility at the expense of other stakeholders. The resource-based view, on the other hand, suggests that some organizations are inherently prone to deceptive and fraudulent behaviors due to their organizational cultures, routines and competitive nature. Kuhn and Ashcraft (2003) mention the third factor as a causal agent, i.e. market capitalism. Accordingly, in an effort to meet financial analysts' demands for positive short-term results, some managements are urged to deceive investors by manipulating the performance reports, and the investors, analysts, and directors may turn a blind eye to such questionable corporate practices in the face of positive investment returns. Similarly, Kochan (2002, p.139) asserts the root cause of the current corporate scandals [in the US context] as "the overemphasis American corporations have been forced to give in recent years to maximizing shareholder value without regard for the effects of their actions on other stakeholders".

Kochan's (2002) argument originates from two distinct viewpoints regarding the basic unit that the brand can be held responsible for ensuring its value proposition. These viewpoints are also discussed in the literature as the justification for such firm actions as brand/corporate scandals. Firstly, shareholder theory asserts that the corporate executive is the agent of the individuals who own the corporation or establish the institution, and he is responsible to them (Friedman, 1970). While positioning shareholders as the main beneficiary of the overall trading activities, the theory does not, however, abandon the ethical considerations that the business is free to design its activities as to increase its profits so long as it engages in open and free competition without deception or fraud (Carson, 2003). Shareholder theory has been criticized in a growing body of literature known as 'stakeholder theory' which was coined by R. Edward Freeman (1994). Treating stakeholders as ends, rather than mere means (Freeman, 1994), the theory argues that a corporation has direct responsibilities to stakeholders such as employees, financiers, suppliers, customers and communities, and not just to shareholders. Adopting a more extensive outlook along the value chain, the theory acts as a control mechanism as to both the short term and long term impacts of firm actions. Regarding the practicality of the theory, Carson (2003, p.390) however, asserts that it includes no mentioning of the prohibition against the fraudulent activity on the side of the corporation.

The executives at Enron and WorldCom might conceivably have "rationalized" their actions by appeal to the stakeholder theory. (The rise in stock prices brought about by creative accounting did, for a time, seem to promote the interests of many stakeholders, including employees who owned stock.)

Thus, the stakeholder theory by Freeman (1994) needs some limitations on the interests of its stakeholders just like the shareholder theory by Friedman does on the interests of its shareholders.

Information Asymmetry in Markets

"Investors look for signs [or signals] to differentiate between high- and low-quality firms" (Jory et al., 2015, p.1724). These signals transmit information from sellers to buyers, or in other words, from those individuals having more information to those having less as a result of the information gap in the market (Spence, 2002). Such signals are important because they reveal information about unobservable characteristics to an uninformed agent (Ndofor & Levitas, 2004). Thus, more signals can be asserted to help in narrowing the information gaps regarding the product quality existing in many markets including consumer durables and capital markets. This also means that firms which possess different knowledge bases do not need to divulge or transfer them directly; they can convey their value by different signals in the market (Ndofor & Levitas, 2004, p.686); and these signals reveal information about unobservable characteristics to an uninformed agent (Ndofor & Levitas, 2004, p.688). This quality identification problem by means of signals is so important that Akerlof (1970) emphasizes in his classic lemons example that purchasers' unwillingness to buy a certain product, used cars in his example, due to their uncertainty about its quality would drive the market out of existence.

These informative signals can be either positive or negative in nature within the context that the market dictates. The existing literature accommodates a consensus that negative informative signals often lead to more severe market results than positive ones do. It may be due to the fact that people tend to prioritize negative information more than positive information in their evaluations of a target (Fong & Wyer, 2012; Lei, Dawar, & Gürhan-Canlı, 2012). Thus, it is reasonable to consider that the effects resulting from a brand scandal involving the firm or its CEO will be harsher than those resulting from good news such as market earnings, corporate success, and higher dividends. For this reason, the signals intended to deal with the negatives at the corporate or brand level differ in nature, thus entail more effort to understand in different market levels.

Bad Apple, Bad Cases or Bad Barrel?

For many years, the unethical behavior on the corporate side was considered to fall into the fields of philosophers, thus overlooked from an organizational viewpoint. With the proliferation of such deeds, and upon the comprehension of their extensive effects onto the industry, economic and legal systems as well as the society, brand scandals have attracted attention across different disciplines, and studies have mounted up. A serious number of such studies tend to probe into the antecedents of, or the factors leading to the corporate misdeeds. More recent and alternative approaches to stakeholder and shareholder theories tend to investigate the issue from a multi-layered perspective, including individual-level, organization-level, and context-level variables. Using a meta-analytical approach, the study by Kish-Gephart, Harrison, and Trevino, (2010) identifies three groups of factors; individual factors (coined as "bad apple"), unethical issue itself ("bad cases"), and organizational environment ("bad barrels"). The bad apple argument says that the corporate scandals arise as a result of a few dishonest individuals whose actions differ by such factors as cognitive moral development, idealism, locus of control besides the demographics of age, gender and education. Highly idealistic individuals, for instance, tend to stand against harming others when faced with an ethical dilemma; or high levels of job satisfaction are generally negatively correlated with workplace deviance (Judge, Scott, & Ilies, 2006). The studies which investigate the effect of demographics especially gender and age, however, differ in their results indicating no specific relation between such demographics and propensity to behave unethically. On the other hand, Breen (2000) extends the bad apple argument into a religion-based context and investigates the corporate scandals that some Catholic priests got involved in in a wider context including individuals, groups, and society as a whole.

The bad case argument offers a context-specific investigation that asserts that the moral issue characteristics differ by the specific contextual factors that the individual faces, such as the concentration of effect, magnitude of consequences, proximity and social consensus. According to Jones (1991), tendency to behave in an unethical way is inversely related to such context-based factors as the total harm to the victims of unethical behavior; the degree of peer agreement against such behavior; the likelihood that the action will be harmful; and time span before the results of unethical actions are realized.

Thirdly, according to the bad barrels argument, a more generalized environment such as egoistic ethical climate, benevolent ethical climate, ethical culture and code of conduct have an effect on the unethical choices. According to Martin and Cullen, (2006), less probability of misdeed is expected in a corporate climate where certain forms of ethical reasoning are accepted as standard by the members, as opposed to that driven by a normative push to make self-interested choices.

No matter how independently each of the three main categories of antecedents for corporate scandals works, they interact to a certain level and form the unethical intention as an antecedent of unethical behavior. Their effect size is also expected to be highly dependent on the organizational culture in that certain cultural setting may be relatively more open to "accept" such misdeeds than others. Culture, in this sense "upholds standards and enforces the following of the rules fostering ethical behavior from employees" (Askew, Beisler, & Keel, 2015, p.110). In other words, it acts as a superior mind that assists or even dictate certain codes of conduct to be shared and implemented in the organization.

REFLECTIONS OF BRAND SCANDALS ON MARKETS

Capital Markets

Among the earliest researchers attracting attention to the implications of negative and positive information on the market, De Bondt and Thaler (1985) explain the situation by the propensity to overreaction. Accordingly, investors show a tendency to overreact to unexpected and bad news, i.e. they overweight recent information and underweight base rate data, which may result in severe losses. Taking the overreaction hypothesis one step further, Dissanaike (1997, p.45) asserts in their empirical study that if investors routinely overreact to news, past stock market losers become winners, and past winners become losers. In another study on the earnings-related disclosures made by a random sample of 93 Nasdaq firms during 1981-90, Skinner (1994) found that the capital market reaction (stock price) to bad news disclosures was greater than that to good news disclosures. Testing the effects of management forecasts of bad and good earnings in the US context, Lacina and Karim (2004) ascertain that the stock market reaction is significantly less negative when management forecasts of bad earnings are followed by management forecasts of improved long-run earnings expectations.

Brand scandals constitute negative signals in nature for investors regarding the quality of the brand and/or corporate entity in question. A good majority of prior works point out that markets react negatively to claims of brand scandals. In his study examining the effect of enforcement actions of the U.S. Securities and Exchange Commission (SEC) against the listed companies, Nourayi (1994) identifies a negative market reaction to the announcement of investigations, which is deducted from the stock price changes as the indicator for the enforcement effect. The violations of disclosures and record-keeping requirements were found to have larger market reactions than violations of other kinds. Long and Rao (1995), on the other hand, investigate the effect of such unethical conduct as bribery, illegal payments, employee discrimination, environmental pollution and insider trading on shareholder wealth. The results reveal that the effects are significantly negative and long-lasting up to approximately one month following the announcement of the misconduct due to possible increases in monitoring costs and risks. In a more recent study, Lee and Fan (2014) probe into a series of scandals in Taiwan between 16 June and 15 September 2004 and empirically prove the distinctive severity of the scandals on the small and medium individual investors. The results show that an outbreak of such continuous scandals leads to a significant number of investors to cease trading altogether in their original portfolios during the scandal period, even if the firms in these portfolios are not directly linked with the scandal.

Consumer Markets

Information asymmetry exists in consumer markets and can affect the relationship between the sided as much as in capital markets. Especially in the markets where consumers cannot verify product quality and producers (or executives) are more advantageous than consumers in information possession, the repercussions of brand scandals can be expected to be more severe. In many consumer markets, consumers do not have access to systematic information and are informed only when a product quality falls below the expected limits, for instance in the case of a product safety call (Freedman, Kearney, & Lederman, 2012, p.499). It may further cause a spillover effect if consumers use the present information in adjusting their expectations from the other products in the market, thus shifting the market dynamics altogether. In the case of Toyota recall, for instance, the effects of the scandal might have further extended if the majority of the consumers had reflected the malfunction onto the Japanese market as a whole and been persistent in their views.

Another impact of a brand scandal occurring in a consumer market is likely to be on the customer-based brand equity of the firm in question. In their study on a product-harm crisis involving a dominant instant coffee brand (discovery of fragments of glass in canisters of instant coffee), Dawar and Pillutla (2000, p.220) revealed that consumers' prior knowledge and expectations of the firm have an effect in their evaluations of the scandal. Purchasers of the crisis brand were found in the study to be more sensitive to firm response than to the risk inherent in the defective product, while purchasers of other brands focused more on product risk perceptions [not firm response]. In either case, the harm that the scandal caused to the brand was through weakening the brand equity.

A more direct outcome of a brand scandal (product-harm crisis in this case) can be on brand performance and market structure. In their study on Nestle's product-harm crisis dated 2005 for their milk powder sales in China, Ma, Zhang, Li, and Wang (2010) found out that the stationary market structure before the crisis did not turn to normal even after 4 months after the outbreak. The observed purchase frequencies, penetration, and market share of the brand were significantly lower than the estimated measures both during and after the crisis period. Besides the significant drop in such market indicators, the researchers further showed that some of the customer portfolios of Nestle were distributed to a number of non-crisis rival brands, as opposed to the arguments about the possible spill-over effects of brand scandals.

Firm-Specific Moderators in Brand Scandal's Effect Size

Although many prior works indicate that market reaction to corporate wrongdoings is most of the time negative, it is difficult to assert that reactions are uniform (Janney & Gove, 2011). This mainly derives from the fact that many factors may alter and even reduce the value and veracity of the signals informing investors about the quality of the brand they invest in (Ndofor & Levitas, 2004, p.698) or consumers about the product that they intend to purchase. Thus, any brand scandal together with the resulting implications should be evaluated within the context of its occurring.

Much of the existing literature tends to look into the effect size of the brand scandals in a multi-layered approach, which includes both micro and macro-level variables. Accordingly, the factors that strengthen or downsize the effects of a brand scandal can differ in nature in that some of them stem from the industry in which they operate such as supply networks, characteristics of delivery agents, rivalry or substitutes while some others originate in more of a macro perspective such as the economic outlook, regulatory system, and ecological perspective. The remaining but equally significant factors are firm-specific, that is, arising from the operations or preferences that firms involved in, such as firm size and industry, corporate social responsibility actions, timing and source of disclosure; in the implications of these operations or preferences, such as brand equity and corporate reputation; and in CEO-related variables such as CEO traits and demographics.

The factors being the subject to this study are the last group, namely firm-specific factors having an impact on the extent of brand scandals in terms of their success or failure. Regarding the methodology behind their selection, a meta-analytical approach has been followed; a number of academic studies published in many leading journals in the field were investigated within a large time frame starting from the 1970s. Only the firm-related variables presented as possible moderators impacting the effect size of brand scandals were grouped and discussed below.

A theoretical model for the discussion point is presented below (Figure 1).

Firm Size

Firm size contributes to a firm reputation through greater name recognition (Willians & Barrett, 2000), which is mentioned in many studies as an asset for the firm to alleviate the negatives of a brand scandal. Larger firms are most probably known by a larger consumer base than smaller ones, which will boost their corporate reputation. This further signals a link between firm size and the effect size of a brand scandal in that firms depending on their size may reveal different practices in their operations, such as more transparency in their public statements, more involvement in SCR activities, positive brand image among customers and larger media coverage.

According to Jory et al. (2015), the size of the firm matters in the propensity to corporate scandals. In their study on the scandals deriving from the CEO's misdeeds, the researchers found out that scandal-prone firms were usually large ones with insiders in critical positions and where the value of options awarded to managers was high. Thus, they conclude that firms with substantial cash as firm resources were less likely to be affected by such scandals; even if they were, they could get rid of the adverse effects more quickly. Similarly, Baucus and Near (1991) tested the illegal acts using event history for a period of 19 years and found that large firms operating in dynamic environments tended to behave illegally more than firms with poor performance. Conducting a research on the link between the corporate values and the scandals in the banking industry, Ehrenhard and Fiorito (2018) also indicated that although the largest banks under investigation seem to focus on clients more than smaller ones, probably due to their international presence, they were less inclined to be transparent in their business operations, with none of them mentioning transparency as a core value in their statements. Out of the 25 largest European banks investigated, only those with social inclusive principles were found not to get involved in large-scale scandals.

Figure 1. Theoretical Model

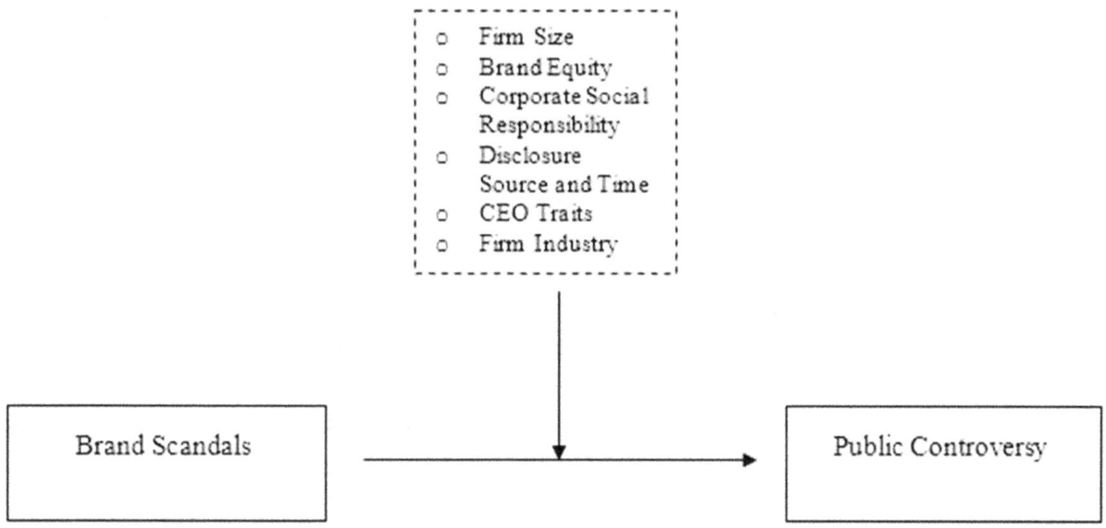

Brand Equity – Corporate Reputation

Defined by Aaker (1991) as the set of assets and liabilities that can be attached to a brand that adds to or subtracts value, brand equity is a function of customer expectations and firm actions. Its significance in terms of firm-customer relations derives to a large extent from its invaluable and fragile nature (Dawar & Pillutla, 2000). This fragility is especially evident in the case of a brand scandal where the initial market response is almost all the time manifested by a sharp and sudden drop in firm value accompanied by a drop in market sales, as an indication of deteriorated firm brand equity.

Albeit its vulnerability at the time of the unexpected disclosure of a firm's misdeed, brand equity that consumers possess for a given firm/brand can also serve as a shield to ward off the negative outcomes of a brand scandal. A recent experimental study on a product-harm crisis involving a personal computer brand (Rea, Wang, & Stoner, 2014) showed that although a significant decrease in customer brand equity level was recorded following the disclosure, its effect size was less for the high-equity brand. Furthermore, the loss in consumer perceptions for this high-equity brand was significantly smaller than that for the low-equity brand. A similar experimental study was conducted in the context of a product-harm crisis for a beer brand (as considered to be relevant and familiar to the experiment setting involving students) by Lei et al. (2012). The researchers revealed that participants attributed less blame and higher brand trustworthiness for the brand for which they had positive prior beliefs if the crisis was said to be similar to others in the industry.

A related concept to brand equity in consumer evaluations of a brand scandal is corporate reputation. Both concepts refer to the prior evaluation of a given firm/brand on the side of consumers (Siomkos & Kurzbard, 1994). The researchers indicated that high levels of a reputation for a firm caused a lesser degree of reduced future sales. Similarly, a study was conducted by Grunwald and Hempelmann (2010) in a fictitious context of product recall situations involving serious health and safety risks to the consumers in Germany. Findings showed that a high reputation of quality positively affected the company's responsibility, and thus protecting the firm from further damage.

The common ground in all these studies is that positive knowledge about the firm through sound brand equity and/or corporate reputation prior the scandal (or "reputational capital" as stated in the study by Coldwell, Joosub, and Papageorgiou, 2012) has a buffering effect in the process following it. Thus, their impact on the brand in terms of mitigating the effects of scandal is expected to be significant especially when the consumers are emotionally involved (Custance et al., 2012).

Firm Engagement in Corporate Social Responsibility

Akerlof (1970) in his influential article titled "The market for "lemons" pays attention to the information asymmetry between the parties in an economic exchange, which overturns the market in the long run in favor of the "lemons" (bad cars). In order to decrease this asymmetry and get protected against the lemons, consumers look for clues that may help them to distinguish between high quality and good quality firms. To this end, engaging in social responsibility projects on the firm side is seen as a good way of giving such a clue to consumers. Recently has there been a growing interest in firms' engaging socially responsible projects as a manifestation of their corporate reputation in the community as well as in the strategic management and marketing literature. There is a good body of literature showing that the social responsiveness of firms is positively linked with their corporate reputation alongside customer willingness to pay price premiums for the products of those firms socially active (Brammer & Pavelin, 2006; Fombrun & Shanley, 1990). In this regard, corporate giving acts as a catalyst to enhance positive corporate identity, which helps to safeguard against the effects of the scandal.

It is, for this reason, reasonable to surmise that this tendency to esteem firms' benevolence for the society will reflect on the market reactions following a scandal revelation. Examining firms' prior ethical stance through their CSR initiatives for the stock option backdating scandals involved, Janney and Gove (2011) found that an enhanced overall reputation for CSR activities helped firms in question to buffer from scandal's negative outcomes. If, however the prior emphasized dimension of the firm's ethical attitude or core identity was the very subject of the scandal, then the market reaction to this was found to be harsher and bear greater negative effects. In a similar vein, Willians and Barrett (2000) indicated, in their study looking at the link between corporate giving and corporate crime that corporate giving acted as a significant moderator. The extent of firm reputation impairment following a brand scandal was diminished through corporate philanthropy. Validating the results of many previous studies about the positive moderating effect of CSR on consumers' crisis evaluation, Klein and Dawar (2004) further extended the topic as to include a significant mediating factor; CSR-sensitivity. Accordingly, regardless of the intensity of the firm CSR activities, the negative effects of the crisis were found to be mitigated only for CSR-sensitive consumers.

Source and Timing of Disclosure

How a market reacts to a brand scandal depends on the actions taken in connection with the scandal besides other factors (Janney & Gove, 2011). As two of these actions are considered to be particularly important; the timing [when the firm makes it public – as soon as it learns it or after some time?], and source of a disclosure [is it a self-disclosure or others break the news?]. First, being proactive for the firm faced with a brand scandal is suggested as the best approach rather than a "wait and see" attitude as experienced in the Volkswagen scandal in 2015 when the management was under harsh criticism for not responding in time. Second, there are certain costs of making the fraudulent act public by the firm such as" potential fracture in shared identity between the firm and an investor". On the other hand, "being 'outed' by a regulatory body can lead to a perception of the firm attempting (and failing) to hide bad news, further damaging the shared identity" (Janney & Gove, 2011, p.1571).

Suggesting a similar approach for the prevention of large stock price declines, Skinner (1994, p.40) justifies the practicality of voluntary and proactive attitude on the firm side when faced with a corporate scandal stating;

if the information is disclosed "voluntarily" (prior to the mandated release date), it is more difficult for the plaintiff, who does not know for sure when the manager first received the bad news, to argue that the manager withheld information. Second, disclosing early limits the period of nondisclosure, thereby reducing the damages that plaintiffs can claim.

Thus, releasing the bad news early may help the firm in two ways; it prevents the arguments that the firm/manager did not inform the public in time, and it reduces the size of the plaintiff as well as the expected cost of the suit. In a similar vein, Mercer (2004) emphasized the timing of the disclosure, - among other disclosure characteristics such as precision, venue, amount of supporting information and inherent plausibility -, as an important element of disclosure credibility.

CEO Traits

Pinto, Leana, and Pil (2008, p.686) define two types of organization-level corruption. One involves the individual or organization as the beneficiary of the corrupt activity, and the other involves a corrupt behavior undertaken by an individual actor or two or more actors. Thus, the researchers make the distinction regarding a brand scandal on the basis of the individual and organization. The individual-involved scandals "refer to the deliberate actions taken by management at any level to deceive, can, swindle, or cheat investors or other key stakeholders" (Zahra, Priem, & Rasheed, 2005, p.804). Although it mentions those individuals at any level of the management, many scandals of this type, especially those occurring in large multinationals, involve CEOs as the main actor and can take such labels as white-collar crime, management fraud, managerial vice or illegal behavior. It is also seen that many studies in the field investigate the effect of CEOs as the antecedent of a brand scandal, where CEOs' personality traits, personal ambitions, management capabilities and/or dispositions are taken as the direct cause of the scandals. Zona, Minoja, and Vittorio (2013) showed in their study on the case of Banca Popolare di Lodi, an Italian bank, that the CEO's personal traits may interact with corporate strategy and stakeholders' cohesion. Instead of asserting that certain environmental contexts drive CEOs having specific traits to unethical behavior, authors emphasize the active role of CEOs in shaping their environments such as securing stakeholders' cohesion in support of their unethical corporate actions. Ashforth, Gioia, Robinson, and Trevino (2008) also attract attention to such CEO traits as moral identity, empathy, and psychopathology as the antecedents of the managerial fraud.

From another perspective, CEO traits can act as a moderator in brand scandals, in that instead of directly related to the fraudulent act itself, they can lessen or augment its effects in the relationship between the antecedents and the scandals. In such a study, Zahra et al. (2005) mention that the individual level moderators, such as the demographics of age, experience, education, gender, and the individual trait of self-control have an effect on the strength of brand scandals. Youth, for instance, is associated with a risk-seeking behavior, thus promoting higher propensity to illegal behavior, while moral development comes with the maturity, thus "senior executives are less likely to make precipitous decisions under the sway of industry or organizational pressures" (Zahra et al., 2005, p.816). Positively correlated with age is the experience factor in that more mobile and short-tenured senior executives are expected to engage in illegal activities more than those more experienced.

Even the functional background is mentioned to be related to the fraudulent act; manufacturing companies headed by CEOs with finance and administrative backgrounds are more likely to engage in antitrust violations than CEOs with other backgrounds (Simpson & Kope, 1997 as cited in Zahra et al., 2005, p.816). Educational background can further be linked to brand scandals as a result of the fact that the level of education is positively correlated to the level of moral development, at least most of the time. However, there are contrasting views on the education effect with some studies emphasizing the business programs increasing self-interest behavior, thus promoting the illegality (Frank, Gilovich, & Regan, 1993 as cited in Zahra et al., 2005, p.816).

Gender is also mentioned as a moderating factor in fraudulent behavior, with some studies indicating the difference in proclivity for illegal activities between male and female students. Lastly, it is expected that that executive officers with less self-control tend to be risk-takers, which increases the likelihood of engaging in wrongdoing. Daboub, Rasheed, Priem, and Gray (1995, p.156) also add the factor of the military service to these moderators, stating that prior military service may be associated such factors as honor, disinterestedness, discipline, and sacrifice, thus impacting the behavior of business executives in the way to brand scandals.

In a more recent study on the executive stock option backdating scandal, Carver, Cline, and Hoag (2013) further showed that managerial power is linked to the decision to backdate. The presence of a founder CEO increased the likelihood of illegal activity. Another study by Grebe (2012) indicated the function of the CEO related factors following the scandal outbreak by emphasizing the importance of being genuinely sorry when apologizing.

Firm's Industry

Besides other factors, the industry where a firm operates may have an impact on the likelihood that it will engage in a brand scandal. It derives from two present situations; corporate wrongdoing is more common in some industries than in others, and legal enforcements may be harsher in some industries than in others (Baucus & Near, 1991, p.15). Furthermore, the reported cases show that "illegal behavior differs across industries" (Simpson, 1986 as cited in Baucus & Near, 1991, p.15); and "violation rates are similar for firms in given industries" (Cressey, 1976 as cited in Baucus & Near, 1991, p.15).

Although under the mentioned conditions it is possible to make some predictions about firms' propensity to brand scandals based on their industry, it is hard to locate specifically which industries are likely to engage in wrongdoing. Nor is there a common theoretical or empirical consensus about the possible industries. The existing studies in the field differ in their empirical findings within their specific contexts and sample groups. For example, Baucus and Near (1991) investigated the effect of the industry as an antecedent of the illegal behavior in their study where a number of other environmental, internal and situational variables also tested. Findings showed that those firms operating in the foods, lumber, petroleum refining and transportation equipment (automobile) industries were more likely to get involved in a brand scandal.

The mentioned firm effect may further be evident in the sub-sectors or the type of product offerings. In a more contemporary study, Chira (2014) tested the strength of the market reaction to bad news about financial institutions during the 2008 crisis. The results revealed that negative news associated with firms in the banking sector was seen as more detrimental to shareholders' wealth than news about firms from other sectors. Although there was a negative market reaction to all financial institutions during the crisis, the negativity was more distinctive for investment banks than for commercial banks.

Although there is no clean-cut background about exactly how or why certain industries are more prone to illegal activity, it may be possible to infer that some cultural factors dictated or popularized by certain industries may drive firms operating there into such illegalities. Thus, the industry may be among those indicators for the inclination to brand scandals on firms' side, with no common view about its implications or limitations.

SOLUTIONS AND RECOMMENDATIONS

Brands may go through hard times involving either corporations as a whole or individuals representing these corporations. In either case, the market reaction to bad news is expected to have large repercussions regardless of operating in a consumer or capital market. It may yet be possible to alleviate the negative consequences of such scandals through successful management of the firm-specific factors, which often moderate the effect size of the scandals increasing or decreasing it.

Although it may not be always possible to foresee and prevent such a corporate crisis, a proactive approach can still be taken on the firm side regarding the weaknesses involving the firm and the industry where it operates. Such factors as CEO traits and social responsibility projects as well as time and source of the disclosure are, for instance, can be controlled to some extent by the firm. The action plans to be taken in the case of such scandals related to these factors are recommended to be included in the firm's strategic planning rather than being handled ad hoc. Other factors that are harder to control such as brand equity and corporate reputation, on the other hand, should be considered of first priority in this action plan along with the firm's financial sustainability. Defining a separate department specifically responsible before, during and after the crisis periods is also suggested especially in high-risk industries such as banking and insurance.

FUTURE RESEARCH DIRECTIONS

It is too risky to have a wait-and-see approach in the case of the scandals in which firms get involved in today's highly competitive business environment. For this reason, more and more firms tend to attribute strategic importance to the issue and to prepare action plans and even to allocate certain budgets just in case. Yet, many such scandals are away from being prevented with prior preparation. In such cases, it becomes highly important to spot the factors which may alleviate the scandal's adverse effects and to make them manageable by the firm.

Future studies are recommended to investigate the issue in an industry-specific way, thereby bringing a more in-depth analysis of such factors. Culture is considered to be another crucial variable at this point. Thus, corporate scandals can be looked at from a cultural point of view by including such contextual factors as sub-culture, social class, and reference groups as well. Lastly, it is further suggested to operationalize the issue generally applying a quantitative research method in order to test the mentioned effects in the field.

CONCLUSION

Brands may encounter a crisis during their lifetime. These may be divided into two broad categories; *product-related* crisis such as product-harm crisis, product failure and backdating; *person-related* crisis such as the illegal activity of an executive, inappropriate personal affairs and even death of a founder (besides other types of environment-oriented, institutional and financial illegalities, corporate misbehavior and service failures). No matter what factor lies at the core of the scandal, they all put the survival of the corporation in jeopardy, thus are handled at the corporate level (Greyser, 2009).

As for the theoretical ground of brand scandals, there are two views differing in their propositions as the focus of corporate responsibility. Firstly, according to the shareholder theory popularized by Friedman (1970), the corporate executive, as the agent of the individuals who owns and/or manages the institution, should pay regard to the benefits of the shareholders in the first place. Stakeholder theory (Freeman, 1994), on the other hand, treats stakeholders including customers, employees, suppliers, financiers, and society as ends rather than just means, and prioritizes their benefits altogether without weighting on any side. Both theories have limitations in many ways such as the extent of the responsibility that they undertake, where it begins and ends, and how the honesty and integrity mentioned in both are operationalized.

As for the underlying causes of brand scandals, there also exist different views. While the transaction cost economics put an emphasis on the creation of transaction value for the firm at the expense of many other factors, while the resource-based view put forward the organizational structure and routines as a possible cause of the crisis (Jory et al., 2015). Kuhn and Ashcraft (2003) further add the third cause to this, i.e. the market capitalism, which asserts that having to survive in the competitive business world, firms/managements are urged to engage in illegal behaviors from time to time.

Whatever the cause of such illegalities is associated with, the main difficulty that firms have to face in such a case is mostly brand-oriented. That is to say, it is the brand image, brand reputation, brand equity and/or brand trust that are badly affected by the crisis, with the resulting drop in sales and profit margins. In any case, the cost of the market reaction to such corporate wrongdoings can be more severe than that of the legal system (Karpoff et al., 2008). Regardless of the type of the brand scandal, this market reaction can be two-fold; felt at the level of consumer markets and that of capital markets, with the differing post-scandal views and expectations of their addressees. Owning no systemic information about the products in many consumer markets, consumers are only informed about the quality when a brand scandal outbreaks (Freedman et al., 2012), as in the case of Toyota recall, product contamination scandal of Coca Coca and recent Volkswagen's emission scandal. In consumer markets, it is not uncommon for the negative effects of such scandals to be persistent for a long time after the crisis. In the product-harm crisis that Nestle involved in China, for instance, the market indicators of sales frequencies, penetration, and market share were recorded to be badly affected; and worse than this, the negative effects were still persistent even 4 months after the crisis. Another outcome of brand scandals in consumer markets is the spillover effect, namely, the transfer of the damaged brand reputation onto the other brands and/or products, thus damaging the industry dynamics in the long run.

The extent of brand scandals can be even more instantaneous at capital markets where the asymmetric information (Akerlof, 1970) between investors and the institution can be even greater in proportion to the amount of money involved. A number of studies show that investors tend to overreact to unexpected bad news in the market (De Bondt & Thaler, 1985; Dissanaike, 1997); stop trading altogether although not being affected directly (Lee & Fan, 2014); the size of the market reaction to bad news is bigger than that of the good news (Skinner, 1994); and the effects can be long-lasting following the scandal (Long & Rao, 1995) just like in consumer markets.

Although brand scandals are expected to have different implications in different market types, many studies show that their effect size can be altered by the inclusion of certain external factors or moderators into the process. Those included in this study are firm-specific factors, directly concerning the firm itself or the CEO as its representative. Firstly, firm size is shown in a number of studies to have an impact on the extent of brand scandals in that large scale firms tend to be less transparent and engage in misconduct more than smaller ones. Moreover, firm size may enhance firm reputation since the firm will be known by a larger audience, which may be an asset during the scandal. Another important moderator is brand equity, handled together with corporate reputation. The negative outcomes of a scandal are generally overcome more easily and in a shorter time span for high-equity brands. A good example is the Volkswagen emission scandal in 2015, to which the market reaction was severe with a significant loss in share prices immediately after its breakout. However, the brand has recovered from the crisis very well, which has, to a large extent, resulted from its reputation as having German engineering superiority and a proven track record. Similarly, firm engagement in corporate social responsibility is shown to have a positive impact on warding off the negatives of brand scandals. Such philanthropic actions intrinsically convey a message to consumers regarding the goodwill and trustworthiness on the firm side. Those disclosures made by the firm itself and immediately after the crisis are further shown to have a relieving effect in the crisis period. For this reason, instead of having a wait and see approach and of being divulged by an outside body, it may be a better idea to take the responsibility and being proactive in the compensation process. Besides timing and source of the disclosure, certain CEO traits such as age, gender, educational background, and self-control are also discussed to smooth out the difficulties during and after brand scandals. Lastly, although the findings vary depending on the context of the studies conducted, the industry where the firm operates is discussed to moderate the crisis's influence in that certain industries may promote fraudulent acts due to their corporate cultures and routines.

REFERENCES

Aaker, D. (1991). *Managing brand equity: Capitalizing on the value of a brand name*. Free Press.

Akerlof, G. A. (1970). The market for "lemons": Qualitative uncertainty and the market mechanism. *The Quarterly Journal of Economics*, *84*(3), 488–500. doi:10.2307/1879431

Ashforth, B. E., Gioia, D. A., Robinson, S. L., & Trevino, L. K. (2008). Re-viewing organizational corruption. *Academy of Management Review*, *33*(3), 670–684. doi:10.5465/amr.2008.32465714

Askew, O. A., Beisler, J. M., & Keel, J. (2015). Current Trends Of Unethical Behavior Within Organizations. *International Journal of Management & Information Systems*, *19*(3), 107–114. doi:10.19030/ijmis.v19i3.9374

Baucus, M., & Near, J. P. (1991). Can Illegal Corporate Behavior Be Predicted? An Event History Analysis. *Academy of Management Journal, 34*(1), 9-36. doı: doi:10.2307/256300

Brammer, S. J., & Pavelin, S. (2006). Corporate Reputation and Social Performance: The Importance of Fit. *Journal of Management Studies*, *43*(3), 435–455. doi:10.1111/j.1467-6486.2006.00597.x

Breen, M. (2000). The Good the Bad and the Ugly: The Media and the Scandals. *An Irish Quarterly Review*, *89*(356), 332–338.

Carson, T. L. (2003). Self-Interest and Business Ethics: Some Lessons of the Recent Corporate Scandals. *Journal of Business Ethics*, *43*(4), 389–394. doi:10.1023/A:1023013128621

Carver, B. T., Cline, B. N., & Hoag, M. L. (2013). Underperformance of founder-led firms: An examination of compensation contracting theories during the executive stock options backdating scandal. *Journal of Corporate Finance, 23*, 294-310. doı: doi:10.1016/j.jcorpfin.2013.09.002

Cheng, S. Y. Y., White, T. B., & Chaplin, L. N. (2012). The effects of self-brand connections on responses to brand failure: A new look at the consumer–brand relationship. *Journal of Consumer Psychology*, *22*(2), 280–288. doi:10.1016/j.jcps.2011.05.005

Chira, I. (2014). Bad news and bank performance during the 2008 financial crisis. *Applied Financial Economics*, *24*(18), 1187–1198. doi:10.1080/09603107.2014.925048

Coldwell, D., Joosub, T., & Papageorgiou, E. (2012). Responsible leadership in organizational crises: an analysis of the effects of public perceptions of selected SA business organizations. *Journal of Business Ethics, 109*(2), 133-144. doı: doi:10.100710551-011-1110-8

Custance, P., Walley, K., & Jiang, D. (2012). Crisis brand management in emerging markets. *Marketing Intelligence & Planning*, *30*(1), 18–32. doi:10.1108/02634501211193895

Daboub, A. J., Rasheed, A. M., Priem, R. L., & Gray, A. D. (1995). Top Management team Characteristics and Corporate İllegal Activity. *Academy of Management Review, 20*(1), 138-170. doı: doi:10.2307/258890

Dawar, N., & Pillutla, M. M. (2000). Impact of product-harm crises on brand equity: The moderating role of consumer expectations. *JMR, Journal of Marketing Research*, *37*(2), 215–226. doi:10.1509/jmkr.37.2.215.18729

De Bondt, W. F., & Thaler, R. (1985). Does the Stock Market Overreact? *Journal of Finance, 40*(3), 793-805. doı: doi:10.2307/2327804

Dissanaike, G. (1997). Do Stock Market Investors Overreact? *Journal of Business Finance & Accounting*, *24*(1), 27–49. doi:10.1111/1468-5957.00093

Ehrenhard, M. L., & Fiorito, T. L. (2018). Corporate values of the 25 largest European banks: Exploring the ambiguous link with corporate scandals. *Journal of Public Affairs*, *18*(1), 1–9. doi:10.1002/pa.1700

Fombrun, C., & Shanley, M. (1990). What's in a name? Reputation building and corporate strategy. *Academy of Management Journal, 33*(2), 233-258. doı: doi:10.2307/256324

Freedman, S., Kearney, M., & Lederman, M. (2012). Product Recalls, Imperfect Informatıon, and Spillover Effects: Lessons from the Consumer Response to the 2007 Toy Recalls. *The Review of Economics and Statistics*, *94*(2), 499–516. doi:10.1162/REST_a_00162

Freeman, R. E. (1994). The politics of stakeholder theory: Some future directions. *Business Ethics Quarterly, 4*(4), 409-421. doı: doi:10.2307/3857340

Friedman, M. (1970). The Social Responsibility of Business is to Increase its Profits. *The New York Times Magazine*, 1-6.

Gberevbie, D., Joshua, S., Excellence-Oluye, N., & Oyeyemi, A. (2017). Accountability for sustainable development and the challenges of leadership in Nigeria, 1999-2015. *SAGE Open*, *7*(4), 1–10. doi:10.1177/2158244017742951

Grebe, S. K. (2012). The importance of being genuinely sorry when organizations apologize: How the Australian Wheat Board (AWB Limited) was damaged even further by its response to a corporate scandal. *Journal of Public Affairs*, *13*(1), 100–110. doi:10.1002/pa.1450

Greyser, S. A. (2009). Corporate brand reputation and brand crisis management. *Management Decision*, *47*(4), 590–602. doi:10.1108/00251740910959431

Grunwald, G., & Hempelmann, B. (2010). Impacts of Reputation for Quality on Perceptions of Company Responsibility and Product-related Dangers in times of Product-recall and Public Complaints Crises: Results from an Empirical Investigation. *Corporate Reputation Review*, *13*(4), 264–283. doi:10.1057/crr.2010.23

Janney, J. J., & Gove, S. (2011). Reputation and corporate social responsibility aberrations, trends, and hypocrisy reactions to firm choices in the stock option backdating scandal. *Journal of Management Studies*, *48*(7), 1562–1585. doi:10.1111/j.1467-6486.2010.00984.x

Jones, T. M. (1991). Ethical decision making by individuals in organizations: An issue-contingent model. *Academy of Management Review, 16*(2), 366-395. doı: doi:10.2307/258867

Jory, S., Ngo, T. N., Wang, D., & Saha, A. (2015). The market response to corporate scandals involving CEOs. *Applied Economics*, *47*(17), 1723–1738. doi:10.1080/00036846.2014.995361

Judge, T. A., Scott, B. A., & & Ilies, R. (2006). Hostility, job attitudes, and workpace deviance: Test of a multilevel model. *Journal of Applied Psychology, 91*(1), 126-138. doı: doi:10.1037/0021-9010.91.1.126

Karpoff, J., Lee, D., & Martin, G. (2008). The cost to firms of cooking the books. *Journal of Financial and Quantitative Analysis*, *43*(3), 581–611. doi:10.1017/S0022109000004221

Kish-Gephart, J. J., Harrison, D. A., & Trevino, L. K. (2010). Bad Apples, Bad Cases, and Bad Barrels: Meta-Analytic Evidence About Sources of Unethical Decisions at Work. *The Journal of Applied Psychology*, *95*(1), 1–31. doi:10.1037/a0017103 PMID:20085404

Klein, J., & Dawar, N. (2004). Corporate social responsibility and consumers' attributions and brand evaluations in a product–harm crisis. *International Journal of Research in Marketing*, *21*(3), 203–217. doi:10.1016/j.ijresmar.2003.12.003

Kochan, T. (2002). Addressing the crisis in confidence in corporations: Root causes, victims, and strategies for reform. *The Academy of Management Executive*, *16*(3), 139–141. doi:10.5465/ame.2002.8540394

Kuhn, T., & Ashcraft, K. L. (2003). Corporate Scandal and the Theory of the Firm: Formulating the Contributions of Organizational Communication Studies. *Management Communication Quarterly*, *17*(1), 20–57. doi:10.1177/0893318903253421

Lacina, M. J., & Karim, K. E. (2004). Tests of Market Reaction and Analysts' Forecast Revisions to the Disclosure of Improved Management Earnings Expectations: A Case of Concurrent Bad News Management Earnings Forecasts. *Review of Quantitative Finance and Accounting*, *23*(2), 123–148. doi:10.1023/B:REQU.0000039508.11607.9d

Lee, J.-H., & Fan, W.-M. (2014). Investors' perception of corporate governance: A spillover effect of Taiwan corporate scandals. *Review of Quantitative Finance and Accounting*, *43*(1), 97–119. doi:10.100711156-013-0366-8

Lei, J., Dawar, N., & Gürhan-Canlı, Z. (2012). Base-Rate Information in Consumer Attributions of Product-Harm Crises. *JMR, Journal of Marketing Research*, *49*(3), 336–348. doi:10.1509/jmr.10.0197

Long, D. M., & Rao, S. (1995). The Wealth Effects of Unethical Business Behavior. *Journal of Economics and Finance*, *19*(2), 65–73. doi:10.1007/BF02920510

Ma, B., Zhang, L., Li, F., & Wang, G. (2010). The effects of product-harm crisis on brand performance. *International Journal of Market Research*, *52*(4), 443–458. doi:10.2501/S1470785309201399

Martin, K. D., & Cullen, J. B. (2006). Continuities and extensions of ethical climate theory: A meta analytic review. *Journal of Business Ethics*, *69*(2), 175–194. doi:10.100710551-006-9084-7

Mendenhall, R. R., & Nichols, W. D. (1988). Bad News and Differential Market Reactions to Announcements of Earlier-Quarters Versus Fourth-Quarter Earnings. *Journal of Accounting Research, 26*, 63-86. doi: doi:10.2307/2491180

Mercer, M. (2004). How Do Investors Assess the Credibility of Management Disclosures? *Accounting Horizons*, *18*(3), 185–196. doi:10.2308/acch.2004.18.3.185

Ndofor, H. A., & Levitas, E. (2004). Signaling the Strategic Value of Knowledge. *Journal of Management*, *30*(5), 685–702. doi:10.1016/j.jm.2004.04.002

Nourayi, M. M. (1994). Stock Price Responses to the SEC's Enforcement Actions. *Journal of Accounting and Public Policy*, *13*(4), 333–347. doi:10.1016/0278-4254(94)90003-5

Pace, S., Balboni, B., & Gistri, G. (2014). The effects of social media on brand attitude and WOM during a brand crisis: Evidences from the Barilla case. *Journal of Marketing Communications*, *23*(2), 135–148. doi:10.1080/13527266.2014.966478

Pinto, J., Leana, C. R., & Pil, F. K. (2008). Corrupt Organizations or Organizations of Corrupt Indiviudlas? Two Types of Organization-Level Corruption. *Academy of Management Review*, *33*(3), 685–709. doi:10.5465/amr.2008.32465726

Rea, B., Wang, Y. J., & Stoner, J. (2014). When a brand caught fire: The role of brand equity in product-harm crisis. *Journal of Product and Brand Management*, *23*(7), 532–542. doi:10.1108/JPBM-01-2014-0477

Roehm, M., & Tybout, A. M. (2006). When Will a Brand Scandal Spill Over, and How Should Competitors Respond? *JMR, Journal of Marketing Research*, *43*(3), 366–373. doi:10.1509/jmkr.43.3.366

Siomkos, G., & Kurzbard, G. (1994). The hidden crisis in product-harm crisis management. *European Journal of Marketing*, *28*(2), 30–41. doi:10.1108/03090569410055265

Sivakumar, N. (2011). Management of financial market scandals – regulatory and values based approaches. *Humanomics*, *27*(3), 153–165. doi:10.1108/08288661111165204

Skinner, D. J. (1994). Why Firms Voluntarily Disclose Bad News. *Journal of Accounting Research*, *32*(1), 38-60. doi: doi:10.2307/2491386

Spence, M. (2002). Signaling in Retrospect and the Informational Structure of Markets. *The American Economic Review*, *92*(3), 434–459. doi:10.1257/00028280260136200

Tanimura, J. K., & Okamoto, M. G. (2013). Reputational Penalties in Japan: Evidence from Corporate Scandals. *Asian Economic Journal*, *27*(1), 39–57. doi:10.1111/asej.12004

Willians, R. J., & Barrett, J. D. (2000). Corporate Philanthropy, Criminal Activity, and Firm Reputation: Is There a Link? *Journal of Business Ethics*, *26*(4), 341–350. doi:10.1023/A:1006282312238

Zaal, R. O., Jeurissen, R. J., & Groenland, E. A. (2019). Organizational architecture, ethical culture, and perceived unethical behavior towards customers: Evidence from wholesale banking. *Journal of Business Ethics*, *158*(3), 825–848. doi:10.100710551-017-3752-7

Zahra, S. A., Priem, R. L., & Rasheed, A. A. (2005). The Antecedents and Consequences of Top Management Fraud. *Journal of Management*, *31*(6), 803–828. doi:10.1177/0149206305279598

Zona, F., Minoja, M., & Vittorio, C. (2013). Antecedents of Corporate Scandals: CEOs' Personal Traits, Stakeholders' Cohesion, Managerial Fraud, and Imbalanced Corporate Strategy. *Journal of Business Ethics*, *113*(2), 265–283. doi:10.100710551-012-1294-6

ADDITIONAL READING

Ailon, G. (2015). From superstars to devils: The ethical discourse on managerial figures involved in a corporate scandal. *Organization*, *22*(1), 78–99. doi:10.1177/1350508413501937

Braxton, D. F., Muehling, D. D., & Joireman, J. (2019). The effects of processing mode and brand scandals on copycat product evaluations. *Journal of Marketing Communications*, *25*(3), 247–267. doi: 10.1080/13527266.2016.1236284

Guckian, M. L., Markowitz, E. M., Chapman, D. A., & Lickel, B. (2018). "A few bad apples" or "rotten to the core": Perceptions of corporate culture drive brand engagement after corporate scandal. *Journal of Consumer Behaviour*, *17*(1), 29–41. doi:10.1002/cb.1672

Guèvremont, A., & Grohmann, B. (2018). Does brand authenticity alleviate the effect of brand scandals? *Journal of Brand Management*, *25*(4), 322–336. doi:10.105741262-017-0084-y

Kurzbard, G., & Siomkos, G. J. (1992). Crafting a Damage Control Plan: Lessons from Perrier. *The Journal of Business Strategy*, *13*(2), 39–43. doi:10.1108/eb039480

Markowitz, E. M., Chapman, D. A., Guckian, M. L., & Lickel, B. (2017). A Corporate Scandal that Hits Close to Home: Examining Owners' Responses to the Volkswagen Diesel Emissions Scandal. *Environmental Communication*, *11*(6), 740–755. doi:10.1080/17524032.2017.1363071

Sengupta, A. S., Balaji, M. S., & Krishnan, B. C. (2015). How customers cope with service failure? A study of brand reputation and customer satisfaction. *Journal of Business Research*, *68*(3), 665–674. doi:10.1016/j.jbusres.2014.08.005

Young, M. N., & Buchholtz, A. K. (2002). Firm Perofrmance and CEO Pay: Relational Demography as a Moderator. *Journal of Managerial Issues*, *14*(3), 296–313.

KEY TERMS AND DEFINITIONS

Brand Equity: The set of assets and liabilities that can be attached to a brand that adds to or subtracts value.

Brand Scandals: Wrongdoings which lead to public controversy and often threaten the corporate identity.

Capital Markets: Financial markets where long or short term securities are traded by professional buyers and sellers.

Consumer Markets: The markets where end-consumers buy or sell in order to meet their own needs in their everyday lives.

Information Asymmetry: The imbalance in the quality identification by means of signals between the different agents that directly get involved in the market operations.

Shareholder Theory to Brand Scandals: The approach which positions shareholders as the main beneficiary of the overall trading activities, yet emphasizes the importance of open and free competition without deception or fraud.

Stakeholder Theory to Brand Scandals: The approach which adopts a more extensive view into scandals incorporating stakeholders such as employees, financiers, suppliers, customers, and communities, as the direct agents in which the firm has direct responsibilities too.

Chapter 8
Corporate Social Responsibility (CSR) and the 2030 Agenda in the Framework of New Trends in Tourism and Hotel Companies' Performance

Raquel García Revila
Universidad a Distancia de Madrid, Spain

Olga Martinez Moure
Universidad a Distancia de Madrid, Spain

ABSTRACT

Sustainable tourism refers to those tourism activities that respect the natural, cultural, and social environment and the values of a community, which allows it to enjoy a positive exchange of experiences between residents and visitors, where the relationship between the tourist and the community is fair and the benefits of the activity are evenly distributed, and where visitors have a truly participatory attitude in their travel experience. One of the main keys to sustainable tourism is the involvement of the visitors and the host and local community.

INTRODUCTION

Today, tourism activity constitutes a sector that has a substantial weight in the global economy of a country. That is, income from spending by tourists in countries contributes significantly to the balance of payments, especially in developing countries. The contribution that tourism makes to a country's economy as a consequence of its ability to generate foreign exchange is usually analyzed. This is evident when the income generated by this concept is compared with other parts of the balance of payments, generally with imports, services of the country's external debt with exports.

DOI: 10.4018/978-1-7998-4543-0.ch008

In the case of Spain, tourism is very important since it has been marked by a very important evolution, which has led to a change of scenery: the tourism passed from a developmental model to a very environmentally friendly (the current paradigm). It is at this stage, precisely, where acquires a specific weight the corporate social responsibility, which is described as a type of direction that planned activities of organizational nature by taking into account the impact on the environment and on the local community.

Spain participates in various international programs to promote sustainable tourism, among them are the FITUR Green Sustainability and Tourism Forum. Among the organizers of this event is the Technological Hotel Institute, a Spanish organization promotes the efficiency and sustainability of companies linked to the hotel and tourism industry. The result is translated into Spanish tourist companies with a marked ecological and sustainable profile. Also, for the protection of its wetlands, Spain participates in the Ramsar Convention or Convention on Wetlands of International Importance which includes more than 70 Spanish natural spaces. They are aquatic bird habitats in which they try to maintain their ecosystem and guarantee their future.

In this chapter it will explain, in a very succinctly way, how has been the evolution that has characterized the most hotel and tourist companies in Spain. Mainly, this work will be focusing specifically on the current situation, which, as it was explained in previous lines, is clearly marked by corporate social responsibility. This way of understanding the tourism business acquires its own dimension at a time of economic and sociological changes as important as the current, also strongly influenced by the international crisis which has seriously affected Spain. Tourism businesses, more than any other organization, have adapted to the turbulent changes produced in this changing scenario, configured as a model to follow for the good practice they have shown in the conduct of their business.

In fact, it can be ensured that one of the strategic lines and business of the hotel and tourist companies in general has been precisely environmental responsibility, which in tourism is framed by the sustainable tourism. It has not always been so, since in the recent past, the tourism phenomenon did not participate in the canons of sustainability and was joined, in many cases, with excessive town planning. Fortunately, this reality is part of the past and today we find a scenario of respect for the environment and commitment to the natural and cultural capital of the people.

Corporate social responsibility has recently been defined by the European Commission (2001) as "the responsibility of companies for their impact on society". This concept includes social, economic and environmental resources. The companies that decide to assume the social responsibility in their daily management, modifying the management of the company, the means of communication, of communication among others etc.) and on the other the need to measure and to reduce their environmental impacts.

In the Charter for Sustainable Tourism, approved by the World Tourism Organization, which marked a before and after, states in its first principle: *Tourism development shall be based on criteria of sustainability, which means that it must be ecologically bearable in the long term, as well as economically viable, and ethically and socially equitable for local communities. (...) As a powerful instrument of development, tourism can and should participate actively in the sustainable development strategy. A requirement of sound management of tourism is that the sustainability of the resources on which it depends must be guaranteed* (UNWTO, 1995).

Sustainable tourism refers to those tourism activities that respect the natural, cultural and social environment and the values of a community, which allows to enjoy a positive exchange of experiences between residents and visitors, where the relationship between the tourist and the community Is fair and the benefits of the activity are evenly distributed, and where visitors have a truly participatory attitude in their travel experience.

One of the main keys to sustainable tourism sustains that it is necessary the involvement of the visitors and the host and local community, so that this new conception of tourist practice have guaranteed future.

However, to understand the full dimensionality of sustainable tourism and how it has acquired naturalization, it is necessary to bring up the work of the Commission of the European Communities, which published a paper in 2001, where a strategy of sustainable development is established - not only for tourism, but development in general - for European countries.

All this critical consciousness - not recent, since enjoys a certain tradition - it also connects to corporate social responsibility. In this regard, the Green Book of the European Commission (2001) points out that the social responsibility of the employer could be defined as: *Companies integrate social and environmental concerns in their business operations and in their interaction with their stakeholders on a voluntary basis.* From this definition, derives the idea of establishing important environmental strategic lines in the shares of companies based in countries of the European Union.

The concern of the European Union for environmental responsibility, sustainable development and good management of tourism businesses, has been reflected, as we have already seen, in multiple documents. It should also be mentioned the Communication from the Commission to the Council, the European Parliament, the Economic and Social Committee and the Committee of the Regions (2003), which focused in particular on the guidelines to be followed by tourism in Member Countries to be considered sustainable. We quote textually some interesting lines in this regard:

- *Sustainable tourism value also means optimizing employment and social benefits, i.e. the sector's enterprises implement the concept of corporate social responsibility.*
- *Regarding initiatives for encouraging the development and adoption of good practice in sustainable production throughout the European tourism sector and among its stakeholders, the Commission favors in particular promoting the principles of governance and fostering Corporate Social Responsibility (CSR) practices as a specific initiative within the European Multi-stakeholder Forum on CSR. Focusing on the enterprises of the sustainable value chain, in particular SMEs and micro-enterprises, this needs to involve, for implementation purposes, appropriate intermediaries to reach these enterprises.*
- *Open governance requires businesses to assume responsibility in conducting their operations in an economically viable manner that takes into account environmental and social issues.*
- *Major objectives regarding good private and public governance for sustainable tourism are, among others,: the integration of sustainable tourism development into overall economic, social and environmental development strategies; integrated sector policies and overall coherence across all levels; among the means to* be *employed are mentioned: the development and adoption of corporate responsibility reporting and sustainability accounting in both the public and private sectors; using Local Agenda 21 specifically for tourist destinations, including at regional level; the use of value chain and destination development monitoring and indicator systems; and the participation of citizens, both as consumers and in the work place.*
- *Better-quality and easily-accessible information on the environment and on practical matters helps shape opinions and thus individual tourists' decisions that support sustainability. The extension of the Community eco-label scheme to services started with the sub-sector of tourist accommodation, the first service sector for which ecological criteria were developed. Likewise, a wide uptake of the Community Eco-Management and Audit Scheme (EMAS) by the tourism sector*

> *to evaluate, report and improve environmental performance, together with rigorous and independently-verified environmental or sustainable development performance reports, is to be favored.*

The various European institutions such as the European Commission are aware of national diversity that exists within the Union, being composed of countries with a particular culture and diverse traditions. Therefore, companies in each nation are embedded in the culture. Thus, European institutions, and, in a very specific and particular way, the Commission have established lines of action on corporate responsibility and respect for the environment, unifying them into a single consensus. That is, it always considers the peculiarity of each area and the global context of the Union. The White Paper states that anyone who polluter should pay. Textually, in the White Paper is contained the following sentence: *Environmental liability aims at making the causer of environmental damage pay for remedying the damage that he has caused.*

In this way, a tourism industry in which environmental responsibility and accountability are an inherent part of the commercialization of tourist services, it is possible to reduce negative impacts on the environment and on local cultures, particularly in areas of rich biodiversity, fragile ecosystems and communities vulnerable.

METHODOLOGY

The research goal is to analyze the evolution that have suffered tourism businesses, specifically in Spain, centering on the current situation, marked by Corporate Social Responsibility. For this aim, a global vision of tourism in Spain will be given in first place, including a brief summary of the importance of tourism in sustainable development at a global level, the context of sustainability explained internationally and characteristics of the current tourism organization in Spain. Then, an empirical study of the situation of Spain in the Global Compact and Global Reporting Initiative (GRI) agreement is realized. This empirical study consists on shown the evolution of the Global Compact Spanish companies and the number of Spanish companies reporting according to GRI over the years of study (2002-2012). Next, a regression function to predict the evolution of the Global Compact Spanish companies and the number of Spanish companies reporting according to GRI in the coming years are estimated. Finally, the importance of tourism organizations is mentioned as final reflection.

THEORETICAL FRAMEWORK

The focus on corporate social responsibility has been in the media in the United States since the 1990s. Since then, it has become a pillar of the arsenal of public relations campaigns of many corporations. In an ideal world, the common assumption is that corporations act in a socially responsible manner as a result of internally or externally motivated ethical obligations (Holcomb, Upchurch, & Okumus, 2007).

To understand the centrality of Corporate Social Responsibility in tourism businesses and the situation in which we currently find ourselves, must be reviewed - albeit in a summarily way - who have been the most important authors who have created a theoretical corpus on this matter. Thus, it is necessary to quote Middleton (1998), who speaks in his scientific production, which factors they were that have led to tourism businesses to advocate and implement the principles of sustainability. He has not focused solely on these aspects, he has also spoken of the importance of reducing costs to reach business success, etc., but the idea is to emphasize the issue of sustainability, as the main theme of this chapter. Meanwhile, Porter and Van der Linde (1995) emphasize the importance of the proper use of natural resources and the constant search for quality. This is especially relevant in the case of hotels - although it is a constant factor for all companies and organizations. An example of how these theories impact on the new hotel management has been the change in the use of non-renewable nature resources by renewable resources. This has brought a benefit to the environment and hotel management.

Corporate social responsibility has been the result of growing interest among academics and practitioners. It has been seen as a philosophy and a policy that brings great benefits to the economy, society and the environment. This is through the idea that companies have broad goals beyond trade. This fact is usually a difficult task, however, the tourism industry seems to have particular and identifiable duties outside the business sphere, due to its close relationship with destination environments and societies that are facets of its products (Henderson, 2007). Corporate social responsibility activities carried out by tourism companies have a positive influence on their market value. Social initiatives for tourism not only generate social benefits for society directly, but also through commercial mechanisms through the increase of benefits that benefit the community, social action (Nicolau, 2008).

The use of sustainable and green buildings to house hotels has been another demonstration of this change of scenario, which calls for eco-efficiency. Nevertheless, for this new scenario solidifies and extends to the entire sector, it is necessary that the managers of the hotel organizations and entrepreneurs have a critical awareness of these issues. It is already a widely debated issue. For example, Ayuso (2005), Ayuso and Argandoña (2009), and Llull (2003) emphasize the importance of the entrepreneur to reach this eco-efficiency. In the same vein, staff awareness - directly linked to human resources - becomes another important factor. Obviously, the environmental concerns of the entrepreneur can only have visibility as long as the public authorities at all levels have a disposition to care for their surroundings and environment - context that is occurring within Europe - establishing mandatory standards for environmental quality, grants for companies and organizations that perform best practices, pricing of natural resources as water, etc.

THE IMPORTANCE OF TOURISM IN SUSTAINABLE DEVELOPMENT AT A GLOBAL LEVEL

As a multiplicity of authors have expressed in recent times, sustainable development is the set of processes to achieve optimal and respectful management of natural resources. In addition, the sustainable development makes these natural resources more durable, with the aim that they are properly enjoyed by future generations. For this reason, tourism activities must always revolve around on sustainability criteria, i.e., long-term durability of the natural and cultural environment and commitment to renewable energies.

In summary, the objective of this - not so new - line of thinking is the preservation of cultural and environmental capital worldwide. Thus, tourism should contribute to sustainable development while preserving the traditions of the people and generating economic inputs that reversing to the local population. In addition, it is necessary to respect the loading capacity of the ground and be particularly respectful of fragile environments. In turn, must involve all participants in the process (visitors and host community) in solidarity so that tourism could be dynamic and always respectful by the two poles.

The public authorities of each country should ensure that this can be fulfilled correctly and effectively - along with the establishment and promotion of suitable environmentally systems and with different tourism management studies. In the same vein, the Environment Program in Tourism of the United Nations points out that sustainable tourism must not only satisfy the needs of visitors, but also the receiving regions - the context in which the touristic experience develops - while future options are generated for the host community.

Precisely, with the aim that tourism is always a sustainable process becomes necessary to be made various codes and actuation systems of Corporate Social Responsibility, as indeed, is happening in Spain and in the countries of the European community. But of course, Corporate Social Responsibility is not only a concern in Europe. Rather, it is a worldwide concern in a collaborative level, in which Iberoamerican countries are quite involved and have hosted congresses and world level meetings on issues related to sustainability. It can be exemplified the case of the XVII Inter-American Travel Congress, which was developed in Costa Rica (specifically, in the city of San José) in 1997. This congress was characterized because Tourism Ministers approved the Declaration and Plan of Action for the sustainable development of tourism, and marking a before and after in sustainable tourism. This global meeting was called Declaration of San José and it states and emphasized the commitment of States to advocate for a respectful development based on tourism. The active role of tourism in the equal development of nations is also highlighted.

THE CONTEXT OF SUSTAINABILITY EXPLAINED INTERNATIONALLY

With current globalization, it is evident that it should be take into account the international political context. This, to understand the full depth that happens with business organizations in each country. This, if anything, becomes more intense in the case of organizations and tourism companies, because from the perspective of the UN (United Nations), tourism is set as one of the economic activities that move a greater amount of economic inputs at worldwide level. Furthermore, it is also a key activity to poverty alleviation in some depressed areas of the earth. That is why it has taken validity one famous phrase, which collects this idea very well: *Tourism for the poor.* In fact, says the Tourism Alliance Against Poverty (collaboration made between the International Centre for Responsible Tourism, the International Institute for Environment and Development and finally, the Institute for Overseas Development, *Tourism for the poor* can be defined as the kind of tourism whose benefits are aimed at increasing the quality of life of persons without resources.

In short, it is to combine tourism with community development. This is one of many examples that make visible the importance of tourism development to alleviate the inequalities in the world and the gap between rich and poor.

Sustainable development consists above all of giving people opportunities to influence their future, to claim their rights and express their concerns. The UN's long-term vision of global sustainability is to eradicate poverty, reduce inequality and make growth inclusive, and make production and consumption more sustainable, while tackling the effects of climate change and respecting others Planetary boundaries. Country economic policies and international economic relations are largely relevant to sustainable development. The revival and acceleration of development require a dynamic and supportive international economic environment, as well as policies decided at national level. The absence of any of these requirements will frustrate the development process. A favorable external economic environment will be decisive. The development process will not gain momentum if the world economy lacks dynamism and stability and is characterized by uncertainty. Nor will it gain momentum if developing countries carry the burden of external debt, if development finance is insufficient, barriers to market access exist, and commodity prices remain low, and terms of trade of developing countries remain unfavorable.

The importance of tourism in macroeconomic figures is so high that the World Economic Forum emphatically said that tourism was responsible for the creation of a very substantial part of jobs in developing countries. Meanwhile, the Sustainable Tourism - Eliminating Poverty Initiative aims to strengthen measures intended at reducing poverty in poor countries, through tourism activities. To this end, institutional coordination at world level is necessary. This international climate makes tourism organizations in our country have a number of preset channels through which they must travel. That is why they enjoy some unique characteristics that we develop in the next lines.

The international economy should provide an enabling international climate for achieving environmental and development goals by promoting sustainable development through trade liberalization. Also, making trade and the environment mutually supportive. In addition, by providing sufficient financial resources to developing countries and addressing the issue of international debt. And finally, encouraging the adoption of macroeconomic policies favorable to the environment and development.

Furthermore, policies and measures aimed at creating an international environment that strongly supports national development efforts are fundamental. International cooperation in this area should be designed to complement and support, not to diminish or subsume, appropriate national economic policies in both developed and developing countries for the world to move towards sustainable development.

Global Compact is an international initiative that promotes the implementation of 10 Universally Accepted Principles to promote Corporate Social Responsibility (CSR) in the areas of Human Rights and Business, Labor Standards, the Environment and Fight against Corruption in the activities and business strategy of the companies. With over 13,000 signatories in more than 145 countries, it is the largest voluntary initiative of corporate social responsibility in the world. Backed by the CEOs of its member companies, the Global Compact is a practical framework for developing, implementing and disseminating corporate sustainability policies and practices, providing its signatories with a wide range of resources and management tools to help them implement Business and sustainable development. Global Compact is considered a framework of action that facilitates the social legitimacy of businesses and markets. Those organizations that adhere to the Global Compact share the conviction that business practices based on universal principles contribute to the creation of a more stable, equitable and inclusive global market and that it fosters more prosperous societies.

The Global Reporting Initiative (GRI) is an independent organization created in 1997 by the convening of the Coalition of Environmentally Responsible Economies (CERES) and the United Nations Environment Program (UNEP). Its mission is to develop and disseminate the Sustainability Reporting Guide, an optional accounting report on sustainability. The GRI has developed the "Guide for the elaboration of a sustainability report", whose first version appeared in 2000, the second in 2002 and the third in 2006. Its mission is to improve the quality, accuracy and usefulness of reports of sustainability to reach a level equivalent to that of financial reports. It is fundamentally based on the implementation of triple bottom line, economic, social and environmental. The GRI counts on the active participation of representatives of human rights organizations, labor rights, research, environmental, corporations, investors and accounting organizations.

DEFINING CHARACTERISTICS OF THE CURRENT TOURISM ORGANIZATION IN SPAIN

Spain is one of the main tourist powers of the world, both for the number of visitors it receives and for the income reported by this activity. The consolidation of Spain as a tourist destination dates back to the 1960s, although it has a worthy background in illustrated travelers and the romantics who visited Spain. Since the eighteenth century, but especially throughout the nineteenth century, many travelers travel through Spain, including naturalists and writers. Both of them were impressed by the diversity offered by the nature of Spain, by the exoticism of landscapes reminiscent of Africa, by the survival of Arab and Eastern heritages, by cities and monuments, by types and customs Popular, for banditry, for bullfights, etc.

The tourist model that has been consolidated in Spain has as main characters the international origin of the visitors, its condition of mass tourism and the concrete demand of sun and beach. The countries that send tourists to Spain are mainly members of the European Union. Germany and the United Kingdom stand out, from which almost half of the tourists visit us annually, followed by France, Benelux, Italy and the Scandinavian countries. Spanish tourism achieves the international podium thanks to the richness of its cultural resources, its infrastructures and "the adaptation to the digital consumption habits", according to the agency, which analyzes the holiday industry of 141 countries around the world. Spain has climbed at a high speed in this world ranking, since in the previous edition of 2013 (the study is done every two years), ranked fourth. And in 2011, the eighth.

In Spain the competences in the matter of tourism are transferred to the Autonomous Communities (article 148 of the Spanish Constitution). The central State, therefore, does not have direct competences in tourist matters, although it can make policies that influence the sector in function of other of its attributes: foreign trade, international relations, legislation of professional titles, international promotion, etc.

Many approaches can be used to define a tourist organization today. Based on the different business theories, a common factor that emphasizes all of them is the pursuit of profits. Today, this profit maximization and cost reduction is accompanied by a very strict code of ethics, in which tourism organizations try to give back to society part of these inputs. Therefore, the newest theories are talking about the existence of a new model of social enterprise. According to Manuela Guzmán Raja and Carmen Maria Martínez Franco (2016, pp.5-6), a social enterprise can be defined in the next terms: *A matter of great importance is the conceptualization of the scope of entities that could enjoy such qualification. In this regard, the definitions developed throughout the 21st century, could be included in this field both non-profit entities such as corporations, as long that their main purpose is the pursuit of social benefit. Therefore, what comes is to combine the creation of economic and social value simultaneously, the raison d'être of such entities, using for the achievement of strategic business tools capable of generating surpluses that allow them to refinance, and not depend on donations or subsidies to ensure their survival, achieving its financial sustainability. In summary, social business generates a business process that provides innovative solutions to social problems.*

As the last point suggests, tourism organizations today as social enterprises, offering innovative solutions to specific social problems. These solutions can be referred to use the expression outlined by the authors above, in a study that also has been awarded by AECA.

Certainly, tourist organizations have opted for the social commitment, bringing in their business and organizational practices the banner of eco-efficiency, and proclaiming itself as a role model to other companies.

Following the characteristics of the current tourism organization, it can be cited innovation, which is necessary in the changing scenario. Today, hotel companies move in an environment of continuous change, which is why making continuous innovation will allow them to adapt competitively to the changes and transformations and succeed in business.

Transparency can be another defining characteristic of the companies, since the climate in which is that of corporate responsibility, so that transparency in practice becomes as demand from society to current companies. According to Guzmán Raja and Martínez Franco (2016, p.8): *Transparency and visibility for these businesses is essential, mainly because the creation of social value cannot be measured by economic profitability.*

Another characteristic - which would not deplete, in any way, all the definitive features - is the commitment to historical time: indeed, the importance of conjugation of competitiveness, efficiency and cost reduction with respect for the environment has made the scenario of social responsibility the *forced* context for a tourist company to succeed in business. In part, this is because the social awareness that exists, not only public authorities, but also the people - customers of the touristic company -.

Finally - and with no desire of exhaust the characteristics of the current tourism organization - it is imbued with the concept - so in vogue today – of environmental responsibility and forming a constituent part of the Corporate Social Responsibility. This new construct refers to the importance of not generating any negative effect on the environment in which tourism develops.

DESCRIPTION OF THE TOURISM PLAN 2020

To finish describing the current scenario, it is necessary to explain - albeit so briefly – the Tourism Plan 2020, by the Ministry of Industry, Tourism and Trade (2006) specifically designed to achieve an improvement in the sustainability and competitiveness of the tourism sector.

The objectives of the Tourism Plan 2020 are to increase the social and economic benefits of tourism, to achieve a socio-territorial rebalancing that promotes tourism in new destinations, to improve the quality of the natural and cultural environment, reducing the negative impacts that the Tourist activity. In summary, make public and society aware of the importance of supporting tourism as a guarantee of prosperity and improvement of living conditions.

There are many publications that focus on this issue that are shown next:

1. To achieve a rebalancing of territories through tourism and a de-seasonality of the places. To this end, there are competitiveness plans (which are focused, among other things, to achieve accessibility in the destination), the Senior Tourism Pilot Project in Europe (born by the awareness that currently exists in caring and articulate leisure in elderly population - greater today, because people is in a progressively aging society).
2. Planning and good management of destinations, specifying assessment tools of sustainability.
3. Retraining of tourist destinations classified as obsolete.
4. Other measures.

The Plan is part of the process of modernization of Spain and the great Economic and social transformation that it has experienced in the last 15 years, As a result of its full incorporation into the globalized economy and the European space. Its goal is to achieve that in the 2020, Spanish tourism system is the most competitive and sustainable, providing maximum social welfare. Tourism 2020 defines a strategy agreed upon and shared by the public and private agents of the sector for the coming years, thus laying the foundations for preparing and adapting the tourism industry to the changes it faces, in order to enhance and improve its Position in 2020.

In short, the Spanish Tourism Plan 2020, based on the principle of shared leadership, is the beginning of a set of actions that tourism administrations and entrepreneurs of the sector will develop from the commitment to the environment, New technologies and the consideration of people as the main asset of the Spanish tourism sector. In this way, together we will ensure that Spanish tourism is one of the main sources of employment and social welfare.

EMPIRICAL STUDY

The Position of Spain in the Global Compact and the Global Reporting Initiative Agreement

The second part of this study is an empirical or analytical study of the situation of Spain in the Global Compact and the Global Reporting Initiative (GRI) agreement, based on the theoretical framework above. As the first thing, it can be said that the GRI Model is a good practice guide that provides support for companies to adopt effective policies about Corporate Social Responsibility and social commitment. That is, according to experts in the field, an enormously powerful analytical tool to achieve good collaboration between all stakeholders. In summary, the goal is to achieve in the companies involved a balance in three ways, economic, social and environmental and, at the same time, they are balanced.

The number of signatory companies of the Global Compact and the number of Spanish companies reporting according to GRI are represented in the table below. As it can be seen in Table 1, the number of Spanish companies' signatories of the Global Compact and the number of Spanish companies reporting according to GRI, have increased progressively from 2002 to 2012.

Table 1. The number of Spanish companies' signatories of the Global Compact and the number of Spanish companies reporting according to GRI

From the data in the table above, it is necessary to extrapolate the number of Spanish companies' signatories of the Global Compact for the coming years. For that, in first place the evolution of these values over the years of study (2002-2012) is shown graphically. Secondly, from this graph a regression function to predict spending in the coming years is constructed.

Note that it has been adjust the values by a fourth degree polynomial function, since the adjustment is quite good (coefficient of determination 0.993).

The regression model shown in Figure 2, can be used to estimate the values of number of Spanish companies' signatories of Global Compact for the coming years, as it is shown in Table 2.

In table below, it can be seen how the values will gradually increase in the coming years, as has happened in the last 10 years exponentially.

If a similar analysis is made for the number of Spanish companies reporting according to GRI, similar results are obtained (as seen in the following charts).

Table 1. Number of signatories of the Global Compact Spanish companies and number of Spanish companies reporting according to GRI (Garcia Martin, 2014)

	Number of Spanish companies signatories of the Global Compact	Number of Spanish companies reporting according to GRI
2002	62	7
2003	109	14
2004	146	35
2005	204	61
2006	350	91
2007	314	122
2008	402	132
2009	522	160
2010	666	178
2011	1.034	186
2012	1.381	

Figure 1. Evolution of Spanish companies' signatories of the Global Compact (2002-2012)

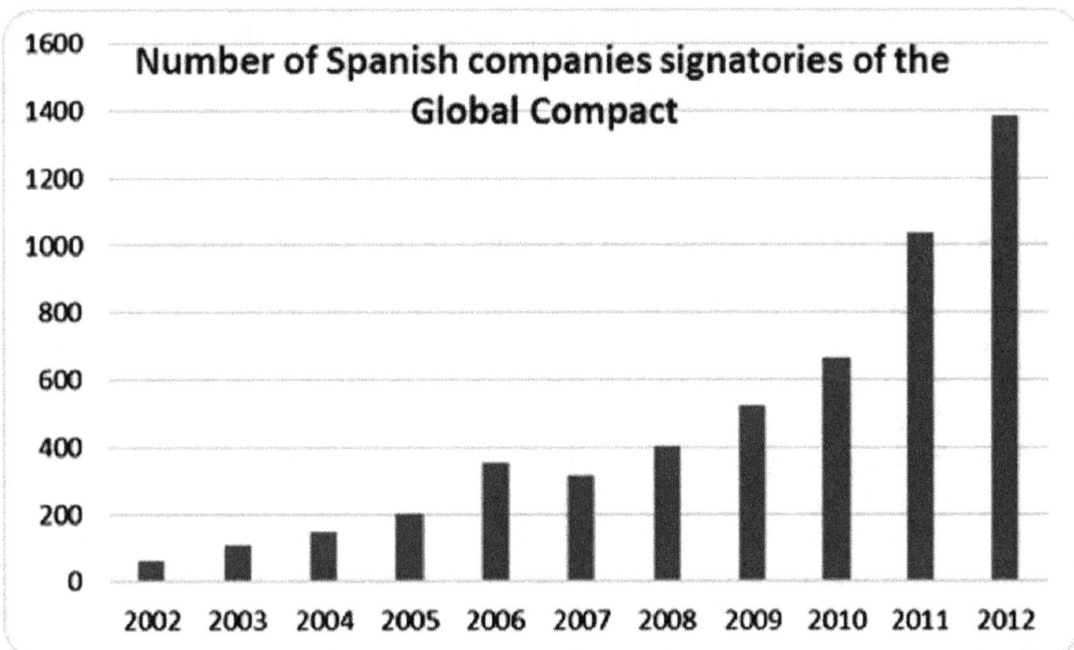

Figure 2. Fourth degree polynomial adjust

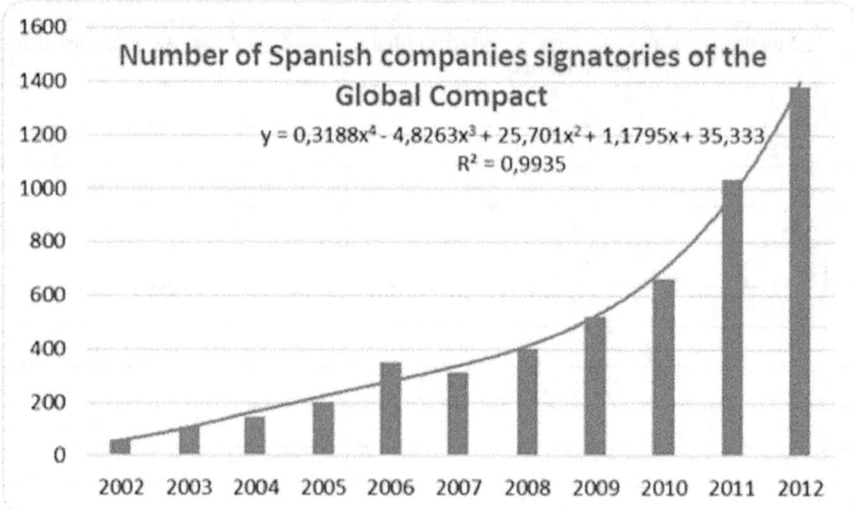

Table 2. Data of Spanish companies' signatories of the Global Compact (2002-2012)

Year	2013	2014	2015	2016	2017	2018	2019	2020
Spanish companies	2.020	2.895	4.091	5.684	7.756	10.395	13.699	17.774

The Importance of Tourism Organizations in the Global Compact

The World Tourism Organization (UNWTO) and the United Nations Global Compact are private sector interlocutors for the achievement of the Sustainable Development Goals (ODS) and the Development Agenda 2030 for what is called for action. This sector is key to the economy and social welfare and has actors who are aware and able to exemplify the true impact of Corporate Social Responsibility (CSR). The Global Compact is the largest voluntary initiative of corporate responsibility and sustainable development in the world, aimed at generating shared value among its members.

Companies in the tourism sector play an important role in transforming the sector's approach and introducing sustainability criteria into its operations. These can promote responsible tourism, which respects the natural, cultural and social environment and promotes the sustainable development of tourist destinations.

Companies are vital in this Global Compact because they express their commitment to work for sustainable development in the hands of leading organizations in the sector with which to enhance their opportunities. The United Nations Global Compact is the largest global public-private partnership for development in which 12,500 companies from 145 different countries come together to promote Ten Principles based on universal declarations and conventions related to human rights, labor standards, the environment and the fight against corruption.

Figure 3. Evolution of the number of Spanish companies reporting according to GRI (2002-2011)

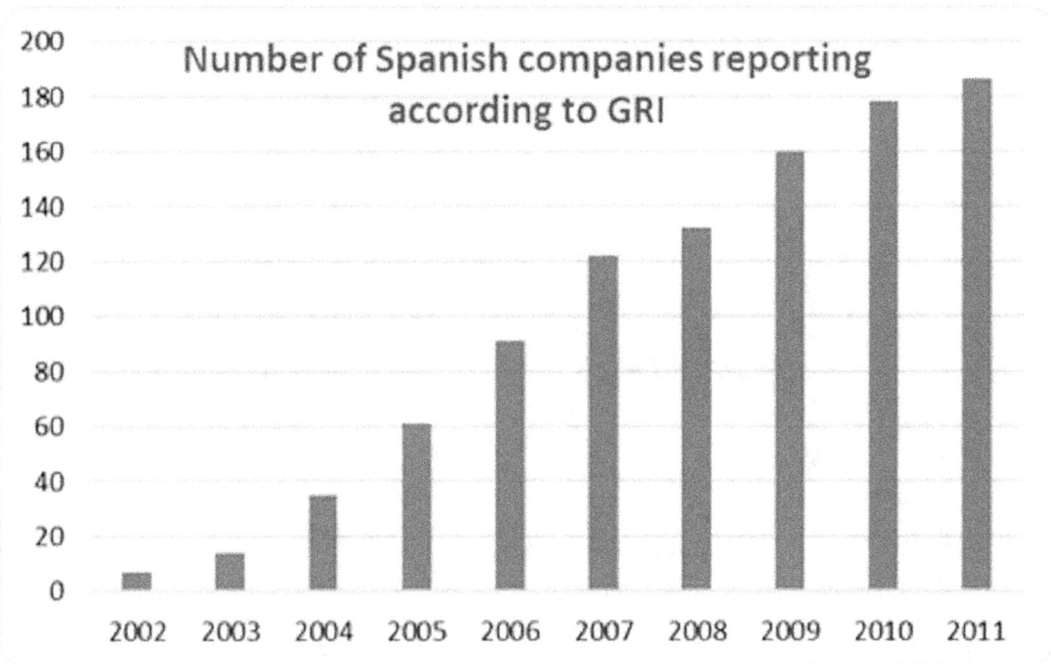

Figure 4. Second degree polynomial adjustment

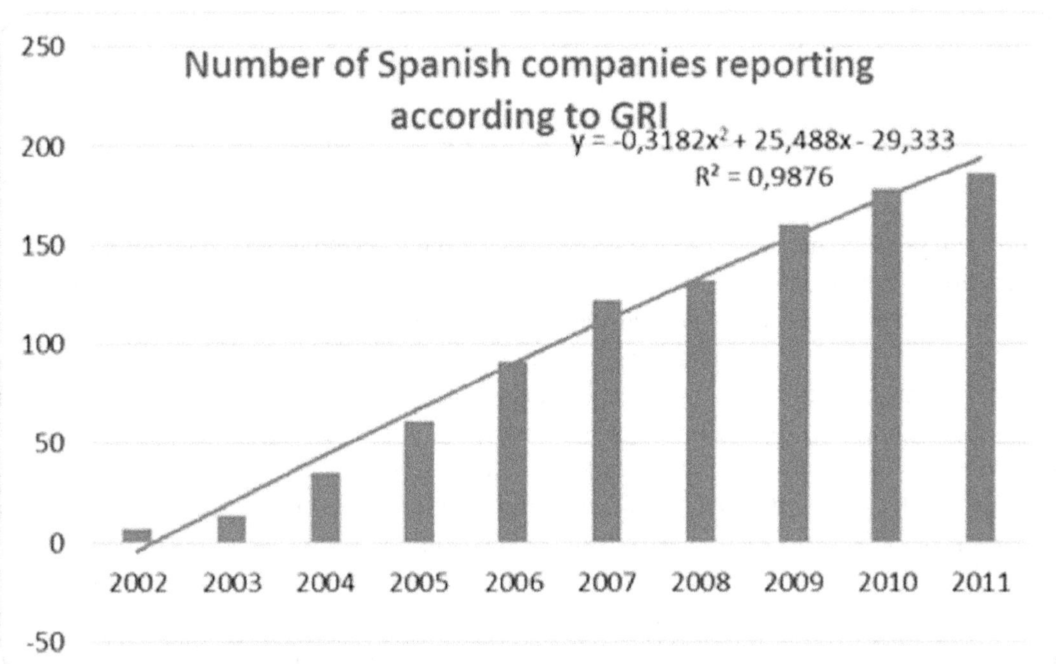

Figure 5. The pillars of sustainability

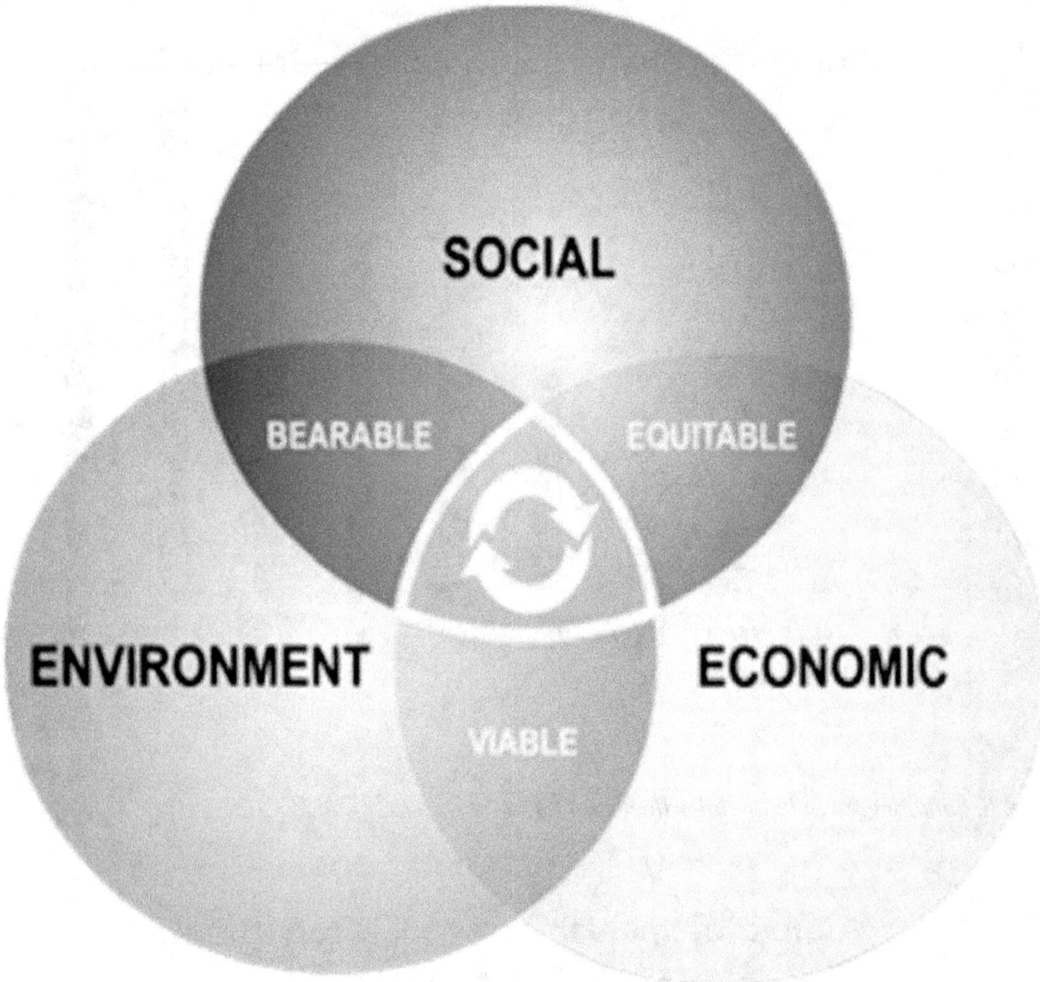

Tourism plays a key role in the EU, because of its economic potential and job creation, as well as its social and environmental implications. Statistics on tourism are not only used for EU tourism policies but also for monitoring regional policy and sustainable development.

As it was advanced at the beginning of this chapter, organizations and hotel and tourism enterprises are set up as a demonstrative example of responsible activity with the environment and socially sustainable practices, establishing itself as a role model. An example of this reality can be the collaboration established by the UNWTO (United Nations World Tourism Organization) and the Spanish Global Compact Network, in which a total of thirteen organizations located in our country - number that is growing right now - participate in the objectives of establishing and solidifying various practices of CSR (Corporate Social Responsibility), aimed, as is well known, to the constant increase of sustainable tourism.

It is important to remark that the working paper entitled "Responsible Tourism: a commitment by all", document that the authors have managed to prepare this chapter, in which a decalogue of good practices for hotel and tourism companies in general, aimed to complete the various objectives of sustainable development (specify irrefutably the three pillars of sustainable tourism - economic, environmental and socially -), as set out in the following illustration.

In this way, businesses and tourism organizations contribute not only to their activities, but also the mechanisms of social awareness to create and achieve a more balanced society where preserving the resources of nature and creation an equalitarian society are configured as key objectives. As mentioned in previous lines, are thirteen Spanish companies that are part of the agreement between the World Tourism Organization and the Spanish Network of Global Compact, a reality that, according to the data, will grow and becoming more intense in the upcoming years. In this propitious scenario, it has had much to do the publication of Global Code of Ethics for Tourism and the 10 Principles of the Global Compact. Notice that the chapter addresses issues so important as education, employment and, of course, human rights. It is important to remark the words of the President of the Spanish Global Compact Network, Ángel Pes (2016): *This initiative is a pioneer not only by the involvement of the private sector in the Agenda of 2030, but also by the need to involve key players in achieving a sector of responsible and sustainable tourism. To put a challenge of its kind in the third most visited country in the world it offers interesting possibilities to replicate this project globally.*

In the case of Spain, thanks to the collaboration agreement reached by the World Tourism Organization (WTO) and the Spanish Global Compact Network, thirteen Spanish companies have joined the commitment to develop corporate social responsibility practices that advocate sustainable tourism. Under the title 'Responsible Tourism: A Commitment for All', the initiative launched on 19 September highlights the role of tourism companies in achieving the Sustainable Development Goals (ODS).

As we finish this article, the twenty-fifth edition of the UN Climate Change Conference is opening in Madrid. The main goal of this convention is to deal with the climate crisis by consensus in order to address the risks involved. This climate summit takes the form of a political forum and includes companies, civil society stakeholders and other social entities with the objective of reducing the effects of climate change. It's basically continuation of the Paris Agreement and the Kyoto Protocol.

Among the most important activities of this major convention is the so-called "Global Climate Action Agenda", which focuses on events carried out by NGOs. In short, this climate summit showcases the huge concern on a global scale when it comes to the environment and sustainability, an issue that fits in with the 2030 Agenda. The 2030 Agenda for Sustainable Development is a decisive action plan resulting from concerns aired by the United Nations, with the key goals being the protection of the environment and people, as inhabitants of 'Mother Earth'.

This Agenda already has somewhat of a tradition, as United Nations member countries met in 2012 to set the MDGs, i.e. the Millennium Development Goals, for the year 2015, which was when a new global agreement on climate change was created. In that sense, on 25 September 2015, the member countries adopted the agreement to implement the 2030 Agenda, which is basically a programme of measures sponsored by the United Nations and encompassing a total of seventeen Sustainable Development Goals that are in turn divided into 169 targets to facilitate compliance. Within these goals and targets, centre stage is given to the poorest or most vulnerable regions and the most fragile population groups. These goals are, in short, pathways to overcome current environmental problems and thus build a more sustainable world from a social, economic and - of course - environmental point of view. Government partnerships and citizen engagement, together with the important work carried out by non-governmental organisations (NGOs), are necessary (but not sufficient) conditions to achieve sustainability. The idea is for the agreed commitments to be fulfilled in a transition from theory to action. In this sense, innovation is necessary and paramount, particularly because it influences all industries and all spheres of society today. Innovation is key to fulfilling and cementing these goals, for which it is necessary to take into account the level of progress of every nation across the world. Frank collaboration between the public and private sectors is a very important and decisive incentive for this reality to become more and more plausible. Civil society, as mentioned above, also plays a vital role in this whole process. In short, it's about guaranteeing a prosperous and sustainable world in terms of present and future. We need to learn from past mistakes, so that they don't happen again and so we can constructively guarantee a better world for the generations to come. Not just the environment, but also social equity, employment, justice, protection of the most disadvantaged, healthcare and education are crucial factors to achieve a more prosperous and equitable world.

In the fulfilment of the goals set in the 2030 Agenda which, as we'll recall, is a consensual climate action plan organised and promoted by the United Nations, tourism plays an absolutely vital role, which is an important incentive for corporate social responsibility. Tourism, as an economic activity with a great reach (in the sense that it favours and positively impacts activities such as retail, transport, etc.) plays a decisive role in social development and progress, in the promotion of economic and sustainable development and in the enhancement of peace and harmonious living in the nations receiving tourist flows.

With tourism models having surpassed developmentalist models and formulas, the new branches of tourism lead to decent employment, granting job opportunities to once excluded groups and making tourism activities foster an awareness of being "at the core of self-development". Specifically, the most important contributions made by tourism to job creation are condensed in target 8.9, which reads as follows: *"By 2030, devise and implement policies to promote sustainable tourism which creates jobs, promotes local culture and products"*.

The important contribution of tourism to the promotion of ethical consumerism is well-known (and has already been mentioned in this article). Sustainable production is linked with ethical consumerism, which triggers and fosters critical and environmentally conscious awareness. Rethinking global tourism, i.e. on a worldwide level, has been key in reaching a consensus of governments and nations to implement joint actions that favour the environment. We have seen the major input of tourism in encouraging local, ethical and artisanal production and in cementing ethical consumerism with the environment, which protects the current generations and guarantees an intact environment for the coming generations. Target 12b of SDG 12 underlines the need to - we quote verbatim - *"develop and implement tools to monitor sustainable development impacts for sustainable tourism which creates jobs, promotes local culture and products"*. In harmony with the goal mentioned, let's now look at target 14.7, which reads *"By 2030, increase the economic benefits to small island developing States and least developed countries from the sustainable use of marine resources, including through sustainable management of fisheries, aquaculture and tourism"*.

Respectful formulas of tourism help preserve the oceans, marine resources and all natural ecosystems. If we specifically focus on maritime and coastal tourism, we'll see that many small island states are greatly benefiting from the inputs derived from this type of tourism in terms of economic and social progress. These are also very environmentally friendly activities and always carried out under the parameters set by the cornerstones of sustainability. Only in this way can truly sustainable and inclusive development and growth be achieved.

CONCLUSIONS

Tourism is configured as an important activity in the economy of a country, this being especially palpable in the case of Spain, since tourism activities in our country have undergone a major evolution, from very developmental models to other paradigms markedly environmentally respectful and that are very much alive today. It is in this scenario that takes a leading role Corporate Social Responsibility. In this contribution it was analyzed the evolution of tourism businesses in our country. Furthermore, it was explained in detail in this chapter what the current situation is. Notice that, this reality is clearly tinted by Corporate Social Responsibility. Thus, one of the strategic and business lines of hotel and tourist companies in general has been precisely environmental responsibility.

Tourism has become today a model example, i.e., serving as an example for other sectors, the well-doing of business practices and management. In this way, new typologies of tourism have acquired an international reputation, such as "tourism for the poor", characterized by channel towards the most disadvantaged populations an important part of the inputs generated by tourism. The sector has enormous potential for the creation of decent work and the promotion of entrepreneurship, helping to empower disadvantaged groups, in particular young people and women. In addition, tourism promotes exchange between people from different parts of the world, enhancing understanding between cultures and promoting peace between communities and nations. Tourism is, therefore, one of the most dynamic and far-reaching economic sectors.

Many approaches can be used to define a tourist organization today. In Spain, hotel companies come characterized by constant innovation, flexibility, transparency and Corporate Social Responsibility. Today, hotel companies move in an environment of continuous change, making continuous innovation will allow them to adapt competitively to the changes and transformations and succeed in business.

In addition, sustainable tourism contributes to generating long-term benefits, investing in measures to combat deforestation and desertification, to maintain tourist destinations in optimum conditions and to generate a greater flow of visitors and benefits to the environment and local communities. Companies that are committed to sustainable tourism can create programs for tourists focused on how to preserve and care for the environment to help local communities manage their visits in order to obtain the greatest possible benefit with a minimum of risks to their ecosystems, Its biological diversity and its flora and fauna. Responsible production and consumption are also considered key challenges, both in terms of the supply chain of companies in the sector, and in the promotion of patterns of sustainable consumption among tourists. In addition, it is important to preserve the destination and promote sustainable and intelligent cities that benefit the local population and tourists.

The empirical study of the situation of Spain in the Global Compact and GRI agreement over the years of study (2002-2012) was performed. Specifically, regression models were constructed of these cases to predict spending in the coming years. These models shown that the number of Spanish companies' signatories of the Global Compact and the number of Spanish companies reporting according to GRI gradually increase in the coming years.

In this way, it has been seen throughout this chapter that Spain is aware of the importance of tourism and its role in the development model, the short-term successes, and that is the key to real opportunities. Therefore, the country must try to adapt progressively to the structural changes that occur in the global context and that directly affect the tourist market and that condition our competitiveness in the immediate future. These are changes that have to be answered in a creative and innovative way, in the face of the inertia of the past unviable, at least dubious, in the real tourist scenario.

In the last part of our chapter, it was shown specifically on the contribution of hotel and tourism organizations in sustainable development and Corporate Social Responsibility. In conclusion, companies within the hotel industry are examples to follow of responsible activity with the environment and socially sustainable practices. Promoting sustainable and intelligent cities is fundamental to guarantee destinations that attract tourists and promote the quality of life of local communities. The Sustainable Development Objectives require the construction of strategic alliances between the different actors that have an impact on the sector. In short, they require the commitment of society as a whole.

REFERENCES

Ayuso, S. (2003). *Gestión sostenible en la industria turística. Retórica y práctica en el sector hotelero español* (Unpublished doctoral dissertation). Universidad Autónoma de Barcelona, Spain.

Ayuso, S. (2005). Turismo y desarrollo sostenible. *Revista Cultural. Ejemplar dedicado a Cultura Sostenible, 40*, 101-104.

Ayuso, S., & Argandoña, A. (2009). Responsible Corporate governance: Towards a stakeholder board of directors? *Corporate Ownership and Control, 6*(4), 9–19. doi:10.22495/cocv6i4p1

European Commission. (2001). *Green Paper: Promoting a European framework for Corporate Social Responsibility. COM(2001)366*. European Commission.

European Commission. (2002). *Corporate Social Responsibility: A business contribution to Sustainable Development. COM(2002)347*. European Commission.

European Commission. (2003). Opinion of the Committee of the Regions on the 'Communication from the Commission to the Council, the European Parliament, the European Economic and Social Committee and the Committee of the Regions — Basic orientations for the sustainability of European tourism'. COM(2003) 716 final. Brussels: European Commission.

Garcia Martin, M. A. (2014). *La responsabilidad social corporativa en las entidades públicas y el proceso de reforma de las Administraciones Públicas*. Retrieved November 15, 2016 from http://www.pap.minhap.gob.es/sitios/140aniversario/Documents/DEBATEMiguelAngelGarciaMartin.pdf

Guzmán Raja, M., & Martínez Franco, C. M. (2016). Un nuevo paradigma de negocio: La empresa social. *Revista AECA, 102*, 5–8.

Henderson, J. C. (2007). Corporate social responsibility and tourism: Hotel companies in Phuket, Thailand, after the Indian Ocean tsunami. *International Journal of Hospitality Management, 26*(1), 228–239. doi:10.1016/j.ijhm.2006.02.001

Holcomb, J. L., Upchurch, R. S., & Okumus, F. (2007). Corporate social responsibility: What are top hotel companies reporting? *International Journal of Contemporary Hospitality Management, 19*(6), 461–475. doi:10.1108/09596110710775129

Llull, A. (2003). *Contabilidad medioambiental y desarrollo sostenible en el sector turístico* (Unpublished doctoral dissertation). Palma de Mallorca: Govern de les Illes Balears/Conselleria d'Economia, Comerç i Industria.

Middleton, V. (1998). *Sustainable Tourism. A Marketing Perspective*. Butterworth-Heinemann.

Ministry of Industry, Tourism and Trade. (2006). Plan Nacional de Adaptación al Cambio Climático. Madrid: Oficina Española de Cambio Climático, Ministry of Industry, Tourism and Trade.

Nicolau, J. L. (2008). Corporate Social Responsibility: Worth-Creating activities. *Annals of Tourism Research*, *35*(4), 990–1006. doi:10.1016/j.annals.2008.09.003

Pes, A. (2016, December). *La economía será digital o no será sostenible*. Paper presented at the meeting El Protagonismo de las empresas ante la Agenda 2030, Madrid, Spain.

Porter, M. E., & Van der Linde, C. (1995). Green and Competitive: Ending the Stalemate. *Harvard Business Review*, *73*(5), 120–134.

UNWTO. (1995). *Charter for sustainable tourism*. Retrieved November 7, 2016 from http://www.e-unwto.org/doi/pdf/10.18111/unwtodeclarations.1995.21.13.1

KEY TERMS AND DEFINITIONS

Eco-Efficiency: The relationship between the value of the product or service produced by a company and the sum of environmental impacts throughout its life cycle.

Ecological Crisis: A situation that arises when the environment of a species or a population undergoes critical changes that destabilize its continuity.

Environmental Responsibility: A damage caused to other species, nature as a whole to future generations, by the actions or non-actions of another individual or group.

Natural Resources: Material goods and services provided by nature without altering the part of the human being and contributing to the welfare and development of society directly (raw materials, minerals, food) or indirect.

Social Responsibility: Burden, commitment, or obligation of members of a society either as individuals or as a member of a group, both with each other and for society as a whole.

Sustainability: The balance of a species with the resources of its environment. Describes how biological systems remain diverse, material, and productive over time.

Tourism: Trips and stays made by people in places other than their usual environment within a period of less than 365 days, for leisure, business, or other reasons.

Chapter 9
Corporate Social Responsibility as a Part of the Strategies for Business Sustainability Based on the Innovative Activity Development

Iveta Ubrežiová
Department of Management in Poprad, Catholic University in Ružomberok, Poprad, Slovakia

Oksana Sokil
Faculty of Economics and Management, Slovak University of Agriculture in Nitra, Slovakia

Mária Janošková
https://orcid.org/0000-0002-5975-753X
Department of Management in Poprad, Catholic University in Ružomberok, Poprad, Slovakia

ABSTRACT

This chapter identifies the most effective measures of corporate social responsibility pillars that prompt the CSR implementation as an innovative tool for modern business. Differences between the respondents' education level and the level of their awareness with the concept of CSR are researched. Primary data were collected by conducting the survey in 2019; statistical analysis of data was performed using software SAS: analytics, business intelligence, and data management. The results showed that research and development in the field of environmental protection, development of qualification, skills of employees and conducting a systematic stakeholders' survey about the company's activities are the most effective measures to improve innovation through CSR. The research found that the level of education affects the level of knowledge about CSR, and the job title of the respondents has no effect on the level of CSR concept awareness. The study also provides significant recommendations for improving the level of CSR implementation that can be used by all kinds of business.

DOI: 10.4018/978-1-7998-4543-0.ch009

INTRODUCTION

The interests of each company require solving strategic development problems through various tasks and issues that are related to the harsh competitive struggle that already takes place in the domestic and foreign markets. Nowadays, sustainable economic development is not determined by the availability of raw materials or markets, but an opportunity for enterprises to enter the market of highly skilled labor resources, scientific inventions and new technologies, which is impossible without the creation of an innovative model of development and principles of Corporate Social Responsibility (Bolzan, Bitencourt, & Volkmer Martins, 2019; Grydzhuk, 2008; Ubrežiová & Gurská, 2012; Ubrežiová & Horská, 2011). Previous researches show that these two concepts are extremely important for each company, as CSR and practice in the innovation sphere help to function normally in the conditions of deep, radical reformation of the economy (Grydzhuk, 2008; MacGregor & Fontrodona, 2008; Rexhepi, 2013). The main purpose of such reformation is not only the profitability of the business and the economic growth of enterprises, but, first of all, satisfying the needs of stakeholders (Voloskovets, 2010). Besides, the development of new market opportunities, marketing research, financial management, resource utilization, investment attraction, and socially responsible business awake the need to provide innovative ways of expanding (Lii & Lee, 2019; Marin, 2017; Song, 2018).

Nevertheless, the issue of combining two radically important components as an innovation activity and corporate social responsibility of entrepreneurship is still not sufficiently researched in the scientific environment (Voloskovets, 2010). The relationship between CSR and innovative activities is a new concept and, accordingly, is not sufficiently developed in the theoretical and empirical aspects (Bocquet & Mothe, 2013; Chala, 2014). This kind of research remains scarce especially in the case of small and medium-sized enterprises (Bocquet & Mothe, 2013; Jenkins, 2006; Murillo & Lozano, 2006).

The purpose of the chapter is to identify the most effective measures of three Corporate Social Responsibility pillars which are prompted the CSR implementation as an innovative tool for modern business. The research also aims to identify the relationship between the level of education/the job title of the respondent at the enterprise and the level of his/her awareness with the CSR concept. To achieve the goal, it is necessary to find out answers to the following questions:

- RQ1. Are the CSR measures important for innovation activity development?
- RQ2. What are the main CSR activities which help to improve the innovative activity of the enterprise?
- RQ3. What is the level of awareness about CSR among employees working in creating innovative technologies and products area?

The second section reviews literature describing the essence of CSR and innovation, and also explains the interrelation between these two concepts. The third section represents the hypothesis of the study. The next part describes methodological issues that include research design and sample identification. The empirical results are presented and discussed in the fifth section. The last parts represent proposals for further research.

THEORETICAL BACKGROUND

This part of the article describes the thoughts of scientists, whose research is closely related to the concepts of innovation activity and CSR.

The Attitude of Scientists to the Concept of CSR

Today, the concept of Corporate Social Responsibility is not a new or unknown phenomenon. But it should be noted that this field of study is increasingly explored among well-known researchers, leading companies, governments, and non-governmental organizations (Lee, 2008; Secchi, 2007; van Marrewijk, 2003; Veiga Ávila et al., 2019; Zinchenko, 2017). Most companies have already realized the importance of CSR activities and thus have long been implementing measures in such area in their business strategies (Aßländer, 2011; Janošková & Palaščáková, 2018). From this point of view, the authors are paid the attention to the sustainable development of business activities towards to the implementation of business strategy (Chebeň, Lančarič, Savov, Tóth, & Tluhoř, 2015; Chládková & Formánková, 2016; Halasi, Schwarcz, Mura, & Roháčiková, 2019). Based on Bylok (2016), in defining the Corporate Social Responsibility in the subject – related literature the macro and micro–social approaches are in evidence. In the macro-social approach, the authors place emphasis on one personal engagement of the owner/entrepreneur with regard to the surroundings, while in the macro–social approach CSR is treated as an element of the strategy of sustainable development. In the micro-social approach, the emphasis is placed on the socially broader consequences of the business activities of enterprises. While we can generally see a decline of the share of industry, parallel to this trend the Visegrad countries are taking over more industrial production (mainly assembly). This will reduce the requirements for innovative knowledge workers. This "over-industrialization" has led to a dual economy, in which domestic companies compete by utilizing the comparative advantages of a cheaper labor force. In fact, products whose comparative advantages do not decrease as the development gap narrows are needed for sustainable economic development. If we continue to hinder the development of non-material services this way, then by decreasing innovative capacities we shall get deeper into the trap of dependent market economies (György, 2017).

However, there are still companies that believe that CSR activities are nothing more than a move to improve their image (Alvarez Dominguez, 2011; Bhattacharya, 2006). In our opinion, if firms think that CSR is the same as philanthropy, or nothing more than charity, then this means that such companies still clearly do not understand the essence of Corporate Social Responsibility (Baines, 2016).

Since the expectations of the stakeholders have changed, being a socially responsible company has become much more important than before. Businesses should remember that the time of globalization makes it impossible to conduct unethical business. Companies can no longer ignore the requirements for labor relations with employees, or restrictions on environmental pollution because failure to comply with these rules will necessarily lead to a negative reaction from the public (Diačiková & Daňková, 2019; Fassin & Buelens, 2011).

In our opinion, we should analyze the attitude of scientists to the concept of CSR. In particular, Pin-Chao et al. (2018) and also Ubrežiová and Horská (2011) believe that every year CSR becomes more attractive for social attention. The authors argue that the improvement of CSR models can contribute to the development of external markets, improve social efficiency and resolve conflicts more quickly. Ulutaş, Giritli, and Mcdermott (2016) argue that most definitions describe CSR as one of the most important methods that companies use as a way to improve loyalty to the company. Also, the authors state that CSR can meet the requirements of stakeholders in social, economic and environmental directions (Antošová & Csikósová, 2016). Therefore, we can agree with the authors and point out that CSR reflects the positive aspects of the enterprise's activities to improve the overall social environment. In turn, Moon (2007) believes that in the future, the improvement of the natural environment will be one of the most important incentives for enterprises. This situation will encourage the company to develop CSR activities in such a direction. The author states that an environmentally responsible company will always be more dominant in the market and has more competitive advantages. Oginni and Omojowo (2016) follow the same opinion and argue that the uninterrupted activity of the company in the sphere of CSR will help to develop more interest in the business from the side of stakeholders. Consequently, we can conclude that socially responsible firms receive significant competitive advantages, which ensure positive growth and stable development of the company. Montecchia, Giordano, and Grieco (2016) describe that today there are many ways to effectively communicate with CSR. These channels can take the form of annual reports, company websites, CSR reports, or by organizing social events (Kunz, Ferencová, Hronová, & Singer, 2015; Sutherland, 2016). However, the authors point out that the CSR report is one of the most used and most effective methods of communicating with CSR. The advantage of this method is that its content helps researchers to reduce the time of searching for information about the company's activities in the sphere of CSR.

The Investigation of the Concept of "Innovative Activity"

Regarding innovation activity, we can see that a significant number of fundamental research is devoted to this concept. In particular, Tarasova (2012) argues that innovation activity is a set of practical actions aimed at using scientific and technical results to obtain new or improved existing products, technologies, management methods, etc. Scientist Faychuk (2013) believes that innovation activity is aimed at updating the existing, creating and using a new competitive product (product, the technology of production method) in order to better meet public needs (the increase of labor productivity, quality of products, the decrease of its cost, etc.). Besides, Koyuda and Sheyko (2013) have a similar view of this kind of activity and argue that it is aimed at the development, use and commercialization of scientific, technological and technological results of the innovation process for the production of products, expansion of the nomenclature (range), implementation of the latest technology (organization of management or improvement, etc.) and the competitive products (works, services) in order to obtain economic efficiency. There is also the opinion that innovative activity is a process that is focused on realizing the results of completed researches or other scientific and technological advances in a new or improved product, implemented in the market, in a new or improved process used in practice (Ervits, 2018; Kovalenko, 2015). Chukhray and Lisovska (2015) in their work have described the main factors that prevent or promote the implementation of innovation activities in the enterprise's activity (see Table 1).

Table 1. The main factors that prevent or promote the implementation of innovation activities in the enterprise's activity

Group of factors	Factors that prevent	Factors that promote
Economic, technological	Lack of funds for investment projects, weak material, scientific and technical base, outdated technology, lack of reserve capacities, the domination of current production interests.	Availability of financial and logistical resources, advanced technologies, necessary economic, scientific and technical infrastructure; material incentives for innovation activities.
Political, legal	Limitations on antimonopoly, tax, patent and licensing legislation.	Legislative measures (especially incentives) that encourage innovation activity; state support for innovation.
Organizational and managerial	Excessive centralization; the authoritarian style of management; the predominance of vertical information flows; the complexity of inter-branch and inter-organizational interactions; rigidity of planning; orientation to existing markets; orientation to short-term payback; the difficulty in coordinating the interests of participants in innovative processes.	The flexibility of organizational structures, democratic style of management, the predominance of horizontal flows of information, self-planning, admission of correction, decentralization, autonomy, the formation of target and problem groups, reengineering.
Socio-psychological and cultural	Counteraction to changes that may have consequences such as changing of status, the need for a new job, the restructuring of old methods of activity, the violation of behavioral stereotypes and established traditions; timidity of uncertainty; fear of punishment for failure; counteraction to everything that comes from outside.	Moral encouragement, public recognition, provision of opportunities for self-realization and creative work, the normal psychological climate in the team.

Source: Chukhray and Lisovska (2015)

In addition, among the most important factors that influence the success of innovation are market orientation, compliance with the goals of the organization, effective system of selection and evaluation of projects, effective project management, and control, the source of creative ideas, the sensitivity of organizations to innovations, individual and collective responsibility.

The Interconnection Between CSR and Innovation Activity

In today's conditions of a market economy, more and more managers of various business structures consider their main task to search and develop innovative mechanisms that allow ensuring the competitiveness and socio-economic stability of organizations in the long-term. Currently, Corporate Social Responsibility (CSR) is one of such effective innovations. The main characteristic of CSR is that it aims not only at the sustainable strategic development of the business itself but also in satisfying the interests of society and the state as a whole. Synergetic of such interaction is the key to successful promotion, the stability of enterprises and business structures (Khrushch, 2016). For example, The UN Global Compact-Accenture CEO Study on Sustainability 2013 has conducted research between more than 1,000 executives from the largest multinational corporations.

The results show that 78% of them believe that CSR activities contribute to the development of innovative solutions and create competitive advantages (United Nations Global Compact, 2013). On the other hand, Harvard Business Review has published research findings that show that CSR policies and related programs can increase the organization's innovation. The research has made it possible to establish a link between participation in Corporate Social Responsibility projects and a certain number of new products launched on the market. Scientists studied 128 firms in all major industry sectors. One-third of the companies that ranked first in the level of CSR activity, launched an average of 47 new products in one year. The rest of the companies which were at the end of the rating launched only 12 new products. The authors of the report believe that the CSR policy also guarantees access to a wide range of knowledge for the organization in the process of building relationships with external stakeholders (clients, suppliers, non-profit organizations and public authorities). This way, it allows the company to keep pace with changing market, technology trends and promote the creation of "creative jumps" (Luo & Du, 2012). Besides, the reason for the interest increasing in combining of these two concepts is that companies always strive to raise profit by the implementation of innovations into their activities, and CSR measures can be used as innovative ways, which contribute improvement of productivity, efficiency, and competitiveness of the enterprise (Khrushch, 2016). For example, MacGregor and Fontrodona (2008) state that in general innovations have risky nature, and CSR can be used as a risk reduction method. Hockerts and Morsing (2008) in their research confirmed that companies that take the top places in the rating of social activities, perceive CSR as an efficient tool of innovation activities development of the company. Corporate Social Responsibility practices are typically used as an instrument to improve stakeholder interaction. CSR indicates that companies have to take into account the needs and requirements of stakeholders. This interaction can become a way of implementing or improving the innovation enterprise activity since the goal of innovation is to maximize the satisfaction of the needs of the stakeholders in general and, in particular, to increase the number of consumers (Reinlie, 2017). However, innovation does not always relate to commercial markets and consumer requires, it may be a social requirement that connects process, product, organizational or marketing innovations. For example, CSR can be a social need that will be used to ensure the employee's right to a safe workplace, and the satisfaction of this need might accelerate the implementation of innovations in the company's activities. Besides, companies may feel pressure from environmental protection activist groups. Such kind of pressure can push an organization to invent innovative solutions that can help to reduce or eliminate conflicts related to environmental protection (Tidd & Bessant, 2013).

Summarizing the above, we can agree that current research in the field of combining CSR and innovation is insufficient. Researchers are trying to explain the connection between these two concepts, but because of the conceptual difference between CSR and innovation, the interpretations of the results are always different.

Methodology

Hypotheses

Skills, experience, and education of employees can positively affect the innovation activities development of the enterprise. Studies show that employee engagement in CSR activities has an undoubted impact on business development, the environment, and society (Rosati, 2018). Therefore, firms need to understand the employee knowledge level about CSR. In this connection, many studies show that the level of CSR awareness depends on the employee 's individual characteristics (Asrar-ul-Haq, 2017; Rahman, 2019; Sengupta, 2016). For example, Saxena (2017) believes that the perception of CSR depends on the education level. Besides, some authors believe that employees who hold higher positions have a better understanding of the CSR concept and its importance (Kovalenko, 2015; Voloskovets, 2010).

- H1: There is a significant difference between the educational level of the respondent and his/her level of CSR concept awareness.
- H2: There is a significant difference between the job title of the respondent and his/her level of CSR concept awareness.

Data Collection

The aim of the research is to identify the main areas of CSR that can contribute to the development of enterprise innovation activities. The survey was conducted using the questionnaire method. The questionnaire sample is an original proposal. The questionnaire was filled by 217 respondents working in the area of innovation products and technologies creation. The research was conducted during October-November 2018. The questionnaire consists of the following main parts:

- I. General information about the respondent. This part includes questions about the respondent's position at the company and education degree
- II. Awareness of the term CSR and the company's activities in this area.
- III. Selection of the most important activities within CSR three pillars (economic, environmental and social pillar)

Respondents were required to identify which CSR measures are the most effective for improving company innovation activity. The questionnaire template made it possible to select several suggested options. Likert scale was used for the questionnaire's formulation. According to this, the respondent evaluates the degree of his/her agreement or disagreement with judgment. The level of the respondent's awareness about CSR content was evaluated by using this rating scale (1- "not at all", 5 - "a lot"). The Likert scale was also used in part III, where respondents express their opinion about the importance of the CSR measures to facilitate innovation activities development (1- "not important", 5 - "important").

Data Analysis

The investigation of the CSR phenomenon requires the use of a wide range of general and special methods for data mining. Thus, for the study of this problem, it was mandatory to apply the following methods of data analysis: analysis, synthesis, induction, deduction, complex, comparative. Besides, descriptive analysis and graphics were made using Microsoft Excel. XLSTAT: Statistical software and data analysis add-on for Excel was used to analyze our data. In order to refute or confirm H1 and H2, it was used the Kruskal–Wallis test and Dunn's test.

RESULTS

A total of 217 surveys were collected. Table 2 shows general information about respondents. According to respondents' answers, it can be seen, that the largest number of respondents hold positions of a technician and software innovation engineer (42, 4% (92 respondents) and 30% (65 respondents) respectively). Besides, the questionnaire was filled by 9 managers of the departments, 16 team leaders and 35 product development engineers.

Table 2. General information about respondents

Characteristic		Respondents' part
Work position	Manager of the department	4,1%
	Product development engineer	16,1%
	Software innovation engineer	30%
	Team leader	7,4%
	Technician	42,4%
Education degree	Secondary education	15,7%
	Bachelor or equivalent level	50,9%
	Master or equivalent level	29,2%
	PhD or equivalent level	4,2%

Source: own research

Besides, the respondents' education degree was the following: secondary education – 15, 7% (34 respondents), bachelor or equivalent level – 50, 9% (110 respondents), master or equivalent level – 29, 2% (63 respondents) and PhD or equivalent level – 4, 2% (9 respondents).

Attitude Toward CSR

The next part of the questionnaire was aimed to explore the attitude of the respondents toward CSR. Thus, 73, 3% (159 respondents) pointed out that the CSR measures are important for innovation activity development. This fact may have a positive impact on enterprise activity development, because, employees' understanding of the CSR importance may become an impetus of new ideas to improve the company's innovation activity. On the other hand, 62, 2% of the respondents are familiar with CSR activities within the investigated company. In this case, it is recommended to organize additional meetings or workshops that may help employees improve their knowledge about the significance of Corporate Social Responsibility and familiarize workers with CSR company's activities. The Likert scale helped us with further investigation within respondents. Table 3 explicitly shows the extent to which respondents agree or disagree with the following statement: "I am aware of the CSR concept and how it is implemented in the company's activities".

Table 3. Respondents' agreement/disagreement with statements toward CSR

Mark Statement	1 - strongly disagree	2	3	4	5 - strongly agree
I am aware of the CSR concept and how it is implemented in the company's activities	1,4%	16,6%	27,6%	33,6%	20,7%

Source: own research

The results show that most employees highly evaluate their knowledge of CSR and the company's activity in the field. In particular, 73 surveyed workers gave a mark 4, and 45 gave a mark 5. Moreover, respondents had to assess the importance of listed CSR measures for improving the innovation activity of the enterprise. Table 4 represents the results of this survey part.

Table 4. The evaluation of CSR activities

Mark Statement	1 - not important	2	3	4	5 - important
Research and development in the field of environmental protection	0	1,4%	17%	42,4%	39,2%
Purchase of environmentally friendly machinery and equipment	13,4%	21,7%	28,1%	13,8%	23%
Improving the sales business activities, taking into account the ethical principles of trade	6%	29,5%	53,9%	5,5%	5,1%
Providing customer service after the sale of products and services	7,4%	36%	50,2%	3,2%	3,2%
Solving complaints with shareholders, suppliers and business partners	3,2%	10,7%	40%	34,6%	11,5%
Development of qualification and skills of employees	0	0,5%	10,5%	24%	65%
Protection of intellectual property	4,6%	31,8%	49,8%	10,1%	3,7%
Work benefits (e.g. Home office, additional insurance, …)	2,8%	25,8%	59%	9,2%	3,2%
Conducting a systematic stakeholders questionnaire survey about the company's activities	0	1,8%	26,3%	42,4%	29,5%

Source: own research

Consequently, it can be concluded that, according to respondents' answers, the research and development in the field of environmental protection is one of the most important CSR measures that contribute to the development of innovation activities. The respondents' chose may be explained by the fact that constant searches to improve the level of environmental protection can encourage employees to look for new ways to solve this problem. Besides, the majority of the respondents pointed out that the development of the qualification and skills of employees is an important factor in novelty creating. This may be due to the fact that more knowledgeable and skilled workers usually have better ideas which help to increase innovation activities in the business. Moreover, systematic monitoring of the stakeholders' desires enables the company to find innovative ways to meet these requirements more quickly than competitors. Survey results show that most respondents agree with this statement. Thus, 29,5% of the respondents gave a mark 5 and 42,4% - 4.

Statistical Data Processing

Proving/Refuting of H1

During the study, it was necessary to examine the difference between the educational level of the respondent and his/her level of CSR concept awareness. The use of the Kruskal–Wallis test helps to prove that such a difference is statistically significant (p-value < 0,0001, alpha = 0,01). Consequently, it can be concluded that the level of education affects the level of knowledge about CSR. Besides, multiple pairwise comparisons by Dunn's procedure was used (see Table 5).

Table 5 shows that respondents with a master and Ph.D. level of education (or equivalent levels) gave a high assessment of their awareness about the CSR concept. Employees with a bachelor's level (or equivalent level) demonstrated a slightly worse result. And at last, employees who have finished a secondary school presented the lowest level of knowledge about the CSR essence.

Table 5. Multiple pairwise comparisons using Dunn's procedure

Sample	Frequency	Groups		
Secondary school	34	A		
Bachelor / Engineer	110		B	
Master	64			C
PhD	9			C

Source: own research

Proving/Refuting of H2

Hypothesis 2 states that there is a significant difference between the job title of the respondent and his/her level of CSR concept awareness. As in the previous case, we use the Kruskal–Wallis test for confirming/refuting the H2. In this situation, statistical data processing has shown that p-value = 0,035 (alpha = 0,01). It means that the Kruskal–Wallis test refutes H2 and it can be concluded that the job title of the respondents has no effect on the level of CSR concept awareness.

DISCUSSION

In this work, it was conducted the research directed to find out the interconnection between CSR and innovation activity. Based on preliminary studies of this area, it was aimed a purpose to identify the most effective measures of three Corporate Social Responsibility pillars which prompt the CSR implementation as an innovative tool for modern business. The study allows us to find out answers to the questions pointed out during our research. Answers of respondents to the RQ1 make it possible to understand that CSR measures are important for the innovation development in an enterprise. According to the survey results, 73,3% of respondents gave a positive answer to this question. These facts corroborate our results of literary analysis, which argued that CSR is important for this kind of company's activity and that these two concepts are interconnected (Khrushch, 2016; Luo & Du, 2012). The respondents' answers to the RQ2 show us that conducting systematic stakeholders' questionnaire survey about the company's activities one of the main CSR activities which help to improve the innovative activity of the enterprise. According to the obtained results, it is possible to agree with the conclusions of the processed literature, which states that Corporate Social Responsibility practices are typically used as an instrument to improve stakeholder interaction (Reinlie, 2017). Besides, surveyed employees pointed out that the development of qualification, skills of employees play a significant role during the innovation creating process. Due to this fact during our study, it was also confirmed that ensuring employee rights to a safe workplace, developing workers' knowledge and skills can accelerate the implementation of the innovation in the company's activities (Tidd & Bessant, 2013). The present study claims that there is a significant difference between the educational level of the respondent and his/her level of CSR concept awareness. This conclusion supports our literature analysis findings that the level of CSR awareness depends on and the employee 's individual characteristics (Asrar-ul-Haq, 2017; Rahman, 2019; Saxena, 2017; Sengupta, 2016). On the other hand, the present study disproves the fact that the job title has an influence on the worker's CSR awareness (Kovalenko, 2015; Formánková et al., 2016; Voloskovets, 2010). D`Anselmi (2011) provided a broader interpretation of the stakeholders by defining them as people or groups that were voluntarily or unintentionally exposed to the risk arising from the actions of the firm. The growth of the role of business responsibility in ensuring sustainable development of society requires a revision of corporate strategies in terms of integrating CSR into the corporate governance system.

CONCLUSION

This research analyzed the scientific views of different authors about defining the concepts of "innovation activity" and "Corporate Social Responsibility". Besides, the peculiarities of the interaction of these two concepts are analyzed. It should also be noted that the authors conducted survey questionnaires among employees working in the field of innovative products and technologies creation. The results of the study showed that research and development in the field of environmental protection, development of qualification, skills of employees and conducting a systematic stakeholder questionnaire survey about the company's activities are the most effective measures to improve innovation through CSR. On the other hand, respondents believe that improving the sales business activities, providing customer service after the sale of products and services, protection of intellectual property or work benefits do not have an influence on the innovation activity of the company. Besides, 62,2% of the respondents are familiar with CSR activities within the investigated company. In this case, it is recommended to organize additional meetings or workshops that may help workers improve their knowledge about the significance of CSR and familiarize workers with CSR company's activities. It should be noted that this paper is just a first step toward the complete investigation relationship between innovation activities and CSR measures. Furthermore, in this work were initially used topic limitations (for example, we were focused only on employees who work in creating innovative technologies and products area). Besides, the research was conducted in only one company. Moreover, a limited list of activities related to each of the CSR pillars was given. In future studies, it is not necessary to apply the same topic limitations. First of all, the survey can be conducted among employees who work in other company's areas. Second, future researches can be conducted in more than one company. In addition, a more broad list of CSR activities can be created for the survey. The research findings confirm a significant part of the information received from the literature and help us to make important assumptions. The present work demonstrates that the level of education affects the level of concept awareness. Furthermore, the research shows the job title of the respondents has no effect on the level of knowledge about CSR.

ACKNOWLEDGMENT

The publication of this article is supported by the Slovak Agency KEGA - project 005SPU-4/2019 *"Theory and Practice of the International Management and Entrepreneurship in Multicultural Environment"* and Slovak agency VEGA - project 1/0651/18 *"Research of institutional environment influence to the corporate social responsibility, consumers´ satisfaction and performance of the company"* and project 1/0280/21 *"Expansion of research in the area Corporate Social Respoinsibility to sustainable Human Resource Management, with an emphasis on Intellectual capital"*. Financial support from this Ministry of Education's scheme is also gratefully acknowledged.

REFERENCES

Alvarez Dominguez, A. (2011). The impact of human resource disclosure on corporate image. *Journal of Human Resource Costing & Accounting*, *15*(4), 279–298. doi:10.1108/14013381111197225

Antošová, M., & Csikósová, A. (2014). Social behavior of companies in Slovakia and their support by European Union. *Procedia Social and Behavioral Sciences, 109,* 307–311. doi:.2013.12.462 doi:10.1016/j.sbspro

Antošová, M., & Csikósová, A. (2016). Corporate Social Responsibility in small and medium enterprises in Slovakia. *Actual Problems of Economics*, *175*, 217–224.

Asrar-ul-Haq, M., Kuchinke, K. P., & Iqbal, A. (2017). The relationship between corporate social responsibility, job satisfaction, and organizational commitment: Case of Pakistani higher education. *Journal of Cleaner Production*, *142*(4), 2352–2363. doi:10.1016/j.jclepro.2016.11.040

Aßländer, M. S. (2011). Corporate Social Responsibility as subsidiary co-responsibility: A macroeconomic perspective. *Journal of Business Ethics*, *99*(1), 115–128. doi:10.100710551-011-0744-x

Baines, P. (2016). Philanthropy vs. Corporate Social Responsibility. *CEO Magazine.* Retrieved on November 17, 2019, from www.theceomagazine.com/business/philanthropy/philanthropy-vs-corporate-social-responsibility/

Bhattacharya, C. B., Sen, S., & Korschun, D. (2006). Using corporate social responsibility to win the war for talent. *MIT Sloan Management Review*, *49*(2), 37–44.

Bocquet, R., & Mothe, C. (2011). Exploring the relationship between CSR and innovation: A comparison between small and largesized French companies. *Revue Sciences de Gestion. Institut de Socio-Economie des Entreprises et des Organisations*, *2011*, 101–119.

Bolzan, L., Bitencourt, C., & Volkmer Martins, B. (2019). Exploring the scalability process of social innovation. *Innovation & Management Review*, *16*(3), 218–234. doi:10.1108/INMR-05-2018-0029

Bylok, F. (2016). The Concept of Corporate Social Responsibility in Strategies of SMEs. *Club of Economics in Miskolc TMP*, *1*(12), 19–26. doi:10.18096/TMP.2016.01.03

Chala, Y. V. (2014). Sotsial′na vidpovidal′nist′ pidpryyemstv yak osnova innovatsiynoho rozvytku suchasnoyi ekonomiky. In *Zbirnyk naukovykh prats, „Problemy i perspektyvy rozvytku bankivs'koyi systemy Ukrayiny* (pp. 275–285). Kirovohrad National Technical University.

Chebeň, J., Lančarič, D., Savov, R., Tóth, M., & Tluhoř, J. (2015). Towards Sustainable Marketing: Strategy in Slovak Companies. *Amfiteatru Economic*, *17*(40), 855–871.

Chládková, H., & Formánková, S. (2016). Strategy for SMEs in the area of primary agricultural production. *Agricultural Economics, 9*(62), 395-406. doi:/2015-AGRICECON doi:10.17221/260

Chukhray, N. I., & Lisovs′ka, L. S. (2015). *Upravlinnya innovatsiyamy. Navchal'nyy posibnyk*. L′viv: Vydavatelsvo L′viv. politekhniky.

D'Anselmi, P. (2011). *Values and Stakeholders in an Era of Social Responsibility*. New York: Free Press.

Diačiková, A., & Daňková, A. (2019). Green Marketing Communication. In P. Madzík (Ed.), *Conference Proceedings „Current trends and challenges in businesses management"* (pp. 241-249). Ružomberok, Slovakia: VERBUM.

Ervits, I. (2018). Geography of corporate innovation: Internationalization of innovative activities by MNEs from developed and emerging markets. *Multinational Business Review*, *26*(1), 25–49. doi:10.1108/MBR-07-2017-0052

Fassin, Y., & Buelens, M. (2011). The hypocrisy-sincerity continuum in corporate communication and decision making: A model of corporate social responsibility and business ethics practices. *Management Decision*, *49*(4), 586–600. doi:10.1108/00251741111126503

Faychuk, O. M. (2013). Innovatsiynyy protses yak rushiyna syla ekonomichnoho zrostannya. *Bìznes Ìnform*, *10*, 66–70.

Formánková, S., Kučerová, R., & Prísažná, M. (2016). ISO 26 000: Concept of Social Responsibility at Czech University. In *International Conference on Management "Trends of Management in the Contemporary Society"* (pp. 97-101). Brno, Czech Republic: Mendel University.

Grydzhuk, I. (2008). Innovatsiyna skladova stiykoho rozvytku ekonomiky rehioniv. In Teoriyi mikro-makroekonomiky, Zbirnyk naukovykh prats, Akademiya munitsypal′noho upravlinnya (pp. 239-240). Academic Press.

György, B. (2017). To What Extend is Hungary a Knowledge Based Economy? *Club of Economics in Miskolc TMP*, *1*(13), 69–84. doi:10.18096/TMP.2017.01.06

Halasi, D., Schwarcz, P., Mura, L., & Roháčiková, O. (2019). The impact of EU support resources on business success of family-owned businesses. *Potravinarstvo Slovak Journal of Food Sciences*, *13*(1), 846–853. doi:10.5219/1167

Hockerts, K., & Morsing, M. (2008). *A literature review on corporate social responsibility in the innovation process*. Center for Corporate Social Responsibility.

Janošková, M., & Palaščáková, D. (2018). Corporate social responsibility as a strategic goal in business: A case study. In C. R. Baker (Ed.), Corporate Social Responsibility (CSR): Practices, Issues and Global Perspectives (pp. 109-144). New York, NY: Nova Science Publishers.

Jenkins, H. (2006). Small Business Champions for Corporate Social Responsibility. *Journal of Business Ethics*, *67*(3), 241–256. doi:10.100710551-006-9182-6

Khrushch, O. V. (2016). Innovatsiyni pidkhody u formuvanni stratehiyi korporatyvnoyi sotsial′noyi vidpovidal′nosti pidpryyemstva. *Visnyk Khmel'nyts'koho natsional'noho universytetu. Ekonomichni nauky, 4*(2), 261-265.

Kovalenko, O. V. (2015). Problemni aspekty stanovlennya innovatsiynoyi systemy Ukrayiny v konteksti teoriyi tekhnolohichnoho rozvytku. *Efektyvna ekonomika, 3*, 31-33.

Koyuda, P. M., & Sheyko, I. A. (2013). *Efektyvnist' ekonomichnoyi diyal'nosti pidpryyemstv: teoriya ta praktyka*. Kompaniya SMIT.

Kunz, V., Ferencová, M., Hronová, Š., & Singer, M. (2015). Researching of socially responsible behaviour in selected companies and organizations through their corporate websites. *Polish Journal of Management Studies*, *12*(2), 91–102.

Lee, M. D. P. (2008). A review of the theories of corporate social responsibility: Its evolutionary path and the road ahead. *International Journal of Management Reviews*, *10*(1), 53–73. doi:10.1111/j.1468-2370.2007.00226.x

Lii, Y.-S., & Lee, M. (2012). Doing right leads to doing well: when the type of CSR and reputation interact to affect consumer evaluations of the firm. *Journal of Business Ethics, 105*(1), 69-81. doi:s10551-011-0948-0

Luo, X., & Du, S. (2012). "Good" Companies Launch More New Products. *Harvard Business Review*, *90*(4), 28.

MacGregor, S. P., & Fontrodona, J. (2008). Exploring the fit between CSR and Innovation. *IESE Business School – University of Navarra*. Retrieved on November 17, 2019, from https://pdfs.semanticscholar.org/ 619d/e1d0acce38bdd8568159939661555bf6bf0f.pdf

Marin, L., Martín, P. J., & Rubio, A. (2017). Doing Good and Different! The Mediation Effect of Innovation and Investment on the Influence of CSR on Competitiveness. *Corporate Social Responsibility and Environmental Management*, *24*(2), 159–171. doi:10.1002/csr.1412

Montecchia, A., Giordano, F., & Grieco, C. (2016). Communicating CSR: Integrated approach or selfie? evidence from the milan stock exchange. *Journal of Cleaner Production*, *136*, 42–52. doi:10.1016/j.jclepro.2016.01.099

Moon, J. (2007). The contribution of corporate social responsibility to sustainable development. *Sustainable Development*, *15*(5), 296–306. doi:10.1002d.346

Murillo, D., & Lozano, J. M. (2006). SMEs and CSR: An Approach to CSR in their Own Words. *Journal of Business Ethics*, *67*(3), 227–240. doi:10.100710551-006-9181-7

Oginni, O. S., & Omojowo, A. D. (2016). Sustainable development and corporate social responsibility in sub-Saharan Africa: Evidence from industries in Cameroon. *Economies*, *4*(2), 1–15. doi:10.3390/economies4020010

Pin-Chao, L., Jing-Qiu, L., Guangdong, W., Chun-Lin, W., Xiao-Ling, Z., & Meng-Chen, M. (2018). Comparing international contractors' CSR communication patterns: A semantic analysis. *Journal of Cleaner Production*, *203*, 353–366. doi:10.1016/j.jclepro.2018.08.218

Pin-Chao, L., Ni-Ni, X., Chun-Lin, W., Xiao-Ling, Z., & Jui-Lin, Y. (2017). Communicating the corporate social responsibility (CSR) of international contractors: Content analysis of CSR reporting. *Journal of Cleaner Production*, *156*, 327–336. doi:10.1016/j.jclepro.2017.04.027

Pzytuła, S., Formánková, S., Ubrežiová, I., & Dunay, A. (2019). Corporate Social responsibility in Visegrad countries (Poland, Czech Republic, Slovakia, Hungary). In A. Dlugopolska-Mikonowicz, S. Przytula, & C. Stehr (Eds.), *Corporate Social Responsibility in Poland. Strategies, Opportunies and Challenges* (pp. 325–353). Springer. doi:10.1007/978-3-030-00440-8_20

Rahman, A. A., Castka, P., & Love, T. (2019). Corporate social responsibility in higher education. *Corporate Social Responsibility and Environmental Management*, *26*(4), 916–928. doi:10.1002/csr.1731

Reinlie, M. B. (2017). *Corporate Social Responsibility (CSR) and Innovation* (Master thesis). University of Oslo. Retrieved on November 21, 2019, from https://www.duo.uio.no/bitstream/handle/10852/57995/CSR-and-Innovation--ESST-Master-thesis--Maria-Borgeraas-Reinlie.pdf?sequence=1&isAllowed=y

Rexhepi, G., Kurtishi, S., & Bexheti, G. (2013). Corporate Social Responsibility (CSR) and Innovation–The Drivers of Business Growth? *Procedia: Social and Behavioral Sciences*, *75*, 532–541. doi:10.1016/j.sbspro.2013.04.058

Rosati, F., Costa, R., Calabrese, A., & Pedersen, E. R. G. (2018). Employee attitudes towards corporate social responsibility: A study on gender, age and educational level differences. *Corporate Social Responsibility and Environmental Management*, *25*(6), 1306–1319. doi:10.1002/csr.1640

Saxena, M., & Mishra, D. K. (2017). CSR perception: A global opportunity in management education. *Industrial and Commercial Training*, *49*(5), 231–244. doi:10.1108/ICT-12-2016-0085

Secchi, D. (2007). Utilitarian, managerial and relational theories of corporate social responsibility. *International Journal of Management Reviews*, *9*(4), 347–373. doi:10.1111/j.1468-2370.2007.00215.x

Sengupta, M. (2016). Impact of CSR on Education Sector. In N. Mitra & R. Schmidpeter (Eds.), *Corporate Social Responsibility in India: Cases and Developments After the Legal Mandate* (pp. 33–50). Springer.

Song, W., Ren, S., & Yu, J. (2018). Bridging the gap between corporate social responsibility and new green product success: The role of green organizational identity. *Business Strategy and the Environment*, *28*(1), 88–97. doi:10.1002/bse.2205

Sutherland, E. (2016). Corporate social responsibility: the case of the telecommunications sector. *Info*, *18*(5), 24-44. doi:10.1108/info-05-2016-0022

Tarasova, O. V. (2012). Teoretyko-metodolohichni osnovy innovatsiynoyi diyal′nosti pidpryyemstv. *Ekonomika kharchovoyi promyslovosti*, *1*, 37-41.

Tidd, J., & Bessant, J. (2013). *Managing Innovation. Integrating Technological, Market and Organizational Change*. University of London.

Ubrežiová, A., & Horská, E. (2011). *Perception and Approach towards Corporate Social Responsibility in SMEs: Case Study of Slovak and Czech Republic*. Paper presented at the PEFnet 2011 "European Scientific Conference of Ph.D. Students.

Ubrežiová, I., & Gurská, S. (2012). *International Management and Entrepreneurship*. Wolters Kluwer ČR.

Ubrežiová, I., & Sokil, O. (2018). The evaluation of three pillars of corporate social responsibility in practise. In E. Horská, Z. Kapsdorferová, & M. Hallová (Eds.), *International scientific days 2018. Towards productive, sustainable and resilient global agriculture and food systems* (pp. 1331–1343). Wolters Kluwer ČR.

Ulutaş, D. D., Giritli, H., & Mcdermott, P. (2016). Corporate social responsibility in construction industry: A comparative study between UK and Turkey. *Built Environment Project and Asset Management*, *6*(2), 218–231. doi:10.1108/BEPAM-08-2014-0039

United Nations Global Compact. (2013). The UN Global Compact-Accenture CEO Study on Sustainability 2013. *Architects of a Better World*. Retrieved on December 3, 2019, from https://www.unglobalcompact.org/library/451

van Marrewijk, M. (2003). Concepts and Definitions of CSR and Corporate Sustainability: Between Agency and Communion. *Journal of Business Ethics*, *44*(2–3), 95–105. doi:10.1023/A:1023331212247

Veiga Ávila, L., Beuron, T., Brandli, L., Damke, L., Pereira, R., & Klein, L. (2019). Barriers to innovation and sustainability in universities: An international comparison. *International Journal of Sustainability in Higher Education*, *20*(5), 805–821. doi:10.1108/IJSHE-02-2019-0067

Voloskovets, N. Y. (2010). Korporatyvna sotsial'na vidpovidal'nist' pidpryyemstv yak osnova innovatsiynoho rozvytku suchasnoyi ekonomiky. *Naukovi pratsi Kirovohrads'koho natsional'noho tekhnichnoho universytetu. Ekonomichni nauky, 17,* 125-130.

Zinchenko, A., & Saprykina, M. (2017). *Rozvytok KSV v Ukrayini: 2010–2018*. Kyiv, Ukraine: Yuston.

ADDITIONAL READING

Antošová, M., & Csikósová, A. (2013). *Corporate Social Responsibility in context of regional development*. LAP Lambert Academic Publishing.

Hillestad, T., Xie, C., & Haugland, S. (2010). Innovative corporate social responsibility: The founder's role in creating a trustworthy corporate brand through "green innovation". *Journal of Product and Brand Management*, *19*(6), 440–451. doi:10.1108/10610421011085758

Janošková, M., & Csikósová, A. (2018). About Corporate Social Responsibility in small and medium enterprises in Slovakia. In *New trends in process control management* (pp. 165–185). VŠB – TU Ostrava.

Sokil, O., & Ubrežiová, I. (2017). The opportunity and threats for the selected Ukraine company in the entering the international markets. In I. Košičiarová & Z. Kádeková (Eds.), *Managerial trends in the development of enterprises in globalization ERA. Nitra: Slovak University of Agriculture* (pp. 219–226). Slovak University of Agriculture.

Ubrežiová, I., Horská, E., & Krasnodębski, A. (2017). How can corporate social responsibility be perceived in multinational companies? A case study. In B. C. Illés, M. Nowicka-Skowron, E. Horská, & A. Dunay (Eds.), *Management and organization: concepts, tools and applications* (pp. 129–144). Pearson., doi:10.18515/dBEM.M2017.n02.ch11

Ubrežiová, I., Kráľová, T., & Kozáková, J. (2019). Factors influencing interest of Slovak consumers' in organic dairy products. *Potravinárstvo, 13*(1), 538–546. doi:10.5219/1137

Ubrežiová, I., Kučová, R., & Hováthová, J. (2017). How can we see the corporate social responsibility within its application in business practice? *Acta Universitatis Agriculturae et Silviculturae Mendelianae Brunensis, 65*(1), 339–346. doi:10.11118/actaun201765010339

Ubrežiová, I., & Moravčíková, K. (2017). How to perceive the corporate social responsibility in the agro-food companies? *Serbian journal of management, 1*(2), 201-215.

Yang, R., Zhu, W., Marinova, D., & Wei, J. (2019). Time to take corporate innovation initiatives: The consequence of safety accidents in China's manufacturing industry. *Career Development International, 24*(5), 404–419. doi:10.1108/CDI-10-2018-0270

KEY TERMS AND DEFINITIONS

Activity: A definition is a quality or state of being active: behavior or actions of a particular kind.

Company: A company, abbreviated as co., is a legal entity made up of an association of people, be they natural, legal, or a mixture of both, for carrying on a commercial or industrial enterprise. Company members share a common purpose, and unite to focus their various talents and organize their collectively available skills or resources to achieve specific, declared goals.

Corporate Social Responsibility (CSR): The concept of CSR basically means a voluntary decision to support a better society and making the environment cleaner.

Development: It means an ongoing process to achieve a better outcome in the future.

Innovation: In its modern meaning is "a new idea, creative thoughts, new imaginations in the form of device or method". Innovation is often also viewed as the application of better solutions that meet new requirements, unarticulated needs, or existing market needs.

Research: Is defined as the creation of new knowledge and/or the use of existing knowledge in a new and creative way so as to generate new concepts, methodologies, and understandings. This could include synthesis and analysis of previous research to the extent that it leads to new and creative outcomes.

Strategy: It is important because the resources available to achieve these goals are usually limited. Strategy generally involves setting goals, determining actions to achieve the goals, and mobilizing resources to execute the actions.

Sustainable Business: Sustainable business believes that every business can improve their economic, social, and environmental bottom line by implementing meaningful sustainability practices and programs.

Section 2

Business Sustainability From the Internal Stakeholder Perspective

Chapter 10
Addressing Sustainability and Industry 4.0 to the Business Model

Maria do Rosário Cabrita
Department of Mechanical and Industrial Engineering (UNIDEMI), NOVA School of Science and Technology, Universidade NOVA de Lisboa, Caparica, Portugal

Susana Duarte
Department of Mechanical and Industrial Engineering (UNIDEMI), NOVA School of Science and Technology, Universidade NOVA de Lisboa, Caparica, Portugal

ABSTRACT

Industry 4.0 drivers and sustainability are topics increasingly referred to as part of the firm's strategy. Business value creation must be linked to sustainability and be designed on the road to the Industry 4.0. Technological advancements can bring about countless opportunities for growth and success in achieving humanity's set goals fitting the challenges of sustainability. This seminal work attempts to explore how Industry 4.0 creates opportunities to promote business sustainability. Based on the concepts of sustainability, business model, and the Industry 4.0 drivers, this chapter aims to provide insightful information on the potentials of exploring business model in the age of Industry 4.0.

INTRODUCTION

The global industrial landscape has changed deeply in the last few years due to increasing technological developments and innovations in manufacturing processes. The Industry 4.0 concept has emerged, and the academic literature has paid increased attention to this topic, which remains non-consensual. Nevertheless, there is a common understanding that the emergence of a new industrial paradigm will lead to novel business models. Little is known about which elements structure and shape the new digital business models. However, it is, at least, consensual that new business models must accomplish the mechanism underlying integration amongst the economic, environmental, and social components of business sustainability (BS).

DOI: 10.4018/978-1-7998-4543-0.ch010

Today, economies across the world are facing unprecedented challenges crossing social, economic and environmental dimensions of sustainability including climate change, natural disasters, loss of biodiversity, water scarcity, inequality, social insecurity and so on. These issues involve all stakeholders - citizens, governments, civil society, institutions - and they also involve businesses. A common response is needed as a matter of urgency in order to make sustainability a mainstream topic in business history where businesses and societies can find approaches that will move towards all three goals - environmental protection, social wellbeing, and economic development - at the same time.

Some authors (Bonvoisin, Stark, & Seliger, 2017; Dyllick, 2015; Haanaes et al., 2012) argue that benefits of addressing sustainability issues accrue not only to the society and environment but also to the enterprises themselves, throughout tangible benefits in the form of reduced costs from resource efficiency and regulatory compliance improvement, less labour turnover and reducing risks, as well as in the form of better reputation and image, increased competitiveness, better access to financing and increased attractiveness to talent.

Our world does not only face sustainability challenges but also faces technological advancements in digitalization and automation that are transforming the industrial production systems. In the last years, opportunities created by the Industry 4.0 (I4.0), with the use of emerging technologies, are transforming business and engineering processes in a way that they are deeply integrated making production operate in a flexible, efficient, and sustainable way with constantly high quality and low cost (Wang, Wan, Li, & Zhang, 2016). Some studies show that companies are starting to capitalize on the potential of emerging technologies to rearrange production, services, business models or the whole organization in a more sustainable way. In sum, Industry 4.0 could be an enabler to sustainable business models.

The topic "Business Model" (BM) has been the subject of a growing number of studies and published articles. Interest in business models as a distinct management research topic is relatively recent and some scholars argue that the increasing usage of the BM concept, which began in the mid-1990's, may have been driven by the advent of the Internet and by the emergence of the "new economy" (Baden-Fuller & Morgan, 2010; Morris, Schindehutte, & Allen, 2005; Zott, Amit, & Massa, 2011). Moreover, the concept is relevant for firms of all sorts, and progress in the field has been still fuzzy and vague by lack of consensus over the key components of a BM (Osterwalder, 2004).

Recent advances in Information and Communication Technologies (ICTs) and business conducted over the internet, with its dynamic, and rapidly competitive characteristics, promises new avenues for reflection on the creation of wealth (Afuah & Tucci, 2001; Amit & Zott, 2001). Introducing the I4.0 levers, new BMs that were unheard of, or very rare decades ago, will lead to organizations experimenting with new ways of achieving their goals, providing a great source of wealth and opportunity in today's economy.

As I4.0 progresses, BM for traditional manufacturing is changing, and new models are emerging. Little is known about which elements structure and shape the new digital BMs. It is expected that the value generated from the fourth industrial revolution goes beyond the value that can be created through the configuration of the value chain (Porter, 1985), or from the exploitation of unique resources (Barney, 1991). New BMs innovate through new mechanisms structures, automation and big data exchange not present in traditional businesses.

Based on the concept of a business model, this paper will explore the intersections between the opportunities provided by the development of I4.0 and the challenges to business sustainability. To do so, we focus on the business model compositional facets integrating the sustainability issues and the Industry 4.0 challenges. In this paper, we present initial approaches for adapting business models to the new business environment. This analysis, based on the concepts, principles, and drivers of Industry 4.0 can provide the basis to reflect on the creation and capture of value. The main conclusion of this research is that there is a high potential for Industry 4.0 to ensure a more sustainable business. This is shown by analyzing business sustainability drivers, business models components and I4.0 technological opportunities.

SUSTAINABLE DEVELOPMENT, BUSINESS SUSTAINABILITY AND SUSTAINABLE VALUE

Sustainability is a multi-dimensional concept encompassing environmental, social, and economic dimensions. Such dimensions form the Triple Bottom Line (TBL) view of sustainability. Awareness about Sustainable Development (SD) in business organizations has increased, over the last decades and sustainability strategies may require some adjustment of business models, where sustainable value emerges as the intersection of economic, social and environmental requirements and decisions.

Sustainable Development

The United Nations General Assembly adopted the Agenda 2030 Sustainable Development Goals (SDGs) on September 25, 2015, which includes 17 self-sustaining goals, with 169 targets. These so-called SDGs are intended to serve as a foundation for a transformation of the global economies towards sustainable development (United Nations, 2015) by addressing the root causes of poverty and the universal need for development that works for all people. The goals cover the three dimensions of sustainable development: economic growth, social inclusion, and environmental protection. Agenda 2030 has five topics known as the five Ps: people, planet, prosperity, peace, and partnerships, which span across the 17 SDGs (Zhai & Chang, 2019). We can support the argument that sustainable development aims at achieving social progress, environmental equilibrium, and economic growth. In this sense, proper decisions on sustainable resource management have an impact on sustainable growth for a sustainable society (Yang, 2019). Sustainability of society includes decisions against poverty, gender equality, quality education, and health systems, while the sustainability of the economy depends on the adoption of proper production, distribution and consumption systems. On the other hand, the sustainability of the environment includes decisions on land use, energy management, recycling, and waste management activities, reuse, and renewable programs, as well as conservation of ecology or biodiversity (Mensah, 2019).

Business Sustainability

In a time when more and more firms claim to manage sustainably, it is imperative to distinguish between those firms that do and those that do not make effective contributions to economic, social and environmental sustainability issues (Dyllick & Muff, 2015). Indeed, sustainability becomes part of the firm's heart of business (Broek, 2010). Firms should understand the impact of the business network on critical sustainability issues. The term business sustainability or sustainable business means conducting business to meet human needs without rapidly depleting resources, degrading the environment, or compromising nature conservation efforts at the same time generate profit (Broek, 2010; Duarte & Cruz-Machado, 2016). Svensson and Wagner (2015) refer to BS as a company's or an organization's economic, social and environmental efforts to implement and manage both its own and its business network's impact on earth's life and ecosystems. In addition, Usha and Devakumar (2019) assert some initiatives taken to manage an organization and its relationships in quest of social, economic and environmental associated performance enhancement along with the organization's network of relationships have been termed as BS. Mahajan and Bose (2018) appreciate that it may also be referred to as the TBL approach (People, Planet and Profit) and emphasizes that the concept of BS is based on long-term thinking, not a short-term perspective.

We are aware of the variety of frameworks that are based on the three pillars of sustainability. BS perspective suggests the use of drivers and indicators to measure business models' performance in economic,

Figure 1. Business drivers, value forms and indicators of business sustainability

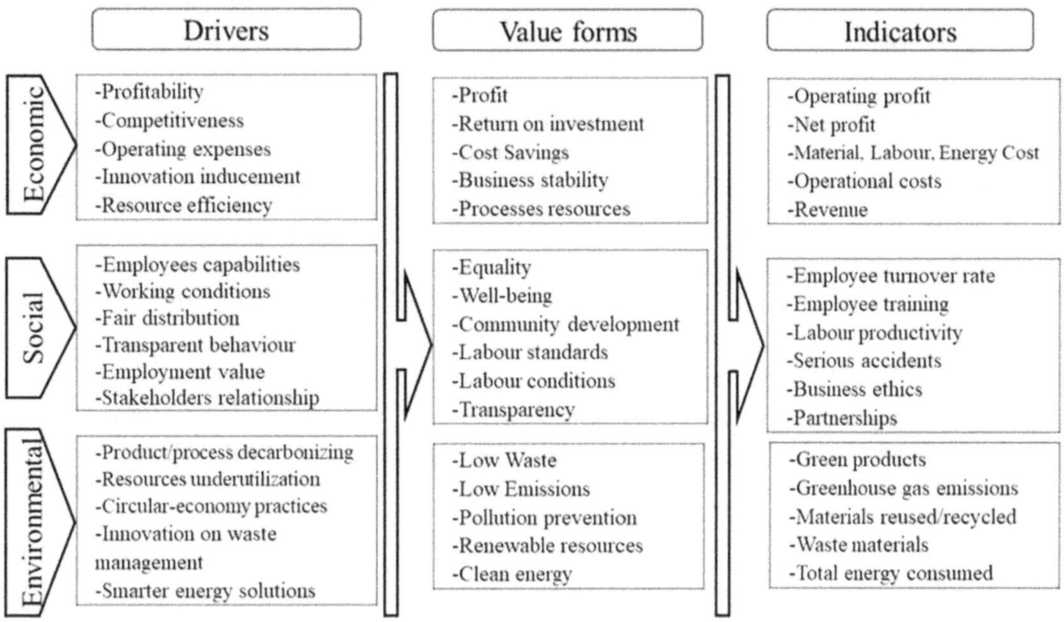

social and environmental areas. Indeed, the awareness about BS has increased among stakeholders, and increasingly is making part of the action plan of the firm (Duarte & Cruz-Machado, 2016). The values to evaluate this action plan can be defined as sustainable value. According to Evans et al. (2017) and Boons and Lüdeke-Freund (2013), sustainable value is the merging of economic value, social value, and environmental value. In addition, Evans et al. (2017) mentioned that sustainability drivers can take forward the creation of sustainable value for the business. There are several drivers (Evans et al., 2017; Hurtado-Jaramillo, Chiu, Arimany-Serrat, Ferràs, & Meijide, 2018), sustainable values (Evans et al., 2017) and indicators (Feil, Quevedo, & Schreiber, 2015; Watanabe, Silva, Junqueira, Santos, & Miyagi, 2016) for measure the sustainable performance in the context of BS. An example from the environmental perspective is the smarter energy solution (driver) helps to have clean energy (value) which can be measured through total energy consumed (indicator). From a social perspective, transparent behavior will lead to transparency in business and can be measured through a business ethics indicator. Figure 1 integrates some business drivers, value forms, and indicators of sustainable performance.

Businesses should consider sustainability in all activities and relationships, which includes not only customers, suppliers and partners involved in activities as conception, design, manufacturing and providing even service after the use and the disposal of the products (Watanabe et al., 2016) but firms' behavior, business strategy, operations management, accounting, finance, economics, environmental science, ethics, and social psychology (Pojasek, 2007). This induces the emergence of a new business model (Watanabe et al., 2016). According to Usha and Devakumar (2019), to reach business sustainability, it is necessary for the business model to take care of the stakeholder's economic, social and environmental benefits. The sustainable business model can support managers to better understand how it can contribute to sustainability through a firm's value proposition and including methods of value creation, delivery, and capture (Morioka, Evans, & Carvalho, 2016).

Sustainable Value

To effectively integrate sustainability decisions into business models, organizations must consider benefits to both the environment and society. This means that sustainable value includes economic, social and environmental benefits. Hope (2018) identifies some tools that can help to develop sustainable business models. Among these tools are: i) the Cambridge Value Mapping Tool (Vladimirova, 2016) and; ii) the Sustainable Value Analysis Tool (Yang, Vladimirova, & Evans, 2017). More recently, Vladimirova (2019) explored another tool, the Sustainable Value Proposition Builder to support the development and communication of value propositions to multiple stakeholders participating in the process of sustainable business model innovation. We will use the Sustainable Value Analysis Tool (Figure 2), because of its simplicity and the fact that this study adopts the notion of sustainable value that "incorporates economic, social and environmental benefits conceptualized as value forms" (Yang et al., 2017).

Business Models

Business Model, as a manifestation of strategy (Casadesus-Masanell & Ricart, 2010), is a term often used to describe the key components of a business, providing a tool to analyze and communicate strategic choices (Shafer, Smith, & Linder, 2005), and articulate how a firm creates and captures value (Magretta, 2002). Despite the plethora of research on BMs, scholars do not agree on a unique definition that fits all the necessary purposes. There is no universal consensus on what a BM actually is and what its structure is (Lambert & Davidson 2013; Morris et al., 2005; Zott et al., 2011). Given that interest in the concept has only recently emerged, it is not surprising that the literature is currently characterized by a lack of consensus. This lack of consensus may in part be attributed to interest in the concept from a wide range of disciplines. Throughout the literature review, we can found that the BM has been used to address different concerns in different contexts and in different management areas. Researchers have looked at the BM concept in the context of different domains, such as e-commerce and e-business (Amit & Zott, 2001), business management and strategy (Casadesus-Masanell & Zhu, 2013), technology and innovation management (Massa & Tucci, 2014), environmental sustainability (Schaltegger, Ludeke-Freund, & Hansen, 2012). In addition, the BM concept has also been challenged by traditional theories of value creation and value capture, two terms that are often used to describe BMs.

Figure 2. Sustainable Value Analysis Tool
Source: Yang et al. (2017)

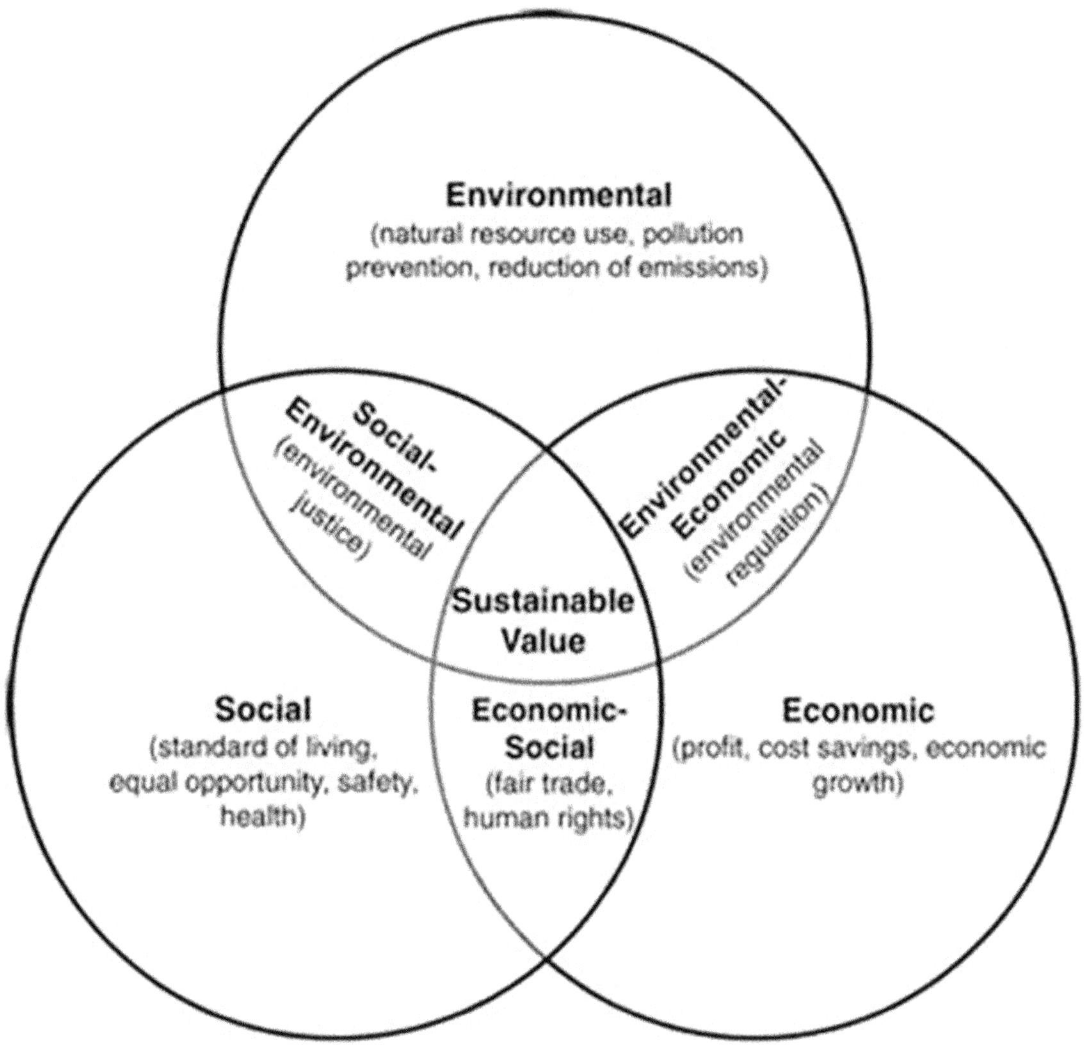

Business Model: Definitions and Concept

Business Model is not just one concept, it can be defined as a multifaceted concept (Lambert & Davidson, 2013). Some authors (Morris et al., 2005) have tried to create a consensus about the BM concept. Morris et al. (2005) investigated thirty definitions of BM and found three major classes of a BM. The first class of BM based on the economic definition, directed to a profit generation through variables as revenue streams and cost structures. The second class of BM anchored in the operational terms, directed to the architectural configurations by aiming at creating value through the infrastructural design of a business. The third class of BM grounded in the strategic view, which definition is directed to the positioning of a firm, considering factors such as market position and growth opportunities.

Table 1. Business model definitions

Authors	Definition: What is the business model?
Timmers (1998, p.2)	"is an architecture for the product, service and information flows, including a description of the various business actors and their roles; and a description of the potential benefits for the various business actors; and a description of the sources of revenues."
Afuah and Tucci (2001, pp.3-4)	"is the method by which a firm builds and uses its resources to offer its customers better value than its competitors and to make money doing so. It details how a firm makes money now and how it plans to do so in the long term. The model is what enables a firm to have a sustainable competitive advantage, to perform better than its rivals in the long term."
Magretta (2002, pp.4-6)	"is a story that explains how enterprises work." And are also a "planning tool that focuses attention on how all the elements of the business fit into a working whole."
Chesbrough and Rosenbloom (2002, p.532)	"is an architecture of organizational and financial structures of a business."
Morris et al. (2005, p.727)	"is a concise representation of how an interrelated set of decision variables in the areas of venture strategy, architecture, and economics are addressed to create sustainable competitive advantage in defined markets."
Osterwalder and Pigneur (2010, p.14)	"it describes the rationale of how an organization creates, delivers, and captures value."
Teece (2010, p.173)	"it articulates the logic and provides data and other evidence that demonstrates how a business creates and delivers value to customers. It also outlines the architecture of revenues, costs, and profits associated with the business enterprise delivering that value."
Baden-Fuller and Morgan (2010, p.167)	"it defines the business's characteristics and its activities in a way that matches the generic level that defines a kind or type of behavior but that also suggests why it works, because it embodies the essential elements and how they are to be combined to make them work."
Zott and Amit (2010, p.222)	"a template of how a firm conducts business, how it delivers value to stakeholders (e.g., the focal firms, customers, partners, etc.), and how it links factor and product markets."
Jensen (2013, p.67)	"a focal firm's core logic for creating, delivering and capturing value within a stakeholder network."
Fielt (2013, p.92)	"describes the value logic of an organization in terms of how it creates and captures customer value."
Euchner and Ganguly (2014, p.33)	"the means by which a firm creates and sustains margins or growth...the ability to create margins and growth is dependent on what competitors are doing to create margins and growth for themselves. The business model is not simply the means by which a firm creates and captures customer value."
Roome and Louche (2016)	"the way firms do business, creating and capturing value within a value network"
Geissdoerfer, Vladimirova, and Evans (2018)	"…simplified representations of the value proposition, value creation, and delivery, and value capture elements and the interactions between these elements within an organizational unit."

A BM can be understood as the logic for creating value (Linder & Cantrell, 2000), and the logic that connects operational potential with the realization of economic value (Chesbrough & Rosenbloom, 2002). Following this logic, the BM can be used to define how firms should structure their resources, capabilities, and processes to create and capture value from the possibilities offered by the context. Table 1 provides an overview of some of the most used definitions over time according to several authors.

From the revision above, it is possible to understand that BMs are about how a business works and what kind of value a business is delivering and how this is communicated and transferred to the customers.

Business Model Components

Some literature also focuses on BM's components, dimensions or building blocks. For Weill, Malone, D'Urso, Herman, and Woerner (2005), a BM is composed of two elements: a) what the business does; b) and how the business makes money. These two dimensions are translated into assets and relationships. The assets are divided into physical, financial, intangible and human assets and relationships, combined with assets, represent the relationship with buyers. Baden-Fuller and Morgan (2010) suggest that a BM is a combination of characteristics and its business activities capture how the essential elements work together. With these elements, several building blocks can be created. In turn, Teece (2010) considers that "in essence, a business model embodies nothing less than the organizational and financial 'architecture' of a business". A BM is more of a conceptual model than a financial statement. It depicts the business logic and makes assumptions about the participants (customers, suppliers, and partners) and value exchanges between them (tangible and intangible benefits and knowledge) (Zott et al., 2011).

Many definitions and component breakdowns of the BM have been proposed over the last decade (Amit & Zott, 2001; Casadesus-Masanell & Ricart, 2010; Chesbrough & Rosenbloom, 2002; Magretta, 2002; Morris et al., 2005; Osterwalder & Pigneur, 2010; Teece, 2010; Zott & Amit, 2010). Table 2 presents a selective overview of business model frameworks according to several authors. Each of the following frameworks is based on different perspectives thus none of them is more correct than the other.

In sum, there are notable similarities regarding the elements which can be used to represent how an enterprise creates and captures customer value. Nevertheless, there is more than one way to design a BM, and so the question of how to develop a BM remains unanswered (Fliegner, 2017). In any case, most perspectives on BMs include the firm's offerings and activities undertaken to produce them. From the literature revision, managers must consider the firm's value proposition, choose the activities it will undertake within the firm, and determine how the firm fits into the value creation network.

However, new features of the new industrial era are affecting the business models and business model innovation are derived in consequence (Ibarra, Ganzarain, & Igartua, 2018).

Integrating Sustainability Initiatives into Business Models

According to Osterwalder and Pigneur's, (2010) framework, a company's BM consists of four main pillars: product/value proposition, customer interface, infrastructure management, and financial aspects. The first two pillars (product and customer interface) are external in nature, as they relate to the company's external context. The other two components (infrastructure management and financial aspects) are internal in nature, as they are related to the company´s resources and activities (Osterwalder, 2004, p.42). This conceptualization is based on the following logic: A business model focuses the value being created for target customers (product); therefore, a firm has to manage its partnerships, resources, and capabilities to find adequate value configurations for products and services (infrastructure management); to address market segments and target customers, communication and distribution channels as well as diverse customer relationships have to be established (customer interface); finally, the goal of a firm is to appropriate as much of the created value as possible which refers to the underlying financial performance (financial aspects).

Table 2. Components of a business model

Authors	Components of a business model
Afuah and Tucci (2001)	· Customer value · Scope · Price · Revenue sources · Connected activities · Implementation · Capabilities · Sustainability
Amit and Zott (2001)	· Activity system content · Activity system structure · Activity system governance
Chesbrough and Rosenbloom (2002)	· Value proposition · Market segment · Value chain · Cost structure and profit potential · Value network · Competitive strategy
Magretta (2002)	· Customer · Value propositions; · How money are made; · Value delivery; · Costs.
Hedman and Kalling (2003)	· Customers · Competitors · Offering · Activities and organization · Resources · Supply of factor and production inputs
Moris et al. (2005)	· Factors related to the offering · Market factors · Internal capability factors · Competitive strategy factors · Economic factors · Personal/investor factors
Osterwalder and Pigneur (2010)	· Customer Segments · Value Propositions · Channels · Customer Relationships · Revenue Streams · Key Resources · Key Activities · Key Partnerships · Cost Structure
Gauthier and Gilomen (2016)	· Business logic of a company; · The way the company makes money; · What the company offers; · To whom the company offers this; · How the company can accomplish this.

Combining the sustainability drivers described in Figure 1 with the four BM pillars described above, allowed us to develop our sustainable value matrix, as depicted in Table 3:

Table 3. Sustainable Value Matrix

BM Components	Definition	Sustainability Initiatives
Product/Value proposition	Product refers to all aspects of what a firm offers to its customers. This comprises not only the company's bundles of products and services but the way it differentiates itself from its competitors.	Sustainability initiatives related to aspects of product and value proposition that answer to questions of how environmental, social and economic issues frame the organization's offering and the value proposition offered to the market?
Customer interface	The customer interface describes how and to whom it delivers its value proposition, which is the firm's bundle of products and services.	Sustainability related to aspects of relationships, customers and channels that answer to questions of how environmental, social and economic issues target the organization's customers, its delivery systems and its customer loyalty?
Infrastructure management	Infrastructure management describes how certain activities, resources, and partnerships drive the organization's value creation process	Sustainability actions related to aspects that answer to questions of how resources, activities, and partnerships related to environmental, social and economic issues are managed by the organization.
Financial aspects	Revenue model and cost structure illustrate how the organization's value proposition turns into financial performance	Sustainability related to aspects answer to questions of how environmental, social and economic issues affect the revenue model and cost structure.

INDUSTRY 4.0

"Industry 4.0" (I4.0) was first coined in 2011 to promote the idea as an approach to strengthening the competitiveness of the German manufacturing industry, and, since then, the term has drawn great attention from academics, practitioners, governmental officials, and politicians all over the world. In general, I4.0 has been compared to and used interchangeably with the fourth industrial revolution. Overall, the vision of I4.0 describes a whole new approach to business operations. In their publication, Kagermann, Wahlster, and Helbig (2013, p.5) describe their vision of I4.0 as follows:

In the future, businesses will establish global networks that incorporate their machinery, warehousing systems and production facilities in the shape of Cyber-

Physical Systems (CPS). In the manufacturing environment, these Cyber-Physical Systems comprise smart machines, storage systems and production facilities capable of autonomously exchanging information, triggering actions and controlling each other independently. This facilitates fundamental improvements to the industrial processes involved in manufacturing, engineering, material usage and supply chain and life cycle management. The Smart Factories that are already beginning to appear to employ a completely new approach to production. Smart products are uniquely identifiable, may be located at all times and know their own history, current status and alternative routes to achieving their target state. The embedded manufacturing systems are vertically networked with business processes within factories and enterprises and horizontally connected to dispersed value networks that can be managed in real-time – from the moment an order is placed right through to outbound logistics. In addition, they both enable and require end-to-end engineering across the entire value chain.

Industry 4.0: Definitions and Concept

I4.0 is based on the concept of cyber-physical systems (CPS) – the fusion of the physical and the virtual world - which is mainly a technological approach. Deloitte (2014) describes CPS as online networks of social machines that are organized in a similar way to social networks. Aspects such as the changes in organizational structures and processes, the adaption of existing business models, or the development of necessary employee-skills and qualifications are neglected. I4.0 is seen as a collective term for technologies and concepts of value chain organization that reflects the change of manufacture from centralized mode to distributed mode. Technologies that are driving the fourth industrial revolution fall into two distinct categories, as depicted in Table 4.

Table 4. Technologies driving Industry 4.0

Technologies changing the physical world	Technologies changing the digital world
· Biotechnology · Robotics · 3D Printing · New materials · Internet of Things (IoT) · Energy capture, storage, and transmission	· Artificial Intelligence (AI) · Blockchain applications · New computational technologies · Virtual and augmented reality

Industry 4.0: Challenges of the New Paradigm

I4.0 has been very much driven by changes concerned with technological capabilities and processes, impacting the way we do business. Digitization is the major driver of changes throughout the value chain putting pressure on traditional BMs and leading to the emergence of new models. According to Deloitte (2014) the increased emphasis on open innovation processes, along with the integration of customers in the production process in combination with big data analytics opens up possibilities for new BMs. However, technological changes may also mean further delimitation of work, acceleration, more intense work and other new challenges to work-life balance. There are other sensitive areas to keep in mind, such as protection, privacy, and security.

As a consequence of the intense network of people and machines within I4.0, job content, work processes, work environment, and the required skills will change significantly (Ford, 2009). According to the author, technologies such as artificial intelligence, machine learning, and software automation applications would increasingly enable computers to fulfill jobs that require significant training and education. Bonekamp and Sure (2015) analyze the implications of I4.0 and cyber-physical systems on human labor and work for the organization and found that I4.0 would lead to a substantial decrease in standardized low-skill and an increase in high-skill activities, embracing planning, control, and IT-related tasks. They also expect a growing complexity in many job profiles, along with cross-company partner networks. We will need people who can manage new operations, manage the robotics, program them and maintain them. It is envisaged the growing importance of learning, training, and education in order for the workers to be prepared to adapt to future qualification requirements derived from I4.0 technologies.

While some argue that collaboration is the key to achieving a complete 4.0 network, others, like Bouncken and Kraus (2013) state that companies will have to compete and "protect themselves" against competitors. Brettel, Friederichsen, Keller, and Rosenberg (2014) state that companies have to focus on their core competencies and create a network of collaboration to outsource other activities. Rogers, Ojha, and White (2011) say that collaboration is only necessary when competences and capabilities are not enough.

SUSTAINABILITY REQUIREMENTS FOR INDUSTRY 4.0

Established business models will become more data-based, and customer-focused due to the increased connectivity and use of analytical data processes. At this early development phase, there is very scarce research on the potential use of Industry 4.0, and it is still unclear what important factors influence such potential. For instance, Bonilla, Silva, Silva, Gonçalves, and Sacomano (2018) studied how inherent characteristics of I4.0 and the changes it promotes, affect the flows of raw material, energy, products, waste, assets and information, and how their modification consequently impacts either positively or negatively on environmental sustainability. The authors found evidence of a predominance of positive impacts in qualitative terms. However, the advert that in the long term, the way that I4.0 will impact environmental sustainability is not straightforward. The reaction of society, business, and governments to the new paradigm will be critical in directing the types of impact.

Kamble, Gunasekaran, and Gawankar (2018) recommend a holistic approach when designing a conceptual framework linking sustainability and I4.0 features, including not only I4.0 technologies but also machine-equipment interactions; human-machine interactions; sustainability and trend technology of I4.0. Varela, Araújo, Ávila, Castro, and Putnik (2019) studied the relationships between I4.0 and the three sustainability pillars and found a strong correlation among them. According to the authors, it is expected that I4.0 will drive companies, for instance, industrial ones, to more favorable economic situations (e.g., flexibility, productivity, competitiveness); to positive impacts on environmental dimension (e.g., decrease industrial waste; increase practice of circular economy; decrease resources consumption), and; to more positive influence in the social dimension of sustainability (e.g., increase participation of employees in decision-making).

According to Ibarra et al. (2018), despite the lack of common definitions, it seems to be a consensus on the description of the features of the I4.0, since all studies take them into account. Based on the literature review, features and requirements of the I4.0 are mentioned in Table 5.

In addition, sustainability and I4.0 (through the concept of digitalization) are transversal themes crossing all parts of the value chain (Machado, Winroth, and Silva, 2019). According to Ibarra et al. (2018), I4.0 will be the most powerful driver of innovation for the near future, where the business world's rapid digitalization is breaking down the traditional barriers of the industry. Therefore, innovative solutions to improve practices and processes are attained by exploring novel technologies (Watanabe et al., 2016). By this way, Bradley, Parry, and O'Regan (2020) refer "Business model frameworks for sustainability need to identify profit centres, and help unpick the full range of other value that a business model is able to create and capture and for whom, as such an exploration is key to understanding the organizations sustainable development contribution." Also, Velter et al. (2019) consider that linking sustainability to Business models must take considerations as for example: (1) the value priority must be considered both equal economic, social and environmental; (2) the value horizon must be direct, short- or medium-term but also indirect, long-term; (3) Sustainable customer value and co-benefits through value for society & environment; (4) Value creation and delivery network through Business and interlinked value chains plus value network including new and possibly non-traditional partners and (5) Value capture with economic, social and environmental business value and earth value.

Table 5. Features and requirements of the Industry 4.0

Main Features of the Industry 4.0	Main issues affecting traditional Business Model	Main requirements to face the digital transformation
Interoperability Virtualization Decentralization of decision making Real-time capability Service orientation Modularity	Networking and reduction of barriers Flexibility and personalization Individualized mass production Local production Low price Smart goods and services Fragmentation of the value chain Globalization and decentralization of production V-H integrated production systems	Standardization Work organization Availability of products New Business Models Know-how protections Availability of skilled workers Research investment Professional development Legal frameworks

Therefore, and according to Morioka et al. (2016) the term of sustainable business model innovations involves "the challenge of innovating (developing and implementing new solutions for products, processes, marketing and/or organization), in order to improve corporate sustainability performance (firm's contribution to global sustainable development), that is embedded in firm's core business model (firm's configuration to propose, create, deliver and capture value)." Also Bocken, Short, Rana, and Evans (2014) defined the term as "innovations that create significant positive and/or significantly reduced negative impacts for the environment and/or society, through changes in the way the organization and its value-network create, deliver value and capture value (i.e. create economic value) or change their value propositions."

Therefore, the novel business model considering the sustainable requirements for I4.0 reflects the linkage of physical-products with cyber-services, meeting the customer needs through smart data for offering new services and a sustainable-oriented decentralized organization (Machado et al., 2019).

Addressing Sustainability and Industry 4.0 to the Business Model

With the concepts of sustainability and industry 4.0, new evolving business models are highly driven, not only by selling the functionality and availability of products but contribute to solving a social or environmental problem (Stock & Seliger, 2016). In their research, Bocken et al. (2014) introduced 3 different components that may contribute to building up the business model and are as follows: (1) Technology (maximize material and energy efficiency, create value from waste and substitute with renewables and natural processes); (2) Social (deliver functionality rather than ownership, adopt a stewardship role and encourage sufficiency) and (3) Organizational (re-purpose the business for society/environment, develop scale-up solutions). In addition, Watanabe et al. (2016) proposed a framework considering sustainability with four components: technological, economic, social and environmental. Technological innovation can drive to a new business model innovation (Bocken et al., 2014; Parida, Sjödin, & Reim, 2019). The framework proposed by Parida et al. (2019), considers the linkages between digitalization, business model innovation, and sustainability industry. This framework suggests that digitalization (by applying diverse digital technologies) enables business model innovation. In sequence, value creation, value delivery, and value capture are changed allowing benefits on business sustainability. Boons and Lüdeke-Freund (2013) consider a generic business model with four distinct elements: (1) Value proposition (what value is embedded in the product or service offered by the firm) ; (2) Supply chain (how are upstream relationships with suppliers structured and managed); (3) Customer interface (how are downstream relationships with customers structured and managed and (4) Financial model (costs and revenues from the other elements and their distribution across business model stakeholders). More recently, and based on these elements, the authors De Man and Strandhagen (2017), adding the concepts of industry 4.0 and sustainability to the business models, connect the supply chain management with sustainability strategies, supported through industry 4.0, and addresses the customer needs that are financially justifiable.

Focusing on business sustainability requires a framework for understanding how sustainability may generate opportunities for value creation, value delivery, and value capture. Table 6 systematizes crossing references on the sustainability/business model and I4.0/business model.

Table 6. Components of Sustainable Business Models 4.0

Sustainability & Business model	Morioka et al. (2016)	· Sustainable value proposition · Sustainable value creation and delivery · Sustainable value capture
	Bocken et al. (2014)	· Value proposition (product/service, customer segments, and relationships) · Value creation and delivery (key activities, resources, partners, technology) · Value capture (cost structure and revenue streams)
Industry 4.0 & Business model	Ibarra et al. (2018); Parida et al. (2019)	· Value Creation (key activities, resources, and partnerships) focused on · Value Delivery (product and services, distribution, communication and sales channels, customer segments and relationships) · Value Capture (costs and revenues)

At the advent of I4.0, the sustainable value approach in an organization is an intrinsically embedded Cyber-Physical-System. Figure 3 provides an overview of how I4.0 holds a great opportunity for realizing sustainable value on all three sustainability dimensions: economic, social and environmental. I4.0 and its embedded technology diffusion progress are expected to grow exponentially in terms of technical change and socioeconomic impact. Therefore, coping with sustainable value creation requires a holistic approach that encompasses innovative and sustainable systems solutions that consider not only technological advancements but also social innovation, under the sustainability umbrella (Morrar, Arman, & Mousa, 2017).

The concept of social innovation denotes the existence of processes, factors, and methods that lead the society to a sustained positive transformation, and express both the newness and improved responses to societal needs. Social innovation has been defined as new practices used to tackle social challenges; they have a positive influence on individuals, society, and organizations (Hahn & Andor, 2013). Social innovation is also defined as new models, services or products that meet social needs and bring new opportunities and benefits to the people and society. The literature review states that social innovation can take many forms, a principle, law, behavior change, business model, product, process or technology. Usually, social innovations result from a combination of these components.

Figure 3. The framework of potential sustainable value in the age of Industry 4.0

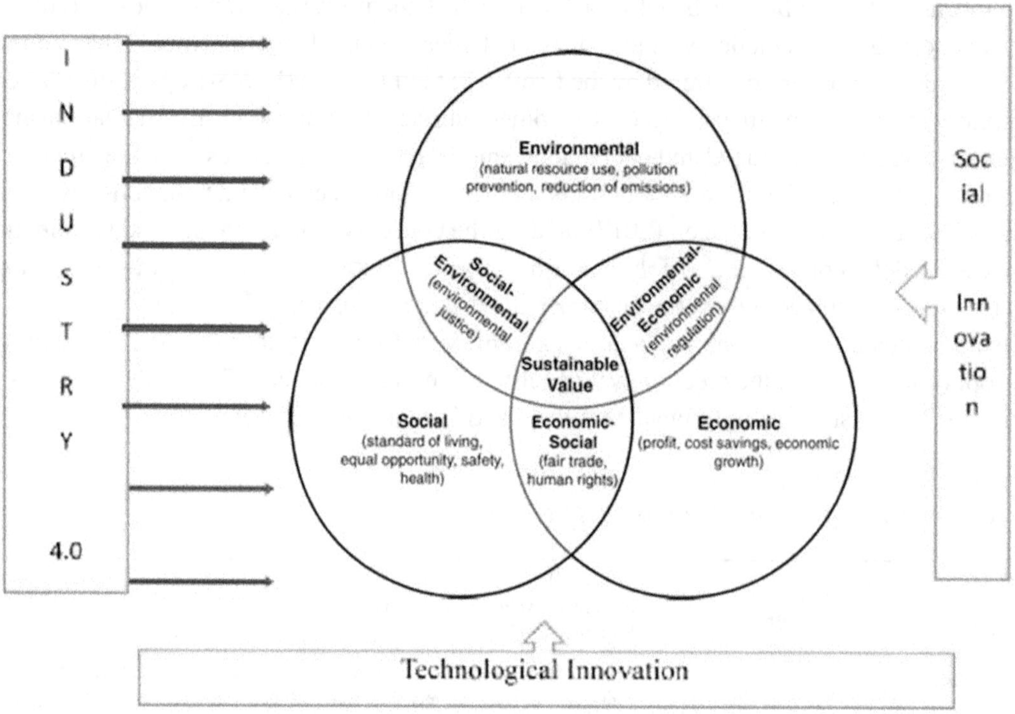

The three key pillars – economic, social, and environmental –form the bases of our simple framework. Technological and social innovation represent the key drivers to be considered in a business model to providing sustainable solutions that meet the three key criteria of sustainability. Including in the framework, the sustainability issues will act as a filter and catalyst when addressing technological and social innovative solutions. Managers should focus on the alignment between technical development and the new practices required to deal with social challenges facing organizations. While technological development can positively affect the diffusion and dissemination of social innovation, it is also accepted that technical innovation often only develop their true potential in combination with social innovation. As mentioned by Morrar et al. (2017) the technological revolution that accompanies the I4.0 achieves its true potential in combination with social innovation.

CONCLUSIONS

The main purpose of this work is to analyze the potential of Industry 4.0 applications to realize a more sustainable business model. I4.0 can have many impacts, positive as well as critical ones. In general, when we talk about I4.0 we focus on a technical context, but the increasing digitization and interconnection of products, value chains, and business models have also massive impacts on society and the environment. Technological innovation should interact with social innovation to shape the future of society. The development of I4.0 technologies can be exploited for the creation of new business models addressing sustainability issues. But not only I4.0 present the opportunity to conceive new business models but also the concept of sustainability provides innovative changes.

This study contributes to the literature on I4.0 as well as on new business models and sustainability. By addressing sustainability and I4.0 to BM, we shed light on an important research gap. This work contributes to advances in I4.0 research indicating that the use of the new technologies can enable I4.0 to have positive impacts on all the sustainability dimensions in an integrated way, and also supporting the development of sustainable business models.

The paper provides a framework to explore and specify critical elements for sustainable value creation in dynamic and complex settings of sustainable environments. The study also suggests that sustainable value creation in the context of the I4.0 requires not only the consideration of economic, environmental, social and public benefits and challenges but also, even more, their integrative combination and holistic harmonization. Management's focus on just a single dimension or a subset of these dimensions does not develop the I4.0 to its full sustainability potential.

While this work provides new theoretical and conceptual perspectives, more research on business models for sustainability is needed to further develop more integrative theories of sustainability management that can effectively contribute to business sustainability.

ACKNOWLEDGMENT

This work was supported by UNIDEMI [UIDB/00667/2020].

REFERENCES

Afuah, A., & Tucci, C. L. (2001). *Internet business models and strategies*. McGraw-Hill, Irwin.

Amit, R., & Zott, C. (2001). Value creation in e-business. *Strategic Management Journal*, *22*(6-7), 493–520. doi:10.1002mj.187

Baden-Fuller, C., & Morgan, M. S. (2010). Business models as models. *Long Range Planning*, *43*(2-3), 156–171. doi:10.1016/j.lrp.2010.02.005

Bocken, N. M. P., Short, S. W., Rana, P., & Evans, S. (2014). A literature and practice review to develop sustainable business model archetypes. *Journal of Cleaner Production*, *65*, 42–56. doi:10.1016/j.jclepro.2013.11.039

Bonilla, S. H., Silva, H. R. O., da Silva, M. T., Gonçalves, R. F., & Sacomano, J. B. (2018). Industry 4.0 and sustainability implications: A scenario-based analysis of the impacts and challenges. *Sustainability*, *10*(10), 3740. doi:10.3390u10103740

Bonvoisin, J., Stark, R., & Seliger, G. (2017). Field of Research in Sustainable Manufacturing. In R. Stark, G. Seliger, & J. Bonvoisin (Eds.), *Sustainable Manufacturing: Challenges, Solutions and Implementation* (pp. 3–20). Springer. doi:10.1007/978-3-319-48514-0_1

Boons, F., & Lüdeke-Freund, F. (2013). Business models for sustainable innovation: State-of-the-art and steps towards a research agenda. *Journal of Cleaner Production*, *45*, 9–19. doi:10.1016/j.jclepro.2012.07.007

Bouncken, R. B., & Kraus, S. (2013). Innovation in knowledge-intensive industries: The double-edged sword of coopetition. *Journal of Business Research*, *66*(10), 2060–2070. doi:10.1016/j.jbusres.2013.02.032

Bradley, P., Parry, G., & O'Regan, N. (2020). A framework to explore the functioning and sustainability of business models. *Sustainable Production and Consumption*, *21*, 57–77. doi:10.1016/j.spc.2019.10.007

Brettel, M., Friederichsen, N., Keller, M., & Rosenberg, M. (2014). How virtualization, decentralization and network building change the manufacturing landscape: An Industry 4.0 perspective. *International Journal of Mechanical, Aerospace, Industrial. Mechatronic and Manufacturing Engineering*, *8*(1), 37–44.

Broek, F. V. D. (2010). *Green Supply Chain Management, Marketing Tool or Revolution?* Retrieved on December 10, 2019, from http://www.yieldopedia.com/paneladmin/reports/f744f7e72bd9617b57e-09809a21042e8.pdf

Casadesus-Masanell, R., & Ricart, J. (2010). From strategy to business models and to tactics. *Long Range Planning*, *43*(2-3), 195–215. doi:10.1016/j.lrp.2010.01.004

Casadesus-Masanell, R., & Zhu, F. (2013). Business model innovation and competitive imitation: The case of sponsor-based business models. *Strategic Management Journal*, *34*(4), 464–482. doi:10.1002mj.2022

Chesbrough, H., & Rosenbloom, R. S. (2002). The role of the business model in capturing value from innovation: Evidence from Xerox Corporation's technology spin-off companies. *Industrial and Corporate Change*, *11*(3), 529–555. doi:10.1093/icc/11.3.529

De Man, J. C., & Strandhagen, J. O. (2017). An Industry 4.0 Research Agenda for Sustainable Business Models. *Procedia CIRP*, *63*, 721–726. doi:10.1016/j.procir.2017.03.315

Deloitte. (2014). *Industry 4.0: Challenges and solutions for the digital transformation and use of exponential technologies*. Deloitte.

Duarte, S., & Cruz-Machado, V. (2017). Green and Lean Model for Business Sustainability. In J. Xu, A. Hajiyev, S. Nickel, & M. Gen (Eds.). *Proceedings of the Tenth International Conference on Management Science and Engineering Management. Advances in Intelligent Systems and Computing* (pp. 1281-1292). Singapore: Springer. 10.1007/978-981-10-1837-4_105

Dyllick, T. (2015). Responsible management education for a sustainable world: The challenges for business schools. *Journal of Management Development*, *34*(1), 16–33. doi:10.1108/JMD-02-2013-0022

Dyllick, T., & Muff, K. (2015). Clarifying the Meaning of Sustainable Business: Introducing a Typology from Business-as-Usual to True Business Sustainability. *Organization & Environment*, *29*(2), 156–174. doi:10.1177/1086026615575176

Euchner, J., & Ganguly, A. (2014). Business model innovation in practice. *Research Technology Management*, *57*(6), 33–39. doi:10.5437/08956308X5706013

Evans, S., Vladimirova, D., Holgado, M., Fossen, K. V., Yang, M., Silva, E. A., & Barlow, C. Y. (2017). Business Model Innovation for Sustainability: Towards a Unified Perspective for Creation of Sustainable Business Models. *Business Strategy and the Environment*, *26*(5), 597–608. doi:10.1002/bse.1939

Feil, A. A., Quevedo, A. M., & Schreiber, D. (2015). Selection and identification of the indicators for quickly measuring sustainability in micro and small furniture industries. *Sustainable Production and Consumption*, *3*, 34–44. doi:10.1016/j.spc.2015.08.006

Fielt, E. (2013). Conceptualising Business Models: Definitions, Frameworks and classifications. *Journal of Business Models*, *1*(1), 85–105. doi:10.5278/ojs.jbm.v1i1.706

Fliegner, W. (2017). Analysis of the business model elements and their relationships. *Research Papers of the Wroclaw University of Economics*, *474*(474), 54–64. doi:10.15611/pn.2017.474.05

Ford, M. (2009). *The lights in the tunnel*. Acculant Publishing.

Gauthier, C., & Gilomen, B. (2016). Business models for sustainability: Energy efficiency in urban districts. *Organization & Environment*, *29*(1), 124–144. doi:10.1177/1086026615592931

Geissdoerfer, M., Vladimirova, D., & Evans, S. (2018). Sustainable business model innovation: A review. *Journal of Cleaner Production*, *198*, 401–416. doi:10.1016/j.jclepro.2018.06.240

Guo, F. (2017). The spirit and characteristic of the general provisions of civil law. *Law and Economics*, *3*, 5–16.

Haanaes, K., Reeves, M., von Streng Velken, I., Audretsch, M., Kiron, D., & Kruschwitz, N. (2012). *Sustainability nears a tipping point*. Boston Consulting Group.

Hahn, J., & Andor, L. (2013). *Guide to Social Innovation*. European Commission.

Høgevold, N. M., Svensson, G., Padin, C., & Dos Santos, M. (2016). A comparison of sustainable business models between goods and service industries: Similarities and differences. *International Journal of Business Excellence*, *10*(1), 20–36. doi:10.1504/IJBEX.2016.077616

Hope, A. (2018). Sustainable business model design: A review of tools for developing responsible business models. In L. Moratis, F. Melissen, & S. O. Idowu (Eds.), *Sustainable Business Models: Principle, Promise and Practice* (pp. 377–394). Springer. doi:10.1007/978-3-319-73503-0_17

Hurtado-Jaramillo, C. H., Chiu, M.-C., Arimany-Serrat, N., Ferràs, X., & Meijide, D. (2018). Identifying Sustainability-Value Creation Drivers for a Company in the Water Industry Sector: An Empirical Study. *Water Resources Management*, *32*(3), 3961–3978. doi:10.100711269-018-2030-5

Ibarra, D., Ganzarain, J., & Igartua, J. I. (2018). Business model innovation through Industry 4.0: A review. *Procedia Manufacturing*, *22*, 4–10. doi:10.1016/j.promfg.2018.03.002

Jensen, A. B. (2013). Do we need one business model definition? *Journal of Business Models*, *1*(1), 61–84. doi:10.5278/ojs.jbm.v1i1.705

Kagermann, H., Wahlster, W., & Helbig, J. (2013). *Securing the future of German manufacturing industry: Recommendations for implementing the strategic initiative INDUSTRIE 4.0: Final report of the Industrie 4.0 Working Group*. National Academy of Science and Engineering.

Kamble, S. S., Gunasekaran, A., & Gawankar, S. A. (2018). Sustainable Industry 4.0 framework: A systematic literature review identifying the current trends and future perspectives. *Process Safety and Environmental Protection, 117*, 408–425. doi:10.1016/j.psep.2018.05.009

Lambert, S. C., & Davidson, R. A. (2013). Applications of the business model in studies of enterprise success, innovation and classification: An analysis of empirical research from 1996 to 2010. *European Management Journal, 31*(6), 668–681. doi:10.1016/j.emj.2012.07.007

Machado, C. G., Winroth, M. P., & Silva, E. H. D. (2019). Sustainable manufacturing in Industry 4.0: An emerging research agenda. *International Journal of Production Research.* Advance online publication. doi:10.1080/00207543.2019.1652777

Magretta, J. (2002). Why business models matter. *Harvard Business Review, 80*(5), 86–92. PMID:12024761

Mahajan, R., & Bose, M. (2018). Business sustainability: Exploring the meaning and significance. *IMI Konnect, 7*(2), 8–13.

Massa, L., & Tucci, C. (2014). Business model innovation. In M. Dodgson, D. M. Gann, & N. Phillips (Eds.), *The Oxford handbook of innovation management* (pp. 420–441). Oxford University Press.

Mensah, J., & Ricart Casadevall, S. (2019). Sustainable development: Meaning, history, principles, pillars, and implications for human action: Literature review. *Cogent Social Sciences, 5*(1). Advance online publication. doi:10.1080/23311886.2019.1653531

Morioka, S. N., Evans, S., & Carvalho, M. M. (2016). Sustainable business model innovation: Exploring evidences in sustainability reporting. *Procedia CIRP, 40*, 659–667. doi:10.1016/j.procir.2016.01.151

Morrar, R., Arman, H., & Mousa, S. (2017). The Fourth Industrial Revolution (Industry 4.0): A social innovation perspective. *Technology Innovation. Management Review, 7*(11), 12–20. doi:10.22215/timreview/1117

Morris, M., Schindehutte, M., & Allen, J. (2005). The entrepreneur's business model: Toward a unified perspective. *Journal of Business Research, 58*(6), 726–735. doi:10.1016/j.jbusres.2003.11.001

Osterwalder, A. (2004). *The business model ontology – a proposition in a design science approach* (PhD. Thesis). University of Lausanne: Ecole des Hautes Etudes Commerciales HEC. Retrieved on December 15, 2019, from http://www.hec.unil.ch/aosterwa/Phd/Osterwalder_PhD _BM_Ontology.pdf

Osterwalder, A., & Pigneur, Y. (2010). *Business model generation.* Wiley.

Parida, V., Sjödin, D., & Reim, W. (2019). Reviewing Literature on Digitalization, Business Model Innovation, and Sustainable Industry: Past Achievements and Future Promises. *Sustainability, 11*(2), 391. doi:10.3390u11020391

Pojasek, R. B. (2007). A framework for business sustainability. *Environmental Quality Management, 17*(2), 81–88. doi:10.1002/tqem.20168

Rogers, P., Ojha, D., & White, R. (2011). Conceptualizing complementarities in manufacturing flexibility: A comprehensive view. *International Journal of Production Research, 49*(12), 3767–3793. doi:10.1080/00207543.2010.499116

Roome, N., & Louche, C. (2016). Journeying toward business models for sustainability: A conceptual model found inside the black box of organizational transformation. *Organization & Environment*, *29*(1), 11–35. doi:10.1177/1086026615595084

Schaltegger, S., Ludeke-Freund, F., & Hansen, E. G. (2012). Business cases for sustainability: The role of business model innovation for corporate sustainability. *International Journal of Innovation and Sustainable Development*, *6*(2), 95–119. doi:10.1504/IJISD.2012.046944

Shafer, S. M., Smith, H. J., & Linder, J. (2005). The power of business models. *Business Horizons*, *48*(3), 199–207. doi:10.1016/j.bushor.2004.10.014

Stock, T., & Seliger, G. (2016). Opportunities of Sustainable Manufacturing in Industry 4.0. *Procedia CIRP*, *40*, 536–541. doi:10.1016/j.procir.2016.01.129

Svensson, G., Høgevold, N., Ferro, C., Varela, J. C. S., Padin, C., & Wagner, B. (2016). A Triple Bottom Line Dominant Logic for Business Sustainability: Framework and Empirical Findings. *Journal of Business-To-Business Marketing*, *23*(2), 153–188. doi:10.1080/1051712X.2016.1169119

Svensson, G., & Wagner, B. (2015). Implementing and managing economic, social and environmental efforts of business sustainability: Propositions for measurement and structural models. *Management of Environmental Quality*, *26*(2), 195–213. doi:10.1108/MEQ-09-2013-0099

Teece, D. J. (2010). Business Models, Business Strategy and Innovation. *Long Range Planning*, *43*(2-3), 172–194. doi:10.1016/j.lrp.2009.07.003

Timmers, P. (1998). Business models for electronic markets. *Electronic Markets*, *8*(2), 3–8. doi:10.1080/10196789800000016

United Nations. (2015). *Transforming our world: the 2030 Agenda for Sustainable Development*. United Nations.

Usha, N., & Devakumar, G. (2019). Modelling Business Sustainability in Agri Engineering Manufacturing Companies: Effect of Innovation, Technology and Business Model. *International Journal of Recent Technology and Engineering*, *8*(1C), 341–345.

Varela, L., Araújo, A., Ávila, P., Castro, H., & Putnik, G. (2019). Evaluation of the relation between lean manufacturing, industry 4.0, and sustainability. *Sustainability*, *11*(5), 1439. doi:10.3390u11051439

Vladimirova, D. (2016). The Cambridge Value Mapping Tool. *IfM Review*. Retrieved on December 18, 2019, from https://www.ifm.eng.cam.ac.uk/news/the-cambridge-value-mapping-tool/

Vladimirova, D. (2019). Building sustainable value propositions for multiple stakeholders: A practical tool. *Journal of Business Models*, *7*(1), 1–8. doi:10.5278/ojs.jbm.v7i1.2103

Wang, S., Wan, J., Li, D., & Zhang, C. (2016). Implementing smart factory of Industrie 4.0: An outlook. *International Journal of Distributed Sensor Networks*, *12*(1), 3159805. Advance online publication. doi:10.1155/2016/3159805

Watanabe, E. H., Silva, R. M., Junqueira, F., Santos, D. J., & Miyagi, P. E. (2016). An Emerging Industrial Business Model considering Sustainability Evaluation and using Cyber Physical System Technology and Modelling Techniques. *IFAC-PapersOnLine*, *49*(32), 135–140. doi:10.1016/j.ifacol.2016.12.203

Weill, P., Malone, T. W., D'Urso, V. T., Herman, G., & Woerner, S. (2005). *Do some business models perform better than others? A study of the 1000 largest US firms.* Working Paper 226. Sloan School of Management Massachusetts Institute of Technology. Retrieved on January 12, 2020 from https://mpra.ub.uni-muenchen.de/4752/1/MPRA_paper_4752.pdf

Yang, L. (2019). From general principles of civil law to general provisions of civil law: A historical leap in contemporary Chinese civil law. *Social Sciences in China*, *2*, 85–91.

Yang, M., Vladimirova, D., & Evans, S. (2017). Creating and capturing value through sustainability: The Sustainable Value Analysis Tool. *Research Technology Management*, *60*(3), 30–39. doi:10.1080/08956308.2017.1301001

Zhai, T., & Chang, Y. C. (2019). Standing of environmental public-interest litigants in China: Evolution, obstacles and solutions. *Journal of Environmental Law*, *30*(3), 369–397. doi:10.1093/jel/eqy011

Zott, C., & Amit, R. (2010). Business model design: An activity system perspective. *Long Range Planning*, *43*(2-3), 216–226. doi:10.1016/j.lrp.2009.07.004

Zott, C., Amit, R., & Massa, L. (2011). The business model: Recent developments and future research. *Journal of Management*, *37*(4), 1019–1042. doi:10.1177/0149206311406265

Chapter 11
Developing Strategies in the Sharing Economy:
Human Influence on Artificial Neural Networks

Ramona Diana Leon
https://orcid.org/0000-0002-1448-0522
National School of Political and Administrative Studies, Romania

ABSTRACT

The sharing economy is challenging the traditional business models and strategies by encouraging collaboration, non-ownership, temporal access, and redistribution of goods and/or services. Within this framework, the current chapter aims to examine how managers influence, voluntarily or involuntarily, the reliability of a managerial early warning system, based on an artificial neural network. The analysis focuses on seven Romanian sustainable knowledge-based organizations and brings forward that managers tend to influence the results provided by a managerial early warning system based on artificial neural network, voluntarily and involuntarily. On the one hand, they are the ones who consciously decide which departments and persons are involved in establishing the structure of the managerial early warning system. On the other hand, they unconsciously influence the structure of the managerial early warning system through the authority they exercise during the managerial debate.

INTRODUCTION

The concept of "sustainability" has its roots in the social sciences, more exactly, in the ecological paradigm (O'Riordan, 1976), and it is used for the first time by George Ludwig Hartig, in 1785. He argues that forestry can be sustainable only if the future generations will be able to obtain the same benefits from its exploitation as the current generation. However, the perspective from which it is approached changed radically in the last centuries (Table 1). Thus, the theories developed in the 19th and the early 20th centuries (namely, the classical theory, the stakeholder theory, etc.) adopt an economic perspective

DOI: 10.4018/978-1-7998-4543-0.ch011

and claim that a firm's sustainability is ensured through profit maximization and shareholders' satisfaction. Furthermore, the theories promoted during the 20th and 21st centuries (like, neo-institutional theory, the knowledge-based theory of the firm, the holistic theory etc.) bring forward two more perspectives, namely: the social and ecological ones; as a consequence, three pillars of company's sustainability are emphasized, such as: profitability, stakeholders' satisfaction, and natural environment (Fiksel, 2006; Leon, 2018a; Lozano, 2008). Nevertheless, these perspectives are combined and the borders of sustainability are extended by the sharing economy which describes a socio-economic environment dominated by non-ownership (Belk, 2014; Botsman & Rogers, 2011), intra- and inter-organizational collaboration (Leon, Rodriguez-Rodriguez, Gomez-Gasquet, & Mula, 2017; Mantymaki, Baiyere, & Islam, 2019; Sthapit, 2019), temporary access (Habibi, Davidson, & Laroche, 2017; Yang, Bi, & Liu, 2020), and sharing of under-utilized or idle goods and/or services (Hong, Kim, & Park, 2019; Lee & Kim, 2019).

Table 1. The perspectives from which the concept of "sustainability" is approached

Perspective	Sustainability as...	Author/-s (Year)
Environmental	*A duty*	Barkemeyer, Holt, Preuss, and Tsang (2011); Pearce, Markandya, and Barbier (1989)
	A process	Braat (1991)
	An ability	Bansal (2005); Jennings and Zandbergen (1995)
	A capacity	Ariansen (1999)
	A component of the social and ethical responsibility	Landrum and Ohsowski (2018); Ng and Burke (2010); Richardson (2009); Schwartz and Carroll (2008)
Social	*A condition*	Torjman (2000)
	A level	Black (2004)
Economic	*A general goal*	Anderson (1991); Saunila, Nasiri, Ukko, and Rantala (2019)
	A specific objective	Daily and Walker (2000); Maddox (2000)
	A change factor	Blum-Kusterer and Hussain (2001); Bos-Brouwers (2010)
	A way to satisfy stakeholders' needs	Dyllick and Hockerts (2002); Hahn, Figge, Pinkse, and Preuss (2010)
	An image of productivity	Dunphy, Griffiths, and Benn (2003); Holliday, Schmidheiny, and Watts (2002)
	An adaptive capacity	Kira and van Eijnatten (2008)
	A stage of development	Ketola (2010)
	A process	Cândea (2006)
	A result	Vaida and Cândea (2010)

Within this framework, managers realize that the traditional strategies and business models, such as: the powerful input of resources into the supply sector (Böcker & Meelen, 2017; Fan, Xia, Zhang, & Chen, 2019), platform competition and price-setting (Armstrong, 2006; Eisenmann, Parker, & van Alstyne, 2006), and network externalities (Parker & van Alstyne, 2005) are no longer viable. Therefore, they have to focus not only on increasing shareholders' satisfaction but also on augmenting their internal and external stakeholders' satisfaction, improving the quality of life, and protecting the environment. In other words, they have to address the challenges from the micro- and macro-environment, having their stakeholders' best interest in mind.

Against this backdrop, managers look for potential solutions and tools that could provide them some "early warnings". Therefore, for the last 50 years, various early warning systems have been developed. Some of them use abstract tools, like: statistical analysis (Laitinen & Chong, 1999; Salzano, Garcia Agreda, Di Carluccio, & Fabbrocino, 2009) or artificial neural networks (Yang, 2012; Zheng, Zhu, Tim, Chen, & Sun, 2012) while others focus on managers' involvement and mitigate for the use of managerial debates (Day & Schoemaker, 2005; Kotler & Caslione, 2009). Only a few researchers (Bertoncel, Erenda, Pejić Bach, Roblek, & Meško, 2018; Haji-Kazemi & Andersen, 2013; Leon, 2018b) take into account the challenges brought forward by the sharing economy and the fact that this is usually focusing on the external stakeholders (Frenken & Schor, 2017; Li, Ding, Cui, Lei, & Mou, 2019; Niemimaa, Järveläinen, Heikkilä, & Heikkilä, 2019; Stofberg & Bridoux, 2019). Thus, they state that, in the current environment, a successful strategic tool should combine the subjective character of a managerial debate with the abstract character of various business intelligence tools.

Despite the valuable insights provided by this mixt approach of the managerial early warning system, its findings may be limited by several biases. According to Elbanna (2010), managers can influence strategy's development through coalition formation, agenda control, tactics of timing, and tactics concerning the control and manipulation of information. Besides, several scholars (Curşeu, Schruijer, & Fodor, 2016; Hollenbeck, Beersma, & Schouten, 2012; Parayitam & Papenhausen, 2016) argue that the results of a managerial early warning system can also be influenced by company's size, group diversity, agreement-seeking behavior, and knowledge sharing behavior. Each of these may have an impact on the identification of weak signals since they limit managers' perspective, and influence the way in which managers act during debates, factors selection, scenarios development, and strategy development. Starting from these, the current chapter aims to examine how managers influence, voluntarily or involuntarily, the reliability of a managerial early warning system, based on an artificial neural network.

The content of this chapter is organized around four sections. Section 2 describes the conceptual framework, emphasizing the tools used by the management teams to foresight the company's potential threats and opportunities. Then, the research design is highlighted; a qualitative-quantitative approach is employed in order to examine how the managers from 7 Romanian sustainable knowledge organizations influence, voluntarily or involuntarily, the reliability of a managerial early warning system, based on an artificial neural network. The results of this analysis are presented in Section 4 and they prove that managers influence, consciously and unconsciously, the reliability of a managerial early warning system. On the one hand, they are the ones who consciously decide which departments and persons are involved in establishing the structure of the managerial early warning system. On the other hand, they unconsciously influence the structure of the managerial early warning system through the authority they exercise during the managerial debate. Last but not least, the chapter closes by synthesizing the main findings and providing further research directions.

MANAGERIAL EARLY WARNING SYSTEMS – NEW SOLUTIONS TO OLD PROBLEMS

A managerial early warning system is a strategic tool that fosters the anticipation of the weak signals and the development of various responses to turbulence. Thus, it is seen as a specific information system, based on a cause-effect analysis (Ohatka & Fukazawa, 2009; Williams, Klakegg, Walker, Andersen, & Magnussen, 2012) and capable of extending the time available to react to unforeseen events (Genc, Duffie, & Reinhart, 2014).

The development of a managerial early warning system includes three phases, namely:

1. *Environment scanning* – focuses on selecting the elements from the micro- and macro-environment that could influence directly or indirectly the company's evolution and sustainability. At this level, managers tend to choose between adopting an inside or outside approach. The former reduces the volume of information that has to be processed further while offering a limited perspective on what may happen. The latter provides a complete image of the environment due to its 360° perspective while generating information overload. Although managers tend to choose between the two approaches, they neglect the fact that these are complementary and a state of equilibrium can be achieved between them.
2. *Diagnosis* – concentrates on collecting and analyzing historical data in order to determine trends and patterns. Several scholars recommend adopting an abstract approach and applying statistical methods and techniques (Bisson & Diner, 2017; Cao et al., 2011; Laitinen & Chong, 1999; Li & Davies, 2001; Schwarz, 2005; Tsai, 2013) while others state that the solution lies in adopting a subjective approach and using a managerial debate (Day & Schoemaker, 2005; Kotler & Caslione, 2009). Only a few researchers emphasize the advantages provided by both perspectives and argue that these could be combined (Bertoncel et al., 2018; Haji-Kazemi & Andersen, 2013; Leon, 2018b).
3. *Strategy formulation* – is the most subjective phase of the managerial early warning system and it involves using long-term orientation, strategic thinking, creativity and thinking outside the box. Within this framework, future evolutions are predicted, scenarios are built and strategic response is provided for what may come.

Against the backdrop of the sharing economy and the increased interest in developing smart firms, economies, communities, and cities, various abstract models of managerial early warning systems are developed (Table 2). These models use classical statistical techniques (such as, logit regression, fragility analysis, structural modeling, Kolmogorov – Smirnov test, Mann – Whitney – Wilcoxon test, etc.), are excellent when it comes to evaluating the influence factors from the environment but they do not comply with all the requirements for being labeled as a "managerial early warning system". Thus, they support the identification of weak signals and neglect the importance of developing various strategic responses. In other words, they lack a strategic approach; therefore, their utility stops at the second phase of the managerial early warning system. Furthermore, they tend to focus on financial performance and ignore the indicators that describe a company's social and environmental perspective.

Table 2. Abstract models of managerial early warning systems, based on classical statistical techniques

Author/-s (Year)	Managerial Early Warning System	
	Goal	**Tools**
Laitinen and Chong (1999)	To predict the firm's bankruptcy.	- time-series analysis
Schwarz (2005)	To anticipate the challenges from the internal and external business environment.	- trend analysis
Lieu, Lin, and Yu (2008)	To forecast the probability of a company experiencing financial distress.	- Kolmogorov – Smirnov test; - Mann-Whitney-Wilcoxon test; - logit regression.
Dikmen, Talat Birgonul, Ozorhon, and Egilmezer Sapci (2010)	To predict the failure likelihood of construction companies by assessing their current situation based on both company-specific and external factors.	- analytical network process; - Delphi method.
Tsai (2013)	To predict the company's financial distress.	- multinomial logit model; - probability forecast; - bootstrapping.
Li, Xia, Li, and Zheng (2015)	To forecast the evolution of the vegetable price.	- regression analysis
Hernandez Ticono, Holmes, and Wilson (2018)	To predict corporate financial distress/bankruptcy.	- polytonomous response logit regression
Boonnnan, Jacobs, Kuper, and Romero (2019)	To predict the financial crisis.	- the logit model.
Dekker, Panja, Dijkstra, and Dekker (2019)	To identify the "rest" and "disrupted" states of the Dutch railways.	- Principal Component Analysis; - Louvain model and Bries score.

The managerial early warning systems based on artificial neural networks take the advantage of the faster pace of the technological progress and try to fill the gap by using modern statistical techniques, like fuzzy logic or neural networks (Table 3). These work similar to the human brain and facilitate not only data analysis and patterns identification but also the development of potential strategic responses. Although these models aim to provide valuable insights and to ensure a high level of objectivity, the process is still under managers' influence due to the fact that the inputs describing the decisional situation are selected either by the management team (Li & Davies, 2001) or an employee (Cao, Chen, Wu, & Mao, 2011; Schwarz, 2005). These studies support the idea that people should be involved in strategy development since a strategy is implemented by human resources, its success depends on their involvement and is reflected by stakeholders' satisfaction. As Leon (2018b, p.105) state, *a managerial early warning system can provide fabulous solutions for what may come and plans may look great on paper but if human resources do not know what is expected from them and why should they do it, then it would be very difficult for the management team to exploit their full potential. Company's efforts for being sustainable, satisfying the interest of all the categories of stakeholders, may prove to be a real fiasco.*

Table 3. Abstract models of managerial early warning systems, based on modern statistical techniques

Author/-s (Year)	Managerial Early Warning System	
	Goal	Tools
Li and Davies (2001)	To build an intelligent hybrid system for developing global marketing strategies.	- expert system; - fuzzy logic; - artificial neural network.
Tan and Dihardjo (2001)	To predict financial distress in Australian credit unions.	- artificial neural network.
Cao et al. (2011)	To anticipate the moment when a firm will enter into the decline stage.	- Pawlak rough set theory; - artificial neural network.
Li, Qin, Li, and Hou (2016)	To prevent accidents from iron and steel enterprises.	- Analytic Hierarchy Process; - Entropy Weight Method; - Grey System Theory GM (1,1)
Bisson and Diner (2017)	To determine the drivers of change from the milk market competitive environment.	- Delphi method; - graph analysis.
Huang, Wang, and Kochenberger (2017)	To detect the financial deterioration of Chinese companies.	- random-forest; - support vector machine; - neural network.
Li, Wei, and Zhou (2017)	To predict delayed customer orders that will allow for measures to be taken to minimize the risk.	- active learning transductive support vector machine
Hu and Liu (2019)	To anticipate the crisis situation of the supply chain quality.	- fuzzy inference system
Vafaei, Ribeiro, and Camarinha-Matos (2019)	To improve proactive decision making in condition-based maintenance strategies.	- fuzzy logic

Although the development of sharing economy encourages communication and collaboration among stakeholders (Abhari, Davidson, & Xiao, 2019; Davlembayeva, Papagiannidis, & Alamanos, 2019; Mishra, Chiwenga, & Ali, 2019) and treats information and communication technologies as a means to achieve organizational goals, only a few researchers state that the managerial early warning systems should be based on debates (Day & Schoemaker, 2005; Kotler & Caslione, 2009; Philip & Schwabe, 2018). They argue that in order to determine the weak signals, to react properly to the challenges that occur in the internal and external environment, the management team has to answer to the following questions:

1. What were our past blind spots? What is happening in these areas now?
2. Is there any instructive analogy for us in another sector?
3. Which important signals are we ignoring without having a rational argument?
4. In our business sector, who is the best at identifying the weak signals and at reacting to these ahead of everyone else?
5. What are our mavericks and outliers trying to tell us?
6. What future surprises could really affect (help) us?
7. What emerging technologies could change the business rules that we know?
8. *Is there any unbelievable scenario?* (Day & Schoemaker, 2005)

Using a managerial debate as an early warning system provides the proper framework for increasing the quality of managers' decision (Raes, Heijltjes, Glunk, & Roe, 2011), improving resource allocations (Cadez & Guilding, 2008), and augmenting managers' involvement in strategy development and implementation (Olsson, Aronsson, & Sandberg, 2017; Ogbeide & Harrington, 2011; Sölvell, 2018). In other words, a managerial debate allows them to explore and manipulate the environment (Vansteenkiste, Niemiec, & Soenens, 2010), to adapt strategic foresight based on their assumptions and mental models (Ringland, 2010), and to understand how and why things are done (Leon, 2018b). However, this model is time-consuming and strongly influenced by the organizational culture and climate. Last but not least, it can be influenced by the company's size. As García Martín and Herrero (2018) and Rashid (2018) show, the size of the company is directly related to the characteristics of the board and the company's performance. Starting from the aforementioned aspects, it can be stated that:

Hypothesis 1: The company's size has an impact on the reliability of the managerial early warning system.

Furthermore, only a few researchers (Bertoncel et al, 2018; Haji-Kazemi & Andersen, 2013; Leon, 2018b) use the development of the sharing economy as a cornerstone and claim that the abstract and subjective approaches of a managerial early warning system could be combined in a strategic tool. Haji-Kazemi and Andersen (2013) combine the debate with post-mortem analysis while Bertoncel et al. (2018) and Leon (2018b) use a managerial debate and an intelligent business system in the diagnosis phase and place the strategy formulation under the responsibility of the management team. Despite the various advantages provided by this type of managerial early warning system, one issue remains under-explored, namely: managers' influence on the system's reliability.

Managerial groups are considered to be the cornerstone of modern organizations (Curşeu et al., 2016; Hollenbeck et al., 2012) due to the fact that they are able to integrate the explicit and tacit knowledge of the members, to make rational decisions, and to foster strategies implementation. Nevertheless, several issues remain debatable among academics and practitioners, and they tend to focus on group diversity, knowledge sharing behavior, and agreement-seeking behavior.

First of all, most studies (Goyal, Kakabadse, & Kakabadse, 2019; Kipkirong Tarus & Aime, 2014; Parayitam & Papenhausen, 2016; Van der Walt, Ingley, Shergill, & Townsend, 2006) emphasize the positive effect of group diversity on decision quality. Thus, Parayitam and Papenhausen (2016) argue that managers who have different functional backgrounds focus more on decision outcomes than on members' satisfaction; in other words, they are more oriented to tasks than relationships. However, group diversity does not guarantee decision quality since various variables mediate this relationship. On the one hand, individuals' variables like personality, emotional intelligence, etc. should be taken into account; thus, Tuwey and Tarus (2016) prove that chairman's leadership efficacy, members' personal motivation and background have a positive effect on board strategy involvement while Azouzi and Jarboui (2013) reveal that a CEO emotional intelligence is not always positively correlated with board efficiency. On the other hand, organizational variables like size, organizational culture, and climate must be considered; hence, Bridges (2018) claim that the organizations led by more outcome-oriented managers have strong paternalistic cultures while the ones led by more process-oriented managers value diversity. Taking these into account, it can be stated that:

Hypothesis 2: Company's size has an impact on managers' influence.

Secondly, the knowledge sharing behavior is usually brought forward when it comes to managerial group decisions since the group's main purpose is to foster knowledge dissemination and re-combination. Nevertheless, Mojzisch, Grouneva, and Schultz-Hardt (2010) state that three biases may affect this process, namely: (i) manager's preferences, (ii) the importance of external validation, and (iii) uncertainty avoidance. The former highlights the fact that managers evaluate new information based on their initial preferences and discharge everything that is not consistent with these; in other words, managers' mental models which represent the main *sources of expertise, action, and cooperation of individuals in the group* (Hautala, 2011, p.603) are challenged. Furthermore, Mojzisch et al. (2010) prove that the information that can be corroborated by others is considered to be more accurate and relevant than uncorroborated information. Managers' tendency to avoid uncertainty affects the way they perceive and process information; thus, they trust existing information more than the new one (Eisenbart, Garbuio, Mascia, & Morandi, 2016).

Last but not least, the knowledge sharing behavior is linked with agreement-seeking behavior. According to Parayitam and Papenhausen (2016), this provides a solid platform behavior and lowers the levels of process conflict. Still, Finkelstein et al. (2010) state that, at this level, several pitfalls may appear due to inappropriate prejudgments, inappropriate experience, and attachments. These influence the perspective from which managers approach the discussed issues and also the choices they make. They can rarely be objective and impartial when it comes to scanning the environment, identifying the weak signals, and deciding the firm's future. For example, during debates, they may feel the need to align with the CEO's opinion if their past experiences have taught them that this is the right thing to do. As Curşeu et al. (2016) claim, when the responsibility resides with the group leader, the members may exhibit less escalating tendencies. Besides, they can also be tempted to align to the opinion of the majority if they do not experience high psychological safety and they have noticed that the outsiders (those who "dare" to disagree with the majority) are treated differently. As a consequence, they will not share their opinions, ideas, thoughts; instead, they will agree with whatever the majority of the CEO decides. Given these, the following assumption can be made:

Hypothesis 3: Managers' influence affects the reliability of the managerial early warning system.

RESEARCH METHODOLOGY

This chapter aims to examine how managers influence, voluntarily or involuntarily, the reliability of a managerial early warning system, based on an artificial neural network.

Since the research deals with "how" issues, a case-study strategy is employed (Yin, 2014). According to Mariotto, Zanni, and Marcondes de Moraes (2014), this can facilitate theory development if *the particulars of the case are seen as opportunities to make further adjustments in an already crystallized understanding of reality*. Furthermore, a multiple case study approach is developed and the focus is on the sustainable knowledge-based organization which is described as *a complex and adaptive economic entity in which managers are oriented towards achieving multiple objectives (knowledge, economic, environmental and social) by planning on short, medium and long term, adapting to the economic environment challenges in a timely manner, and by adopting an ethic attitude towards all the stakeholders* (Leon, 2013a, 2018a).

In order to select the case study units, a documentary study is employed. According to the Chamber of Commerce, there are 49 potentials sustainable knowledge-based organizations in Iasi. Further, the annual informs of each of these companies is analyzed in order to determine if they meet all the required conditions; the documentary study concentrates on the following criteria: (i) establishing multiple objectives (economic, social, environmental, etc.); (ii) planning on short, medium and long term; (iii) developing an open organizational culture; (iv) investing in human resources; (v) collaborating with other firms; and (vi) reduced number of first-line and middle managers (Leon, 2013b, 2018a). After applying these selection criteria, the research population was reduced to 7 companies.

Table 4. The cornerstone of a managerial early warning system

Factors	Artificial neural network layer	Code
Inflation	Input	F1
Legal system efficiency	Input	F2
Interest rate	Hidden	F3
Foreign direct investment	Hidden	F4
Unemployment	Hidden	F5
Corruption	Hidden	F6
Market deregulation	Hidden	F7
Economic growth	Hidden	F8
Fiscal pressure	Hidden	F9
Bureaucracy	Hidden	F10
Population distribution by age and education	Hidden	F11
Industry atomization	Hidden	F12
Investments in education and research, development and innovation	Hidden	F13
Entrance barriers	Hidden	F14
Employees' professional development	Hidden	F15
Minimum wage	Hidden	F16
Innovations' growth rate	Hidden	F17
Market size	Hidden	F18
Human resources expenses	Hidden	F19
Quality – price ratio	Hidden	F20
Market share	Hidden	F21
Sales variation	Hidden	F22
Customers' satisfaction	Hidden	F23
Dependency of certain clients	Hidden	F24
Variable expenses	Hidden	F25
Revenues	Hidden	F26
Total expenses	Hidden	F27
Profit	Output	F28

Source: (Leon, 2018b)

Further, following Leon (2018b) approach, a multi-stage process is developed, where the outputs of one serve as inputs for the next one. First of all, the external consultant reunites with the person(s) encharged with developing the company's strategy. At this stage, the following variables are considered: (i) the number of persons involved; (ii) the number of departments involved in the process; (iii) CEO's impact on establishing the strategic factors; and (iv) the share of factors that belong to the already validated structure of the managerial early warning system, designed for sustainable knowledge-based organizations. The third variable is codified as a dummy variable where "1" signifies that the CEO decides which factors should be taken into consideration and the others (if any) align to CEO's opinion, and "0" reflects that the list including the strategic factors is the result of a debate. For measuring the last variable, the structure proposed by Leon (2013b) is used as a starting point since it proves that a managerial early warning system should include at least 28 factors (Table 4), describing various events from the micro- and macro-environment.

Table 5. Managers' involvement in strategic planning

Company	Size	No. of persons involved	No. of departments involved	CEO's impact	Share of common factors (%)
1	SME	3	3	1	100.00
2	Large	7	5	0	71.43
3	SME	3	2	1	53.57
4	SME	2	2	0	96.43
5	Large	2	1	0	67.86
6	Large	5	5	1	82.14
7	Large	9	9	1	100.00

Source: (Leon, 2018b)

After choosing the strategic factors that should be taken into consideration, data regarding their evolution are collected from internal and external sources and included in a multi-layer artificial neural network, based on the back-propagation principle. The network is trained using a learning rate of 0.7, a momentum of 0.8 and a target error of 0.01. Further, the artificial neural network is used for forecasting the company's profitability for the next three years.

Once the forecasted values are obtained, the relationships established among the company's size, managers' influence and system's reliability are tested using structural equation modeling, especially partial least square technique (PLS-SEM). This is recommended whenever: (i) the sample size is small; (ii) the research is exploratory; (iii) the predictive accuracy is paramount; and (iv) a correct model specification cannot be provided (Gatautis, Vaiciukynaite, & Tarute, 2019; Shmueli et al., 2019; Wong, 2013).

MAIN RESULTS

According to data presented in Table 5, strategic planning and development are treated as a collective action in both types of companies, SME and large firms; thus, in each organization, more than 2 people are involved in deciding the strategic factors from the micro- and macro-environment. Apparently, all the analyzed firms try to avoid having a limited perspective upon their future and the factors that may influence it; therefore, various people from different departments are involved in strategic planning.

Nevertheless, there is an exception; in a large company from the textile industry, the company's future is decided by two persons who work in the Strategic Management department. The activities are organized based on a matrix organizational chart and the manager and vice-manager of the department are scanning the environment, identifying the weak signals, building scenarios, finding potential solutions, and establishing the most appropriate strategy. Although their analysis is based on the reports delivered by other departments and the CEO is not actively involved in the process, they do not debate; they are more likely to complement each other than to oppose one another.

Table 6. The reliability of the managerial early warning system

Company	Learning cycles	Probability	Average error
1	732	95.00	0.00323
2	3176	92.30	0.00429
3	4174	86.50	0.00736
4	111	95.00	0.00418
5	3245	89.45	0.00672
6	3275	93.50	0.00451
7	1786	97.40	0.00372

Source: (Leon, 2018b)

The situation is different in SMEs where the CEO is practically the one who decides what is important and what is not. For example, in one of the analyzed SMEs, from the consulting services industry, the strategic factors and the relationships established among them were discussed with the management team in a reunion that lasted more than 2 hours. Four persons attended the reunion, namely: the external consultant, the CEO, and two members of the administrative department (the manager of the administrative department, and the human resources specialist), and the discussions concentrated on determining the elements that may influence firm's profitability, based on a "cause-effect" approach. During the reunion, the managers focused mainly on the factors from the internal environment and neglected the influence of the external factors. As the CEO stated right from the beginning:

We are protected from what happens outside … we are too small to be affected by the macro-economic events and we are protected from the national crises since all our contracts are negotiated in euro. Besides, our success depends on our employees' capacity to work on various projects at the same time and satisfying customers' expectations.

For almost 2 hours, the other two participants were eager to support the CEO's opinion. As a consequence, several factors from the standard version were removed (almost 50%) and other elements were proposed; however, most of the factors that were removed described elements from the external environment while most of the ones that were proposed belonged to the internal environment.

Synthesizing, at the end of each reunion that the external consultant had with the management team, the structure of the managerial early warning system is developed. Then, data regarding factors evolution during 1998 – 2015 are collected from internal and external sources. Information upon the external factors is retrieved from Eurostat, National Institute of Statistics, World Bank and OECD databases while data regarding the evolution of the internal factors are collected from the annual reports and confidential internal documents, such as marketing studies, employees' evaluation, etc.

Further, the information is included in an artificial neural network, designed using Alyuda NeuroIntelligence®, in order to forecast the company's profitability during 2016 – 2018 and to identify the potential weak signals. The system's reliability (Table 6) is reflected by the learning cycles, the probability of obtaining the forecasted values and the average error. The first one brings forward how fast does the learning occur; in this case, the output values are computed and compared with the correct answers until the value of the error function is reduced significantly. In other words, when the number of learning cycles is higher, it means that it takes longer for the managerial early warning system to identify the patterns.

Table 7. Convergent validity analysis

Variable	Item	Cronbach's Alpha	CR	AVE
Managers' influence	No. of persons involved No. of departments involved CEO's impact Share of common factors	0.736	0.825	0.561
Managerial early warning system reliability	Learning cycles Probability Average error	0.785	0.875	0.701
Company size	Company size	1.000	1.000	1.000

Source: (Leon, 2018b)

As it can be observed from Table 7, the managerial early warning system developed for Company number 3 registered the highest number of learning cycles (4174), almost 40 times higher than Company number 1, and the lowest confidence interval; thus, after 4174 learning cycles, the forecasted results provided by the managerial early warning system can be guaranteed with an 86.50% probability. On the other hand, the best situation encountered is Company number 1; this time, after 111 learning cycles, the forecasted results can be guaranteed with a 95.00% probability.

Once all the variables of the model's constructs (company's size, managers' influence, and the reliability of the managerial early warning system) are measured, the relationships established among them are tested using the PLS-SEM technique. In line with Hair, Black, and Babin (2012), convergent validity is used for ensuring the correlation between formative and reflective, theoretical and empirical models. Furthermore, the reflective model's validity is highlighted by the convergent and discriminant validity. Thus, the proposed model is valid since Cronbach's Alpha and the composite reliability (CR) are higher than 0.7, and the average variance extracted (AVE) is higher than 0.5 (Table 7). The former proves the internal consistency of the analyzed constructs while the latter emphasizes that the variance explained by the analyzed indicators exceeds the variance generated by the error.

Last but not least, as it can be remarked in Figure 1, the reliability of the managerial early warning system is influenced by both the company's size and managers' influence. In fact, 78.10% of the variability of the managerial early warning system reliability can be explained by managers' influence and company size while 13.30% of managers' influence is positively correlated with the company's size.

Figure 1. The relationships established among the company's size, managers' influence and the reliability of the managerial early warning system

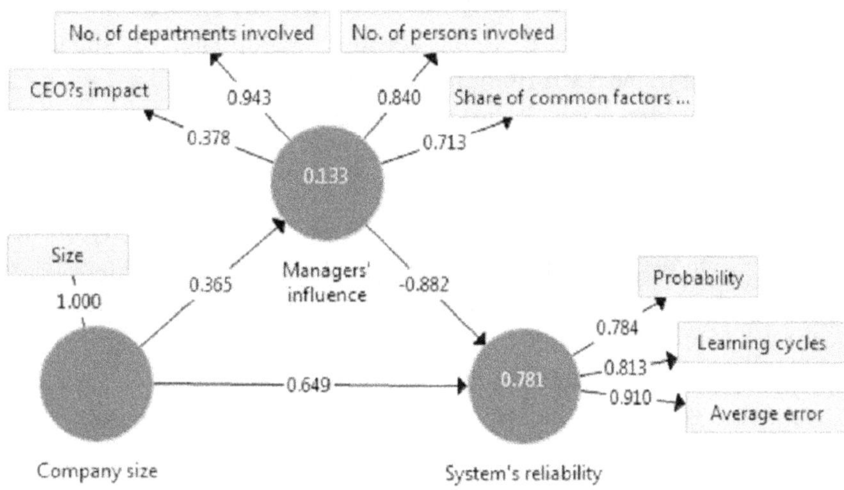

When analyzing the relationships established among the company's size, managers' influence and the reliability of the managerial early warning system, the following elements should be taken into consideration:

- there is a weak positive correlation between company's size and managers' influence ($\beta = 0.365$; $p < 0.05$); therefore, if the company size increases by one standard deviation from its mean, managers' influence would be expected to increase by 0.365 its own standard deviation from its own meanwhile all the other constructs remain constant. In other words, the larger the company gets, the powerful managers' influence becomes.
- there is a strong positive correlation between company's size and the reliability of the managerial early warning system ($\beta = 0.649$; $p < 0.05$); therefore, if the company size increases by one standard deviation from its mean, the reliability of the managerial early warning system would be expected to increase by 0.649 its own standard deviation from its own meanwhile all the other constructs remain constant. Therefore, the larger the company gets, the more reliable the managerial early warning system becomes. As the firm grows, managers' perspective enlarges; they are forced to analyze more elements in order to ensure the company's sustainability. Therefore, various factors are included in the structure of the managerial early warning system which becomes more reliable; it manages to better reflect what is happening inside and outside the organizational boundaries.
- there is a strong negative correlation between managers' influence and the reliability of the managerial early warning system ($\beta = -0.882$; $p < 0.05$); therefore, if managers' influence increases by one standard deviation from its mean, the reliability of the managerial early warning system would be expected to decrease by 0.882 its own standard deviation from its own meanwhile all the other

constructs remain constant. As mentioned before, when it comes to making decisions, managers tend to depart from rationality and to adopt a political behavior. In other words, if managers' influence increases so does their thirst for power and their desire to control the environment. Due to these, they will be tempted to modify the structure of the managerial early warning system by including only those factors that they consider to be appropriate. The situation will be similar to the one encountered in the SME from the consulting services industry where almost 50% of the managerial early warning system's structure was radically changed. As a consequence, the reliability of the managerial early warning system will decrease and the future strategy will be defined based on inappropriate results.

- the company's size has a direct and indirect influence on the reliability of the managerial early warning system. On the one hand, as the firm gets larger, the influence of the management team becomes more powerful; as mentioned previously, as the influence of the management team increases, the reliability of the managerial early warning system decreases. However, the company's size also has a positive impact on the reliability of the managerial early warning system; in other words, as the firm gets larger, the managerial early warning system becomes more reliable.

CONCLUSION AND FUTURE RESEARCH DIRECTIONS

The analysis focuses on 7 Romanian sustainable knowledge-based organizations and brings forward that managers tend to influence the results provided by a managerial early warning system based on artificial neural network, voluntarily and involuntarily. On the one hand, they are the ones who consciously decide which departments and persons are involved in establishing the structure of the managerial early warning system. On the other hand, they unconsciously influence the structure of the managerial early warning system through the authority they exercise during the managerial debate. Thus, it was emphasized that 78.10% of the variability of the managerial early warning system reliability can be explained by managers' influence and the company's size; the former is negatively correlated with the system's reliability while the latter is positively correlated with system's reliability.

These findings have both theoretical and practical implications. On the one hand, they extend the literature from the strategic management field by emphasizing how CEOs may influence the process of strategic planning even when an artificial neural network is used for identifying the future weak signals. On the other hand, they offer a better understanding of how managers may influence, voluntarily and involuntarily, strategic planning and development.

REFERENCES

Abhari, K., Davidson, E., & Xiao, B. (2019). Collaborative innovation in the sharing economy. *Internet Research, 29*(5), 1014–1039. doi:10.1108/INTR-03-2018-0129

Anderson, V. (1991). *Alternative Economic Indicators*. Routledge.

Ariansen, P. (1999). Sustainability, morality and future generations. In W. M. Lafferty & O. Langhelle (Eds.), *Towards Sustainable Development and the Conditions of Sustainability* (pp. 84–96). McMillian. doi:10.1057/9780230378797_5

Armstrong, M. (2006). Competition in two-sided markets. *The RAND Journal of Economics*, *37*(3), 668–691. doi:10.1111/j.1756-2171.2006.tb00037.x

Azouzi, M., & Jarboui, A. (2013). CEO emotional intelligence and board of directors' efficiency. *Corporate Governance*, *13*(4), 365–383. doi:10.1108/CG-10-2011-0081

Bansal, P. (2005). Evolving sustainability: A longitudinal study of corporate sustainable development. *Strategic Management Journal*, *26*(3), 197–218. doi:10.1002mj.441

Barkemeyer, R., Holt, D., Preuss, L., & Tsang, S. (2011). What Happened to the 'Development' in Sustainable Development? Business Guidelines Two Decades after Brundtland. *Sustainable Development*. Retrieved on August 15, 2011 from http://onlinelibrary.wiley.com.ux4ll8xu6v.useaccesscontrol.com/doi /10.1002/sd.521/pdf

Belk, R. (2014). You are what you can access: Sharing and collaborative consumption online. *Journal of Business Research*, *67*(8), 1595–1600. doi:10.1016/j.jbusres.2013.10.001

Bertoncel, T., Erenda, I., Pejić Bach, M., Roblek, V., & Meško, M. (2018). A Managerial Early Warning System at a Smart Factory: An Intuitive Decision-making Perspective. *Systems Research and Behavioral Science*, *35*(4), 406–416. doi:10.1002res.2542

Bisson, C., & Diner, O. Y. (2017). Strategic Early Warning System for the French milk market: A graph theoretical approach to foresee volatility. *Futures*, *87*, 10–23. doi:10.1016/j.futures.2017.01.004

Black, A. (2004). *The quest for sustainable, healthy communities*. Paper presented at the Effective Sustainability Education Conference, NSW Council on Environmental Education, UNSW, Sydney.

Blum-Kusterer, M., & Husain, S. S. (2001). Innovation and corporate sustainability: An investigation into the process of change in the pharmaceutical industry. *Business Strategy and the Environment*, *10*(5), 300–316. doi:10.1002/bse.300

Böcker, L., & Meelen, T. (2017). Sharing for people, planet or profit? Analysing motivations for intended sharing economy participation. *Environmental Innovation and Societal Transitions*, *23*, 28–39. doi:10.1016/j.eist.2016.09.004

Boonnnan, T. M., Jacobs, J. P. A. M., Kuper, G. H., & Romero, A. (2019). Early Warning Systems for Currency Crises with Real-Time Data. *Open Economies Review*, *30*(4), 813–835. doi:10.100711079-019-09530-0

Bos-Brouwers, H. E. J. (2010). Corporate Sustainability and Innovation in SMEs: Evidence of Themes and Activities in Practice. *Business Strategy and the Environment*, *19*(7), 417–435. doi:10.1002/bse.652

Botsman, R., & Rogers, R. (2011). *What's mine is yours: How collaborative consumption is changing the way we live*. Collins.

Braat, L. (1991). The Predictive Meaning of Sustainability Indicators. In O. Kuik & H. Verbruggen (Eds.), *Search of Indicators of Sustainable Development* (pp. 57–70). Kluwer Academic Publishers. doi:10.1007/978-94-011-3246-6_6

Bridges, E. (2018). Executive ethical decisions initiating organizational culture and values. *Journal of Service Theory and Practice*, *28*(5), 576–608. doi:10.1108/JSTP-07-2017-0106

Cadez, S., & Guilding, C. (2008). An exploratory investigation of an integrated contingency model of strategic management accounting. *Accounting, Organizations and Society*, *33*(7-8), 836–863. doi:10.1016/j.aos.2008.01.003

Cândea, D. (2006). De la dezvoltarea durabilă la întreprinderea sustenabilă. *Întreprinderea sustenabilă*, *1*, iii-vi.

Cao, Y., Chen, X., Wu, D. D., & Mao, M. (2011). Early warning of enterprise decline in a life cycle using neural networks and rough set theory. *Expert Systems with Applications*, *38*(6), 6424–6429. doi:10.1016/j.eswa.2010.09.138

Curşeu, P. L., Schruijer, S. G. L., & Fodor, O. C. (2016). The influences of knowledge loss and knowledge retention mechanisms on the absorptive capacity and performance of a MIS department. *Management Decision*, *54*(7), 1757–1787. doi:10.1108/MD-02-2016-0117

Daily, G. C., & Walker, B. H. (2000). Seeking the great transition. *Nature*, *403*(6767), 243–245. doi:10.1038/35002194 PMID:10659827

Davlembayeva, D., Papagiannidis, S., & Alamanos, E. (2019). Mapping the economics, social and technological attributes of the sharing economy. *Information Technology & People*, ITP-02-2018-0085. Advance online publication. doi:10.1108/ITP-02-2018-0085

Day, G. S., & Schoemaker, P. J. H. (2005). Scanning the Periphery. *Harvard Business Review*, *83*(11), 135–150. PMID:16299966

Dekker, M. M., Panja, D., Dijkstra, H. A., & Dekker, S. C. (2019). Predicting transitions across macroscopic states for railway systems. *PLoS One*, *14*(6), e0217710. doi:10.1371/journal.pone.0217710 PMID:31170230

Dikmen, I., Talat Birgonul, M., Ozorhon, B., & Egilmezer Sapci, N. (2010). Using analytic network process to assess business failure risks of construction firms. *Engineering, Construction, and Architectural Management*, *17*(4), 369–386. doi:10.1108/09699981011056574

Dunphy, D., Griffiths, A., & Benn, S. (2003). *Organizational Change for Corporate Sustainability*. Routledge.

Dyllick, T., & Hockerts, K. (2002). Beyond the business case for corporate sustainability. *Business Strategy and the Environment*, *11*(2), 130–141. doi:10.1002/bse.323

Eisenbart, B., Garbuio, M., Mascia, D., & Morandi, F. (2016). Does scheduling matter? When unscheduled decision making results in more effective meetings. *Journal of Strategy and Management*, *9*(1), 15–38. doi:10.1108/JSMA-03-2014-0017

Eisenmann, T., Parker, G., & van Alstyne, M. W. (2006). Strategies for two-sided markets. *Harvard Business Review*, *84*(10), 92–101.

Fan, Y., Xia, M., Zhang, Y., & Chen, Y. (2019). The influence of social embeddedness on organizational legitimacy and the sustainability of the globalization of the sharing economic platform: Evidence from Uber China. *Resources, Conservation and Recycling*, *151*, 104490. doi:10.1016/j.resconrec.2019.104490

Fiksel, J. (2006). Sustainability and resilience: toward a system approach. *Sustainability: Science. Practice & Police*, *2*, 14–21.

Frenken, K., & Schor, J. (2017). Putting the sharing economy into perspective. *Environmental Innovation and Societal Transitions*, *23*, 3–10. doi:10.1016/j.eist.2017.01.003

García Martín, J. C., & Herrero, B. (2018). Boards of directors: Composition and effects on the performance of the firm. *Economic Research-Ekonomska Istraživanja*, *31*(1), 1015–1041. doi:10.1080/1331677X.2018.1436454

Gatautis, R., Vaiciukynaite, E., & Tarute, A. (2019). Impact of business model innovations on SME's innovativeness and performance. *Baltic Journal of Management*, *14*(4), 521–539. doi:10.1108/BJM-01-2018-0035

Genc, E., Duffie, N., & Reinhart, G. (2014). Event-based supply chain early warning system for an adaptive production control. *Procedia CIRP*, *19*, 39–44. doi:10.1016/j.procir.2014.04.076

Goyal, R., Kakabadse, N., & Kakabadse, A. (2019). Improving corporate governance with functional diversity on FTSE 350 boards: Directors' perspective. *Journal of Capital Markets Studies*, *3*(2), 113–136. doi:10.1108/JCMS-09-2019-0044

Habibi, M. R., Davidson, A., & Laroche, M. (2017). What managers should know about the sharing economy? *Business Horizons*, *60*(1), 113–121. doi:10.1016/j.bushor.2016.09.007

Hahn, T., Figge, F., Pinkse, J., & Preuss, L. (2010). Trade-Offs in Corporate Sustainability: You can't Have Your Cake and Eat It. *Business Strategy and the Environment*, *19*(4), 217–229. doi:10.1002/bse.674

Hair, J. F. Jr, Black, W. C., & Babin, B. J. (2012). *Multivariate data analysis*. Prentice Hall.

Haji-Kazemi, S., & Andersen, B. (2013). Application of performance measurement as an early warning system. *International Journal of Managing Projects in Business*, *6*(4), 714–738. doi:10.1108/IJMPB-04-2012-0015

Hautala, J. (2011). Cognitive proximity in international research groups. *Journal of Knowledge Management*, *15*(4), 601–624. doi:10.1108/13673271111151983

Hernandez Ticono, M., Holmes, P., & Wilson, N. (2018). Polytomous response financial distress models: The role of accounting, market and macroeconomic variables. *International Review of Financial Analysis*, *59*, 276–289. doi:10.1016/j.irfa.2018.03.017

Hollenbeck, J. R., Beersma, B., & Schouten, M. E. (2012). Beyond team types and taxonomies: A dimensional scaling conceptualization for team description. *Academy of Management Review*, *37*(1), 82–106. doi:10.5465/amr.2010.0181

Holliday, C. O. J., Schmidheiny, S., & Watts, S. P. (2002). *Walking the Talk: The Business Case for Sustainable Development*. World Business Council for Sustainable Development.

Hong, J. H., Kim, B. C., & Park, K. S. (2019). Optimal risk management for the sharing economy with stranger danger and service quality. *European Journal of Operational Research*, *279*(3), 1024–1035. doi:10.1016/j.ejor.2019.06.020

Hu, X., & Liu, D. (2019). The research into screening crisis early warning indicators of supply chain quality based on fuzzy inference system. *Journal of Intelligent & Fuzzy Systems*, *36*(2), 935–942. doi:10.3233/JIFS-169870

Huang, J., Wang, H., & Kochenberger, G. (2017). Distressed Chinese firm prediction with discretized data. *Management Decision*, *55*(5), 786–807. doi:10.1108/MD-08-2016-0546

Jennings, P. D., & Zandbergen, P. A. (1995). Ecologically sustainable organizations: An institutional approach. *Academy of Management Review*, *20*(4), 1015–1052. doi:10.5465/amr.1995.9512280034

Ketola, T. (2010). Five Leaps to Corporate Sustainability through a Corporate Responsibility Portfolio Matrix. *Corporate Social Responsibility and Environmental Management*, *17*(6), 320–336. doi:10.1002/csr.219

Kipkirong Tarus, D., & Aime, F. (2014). Board demographic diversity, firm performance and strategic change: A test of moderation. *Management Research Review*, *37*(12), 1110–1136. doi:10.1108/MRR-03-2013-0056

Kira, M., & van Eijnatten, F. M. (2008). Socially Sustainable Work Organizations: A Chaordic System Approach. *Systems Research and Behavioral Science*, *25*(6), 743–756. doi:10.1002res.896

Kotler, P., & Caslione, J. A. (2009). *Chaotics: The Business of Managing and Marketing in the Age of Turbulence*. AMACOM.

Laitinen, E. K., & Chong, H. G. (1999). Early warning system for crisis in SMEs: Preliminary evidence from Finland and the UK. *Journal of Small Business and Enterprise Development*, *6*(1), 89–102. doi:10.1108/EUM0000000006665

Landrum, N. E., & Ohsowski, B. (2018). Identifying Worldviews on Corporate Sustainability: A Content Analysis of Corporate Sustainability Reports. *Business Strategy and the Environment*, *27*(1), 128–151. doi:10.1002/bse.1989

Lee, K.-H., & Kim, D. (2019). A peer-to-peer (P2P) platform business model: The case of Airbnb. *Service Business*, *13*(4), 647–669. doi:10.100711628-019-00399-0

Leon, R. D. (2013a). Sustainable knowledge based organization from an international perspective. *International Journal of Management Science and Information Technology*, *10*, 166–181.

Leon, R. D. (2013b). A managerial early warning system for the sustainable knowledge based organization. *Ovidius University Annals. Economic Sciences Series*, *13*(1), 842–847.

Leon, R. D. (2018a). The sustainable knowledge based organizations – definitions and characteristics. *Environmental Engineering and Management Journal*, *17*(6), 1425–1437. doi:10.30638/eemj.2018.141

Leon, R. D. (2018b). A Managerial Early Warning System: From an Abstract to a Subjective Approach. In R. D. Leon (Ed.), *Managerial Strategies for Business Sustainability during Turbulent Times* (pp. 100–121). Information Science Publishing., doi:10.4018/978-1-5225-2716-9.ch006

Leon, R. D., Rodriguez-Rodriguez, R., Gomez-Gasquet, P., & Mula, J. (2017). Social network analysis: A tool for evaluating and predicting future knowledge flows from an insurance organization. *Technological Forecasting and Social Change*, *114*, 103–118. doi:10.1016/j.techfore.2016.07.032

Li, C. P., Qin, J. X., Li, J. J., & Hou, Q. (2016). The accident early warning system for iron and steel enterprises based on combination weighting and Grey Prediction Model GM (1,1). *Safety Science*, *89*, 19–27. doi:10.1016/j.ssci.2016.05.015

Li, Q., Wei, F., & Zhou, S. (2017). Early warning systems for multi-variety and small batch manufacturing based on active learning. *Journal of Intelligent & Fuzzy Systems*, *33*(5), 2945–2952. doi:10.3233/JIFS-169345

Li, S., & Davies, B. J. (2001). GloStra – a hybrid system for developing global strategy and associated Internet strategy. *Industrial Management & Data Systems*, *101*(3), 132–140. doi:10.1108/02635570110386643

Li, Y., Ding, R., Cui, L., Lei, Z., & Mou, J. (2019). The impact of sharing economy practices on sustainability performance in the Chinese construction industry. *Resources, Conservation and Recycling*, *150*, 104409. doi:10.1016/j.resconrec.2019.104409

Li, Y. Z., Xia, J. B., Li, C. G., & Zheng, M. Y. (2015). Construction of an Early-Warning System for Vegetable Prices Based on Index Contribution Analysis. *Sustainability*, *7*(4), 3823–3837. doi:10.3390u7043823

Lieu, P. T., Lin, C. W., & Yu, H. F. (2008). Financial early-warning models on cross-holding groups. *Industrial Management & Data Systems*, *108*(8), 1060–1080. doi:10.1108/02635570810904613

Lozano, R. (2008). Developing collaborative and sustainable organizations. *Journal of Cleaner Production*, *16*(4), 499–509. doi:10.1016/j.jclepro.2007.01.002

Maddox, J. (2000). Positioning the goalposts. *Nature*, *403*(6766), 139–140. doi:10.1038/35003065 PMID:10646578

Mantymaki, M., Baiyere, A., & Islam, A. K. M. N. (2019). Digital platforms and the changing nature of physical work: Insights from ride-hailing. *International Journal of Information Management*, *49*, 452–460. doi:10.1016/j.ijinfomgt.2019.08.007

Mariotto, F. L., Zanni, P. P., & Marcondes de Moraes, G. H. S. (2014). What is the use of a single-case study in management research? *Revista de Administração de Empresas*, *54*(4), 358–369. doi:10.1590/S0034-759020140402

Mishra, J., Chiwenga, K., & Ali, K. (2019). Collaboration as an enabler for circular economy: A case study of a developing country. *Management Decision*, MD-10-2018-1111. Advance online publication. doi:10.1108/MD-10-2018-1111

Mojzisch, A., Grouneva, L., & Schultz-Hardt, S. (2010). Biased evaluation of information during discussion: Disentangling the effects of preference consistency, social validation, and ownership of information. *European Journal of Social Psychology*, *40*(6), 946–956. doi:10.1002/ejsp.660

Ng, E. S., & Burke, R. J. (2010). Predictor of Business Student's Attitudes toward Sustainable Business Practices. *Journal of Business Ethics*, *95*(4), 603–615. doi:10.100710551-010-0442-0

Niemimaa, M., Järveläinen, J., Heikkilä, M., & Heikkilä, J. (2019). Business continuity of business models: Evaluating the resilience of business models for contingencies. *International Journal of Information Management*, *49*, 208–216. doi:10.1016/j.ijinfomgt.2019.04.010

O'Riordan, T. (1976). *Environmentalism*. Pion Limited.

Ogbeide, G., & Harrington, R. (2011). The relationship among participative management style, strategy implementation success, and financial performance in the foodservice industry. *International Journal of Contemporary Hospitality Management*, *23*(6), 719–738. doi:10.1108/09596111111153448

Ohatka, F., & Fukazawa, Y. (2009). Managing risks symptom: A method to identify major risks of serious problem projects in SI environment using cyclic causal model. *Project Management Journal*, *41*(1), 51–60. doi:10.1002/pmj.20144

Olsson, O., Aronsson, H., & Sandberg, E. (2017). Middle management involvement in handling variable patient flows. *Management Research Review*, *40*(9), 1007–1024. doi:10.1108/MRR-05-2016-0114

Parayitam, S., & Papenhausen, C. (2016). Agreement-seeking behavior, trust, and cognitive diversity in strategic decision making teams: Process conflict as a moderator. *Journal of Advances in Management Research*, *13*(3), 292–315. doi:10.1108/JAMR-10-2015-0072

Parker, G., & van Alstyne, M. W. (2005). Two-sided network effects: A theory of information product design. *Management Science*, *51*(10), 1494–1504. doi:10.1287/mnsc.1050.0400

Pearce, D., Markandya, A., & Barbier, E. B. (1989). *Blueprint for a Green Economy*. Earthscan.

Philip, T., & Schwabe, G. (2018). Understanding early warning signs of failure in offshore-outsourced software projects at team level. *Journal of Global Operations and Strategic Sourcing*, *11*(3), 337–356. doi:10.1108/JGOSS-12-2017-0057

Raes, A. M. L., Heijltjes, M. G., Glunk, U., & Roe, R. A. (2011). The interface of the top management team and middle managers: A process model. *Academy of Management Review*, *36*(1), 192–126. doi:10.5465/amr.2009.0088

Rashid, A. (2018). Board independence and firm performance: Evidence from Bangladesh. *Future Business Journal*, *4*(1), 34–49. doi:10.1016/j.fbj.2017.11.003

Richardson, B. J. (2009). Keeping Ethical Investment Ethical: Regulatory Issues for Investing for Sustainability. *Journal of Business Ethics*, *87*(4), 555–572. doi:10.100710551-008-9958-y

Ringland, G. (2010). The role of scenarios in strategic foresight. *Technological Forecasting and Social Change*, *77*(9), 1493–1498. doi:10.1016/j.techfore.2010.06.010

Salzano, E., Garcia Agreda, A., Di Carluccio, A., & Fabbrocino, G. (2009). Risk assessment and early warning systems for industrial facilities in seismic zones. *Reliability Engineering & System Safety*, *94*(10), 1577–1584. doi:10.1016/j.ress.2009.02.023

Saunila, M., Nasiri, M., Ukko, J., & Rantala, T. (2019). Smart technologies and corporate sustainability: The mediation effect of corporate sustainability strategy. *Computers in Industry*, *108*, 178–185. doi:10.1016/j.compind.2019.03.003

Schwartz, M. S., & Carroll, A. B. (2008). Integrating and Unifying Competing and Complementary Frameworks: The Search for a Common core in the Business and Society Field. *Business & Society*, *47*(2), 148–186. doi:10.1177/0007650306297942

Schwarz, J. O. (2005). Pitfalls in implementing a strategic early warning system. *Foresight*, *7*(4), 22–30. doi:10.1108/14636680510611813

Shmueli, G., Sarstedt, M., Hair, J. F., Cheah, J. H., Ting, H., Vaithilingam, S., & Ringle, C. M. (2019). Predictive model assessment in PLS-SEM: Guidelines for using PLSpredict. *European Journal of Marketing*, *53*(11), 2322–2347. doi:10.1108/EJM-02-2019-0189

Sölvell, I. (2018). Managers' silent whisper innovation involvement and role-modeling in service firms. *European Journal of Innovation Management*, *21*(1), 2–19. doi:10.1108/EJIM-02-2017-0020

Sthapit, E. (2019). My bad for wanting to try something unique: Sources of value co-destruction in the Airbnb context. *Current Issues in Tourism*, *22*(20), 2462–2465. doi:10.1080/13683500.2018.1525340

Stofberg, N., & Bridoux, F. (2019). Consumers' choice among peer-to-peer sharing platforms: The other side of the coin. *Psychology and Marketing*, *36*(12), 1176–1195. doi:10.1002/mar.21265

Tan, C., & Dihardjo, H. (2001). A study of using artificial neural networks to develop an early warning predictor for credit union financial distress with comparison to the probit model. *Managerial Finance*, *27*(4), 56–77. doi:10.1108/03074350110767141

Torjman, S. (2000). *The social dimension of sustainable development*. Caledon Institute of Social Policy.

Tsai, B. H. (2013). An Early Warning System of Financial Distress Using Multinomial Logit Models and a Bootstrapping Approach. *Emerging Markets Finance & Trade*, *49*(2), 43–69. doi:10.2753/REE1540-496X4902S203

Tuwey, J., & Tarus, D. (2016). Does CEO power moderate the relationship between board leadership and strategy involvement in private firms? Evidence from Kenya. *Corporate Governance*, *16*(5), 906–922. doi:10.1108/CG-01-2016-0010

Vafaei, N., Ribeiro, R. A., & Camarinha-Matos, L. M. (2019). Fuzzy Early Warning Systems for Condition Based Maintenance. *Computers & Industrial Engineering*, *128*, 736–746. doi:10.1016/j.cie.2018.12.056

Vaida, A., & Cândea, D. (2010). Model pentru internalizarea sustenabilităţii în organizaţii. *Întreprinderea sustenabilă, 5*, 1-62.

Van der Walt, N., Ingley, C., Shergill, G., & Townsend, A. (2006). Board configuration: Are diverse boards better boards? *Corporate Governance*, *6*(2), 129–147. doi:10.1108/14720700610655141

Vansteenkiste, M., Niemiec, C. P., & Soenens, B. (2010). The development of the five mini-theories of self-determination theory: an historical overview, emerging trends, and future directions. In T. C. Urdan & S. A. Karabenick (Eds.), *The decade ahead: theoretical perspectives on motivation and achievement* (Vol. 16, pp. 105–165). Emerald Group Publishing., doi:10.1108/S0749-7423(2010)000016A007

Williams, T., Klakegg, O. J., Walker, D. H. T., Andersen, B., & Magnussen, O. M. (2012). Identifying and acting on early warning signs in complex projects. *Project Management Journal*, *43*(2), 37–53. doi:10.1002/pmj.21259

Wong, K. K.-K. (2013). Partial Least Squares Structural Equation Modeling (PLS-SEM) Techniques Using SmartPLS. *Marketing Bulletin*, *24*, 1–32.

Yang, C. (2012). Research on internet public opinion detection system based on domain ontology. In F. L. Wang, J. Lei, Z. Gong, & X. Luo (Eds.), *WISM'12 Proceedings of the 2012 international conference on Web Information Systems and Mining* (pp. 105-110). Berlin: Springer-Verlag. 10.1007/978-3-642-33469-6_15

Yang, Y., Bi, G. B., & Liu, L. D. (2020). Profit allocation in investment-based crowdfunding with investors of dynamic entry times. *European Journal of Operational Research*, *280*(1), 323–337. doi:10.1016/j.ejor.2019.07.016

Yin, R. K. (2014). *Case Study Research Design and Methods*. Sage.

Zheng, G., Zhu, N., Tim, Z., Chen, Y., & Sun, B. (2012). Application of a trapezoidal fuzzy AHP method for work safety evaluation and early warning rating of hot and humid environments. *Safety Science*, *50*(2), 228–239. doi:10.1016/j.ssci.2011.08.042

KEY TERMS AND DEFINITIONS

Artificial Neural Network: An ICT tool that imitates the real environment, providing various estimations and emphasizing how the system could react under certain circumstances.

Inappropriate Experience: The use of standard rules in various situations with the hope that they will always provide the same result. It goes hand in hand with individuals' resistance to change.

Inappropriate Prejudgments: A belief that one's assumption is the most appropriate one and all the other ideas that may contradict it should be ignored. It supports managerial myopia.

Managerial Early Warning System: An organizational tool based on data collection, analysis, and communication that supports the anticipated identification of weak signals and the development of the future business strategy. It involves analyzing the micro- and macro-environment, diagnosing the situation and determining the best way to react to the identified challenges.

Sustainability: The capacity of a system to develop various activities on short and long term without negatively influencing the systems with which it is connected.

Sustainable Knowledge-Based Organization: A complex and adaptive economic entity in which managers are oriented towards achieving multiple objectives (knowledge, economic, environmental and social) by planning on short, medium and long term, adapting to the economic environment challenges in timely manner, and by adopting an ethic attitude towards all the stakeholders.

Sustainable Organization: An ethic and authentic firm that is able to achieve its economic, social and environmental objectives, on short, medium, and long term through the rational use of its resources.

Weak Signal: An element from the micro- or macro-environment that comes out of the blue and forces the organization to react one way or another.

Chapter 12
The Response of Trading Volume to Borsa Istanbul Sustainability Index Inclusions and Exclusions

Ibrahim Yasar Gok
Suleyman Demirel University, Turkey

Handan Goksen
Suleyman Demirel University, Turkey

ABSTRACT

Borsa Istanbul Sustainability Index (XUSRD) was launched on November 4, 2014. Initially, there were 15 firms in the index. This number grew to 56 as of December 2019. This study aims to investigate whether the firms' inclusion in or exclusion from XUSRD affect their trading volume. Both the effects of the announcement days and the effective days of the index changes were considered, and six index events that occurred between Nov 2014 and Dec 2019 were studied. On the effective days and their subsequent days, there were no significant trading volume changes for both included and excluded firms. On the announcement days, the trading volume increased for the included firms and decreased for the excluded firms, though only the experience of the deleted firms was statistically significant. Therefore, there was an asymmetric response to additions and deletions. In addition, the index effect on the included and excluded firms was temporary, which supports the price pressure hypothesis.

INTRODUCTION

Efficient market hypothesis assumes that a firms' inclusion in an index should not affect its stock prices (Gregoriou, 2011). However, in practice, index revisions can affect the firms' stock prices and trading volumes either temporarily or permanently. Though some traditional stock indices do not change their constituents in relation to performance criteria like Egypt's EGX30 (Ahmed & Bassiouny, 2018), and

DOI: 10.4018/978-1-7998-4543-0.ch012

index changes like in S&P 500 may be considered information-free events (Clacher & Hagendorff, 2012), sustainability indices are revised in terms of firms' compliance to environment, social and governance (ESG) criteria. Hence, the events related to sustainability index may contain meaningful information (Clacher & Hagendorff, 2012). In this respect, being included in the sustainability indices would result in prominent impacts on prices and trading activity of listed firms.

There are some previous studies investigated the effect of Borsa Istanbul Sustainability Index (XUSRD) related events on firms' returns. Çıtak and Ersoy (2016) found that there was no significant difference between the returns of XUSRD firms and the control group. Gündüz (2018) showed that being included in the XUSRD did not affect the value of stocks. Temiz and Acar (2018) demonstrated that the inclusion announcements revealed limited effects on returns. By examining the effect of XUSRD inclusion announcements on Turkish banks' returns, Gök and Gökşen (2020) evidenced that while there were negative abnormal returns before the announcements, positive abnormal returns were observed following the announcements.

However, investigating the index events in the perspective of returns is one of the research questions. The other one is whether the index events affect the trading volume. In this study, it is particularly aimed to detect whether the inclusion in or exclusion from XUSRD has any significant impact on firms' trading volume. To our knowledge, this is the first study focusing on firms' trading volume changes related to XUSRD events and will fill a gap in the CSR literature.

The remaining of the study is organized as follows: Section 2 explains corporate social responsibility strategy, Section 3 reviews the literature on the effects of index revisions, Section 4 presents the data and methodology, Section 5 provides the empirical results, and last section concludes the chapter.

Corporate Social Responsibility Strategy

Corporate social responsibility (CSR) is no longer just a philanthropic endeavor but an integral part of corporate strategy (Galbreath, 2006; Lamberti & Noci, 2012). To create sustainable business models, firms need to integrate CSR into corporate strategy (Jhunjhunwala, 2014). Adopting a CSR strategy contributes the firms in many ways. For instance, a good signaling effect may be created through CSR activities, and accordingly, a reliability and reputability certification can be earned (Lin, Hung, Chou, & Lai, 2019). Firms can successfully manage corporate reputation (CR) through CSR activities by doing good and avoiding bad, and CSR practices in the perspective of avoiding bad should be implemented foremost, because stakeholder can forgive a weak CSR performance in terms of doing good (Lin-Hi & Blumberg, 2018). Hun et al. (2014) found that CSR practices positively and directly influenced the reputation and brand credibility in Korea. Similarly, Liu, Wong, Shi, Chu, and Brock (2014) suggested that CSR performance positively affected the brand preference of customers in China. By focusing on banking customers in India, Fatma, Rahman, and Khan (2015) revealed that CSR activities enhanced consumer trust, which mediates the positive link between CSR and CR as well as CSR and brand equity. In addition, employees are one of the primary stakeholders, and their needs for safety/security, distinctiveness, belongingness and meaning can be satisfied by CSR activities (Bauman & Skitka, 2012). By using data of nearly 85,000 questionnaires from 381 Brazilian firms, Barakat, Isabella, Boaventura, and Mazzon (2016) found that CSR activities revealed a good organizational image, which led to positive employee assessments. Skudiene and Auruskeviciene (2012) reported that both internal and external CSR practices were positively associated with employee motivation. Edmans (2011) demonstrated that the higher the employee satisfaction, the greater the shareholders return. CSR activities can also affect the brand credibility.

Implementing CSR in a correct and strategic way may enable firms to develop innovative approaches, which contribute to value creation (Rexhepi, Kurtishi, & Bexheti, 2013). By studying 213 firms, Bocquet, Le Bas, Mothe, and Poussing (2013) revealed that higher strategic CSR adoption was more likely associated with innovating in products and processes. This positive CSR-innovation relationship was also supported by the findings of Luo and Du (2015), who found that more new products were launched by CSR firms. Engaging in CSR activities may also contribute to decreases in the level of information asymmetry (Cui, Jo, & Na, 2018; Nguyen, Agbola, & Choi, 2019). It was also documented that international expansion can be speed up by practicing environmental CSR (Xu, Zeng, & Chen, 2018). The positive link between CSR and customers' purchase intention was revealed as well (Lee & Shin, 2010). Furthermore, increasing CSR activities may lower the debt financing cost (Ye & Zhang, 2011). In addition, corporate financial performance (CFP) can be positively affected by CSR practices (Su, Peng, Tan, & Cheung, 2016). The positive effects of CSR on CFP were identified in US firms by Peters and Mullen (2009), in Taiwanese firms especially in the long-term by Lin, Yang, and Liou (2009), in Chinese firms by Chen and Wang (2011), in Australian firms by Torugsa, O'Donohue, and Hecker (2012), in Spanish firms by Muñoz, de Pablo, and Peña (2015), in Korean firms by Oh and Park (2015), and in Nigerian firms by Uadiale and Fagbemi (2012). In a broader study, Su et al. (2016) reported that among ten emerging Asian markets, the positive CSR-CFP link was stronger in less developed countries than more developed markets. Hou, Liu, Fan, and Wei (2016) focused on East Asian firms and conducted a meta-analysis by considering more than 30,000 firms reported in 28 studies. They found that the impact of environmental CSR practices on business performance was stronger than the effect of social CSR practices. It was also noted that the effect of CSR was more pronounced on operational performance than financial performance.

On the other hand, a CSR strategy is not always perceived positively by the investors, especially because the negative relationship between CSR and CFP were documented in some previous studies. For instance, the findings of Becchetti, Di Giacomo, and Pinnacchio (2008) on US firms partially showed that CSR led the firms to move away from maximization of the shareholders wealth to targeting of multi-stakeholder wealth. Lima Crisóstomo, de Souza Freire, and Cortes de Vasconcellos (2011) found that the impacts of CSR on firm value were negative for Brazilian firms. Inoue, Kent, and Lee (2011) detected non-positive effects of CSR on CFP in US sport industry. Rutledge, Karim, Aleksanyan, and Wu (2014) reported a negative CSR and CFP link for Chinese state owned enterprises. Fiori, di Donato, and Izzo (2015) revealed that better CSR performance was associated with a decrease in stock returns for Italian firms. In the perspective of European firms, Quéré, Nouyrigat, and Baker (2018) documented that CSR ratings were inversely related to subsequent equity market performance. Besides, Usman and Amran (2015) noted that while some disclosures like human resources enhanced CFP, there was a negative relationship between environmental disclosure and CFP in Nigerian companies. Lin, Chang, and Dang (2015) documented that the industry type (environmentally sensitive or environmentally non-sensitive industries) moderated the direct effect of CSR on CFP. Moreover, CSR-CFP link can differentiate between developed and developing country firms (Wang, Dou, & Jia, 2016). Some studies, on the one hand, reported that the effects of CSR on CFP are mixed, and sustainable firms' financial performance may not significantly differ from non-sustainable ones (Gok, Ozdemir, & Unlu, 2019a).

In addition, CSR activities can be perceived differently even among employees. Wisse, van Eijbergen, Rietzschel, and Scheibe (2018) found that the positive effect of CSR was more pronounced on older employees than younger ones. Moreover, though possible innovations are provided by CSR activities, whether these innovations increase the competitiveness and create value is not a given, furthermore, even CEOs sometimes privately admit that they are not sure if the CSR projects benefit (Husted & Allen, 2007). Besides, if a firm's innovativeness capability is low, CSR practices may even negatively affect customer satisfaction, which in turn has a negative effect on market value (Luo & Bhattacharya, 2006). Also, CSR exercises may increase the firms' expenditures like donations to charities, taking environmental protection measures and providing social development programs (Javeed & Lefen, 2019). While the synergy and benefits of CSR implementation may not appear in the short term, increasing CSR expenditures may damage business performance and cause an increase in operation costs (Feng, Wang, & Huang, 2015). Besides, adopting responsive but not strategic CSR practices may even limit innovation (Bocquet et al., 2013). Also, in some sectors like restaurant, implementing CSR strategy along with internationalization may cause an increase in operational complexity, which may affect synergy, risk and performance negatively (Jung, Lee, & Dalbor, 2016). By implementing CSR, in some cases, an over-investing can occur due to the incentives of insiders like corporate managers and large blockholders, and accordingly, a conflict between insiders and outsiders may arise (Barnea & Rubin, 2010). Besides, investing in CSR activities more than the optimal level may increase the debt financing costs (Ye & Zhang, 2011). Systematic risk behavior of CSR firms may also negatively differentiate, compared to non-responsible firms (Charlo, Moya, & Muñoz, 2015). Therefore, some investors may react negatively to the CSR-related events.

Despite of positive and negative CSR perceptions among investor community, socially responsible investors do not only consider the firms' business performance in their investment decisions but also the firms' commitments to ESG criteria. They would like to invest in the firms, which are not participating in nuclear energy, mining, gambling, tobacco, alcohol, weapons and so on. Their awareness regarding gender and racial discriminations, human and labor rights violations, countering bribery and corruptions, environmental pollution, biodiversity, climate change and so on are reflected in their trading behavior. They aim to increase the goodness in the society through trading (Hudson, 2005). Since the ethical failures cause some of the biggest bankruptcies in US like Enron and WorldCom, they monitor the companies about their corporate governance practices. Because it was noted that excessive corporate social irresponsibility led tax avoidance (Hoi, Wu, & Zhang, 2013), it is expected that such actions would not be observed in CSR-oriented firms. By taking into account the listed firms in sustainability indices, socially responsible investors can easily track the firms, which demonstrate CSR practices. Nevertheless, because socially responsible investment (SRI) portfolios constitute CSR firms, their investment universe is smaller than conventional investors, hence, some studies examined whether the performances of conventional and SRI portfolios differ each other (Gök & Özdemir, 2017). One other issue regarding SRI portfolios is exploring the international portfolio diversification opportunities for international investors. Gok, Duranay, and Uzunoglu Unlu (2019b) found that international socially responsible investors may benefit by including various countries' sustainable firms into their portfolios.

Literature Review on Index Revisions

There are 'index effect' theories to explain the impacts of index additions and deletions. These theories have specific characteristics in terms of return and trading volume. One of them is price pressure hypothesis (PPH). Regarding PPH, Harris and Gurel (1986) stated that while there is perfect elasticity in the long-term demand, in the short run the demand curve is downward sloping. They expressed that the announcements of events do not convey information, and the shift in the demand is temporary. They investigated the impacts of list changes for the S&P 500 index on price and volume. It was found that while there was a significant price increase on the day of the inclusion announcements, the prices bounced back in the 2-week period. In the period of 1973-1983, the average volume on the day of the announcement was '1.89' times larger than compared to the trading volume before 8 weeks of the announcement. In the period of 1978-1983, the mean volume ratio (MVR) was '2.81' on day 1, and it decreased consistently through 5-day period and was '1.16' on day 5.

Other explanations were brought by imperfect substitutes, information content, liquidity effect and investor recognition hypotheses. The imperfect substitute hypothesis posits that stocks have a long-term downward sloping demand curve, and because of imperfect substitutability, an excess return following an index change arise, which was created by excess demand of index funds to buy added and sell deleted stocks (Chen, Noronha, & Singal, 2004). The findings of Hanaeda and Serita (2003) and Liu (2006) regarding Nikkei 225 index supported this hypothesis. Liquidity effect hypothesis claims that because the included stocks are more actively traded, the prices of these stocks permanently increase, and conversely, permanent decline in the liquidity decreases the prices of deleted stocks (Baran & King, 2012). Hegde and McDermott (2003) found that liquidity of the included stocks in S&P 500 permanently increased, which was mostly attributed to a decrease in direct transaction costs.

Information content hypothesis assumes that the inclusions to the index contain information in favor of included stocks, and this new information increases the prices (Cai, 2007). Though S&P US indices methodology clearly states that the addition to the indices does not mean any investing advice (S&P DJI, 2019), Cai (2007) found that there was information content for S&P 500 inclusions, and the included firms' stock prices increased significantly, as it was not the case for the volume. Investor awareness hypothesis also provides explanations. It posits that although the investors' attention is drawn by the inclusion in the index, the attention for the exclusion from the index was not immediately drawn back (Baran & King, 2012).

Briefly, while the imperfect substitutes and information content's empirical characteristics imply that the effects on stock prices and trading volume are permanent and temporary, respectively, liquidity effect supports permanent changes in both stock prices and trading volume (Kappou & Oikonomou, 2016). For the investor awareness hypothesis, there is permanent price effect for additions but temporary price effect for deletions (Baran & King, 2012), and temporary effects for the trading volume (Kappou & Oikonomou, 2016).

In the literature, though conventional stock indices were widely investigated in terms of index effect, there are limited studies, which have been concentrated on sustainability indices, especially on the ones in the emerging markets. Since the focus of this chapter is on trading volume, the previous studies, in which the index effect on trading volume was empirically examined, were presented.

Regarding Dow Jones Sustainability Stoxx Index (DJSSI), Consolandi, Jaiswal-Dale, Poggiani, and Vercelli (2009) investigated the effects of inclusions (deletions) on the firms' return and trading volume. They reported that the included firms' MVR was '1.05' but statistically indifferent from '1' in the period between the announcement day and the day before the effective day. The MVR was '1.13' and significantly different from '1' during the 10-day period following the effective day. The deleted firms' MVR was '0.93' but statistically indifferent from '1' between the announcement day and the day before the effective days. However, it increased to '1.08' in the 10-day period after the effective day. Lackman, Ernstberger, and Stich (2012) examined the reactions to the firms' inclusion in DJSSI. Regarding MVR of day T, they calculated that it had the value of '0.999' for 334 observations for the period of 2001 and

2008. The MVR was found to be '0.996' in the (-2, 2) event window. Contrary to the PPH, they noted that there were neither immediate increases in the trading volume nor price reversals after the index additions.

On the Dow Jones Sustainability World Index (DJSI), Cheung (2011) explored whether the changes in the composition of the index affect the firms' return, risk and liquidity. It was documented that both the included and deleted firms' trading volumes decreased on the announcement day and its subsequent days, and cumulative abnormal volume (CAV) was significantly lower than '1'. However, the volume recovered after the change day, and the average CAV was '1.028' during the 5-day period including the day of change. Durand, Paugam, and Stolowy (2019) investigated the impacts of variations in CSR visibility, which were captured by DJSI events, on the firms' equity price and trading volume. They noted that the events did not cause a prominent effect on market activity.

By considering the additions to the FTSE4Good UK index, Clacher and Hagendorff (2012) revealed that market adjusted mean trading volume significantly increased on the day of the announcement indicating the positive reaction of investors. Regarding the effect on the abnormal return, they found that there was a positive and significant increase on the day of the announcement, however it was not the case in the longer event periods. Therefore, they concluded that although being classified as a socially responsible firm was not viewed as harming the shareholders benefits, it was rather not created value for shareholders.

Regarding the changes in listed firms of the MSCI KLD 400 index, Kappou and Oikonomou (2016) found that the firms' deletion was associated with an increase in the trading volume (the MVR was '1.93' and significant at 5% level) on the day of the event. However, the deleted firms' MVR was reversed in the long-term. Hence, they reported that there was a temporary change in the trading volume of the deleted firms. Although the firms' addition to the index also increased the MVR which was '1.30', it was statistically indifferent from '1'. They also noted that the market anticipated the upcoming deletion event but not the coming addition event.

Data and Methodology

XUSRD was launched on November 4, 2014, and it has one index period from November to October. Firms are selected by Ethical Investment Research Services (EIRIS) Limited in the perspective of its ESG criteria. For the first index period, from November 2014 to October 2015, 15 firms were included in the index. For the second, third, fourth and fifth index periods, 14, 14, 5 and 6 firms were selected, respectively. For the most recent index period, which has started on November 1, 2019 and will end at the end of October 2020, 7 firms were determined as sustainable companies and included in the XUSRD. On the other hand, some firms demonstrated lower sustainability performance and consequently, excluded from the index. Three firms in 2017 and one firm in 2019 were deleted from XUSRD. There was only one firm, which was excluded from and then reincluded in the index. Also, one firm has delisted from Borsa Istanbul and in the meantime from XUSRD in 2017. Over the years, 60 firms in total were included in, 4 firms were excluded from, and 1 firm was reincluded in the XUSRD. As of December 2019, there are 56 firms in the index, of which 24 of them take part in manufacturing sector, 4 of them in electricity, gas and water sector, 17 of them in financial institutions sector, 2 of them in construction and public work sector, 3 of them in technology sector, 3 of them in wholesale, retail trade, hotel and restaurant sector, and 3 of them in transportation, communication and storage sector.

To measure the effects of these inclusions and exclusions on trading volume, the methodology of Harris and Gurel (1986) was followed. They used the following formula;

$VR_{it} = \frac{V_{it}}{V_{mt}} \cdot \frac{V_m}{V_i}$ .where, VR_{it} .is the volume ratio, V_{it} .is the trading volume for the security i on the day t (the event day about the inclusion or exclusion), V_{mt} .is the total trading volume of the market on day t, V_m .is the market's average trading volume for the 40 trading days before the event day, and V_i .is the security i's average trading volume for the 40 trading days before the day t.

This standardized measure is adjusted for the changes in the market (Harris & Gurel, 1986) and considers the trading volume for both the event day and the 40-day period before the events. Accordingly, if the VR_{it} .is higher than '1', it indicates that the trading volume is positively affected by the event. In this study, Borsa Istanbul All (XUTUM) index was used to represent the Borsa Istanbul equity market.

After calculating the VR_{it} . the mean volume ratio was obtained by the following formula (Harris and Gurel, 1986):

$$MVR = \frac{1}{N} \sum VR_{it}$$

The MVR sheds light on the general trend about the trading volume and can be interpreted by comparing '1'. On the other hand, to get statistically significant results, one sample t-test was employed. By determining the test value as '1', the following hypothesis was tested:

H_0= The difference between the VR values and '1' is equal to zero.

H_a= The difference between the VR values and '1' is not equal to zero.

For the analysis, two different event days were used. The first one is the announcement days of the inclusion in or exclusion from the XUSRD. The second one is the effective days of the changes in the XUSRD. In 2014, the announcement and the effective days were the same. The announcements days for the 2015, 2016, 2017, 2018 and 2019 were October 23, October 24, October 27, October 26 and October 25, respectively. The announcements were derived from Public Disclosure Platform of Turkey. The effective days for the 2014 and 2015 were November 4 and November 2, respectively. For 2016, 2017, 2018 and 2019, the effective day was November 1. Consequently, there were 5, 6, 3, 3, and 4 trading days between the announcements and effective days of 2015, 2016, 2017, 2018 and 2019, respectively. Daily traded lot sizes for each of the securities and XUTUM was used. Historical daily trading volumes were obtained from Matriks Data Terminal.

Results

Table 1 shows the results that were obtained by considering the event day as the announcement day, which took place before the effective day of the index changes. The effects of the inclusions were reported for each of the year and also separately examined as a whole for the 2014-2019 period. However, since there were only a few deleted firms, the effect of exclusions was only investigated in terms of 2014-2019 period. In the Table 1, while the AD represents the announcement days, (AD, ED-1) refers to the period between the announcement day and the day before the effective day (ED) for index changes.

For the inclusion announcements, it was found that the MVR was higher than '1' in 2014, 2016, 2018 and 2019. Conversely, in 2015 and 2017, the MVR was lower than '1'. For the period of 2014-2019, the MVR was '1.0424'. As a result, in general, it was understood that the inclusion announcements had a positive impact on the included firms' trading volume. However, according to one sample t-test results, the null hypothesis was not rejected for 2014 (t = 0.2833, p>0.05), 2016 (t = 1.2182, p>0.05), 2018 (t = 0.8332, p>0.05), 2019 (t = 0.0992, p>0.05) and the 2014-2019 period (t = 0.4233, p>0.05). Consequently, the volume ratios in these years were not significantly different from '1', although they were generally slightly higher than '1'.

Interestingly, all the MVR values in the (AD, ED-1) period decreased while they were higher than '1' in the day AD. Thus, it can be inferred that the reactions of investors to the inclusion news were temporary in 2014[1], 2016, 2018, 2019, and 2014-2019 period. On the other hand, in 2015 and 2017, the MRV values increased after the announcement days, and the MVR almost reached '1' in 2015. Therefore, in 2015, an increasing trend in trading volume was observed in the subsequent days, though it was still not higher than '1'.

For the exclusion announcements, it was reported that the MVR of 2014-2019 period was '0.5830', which was prominently lower than '1'. According to the one-sample t-test results, the null hypothesis was rejected at 10% significance level (t = -3.0829, p<0.1). As a result, it was understood that the trading volumes of excluded firms significantly decreased. However, this situation was temporary, since the trading volumes increased after the exclusion announcements and reached to '0.8262' in the period of (AD, ED-1). Overall, the trading volume for the included and excluded firms demonstrated changes in favor of PPH.

Table 1. Exploring the Impacts on/after the Announcement Days

Period	N	AD			AD, ED-1		
		MVR	*t*-Value	*p*	MVR	*t*-Value	*p*
The Included Firms							
2014	15	1.0677	0.2833	0.7810	-*	-	-
2015	14	0.8769	-0.7107	0.4897	0.9798	-0.1954	0.8480
2016	14	1.3092	1.2182	0.2447	0.8948	-1.2306	0.2402
2017	5	0.5177	-3.8817	0.0178	0.6323	-5.8378	0.0042
2018	6	1.2006	0.8332	0.4426	0.8680	-0.6924	0.5195
2019	7	1.0248	0.0992	0.9241	0.9137	-0.3979	0.7044
2014-2019	61	1.0424	0.4233	0.6735	0.9349	-0.8988	0.3723
The Excluded Firms							
2014-2019	4	0.5830	-3.0829	0.0540	0.8262	-0.7411	0.5123

* The announcement and effective days were the same for 2014.

Figure 1 depicts the average change of trading volume before and after the announcement days for 61 included firms. Logarithmic daily trading volume change [for instance, $day\, t = \ln\left(\frac{Vol_t}{Vol_{t-1}}\right)$] was calculated ten days before and after the announcement days for each of the firms, and then the firms' volume changes were averaged for each of the days. The figure clearly displayed that the volume change was positive on day T, though it was negative for the day T-1 and T+1. Hence, the figure visually supports the temporary change argued by PPH.

Figure 1. Average Logarithmic Change of Trading Volume for the Included Firms

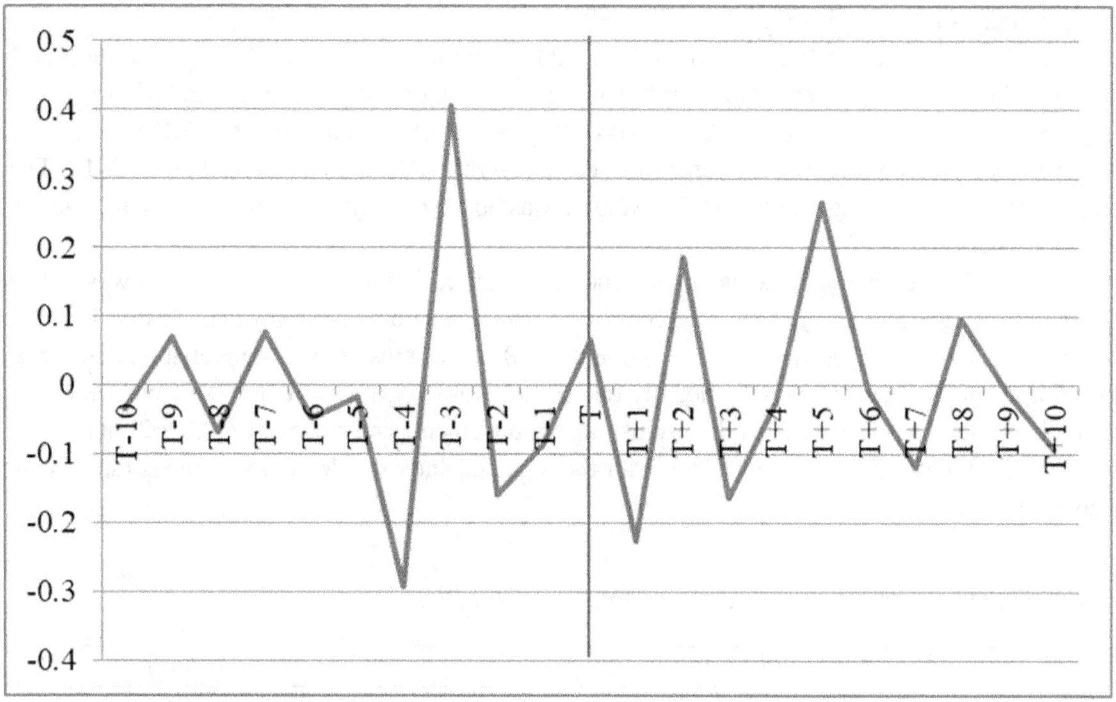

Figure 2 shows how the excluded firms' average trading volume changed over the course of ten days before and after the announcement days. There was a negative volume change on day T, though it was positive on day T-1. The negativity remained on day T+1, but it turned to positive on day T+2. Therefore, the chart evidently displayed the temporary volume change for the four excluded firms.

Table 2 presents the results, in which the event day was considered as the effective day of the index changes. While the ED refers to the effective day of the index changes, the (ED, ED+5) and (ED, ED+10) represent the after event 6-day and 11-day periods including ED.

Regarding the included firms' MVR on ED, it was documented that the only value higher than '1' was in 2017. Interestingly and conversely, on the announcement day of 2017, the MVR was found to be less than '1'. Therefore, it was demonstrated that the positive reaction to the firms' inclusion to the XUSRD was performed on the effective day rather than the announcement day in 2017. However, the null hypothesis was not rejected for 2017 ($t = 0.1780$, $p>0.05$). Hence, the VR values in 2017 were not significantly different from '1'. Overall, these findings indicated that the effects of inclusion in the index were mostly revealed on the announcement days, not on the effective day.

The deleted firms' MVR value for the 2014-2019 period was '0.7640'. However, it was not significantly different from '1', since the null hypothesis was not rejected at 5% significance level ($t = -1.4797$, $p>0.05$). Although the MVR was lower than '1' on ED, in the subsequent days it increased overwhelmingly. The MVR were '1.0892' and '1.4023' in the 6- and 11-day periods, respectively. These findings are in parallel with PPH.

Figure 2. Average Logarithmic Change of Trading Volume for the Excluded Firms

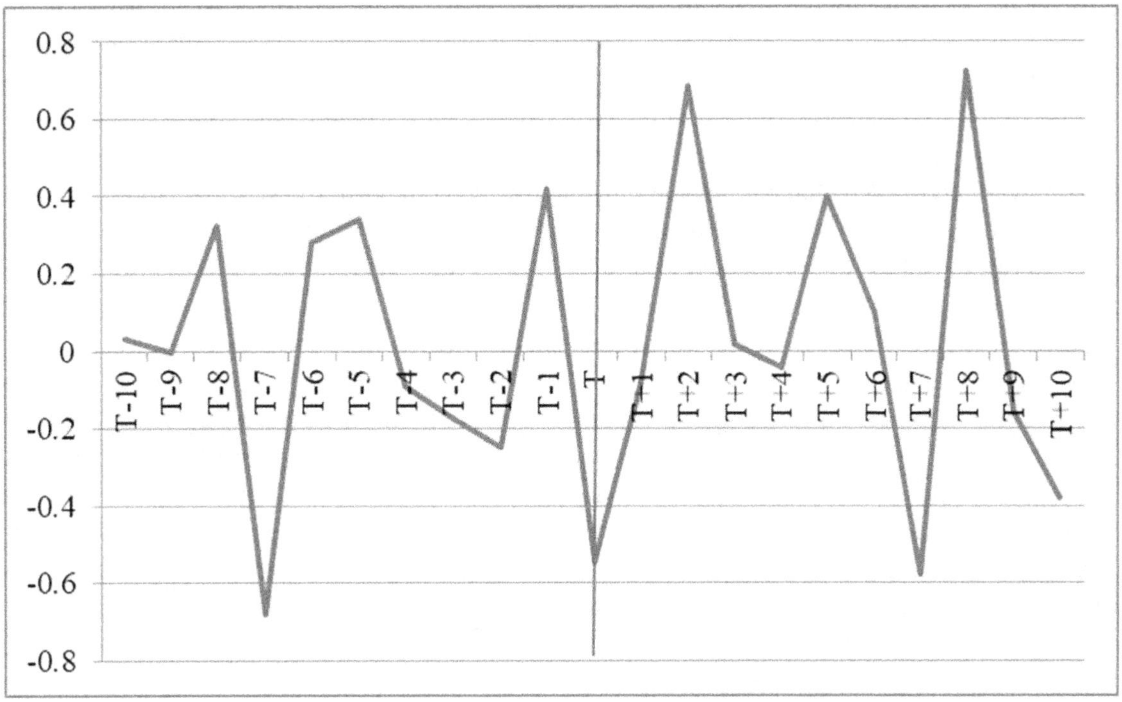

Table 2. Exploring the Impacts on/after the Effective Days of the Index Changes

Period*	N	ED			ED, ED+5			ED, ED+10		
		MVR	*t*-Value	*p*	MVR	*t*-Value	*p*	MVR	*t*-Value	*p*
The Included Firms										
2014		1.0677	0.2833	0.7810	0.8195	-2.4234	0.0295	0.8107	3.8698	0.0017
2015	14	0.8780	-1.3345	0.2049	1.0227	0.2732	0.7889	1.0528	0.5263	0.6075
2016	14	0.7325	-3.7709	0.0023	0.7122	-3.6728	0.0028	0.7516	-2.6374	0.0204
2017	5	1.0951	0.1780	0.8673	1.0890	0.2531	0.8126	0.9995	-0.0022	0.9983
2018	6	0.8208	-2.1282	0.0865	0.7669	3.1635	0.0249	0.7076	-4.4165	0.0069
2019	7	0.8870	-0.3138	0.7642	0.8740	-0.6145	0.5614	0.8355	-1.2274	0.2656
2014-2019	61	0.9044	-1.1153	0.2691	0.8607	-2.7888	0.0070	0.8538	-3.4144	0.0011
The Excluded Firms										
2014-2019	4	0.7640	-1.4797	0.2355	1.0892	1.0099	0.3869	1.4023	2.0955	0.1271

*Since the effective and the announcement days were the same in 2014, the findings for 2014 can be seen in Table 1.

DISCUSSION AND CONCLUSION

XUSRD was launched on November 2014, and it has one index period per year between November and October. Therefore, as of December 2019, six index events occurred. In the first event, 15 firms were included in the index. In the following events, the number of constituents increased to 29, 43, 45, 50 and 56, respectively. In total, 61 firms were included and 4 firms were deleted from the index. Index events have a potential to affect the listed and delisted firms' trading dynamics. Although conventional stock indices like S&P 500 and Nikkei 225 were widely investigated in terms of index effect, sustainability indices were rarely examined, especially in the perspective of how the included or deleted firms' trading volumes were affected. Besides, the limited existing literature regarding the effects of sustainability index events on trading volume was mostly conducted on developed markets.

By providing the CSR literature of the emerging markets, this study examines the effects of the XUSRD events on the firms' trading volume. Moreover, this study completed one of the missing parts of the Turkish CSR literature. Although Gök and Gökşen (2020) reported that the XUSRD inclusions positively affected the Turkish banks' returns, which indicated that the investors perceived the entering as a value creation, the effects of index events on volume have not been addressed before.

To examine the index effect, the methodology of Harris and Gurel (1986), which is the most common approach in the literature, was used, and one sample t-test was employed. Both the announcement day and effective day of the index changes were considered as the event days. The index effect was particularly observed on the day of the announcements. While the included firms' trading volume increased, the excluded firms' trading volume decreased. Therefore, these results suggested that the investors reacted to XUSRD events. However, only the decrease in the deleted firms was statistically significant, which indicated that there was an asymmetric reaction to additions and deletions. This finding was in line with the findings of Consolandi et al. (2009). In the subsequent days of announcements, the reversals were observed. As a result, it was concluded that the effect was temporary, in parallel with the price pressure hypothesis.

The XUSRD is a relatively new index. Because there were only a few deletions, the results for the excluded firms should be cautiously interpreted. Since the Turkish firms' interest in corporate sustainability practices has been growing, it is expected that the number of constituents in XUSRD will exceed 100 in the near future. Therefore, future studies can investigate the index effect with a larger sample in the following years by considering the response of both volume and return.

REFERENCES

Ahmed, N., & Bassiouny, A. (2018). The Effects of Index Changes on Stock Trading: Evidence from the EGX. *Review of Economics & Finance*, *11*(1), 55–66.

Barakat, S. R., Isabella, G., Boaventura, J. M. G., & Mazzon, J. A. (2016). The Influence of Corporate Social Responsibility on Employee Satisfaction. *Management Decision*, *54*(9), 2325–2339. doi:10.1108/MD-05-2016-0308

Baran, L., & King, T.-H. D. (2012). Cost of Equity and S&P 500 Index Revisions. *Financial Management*, *41*(2), 457–481. doi:10.1111/j.1755-053X.2012.01186.x

Barnea, A., & Rubin, A. (2010). Corporate Social Responsibility as a Conflict Between Shareholders. *Journal of Business Ethics*, *97*(1), 71–86. doi:10.100710551-010-0496-z

Bauman, C. W., & Skitka, L. J. (2012). Corporate Social Responsibility as a Source of Employee Satisfaction. *Research in Organizational Behavior*, *32*, 63–86. doi:10.1016/j.riob.2012.11.002

Becchetti, L., Di Giacomo, S., & Pinnacchio, D. (2008). Corporate Social Responsibility and Corporate Performance: Evidence from a Panel of US Listed Companies. *Applied Economics*, *40*(5), 541–567. doi:10.1080/00036840500428112

Bocquet, R., Le Bas, C., Mothe, C., & Poussing, N. (2013). Are Firms with Different CSR Profiles Equally Innovative? Empirical Analysis with Survey Data. *European Management Journal*, *31*(6), 642–654. doi:10.1016/j.emj.2012.07.001

Cai, J. (2007). What's in the News? Information Content of S&P 500 Additions. *Financial Management*, *36*(3), 113–124. doi:10.1111/j.1755-053X.2007.tb00083.x

Charlo, M. J., Moya, I., & Muñoz, A. M. (2015). Sustainable Development and Corporate Financial Performance: A Study Based on the FTSE4Good IBEX Index. *Business Strategy and the Environment*, *24*(4), 277–288. doi:10.1002/bse.1824

Chen, H., Noronha, G., & Singal, V. (2004). The Price Response to S&P 500 Index Additions and Deletions: Evidence of Asymmetry and a New Explanation. *The Journal of Finance*, *59*(4), 1901–1929. doi:10.1111/j.1540-6261.2004.00683.x

Chen, H., & Wang, X. (2011). Corporate Social Responsibility and Corporate Financial Performance in China: An Empirical Research from Chinese Firms. *Corporate Governance*, *11*(4), 361–370. doi:10.1108/14720701111159217

Cheung, A. W. K. (2011). Do Stock Investors Value Corporate Sustainability? Evidence from an Event Study. *Journal of Business Ethics*, *99*(2), 145–165. doi:10.100710551-010-0646-3

Çıtak, L., & Ersoy, E. (2016). Firmaların BIST Sürdürülebilirlik Endeksine Alınmasına Yatırımcı Tepkisi: Olay Çalışması ve Ortalama Testleri ile Bir Analiz. *International Journal of Alanya Faculty of Business*, *8*(1), 43–57.

Clacher, I., & Hagendorff, J. (2012). Do Announcements About Corporate Social Responsibility Create or Destroy Shareholder Wealth? Evidence from the UK. *Journal of Business Ethics*, *106*(3), 253–266. doi:10.100710551-011-1004-9

Consolandi, C., Jaiswal-Dale, A., Poggiani, E., & Vercelli, A. (2009). Global Standards and Ethical Stock Indexes: The Case of the Dow Jones Sustainability Stoxx Index. *Journal of Business Ethics*, *87*(1), 185–197. doi:10.100710551-008-9793-1

Cui, J., Jo, H., & Na, H. (2018). Does Corporate Social Responsibility Affect Information Asymmetry? *Journal of Business Ethics*, *148*(3), 549–572. doi:10.100710551-015-3003-8

Durand, R., Paugam, L., & Stolowy, H. (2019). Do Investors Actually Value Sustainability Indices? Replication, Development, and New Evidence on CSR Visibility. *Strategic Management Journal*, *40*(9), 1471–1490. doi:10.1002mj.3035

Edmans, A. (2011). Does the Stock Market Fully Value Intangibles? Employee Satisfaction and Equity Prices. *Journal of Financial Economics*, *101*(3), 621–640. doi:10.1016/j.jfineco.2011.03.021

Fatma, M., Rahman, Z., & Khan, I. (2015). Building Company Reputation and Brand Equity Through CSR: The Mediating Role of Trust. *International Journal of Bank Marketing*, *33*(6), 840–856. doi:10.1108/IJBM-11-2014-0166

Feng, Z.-Y., Wang, M.-L., & Huang, H.-W. (2015). Equity Financing and Social Responsibility: Further International Evidence. *The International Journal of Accounting*, *50*(3), 247–280. doi:10.1016/j.intacc.2015.07.005

Fiori, G., di Donato, F., & Izzo, M. F. (2015). Corporate Social Responsibility and Stock Prices: A Study on the Italian Market. *Corporate Ownership & Control*, *12*(2), 608–617. doi:10.22495/cocv12i2c6p3

Galbreath, J. (2006). Corporate Social Responsibility Strategy: Strategic Options, Global Considerations. *Corporate Governance*, *6*(2), 175–187. doi:10.1108/14720700610655178

Gok, I. Y., Duranay, S., & Uzunoglu Unlu, H. (2019b). Co-movement Dynamics of Sustainability Indices: Investigating the Diversification Opportunities Through FTSE4Good Index Family and Borsa Istanbul Sustainability Index. *Social Responsibility Journal*, *ahead-of-print*(ahead-of-print). Advance online publication. doi:10.1108/SRJ-02-2019-0073

Gök, İ. Y., & Gökşen, H. (2020). *Bankaların Sürdürülebilirlik Endeksine Dahil Edilmelerinin Getiri Üzerindeki Etkisinin Araştırılması*. Süleyman Demirel Üniversitesi Vizyoner Dergisi.

Gök, İ. Y., & Özdemír, O. (2017). Borsa İstanbul Sürdürülebilirlik Endeksinin Performans Karakteristiği. *Sosyoekonomi*, *25*(34), 87–105.

Gok, I. Y., Ozdemir, O., & Unlu, B. (2019a). The Effect of Corporate Sustainability Practices on Financial Performance: Evidence From Turkey. In A. Antonaras & P. Dekoulou (Eds.), *Cases on Corporate Social Responsibility and Contemporary Issues in Organizations* (pp. 52–70). IGI Global. doi:10.4018/978-1-5225-7715-7.ch004

Gregoriou, A. (2011). The Liquidity Effects of Revisions to the CAC40 Stock Index. *Applied Financial Economics*, *21*(5), 333–341. doi:10.1080/09603107.2010.530216

Gündüz, Ç. (2018). Sürdürülebilirlik Endeksi Kapsamına Alınmanın Hisse Senedi Değerine Etkisi: BIST Uygulaması. *Bankacılar Dergisi*, *106*, 37–58.

Hanaeda, H., & Serita, T. (2003). Price and Volume Effects Associated with a Change in the Nikkei 225 Index List: New Evidence from the Big Change on April 2000. In J. J. Choi, & T. Hiraki (Eds.), International Finance Review Vol. 4- The Japanese Finance: Corporate Finance and Capital Markets in Changing Japan (pp. 199-225). Bingley: Emerald Group Publishing Limited.

Harris, L., & Gurel, E. (1986). Price and Volume Effects Associated with Changes in the S&P 500 List: New Evidence for the Existence of Price Pressures. *The Journal of Finance*, *41*(4), 815–829. doi:10.1111/j.1540-6261.1986.tb04550.x

Hegde, S. P., & McDermott, J. B. (2003). The Liquidity Effects of Revisions to the S&P 500 Index: An Empirical Analysis. *Journal of Financial Markets*, *6*(3), 413–459. doi:10.1016/S1386-4181(02)00046-0

Hoi, C. K., Wu, Q., & Zhang, H. (2013). Is Corporate Social Responsibility (CSR) Associated Tax Avoidance? Evidence from Irresponsible CSR Activities. *The Accounting Review*, *88*(6), 2025–2059. doi:10.2308/accr-50544

Hou, M., Liu, H., Fan, P., & Wei, Z. (2016). Does CSR Practice Pay Off in East Asian Firms? A Meta-Analytic Investigation. *Asia Pacific Journal of Management*, *33*(1), 195–228. doi:10.100710490-015-9431-2

Hudson, R. (2005). Ethical Investing: Ethical Investors and Managers. *Business Ethics Quarterly*, *15*(4), 641–657. doi:10.5840/beq200515445

Hur, W.-M., Kim, H., & Woo, J. (2014). How CSR Leads to Corporate Brand Equity: Mediating Mechanisms of Corporate Brand Credibility and Reputation. *Journal of Business Ethics*, *125*(1), 75–86. doi:10.100710551-013-1910-0

Husted, B. W., & Allen, D. B. (2007). Strategic Corporate Social Responsibility and Value Creation among Large Firms: Lessons from the Spanish Experience. *Long Range Planning*, *40*(6), 594–610. doi:10.1016/j.lrp.2007.07.001

Inoue, Y., Kent, A., & Lee, S. (2011). CSR and the Bottom Line: Analyzing the Link Between CSR and Financial Performance for Professional Teams. *Journal of Sport Management*, *25*(6), 531–549. doi:10.1123/jsm.25.6.531

Javeed, S. A., & Lefen, L. (2019). An Analysis of Corporate Social Responsibility and Firm Performance with Moderating Effects of CEO Power and Ownership Structure: A Case Study of the Manufacturing Sector of Pakistan. *Sustainability*, *11*(1), 248. doi:10.3390u11010248

Jhunjhunwala, S. (2014). Intertwining CSR with Strategy – The Way Ahead. *Corporate Governance*, *14*(2), 211–219. doi:10.1108/CG-03-2011-0021

Jung, S.-Y., Lee, S., & Dalbor, M. (2016). The Negative Synergistic Effect of Internationalization and Corporate Social Responsibility on US Restaurant Firms' Value Performance. *International Journal of Contemporary Hospitality Management*, *28*(8), 1759–1777. doi:10.1108/IJCHM-07-2014-0361

Kappou, K., & Oikonomou, I. (2016). Is There a Gold Social Seal? The Financial Effects of Additions to and Deletions from Social Stock Indices. *Journal of Business Ethics*, *133*(3), 533–552. doi:10.100710551-014-2409-z

Lackmann, J., Ernstberger, J., & Stich, M. (2012). Market Reactions to Increased Reliability of Sustainability Information. *Journal of Business Ethics, 107*(2), 111-128. doi: 1-1026-3 doi:10.100710551-01

Lamberti, L., & Noci, G. (2012). The Relationship Between CSR and Corporate Strategy in Medium-Sized Companies: Evidence from Italy. *Business Ethics (Oxford, England)*, *21*(4), 402–416. doi:10.1111/beer.12002

Lee, K.-H., & Shin, D. (2010). Consumers' Responses to CSR Activities: The Linkage Between Increased Awareness and Purchase Intention. *Public Relations Review*, *36*(2), 193–195. doi:10.1016/j.pubrev.2009.10.014

Lima Crisóstomo, V., de Souza Freire, F., & Cortes de Vasconcellos, F. (2011). Corporate Social Responsibility, Firm Value and Financial Performance in Brazil. *Social Responsibility Journal*, *7*(2), 295–309. doi:10.1108/17471111111141549

Lin, C. H., Yang, H. L., & Liou, D. Y. (2009). The Impact of Corporate Social Responsibility on Financial Performance: Evidence from Business in Taiwan. *Technology in Society*, *31*(1), 56–63. doi:10.1016/j.techsoc.2008.10.004

Lin, C.-S., Chang, R.-Y., & Dang, V. T. (2015). An Integrated Model to Explain How Corporate Social Responsibility Affects Corporate Financial Performance. *Sustainability*, *7*(7), 8292–8311. doi:10.3390u7078292

Lin, L., Hung, P.-H., Chou, D.-W., & Lai, C. W. (2019). Financial Performance and Corporate Social Responsibility: Empirical Evidence from Taiwan. *Asia Pacific Management Review*, *24*(1), 61–71. doi:10.1016/j.apmrv.2018.07.001

Lin-Hi, N., & Blumberg, I. (2018). The Link Between (Not) Practicing CSR and Corporate Reputation: Psychological Foundations and Managerial Implications. *Journal of Business Ethics*, *150*(1), 185–198. doi:10.100710551-016-3164-0

Liu, M. T., Wong, I. A., Shi, G., Chu, R., & Brock, J. L. (2014). The Impact of Corporate Social Responsibility (CSR) Performance and Perceived Brand Quality on Customer-Based Brand Preference. *Journal of Services Marketing*, *28*(3), 181–194. doi:10.1108/JSM-09-2012-0171

Liu, S. (2006). The Impacts of Index Rebalancing and Their Implications: Some New Evidence from Japan. *Journal of International Financial Markets, Institutions and Money*, *16*(3), 246–269. doi:10.1016/j.intfin.2005.02.006

Luo, X., & Bhattacharya, C. B. (2006). Corporate Social Responsibility, Customer Satisfaction, and Market Value. *Journal of Marketing*, *70*(4), 1–18. doi:10.1509/jmkg.70.4.001

Luo, X., & Du, S. (2015). Exploring the Relationship Between Corporate Social Responsibility and Firm Innovation. *Marketing Letters*, *26*(4), 703–714. doi:10.100711002-014-9302-5

Muñoz, R. M., de Pablo, J. D. S., & Peña, I. (2015). Linking Corporate Social Responsibility and Financial Performance in Spanish Firms. *European Journal of International Management*, *9*(3), 368–383. doi:10.1504/EJIM.2015.069133

Nguyen, V. H., Agbola, F. W., & Choi, B. (2019). Does Corporate Social Responsibility Reduce Information Asymmetry? Empirical Evidence from Australia. *Australian Journal of Management*, *44*(2), 188–211. doi:10.1177/0312896218797163

Oh, W., & Park, S. (2015). The Relationship Between Corporate Social Responsibility and Corporate Financial Performance in Korea. *Emerging Markets Finance and Trade, 51*(sup3), 85-94. doi:10.1080/1540496X.2015.1039903

Peters, R., & Mullen, M. R. (2009). Some Evidence of the Cumulative Effects of Corporate Social Responsibility on Financial Performance. *Journal of Global Business Issues*, *3*(1), 1–14.

Quéré, B. P., Nouyrigat, G., & Baker, C. R. (2018). A Bi-Directional Examination of the Relationship Between Corporate Social Responsibility Ratings and Company Financial Performance in the European Context. *Journal of Business Ethics*, *148*(3), 527–544. doi:10.100710551-015-2998-1

Rexhepi, G., Kurtishi, S., & Bexheti, G. (2013). Corporate Social Responsibility (CSR) and Innovation–The Drivers of Business Growth? *Procedia: Social and Behavioral Sciences*, *75*, 532–541. doi:10.1016/j.sbspro.2013.04.058

Rutledge, R. W., Karim, K. E., Aleksanyan, M., & Wu, C. (2014). An Examination of the Relationship Between Corporate Social Responsibility and Financial Performance: The Case of Chinese State-Owned Enterprises. In *Accounting for the Environment: More Talk and Little Progress* (pp. 1–22). Emerald Group Publishing Limited. doi:10.1108/S1479-359820140000005001

Skudiene, V., & Auruskeviciene, V. (2012). The Contribution of Corporate Social Responsibility to Internal Employee Motivation. *Baltic Journal of Management*, *7*(1), 49–67. doi:10.1108/17465261211197421

S&P DJI. (2019). *S&P U.S. Indices Methodology*. Author.

Su, W., Peng, M. W., Tan, W., & Cheung, Y.-L. (2016). The Signaling Effect of Corporate Social Responsibility in Emerging Economies. *Journal of Business Ethics*, *134*(3), 479–491. doi:10.100710551-014-2404-4

Temiz, H., & Acar, M. (2018). Sürdürülebilirlik Endeksinde İşlem Gören Firmaların Finansal Performansı: Olay Çalışması Örneği. *Hitit Üniversitesi Sosyal Bilimler Enstitüsü Dergisi*, *11*(3), 1971–1987.

Torugsa, N. A., O'Donohue, W., & Hecker, R. (2012). Capabilities, Proactive CSR and Financial Performance in SMEs: Empirical Evidence from an Australian Manufacturing Industry Sector. *Journal of Business Ethics*, *109*(4), 483–500. doi:10.100710551-011-1141-1

Uadiale, O. M., & Fagbemi, T. O. (2012). Corporate Social Responsibility and Financial Performance in Developing Economies: The Nigerian Experience. *Journal of Economics and Sustainable Development*, *3*(4), 44–54.

Usman, A. B., & Amran, N. A. B. (2015). Corporate Social Responsibility Practice and Corporate Financial Performance: Evidence from Nigeria Companies. *Social Responsibility Journal*, *11*(4), 749–763. doi:10.1108/SRJ-04-2014-0050

Wang, Q., Dou, J., & Jia, S. (2016). A Meta-Analytic Review of Corporate Social Responsibility and Corporate Financial Performance: The Moderating Effect of Contextual Factors. *Business & Society*, *55*(8), 1083–1121. doi:10.1177/0007650315584317

Wisse, B., van Eijbergen, R., Rietzschel, E. F., & Scheibe, S. (2018). Catering to the Needs of an Aging Workforce: The Role of Employee Age in the Relationship Between Corporate Social Responsibility and Employee Satisfaction. *Journal of Business Ethics*, *147*(4), 875–888. doi:10.100710551-015-2983-8

Xu, X., Zeng, S., & Chen, H. (2018). Signaling Good by Doing Good: How Does Environmental Corporate Social Responsibility Affect International Expansion? *Business Strategy and the Environment*, *27*(7), 946–959. doi:10.1002/bse.2044

Ye, K., & Zhang, R. (2011). Do Lenders Value Corporate Social Responsibility? Evidence from China. *Journal of Business Ethics*, *104*(2), 197–206. doi:10.100710551-011-0898-6

ENDNOTE

1. Since the announcement and effective days were the same for 2014, the mvr of (ed, ed+5) and (ed, ed+10) in the table 2 can be considered to understand the effects after the announcement day.

Chapter 13
Creative Problem Solving in Online Innovation Contests:
What Motivates Top Solvers to Participate in the New Collaborative Economy?

Rolf K. Baltzersen
Østfold University College, Norway

ABSTRACT

Online innovation contests represent one of the most interesting new ways of utilizing creative skills in the new collaborative economy, but we still know very little about what motivates the problem solvers. Previous studies suggest that the economic reward is not the only motivational factor, but there are many other motives too. The aim of this research study is to identify the core motivational dimensions based on the experiences of top solvers in three different types of online innovation contests. The empirical findings are used to construct a motivational typology for creative problem solving that can guide future research.

INTRODUCTION

To develop the new collaborative economy, it is important to understand what motivates individuals to participate in creative problem-solving activities. Online innovation contests represent an important example of the more creative work done within this economy. By analyzing various solver profiles in three different contest environments, this chapter provides a comprehensive motivational typology, allowing us to understand better how to organize creative problem-solving processes in the new collaborative economy.

DOI: 10.4018/978-1-7998-4543-0.ch013

BACKGROUND

Crowdwork in the New Collaborative Economy

The 'new collaborative economy' remains an ambiguous term to both scholars and the public, with various definitions. Several different terms are also used to describe more or less the same phenomenon, such as "sharing economy" (Frenken & Schor, 2019), "collaborative consumption" (Hamari, Sjöklint, & Ukkonen, 2016), "peer-to-peer economy" (Sundararajan, 2016), or "access economy" (Denning, 2014). However, most terms share a common understanding of an emerging marketplace where consumers rely on each other instead of large companies – giving, swapping, borrowing, trading, and renting both products and services in an online setting. Typically, access is more important than exclusive ownership, which suits Generation Z, assumed to prefer lower-cost options that offer temporary access to different assets, like, for example, home and car sharing (Denning, 2014; Frenken & Schor, 2019; Hamari et al., 2016). Usually, a "web-based middleman" or online intermediary will ensure that the transaction is performed properly, but without directly controlling the consumer interaction (Frankenfield, 2018; Hamari et al., 2016). In addition, these new economic solutions often aim to serve a broader collective purpose or common good, like the alleviation of societal problems, such as hyper-consumption, pollution, and poverty (Hamari et al., 2016). "Green values" are especially important, and many online platforms advertise that they contribute to reducing CO2 emissions. Although the environmental effects remain difficult to measure, sharing is expected to reduce the demand for new goods or facilities (Frenken & Schor, 2019).

Crowdwork is increasingly important in this collaborative economy, allowing thousands of people to work on the same project in an online setting. A large group can now perform separate "tasks" on short-term contracts in ways not previously possible. For example, in Amazon's Mechanical Turk, workers bid to complete microtasks or very small units of work. A growing number of platforms also offer more complex project work that covers a wide range of professions (e.g. Upwork and Thumbtack) (Sundararajan, 2018). In addition, companies and other organizations increasingly seek external expertise when they are unable to solve problems (Chesbrough, 2017).

Online Innovation Contests

In recent years, it has become more popular to receive outside help by arranging online innovation contests (ICs). Typically, a solution-seeking organization will attempt to recruit a large number of online "solvers" to join a contest and win prize money, ranging from a few hundred to millions of dollars. Only solvers who provide successful solutions will receive the money, transferring the risk of failure from the organization to the solver. While large companies previously organized these contests themselves, it has now become more common to use innovation intermediaries that support the solution-seeker in hosting the contest. Seekers can be large and small firms, governments, and other organizations. Some intermediaries have existed for over a decade, with InnoCentive (founded in 2001), IdeaConnection (2007), and Topcoder (2001) among the first. They aim to make it easy for a solution-seeking organization to utilize the knowledge of a large and diverse pool of experts worldwide. For example, InnoCentive claims to have access to a global network of over 400,000 solvers, with nearly 60% educated to masters level or above. Topcoder offers both ICs and paid crowdwork to its over one million members. While most platforms are orientated toward research and developmental work, others, like eÿeka, focus on marketing. The innovation intermediaries usually offer a "package" of support, like guidance in formulating an appropriate challenge, connecting seeking companies with problem solvers, finding relevant technology, or help strengthening innovation networks. Several intermediaries host hundreds of ICs every year for their clients (Agogué et al., 2017; Terwiesch & Xu, 2008).

Although the ICs are organized in different ways, all intermediaries require that solvers come up with proposals within a relatively short time period. Some researchers claim these online ICs are especially interesting because they showcase a new type of large-scale collective intelligence (CI) made possible by the internet (Lévy, 1999; Malone, 2018). While large-scale online collective work arguably represents the next important step in human evolution, we still struggle to organize large groups to produce better scientific, economic, and political solutions. Online ICs demonstrate how a crowd or large group can actually do creative work in the new collaborative economy. However, we know little about what motivates the key persons – the top solvers – who participate in these contests.

The aim of this study is to explore what motivates creative problem-solving in ICs. By analyzing various solver profiles in three different contest environments, this chapter provides a comprehensive motivational typology for creative problem-solving in the new collaborative economy, allowing us to understand better how to organize creative problem-solving in an online setting.

Motivation in Online Innovation Contests: A Literature Review

A search of papers with relevant key terms on Google Scholar ("motivation+innovation contests," "motivation+innovation intermediaries," "motivation+open innovation") identified only four recent publications on solver motivation in online ICs (Hofstetter, Zhang, & Herrmann, 2018; Hossain, 2018; Innocent, Gabriel, & Divard, 2017; Shafiei Gol, Stein, & Avital, 2018). All four studies build on data about the solvers from innovation intermediaries. Shafiei Gol et al.'s (2018) exploratory qualitative study, based on interviews with solvers on the Topcoder platform, found that they are motivated by a sense of psychological safety and autonomy, as well as by self-growth opportunities. Innocent et al.'s (2017) study, based on 93 online interviews with top contributors from three major crowdsourcing platforms, identified learning and social interaction as important motivators. Hossain (2018) analyzed 82 interviews of successful solvers at IdeaConnection, outlining their motivations, challenges, and opportunities. In the only quantitative study, Hofstetter et al. (2018) collected data from another innovation intermediary within creative marketing (Atizo). Initially, experimental data were collected from 301 individuals; next, participatory field data were collected from 6101 individuals in 261 contests (Hofstetter et al., 2018).

Other studies also underline motivational issues as being very important to solvers' participation in ICs. For example, Bakici & Almirall (2017) find a major tension in online ICs between the use of monetary incentives and non-monetary incentives, like the enjoyment of the task. However, there has been surprisingly little research in IC solvers' motivations. One reason for this may be that intermediary companies cautiously protect both the problem seekers and problem solvers, making it difficult to access data. Yet most intermediaries publish numerous successful profile stories on their websites, including interviews with top contributors. The studies by Innocent et al. (2017) and Hossain (2018) use these online interviews as data. On the one hand, these stories are a part of a marketing strategy to recruit seekers and solvers; hence, cherry picking and positive bias should make one cautious about assuming they give the full picture. On the other hand, they are narratives that provide valid information about identifiable persons who report what motivates them and why they compete.

In principle, anyone can participate in ICs, regardless of age, gender, location, skill level, education, or experience. For instance, at IdeaConnection, the pool of solvers includes students, retired scientists, and scientists in part-time employment. Although most winners are professionals, some are also "amateur scientists" (Hossain, 2018). However, all the interview studies describe solvers with advanced skills, including relevant formal education and working experience (Hossain, 2018; Innocent et al., 2017).

Furthermore, existing studies indicate that solvers are motivated not only by money but also by a complex mixture of motivational factors (Hossain, 2018; Innocent et al., 2017; Shafiei Gol et al., 2018). Nevertheless, the existing motivational models that describe solvers appear too simplistic to encompass this complexity. For example, in his conclusion, Hossain (2018) acknowledges this motivational complexity by mentioning the importance of both intrinsic and extrinsic motivation, but he does not elaborate on specific motivational factors or dimensions, concluding only that "extrinsic motivation is dominant, whereas intrinsic motivation works as a complement to extrinsic motivations" (Hossain, 2018). There have been few other attempts to construct a more comprehensive motivational framework or typology to guide research within this field.

However, as described in an interesting and highly cited qualitative study, Brabham (2010) interviewed 17 solvers who participate regularly in design t-shirt competitions hosted by Threadless, identifying four primary motivators: making money, developing creative skills, the appeal of freelance work, and love of the community. Hossain's (Hossain, 2018) empirical findings also point to similar motivational categories, which can be used as a framework for a deeper understanding of creative problem-solving in ICs. In this chapter, six topics mentioned in Hossain's (2018) study will be discussed in further detail.

First, as explored in this chapter's section "perceived learning as motivation," previous studies show that learning is a key motivation for IC problem solvers (Hossain, 2018; Shafiei Gol et al., 2018). Although Hossain (2018) does not distinguish between different types of learning, aspects of cognitive learning are addressed in his description of how solvers are drawn to tackling challenges that are intellectually stimulating and can improve their skills. Brabham (2010) also reports that many solvers participate to improve their skills within a supportive community, with some even learning with no previous experience. Although collaborative learning is not explicitly mentioned in any studies, Hossain (2018) notes that solvers' varied backgrounds provide opportunities to learn from each other. Hossain (2018) addresses transformative learning dimensions specifically only briefly and then in broader terms regarding how solvers grow as professional scientists. Similarly, in Brabham's (2010) study, one solver claims the participation made him realize he had creative skills, indicating a sense of personal growth.

Second, as investigated in the section "being immersed," Hossain (2018) finds many solvers show related positive feelings like enjoyment, excitement, and pleasure. Likewise, in Brabham's (2010) study, several participants describe their love of the contest format in Threadless as generating an addictive motivation. Hofstetter et al. (2018) also claim that enjoyment of the task appears to be particularly relevant for ICs that emphasize creative problem-solving.

Third, as analyzed in the section "being part of a community," Hossain (2018) finds that most solvers are motivated by opportunities to interact with other solvers. Likewise, Brabham (2010) finds that the participants enjoy being in community with likeminded art enthusiasts and do not look upon themselves as customers. Many highlight the humorous dialogue in the blog forum as a reason for continually returning to the site. Hofstetter et al. (2018) also suggest that social factors play a role in innovation communities.

Fourth, as discussed in the section "being recognized for your work," some solvers report that they participate in challenges to receive feedback and validate their own level of knowledge; money is less important than contributing to the greater social good and sharing their skills for others' benefits (Hossain, 2018). Likewise, in Brabham's (2010) study, some participants specifically mention that they enjoy receiving feedback on their work. Hofstetter et al. (2018) also find that performance feedback, such as high rankings, high ratings, or positive comments, is likely to increase one's feelings of competence. Receiving likes from other users also stimulates further participation and creative effort.

Fifth, as analyzed in the section "the prize money," both Hossain (2018) and Brabham (2010) find that the main motivation for most solvers is money, which is typically added to other income. ICs are usually organized with a predetermined reward structure, which either focuses all the prize money at the top rank (e.g. IdeaConnection) or provides multiple prizes to the best solvers (e.g. ëyeka and Topcoder). However, Hofstetter et al. (2018) find that the use of multiple prizes more effectively sustains participation across contests because the prize money also symbolizes achievement and increases the solver's self-perception of competence (Hofstetter et al., 2018).

Sixth, as examined in the section "the solver personality," Hossain (2018) finds that solvers enjoy the flexibility of the projects and the freedom to choose what they want to work with. Many different social groups participate, including retired people and students. Likewise, Brabham (2010) finds that Threadless attracts several different groups of solvers that want exposure, both hobbyists and freelancers.

THE RESEARCH METHOD

Selection of Online Innovation Intermediaries

This explorative study maps and describes the most important motivational factors in online ICs, by analyzing why top solvers are motivated to participate in these contests. Today, a significant number of online innovation intermediaries exist and cover a wide range of ICs. Still, few sites provide an overview of this new sector within the collaborative economy. One exception is IdeaConnection, which provides a helpful overview on their website (https://www.ideaconnection.com/outsourcing/). Search terms like "Innovation intermediaries" were also used to identify recently published papers on Google scholar that could summarize innovation intermediaries (e.g Bakici & Almirall, 2017). Using this information, ten innovation intermediaries were identified as relevant. The table below provides an overview with key information.

Using purposeful sampling (Patton, 2002), three intermediaries – Topcoder, ëyeka, and IdeaConnection – were selected for closer study according to the following criteria: 1) established more than five years ago; 2) among the top companies concerning revenue; 3) provide solver data. These intermediaries offer different contest formats regarding how and what type of work is to be done. IdeaConnection is orientated toward challenges that require cross-disciplinary research, while Topcoder covers challenges within IT. eÿeka is different from Topcoder and IdeaConnection because it focuses only on ICs within graphic creation and content marketing. There is also significant variation concerning the prize money amounts and how the contests are organized. Topcoder is largely a crowdwork platform that focuses on complex projects and requires skillful, creative workers for projects in which there is a greater likelihood of winning smaller amounts of money than with IdeaConnection and eÿeka. IdeaConnection, on the other hand, emphasizes teamwork and larger, collective problem-solving events, like Idea Rallies. Examining these three intermediaries, the study aims to generalize findings on motivation that are important for all types of online ICs.

Table 1. Key organizational information about online innovation intermediaries

	Founded	Headquarters	Challenges	From zoominfo.com (checked 02.01.2020)	Information about top solvers
Agorize	2011	Paris, France	Cross-disciplinary Startups challenges Students challenges Online hackathons	Revenue: 25M (Employees: 130)	No
Ennomotive	2014	Madrid, Spain	Engineering challenges	Revenue: 400K (Employees: 2)	No
IdeaConnection	2007	Victoria, British Columbia, Canada	Cross-disciplinary R&D challenges	Revenue: 6.1M (Employees: 32)	Yes
InnoCentive	2001	Waltham, Massachusetts, United States	Cross-disciplinary R&D challenges.	Revenue: 10M (Employees: 79)	No
ëyeka	2001	Paris, France	Product design challenges (marketing)	Revenue: 13.1M (Employees: 68)	Yes
Topcoder	2001	Indianapolis, Indiana, United States	IT	Revenue: 34.5M (Employees: 180)	Yes
HeroX	2013	Valley Cottage, New York, United States	Cross-disciplinary R&D challenges	Revenue: 5.4M (Employees: 28)	No
Hypios Crowdinnovation	2015	Paris, France	Cross-disciplinary R&D challenges	Revenue: 4.8M Employees: 25	No
Jovoto	2007	New York City, United States.	Product design challenges (marketing)	Revenue: 8.3M (Employees: 38)	Yes
Mindsumo	2011	Durham, North Carolina, United States	Product design challenges (marketing)	Revenue: 13.7M (Employees: 63)	Yes (video)

Solver Profiles

The data consist of solver profiles, such as interviews or stories, on the websites of three different intermediaries: eÿeka, IdeaConnection, and Topcoder. In total, 33 solver profiles were included in the data corpus with approximately 10 stories from each intermediary. Note that 10 of 17 profile stories in Topcoder and 13 of over 80 profile stories in IdeaConnection were randomly selected. All the solvers in the data corpus have won a contest, so they are not representative of the large member database, which includes many who have not won any contests. As the profiles only include winners, there is a potential bias in not including the larger majority of non-winners, who may have different motives. The table below provides an overview of the solver profile data.

Table 2. Solver profile data

Solver profiles	Number of profiles
Topcoder (TC) – stories written by the solvers with their usernames.	10 of 18 profile stories (7500 words)
eÿeka (ey) – testimonials written by solvers with their usernames.	All 10 profiles on part of the website (2100 words)
IdeaConnection (ID) – interviews of top solvers who are referred to by personal name. Written by IdeaConnection	13 of over 90 profiles (11900 words)

The solver profile data are presented in slightly different formats, as essays, interviews, or testimonials, but they all report on the solvers' personal motivations to participate, the challenges they face, and the benefits they receive by participating in ICs. The data are biased in the sense that they downplay the negative aspects of being a solver or seeker; on the company website, the emphasis will naturally be on the success stories to recruit new members to the site. However, because many of the profile stories display authentic names or usernames, there is no reason to believe that the published content is untrue. As this chapter's aim is to establish a comprehensive motivational framework and not to map inhibitory factors, potential bias in the data is less problematic. The data are primarily included to provide rich descriptions of motivation that can provide the foundation for a complex, tentative, motivational typology.

At Topcoder, a large majority of solvers are male (seven males and two females) and all are young adults in their twenties. Five of six solvers report being college or university students when joining TopCoder, while only one was in a full-time job. All the solver profiles were published between 2010 and 2014, with the solver participation then ranging from one year up to 10 years. The length of the profile stories vary from 500 to 1289 words, with a total of 7500 words comprising the Topcoder data.

Of the 10 solvers at eÿeka, eight are male and two are female. Five are young adults around 30, while two are middle-aged. All have been participating in the contests for several years. Three report being freelancers, while two of five are art directors. The profile stories are quite short, varying from 126 to 340 words, with a total amount of 2100 words.

At IdeaConnection, the demographic background is quite similar. All thirteen solvers are male. The majority, nine are middle-aged, while two are young adults and two are seniors. Almost all the solvers are highly qualified experts, with eight claiming a research background and six currently working as researchers. Four work as managing directors and are independent consultants. On this website, the interviews are longer, ranging from 588 to 1289 words, comprising a total of 11900 words.

Comparing the profiles across the three intermediaries, we see that both Topcoder and ëyeka have solvers who are primarily young adults, while IdeaConnection's solvers are largely middle-aged. At Topcoder, several of the solvers began to participate when they were students, while at IdeaConnection, individuals began when they are already working as researchers or had become experts in a field. A large majority of the solvers are male at all the intermediaries, indicating that this may be a typical characteristic of most online ICs.

Data Analysis

The profile data were copied from the websites in November 2019 and constitute the complete data. Following the systematic procedure of Yin (2009), this explorative case study comprised two distinct, analytical steps. In the first step, the researcher read the 33 solver profiles and coded them inductively according to what the solvers stated motivates them to participate in online ICs, including both explanations of why they participate and what they enjoy about this work (Elo & Kyngäs, 2008; Mayring, 2004). Here, an open coding approach was used, creating tentative themes that describe different motivational factors (Marshall & Rossman, 2011: 214-215). As part of this initial coding, themes were produced and compared. The analysis focused on identifying similarities, rather than differences, between solvers in the different intermediaries in an attempt to locate the general motivations that characterize top solvers. This first step is an inductive, or data-driven, explorative approach, where the coding is performed separately from matrixes or predetermined analytical categories (Yin, 2009).

In the next phase of the data analysis, the categories from the review were used as a framework to reorganize the data. The data themes were compared with the initial categories from the review and adjusted to better fit the concepts from the literature review (e.g. Marshall & Rossman, 2011). The themes were important in the formulation of the motivational framework's sub-dimensions. Both data and theory are important in capturing a larger variation of motivational factors that influence solvers. This interplay builds on abductive reasoning (Van de Ven, 2007), with an emphasis on using both data and relevant studies to develop appropriate categories.

In the discussion, the six major motivational dimensions are described as part of a comprehensive motivational typology and are analyzed in relation both to other empirical studies of the new collaborative economy and to broader motivational theories (e.g. Csikszentmihalyi, 1990; Maslow, 2013). This composite typology is key as most solver profiles reveal a complex motivational mix that drives online IC participation. Various quotations from the profiles are included in the analysis because they represent rich, informative statements, illustrating the complex solver motives. As these quotations are often informal statements, they frequently contain grammatical errors; the statements are copied in their original form into this study. Note that some of the statements about motivation have been left out in the final report because they are redundant and do not offer new information regarding the motivational framework.

MAIN FOCUS OF THE CHAPTER

Perceived Learning as Motivation

Cognitive Learning as Motivation

In accordance with the findings from the literature review, this study shows that many solvers underline learning as a motivational factor, indicating the importance of *improving their own cognitive learning*. For example, one solver at IdeaConnection explains how participation improves his problem-solving skills, "The process of attempting to solve the problems is shaping my ability. So I have been honing my talent and making myself better at solving problems for a long while". A solver at Topcoder similarly claims that the "extremely high standards will permeate from the competitions you work on into other projects as well, making you a much more valuable engineer and worker". Even without winning the contest, this way of working and solving problems will benefit your ordinary work. According to another solver at Topcoder, you become a better programmer because you work with much harder problems, "I think one of the major reasons is because we are challenged to solve much more difficult problems than what we usually solve in our day jobs. When you start solving those problems, the easier problems you encounter on a day-to-day basis seem to get a lot easier". A study of Innocentive similarly shows that solvers report learning new skills (Innocent et al., 2017). Learning is very important as the solvers know that they will often not receive any payment. Likewise, in another Topcoder study, a solver is motivated by challenges he has never met before and learning about new technologies (Shafiei Gol et al., 2018), suggesting that the technological challenges develop the solvers' competence in a way that it is helpful for their professional work. Another solver highlights that learning happens all the time:

There's always a learning curve and we keep on learning. I used to tell my students that every scientist and every researcher should think of themselves as a student. If I don't think of myself as a student then I can never be a scientist. (ID)

The solver has a profound view of learning in which even the expert learns all the time. Knowledge is never a waste, and may be relevant on another occasion:

The way I look at things is that if people lose a particular challenge, instead of saying 'I lost' they should focus on what they have learned. For example, they may have learned what not to do or how to do something better the next time. (ID)

At one level, most solvers acknowledge that they acquire new skills through participating in different online contests. For example, one solver at Topcoder claims that his motivation for competition prompted him to learn most of his technical skills. Another solver claims that the programming competitions help improve your programming skills, which is especially important when writing code because after some time one will otherwise often stop improving (TC). As one solver states, "For example, with the introduction of wireframe contests, I learnt how to make prototypes in Axure completely from scratch, constantly looking up resources online, if only to keep up with the competition" (TC). The learning process, which in this case starts from scratch, happens under strong time pressure to keep up with the competition. The solver is also excited about being able to join a project at any stage, anywhere (TC), indicating a strong degree of task self-selection.

A solver at eÿeka states that he has struggled to find his personal creative style, but participation in eÿeka helped him to decide to specialize in stop-motion paper animation; today, this choice allows him to design various creative products (ey). On the other hand, some solvers highlight the development of a broader set of skills. For example, before joining eÿeka, a certain copywriter did not care much about his layout abilities, but participation in various contests made him think further about good product designs and so expanded his creative repertoire. A solver at IdeaConnection also underlines that this type of problem-solving forces you to practice your knowledge and test it actively, helping you not to forget it (ID).

Collective Learning as Motivation

The findings also suggest a *second perspective on learning by motivation.* As IdeaConnection is centered on team work, several of the solvers highlight the value of *collective learning*. For example, one solver highlights the value of learning something from other team members "and using other people's knowledge to increase my own" (ID). Knowledge sharing in the team happens during the problem-solving process. Another solver underlines that everyone learns from everyone in the team, "Everybody came from a different background, and so we all learnt from each other about lots of different aspects. And I think everybody felt that way" (ID). The multidisciplinary teams create a feeling of learning through diversity because each member brings a unique contribution. A third solver highlights the value of observing the contributions of people from other areas:

I think it was interesting from an intellectual perspective to see some information from other people's areas. It gave me some extra depth in an area and I actually came up with a potential invention which was in a related field. So that was an unexpected benefit. (ID)

Here, the solver acquires "some extra depth in an area" or a deeper understanding of the problem through the diverse contributions, which also helped him at a later occasion. At Topcoder, several solvers also highlight the learning value of accessing how others have tried to solve a similar problem. One solver says, "After the match, I saw chokudai's spreadsheet. It had all local testing result from his methods. It struck my head immediately and seemed to light my way forward – I'm still using this methodology when doing every MM" (TC). The phrase "struck my head immediately and seemed to light my way forward" indicates that deep learning can happen by seeing others' solutions, which can strongly impact on the solver's future work. Likewise, another solver is explicit about the learning value of observing other solutions:

One thing that really helped me was the ability to see other people's solutions to the problem. When I would finish coding my problem, and look at the other solutions to the problem, I would always find new ways of using some of the base language or library features that had never occurred to me. (TC)

By observing alternative solutions, the solver almost immediately receives new ideas. A bonus with Topcoder is that the final competitors have the opportunity to see the designs and the codes of the other finalists; this is part of the award and helps competitors to keep improving (Shafiei Gol et al., 2018).

Regarding team skills, another solver describes how this work has improved his ability to work in multidisciplinary and multicultural teams, "Actually I gained a lot of experience in how to work in this kind of team with people from different backgrounds and different cultures" (ID). All these solvers share a conception of team work as integral to an informal learning process, where learning also takes place through problem-solving.

Furthermore, at Topcoder, solvers describe the learning that happens in the online community. One solver says, "The forums were a place to ask questions, and I was encouraged to read up further and look up interesting new technologies and design trends" (TC). In the forums, people motivate and help each other, and some solvers also share a large amount of their work on their own blogs (TC). This coincides with another study of Topcoder solvers, showing that learning opportunities and feedback on their work are considered important (Shafiei Gol et al., 2018). Furthermore, solvers in the present study report that participation in the online community helps to establish professional networks with people outside the contests (TC). Although the environment is competitive, there is a sense of knowledge sharing and helping.

Transformative Learning as Motivation

In addition, the findings indicate the presence of a *third perspective on learning by motivation*, here labeled as transformative learning. Several solvers describe experiences that expand their human capabilities and help fulfill their personal potential. Mike, a solver, explains how winning awards at eÿeka have changed his life in many ways. Winning prizes has influenced how he views himself and transformed his life skills in a positive way:

That has changed my life in many ways. Especially in the perception of the challenges and overcoming problems. Nothing is impossible, fight with all possible disadvantages and do not give up. If you use all your strength to move forward, you arrive where you want. To this day, I am still competing, and I press on. (ey)

With the phrase "nothing is impossible," Mike signals that he is no longer afraid of facing difficult challenges in other areas of life. His personal character is strengthened and able to endure resistance. The formulation of "you arrive where you want" points to a goal-seeking activity and an emphasis on daring to follow your dream and becoming who you want to be. Likewise, another solver thinks that winning a contest has been important for his personal development:

I won the Marathon finals. I definitely didn't feel like a contender for a champion title, so I was both very happy and surprised with the result. This was also the last finals where there was no close race for the first place. So why was this so important for me? It marked the point in time, where I finally started to believe in myself—for quite a long time I thought that I'm able to get decent results in Marathons because I put a lot of time into them, way more than anyone else. (TC)

Winning the Marathon final marked the point when the solver began to believe in himself. His description of receiving a champion title resembles how winners are acknowledged in sport events, boosting their self-confidence to new heights. Not so differently, a solver at eÿeka explains how the contests have made him constantly improve and challenge himself:

Eÿeka also gave me opportunities to push my limits further when creating a video: when you have to make a video for high standing brands, who require high quality videos, you have to meet great persons, you have to find the best places to shoot, you have to ask professionals to shoot with you... you go further... you become better, with some difficulties sometimes, but that's what makes you stronger. The most important thing is not the destination, but the journey. (ey)

The solver has raised his production standards and work quality through the advanced requirements in the ICs. By emphasizing the journey and not the destination, he places a focus on pushing limits and trying to improve all the time.

A solver explains that eÿeka "brought me back on the right track," by revealing the type of work he is really passionate about after winning a contest (ey). Another solver talks about a new desire to do the work that now influences his life, "I need this. This is what makes me alive. This has become an evidence. I can't do without this now" (ey). The phrases "I need this" or "I can't do without this now" describe the work as becoming a basic need, suggesting an addictive, almost obsessive motivation. In describing the work as what makes him alive, the solver illustrates how the contest has touched him in a fundamental way, giving new meaning to his life. Another solver emphasizes the transformation of realizing that he is a creative person, "eÿeka gave me the opportunity to prove myself that I am a creative person. I learned that no matter what everybody tells you, you got to follow your gut and just do what makes you happy" (ey). His description suggests a personal growth that is both about becoming independent and finding yourself

These solver narratives illustrate that winning an IC can trigger a personal transformation that changes the perceived life journey and self-perception and creates a sense of fulfilling one's personal potential.

Being Immersed

Many solvers describe being immersed when they face difficult problems. One eÿeka solver states, "I missed that moment in which you have to think and break your head to come up with a good idea." The phrase "break your head" illustrates the substantial mental energy required to solve the problem she needs to work with. Another solver explains how this work pushes him to the boundaries of his own creative capabilities, "Don't even get me started about how much eÿeka has made my brain explode in the creative category." Both the "breaking of a head" and the "brain explosion" provide vivid descriptions of how solvers meet the toughest problems with enthusiasm and fearlessness. Likewise, another study of IdeaConnection shows that solvers actually want the worst problems and dive into the challenges (Innocent et al., 2017).

This state of mind fuels large amounts of motivation. For example, another solver in the present study explains how he continuously works on the same problem:

I would say that it's the process that I enjoy the most, the process I have to go through. The brain keeps working and going off in different directions and tries to look at things from different perspectives which are needed to come up with a brand new solution that appeals to a seeker. I find this process really amazing. (ID)

The solver seems almost not in charge of his own thinking; the creative process does not rely entirely on intentional control but takes unexpected directions, amazing the solver. By loosening his reflective control, he is more open to "free associations." Under these conditions, even hard and exhausting work is perceived as enjoyable. Similarly, another solver recounts how he thinks about the problem every day:

I participated almost every day, right up until the last moment when I was occupied with my niece's wedding. Up until then, I was working almost around the clock, not sleeping much and waking up with ideas. It was enjoyable and tiring sometimes but you know when something is really enjoyable you just forget about all your tiredness. (ID)

Because the work is perceived as enjoyable, the solver does not notice that he is tired. By working "around the clock" and "waking up with ideas," he shows a strong level of immersion—almost to the level of obsession—that makes an extraordinary effort possible. On the other hand, there are also solvers who scan challenges and only work on problems they think they can solve quickly because they already have the appropriate expertise. Likewise, in a study of Innocentive, another intermediary, solvers highlight the intellectual freedom of the problem-solving process and the fact that there are no limitations or restrictions on how you approach the problem (Innocent et al., 2017). The contest offers the freedom to choose the problems you want to work with according to your interests.

Furthermore, the findings indicate that solvers become immersed because of the contest format. At eÿeka, one solver claims that the contests make your brain produce more creative work than usual, as if the contest triggers an arousal that makes him more creative. One Topcoder solver reports being attracted to the contests because they are really fun. A second Topcoder solver describes participation in programming contests as being a "hell of a lot of fun", with the contests quickly becoming his new hobby. Here, strong passion for the work is closely connected to being part of a contest.

Reaching the finals appears to trigger even more motivation. In one example, two groups are selected for the final round, "Yes, that's exactly right. They let us know they had selected two groups, ours and another and gave us a few questions which gave away more about what they were looking for and so we hit those questions really hard." (ID) When the contest includes a final round, with only two groups left, the likelihood of winning is much higher, thus intensifying the race. The almost addictive motivation to participate in contests is vividly described by a third Topcoder solver:

I got hooked on Algorithm contests immediately. The sweet anticipation of Coding Phase? (...), the adrenaline rush of coding against the clock, the frenzy of Challenge Phase and the wearing wait for the final results... After the first couple of matches I was addicted. Between the competitions I've read every feature article on the site and every thread in the forums, and still it was not enough to satisfy my addiction. A bit later bimonthly Marathon Matches were introduced for people who need more than two hours of competing per week, and they turned out to be even better than SRMs – less adrenaline-filled but more exploratory. (TC)

The match concept indicates a strong degree of gamification with tight deadlines, leaderboards, and a race against the clock. To some solvers, this is highly motivating, and some report dedicating a large amount of time during the contest period. For example, one solver describes the final rounds as requiring non-stop work, with solutions being submitted all the time (TC). As one solver describes:

Over time, participating in Design Studio contests instilled in me a strong sense of discipline and precision. The tightly defined specifications and instructions, the rush to submit mere minutes before a deadline, that facepalm feeling when you fail screening for simple mistakes in font declaration, the anticipation while checking tournament leaderboards, the recognized faces in the forums, the grogginess from staying awake working for ten hours straight on contest after contest, that final thrill of seeing that your submission has won -These are all things that are endearingly familiar and common to any Design Studio competitor. (TC)

Here, the solver describes a contest that create a strong sense of discipline and precision in his work, partly due to time pressure and the need to finish before close deadlines. During the contest, the leaderboard scores also create sustained excitement, as the solver reports working for ten hours straight on contest after contest.

Moreover, several solvers highlight how the collaboration and diversity of the team has positively influenced their motivation. One IdeaConnection solver emphasizes three benefits of being in a team, "The first is that you get different cultures, people from different backgrounds. Second, you get different perspectives. And third is the sharing of the workload and responsibilities" (ID). Concerning diversity, the solver underlines the value of being on a team with both a multicultural and multidisciplinary background. The multidisciplinary diversity also helps avoid "free riders" because all members are assigned a specific role in the team. One solver reports that it is not a problem when the team members are strangers to each other because they all bring unique experiences to the table. When everyone can make a contribution, it helps the team work (ID). Another solver, who also enjoys the diversity in the team work, also distinguishes between multicultural and multidisciplinary diversity, indicating the value both in working with "people from different disciplines" and people from "different parts of the world" (ID). Likewise, another solver highlights the fun and interest of being in multidisciplinary groups:

When a single person works on something you may only get one idea. But this rally which was about chemistry also attracted biochemists and biologists and people from a biotechnology background and so on. Each one viewed the challenge from their own perspective and that's the whole fun and interesting thing because your angle is going to be different from another person's angle. When you start getting different angles you receive a fuller picture. (ID)

As the solver observes, with "different angles you receive a fuller picture," increasing both the benefits of team work and the quality of the solution. In addition, other solvers highlight the value of multicultural diversity between team members, "It is very interesting to work with people who have different talents and who think differently from you. It is great to discuss ideas with other people around the world and figure out a solution" (ID).

However, the team diversity makes several solvers underline the importance of having a facilitator who can help organize the group work (ID) and follow a clearly planned schedule with weekly meetings (ID). One specific challenge is to ensure equal participation and prevent people becoming too aggressive concerning their own ideas (ID). The facilitator often also helps the team in writing down the final solution (ID). At Topcoder, there is no facilitator because of the lack of teamwork, but there is a co-pilot who helps organize the contests and communication with the client (TC).

Being Part of a Community

Several solvers mention the value of being part of a community as a motivational factor. One Topcoder solver reports having met many exceptional people, resulting in long-term friendships. Another solver says, "This is what I want to do. This makes me feel happy. It was then when I realized I had built significant relationships with talented people all around the world thanks to Topcoder." His network of friends make it possible to have at "least one available couch on every continent" (TC). At Topcoder, some individuals underline the establishment of tight social connections, like friendship. At IdeaConnection, solvers are more focused on the quality of relationships during the teamwork:

I also enjoyed the comradery of the group. There was a young person from Nigeria and he and I linked up via this Idea Rally and we got to make a good personal connection. I also encouraged the community spirit of people working together. There were several who collaborated and contributed ideas as part of a group. It was a good feeling to be connected with people from all over the world that you might not otherwise have met. (ID)

Here, the solver highlights the comradery and community spirit of the group working on the same problem. Although the group of solvers does not necessarily become friends, good personal connections in the group allow good discussions.

Furthermore, an important part of being together in a community often involves arranging meetings. One IdeaConnection solver states that successfully reaching final rounds has given him the opportunity to travel to places like Massachusetts Institute of Technology (MIT) and Oak Ridge to compete and "that was great seeing those historic locations." By traveling to compete at a special location, the solver feels that he is part of something important. Another Topcoder solver reports being very motivated to participate in onsite programming tournaments finals, "being in the same room with some of the smartest Topcoders working on the same problems is humbling, exhausting and inspiring at the same time." Brought together with other coders, the individuals experience a stronger sense of community. A Topcoder solver explicitly underlines that these meetings help establish close relations between community members and staff, describing all of them as a "big global family." The contest is not only about the challenge, or growing your skills, "but above all – to make great friends" (ID).

Another Topcoder finalist underlines the joy of informal social events at these tournaments, like parties with other developers, where one can share stories and drinks, and of having time off to walk around downtown in the tournament city (TC). The motivation is less about winning the contest than meeting interesting people and enjoying foreign cultures. As one solver explains:

But the biggest lesson I learned was that I absolutely love those onsite events. You get to travel, meet many interesting people, take part in thrilling contests and enjoy foreign culture. The only sad moment is when everything ends and you have to return to your normal life. So, naturally, my goal was to qualify for as many events as possible. Like a child, I wanted to have as much fun as I could and this was the best way to do it. (ID)

The onsite finals trigger motivation when the solvers feel that they are part of an exciting community, can travel around the world, and share experiences with likeminded others.

Being Recognized for Your Work

Solvers report being proud and more self-confident after winning contests. One solver at eÿeka states, "Thanks to eÿeka now I believe in my strengths and talent even more. It encourages me to participate in online contests and develop my skills." Believing more in his own strengths indicates a positive change in his self-esteem. Another person even joined an eÿeka contest to prove to himself that he was actually a creative person because he was not acknowledged at his old job. In Topcoder, a solver explains that he entered the contest to improve his pride and self-confidence:

Me, some idiot who hardly feels like I know what I am doing managed to take second place in a contest between some of the more prominent programmers in the cloud computing arena. I felt validated. Maybe I could do this? Maybe I am good enough? I told my boss that I had placed. He sent an email to the company letting them know. All day I received congratulations and pats on the back. I was hooked. (…) That is why I compete. It's not about the money. It's not even really about the technology. For me it's a form of validation. To know that I can run with some of the best. That I can solve problems others can't. To know that I am at the cutting edge and pushing it further.

The phrase "I felt validated" indicates a boost in his self-confidence, reinforced by the acknowledgement he receives from his work colleagues. The competition is about trying to test his own skills and being able to compete with some of the best. It illustrates how closely connected self-esteem is with the recognition one receives from others. Although not all contestants win prizes, it can be enough for some to be briefly on the leaderboard. One solver reported that the most memorable moment of an online contest was when he was temporarily in first place—a unique experience that gave him some confidence (TC).

For some solvers, the financial reward is not very important in itself, but it signals appreciation of the solver's solution (ID). Some also experience these contests as fairer and less about internal politics than their other work. Because "it all depends on your creativity" (ey), the contests are perceived as a more objective measure of how creative you are.

Furthermore, solvers include their awards on their CVs, displaying their reputation from such contests when they apply for normal paid work (ey). For example, a solver at Topcoder states that her merits got her several job interviews with companies she would have never dared to apply to otherwise. Another solver, describing programming as his hobby and passion, eventually acquired a job as a software developer after one and a half years of work at Topcoder (TC). Likewise, another study reports that individuals join Topcoder to build a reputation (Shafiei Gol et al., 2018).

Moreover, the social impact of winning a contest can also be an important motivation. One eÿeka solver was proud when the winner video was shown on national television:

"I was one of the happiest men on this planet!! A friend called saying to me: Man!!! This is what we've made both together!!!! And we can see it on the big screen!!!! Wow!!! Watch your TV right now!!! My wife was proud of me… I saw it in her eyes. Magic moment." (ey)

The solver's intense feelings of pride are closely connected to the public recognition of his work, creating a feeling of personal accomplishment closely attached to its societal impact. In addition, his own pride increases when he observes that his wife is proud too, illustrating how self-esteem is closely tied to the desire for respect from significant others.

The Prize Money

Although the size of the prize and the number of winners vary, most ICs offer prize money to the winners. In this study, all the solvers have won financial rewards. However, the economic motivation differs significantly, ranging from being vital to personal income to being a bonus. A solver at eÿeka made a dream come true by using the prize money to finance a study abroad, covering one year of tuition fees in Europe, "I am very happy and still cannot believe it!" In some countries, the economic rewards provide opportunities that may be difficult to obtain otherwise. Several solvers also recount how the award was important income in a difficult life situation. One eÿeka solver explains how the work gave her independence after she began to work by herself; eÿeka provided extra income, and the prize money from the contests made it possible to buy a new car and move to a new house. Another solver explains how eÿeka provided important extra income when she stopped working to be with her daughter when she was one year old. In Topcoder, a solver would also like it to be more prize receivers because this would increase the participation and engagement (TC).

The Solver Personality

Some solvers report having a special personality with a particular interest in solving problems. These people are in search for a context where they can use their talent, and online ICs represent one such area. For example, one solver explains that he is interested in almost every area of science and engineering, being a "real science geek" (ID). He has always wanted to be a freelance inventor, having many ideas and being good at solving problems. However, he struggled to find what needs to be invented; but now, at IdeaConnection, "people are coming to me with problems that I can then try and solve". By describing himself as a "real science geek", he also signals that he has a strong intrinsic motivation to solve any kind of scientific problem. Another solver describes this personality as having an "instinctive" urge to solve problems:

I have more of a background in physics than chemistry but the methodology of solving problems is natural and instinctive to me. So when I see a problem my brain just naturally finds a way to solve it. I searched and read some information related to the challenge and I immersed myself in it to come up with a solution. (ID)

Here, the solver describes the problem-solving process as something that happens automatically without being forced, indicating a strong intrinsic motivation.

At IdeaConnection, which requires team work, several solvers describe themselves as having collaborative personalities in similar terms:

IdeaConnection is a platform where I can use my knowledge to solve the challenges. I know there are websites where you can do this alone but the beauty of IdeaConnection is to do it to together in a team. For me, from my childhood onwards I have always worked with a team so it was a good match for me (…) I'm a people person so I like working with strangers. Out of the 16 people I have worked with I'm still friendly with 15 of them. They don't remain as strangers after one week or so. That's a good part of working on the challenges. (ID)

This solver describes himself as someone who has wanted to work in teams since he was a child. Working with unknown others motivates him, and he finds that the team relationship improves during the work.

Another characteristic of the online ICs is that many people are allowed to do creative work. One solver at eÿeka works as a professional wedding photographer, but by participating in the ICs, he has realized that his passion is capturing moments in real life. Here, the online setting offers him a different type of work that he is passionate about. The challenges are more creative or advanced than those of his daily work. Similarly, another solver finds that eÿeka offers him new types of creative challenges, "For the first time in my career, I have the opportunity to think about product innovations and meaningful package design to my personal creative limits" (ey). At Topcoder, a solver notes that he has had incredible opportunities, working with world-leading organizations like NASA or companies like Facebook and Google, which he would have never imagined before joining Topcoder. Another solver recounts being totally uninterested in his university studies because he could not realize any of his ideas. By joining Topcoder, he had the opportunity to begin relevant work while still a student. Another solver states that eÿeka has helped to boost his professional career:

I am creative audiovisual, but I work as a security guard at night. (…) I never had the chance to show my ability. I've been trying to make what I like in my work for many years. A year ago, when I took for granted that it would be impossible to make a great commercial for a prestigious brand, I was encour-

aged to participate in eÿeka. Till today I have won 3 international awards staying in 1st place for brands such as Close-up. That has changed my life in many ways. (ey)

The solver underlines that he had not been given the chance to "show his ability" and that this is what the ICs permit. Consequently, he won several awards, exceeding the limits of what he previously thought was possible for him to do.

Furthermore, solvers highlight the work autonomy that these ICs provide. One solver at eÿeka likes that he can decide which problems to work on and sometimes even the clients (ey). A solver at Topcoder enjoys that he can work from home and also travel often because the online work is location independent. Another solver reports:

Working for Topcoder has given me immense freedom in terms of how my life can be structured. I have the freedom to work whenever and wherever I want (as long as I have an internet connection), and I can work as much or as little as I want to as well. I get paid more than I ever could in a "normal" job in my geographic area, and the financial freedom has allowed me to travel and do things I wouldn't have been able to do otherwise. (TC)

The solver explains that he can have a much more flexible work schedule compared with having a normal job at the location where he lives. Now he is free to choose where and when he wants to work, making it possible to move to a warmer place in the cold winter climate where he lives. Other solvers have retired, but still want to make societal contributions:

I was bored. The Internet has been a godsend to me being an information freak and living in the less populace west where I don't have the big university libraries next door anymore. (…) One of the real attractions to me as a problem solver is that I can sit here in my little place in New Mexico and enjoy my quiet lifestyle and yet through IdeaConnection I am working with some of the best brains in the world to solve these problems. (…) Being retired I miss the connection with the really active research world. So this gives me the satisfaction of knowing that I'm still helping to contribute to solving some of society's problems. (ID)

As a senior citizen, he misses his active life as a researcher, labeling himself as a bored "information freak." The ICs have given new meaning to his life, and, because he lives in a remote area, this work would not have been possible without its online setting. The solver highlights the opportunity to collaborate with other highly skilled persons, the "best brains in the world." In the phrase "I'm still helping to contribute to solving some of society's problems," one senses the feeling of being important again.

SOLUTION AND RECOMMENDATIONS

A Motivational Typology for Creative Problem-Solving

In conclusion, the six motivational dimensions presented in this chapter provide an overview of the complex motives that drive creative problem-solving in online ICs. The table below summarizes the empirical findings and provides a tentative, comprehensive motivational typology for such problem-solving, showing categories, themes, and other relevant motivational theories.

Table 3. A motivational framework for creative problem-solving in ICs

Main categories (dimensions)	Sub-categories	Themes	Relevant motivational theories
1. Learning as motivation	1.1 Cognitive learning	- Problem-solving skills - New professional skills	Metacognition (Flavell, 1979)
	1.2 Collective learning	- Learning from other team members - Teamwork skills - Learning by observing others - Learning by sharing knowledge - Learning through informal feedback from the community	Situated learning (Lave & Wenger, 1991)
	1.3 Transformative learning	- Resilience - Self-discovery	Self-actualization (Maslow, 2013)
2. Being immersed	- Individual flow - Contest flow - Collaborative flow	- Complete absorption in the work - Strong pleasure and joy - Excitement to be part of a contest - Appreciation for diverse contributions - Need for a facilitator to control the teamwork	Flow (Csikszentmihalyi, 1990)
3. Being part of a community	- Good team relationship - Togetherness at onsite gatherings	- Good professional relations - Friendly relationships - Sharing onsite experiences	Love and belonging (Maslow, 1981)
4. Being recognized	- Pride in creative work - Recognition for creative work	- Pride from being acknowledged as the best among peers - Reputation building - Pride in the societal impact of the work - Recognition from significant others (peers, colleagues, friends)	(i) Esteem for oneself (ii) Desire for reputation or respect from others (Maslow, 1981)
5. Prize money	- Variation in the prize amount and the number of winners - Huge variation in economic motivation	- Important income with high economic value (for those in the Global South and freelancers) - Bonus to sufficient salary	- Safety and physiological needs (Maslow, 1981) - Achievement motivation (Wigfield & Eccles, 2000)
6. The solver personality	- Being a problem solver - Inclusion in creative work	- Collaborative personality - Equal opportunity to solve problems (for students, outsiders, seniors)	Self-actualization (Maslow, 1981)

Learning as Motivation

First, the section on *learning as motivation* shows that solvers are motivated by at least three different types of learning: cognitive learning, collective learning, and transformative learning. As the review has shown, several studies find that participants in online ICs are generally motivated by learning. Further research should address these three specific views on learning in more detail.

The findings show a significant *perception of cognitive learning as motivation.* Several solvers are strongly aware of how creative problem-solving improves their individual learning. Many attempt to overcome their creative limitations and expand on their present professional and cognitive skills. On the one hand, some solvers learn new skills from the beginning, indicating strong self-regulated learning motivated by the contest format. In the contest, solving advanced problems often requires the development of new professional skills. Hence, the solvers do this work to broaden their expertise or skill sets. On the other hand, solvers with substantial expertise participate in the contest to keep their existing skills up-to-date.

Other solvers underline how the contests improve their general abilities to solve problems, with the challenges being more advanced than those they are used to. This training is valuable when they attempt to solve problems in their regular professional work, thus indicating that metacognition or an awareness of how learning to learn can be a motivational factor (Flavell, 1979).

Moreover, among the solvers, there is a significant degree of *perceived collective learning as motivation.* Solvers describe learning that motivates and is different from pure individual learning. Some solvers are excited about learning together in new ways in a team environment. They also discover that learning is motivated by transparent knowledge sharing. For example, solvers at Topcoder are motivated to access to winners' solutions to problems they tried to solve or to discuss problems in online forums. This perception of learning resembles situated learning (Lave & Wenger, 1991), which describes the importance of observational learning at work and how people help each other through near-peer learning.

Furthermore, several solvers describe *perceived transformative learning as an important part of their motivation.* Two personal qualities stand out as essential for motivation. First, the solvers feel that they have become more resilient by pushing themselves to become better and to never give up in the contests. Second, winning the contests has had a large impact on them, helping them discover that they actually are creative people. Some stories show signs of a profound personal awakening, not so much about becoming a solver but about becoming who they are as a person. These transformative learning processes resemble what Maslow described as self-actualization, with an emphasis on realizing personal potential and seeking personal growth (Maslow, 2013). Note that although the solvers in the present study highlight different aspects of learning as motivational factors, they all share a strong awareness of how they learn as solvers.

This finding differs from other studies of motivation in the new collaborative economy, where there is little focus on learning processes. For example, Hamari et al. (2016) highlight enjoyment but do not link it to learning. Although there is a significant focus on sustainability and the adoption of green values, participants are usually assumed to have acquired such values already (Hamari et al., 2016). There is less emphasis on how participation can lead toward more sustainable behavior. The present study also provides no information about sustainable learning because few of the solvers worked with this issue. Here, solvers' perceptions of transformative learning are primarily about individual empowerment, and it is unclear whether this will lead to the adoption of green values in the future.

Being Immersed

Second, in the section on *being immersed*, solvers state that they were completely absorbed in the problem-solving process. They note a strong sense of pleasure from overcoming difficult challenges and that during the experience, "the brain keeps working." These reports match the following statement by Csikszentmihalyi about flow, "The best moments in our lives are not the passive, receptive, relaxing times . . . The best moments usually occur if a person's body or mind is stretched to its limits in a voluntary effort to accomplish something difficult and worthwhile" (1990: 3). This flow occurs in complete concentration on a task, its intrinsically rewarding experience, and the feeling that time is transformed while the solver is immersed.

In addition, there is an element of "contest flow," as the solvers report "the thrill of a contest" and their work being spurred by the game features. Solvers want to be on the leaderboard and push their limits to finish the work within the deadline. If they reach the finals, they work even harder. Although flow describes a balance between skill level and the challenge, these contests appear to push the solvers' skills to a higher level because the difficulty of the challenge is greater than the solver's initial skill level. At IdeaConnection, there is also a "collaborative flow." Both multidisciplinary and multicultural diversity trigger interest and joy, strengthening the immersion with others into the shared group work. In these teams, the facilitator keeps control over the task to ensure the team's creativity.

Likewise, surveying why people participate in the collaborative economy, Hamarai et al. (2016) find that enjoyment is the strongest determinant, characterized as an intrinsic motivation that emerges through the activity itself. It is associated with pleasurable and communal activities and is typical in open-source projects and online information sharing. Here, there are obvious similarities with the solvers' feelings of being immersed in challenging work. However, in the ICs, the pleasure is not related to a simple trading of goods but with the positive feelings of a struggle, which is often a time-consuming, exhausting challenge. Further studies should be conscious about the significant variations in what enjoyment can be in the new collaborative economy.

Being Part of a Community

Third, the section on *being part of a community* shows that most solvers want to be part of a community with good relationships between members. Although the need for friends is not as important as teamwork at IdeaConnection, some solvers still report that they made friends, while others report that they established professional networks. Solvers at Topcoder also highlight the importance of attending onsite meetings to motivate stronger feelings of belonging to the same community, thus increasing the likelihood of establishing long-term professional networks and friendships. This motivational dimension is similar to the love and belongingness needs identified by Maslow (1981).

Similarly, researchers have suggested that the new collaborative economy will replace hierarchies and foster personal ties between users and suppliers (Sundararajan, 2016). Many platforms underline the extra benefit of meeting people, making friends, and getting to know others. For example, some Airbnb hosts engage in social activities with their guests, and, at TaskRabbit, some participants build new social networks and meet people they would not otherwise have met. However, while earlier adopters seem more open to social connection, this motivational factor is now declining as more people participate for economic reasons (Frenken & Schor, 2019). The present study also reveals tensions between solvers who participate to gain friends and partake in a community of likeminded people (e.g. Topcoder) and those who establish relations to increase the likelihood of winning a contest or creating professional networks (e.g. IdeaConnection).

This interaction with strangers is perhaps the most important aspect of the collaborative economy. Historically, people have usually not shared anything with those outside their trusted social networks of family, friends, and neighbors (Frenken & Schor, 2019). While the intimacy of sharing a home or car entails a high degree of risk, participating in ICs is much less risky as it is often done anonymously online.

As the emphasis in online ICs is increasingly orientated toward teamwork, the ability to collaborative with unknown others in an efficient way will be become more important. For example, at IdeaConnection, the team members do not know each other in advance and are only together in an online setting for a limited amount of weeks. In addition, the solvers often communicate anonymously with the seeker.

Being Recognized for Your Work

Fourth, as discussed in the section on *being recognized for your work*, several solvers report being proud and more self-confident after winning contests. Winning a prize often produces a feeling of validation of a person's professional skills in comparison with other highly skilled peers. Therefore, the award can be important for a person's professional identity and self-understanding as a creative person. Awards often build reputation and can be included on a résumé. In addition, the examples show that the boost of pride and self-esteem is closely intertwined with the recognition one receives from others through the contest and praise from significant others, such as colleagues, friends, and family. Another type of recognition is the work's value; if the work has a societal impact, this increases motivation. Such motivation resembles Maslow's identification of esteem needs, which includes both the need for self-esteem and the desire for reputation or respect from others (Maslow, 1981).

Likewise, individuals in the new collaborative economy are often motivated to share information to enhance their personal reputation or status as a part of a self-marketing process (Hamari et al., 2016; Sundararajan, 2016, 2018). However, the primary purpose is not to strengthen motivation, but to establish trust between participants. Rating systems aim to make stranger sharing in trade less risky by indicating how users have behaved previously. Although the ratings are not necessarily very accurate, they have been sufficient to entice many people to engage in new economic activities (Frenken & Schor, 2019). Any specific type of collaborative economy is reliant on the trusted exchange of goods and services, primarily done by integrating social ties into commercial exchange. This is possible both because of all the automatically stored traces of online activities and the increased use of online reviews (Sundararajan, 2016, 2018).

In some innovation intermediaries, like IdeaConnection, reputation is important in selecting team members. However, in the ICs, reputation largely involves demonstrating your skills and receiving acknowledgement, which can help build a personal and professional identity and is useful to becoming an important member in an online community. The present study indicates that the motivation of being recognized both serves individual needs and builds a reputation system, making it key for establishing trust in the collaborative economy.

The Prize Money

Fifth, the section on *prize money* indicates that the value of money differs greatly depending on where a person lives. In the Global South, solvers use the money to buy a house or receive an education. For these solvers, everyday safety and physiological needs provide motivation (Maslow, 1981). For several solvers from Europe and the United States, however, the prize money is just seen as a bonus. Yet some are also freelancers and view the prize money as paid work and an important source of extra income. They more carefully assess the probability of being able to solve the problem and win the contest (Wigfield & Eccles, 2000). However, economic benefits cannot be the only reason for participating as most participants, including the top solvers, often receive no prize money. Hence, the motivation of an enjoyable learning process is important. Similarly, Hamari et al. (Hamari et al., 2016) claim the collaborative economy is less about economic benefits and more about enjoyment and adhering to important societal values.

However, concerning economic gains in the new collaborative economy, there are usually few disadvantages for lenders because the person does not need the product during the lending period, whereas the borrower gains access to it without charge. Hence, the transaction costs are lowered (Frenken & Schor, 2019). Similarly, the terms for the seeker in online ICs are very good because payment is often only necessary if the provided solution is regarded as satisfactory. As a "borrower" of expertise, the transaction costs for the seeker are low because it is not necessary to use time identifying relevant external expertise. Instead, the solvers will attempt to "lend" their expertise to the seeker, providing several possible solutions to choose between. Just as transaction costs in goods lending are reduced in the collaborative economy, the seeker in online ICs incurs less costs in identifying a solver who can provide a solution.

The Solver Personality

Sixth, the section on *the solver personality* highlights that some individuals solve problems as a hobby. While some like to solve problems alone, others have collaborative personalities and enjoy working with others. The online ICs offer new opportunities for such people, making it easier to access authentic problems and practice their hobby.

At a macro level, these contests challenge traditional divisions of when one can and cannot make a valuable contribution, by including students and seniors. In many of the challenges, anyone can join. Instead of allowing society to decide when a person has to work or stop working, this becomes an individual decision. This inclusivity gives people equal opportunities to solve interesting problems. For example, one solver, who is retired, lived a "boring" life in a remote area until his participation in online ICs. He feels valuable and important even though society has defined him as nonvaluable. Other solvers participate to pursue their hobby or passion. These different solver narratives illustrate that the contest contributes to richer and more varied lives. Online ICs represent an important democratization of creative work opportunities. They also give more people access to motivation for self-actualization (Maslow, 1981), allowing them to choose how they want to live and to pursue a meaningful life in which they can reach their full potential.

In relation to the collaborative economy, one could claim that these individuals desire to utilize more of their personal potential by solving more problems than they are currently doing. As mentioned by Frenken et al (2019), this notion of underutilization is key to understanding the new collaborative economy. However, this issue typically refers to increasing the use of physical assets through home-sharing platforms, such as Airbnb. When a houseowner is away, the asset of an unoccupied house is not utilized, creating a temporary idle capacity (Frenken & Schor, 2019). In contrast, the ICs aim to harvest underutilized non-physical assets, which, in this case, is a solver's capacity to perform creative problem-solving for difficult challenges.

Furthermore, the solver profiles show that a significant number of solvers are independent workers. In the future, it is expected that a larger percentage of the workforce will be freelancers and participate in different types of crowdwork (Sundararajan, 2016, 2018). Note also that several solvers at IdeaConnection participate in addition to their full-time paid work, blurring the lines between personal and professional and between fully employed and casual labor (Sundararajan, 2016, 2018). Therefore, it is important to understand the personality traits of these individuals, who are early adopters of the future of work, and how their motivation corresponds with how different ICs are organized.

CONCLUSION AND FUTURE RESEARCH DIRECTIONS

Further studies should continue to address how we can analytically conceptualize and empirically assess motivation in the new collaborative economy. First, the findings in the present study illustrate that the collaborative economy is evolving in various sub-sectors, making it more difficult to describe motivation within the framework of a few core dimensions. For example, in the most cited article (Google scholar) on motivation in the collaborative economy, Hamari et al. (2016) propose four important motivational factors in this new economy, namely sustainability, enjoyment, reputation, and economic benefits. In contrast, the present study suggests the use of six motivational factors, including several sub-dimensions.

Second, the solver profiles in the present study provide evidence that in some sectors, motivation needs to be investigated as a complex mix of complementary rather than mutually exclusive factors. For example, none of the IC top solvers are motivated by the prize money alone but describe various important motivational factors. One should, therefore, be careful of proposing motivational dichotomies, as do Hamari et al. (2016) in pitching altruistic (sustainability) against individualistic (economic benefits) motivational factors. Consequently, future studies should consider measuring the presence of different motivational factors in both ICs and other sectors of the new collaborative economy. It is also important to investigate the motivation of all solvers, not only the top solvers. We know little about the large majority of solvers who have not won any prizes. A survey could map the relative importance of different factors in the proposed motivational framework and provide more demographic information about the group. Here, accessing user data will be an important issue, as platforms are often restrictive about giving such permissions (Frenken & Schor, 2019).

Third, the present study shows that motivations are quite different when trading creative services compared with trading goods or services that require simple skills. There is a need for further theoretical discussions and a better understanding of how online ICs stimulate motivation in different ways. As previously mentioned, we must explore not only our conceptual understanding of enjoyment in the new collaborative economy but also other motivational factors that can supplement economic motives.

REFERENCES

Agogué, M., Berthet, E., Fredberg, T., Le Masson, P., Segrestin, B., Stoetzel, M., Wiener, M., & Yström, A. (2017). Explicating the role of innovation intermediaries in the "unknown": A contingency approach. *Journal of Strategy and Management*, *10*(1), 19–39. doi:10.1108/JSMA-01-2015-0005

Bakici, T., & Almirall, E. (2017). Intervention intermediaries flourish: Matching firms with solutions to complex needs. *The Journal of Business Strategy*, *38*(4), 21–29. doi:10.1108/JBS-04-2016-0039

Brabham, D. C. (2010). Moving the crowd at Threadless: Motivations for participation in a crowdsourcing application. *Information Communication and Society*, *13*(8), 1122–1145. doi:10.1080/13691181003624090

Chesbrough, H. (2017). The Future of Open Innovation. *Research Technology Management*, *60*(1), 35–38. doi:10.1080/08956308.2017.1255054

Csikszentmihalyi, M. (1990). *Flow: The psychology of optimal experience*. Harper & Row.

Denning, S. (2014). An economy of access is opening for business: Five strategies for success. *Strategy and Leadership*, *42*(4), 14–21. doi:10.1108/SL-05-2014-0037

Flavell, J. H. (1979). Metacognition and cognitive monitoring: A new area of cognitive–developmental inquiry. *The American Psychologist*, *34*(10), 906–911. doi:10.1037/0003-066X.34.10.906

Frankenfield, J. (2018, Jun 24). *Collaborative Economy*. Retrieved from https://www.investopedia.com/terms/c/collaborative-economy.asp

Frenken, K., & Schor, J. (2019). Putting the sharing economy into perspective. In O. Mont (Ed.), *A Research Agenda for Sustainable Consumption Governance* (pp. 121–136). Edward Elgar Publishing. doi:10.4337/9781788117814.00017

Hamari, J., Sjöklint, M., & Ukkonen, A. (2016). The sharing economy: Why people participate in collaborative consumption. *Journal of the Association for Information Science and Technology*, *67*(9), 2047–2059. doi:10.1002/asi.23552

Hofstetter, R., Zhang, J. Z., & Herrmann, A. (2018). Successive Open Innovation Contests and Incentives: Winner-Take-All or Multiple Prizes? *Journal of Product Innovation Management*, *35*(4), 492–517. doi:10.1111/jpim.12424

Hossain, M. (2018). Motivations, challenges, and opportunities of successful solvers on an innovation intermediary platform. *Technological Forecasting and Social Change*, *128*, 67–73. doi:10.1016/j.techfore.2017.10.018

Innocent, M., Gabriel, P., & Divard, R. (2017). Understanding the participation experience of the top contributors in a crowdsourcing of inventive activities context. *Recherche et Applications en Marketing*, *32*(1), 2–20. doi:10.1177/2051570716676257

Lave, J., & Wenger, E. (1991). *Situated learning: legitimate peripheral participation*. Cambridge University Press. doi:10.1017/CBO9780511815355

Lévy, P. (1999). *Collective intelligence: Mankind's emerging world in cyberspace*. Perseus Books.

Malone, T. W. (2018). *Superminds: The Surprising Power of People and Computers Thinking Together*. Little, Brown and Company.

Marshall, C., & Rossman, G. B. (2011). *Designing qualitative research* (5th ed.). Sage.

Maslow, A. H. (1981). *Motivation and personality*. Prabhat Prakashan.

Maslow, A. H. (2013). *Toward a psychology of being*. John Wiley & Sons.

Patton, M. Q. (2002). *Qualitative research and evaluation methods*. Sage.

Shafiei Gol, E., Stein, M.-K., & Avital, M. (2018). *Why take the risk? motivations of highly skilled workers to participate in crowdworking platforms*. Paper presented at the 39th International Conference on Information Systems. ICIS 2018 International Conference on Information Systems, San Francisco, CA.

Sundararajan, A. (2016). *The sharing economy: The end of employment and the rise of crowd-based capitalism*. MIT Press.

Sundararajan, A. (2018). Crowd-based capitalism, digital automation, and the future of work. *University of Chicago Legal Forum.* Retrieved from https://chicagounbound.uchicago.edu/cgi/viewcontent.cgi?article=1606&context=uclf

Terwiesch, C., & Xu, Y. (2008). Innovation contests, open innovation, and multiagent problem solving. *Management Science*, *54*(9), 1529–1543. doi:10.1287/mnsc.1080.0884

Wigfield, A., & Eccles, J. S. (2000). Expectancy–value theory of achievement motivation. *Contemporary Educational Psychology*, *25*(1), 68–81. doi:10.1006/ceps.1999.1015 PMID:10620382

Yin, R. K. (2009). *Case study research: design and methods* (4th ed.). Sage.

KEY TERMS AND DEFINITIONS

Collective Intelligence: Group problem-solving, which includes large-scale collaboration in an online setting.

Creative Problem-Solving: The process of solving complex, open-ended problems.

Intermediaries: Companies that organize innovation contests for seekers. They provide services that make it easy for a solution-seeking organization to use the knowledge of a large pool of solvers.

Motivation: The reason(s) for acting in a specific way, for example, individual needs, desires, wants, or drives.

Online Innovation Contests: A contest hosted by an organization seeking help from outsiders to solve an internal problem. A large number of individuals are invited to join online, and the persons who solve the problem win prize money.

Seeker: Any solution-seeking organization that has a problem and tries to solve it through an innovation contest. Seekers can be both large and small firms, governments, and other organizations.

Solver: Any person who participates in an innovation contest and attempts to solve a problem formulated by the seeker.

Chapter 14
Performance Measurement Systems for Healthcare Organisations

Raúl Rodríguez Rodríguez
Universitat Politècnica de València, Spain

Sara Trespalacios Figueroa
Independent Researcher, Spain

Juan-Jose Alfaro-Saiz
Universitat Politècnica de València, Spain

María-José Verdecho
Universitat Politècnica de València, Spain

ABSTRACT

This chapter deals with the performance measurement systems (PMS) for healthcare organisations topic. PMS have been proved to be a widely used management tool to control, monitor, and manage performance and, extensively, organisations. However, most of the developed works have focused on industrial organisations, being the application of this topic to health organisations not fully exploited. This chapter brings, based on scientific literature, some sound reviews that could be the starting point for researching activities in this topic. Then, it shows an overview of performance measurement elements applied to healthcare organisations from different optics such as efficacy, quality, adequateness, use of ICT and sustainability at both intra- and inter-organisational contexts.

INTRODUCTION

Performance measurement systems (PMS) have been widely treated and studied within the scientific literature in the last decades, especially in the industry context. PMS are management systems that help decision-makers to better control, monitor and manage their organizations. Then, a PMS is a homoge-

DOI: 10.4018/978-1-7998-4543-0.ch014

neous group of both financial and non-financial measures able to successfully cope with the complexity inherent to any organization. It is a tool derived from strategy and able to impulse and foster performance measurement from the strategic until the operational level. The development of a new PMS should be seen as a strategic investment and it should then be carefully designed, as it is any other strategic action in an organization. In the last years, many PMS frameworks have appeared, trying to establish, with a higher or lower degree of success, effective PMS to better manage organizations. From a general point of view, performance measures should:

- Be derived from strategy.
- Be developed for different activities and business processes.
- Be dynamic, adaptive to changes and, therefore, useful in the long-term.
- Be realistic and logical.

These PMS came up to be initially applied to the industrial organizations, and it is in this context where more frameworks have been developed and applied.

However, in the last years, PMS are being also adopted by service organizations and, extensively, by healthcare organizations, which seeks for a high level in terms of efficiency, efficacy, and productivity with the constraint of being a pretty complex system, with many important stakeholders such as community, government, and patients who interact among themselves and require to meet certain criteria in order to achieve the stipulated goals.

In order to measure the efficacy of any organization, it is necessary to understand both the exogenous or environmental factors as well as the endogenous or internal ones. Only then it will be possible to define and propose changes in order to reach the desired performance levels. In the healthcare organization context, it is possible to affirm that the main efforts have been in developing and applying performance measurement elements regarding the internal level.

Currently, healthcare organizations have demonstrated to have a good experience in defining key performance indicators (KPIs) and make decisions relying on the values of such KPIs. Performance measurement through the usage of KPIs is an important step in the process of assessing performance in any organization (Vitale & Mavrinac, 1995). Additionally, it is of key importance to relate these KPIs to the organization's strategy in order to evidence both the advances and improvements achieves and is, therefore, able to make better decisions. In the healthcare organization's context, there are many KPIs and large amounts of data gathered in many years of maintaining these KPIs. However, they usually lack having strategic objectives linked to these KPIs and derived from strategy. In other words, the traditional industry-based approach of firstly defining strategic objectives coming from stating strategic lines after having taken into account the organizational philosophic elements (mission, vision, values) and secondly defining KPIs associated with these strategic objectives is not followed in healthcare organizations. Alike this traditional and rational approach, healthcare organizations manage and make decisions based on only KPIs and, if defined, strategic objectives that are usually started after taking into account the KPIs. In other words, the classic top-down definition process is here substituted by a bottom-up one. This may lead to a dysfunctional process and to a loss of efficiency regarding the results of the PMS, which should be properly addressed and treated in future research works.

To sum up, there is a crescent interest in measuring the performance of healthcare organizations, as they need great investments and their results are usually controlled following some standard KPIs instead of applying a solid and robust PMS. Whereas in the industry context there are a lot of performance measurement frameworks and application of these, at the healthcare organization level there is, comparatively, very few ones and these are usually a simplification of the user in the industry. Therefore, this chapter aims to offer readers an overview of this important managerial issue.

The main objective of this chapter is to provide an overview of important issues, as they appear in the scientific literature, of how performance measurement is carried out in health organizations. Therefore, this chapter is structured as follows: It firstly develops a point that presents how performance measurement has been applied in health organizations in terms of efficacy, quality, and adequateness; it also highlights the main drawbacks and points out some future gaps that should be covered. The chapter then presents the situation regarding the usage of Information and Communication Technologies (ICT) within performance measurement in health organizations. It then moves into the inter-organizational context and, more concretively, into the supply chain level, as nowadays it is necessary, from a performance measurement point of view to extend the context of the problem beyond the individual health organization boundaries. Then, it addresses how health organizations are considering and measuring performance from a sustainability approach. Finally, the main conclusions and future research lines are highlighted.

PERFORMANCE MEASUREMENT IN HEALTH ORGANISATIONS

It is widely agreed that patient-centeredness should be the main focus of any healthcare organization, is a must within this business. The management of a healthcare organization should, therefore, design and implement strategies and plans in order to augment as much as possible the performance indicator of customer-patient- satisfaction. However, it is important to take into consideration that these managers face other key points that are usually contrary, in terms of performance achievement, to this performance indicator. The main of these key points is usually cost reduction, which is really important in any business organization and also when regarding healthcare organizations, where the budget is usually coming from public organisms (public healthcare organizations). It is necessary then, from a strategic management point of view, the correct definition of appropriate strategic elements such as objectives and associated key performance indicators (KPIs) that can manage this delicate customer satisfaction- cost reduction trade-off. In this sense, Cosgrove et al. (2013) presented, based on a CEO developed high-value health care checklist, ten key strategies. They applied such strategies to eleven leading healthcare organizations, concluding that it is possible when properly managed, achieved both patient-focused cared and quality improvements and, extensively, costs reduction.

In this sense, quality improvements are one of the key points, when properly developed through sound structures and processes, to achieve a higher level of patient care performance in healthcare organizations. The next would be to know whether the quality programs and initiatives are being effective/efficient and to what extent. Measuring healthcare quality through performance measures and using the results as an input to design and implement improvements that will impact the whole healthcare organization's performance is of key importance. But what are the most important and relevant performance measures to measure quality levels in a healthcare organization? Chassin and Loeb (2011) reviewed the origins and development of the current main standardized and used quality measure in healthcare organizations. They point out that the best choice is to follow a process-based approach when defining quality measures for healthcare organizations for two reasons: a) these are the most common ones in current use; and b) these measures have an additional research challenge when dealing with mixing and adjusting them.

Additionally, McDonald et al. (2014) developed and presented a framework to explore management practices in hospitals, highlighting the most used and adequate ones regarding quality and performance improvement. *They point out that there is a lack of standard and concise set of performance measures that could be applied to any healthcare organization, mainly because of the different environments and heterogeneous management approaches that such organizations take. In order to overcome this problem, they focused on a reduced set of management dimensions and associated performance measures. They pointed out that it is not generally proven that, at the healthcare organization's context, higher competitive environments will lead to higher levels of efficiency, being necessary to improve the understanding of how regulation and competition activities affect management and, extensively, to quality and efficiency. They conclude that the best management approaches for healthcare organizations are these that had been previously well implemented and validated in industry, which makes necessary: a) further implement and prove those industrial management practices in healthcare organizations; and b) healthcare organizations should develop new intrinsic management approaches – or extensions of the current ones- that will lead to a more efficient management and performance results* (Information Resources Management Association, 2019, p.687).

From a strategic definition perspective, Steinke, Webster, and Fontaine (2010) developed an innovative methodology to carry out integral evaluations regarding healthcare organizations' performance. *They illustrated a process to more efficiently link the healthcare organizations' mission with their strategic objectives, providing more consistency to the performance evaluation process. Healthcare organizations lack the industrial organizations' experience when defining strategic objectives coming from the organizations' strategic line and philosophical elements – mission, vision, values- and, therefore, this is a field where researchers might make a contribution* (Information Resources Management Association, 2019, p.687).

From a more concrete performance measures point of view, Groome and Mayeaux (2010) presented a conceptual framework to deal with decreasing patient long waiting times. The hypothesis that statistical process control techniques can be used to identify the extreme values regarding waiting time provides an analysis that might be used to identify the specific causes for such waiting time. It was observed a meaningful reduction in the occurrence of prolonged waiting times after having taken measures to minimize the effects of the identified causes, carrying out also processes changes.

Regarding the data quality of these performance measures in healthcare organizations, Mettler and Rohner (2009) analyzed the adoption state of the performance management and how healthcare organizations will develop their performance management systems in the future. It was found, among others, that, from a process design perspective, important processes such as how data is collected and how analysis and communication processes are carried out, there is an important lack of official design and definition. At this stage, the quality of the data generated by a PMS is questioned so is its efficiency as, for instance, how much time is required to gather and manually analyze these data. Therefore, the efficacy of the PMS can be taken with reservation, being the link between the organizational and the strategic level compromised.

On the other hand, there are many works that develop studies about healthcare organizations' performance and how to assess it. We next highlight some of them, each of one analyzing an important factor that affects healthcare organizations.

Regarding the employees' knowledge of management structures and actions and how important these are for achieving a good performance in healthcare organizations, Chang, Hsu, Li, and Chang (2011) carried out a study that affirms that management knowledge is desired and demanded by employees, is a powerful and positive active, whose comprehension forecast a healthcare organization's performance.

Chang (2009) carried out both a strategic map description and a balanced scorecard (BSC) (Kaplan & Norton, 1992) for healthcare organizations. Such a BSC was dynamic and its main characteristic is that it included some inter-organizational elements such as service suppliers. This was an important point, as PMS applied to healthcare organizations were traditionally internally focused, defining KPIs and then defining, not always, strategic objectives. The fact of including external operations carried out by third parties means that healthcare organizations are expanding their knowledge about performance management and, more concretively, how PMS might be of help to better perform. This issue of inter-organisation PMS is dealt with in the next point of this chapter.

In this sense, Lin, Yu, and Zhang (2014) showed the main results of applying the BSC in Chinese public hospitals, finding that such an application will help in

- Avoiding short-term behaviors inherent to financial performance measures.
- Improve the whole medical staff performance in terms of actions and initiative.
- Effectively improve healthcare organizational performance.
- Augment individual satisfaction level.

They also state that, through the BSC application, healthcare organizations adopting BSC will achieve better performance levels when compared to others that do not adopt them; the main performance measures to be implemented are those related to patient's satisfaction and demands; the non-financial performance measures can be motivated and assessed from multiple perspectives.

Additionally, Chang (2007) developed research aiming to explore both the limitations and implications of implementing a PMS, a Balanced Scorecard (BSC) (Kaplan & Norton, 1992), in healthcare organizations. Even though Kaplan and Norton (1992) affirmed that the BSC could get adapted to cover the needs in terms of performance measurement of a public sector organization, this study states that the BSC does not consider the political context within a public sector organization operates. It is demonstrated that the KPIs developed are unable to link-local operations with the government's long-term objectives. These KPIs were high-level ones and, therefore, nor reflecting the clinic standard based on evidence. Health organization managers perceived that the imposed KPIs were incompatible with their local operations, having, therefore, a low impact over the individual health organizations.

Regarding the problems of implementing performance dashboards in service organizations, Ogan and Yigitbasioglu (2012) identified that these dashboards should be more flexible in order to get better adapted to the specific characteristics of a service organization. In other words, the traditional industrial dashboards follow a rigid financially focused structure that cannot fully be translated into service organizations. New performance frameworks dealing with the specifics of service organizations are still needed.

In a conclusion, it is possible to affirm that healthcare organizations know of the importance of defining strategic business objectives and associated performance indicators, especially for measuring efficacy, efficiency and costs inherent to the services they offer. However, there is a lack of properly designing processes and the way to apply them is, in many cases, not develop, which questions the performance measurement quality.

From an operational point of view, healthcare organizations are familiar with presenting statistics, analyzing reports and measuring the development and performance of some of their processes via performance indicators. However, healthcare organizations still need to deeper explore the usage of sophisticated tools such as ICT and advanced quantitative ones that will facilitate performance management, its analysis and, extensively, the decision-making processes.

Finally, it is important to address the role than intellectual capital (IC) plays regarding healthcare organizations' performance. Due to its nature, healthcare organizations' performance levels rely very much on the skills and capabilities of their working force. There are many KPIs to measure intellectual capital and some attempts to integrate such KPIs into a PMS and such a PMS into an intellectual capital management model. However, this approach presents limitations when trying to ask how IC efforts – in terms of resources - of an organization are paying off. In other words, what the impact of IC investments is over the organization's results. There is a need for frameworks to quantitatively assess such an impact in the context of a solid PMS that integrates IC management, and not the way around. In this sense, Boj Viudez, Rodríguez-Rodríguez, and Alfaro-Saiz (2014) developed a methodology to link intangible assets and organizational performance in a Balanced Scorecard context. Such a methodology was applying the Analytic Network Process (Saaty, 1996) in order to quantitatively link the impact of IC over an organization's strategic objectives. They offered the results of having applied this methodology to a public research center. Since a public research center is also a service organization, this framework could be directly applied to measure and manage performance in a healthcare organization. Additionally, other techniques such as fuzzy logic and/or multivariate statistical techniques (Principal Component Analysis, Factor Analysis, Multiple Regression, etc.) could complement such a methodology when being applied to healthcare organizations.

ICT IN HEALTH ORGANISATIONS PERFORMANCE

It is necessary to cover the role of ICT usage regarding healthcare organizations' performance management. The incorporation of ICT will make it easier and more effective the whole performance management process in healthcare organizations, being able to obtain better results.

Then, interesting work is the one carried out by Thrasher, Craighead, and Byrd (2010), who analyzed two aspects of the healthcare research that are interrelated: the information technologies and the decision-making processes, as well as their complementarity at the healthcare organizations network context. They state that strategic alliances in the healthcare organization context might provide an initial point for developing alliances between the different health networks. The decision-making process and the introduction and use of ICT integration of the network capacity allow both efficient collaboration and decision-making processes inside and outside among the network's members. They concluded that future research should focus on studying and determining timely issues, complex medical treatments, and patient satisfaction levels. At this point, Currie (2012) developed an integrative model to cover these issues and also to assess ICT in the healthcare organization's context.

Dunn and Westbrook (2011) carried out an interpretation of KPIs based on applying ICT in the context of healthcare organizations' networks. The model TEMPES uses quantitative indicators and the measurements are used to carry out a comparative analysis. Such a model provides a conceptual tool for health organizations decision-makers and other interested parties to understand and assess the implications of adopting technology-based solutions applied to health organizations. In this sense, they affirmed that the health sector must consider the need of integrating some interrelated aspects such as ICT, the role of ICT on decision-making processes, the timely integration of complex treatments, patient satisfaction, and network diversity and complexity. In other words, it is necessary to take into account the analysis synergic effects of ICT, processes and decision-making processes, aiming to integrate them.

Zhou, Oginhara, Nishimura, and Jin (2019) have recently published their work where they have carried out an analysis of changes in health associated with performance indicators applied to the elderly. Then, they have used different health ICT-based devices to monitor, collect and analyze data under a time-series approach, being able to correlate pulse records and health indicators. Moreover, their model consists of associating the number of steps and health problems that may come up, carrying out forecasting of the steps that the individuals should take in order to avoid health problems. When the number of steps came real and there were differences between the real number and the forecasted one, it was possible to affirm that health problems could appear. Therefore, with the usage of ICT devices combined with a structural equation model, it was possible to construct forecasting models to predict the number of steps to take in order to avoid health problems.

In this sense, Tavares (2018) studied the relationship between ICT and eHealth solutions with self-reported health outcomes in the EU context. She defined eHealth according to the definition provided by the European Union (2016) stating that "*eHealth concerns to these tools and services using Information and Communication Technologies that can improve prevention, diagnosis, treatment, monitoring, and management, to the benefit of the entire community by improving access and quality of care and by making the health sector more efficient*". The study concludes that there is no relationship above commented for patients with good health status whereas such a relationship appears for patients with chronic health problems. For the latter, it is possible to affirm that patients suffering from chronic health problems benefit from using both ICT and eHealth technologies. This is the logical result but it shows that investing in ICT and eHealth will probably help people to improve their life quality level. This fact is aligned with the EU health care policy and should be further carried out in the future. The study also focuses on the EU countries and their ICT and eHealth capabilities, stating that there exists a clear difference across EU countries.

It is also worthy of being commented on recent work from Dutta, Gupta, and Sengupta (2019), which brings together ICT and health outcomes in Asian countries. More concretively, it aims to point out the impact of ICT capabilities and usage over the health outcomes of 30 Asian countries. Further, they selected as health outcomes some important and popular KPIs such as chronic disease, longevity, and mortality, quality of life, costs of care, physical functional status or satisfaction with care. In order to identify the impact of ICT on these KPIs, they applied a multivariate technique called Principal Component Analysis (PCA), which reduces the variability of the initial data matrix and gathers real data of the KPIs for a certain period of time – 17 years in this study-, being able to identify relationships between the variables of the study. Further, PCA is able to capture cause-effect relationships between and among these variables or KPIs. From the analysis, they stated that ICT does have a strong impact on health outcomes. Further, they affirmed that fostering ICT infrastructures has got the potential to close some open gaps regarding healthcare activities and results in some of these countries of the study.

Finally, the analysis of social networks is a relatively new topic within the healthcare organization's management context. The healthcare organizations' networks observed are often small in size compared to other disciplines. Such a characteristic makes them special due to the fact the metrics used for analysis are sensitive to changes in both size and density (Shandu, Gill, & Sood, 2016). As a consequence, the comparisons between networks of different sizes and densities might lead to wrongful interpretations if a validation test is not applied. The results of this study show that simple validation techniques are able to strengthen the analysis carried out in small networks and improve the results in terms of interpretation and conclusions formulation.

HEALTH ORGANISATIONS SUPPLY CHAINS

Augmenting the focus on the supply chain of health organizations, it is possible to find several interesting studies. For example, Privett and Gonsalvez (2014), after a survey and interviews-based study, identified the top ten health pharmaceutical supply chain challenges: (1) lack of coordination, (2) inventory management, (3) absent demand information, (4) human resource dependency, (5) order management, (6) shortage avoidance, (7) expiration, (8) warehouse management, (9) temperature control, and (10) shipment visibility. These challenges should be treated, as long as possible, from a global perspective, as many of them are interrelated and future research should take this into account when trying to solve them. Further, they offer some guidelines when the state that researchers should focus firstly on solving 4 of them (lack of coordination, demand information, HR dependency, and shipment visibility), as these are the root causes of all the 10 challenges.

Equally, Falasca and Kros (2018) analyze the supply chains in health organizations in the past, present and expected future. They find that supply chains in health organizations lack not only of information but also of competencies to execute the most adequate business strategy to cope with environmental changes from an economic perspective. ICT technologies to enable data sharing with suppliers and standardize solutions were also missed.

In this sense, a recent study of Verdin (2020) has reviewed different technologies and their impact on health-care supply chains. More concretively, the author has broken into three main streams the technology that could be applied to health-care supply chains: i) Mature technologies such as sensors, cloud computing, telematics or automated storage; ii) Growth technologies such as mobility, wearable devices or social media; iii) Emerging technologies such as 3D printing, blockchain, IoT, virtual reality or artificial intelligence. The usage and potential application of these technologies are widely tackled as well as future feasible exogenous variables such as new competitors and decentralization and their potential impact over health-care supply chains.

Kwon, Kim, and Martin, D.G. (2016) work over the health organizations' KPIs of efficiency regarding unit decision-making at the supply chain context. They find that one of the most influential and important KPI to make better decisions and, therefore, to achieve better results is the satisfaction of the medical personnel and, especially, of the medics. This is interesting, as the medical personnel usually intra-organizational perspective whereas their performance is of great importance and influence over the overall supply chain's performance.

Dooley, Rossetti, and Handfield (2011) carry out a supply chain performance analysis focused upstream the supply chain and, more concretively, at the supplying of medicines level. The pharmaceutics companies should make their best to improve their delivery systems in order to assure a higher product delivery level, avoiding stock-outs in healthcare organizations. In that sense, pharmaceutics should assure the supply chain continuity considering and dealing with stock levels in a more strategic way and also changing their manufacturing processes to become more flexible and demand-adaptive.

Su, Su, Gammelgaard, and Yang (2011) develop and implement some logistic innovation processes and their implications over the healthcare organization and associated supply chain, especially regarding the product and services suppliers. They affirm that:

- The logistic processes should take a global supply chain perspective.
- The logistic innovation process in supplier-buyer relationships is a good alternative to outsourcing activities.
- This logistic innovation process is dynamic and can improve the assessment and relationships with suppliers.

Regarding supply chain innovation, Lee, Lee, and Schniederjans (2011) examine the main processes to improve the overall healthcare organization performance. Supply chain innovation plays a key role in developing products and services to satisfy customers – patients in this case- and their values. It is demonstrated that the health organization must focus on improving both its innovation processes and its own strategy; for instance, they should investigate the applicability of new ICT and resources at the supply chain level in order to achieve competitive advantages, eliminating unnecessary costs and improving supply chain processes.

Cho, Lee, Ahn, and Hwang (2012) developed a service supply chain performance measurement framework. This framework emphasizes the development of KPIs to measure supply chain processes such as demand forecasting, customer relationships, management resources, ICT management, and financial issues.

On the other hand, Supeekit, Somboonwiwat, and Kritchanchai (2016) that health care supply chain performance measurement should take into account that there exists an interdependence between the performance groups of patient safety and the one including within supply chain efficiency: clinical care and supporting process efficiency. In order to identify these relationships, they develop and apply an ANP-based model, working out the weights for different performance aspects. They concluded stating the most important supply chain performance aspects according to their study: Completeness of treatment, absence of delays in both treatment and clinical care process time. They affirm that efforts in the direction of improving these aspects performance will have a direct and clear incidence over the whole health organization supply chain performance. As future research work, they mention the importance of kinking the identified relationships between these groups with the business processes of the health organization supply chain, being able then to define adequate KPIs for each of these processes.

Recently, Leonard and Masatu (2017) carried out a study to check whether the repetition of measurement would bring a qualitative and quantitative change on health care providers' performance level or not. They stated that measuring repeatedly some important variables regarding a specific protocol brought important quality improvements not only in the short but also in the medium-term. This behavior can be seen as the confirmation that applying measurement regularly would turn into benefits but the problem sometimes is to what extent and supervised by who the management of the measured performed should be carried out. In the supply chain health care context, when many of the main actors are public entities, KPIs for measuring not only the hospital or clinic but also the whole supply chain, mainly the main first-tier suppliers should be clearly defined, controlled and monitored. For those health care entities where such a KPIs system is already in use and properly working for some time, the next step would be to define specific strategic objectives, being supported with the knowledge of not only the organization but also of the supply chain it belongs to. In this scenario, health care decision-makers would be able to keep some of the initially defined and managed KPIs and to define new ones, it is necessary to define some both strategic objectives and KPIs that cover inter-organizational activities and operations.

Looking at the expressive role, regarding values and beliefs of members of organizations, and it's potential for Performance Measurement Systems (PMS), Chenhall, Hall, and Smith (2017) carried out a study in the mental health area, to assess the relationships between PMS and the expressive role. This study focused on health care organizations where the members had homogeneous and strong values and beliefs. This resulted in the expressive role as a solid and homogeneous input into the PMS, which turned into being able to easily define KPIs and strategic objectives that were fully aligned with most of the organization's parts and workers. However, when bringing this approach to the supply chain level, it will be possible to find not only heterogeneous characters regarding values and beliefs but also contradictory and even conflicting objectives. This has not an easy solution as different levels and topics are mixed, which sets a really complex situation with health care companies of the same supply chain belonging to other supply chains and with organizational beliefs and values being different from company to company due to their own nature and different activities, i.e. hospital versus an industrial supplier of products.

Finally, Syahrir and Suparno (2015) carried out a comprehensive literature review about the healthcare supply chain and disaster supply chain. Both topics are in their early steps and there are therefore many research opportunities such as research for integrating both topics. The main research carried out was regarding a classic inventory management and control approach in the event of natural disasters. There is a need to design an inventory model that translates the known available to promise and capable to promise approaches used in industry to the planning of medical needs in the context of natural disasters. Additionally, such a model should be dynamic and able to manage the complexity of several distribution channels and locations. As mentioned, the research solutions should be stochastic, with a great quantitative component in the form of mathematical modeling and simulations.

In conclusion, it is possible to affirm that, even though supply chain management and performance have attracted attention from both academics and practitioners in the last decades, health organizations supply chain performance management is still at the initial phase. Additionally, the works developed to focus on processes downstream the chain and almost ignore the upstream levels.

SUSTAINABILITY PERFORMANCE MEASUREMENT FOR HEALTH ORGANISATIONS

An important topic to be considered regarding health organizations' performance is the sustainability one. At this point, many interesting frameworks have been developed in the last years in the industrial context, as sustainability cannot be taken apart anymore and it directly impacts both intra- and inter-organizational performance. Therefore, we next highlight some sustainable works that could be used as an initial point to develop an integrated inter and intra-organizational performance management system in the healthcare context.

In this sense, it is important to take into account that healthcare organizations deal with many potentially environmentally dangerous products. Measuring environmental performance should lead to being able to apply policies and make decisions and resulting in a lower environmental impact. Pasqualini Blass, Gouvêa da Costa, de Lima, and Borges (2016) carried out a study to measure environmental performance in hospitals. Their main conclusion is that more effective frameworks to defined environmentally relevant KPIs were needed. From their literature review, they coincide in the fact that there is a trend in health care organizations' performance measurement of relying on only KPIs; in other words, managing with only KPIs, which provides a strategic focus to KPIs that, in many occasions, they will not just have. They also highlight a lack of relevance and robustness on the chosen and used KPIs as well as difficulties for deploying these KPIs over all the decision-making levels of the healthcare organization. In order to partially fulfill these gaps, they developed a performance framework that followed a process-oriented approach, providing a systematic approach for monitoring and reporting performance in a healthcare organization.

Then, Hassini, Surti, and Searcy (2012) carried out a literature review providing a framework to support sustainable management practices as well as sustainable KPIs. Regarding the latter, it is recognized the difficulty of developing reliable sustainable KPIs, especially at the supply chain level. Some of these obstacles are inherent to their own inter and intra-processes, existing important challenges such as:

- There is a lack of integration of sustainability strategic objectives and associated KPIs within the PMS at both intra and inter-organizational contexts.
- There is a lack of guidance regarding the dynamics of sustainability.
- There is a lack of frameworks to measure and manage Social Innovation

Other authors such as Ding, Wang, and Zheng (2018) have studied the balance between economic results and environmental and social sustainability considering several sustainable constraints in public health and environment contexts. This is a very important topic, as organizations will have to invest in technology that produces less damage to the environment as well as to offer more environmental products and services but also achieving an economic benefit. The authors conclude that this is a very complex issue and that only the intervention of governments is able to manage and govern the enterprises' decisions and activities regarding public health sustainability.

In this sense, Fathollahi-Fard, Govindan, Hajiaghaei-Keshteli, and Ahmadi (2019) focused on studying the logistics process of a home health care supply chain, as location decisions of actors such as pharmacies, labs and their allocation to specific patients are still issues that can be classified, due to their high logistics operations, as inefficient from an emission point of view. Then, they developed a mathematical model that focused on location-allocation-routing operations, aiming to solve the problem, which is an NP-hard one, obtaining interesting results and being able to also carry out sensitivity analyses.

Finally, Have and Rubalcaba (2016) point out Social Innovation as an important emerging topic to be taken into account and, therefore, measure, control, monitored and managed. Social Innovation can be seen as having a sustainability impact on society, and it could be of interest when measuring performance in healthcare organizations. They concluded that there are four intellectual communities highly active in the development of Social Innovation: Community Psychology, creativity research, social and societal challenges, and local development. Thought this Social Innovation topic is in its early stages, it is important, in the frameworks to design, consider it. Additionally, and regarding healthcare organizations, performance measures of how social innovation has got the potential to impact the performance of such organizations are of interest.

FUTURE RESEARCH DIRECTIONS

During the development of the chapter, several future research works have been highlighted. We resume these at this point.

Then, from the quality of the data point of view, health organizations should focus on improving the quality of the data collected, defining and implementing the necessary channels to do so. This data collection process could and should be supported by the implementation and maintenance of ICT tools, as the usage of these tools would enable fewer mistakes, would assure the data quality and would also provide a better way of presenting the performance measurement information, leading to better decisions and management practices. Additionally, the usage of ICT would enable us to integrate different important aspects related to measuring performance in health organizations.

From a PMS structure and content, it has been presented that the order and importance of the performance perspectives are different for health organizations than for industrial ones. It is then necessary to develop effective, solid and flexible enough performance frameworks that, taking into account this circumstance, will also consider, support and standardize the bottom-up PMS definition in health organizations. Therefore, such a framework should study the most suitable role for KPIs in this business environment, as KPIs are being treated as strategic in most of the cases and they are not by definition. The new approach should find a compromise solution to properly reach a proper mixture and classification of KPIs-strategic objectives and organizational decision-making levels (strategic, tactic and operative). Additionally, this framework should also develop some mechanisms to assure a better alignment of objectives between the health organizations and the government (financial source most of the time).

At the supply chain context, a PMS should be able to establish the necessary mechanisms for defining a complete supply chain PMS for health organizations; issues like individual members responsibility allocation regarding action plans and KPIs maintenance, definition of proper and coherent supply chain strategic objectives or higher degree of collaboration on key processes both downstream and upstream the supply chain. Additionally, a method or approach to better align both supply chain and individual organizations' performance main elements – strategic objectives and KPIs- is needed.

On the other hand, at the sustainability PMS for health organizations context, there are many research possibilities, especially regarding the environment and the social dimensions. The main research opportunities identified are: a) Development of frameworks coping with the integration of sustainability strategic objectives within the PMS at both intra and inter-organizational contexts; b) development of mechanisms to cope with the dynamics of sustainability; c) further studies and development of frameworks that deal with Social Innovation from a performance measurement point of view.

CONCLUSION

This chapter has focused on PMS in healthcare organizations, aiming to offer readers a good picture of the main characteristics of this topic supported by scientific literature.

Then, it is possible to affirm, regarding performance measurement in healthcare organizations, that these organizations are aware of the importance of implementing efficient PMS but they find important drawbacks and obstacles such as data collection processes, official and government support, quality of data, complex system, employees' knowledge of management structures, misalignment of objectives between the individual healthcare organization and the authority – government- ones or the absence of high-performance teams. Additionally, the incorporation of ICT would lead to more PMS for healthcare organizations, as data processes would be more secure and efficient. It is also mentioned that the application of social networks could be of interest in order to improve performance in healthcare organizations.

Looking at the supply chain context, many works have focused upstream the supply chain offering studies and associated results of mainly working with service and product suppliers. This integration should lead to more cooperative processes and a reduction in cost for healthcare organizations. However, it is missed more work on the other side of the supply chain, downstream. Regarding sustainability, there are not many frameworks that have been either developed or applied to measure performance from a sustainability point of view. Only some studies in the environmental context showed improvements in the performance of healthcare organizations.

All these factors, joined to the established culture of managing the healthcare organizations based only on some KPIs produce the need of further research on this topic in order to be able to offer to healthcare organizations flexible and adaptable PMS that will suit their needs and will show efficient to help them to make better decisions and, therefore, to better manage the healthcare organization.

REFERENCES

Boj Viudez, J. J., Rodríguez-Rodríguez, R., & Alfaro-Saiz, J. J. (2014). An ANP-multicriteria-based methodology to link intangible assets and organizational performance in a Balanced Scorecard context. *Decision Support Systems*, *68*, 98–110. doi:10.1016/j.dss.2014.10.002

Chan, Y. (2009). How strategy map works for Ontario's health system. *International Journal of Public Sector Management*, *22*(4), 349–363. doi:10.1108/09513550910961628

Chang, L. (2007). The NHS performance assessment framework as a balanced scorecard approach limitations and implications. *International Journal of Public Sector Management*, *2*(20), 101–117. doi:10.1108/09513550710731472

Chang, Y., Hsu, P., Li, M., & Chang, C. (2011). Performance evaluation of knowledge management among hospital employees. *International Journal of Health Care Quality Assurance*, *24*(5), 348–365. doi:10.1108/09526861111139188 PMID:21916089

Chassin, M. R., & Loeb, J. M. (2011). The on going quality improvement journey: Next stop, high reliability. *Health Affairs*, *30*(4), 559–568. doi:10.1377/hlthaff.2011.0076 PMID:21471473

Chenhall, R. H., Hall, M., & Smith, D. (2017). The expressive role of performance measurement systems: A field study of a mental health development project. *Accounting, Organizations and Society*, *63*(C), 60–75. doi:10.1016/j.aos.2014.11.002

Cho, D. W., Lee, Y. H., Ahn, S. H., & Hwang, M. K. (2012). A framework for measuring the performance of the service supply chain management. *Computers & Industrial Engineering*, *62*(3), 801–818. doi:10.1016/j.cie.2011.11.014

Cosgrove, D. M., Fisher, M., Gabow, P., Gottlieb, G., Halvorson, G. C., James, B. C., Toussaint, J. S., & … . (2013). Ten strategies to lower costs, improve quality, and engage patients: The view from leading health system CEOs. *Health Affairs*, *32*(2), 321–327. doi:10.1377/hlthaff.2012.1074 PMID:23381525

Currie, W. (2012). Tempest: An integrative model for health technology assessment. *Health Policy and Technology*, *1*(1), 35–49. doi:10.1016/j.hlpt.2012.01.004

Ding, H., Wang, L., & Zheng, L. (2018). Collaborative mechanism on profit allotment and public health for a sustainable supply chain. *European Journal of Operational Research*, *2017*(1), 478–495. doi:10.1016/j.ejor.2017.11.057

Dooley, K., Rossetti, C., & Handfield, R. (2011). Forces, trends, and decisions in pharmaceutical supply chain management. *International Journal of Physical Distribution & Logistics Management*, *6*(41), 601–622.

Dunn, A., & Westbrook, J. (2011). Interpreting social network metrics in healthcare organisations: A review and guide to validating small networks. *Social Science & Medicine*, *72*(7), 1064–1068. doi:10.1016/j.socscimed.2011.01.029 PMID:21371798

Dutta, U. P., Gupta, H., & Sengupta, P. P. (2019). ICT and health outcome nexus in 30 selected Asian countries: Fresh evidence from panel data analysis. *Technology in Society*, *59*, 101184. doi:10.1016/j.techsoc.2019.101184

European Union. (2016). *Public Health –Policy*. Retrieved on November 29, 2019 from https://ec.europa.eu/health/ehealth/policy/index_en.htm

Falasca, M., & Kros, J. F. (2018). Success factors and performance outcomes of healthcare industrial vending systems: An empirical analysis. *Technological Forecasting and Social Change*, *126*, 41–52. doi:10.1016/j.techfore.2016.06.024

Fathollahi-Fard, A. M., Govindan, K., Hajiaghaei-Keshteli, M., & Ahmadi, A. (2019). A green home health care supply chain: New modified simulated annealing algorithms. *Journal of Cleaner Production*, *240*, 118200. doi:10.1016/j.jclepro.2019.118200

Groome, L., & Mayeaux, E. Jr. (2010). Decreasing extremes in patient waiting time. *Quality Management in Health Care*, *19*(2), 117–128. doi:10.1097/QMH.0b013e3181dafeac PMID:20351538

Hassini, E., Surti, C., & Searcy, C. (2012). A literature review and a case study of sustainable supply chains with a focus on metrics. *International Journal of Production Economics*, *140*(1), 69–82. doi:10.1016/j.ijpe.2012.01.042

Have, R. P., & Rubalcaba, L. (2016). Social innovation research: An emerging area of innovation studies? *Research Policy*, *45*(9), 1923–1935. doi:10.1016/j.respol.2016.06.010

Information Resources Management Association. (2019). *Human Performance Technology: Concepts, Methodologies, Tools, and Applications*. IGI Global.

Kaplan, R. S., & Norton, D. P. (1992). The balanced scorecard – Measures that drive performance. *Harvard Business Review*, *70*(1), 71–79. PMID:10119714

Kwon, I. - W. G., Kim, S-H., & Martin, D. G. (2016). Healthcare supply chain management; strategic areas for quality and financial improvement. *Technological Forecast and Social Change, 113*(B), 422-428. doi:10.1016/j.techfore.2016.07.014

Lee, S., Lee, D., & Schniederjans, M. (2011). Supply chain innovation and organizational performance in the healthcare industry. *International Journal of Operations & Production Management, 11*(31), 1193 1214. doi:10.1108/01443571111178493

Leonard, K. L., & Masatu, M. C. (2017). Changing health care provider performance through measurement. *Social Science & Medicine*, *181*, 54–65. doi:10.1016/j.socscimed.2017.03.041 PMID:28371629

Lin, Z., Yu, Z., & Zhang, L. (2014). Performance outcomes of balanced scorecard application in hospital administration in China. *China Economic Review*, *30*, 1–15. doi:10.1016/j.chieco.2014.05.003

McDonald, K. M., Schultz, E., Albin, L., Pineda, N., Lonhart, J., Sundaram, V., & Davies, S. (2014). *Care coordination measures atlas update* (AHRQ Publication No. 14–0037-EF). Retrieved on November 23, 2019 from https://www.ahrq.gov/professionals/prevention-chronic-care/improve/coordination/atlas2014/index.html

Mettler, T., & Rohner, P. (2009). Performance management in health care: the past, the present, and the future. In *Proceedings of 9th International Conference on Business Informatics* (pp. 699-708). Vienna, Austria: AIS Electronic Library.

Ogan, M., & Yigitbasioglu, O. V. (2012). A review of dashboard in performance management: Implications for design and research. *International Journal of Accounting Information Systems*, *13*(1), 41–59. doi:10.1016/j.accinf.2011.08.002

Pasqualini Blass, A., Gouvêa da Costa, S. E., de Lima, E. P., & Borges, L. A. (2016). Measuring environmental performance in hospitals: A practical approach. *Journal of Cleaner Production*, *141*(1), 279–289. doi:10.1016/j.jclepro.2016.07.213

Privett, N., & Gonsalvez, D. (2014). The top ten global health supply chain issues: Perspectives from the Field. *Operations Research for Health Care*, *3*(4), 226–230. doi:10.1016/j.orhc.2014.09.002

Saaty, T. L. (1996). *The Analytic Network Process: Decision Making with Dependence and Feedback*. RWS Publications.

Shandu, R., Gill, H. K., & Sood, S. K. (2016). Smart monitoring and controlling of Pandemic Influenza A (H1N1) using Social Network Analysis and cloud computing. *Journal of Computational Science*, *12*, 11–22. doi:10.1016/j.jocs.2015.11.001 PMID:32362959

Steinke, C., Webster, L., & Fontaine, M. (2010). Evaluating building performance in healthcare facilities: An organizational perspective. *Journal Citation Reports*, *2*(3), 63–83. doi:10.1177/193758671000300207 PMID:21165871

Su, S., Su, S. I., Gammelgaard, B., & Yang, S. (2011). Logistics innovation process revisited: Insights from a hospital case study. *International Journal of Physical Distribution & Logistics Management*, *6*(41), 577–600.

Supeekit, T., Somboonwiwat, T., & Kritchanchai, D. (2016). DEMATEL-modified ANP to evaluate internal hospital supply chain performance. *Computers & Industrial Engineering*, *102*, 318–330. doi:10.1016/j.cie.2016.07.019

Syahrir, I., Suparno, I. V., & Vanany, I. (2015). Healthcare and disaster supply chain: Literature review and future research. *Procedia Manufacturing*, *4*, 2–9. doi:10.1016/j.promfg.2015.11.007

Tavares, A. I. (2018). eHealth, ICT and its relationship with self-reported health outcomes in the EU countries. *International Journal of Medical Informatics*, *112*, 104–113. doi:10.1016/j.ijmedinf.2018.01.014 PMID:29500007

Thrasher, E., Craighead, C., & Byrd, T. (2010). An empirical investigation of integration in healthcare alliance networks. *Decision Support Systems*, *1*(50), 116–127. doi:10.1016/j.dss.2010.07.007

Verdin, J. (2020). Emerging technologies in the health-care supply chain. In A. Pagano & M. Liotine (Eds.), *Technology in Supply Chain Management and Logistics: Current Practice and Future Applications* (pp. 111–126). Elsevier. doi:10.1016/B978-0-12-815956-9.00006-5

Vitale, M. R., & Mavrinac, S. C. (1995). How effective is your performance measurement system? *Management Accounting*, *77*(2), 43–47.

Zhou, S., Oginhara, A., Nishimura, S., & Jin, Q. (2019). Analysis of health changes and the association of health indicators in the elderly using TCM pulse diagnosis assisted with ICT devices: A time series study. *European Journal of Integrative Medicine*, *27*, 105–113. doi:10.1016/j.eujim.2019.02.010

KEY TERMS AND DEFINITIONS

BSC: Simple tool that somehow has standardized how to measure (and manage) organizational performance.

KPI: Underestimate performance element, which gathers data that, when properly treated, can become informed about the organization's performance.

Performance: Indicates to what extent an organization is doing it well.

Performance Measurement System: Conjoint of performance elements that together, when properly defined, is one of the most powerful tools for supporting decision-making processes at all business levels.

Strategic Objective: Very important goal, which should be reached to contribute to reaching an organization's competitive position.

Strategy: It is an abstract process that requires people from all over the organization in order to foresee and define what the best path is in order to achieve the organization's goals and assure its market position.

Supply Chain Performance Measurement: Difficult and many times conflictive process where organizations members have to negotiate the supply chain strategic objectives with other members.

Chapter 15
Predicting Employee Performance:
An Intergenerational Approach

Ramona Diana Leon
https://orcid.org/0000-0002-1448-0522
National School of Political and Administrative Studies, Romania

Ramona Ioana Tănăsescu
National School of Political Science and Public Administration, Romania

Carmen Elena Tănăsescu
National School of Political Science and Public Administration, Romania

ABSTRACT

The research aims to perform an intergenerational analysis regarding the impact of counterproductive behavior and contextual performance on employees' task performance. The analysis is performed on a convenience sample of 165 employees from three different generations who work in the banking system. The results show that (1) 33.50% of task performance variance is determined by the variance of contextual individual performance and counterproductive behavior, (2) 13% of the variance of contextual individual performance can be explained by the variance in counterproductive behavior, (3) 33.70% of the variance of contextual organizational performance can be explained by the variance of task performance and counterproductive behavior. In addition, significant differences appear regarding the influence of (1) the counterproductive behavior on the contextual performance (Generation X vs. Y), (2) the contextual individual performance on task performance (Generation X vs. Z), and (3) the counterproductive behavior on the contextual individual performance (Generation Y vs. Z).

DOI: 10.4018/978-1-7998-4543-0.ch015

INTRODUCTION

For many years, business sustainability was linked to the company's economic performance. In other words, it involved satisfying shareholders' interests. The perspective switched from shareholders to stakeholders due to Dodd (1932) who started an academic debate regarding the legality of using the company's profit for the public interest. Against this backdrop, Friedman (1970) argued that business sustainability depends not only on shareholders' satisfaction but also on the satisfaction of the internal and external stakeholders. As a consequence, managers started to focus on: (i) rationally exploiting the resources (Kollmus & Agyeman, 2002); (ii) increasing stakeholders' awareness to social and environmental issues (Finksel, 2006); (iii) investing in the development of an open organizational culture (Kollmus & Agyeman, 2002); (iv) encouraging employees' development and empowerment (Lozano, 2008); and (v) developing activities that encourage knowledge sharing among employees and, improve their capacity of making decisions (Leon, 2018). Thus, the importance of human resources increased since they were the only ones capable of transforming all the other organizational resources and enhancing the achievement of competitive advantage. Furthermore, in the current aging society, human resources become a "critical asset" (Blome, Borell, Hakansson, & Nilsson, 2020; Kollmann, Stoeckmann, Kensbock, & Peschl, 2020; Leinonen, Chandola, Laaksonen, & Martikainen, 2020) due to their skills, abilities, ideas, thoughts, and experiences, generally labeled as "tacit knowledge" (Letmathe, & Rossler, 2019; Upadhyay & Kundu, 2019).

Within this framework, the company's performance became a reflection of employees' performance. Therefore, the concept of job performance captured the attention of various scholars and, according to Hosie and Nankervis (2016), it is the most important criterion in occupational, industrial and organizational psychology and human resources management. Despite this, there is still no common framework for considering the underlying performance dimension requirements of jobs (Hossie & Nankervis, 2016) and the intergenerational approach of this issue is missing although at least five generations are currently working together, and each of them has its own value system and its own definition for performance. Thus, Baby Boomers value teamwork and have a psychological need for group acceptance (Dwyer & Azevedo, 2016; Galo, 2011) while Generation X and Generation Y are individualistic, optimistic and goal-oriented (Baily, 2009; Dwyer & Azevedo, 2016; Kaminska & Borzillo, 2017; Rupčic, 2018). As a consequence, the former are more vulnerable to counterproductive behavior while the latter use it as a challenge to improve their task performance and also the individual and organizational contextual performance.

Taking these into account, this chapter aims to perform an intergenerational analysis regarding the impact of counterproductive behavior and contextual performance on employees' task performance. As it is presented further, these variables are interlinked and influenced by the characteristics of each generation. Thus, the following section emphasizes the types of generations that are currently recognized in the labor market and the relationships established among the dimensions of job performance while section three sheds light on the methodological approach that has been followed in order to achieve the research goal. Further, the perspective from which the concept of job performance is approached by the members of Generation X, Y, and Z who work in the banking system is presented and last but not least, the article closes by drawing several conclusions and emphasizing further research directions.

CONCEPTUAL FRAMEWORK

The Multigenerational Labour Market

According to the generational cohort theory, a generation is defined as a group of individuals born around the same time who share the specific attitudes and values that can influence their behavior and expectations at work (Gerpott, Lehmann-Willenbrock, & Voelpel, 2016; Schullery, 2013; Twenge, Freeman, & Campbell, 2012). Nevertheless, given the fact that the individuals work in a diverse environment and interact with various members from different generations, the generational theory focuses not only on the personal and professional values, beliefs and attitudes but also on the relationships that each generation cohort has with other generations (Howe & Strauss, 2007).

Taking into account the fact that the concept of generation is generally used to name cohorts in population, five generations are currently recognized, namely: The Veterans (1922 – 1945), Baby Boomers (1946 – 1965), Generation X (1966 – 1980), Generation Y (1981 – 1995), and Generation Z (1996 – 2012). The characteristics of each of them are presented further.

The Veterans, born between 1922 and 1945, are also known as The Traditionalists, Silent Generation, and Mature Generation (Galo, 2011). Due to the fact that their development occurred during the Great Depression, World War II, and Korean War, they tend to be patriotic, loyal in both personal and professional relationships, and fiscally conservative (Dwyer & Azevedo, 2016; Galo, 2011). Besides, they respect authority (Dwyer & Azevedo, 2016; Galo, 2011), are financially motivated, and seek formalized workplace and hierarchical structure (Dwyer & Azevedo, 2016). Given the fact that their personal and professional development was strongly influenced by economic, political and social instability, they are in search of a stable workplace in which the status-quo is not easily challenged, ethical behavior is encouraged, long-term job security is ensured, and loyalty is both given and received. Therefore, they value hard work (Galo, 2011), are committed to the organization and its leaders (Dwyer & Azevedo, 2016), and have a high level of risk adversity, considering that change is a challenge that requires time and a detailed analysis (Cadmus, 2002; Dois, Landrum, & Wirck, 2010; Hahn, 2009). Last but not least, they favor face-to-face and written communication and are reluctant to use advanced technology (Keepnews, Brewer, Kovner, & Shin, 2010; Kramer, 2010).

Baby Boomers, born between 1946 and 1965, represent the largest population from the labor market (Kramer, 2010). Due to the fact that their development occurred during the Civil Rights Movements, Women's Liberation, the Space Program, the Cold War, and the Vietnam War, they are optimistic workaholics (Galo, 2011), idealistic and egocentrics (Hatfield, 2002; Keepnews et al., 2010; Knouse, 2011). According to Dwyer and Azevedo (2016), they are goal-oriented and determined to make a difference at work and in society. As a consequence, they are active learners (Galo, 2011), highly competitive and inclined to question authority (Dwyer & Azevedo, 2016; Hatfield, 2002; Knouse, 2011), and use their careers to define who they are (Galo, 2011). They value teamwork, honest and considerate feedback, public recognition (Galo, 2011), and the opportunities the company provides for professional development (Dwyer & Azevedo, 2016). Although they are interested in personal health and well-being (Dwyer & Azevedo, 2016), the fact that they are ambitious and place an organization's needs before their own or their family's needs (Galo, 2011) makes them vulnerable to burnout. Furthermore, given the dynamic environment in which they developed, they see change as an opportunity for organizational progress, problem-solving, and personal growth (Galo, 2011). Last but not least, just like the Veterans, they prefer direct, personal face-to-face communication; nevertheless, unlike the members of the previous generation, they are more open to using advanced technology especially if this facilitates their professional development.

Generation X, born between 1966 and 1980, is also known as Music Television (MTV) Generation, Gen X, the Middle Child, Gen Bust, and Karen Generation (Appelbaum, Serena, & Shapiro, 2005; Debrah & Smith, 2000; McNeil, Johnson, & Johnson, 2001). According to Galo (2011), their development was strongly influenced by the major changes in advanced technology, AIDS, the Persian Gulf War, and the fact that both of their parents worked away from home. Therefore, they are self-reliant, self-sufficient, realistic (Galo, 2011; Kogan, 2001), independent and entrepreneurial (Baily, 2009; Dwyer & Azevedo, 2016; Kogan, 2001). Besides, although they are loyal to organizational goals and value systems (Kaminska & Borzillo, 2017; Rupčic, 2018), they lack employer loyalty (Dwyer & Azevedo, 2016), and seek a balance among work, family, and leisure (Galo, 2011; Kogan, 2001). Furthermore, they are achievement-oriented (Dwyer & Azevedo, 2016), multitasking (Galo, 2011), love work (Baily, 2009), concentrate on getting the job done and put an emphasis on details (Rupčic, 2018). They value options for information control in order to preserve traditional functioning (Rupčic, 2018) and also continuous learning (Galo, 2011). Since they are comfortable with technology, their learning preferences include continual feedback and opportunities for autonomy (Dwyer & Azevedo, 2016), and the professional development programs that include high-tech videos or computer-aided instructions, and problem-solving activities (Galo, 2011). Thus, they have a psychological need for understanding how things are done in order to master the organizational processes efficiently and effectively. Despite the fact that they accept change (Galo, 2011) and challenge the hierarchical decision-making structure and status-quo (Dwyer & Azevedo, 2016), they are stressed by the changes that occur frequently in the system (Rupčic, 2018). Just like the members of the aforementioned generations, they prefer a formal code of conduct and engage in formal and respectful face-to-face and written communication (Rupčic, 2018).

Generation Y, born between 1981 and 1995, is also known as The Millennials, Linked Generation, Generation Me, Digital Natives, Internet Generation, iGen, and Net Generation (Anantatmula & Shrivastav, 2012; Galo, 2011; Schullery, 2013). The values and goals of Generation Y were defined in a context marked by violence, terrorism, abuse, and drugs (Galo, 2011). Therefore, the members of this generation are ambitious, talented, and demanding (Baldonado, 2008), dynamic, optimistic, and goal-oriented (Galo, 2011), impatient (Dwyer & Azevedo, 2016), and they have a lack of respect for ethics and values (Baran & Klos, 2014). Besides, they are frequently labeled as the "why" generation due to the fact that they challenge the established order and do not hesitate to voice their critical opinions (Lyon et al., 2005), to question the traditional work structures (Kaminska & Borzillo, 2017), or to challenge authority when there is doubt (Dwyer & Azevedo, 2016). Due to these, they are accustomed and feel comfortable in a changing environment. Still, because of the faster pace in which changes occur, Rupčic (2018) states that they do not invest much time in understanding the principles of a system's operation. In other words, they adopt a short-term and fragmented perspective and concentrate on job content.

Nevertheless, several contradictions appear at the level of Generation Y. First of all, despite the fact that the members of Generation Y are highly individualistic and use the organizational experience and information to build their own career trajectories (Rupčic, 2018), they value peer opinions (Schwieger & Ladwig, 2018), are highly collaborative, team-oriented (Baily, 2009; Dwyer & Azevedo, 2016; Galo, 2011; Schwieger & Ladwig, 2018), and treat everyone as friends (Rupčic, 2018). Thus, they pursue their goals and seek to benefit from professional development programs but they have a psychological need for external validation. They use the group to satisfy their need for attention, and immediate feedback and gratification (Dwyer & Azevedo, 2016; Kaminska & Borzillo, 2017), and are also a source of learning.

Hence, they learn best by collaborating and have a preference for hands-on activities, mentoring, coaching, and internship (Galo, 2011; Schwieger & Ladwig, 2018). Secondly, although they are goal-oriented, savvy technology multitaskers, with a need for self-fulfillment and they aim to make a difference in the world (Baran & Klos, 2014; Dwyer & Azevedo, 2016; Kaminska & Borzillo, 2017; Schwieger & Ladwig, 2018). they are sometimes seen as a liability for the company due to their continuous connectivity. Thus, they use social networks during working hours (Skoludova & Horakova, 2016), and tend to leak information and knowledge in social media both intentionally and unintentionally (Rupčic, 2018).

The members of *Generation Z*, born between 1996 and 2012, are also known as Tweens, The Founders, Plurals, Homeland Generation, Generation 9/11, Generation 2020 and Post-Millennials (Merriman, 2015; Williams, Page, Petrosky, & Hernandez, 2010). According to Seemiller and Grace (2016) and Schwieger and Ladwig (2018), they have been raised in an environment dominated by political tension, school violence, social instability, natural disasters, identity theft, online hacking, and bullying, in which they had the information and communication channels at their fingertips. Therefore, they are independent learners and advocate for social justice, fairness, equality, and the environment (Schwieger & Ladwig, 2018; Seemiller & Grace, 2016; Stillman & Stillman, 2017). As a consequence, they are the most diverse generation in history in terms of race, gender and sexual orientation (Seemiller & Grace, 2016; Shatto & Erwin, 2017; Stillman & Stillman, 2017; Twenge, 2017). Within this framework, they value hard work (Schwieger & Ladwig, 2018), trust, fairness, loyalty and respect for their employer (Stillman & Stillman, 2017), ethical behavior, fair compensation and promotion across all employees, and open and transparent communication (Ernest & Young, 2016; OC&C Strategy Consultants, 2019). Thus, just like the Veterans and Baby Boomers, they are self-sufficient (Merriman & Valerio, 2016), expect to work hard and save for the future, and are motivated by economic security and financial benefits (Lanier, 2017); these predispositions appeared due to the fact that they had to see their parents struggling during the financial crisis and they were taught that in life there are winners and losers and the difference between them is made by the hard work (Stillman & Stillman, 2017; Turner, 2015). Despite these, the members of Generation Z manage to distinguish themselves from the others by the fact that they are: (i) self-starters (Merriman, 2015; Merriman & Valerio, 2016); (ii) creative and interested in personalization (Schwieger & Ladwig, 2018); (iii) driven by a desire to please others (Stillman & Stillman, 2017); (iv) competitive and cognizant that they will start at the bottom of the company (Stillman & Stillman, 2017); and (v) persistent, realistic, innovative, and carrying a desire to make things happen-like betterment of the environment (Merriman, 2015). Furthermore, they learn what they want to know on their own (Beal, 2016; Schwieger & Ladwig, 2018) and see failure as an opportunity to try again (Deep Focus, 2015). Last but not least, they are highly dependent on technology and prefer online communication instead of face-to-face communication (Schwieger & Ladwig, 2018).

All these characteristics influence individuals' perspectives on work and also their work relationships. Therefore, they may be reflected in individuals' task performance, contextual performance or counterproductive behavior. As aforementioned, the members of Generation Y are more individualistic and put their interests above the needs of the organizations while the members of Generation Z are highly competitive and seek to make a change in the world. Therefore, the former may be more oriented towards improving their task performance while the latter may focus on contextual performance. Each of these components is presented in the following section.

Individual Work Performance: From Task Performance to Contextual Performance

Job performance has always captured the attention of both academics and practitioners since it manages to emphasize employees efficiently and effectively. Nevertheless, the perspectives from which this is approached vary from the functionalist to the social constructivist school of thought. Therefore, concepts like task performance, contextual performance, and counterproductive behavior are brought forward.

Some scholars (Borman & Motowidlo, 1993; Gioia & Pitre, 1990; Hosie & Nankervis, 2016; Model, 2005; Morgan & Smircich, 1980) adopt a functionalist perspective and present the concept of "task performance". This emphasizes employees' competencies and it is generally defined as "the effectiveness with which job incumbents perform activities that contribute to its technical core either by directly implementing a part of its technological process or by providing it with needed materials or services" (Broman & Motowidlo, 1993, p.72). Organ and Paine (1999, p.375) go further and describe it as "a part and parcel of the workflow that transforms inputs of energy, information, and materials into outputs in the form of goods and services to the external consistency". Thus, it is a prescribed role (Kiyani, Ayupp, & Rasool, 2018) which reflects job requirements and is easily measured using performance appraisals. Therefore, it is linked to job content and it varies from one job to another.

Other scholars (Cammock, Nilakant, & Dakin, 1995; Conway, 1999; Greenslade & Jimmieson, 2007; Malik, 2018; Motowidlo & Schmit, 1999) concentrate on the social constructivist theory and shed light on the concept of "contextual performance". This is defined as "a set of interpersonal and volitional behaviors that support the social and motivational context in which organizational work is accomplished" (Broman & Motowidlo, 1993, p.73). Furthermore, Van Dyne and Le Pine (1998) present it as a diverse multidimensional concept that "has the effect of maintaining the broader organizational, social and psychological environment in which the technical core must function" (Motowidlo, Borman, & Schmit, 1997, p.75). Thus, according to Rego (2002), its cornerstone is represented by the activities that are not only directly related to one's functions but model the organizational, social, and psychological context in which the work is performed. In other words, it is linked to job relations and extra-role behaviors, and it is similar across jobs.

Its complexity has awakened the interest of various academics (Carlos & Rodrigues, 2016; Greenslade & Jimmieson, 2007; Van Scotter & Motowidlo, 1996). Thus, Van Scotter and Motowidlo (1996) divide the contextual performance into interpersonal facilitation and job dedication; the former concentrates on the interpersonal relationships that should be established in order to facilitate the accomplishment of the organizational goals while the latter brings forward the self-disciplined behaviors. Greenslade and Jimmieson (2007) go further and state that contextual performance is the result of three elements, such as: (i) job-task support which emphasizes employees' devotion and determination; (ii) interpersonal support which focuses on the relationships established among group members; and (iii) organizational support, synthesizing the rules and regulations that increase employees' sense of belonging. If Van Scotter and Motowidlo (1996) and Greenslade and Jimmieson (2007) make the difference between individual and organizational contextual performance, Carlos and Rodrigues (2016) focus on employees' values and abilities and argue that contextual performance incorporates: (i) persistent effort (merged with personal characteristics); (ii) cooperation; (iii) organizational conscientiousness; and (iv) interpersonal and relational skills. Summarizing, these typologies highlight two components of contextual performance, namely: the individual contextual performance that reflects employees' personality, abilities, determination and devotion, and the organizational contextual performance that incorporates the work relationships, collaboration, communication, and climate.

Although Yang and Wei (2017) claim that task performance is more important than contextual performance, none of the previously developed studies analyzes the relationships established between them. Thus, employees' abilities and devotion may influence their efficiency which in turn can affect the relationships established in the work environment. In other words, it can be stated that:

Hypothesis 1: The contextual individual performance positively influences task performance.

Hypothesis 2: The task performance positively influences the contextual organizational performance.

Still, these can also be influenced by the counterproductive behavior which is defined as "any intentional behavior on the part of an organization member viewed by the organization as contrary to its legitimate interest" (Sackett & DeVore, 2001, p.145). According to Aubé, Rousseau, Mama, and Morin (2009) and Aubé, Rousseau, and Tremblay (2011), it has 4 dimensions, namely: parasitism, interpersonal aggression, boastfulness, and misuse of team resources. Although these elements describe employees' personality and the quality of work relationships, aspects that define the individual and organizational contextual performance, previous studies neglect these influences. Therefore, it can be stated that:

Hypothesis 3: The counterproductive behavior positively influences the contextual individual performance.

Hypothesis 4: The counterproductive behavior positively influences the contextual organizational performance.

Lievens, Conway, and De Corte (2008) state that the counterproductive behavior is negatively related to task performance. But not everyone reacts to the same behavior in the same way (Botsford Morgan, Nelson, King, & Mancini, 2018) and the latest generations that entered the labour market are highly competitive, have an interest in challenging the status quo, and see change as an opportunity. Taking these into account and the fact that the latest generations are individualistic and goal-oriented, it can be claimed that:

Hypothesis 5: Counterproductive behavior positively influences task performance.

Synthesizing, the current model aims to connect the coordinates of job performance (such as, counterproductive behavior, individual contextual performance, organizational contextual performance, and task performance) and to emphasize how the employees from different generations perceive these relationships.

RESEARCH METHODOLOGY

The research aims to perform an intergenerational analysis regarding the impact of counterproductive behavior and contextual (organizational and individual) performance on employees' task performance.

Thus, four constructs are taken into account, namely: counterproductive behavior, contextual organizational performance, contextual individual performance, and task performance. These are operationalized using 17 items (4 items measure the counterproductive behavior, 4 items measure the contextual organizational performance, 4 items measure the contextual individual performance, and 5 items measure the task performance), adapted from Koopmans et al. (2012) and based on a 5-point Likert scale where 5 suggests that the respondents strongly agree with the statement while 1 emphasizes a strong disagreement.

The questionnaire was distributed during face to face interactions with the employees from the three most profitable and innovative banks from Bucharest, Romania. These employed, in 2018, 5702 persons from five generations (namely, the Veterans, Baby-Boomers, Generation X, Generation Y, and Generation Z). Since the research concentrates only on the employees from the last three generations, a convenience sample of 165 persons is extracted; this included 55 employees from Generation X (33.33%), 64 from Generation Y (38.79%), and 46 from Generation Z (27.88%). The sample is not statistically representative by volume but by structure.

Given the fact that the research deals with both reflective and formative constructs (Becker, Klein, & Wetzels, 2012; Roldán & Sanchez-Franco, 2012; Sarstedt, Hair, Ringle, Thiele, & Gudergan, 2016), and the focus is on predictive rather than exploratory research (Hair, Hult, Ringle, & Sarstedt, 2014; Hair, Ringle, & Sarstedt, 2011), partial least square (PLS) analyses are employed. Thus, the relationships are tested using SmartPLS 3.0 software developed by Ringle, Wende, and Bucker (2015).

First of all, the model is analyzed using PLS structural equation modeling (PLS-SEM) which is able to estimate a structural model that explains a key construct (Richter, Cepeda, Roldán, & Ringle, 2015; Rigdon, 2012). Therefore, following Hair et al. (2014) procedure, the reliability and validity of all constructs are assessed, and the structural model is tested with path coefficients. Coefficient determination and effect size can also be used but according to Cheah, Ting, Cham, and Memon (2019), this may not provide an accurate estimation. In order to examine the direct and mediated relationships, the path analysis is conducted using the bootstrapping method with 5000 iterations (Aquirre-Urreta & Rönkkö, 2018; Cho, Ali, & Manhas, 2019; Hair, Hult, Ringle, Sarstedt, & Thiele, 2017).

Secondly, the differences among the employees from Generation X, Generation Y, and Generation Z are analyzed using the multiple group analysis procedure (PLS-MGA). This is a non-parametric method that fosters group comparison (Hair et al, 2017; Sarstedt, Henseler, & Ringle, 2011) by combining non-parametric bootstrapping with a rank-sum test (Henseler, Ringle, & Sinkovics, 2009). As suggested by Henseler, Ringle, and Sarstedt (2016), before performing MGA, the measurement invariance of composites (MICOM) is tested; this is a three-step process, involving: (i) configural invariance assessment, (ii) compositional invariance assessment, and (iii) scalar invariance assessment. The former concentrates on the number of constructs from the inner and outer models, the second one brings forward the outer paths between groups while the latter emphasizes the intergroup differences in means and variances for the inner and outer models constructs. Taking these into account, PLS-MGA is performed and the differences between groups are considered to be significant if the p-value is smaller than 0.05 or larger than 0.95 (Henseler et al., 2016; Sarstedt et al., 2011).

Last but not least, PLSPredict is employed at the general and generational level due to the fact that this supports the estimation of complex models (Ali, Rasoolimanesh, Sarstedt, Ringle, & Ryu, 2018) and it allows the assessment of results' predictive capacity (Cheah et al., 2019; Nunkoo, Teeroovengadum, Ringle, & Sunnassee, 2019; Sarstedt, Ringle, & Hair, 2017; Shmueli, Ray, Velasquez Estrada, & Chatla, 2016). According to Shmueli et al. (2016), PLSPredict assumes that *a full training dataset of manifest variables and a partial holdout dataset with new antecedent predictor measurement*, and brings forward three dimensions, namely: (i) predicting construct versus manifest items; (ii) predicting in-sample versus out-of-sample cases; (iii) generating average-case prediction versus case-wise predictions. Furthermore, for those indicators with naïve benchmark $Q^2_{predict}$ higher than zero, the root means squared error (RMSE) values of PLS and naïve linear regression model (LM) benchmark are compared. The predictive power of the model is decided based on the rules of Shmueli et al. (2019) which are summarized in Table 1.

Table 1. The predictive power of the model based on the results of PLS – LM comparison

PLS-SEM < LM for	Predictive power
None of the indicators	Zero
A minority of indicators	Low
A majority of indicators	Medium
All indicators	High

As aforementioned, the analysis is performed at the general level, describing how the counterproductive behavior and the contextual (organizational and individual) performance are influencing the task performance of the employees from three banks subsidiaries and also at the generational level, emphasizing the differences that occur among the employees from Generation X, Generation Y, and Generation Z.

WORK PERFORMANCE IN THE ROMANIAN INTERGENERATIONAL BANKING SYSTEM

General Results

First of all, the PLS-SEM algorithm is performed in order to determine whether all the indicators and constructs meet the reflective measurement criteria; in other words, the model's validity and reliability are tested. Special attention is given to outer loadings, Cronbach's Alpha, composite reliability (CR), and average variance extracted (AVE). As can be noticed from Table 2, most loadings are above 0.708 which means that the indicators are reliable (Chang, Hsu, & Yang, 2018; Hair, Risher, Sarstedt, & Ringle, 2019). However, three exceptions appear, namely "*Displaying excessive negativity*" (0.653), "*Doing things that harm your organization*" (0.703), and "*Working efficiently*" (0.508). Henseler, Ringle, and Sarstedt (2012) suggests that the indicators with loadings between 0.4 and 0.7 should be discharged if this action may increase composite reliability while several scholars (Memon & Rahman, 2014; Sujit & Rajesh, 2016) argue that that the outer loadings between 0.5 and 0.7 should be acceptable since they emphasize the proportion of indicator variance that is explained by the latent variable (Hair et al., 2019). Taking these into account and the fact that the elimination of these indicators does not increase the composite reliability, all the indicators are kept in the model. Furthermore, the internal consistency reliability is assessed using Cronbach Alpha, CR, and rho_A. According to Hair et al. (2019), the former is a conservative and less precise measurement of reliability that focuses on unweighted items, the second is a more liberal measurement in which the items are weighted based on indicators' loadings while the latter is a compromise solution that lies between the two aforementioned approaches. Given the fact that the values, in all three cases, range between 0.7 and 0.9, the constructs are considered reliable. Last but not least, constructs' convergent validity is determined based on the average variance extracted (AVE) for all items on each construct. Since all the values are higher than 0.5, the constructs are considered to be valid; as Hair et al. (2019) claim, the construct explains more than 50 percent of the variance of the items that make up the construct.

Table 2. Convergent validity and internal consistency reliability of the general model

Variables	Indicator	Loadings	Cronbach's Alpha	rho_A	CR	AVE
Contextual individual performance	Taking initiative	0.836	0.849	0.851	0.898	0.689
	Accepting and learning from feedback	0.835				
	Cooperating with others	0.877				
	Communicating effectively	0.786				
Contextual organizational performance	Showing responsibility	0.831	0.829	0.834	0.886	0.660
	Being customer-oriented	0.804				
	Being creative	0.805				
	Taking on challenging work tasks	0.809				
Counter-productive behavior	Displaying excessive negativity	0.653	0.720	0.770	0.821	0.536
	Purposely making mistakes	0.847				
	Doing things that harm your organization	0.703				
	Doing things that harm your co-workers or supervisor	0.713				
Task performance	Work quality	0.780	0.785	0.807	0.855	0.547
	Planning and organizing work	0.778				
	Being result-oriented	0.829				
	Prioritizing	0.760				
	Working efficiently	0.508				

Further, discriminant validity is assessed using the Fornel Larcker criterion (Table 3) and the Heterotrait-Monotrait (HTMT) ratio of correlation criterion (Table 4). In the first case, it can be stated that the model is valid due to the fact that the values from the diagonal are higher than the values presented in the rows and columns. In other words, it proves that there are no correlations higher than the existing AVE.

Table 3. Discriminant validity based on the Fornel Larcker criterion

Variables	Contextual individual performance	Contextual organizational performance	Counterproductive behavior	Task performance
Contextual individual performance	0.830			
Contextual organizational performance	0.779	0.812		
Counterproductive behavior	0.361	0.331	0.732	
Task performance	0.574	0.519	0.141	0.740

Table 4. Discriminant validity based on the Heterotrait-Monotrait Ratio of correlation

Variables	Contextual individual performance	Contextual organizational performance	Counterproductive behavior	Task performance
Contextual individual performance				
Contextual organizational performance	0.892			
Counterproductive behavior	0.426	0.391		
Task performance	0.691	0.626	0.170	

Henseler, Ringle, and Sarstedt (2015) claim that the Fornell Larcker criterion is not reliable and proposes the HTMT ratio of correlation which is defined as the mean value of the item correlations across constructs relative to the geometric mean of the average correlations. As can be observed in Table 4, for most constructs the value of the HTMT ratio is less than 0.85; the only exception is represented by contextual organizational performance and contextual individual performance. Nevertheless, this is below the threshold value of 0.9 which is considered to be acceptable for the constructs that are conceptually very similar (Henseler et al., 2015). Therefore, discriminant validity is not an issue.

Table 5. Assessment of the formative measurement model

Variables	Indicator	Outer VIF
Contextual individual performance	Taking initiative	2.073
	Accepting and learning from feedback	1.999
	Cooperating with others	2.393
	Communicating effectively	1.658
Contextual organizational performance	Showing responsibility	1.786
	Being customer-oriented	1.645
	Being creative	1.840
	Taking on challenging work tasks	1.777
Counterproductive behavior	Displaying excessive negativity	1.477
	Purposely making mistakes	1.626
	Doing things that harm your organization	1.267
	Doing things that harm your co-workers or supervisor	1.301
Task performance	Work quality	1.917
	Planning and organizing work	1.791
	Being result-oriented	1.828
	Prioritizing	1.579
	Working efficiently	1.121

In order to asses the formative measurement model, the collinearity of the formative indicators is evaluated using the variance inflation factor (VIF). As it can be observed from Table 5, the VIF values range from 1.121 to 2.073. Given the fact that the values are below the threshold of 3 (Becker et al., 2012; Hair et al., 2019; Mason & Perreault, 1991), it can be argued that there are no collinearity issues.

Once model's reliability and validity is checked, the focus changes to the structural model. Thus, it is emphasized that: (i) 33.50% of task performance variance is determined by the variance of contextual individual performance, and counterproductive behavior; (ii) 13% of the variance of contextual individual performance can be explained by the variance in counterproductive behavior; and (iii) 33.70% of the variance of contextual organizational performance can be explained by the variance of task performance and counterproductive behavior. Furthermore, four out of five hypotheses are validated (Table 6), namely: (i) contextual individual performance has a positive influence on task performance ($\beta = 0.602$; $t = 10.825 > 1.96$; $p = 0.000 < 0.05$); (ii) counterproductive behavior has a positive influence on the contextual individual performance ($\beta = 0.361$; $t = 5.678 > 1.96$; $p = 0.000 < 0.05$); (iii) counterproductive behavior has a positive influence on the contextual organizational performance ($\beta = 0.262$; $t = 3.878 > 1.96$; $p = 0.000 < 0.05$); and (iv) task performance has a positive influence on the contextual organizational performance ($\beta = 0.482$; $t = 6.640 > 1.96$; $p = 0.000 < 0.05$).

Table 6. Testing the hypothesis

Hypothesis	Standard deviation	t	p
Contextual individual performance -> Task performance	0.056	10.825	0.000
Counterproductive behavior -> Contextual individual performance	0.063	5.678	0.000
Counterproductive behavior -> Contextual organizational performance	0.068	3.878	0.000
Counterproductive behavior -> Task performance	0.063	1.194	0.233
Task performance -> Contextual organizational performance	0.073	6.640	0.000

Furthermore, the out-of-sample predictive power of the model is analyzed using PLSPredict with 10 folds and one repetition, as suggested by Shmueli et al. (2019). The results presented in Table 7 prove that constructs' indicators outperform the naïve benchmark since all the $Q^2_{predict}$ values are above 0. Thus, given the fact that all the indicators are measured on a 5-point Likert scale, it can be stated that the prediction errors will fall within approximately two points on an average of (i) 49 percent, for the contextual individual performance; (ii) 51 percent, for the contextual organizational performance; and (iii) 46 percent, for the task performance.

Last but not least, it can be noticed that PLS-SEM outperforms the naïve LM benchmark, producing fewer errors (Table 7). Thus, the model has a high predictive power since the differences between the RMSE values of PLS-SEM and those of naïve LM are negative for all the indicators. The most pronounced differences appear at the level of "*Being creative*" (PLS-SEM based RMSE = 1.095; LM based RMSE = 1.131), "*Working efficiently*" (PLS-SEM based RMSE = 1.089; LM based RMSE = 1.117), "*Taking initiative*" (PLS-SEM based RMSE = 1.055; LM based RMSE = 1.081), "*Work quality*" (PLS-SEM based RMSE = 0.910; LM based RMSE = 0.935), and "*Planning and organizing work*" (PLS-SEM based RMSE = 0.876; LM based RMSE = 0.900).

Table 7. PLSPredict assessment for the general model

Construct	Indicator	PLS-SEM		LM		PLS-SEM - LM
		RMSE	$Q^2_{predict}$	RMSE	$Q^2_{predict}$	RMSE
Contextual individual performance	Taking initiative	1.055	0.065	1.081	0.018	-0.026
	Accepting and learning from feedback	0.998	0.111	0.999	0.110	-0.001
	Cooperating with others	0.988	0.093	0.996	0.079	-0.008
	Communicating effectively	0.923	0.023	0.926	0.033	-0.003
Contextual organizational performance	Showing responsibility	0.921	0.037	0.938	0.045	-0.017
	Being customer-oriented	0.962	0.056	0.978	0.024	-0.016
	Being creative	1.095	0.039	1.131	0.026	-0.036
	Taking on challenging work tasks	1.124	0.088	1.125	0.091	-0.001
Task performance	Work quality	0.910	0.015	0.935	0.071	-0.025
	Planning and organizing work	0.876	0.003	0.900	0.052	-0.024
	Being result-oriented	0.882	0.016	0.886	0.007	-0.004
	Prioritizing	0.860	0.008	0.873	0.022	-0.013
	Working efficiently	1.089	0.006	1.117	0.046	-0.028

Table 8. Comparative analysis among the employees from Generation X, Generation Y, and Generation Z

Relationships	Generation X vs. Generation Y		Generation X vs. Generation Z		Generation Y vs. Generation Z	
	ß	p	ß	p	ß	p
Contextual individual performance -> Task performance	0.126	0.213	0.314	**0.021**	0.188	0.171
Counterproductive behavior -> Contextual individual performance	0.525	**0.997**	0.123	0.663	0.403	**0.035**
Counterproductive behavior -> Contextual organizational performance	0.379	**0.978**	0.003	0.529	0.376	0.071
Counterproductive behavior -> Task performance	0.119	0.676	0.382	0.896	0.263	0.805
Task performance -> Contextual organizational performance	0.206	0.095	0.177	0.199	0.030	0.612

Table 9. Testing the hypothesis

Hypothesis	Generation X			Generation Y			Generation Z		
	ß	t	p	ß	t	p	ß	t	p
Contextual individual performance -> Task performance	**0.716**	**8.071**	**0.000**	**0.590**	**4.260**	**0.000**	**0.401**	**2.659**	**0.008**
Counterproductive behavior -> Contextual individual performance	0.189	0.681	0.496	**0.714**	**9.571**	**0.000**	0.311	1.036	0.300
Counterproductive behavior -> Contextual organizational performance	0.258	1.241	0.215	**0.638**	**7.306**	**0.000**	0.262	0.928	0.354
Counterproductive behavior -> Task performance	-0.174	1.014	0.311	-0.055	0.276	0.782	0.208	0.915	0.360
Task performance -> Contextual organizational performance	**0.542**	**4.067**	**0.000**	**0.335**	**4.066**	**0.000**	**0.365**	**2.157**	**0.031**

Multigenerational Analysis: Generation X, Generation Y, and Generation Z

The differences that occur among the three generations of employees (Generation X, Generation Y, Generation Z) are analyzed using PLS-MGA analysis. Taking into account the data presented in Table 8 and the fact that a difference is considered to be significant if the p-value is smaller than 0.05 or larger than 0.95 (Henseler et al., 2009; Sarstedt et al., 2011), it can be stated that significant differences appear between: (i) the employees from Generation X and Generation Y when it comes to the influence of the counterproductive behavior on the contextual individual and organizational performance; (ii) the employees from Generation X and Generation Z when it comes to the influence of the contextual individual performance on task performance; and (iii) the employees from Generation Y and Generation Z when it comes to the influence of the counterproductive behavior on the contextual individual performance.

The differences among the employees from various generations are more visible when the analysis is performed at the level of each generation (Table 9). Thus, among the employees from Generation X and Generation Z, two out of five relationships are validated, namely: (i) the contextual individual performance positively influences task performance (for Generation X: $\beta = 0.716$, $t = 8.071 > 1.96$, $p = 0.000 < 0.05$; for Generation Z: $\beta = 0.410$, $t = 2.659 > 1.96$, $p = 0.008 < 0.05$); and (ii) the task performance positively influences the contextual organizational performance (for Generation X: $\beta = 0.542$, $t = 4.067 > 1.96$, $p = 0.000 < 0.05$; for Generation Z: $\beta = 0.365$, $t = 2.157 > 1.96$, $p = 0.031 < 0.05$). The same relationships are validated among the employees from Generation Y. Still, two more relationships are validated among the latter, namely: (i) the counterproductive behavior positively influences the contextual individual performance ($\beta = 0.714$, $t = 9.571 > 1.96$, $p = 0.000 < 0.05$); and (ii) the counterproductive behavior positively influences the contextual organizational performance ($\beta = 0.638$, $t = 7.306 > 1.96$, $p = 0.000 < 0.05$).

Table 10. PLSPredict assessment for Generation X, Generation Y, and Generation Z

Group	Indicator	PLS-SEM		LM		PLS-SEM - LM
		RMSE	$Q^2_{predict}$	RMSE	$Q^2_{predict}$	RMSE
Generation X	Taking initiative	1.255	-0.110	1.315	-0.219	-0.060
	Accepting and learning from feedback	1.195	-0.082	1.239	-0.162	-0.044
	Cooperating with others	1.148	-0.117	1.186	-0.192	-0.038
	Communicating effectively	1.021	-0.171	1.048	-0.235	-0.027
	Showing responsibility	1.066	-0.107	1.088	-0.154	-0.022
	Being customer-oriented	0.975	-0.041	0.995	-0.085	-0.020
	Being creative	1.102	-0.037	1.159	-0.148	-0.057
	Taking on challenging work tasks	1.109	-0.067	1.136	-0.118	-0.027
	Work quality	0.855	-0.091	0.913	-0.242	-0.058
	Planning and organizing work	0.845	-0.119	0.871	-0.192	-0.026
	Being result-oriented	0.953	-0.163	1.040	-0.386	-0.087
	Prioritizing	1.023	-0.128	1.073	-0.242	-0.050
	Working efficiently	1.171	-0.070	1.332	-0.386	-0.161
Generation Y	Taking initiative	0.928	0.314	0.973	0.246	-0.045
	Accepting and learning from feedback	0.872	0.296	0.922	0.213	-0.050
	Cooperating with others	0.863	0.341	0.878	0.318	-0.015
	Communicating effectively	0.752	0.405	0.790	0.343	-0.038
	Showing responsibility	0.825	0.343	0.875	0.260	-0.050
	Being customer-oriented	0.843	0.427	0.856	0.409	-0.013
	Being creative	0.844	0.426	0.847	0.421	-0.003
	Taking on challenging work tasks	1.013	0.354	1.069	0.281	-0.056
	Work quality	1.044	0.118	1.046	0.076	-0.002
	Planning and organizing work	1.061	0.020	1.063	0.022	-0.002
	Being result-oriented	0.876	0.126	0.897	0.202	-0.021
	Prioritizing	0.820	0.086	0.842	0.036	-0.022
	Working efficiently	0.979	0.005	0.981	0.030	-0.002
Generation Z	Taking initiative	1.011	-0.351	1.190	-0.873	-0.179
	Accepting and learning from feedback	0.985	-0.333	1.184	-0.927	-0.199
	Cooperating with others	0.985	-0.246	1.054	-0.424	-0.069
	Communicating effectively	1.100	-0.399	1.230	-0.749	-0.130
	Showing responsibility	0.890	-0.251	0.920	-0.335	-0.030
	Being customer-oriented	0.944	-0.169	1.154	-0.746	-0.210
	Being creative	1.274	-0.208	1.294	-0.161	-0.020
	Taking on challenging work tasks	1.219	-0.210	1.279	-0.313	-0.060
	Work quality	0.858	-0.195	0.972	-0.532	-0.114
	Planning and organizing work	0.720	-0.109	0.774	-0.283	-0.054
	Being result-oriented	0.821	-0.245	1.025	-0.938	-0.204
	Prioritizing	0.857	-0.236	1.016	-0.737	-0.159
	Working efficiently	1.208	-0.008	1.383	-0.321	-0.175

If the predictive power of the model is analyzed at the generational level, it can be noticed that, for Generation X and Generation Z, the $Q^2_{predict}$ value is below zero for all the analyzed indicators (Table 10). Thus, for the employees from Generation X and Generation Z, the predictive relevance of the model is not confirmed. Still, when it comes to Generation X, it can be noticed that the highest differences appear at the level of: "*Working efficiently*" (PLS-SEM based RMSE = 1.171; LM based RMSE = 1.332), "*Being result-oriented*" (PLS-SEM based RMSE = 0.953; LM based RMSE = 1.040), "*Taking initiative*" (PLS-SEM based RMSE = 1.255; LM based RMSE = 1.315), "*Work quality*" (PLS-SEM based RMSE = 0.855; LM based RMSE = 0.913), and "*Being creative*" (PLS-SEM based RMSE = 1.102; LM based RMSE = 1.159). On the other hand, when it comes to Generation Z, the most powerful differences are registered by: "*Being customer-oriented*" (PLS-SEM based RMSE = 0.994; LM based RMSE = 1.154), "*Being result-oriented*" (PLS-SEM based RMSE = 0.821; LM based RMSE = 1.025), "*Accepting and learning from feedback*" (PLS-SEM based RMSE = 0.985; LM based RMSE = 1.184), "*Taking initiative*" (PLS-SEM based RMSE = 1.011; LM based RMSE = 1.190), and "*Working efficiently*" (PLS-SEM based RMSE = 1.208; LM based RMSE = 1.383).

The situation changes among the employees from Generation Y, where the model has a high predictive power given the fact that the $Q^2_{predict}$ values are higher than zero, and the differences between the RMSE of PLS-SEM and the ones of naïve LM benchmark are negative for all the indicators. The most pronounced differences appear at the level of "*Taking on challenging work tasks*" (PLS-SEM based RMSE = 1.013; LM based RMSE = 1.069), "*Showing responsibility*" (PLS-SEM based RMSE = 0.825; LM based RMSE = 0.875), "*Accepting and learning from feedback*" (PLS-SEM based RMSE = 0.872; LM based RMSE = 0.922), and "*Taking initiative*" (PLS-SEM based RMSE = 0.928; LM based RMSE = 0.973).

CONCLUSION AND FURTHER RESEARCH DIRECTIONS

The current chapter focused on emphasizing the impact of the counterproductive behavior and contextual (individual and organizational) performance on employees' task performance, from an intergenerational approach. Therefore, the analysis was performed in three banks' subsidiaries from Bucharest, Romania, due to the fact that this is the most dynamic economic sector which incorporates employees from five generations, namely, the Veterans, Baby-Boomers, Generation X, Generation Y, and Generation Z. At the general level, the results proved that, among the employees from the Romanian banking subsidiaries: (i) the contextual individual performance has a positive influence on task performance ($ß = 0.602$; $t = 10.825 > 1.96$; $p = 0.000 < 0.05$); (ii) the counterproductive behavior has a positive influence on the contextual individual performance ($ß = 0.361$; $t = 5.678 > 1.96$; $p = 0.000 < 0.05$); (iii) the counterproductive behavior has a positive influence on the contextual organizational performance ($ß = 0.262$; $t = 3.878 > 1.96$; $p = 0.000 < 0.05$); and (iv) the task performance has a positive influence on the contextual organizational performance ($ß = 0.482$; $t = 6.640 > 1.96$; $p = 0.000 < 0.05$).

Still, the perspective changed when an intergenerational approach was employed. On the one hand, it was brought forward that significant differences appear between: (i) the employees from Generation X and Generation Y when it comes to the influence of the counterproductive behavior on the contextual individual and organizational performance; (ii) the employees from Generation X and Generation Z when it comes to the influence of the contextual individual performance on task performance; and (iii) the employees from Generation Y and Generation Z when it comes to the influence of the counterproductive behavior on the contextual individual performance.

On the other hand, it was emphasized that various similarities occur between Generation X and Generation Z. Thus, among the employees from Generation X and Generation Z, it was proved that: (i) the contextual individual performance positively influences task performance (for Generation X: ß = 0.716, $t = 8.071 > 1.96$, $p = 0.000 < 0.05$; for Generation Z: ß = 0.410, $t = 2.659 > 1.96$, $p = 0.008 < 0.05$); and (ii) the task performance positively influences the contextual organizational performance (for Generation X: ß = 0.542, $t = 4.067 > 1.96$, $p = 0.000 < 0.05$; for Generation Z: ß = 0.365, $t = 2.157 > 1.96$, $p = 0.031 < 0.05$). The same relationships were validated among the employees from Generation Y, and in addition, two more aspects were reflected, namely: (i) the counterproductive behavior positively influences the contextual individual performance (ß = 0.714, $t = 9.571 > 1.96$, $p = 0.000 < 0.05$); and (ii) the counterproductive behavior positively influences the contextual organizational performance (ß = 0.638, $t = 7.306 > 1.96$, $p = 0.000 < 0.05$). The similarities between Generation X and Generation Z may occur due to the fact that the members of Generation X were frequently in charged with the education of the latter. Besides, the members of both generations are competitive, driven by change and goal oriented.

These findings have both theoretical and practical implications. On the one hand, they extend the theory from the human resources management and performance management fields by providing an intergenerational analysis on the impact of the counterproductive behavior and contextual performance on employees' task performance. On the other hand, they help the managers to understand how the relationships established among the counterproductive behavior, contextual individual and organizational performance, and task performance can be perceived differently by the employees who belong to various generations, like Generation X, Generation Y, and Generation Z.

ACKNOWLEDGMENT

This work is part of the research project entitled „Strategic development of Intellectual capital. The human resources management practices that foster intergenerational learning" and supported by the Multidisciplinary Doctoral School of SNSPA (Decision 47/04.06.2019).

REFERENCES

Aguirre-Urreta, M., & Rönkkö, M. (2018). Statistical inference with PLSc using bootstrap confidence intervals. *Management Information Systems Quarterly*, *42*(3), 1001–1020. doi:10.25300/MISQ/2018/13587

Ali, F., Rasoolimanesh, S., Sarstedt, M., Ringle, C., & Ryu, K. (2018). An assessment of the use of partial least squares structural equation modeling (PLS-SEM) in hospitality research. *International Journal of Contemporary Hospitality Management*, *30*(1), 514–538. doi:10.1108/IJCHM-10-2016-0568

Anantatmula, V., & Shrivastav, B. (2012). Evolution of project teams for generation Y workforce. *International Journal of Managing Projects in Business*, *5*(1), 9–26. doi:10.1108/17538371211192874

Appelbaum, S., Serena, M., & Shapiro, B. (2005). Generation "X" and the boomers: An analysis of realities and myths. *Management Research News*, *28*(1), 1–33. doi:10.1108/01409170510784751

Aubé, C., Rousseau, V., Mama, C., & Morin, E. M. (2009). Counterproductive behaviors and psychological well-being: The moderating effect of task interdependence. *Journal of Business and Psychology*, *24*(3), 351–361. doi:10.100710869-009-9113-5

Aubé, C., Rousseau, V., & Tremblay, S. (2011). Team size and quality of group experience: The more the merrier? *Group Dynamics*, *15*(4), 357–375. doi:10.1037/a0025400

Baily, C. (2009). Reverse intergenerational learning: A missed opportunity? *AI & Society*, *23*(1), 111–115. doi:10.100700146-007-0169-3

Baldonado, A. (2008). *Exploring Workplace Motivational and Managerial Factors associated with Generation Y*. Northcentral University.

Baran, M., & Klos, M. (2014). Managing an intergenerational workforce as a factor of company competitiveness. *Journal of International Studies*, *7*(1), 94–101. doi:10.14254/2071-8330.2014/7-1/8

Beal, G. (2016). 8 Key Differences between Gen Z and Millennials. *HuffPost*. Retrieved on August 13, 2019 from https://www.huffingtonpost.com/george-beall/8-key-differences-between_b_12814200.html

Becker, J. M., Klein, K., & Wetzels, M. (2012). Hierarchical latent variable models in PLS-SEM: Guidelines for using reflective–formative type models. *Long Range Planning*, *45*(5), 359–394. doi:10.1016/j.lrp.2012.10.001

Blome, M. W., Borell, J., Hakansson, C., & Nilsson, K. (2020). Attitudes toward elderly workers and perceptions of integrated age management practices. *International Journal of Occupational Safety and Ergonomics*, *26*(1), 112–120. doi:10.1080/10803548.2018.1514135 PMID:30130462

Borman, W. C., & Motowidlo, S. J. (1993). Expanding the criterion domain to include elements of contextual performance. In N. Schmitt & W. C. Borman (Eds.), *Personnel Selection in Organizations* (pp. 71–98). Jossey-Bass.

Botsford Morgan, W., Nelson, J., King, E., & Mancini, V. (2018). Reactions to men's and women's counterproductive work behavior. *Equality, Diversity and Inclusion*, *37*(6), 582–599. doi:10.1108/EDI-08-2017-0161

Cadmus, E. (2002). Defining generations in succession planning: There are four. *Seminars for Nurse Managers*, *10*(4), 246–253. PMID:12526620

Cammock, P., Nilakant, V., & Dakin, S. (1995). Developing a lay model of managerial effectiveness: A social constructionist perspective. *Journal of Management Studies*, *32*(4), 443–474. doi:10.1111/j.1467-6486.1995.tb00784.x

Carlos, V. S., & Rodrigues, R. G. (2016). Development and validation of a self-reported measure of job performance. *Social Indicators Research*, *126*(1), 279–307. doi:10.100711205-015-0883-z

Chang, Y. W., Hsu, P. Y., & Yang, Q. M. (2018). Integration of online and offline channels: A view of O2O commerce. *Internet Research*, *28*(4), 926–945. doi:10.1108/IntR-01-2017-0023

Cheah, J. H., Ting, H., Cham, T. H., & Memon, M. A. (2019). The effect of selfie promotion and celebrity endorsed advertisement on decision-making processes: A model comparison. *Internet Research*, *29*(3), 552–577. doi:10.1108/IntR-12-2017-0530

Cho, S. H., Ali, F., & Manhas, P. S. (2019). Examining the impact of risk perceptions on intentions to travel by air: A comparison of full-service carriers and low-cost carriers. *Journal of Air Transport Management*, *71*, 20–27. doi:10.1016/j.jairtraman.2018.05.005

Conway, J. M. (1999). Distinguishing contextual performance from task performance for managerial jobs. *The Journal of Applied Psychology*, *84*(1), 3–13. doi:10.1037/0021-9010.84.1.3

Debrah, Y., & Smith, I. (2000). Globalization, employment and the workplace: responses for the millennium. *Management Research News, 23*(2/3/4), 1-16. doi:10.1108/01409170010782019

Deep Focus. (2015). *Deep Focus Cassandra Report: Gen Z Uncovers Massive Attitude Shifts Toward Money, Work and Communication Preferences*. Retrieved on August 29, 2019 from http://www.marketwired.com/press-release/deep-focus-cassandra-report-gen-z-uncovers-massive-attitude-shifts-toward-money-work-2004889.html

Dodd, E. M. Jr. (1932). For whom are corporate managers trustees? *Harvard Law Review*, *45*(7), 1145–1163. doi:10.2307/1331697

Dois, J., Landrum, P., & Wirck, K. L. (2010). Leading and managing an intergenerational workforce. *Creative Nursing*, *16*(2), 68–74. doi:10.1891/1078-4535.16.2.68 PMID:20486642

Dwyer, R. J., & Azevedo, A. (2016). Preparing leaders for the multi-generational workforce. *Journal of Enterprising Communities: People and Places in the Global Economy*, *10*(3), 281–305. doi:10.1108/JEC-08-2013-0025

Ernst & Young. (2016). *From Innovation to Expectation – How M & E Leaders are Responding to Gen Z.* Retrieved on August 30, 2019 from https://www.ey.com/Publication/vwLUAssets/ey-media-entertainment-leaders-respond-to-gen-z/$FILE/ey-media-entertainment-leaders-respond-to-gen-z.pdf

Fiksel, J. (2006). Sustainability and resilience: toward a system approach. *Sustainability: Science. Practice & Policy*, *2*(2), 14–21. doi:10.1080/15487733.2006.11907980

Friedman, M. (1970, Sept. 13). The responsibility of business is to increase its profits. *The New York Times Magazines*, 32-33.

Galo, A. M. (2011). Beyond the Classroom. Using Technology to Meet the Educational Needs of Multigenerational Perinatal Nurses. *The Journal of Perinatal & Neonatal Nursing*, *25*(2), 195–199. doi:10.1097/JPN.0b013e3182163993 PMID:21540699

Gerpott, F. H., Lehmann-Willenbrock, N., & Voelpel, S. C. (2016). A phase model of intergenerational learning in organizations. *Academy of Management Learning & Education*, *16*(2), 193–216. doi:10.5465/amle.2015.0185

Gioia, D. A., & Pitre, E. (1990). Multiparadigm perspectives on theory building. *Academy of Management Review*, *15*(4), 584–602. doi:10.5465/amr.1990.4310758

Greenslade, J. H., & Jimmieson, N. L. (2007). Distinguishing between task and contextual performance for nurses: Development of a job performance scale. *Journal of Advanced Nursing*, *58*(6), 602–611. doi:10.1111/j.1365-2648.2007.04256.x PMID:17442026

Hahn, J. (2009). Effectively manage a multigenerational staff. *Nursing Management*, *40*(9), 8–10. doi:10.1097/01.NUMA.0000360765.52105.ed PMID:19734749

Hair, J. F., Hult, G. T. M., Ringle, C. M., & Sarstedt, M. (2014). *A primer on partial least squares structural equation modeling (PLS-SEM)*. SAGE Publications.

Hair, J. F., Hult, G. T. M., Ringle, C. M., Sarstedt, M., & Thiele, K. (2017). Mirror, mirror on the wall: A comparative evaluation of composite-based structural equation modeling methods. *Journal of the Academy of Marketing Science*, *45*(5), 616–632. doi:10.100711747-017-0517-x

Hair, J. F., Ringle, C. M., & Sarstedt, M. (2011). PLS-SEM: Indeed a silver bullet. *Journal of Marketing Theory and Practice*, *19*(2), 139–152. doi:10.2753/MTP1069-6679190202

Hair, J. F., Risher, J. J., Sarstedt, M., & Ringle, C. M. (2019). When to use and how to report the results of PLS-SEM. *European Business Review*, *31*(1), 2–24. doi:10.1108/EBR-11-2018-0203

Hatfield, S. L. (2002). Understanding the four generations to enhance workplace management. *AFP Exchange*, *22*(4), 72–74.

Henseler, J., Ringle, C. M., & Sarstedt, M. (2012). Using partial least squares path modeling in advertising research: Basic concepts and recent issues. In S. Okazaki (Ed.), *Handbook of research on international advertising* (pp. 252–276). Edward Elgar. doi:10.4337/9781781001042.00023

Henseler, J., Ringle, C. M., & Sarstedt, M. (2015). A New Criterion for Assessing Discriminant Validity in Variance-based Structural Equation Modeling. *Journal of the Academy of Marketing Science*, *43*(1), 115–135. doi:10.100711747-014-0403-8

Henseler, J., Ringle, C. M., & Sarstedt, M. (2016). Testing measurement invariance of composites using partial least squares. *International Marketing Review*, *33*(3), 405–431. doi:10.1108/IMR-09-2014-0304

Henseler, J., Ringle, C. M., & Sinkovics, R. R. (2009). The use of partial least squares path modeling in international marketing. *Advances in International Marketing*, *20*(1), 277–319. doi:10.1108/S1474-7979(2009)0000020014

Hosie, P., & Nankervis, A. (2016). A multidimensional measure of managers' contextual and task performance. *Personnel Review*, *45*(2), 419–447. doi:10.1108/PR-02-2014-0038

Howe, N., & Strauss, W. (2007). The next 20 years: How customer and workforce attitudes will evolve. *Harvard Business Review*, *85*(7/8), 41–52. PMID:17642125

Kaminska, R., & Borzillo, S. (2017). Challenges to the learning organization in the context of generational diversity and social networks. *The Learning Organization*, *25*(2), 92–101. doi:10.1108/TLO-03-2017-0033

Keepnews, D., Brewer, C., Kovner, C., & Shin, J. (2010). Generational difference among newly licensed registered nurses. *Nursing Outlook*, *58*(3), 155–163. doi:10.1016/j.outlook.2009.11.001 PMID:20494691

Kiyani, A. A., Ayupp, K., & Rasool, S. (2018). Exploring the construct of task performance of academicians in an Asian context: teaching is different from research. *Evidence-based HRM: A Global Forum for Empirical Scholarship, 6*(1), 25-38. doi:10.1108/EBHRM-03-2016-0008

Knouse, S. B. (2011). Managing generational diversity in the 21st century. *Competition Forum, 9*(2), 255-260.

Kogan, M. (2001). Bridging the gap. *Government Executive, 33*(12). Retrieved on August 15, 2019 from https://www.govexec.com/magazine/magazine-human-resources-management/2001/09/bridging-the-gap/9752/

Kollmann, T., Stoeckmann, C., Kensbock, J. M., & Peschl, A. (2020). What satisfies younger versus older employees, and why? An aging perspective on equity theory to explain interactive effects of employee age, monetary rewards, and task contributions on job satisfaction. *Human Resource Management, 59*(1), 101–115. doi:10.1002/hrm.21981

Kollmus, A., & Agyeman, J. (2002). Mind the gap: Why do people act environmentally and what are the barriers to pro-environmental behavior. *Environmental Education Research, 8*(3), 239–260. doi:10.1080/13504620220145401

Koopmans, L., Bernaards, C., Hildebrandt, V., van Buuren, S., van der Beek, A., & de Vet, H. (2013). Development of an individual work performance questionnaire. *International Journal of Productivity and Performance Management, 62*(1), 6–28. doi:10.1108/17410401311285273

Kramer, L. (2010). Generational diversity. *Dimensions of Critical Care Nursing, 29*(3), 125–128. doi:10.1097/DCC.0b013e3181d24ba9 PMID:20395729

Lanier, K. (2017). 5 things HR professionals need to know about Generation Z: Thought leaders share their views on the HR profession and its direction for the future. *Strategic HR Review, 16*(6), 288–290. doi:10.1108/SHR-08-2017-0051

Leinonen, T., Chandola, T., Laaksonen, M., & Martikainen, P. (2020). Socio-economic differences in retirement timing and participation in post-retirement employment in a context of a flexible pension age. *Ageing and Society, 40*(2), 348–368. doi:10.1017/S0144686X18000958

Leon, R. D. (2018). Sustainable Knowledge Based Organizations: Definition and Characteristics. *Environmental Engineering and Management Journal, 17*(6), 1425–1437. doi:10.30638/eemj.2018.141

Letmathe, P., & Rossler, M. (2019). Tacit knowledge transfer and spillover learning in ramp-ups. *International Journal of Operations & Production Management, 39*(9/10), 1099–1121. doi:10.1108/IJOPM-08-2018-0508

Lievens, F., Conway, J. M., & De Corte, W. (2008). The relative importance of task, citizenship and counterproductive performance to job performance ratings: Do rater source and team-based culture matter? *Journal of Occupational and Organizational Psychology, 81*(1), 11–27. doi:10.1348/096317907X182971

Lozano, R. (2008). Developing collaborative and sustainable organizations. *Journal of Cleaner Production, 16*(4), 499–509. doi:10.1016/j.jclepro.2007.01.002

Malik, N. (2018). Authentic leadership – an antecedent for contextual performance of Indian nurses. *Personnel Review*, *47*(6), 1244–1260. doi:10.1108/PR-07-2016-0168

Mason, C. H., & Perreault, W. D. Jr. (1991). Collinearity, power, and interpretation of multiple regression analysis. *JMR, Journal of Marketing Research*, *28*(3), 268–280. doi:10.1177/002224379102800302

McNeil, K., Johnson, O., & Johnson, A. (2001). "Did you hear what Tommy Hilfiger said?" Urban legend, urban fashion and African-American generation Xers. *Journal of Fashion Marketing and Management*, *5*(3), 234–240. doi:10.1108/EUM0000000007289

Memon, A. H., & Rahman, I. A. (2014). SEM-PLS analysis of inhibiting factors of cost performance for large construction projects in Malaysia: Perspective of clients and consultants. *TheScientificWorldJournal*, *165158*, 1–9. Advance online publication. doi:10.1155/2014/165158 PMID:24693227

Merriman, M. (2015). What if the Next Big Disruptor Isn't a What but a Who? *Ernst & Young*. Retrieved on August 28, 2019 from https://www.ey.com/Publication/vwLUAssets/EY-rise-of-gen-znew-challenge-for-retailers/$FILE/EY-rise-of-gen-znew-challenge-for-retailers.pdf

Merriman, M., & Valerio, D. (2016). One Tough Customer: How Gen Z is Challenging the Competitive Landscape and Redefining Omnichannel. *Ernst & Young*. Retrieved on August 29, 2019. https://www.ey.com/Publication/vwLUAssets/EY-one-tough-customer/$FILE/EY-one-tough-customer.pdf

Model, S. (2005). Triangulation between case study and survey methods in management accounting research: An assessment of validity implications. *Management Accounting Research*, *16*(2), 231–254. doi:10.1016/j.mar.2005.03.001

Morgan, G., & Smircich, L. (1980). The case of qualitative research. *Academy of Management Review*, *5*(4), 491–500. doi:10.5465/amr.1980.4288947

Motowidlo, S. J., Borman, W. C., & Schmit, M. J. (1997). A theory of individual differences in task and contextual performance. *Human Performance*, *10*(2), 71–83. doi:10.120715327043hup1002_1

Motowidlo, S. J., & Schmit, M. J. (1999). Performance assessment in unique jobs. In D. R. Llgen & E. D. Pulakos (Eds.), *The Changing Nature of Performance* (pp. 56–86). Jossey-Bass.

Nunkoo, R., Teeroovengadum, V., Ringle, C. M., & Sunnassee, V. (2019). Service quality and customer satisfaction: The moderating effects of hotel star rating. *International Journal of Hospitality Management*, 102414. Advance online publication. doi:10.1016/j.ijhm.2019.102414

OC&C Strategy Consultants. (2019). *A generation without borders. Embracing Generation Z*. Retrieved on June 21, 2019 from https://www.occstrategy.com/media/1806/a-generation-without-borders.pdf

Organ, D. W., & Paine, J. (1999). A new kind of performance for industrial and organizational psychology: recent contributions to the study of organizational citizenship behavior. In C. L. Cooper & I. T. Robertson (Eds.), *International Review of Industrial and Organizational Psychology* (pp. 338–368). Wiley.

Rego, A. (2002). *Comportamentos de Cidadania nas Organizações*. McGraw Hill.

Richter, N. F., Cepeda, G., Roldán, J. L., & Ringle, C. M. (2015). European management research using partial least squares structural equation modeling (PLS-SEM). *European Management Journal*, *33*(1), 1–3. doi:10.1016/j.emj.2014.12.001

Rigdon, E. E. (2012). Rethinking partial least squares path modeling: In praise of simple methods. *Long Range Planning*, *45*(5–6), 341–358. doi:10.1016/j.lrp.2012.09.010

Ringle, C. M., Wende, S., & Becker, J. M. (2015). *SmartPLS 3*. Retrieved November, 15, 2019, from http://www.smartpls.com

Roldán, J. L., & Sánchez-Franco, M. J. (2012). Variance-based structural equation modeling: Guidelines for using partial least squares. In M. Mora, G. Ovsei, A. Steenkamp, & M. S. Raisinghani (Eds.), *Research methodologies, innovations and philosophies in software systems engineering and information systems* (pp. 193–221). Information Science Reference. doi:10.4018/978-1-4666-0179-6.ch010

Rupčic, N. (2018). Intergenerational learning and knowledge transfer – challenges and opportunities. *The Learning Organization*, *25*(2), 135–142. doi:10.1108/TLO-11-2017-0117

Sackett, P. R., & DeVore, C. J. (2001). Counterproductive behaviors at work. In N. Anderson, D. S. Ones, H. K. Sinangil, & C. Viswesvaran (Eds.), *Handbook of Industrial, Work and Organizational Psychology: Personnel Psychology* (Vol. 1, pp. 145–164). Sage Publications. doi:10.4135/9781848608320.n9

Sarstedt, M., Hair, J. F., Ringle, C. M., Thiele, K. O., & Gudergan, S. P. (2016). Estimation issues with PLS and CBSEM: Where the Bias Lies! *Journal of Business Research*, *69*(10), 3998–4010. doi:10.1016/j.jbusres.2016.06.007

Sarstedt, M., Henseler, J., & Ringle, C. (2011). Multigroup Analysis in Partial Least Squares (PLS) Path Modeling: Alternative Methods and Empirical Results. In M. Sarstedt, M. Schwaiger, & C. Taylor (Eds.), *Measurement and Research Methods in International Marketing* (Vol. 22, pp. 195–218). Emerald Group Publishing Limited., doi:10.1108/S1474-7979(2011)0000022012

Sarstedt, M., Ringle, C. M., & Hair, J. F. (2017). Partial least squares structural equation modeling. In C. Homburg, M. Klarmann, & A. Vomberg (Eds.), *Handbook of Market Research* (pp. 1–40). Springer. doi:10.1007/978-3-319-05542-8_15-1

Schullery, N. M. (2013). Workplace engagement and generational differences in values. *Business Communication Quarterly*, *76*(2), 252–265. doi:10.1177/1080569913476543

Schwieger, D., & Ladwig, C. (2018). Reaching and Retaining the Next Generation: Adapting to the Expectations of Gen Z in the Classroom. *Information Systems Education Journal*, *16*(3), 45–53.

Seemiller, C., & Grace, M. (2016). *Generation Z Goes to College*. Jossey-Bass.

Shatto, B., & Erwin, K. (2017). Teaching Millennials and Generation Z: Bridging the generational divide. *Creative Nursing*, *23*(1), 24–28. doi:10.1891/1078-4535.23.1.24 PMID:28196564

Shmueli, G., Ray, S., Velasquez Estrada, J. M., & Chatla, S. B. (2016). The elephant in the room: Evaluating the predictive performance of PLS models. *Journal of Business Research*, *69*(10), 4552–4564. doi:10.1016/j.jbusres.2016.03.049

Shmueli, G., Sarstedt, M., Hair, J., Cheah, J., Ting, H., Vaithilingam, S., & Ringle, C. (2019). Predictive model assessment in PLS-SEM: Guidelines for using PLSpredict. *European Journal of Marketing, 53*(11), 2322–2347. doi:10.1108/EJM-02-2019-0189

Skoludova, J., & Horakova, L. (2016). *The impact of motivating and stimulating generation Y employees on company performance.* Paper presented at the 17th International Scientific Conference on Economic and Social Development, Warsaw, Poland.

Stillman, D., & Stillman, J. (2017). *Gen Z @ Work: How the Next Generation Is Transforming the Workplace.* Harper Collins Publishers.

Sujit, K. S., & Rajesh, B. K. (2016). Determinants of Discretionary Investments: Evidence from Indian Food Industry. *SAGE Open, 6*(1). Advance online publication. doi:10.1177/2158244016636429

Turner, A. (2015). Generation Z: Technology and Social Interest. *Journal of Individual Psychology, 71*(2), 103–113. doi:10.1353/jip.2015.0021

Twenge, J. M. (2017). *IGen: Why Today's Super-Connected Kids Are Growing Up Less Rebellious, More Tolerant, Less Happy - Completely Unprepared for Adulthood.* Atria Books.

Twenge, J. M., Freeman, E. C., & Campbell, W. (2012). Generational differences in young adults' life goals, concern for others, and civic orientation, 1966-2009. *Journal of Personality and Social Psychology, 102*(5), 1045–1062. doi:10.1037/a0027408 PMID:22390226

Upadhyay, P., & Kundu, A. (2019). Linkage between business sustainability and tacit knowledge management in MSMEs A case-based study. *VINE Journal of Information and Knowledge Management Systems, ahead-of-print*(ahead-of-print). Advance online publication. doi:10.1108/VJIKMS-08-2019-0133

Van Dyne, L., & Le Pine, J. A. (1998). Helping and voice extra-role behaviors: Evidence of construct and predictive validity. *Academy of Management Journal, 41*(1), 108–119. doi:10.2307/256902

Van Scotter, J. R., & Motowidlo, S. J. (1996). Interpersonal facilitation and job dedication as separate facets of contextual performance. *The Journal of Applied Psychology, 81*(5), 525–531. doi:10.1037/0021-9010.81.5.525

Williams, K. C., Page, R. A., Petrosky, A. R., & Hernandez, E. H. (2010). Multi-generational Marketing: Descriptions, Characteristics, Lifestyles, and Attitudes. *The Journal of Applied Business and Economics, 11*(2), 21–36.

Yang, Q., & Wei, H. (2017). Ethical leadership and employee task performance: Examining moderated mediation process. *Management Decision, 55*(7), 1506–1520. doi:10.1108/MD-09-2016-0627

KEY TERMS AND DEFINITIONS

Contextual Individual Performance: The emotional and spiritual knowledge (devotion, determination, etc.) that the employees decide to use in the organizational environment in order to foster their professional development.

Contextual Organizational Performance: The quality of the working relationships established within the organization in order to support the employees' professional development and the company's sustainable development.

Counterproductive Behavior: A behavior that stimulates competition among the employees and challenges the status quo.

Generation X: A cohort of population that usually adopts a speculative behavior, using the team and the organization for their own personal and professional purposes.

Generation Y: A cohort of population that witnessed the faster pace of technological progress, is informed and demanding, has a high level of self-esteem, and values the equilibrium between the personal and professional life.

Generation Z: A cohort of population that was raised with the information and communication channels at its fingertip, competitive, interested in the economic, social, and environmental sustainability, very well informed but scared by the future.

Task Performance: The concrete results obtained by the employees at the workplace.

Chapter 16
Strategies for Business Sustainability in a Collaborative Economy:
Building the Career Resilience of Generation Z

Naomi Borg
RMIT University, Australia

Christina M. Scott-Young
RMIT University, Australia

Nader Naderpajouh
https://orcid.org/0000-0001-9628-9766
RMIT University, Australia

ABSTRACT

The increasingly complex and turbulent 21st century work environment poses challenges for businesses that can threaten their long-term sustainability. Given the rapid developments in technology, increasing rates of employee turnover, skills shortages, and changing expectations from Generation Z, the youngest generation now entering the workforce, organizations are recognizing the importance of developing a career resilient workforce. Individual employees' career resilience frames their capacity to respond when faced with career challenges, allowing them to continue functioning effectively, adapt in a flexible manner, and to successfully deliver work outcomes. To sustain a resilient workforce, managers must actively plan, develop, and deploy human resource management initiatives aimed at instilling career resilience in the youngest workplace entrants. By strategically designing generationally-appropriate management practices to maximize Generation Z talent, organizations can bolster their business sustainability to remain competitive in the changing economy.

DOI: 10.4018/978-1-7998-4543-0.ch016

INTRODUCTION

Organizations in the 21st Century operate in an increasingly volatile, uncertain, complex and ambiguous (VUCA) environment (Mack, Khare, Kramer & Burgatz, 2016) which presents challenges that threaten business survival. This fluid VUCA environment is characterized by shocks and stressors in the form of managing multiple generations in the workforce, increasing globalization and burgeoning digitalization (Lee, Huang & Ashford, 2018). In recent years organizational sustainability has been challenged by the loss of valuable company-specific knowledge and experience as the large Baby Boomer (born 1943-1960) component of the workforce retires. Ageing populations in developed nations like Japan, the U.S. and Australia (Sandhu, Sastrowardoyo, Benson & Scott-Young, 2016) also pose significant labor force stressors (McDonald & Kippen, 2001; Dixon, 2003; Burke & Ng, 2006). Organizations now face risks associated with the "major global skills shortages [which] exist in a wide range of industries and sectors" (Holbeche, 2015, p.43). Adding to this risk is the increased mobility and job-hopping of Generation Y employees (born 1980-1994) (Benson, Sandhu, Sastrowardoyo & Scott-Young, 2015). A world-wide survey conducted by KPMG (2014) ranked finding skilled employees one of the most pressing business challenges facing contemporary chief executives, second only to achieving profitable growth.

The recent entry into the workplace of the youngest generation, Generation Z, also known as the Internet Generation (Tapscott & Williams, 2010) or IGen (Twenge, 2017), constitutes another of the many shocks contemporary organizations are experiencing. The sociological concept of generations was developed by Karl Mannheim (1928) to categorize same-aged cohorts who share their birth and formative years in a particular time in history in a particular geographical, cultural and socio-economic location. The generation concept is used to classify different age cohorts into relatively homogeneous categories that display a common world view, value system and set of social behaviors that differentiate them from other age groups and that remain relatively stable throughout their lives (Howe & Strauss, 2000). Although age cut-offs vary between authors, Generation Z is generally considered to include those born in or after 1995 (Scholz & Rennig, 2019) and is the youngest generation following on from the highly-researched Generation Y (also known as Millennials), born between 1980 and 1994 (Howe & Strauss, 2000). As the newest entrant in the workplace, Generation Z has been less-well studied, but early research suggests that they are markedly different to Generation Y (Nielson, 2015). The differences are so stark that generational experts recommend that organizations give priority to adapting their human resource management practices to cater for this new generation's special needs and preferences (Scholz et al., 2018), arguing that they have the potential to ruin businesses that fail to adopt new ways of working (Van Wyk, 2015).

According to Cascio (2019, p.285) "emerging adults typically change jobs at least seven times by their late 20s" highlighting the challenge that organizations face in retaining talented and skilled employees. The entrance of this new generation into the contemporary VUCA environment necessitates that organizations must focus renewed attention on their talent management strategies in order to create a competent workforce which is able not only to respond to arising challenges, but also has the capacity to adapt and be forward-thinking to maintain business agility and sustainability (Seibert, Kraimer & Heslin, 2016). One important attribute which shows promise to assist in the development of a sustainable, enduring skilled workforce is career resilience, which refers to an employee's capacity to respond with fortitude when faced with career challenges, allowing them to continue effective functioning, adapt in a flexible manner, and to successfully deliver outcomes (Seibert et al., 2016). However, there is only limited understanding of resilience in the context of employee careers due to a lack of sustained research in the management literature (Bimrose & Hearne, 2012; Lyons, Schweitzer & Ng 2015). Moreover, to date, there has been no attention paid to building the career resilience of the most vulnerable (Twenge, 2017) and youngest segment of the workforce, Generation Z.

This chapter is conceptual in nature and outlines the strategic importance of building a career-resilient workforce to maintain business sustainability. Organizations that adopt a strategic view of human resource management consider their employees to be human assets that can be made valuable through adopting systems (known as human resource management practices) to explicitly motivate, manage and shape desirable behaviors and produce optimal performance of these assets (Mello, 2011). The investment that organizations make in employee development, in terms of time and money rests on their acknowledgement that employees comprise the fabric and success of the organization's operations and sustainability (Kraimer, Seibert, Wayne, Liden & Bravo, 2011). This chapter presents a new conceptual framework for fostering employees' career resilience based on the Resource-Based View (RBV) of the firm (Barney 1991) which emphasizes the critical role of an organization's internal human resources in sustaining competitive advantage. The framework consists of a suite of specific human resource management practices which organizations can adopt to strategically develop and retain a career-resilient workforce. Specifically, the chapter emphasizes the need to understand the unique characteristics of Generation Z, the latest entrants into the workforce, in order to revisit and strategically tailor human resource management initiatives to develop this new generation's career resilience. Drawing on the limited available research on what Generation Z requires and how workplaces need to adapt, this chapter integrates fragmented knowledge to identify a set of generationally-appropriate practices to guide managers in developing their young entry-level employees.

BACKGROUND: THE CHANGING NATURE OF CAREERS

The late 20th Century saw a radical shift in the employer-employee contract. Traditionally, this psychological contract had placed a paternalistic responsibility on employers to provide their employees with the security, stability and assurance of a life-long job in return for workers' loyalty, efficiency and motivation. The responsibility for employees' career development has since shifted with the new 21st century employer-employee contract creating a partnership of shared obligations between employers and employees (Brown, 1996). The new focus on employee self-directedness and self-management of their own careers in the 1990s catalyzed the emergence of new career paradigms, most notably the protean and boundaryless careers (Hall, 1996; Arthur & Rousseau, 1996). These new models emphasize the shared responsibility of career planning and management (Akkermans, Seibert & Mol, 2018), but place more onus on the employee to assume individual agency in their career development (Watermann et al., 1994; Birchall & Lyons, 1995). According to Hall (1996), the protean career involves employees making lifelong adjustments based on their experience, learning and transitions, whilst the boundaryless career applies an opportunistic lens, focusing on the advantages and prospects associated with an individual employee's higher degree of free agency (Akkermans et al., 2018). The critical importance of human capital to business success necessitates that employers offer ongoing opportunities to assist their workforce to update their skills to ensure they remain satisfied, motivated and productive. Under this new contract "it is the employee's responsibility to manage his or her own career", whilst employers are responsible to "provide employees the tools, the open environment, and the opportunities for assessing and developing their skills" (Watermann, Watermann & Betsy, 1994, p.88). Through fulfilling their responsibilities, employers can expect to gain benefits including high productivity and commitment (Harari, 1995) which will ensure the sustainability of their operations.

CAREER RESILIENCE

The changing nature of the global environment has resulted in additional strain imposed on both employees and employers and their ability to sustain their careers and business operations, respectively. In order to effectively respond to the ongoing challenges and the range of experiences in a dynamic work environment, career resilience is regarded as an "essential survival skill in the 21st Century" (Cascio, 2007, p.552). The concept of career resilience grew from a seminal study by London (1983) which considered career resilience as an element which (together with career insight and career identity) formed the broader construct of career motivation. As originally defined by London (1983, p.628) career resilience is an "individual's resistance to career disruption in a less than optimal environment". The definition has since undergone multiple modifications and to date, there is still no universally accepted form. Following his original definition, London (1983) redefined career resilience as "the ability to adapt to change, even when the circumstances are discouraging or disruptive" (London, 1997, p.34). This new definition saw the replacement of the notion of 'resistance' with 'adaptation' in overcoming challenges and disruptions to careers.

There has also been debate over whether career resilience should be classified as an attribute, a process, or an outcome. Some scholars conceptualize career resilience as an attribute or ability that is not fixed or constant, but one that fluctuates depending on the challenges and disruptions presented in the work environment at a particular point in time (Mishra & McDonald, 2017). In contrast, other researchers (e.g., Van Vuuren & Fourie, 2000) conceptualize career resilience as a 'process' that instills in individuals the capability to overcome persistent and episodic career obstacles arising from loss of supportive workplace relationships, stress, work-life conflicts or job insecurity. This process occurs through the interaction of the individual's private life and support systems with their career, and concerns how the individual uses behaviors, skills and knowledge to overcome disruptions and adapt to new conditions (Mansfield, Beltman, Price & McConney, 2012). The maintenance of career resilience is not guaranteed for individuals who have shown career resilience previously, but it is subject to the ongoing process which tests the individual's ability to respond to and overcome work challenges. Whilst the deliberation on the correct classification of career resilience is still ongoing, it is generally regarded as "an ability, process and outcome that is something that people possess...something that is developed...something that can arise as a consequence of experiences" (Burke & Scurry, 2019, p.18). Based on the existing literature, in this chapter career resilience is defined as the capacity of an individual to adapt to career-related challenges and move towards a positive career trajectory.

CAREER RESILIENCE IN A VUCA WORK ENVIRONMENT

The turbulent environment in which organizations exist today contains a wide array of shocks and stressors which contribute to risks and uncertainties for employees. Career shocks encompass events which may be either anticipated or unanticipated. According to Akkermans et al. (2018), the literature on career shocks originated from studies on the effects of chance events on employee turnover and has since gained traction due to the expectation that amid the dynamism of the 21st century, employees and employers can expect to face multiple shocks. Such shocks arise from various sources from employees' professional and personal lives (Morell, Loan-Clarke & Wilkinson, 2004). These shocks can impact workers which "trigger deliberation about potential career transitions such as acquiring new skills, searching for a new job, changing occupations or retiring" (Seibert et al., 2016, p.245). In some cases, the severity of the shocks may also initiate thoughts about leaving the organization (exit cognitions) (Kulik, Treuren & Bordia, 2012), adding strain on an organization's capacity to retain a stable, experienced workforce.

Career shocks vary in both in their severity and impact on an employee's career trajectory. There are two main classifications of career shocks; positive and negative shocks. Positive career shocks are favorable in nature and commonly take the form of unexpected pay rises or rewards, praise for performing well and recognition for the employee's efforts (Seibert et al., 2016). Conversely, negative career shocks unleash a high degree of stress and challenge on employees and can take various forms, most commonly; work instability, mentor departure, failure to obtain expected rewards or promotions, or organizational changes (mergers and acquisitions) (Seibert et al., 2016). Career shocks challenge both employees and employers who must act to overcome and bounce back from such events. Shocks have been found to contribute to 60% of turnover cases (Holtom et al., 2005), hence, the ability of employers to support employees to be resilient in the face of shocks presents the opportunity to reduce risks of high turnover, which currently threatens business sustainability. One of the initial negative career shocks experienced by early career employees is 'reality shock', characterized by a disconnect between a new worker's expectations and the workplace reality (Kramer, 1974). Studies show that reality shocks pose risks for early career development and contribute to the high rate of early turnover (Kodama, 2017). Supporting new recruits through this initial disenchantment phase is crucial for helping Generation Z to not only survive in their first job role, but also to thrive in their early career phase.

On the other hand, career stressors are more ongoing and persistent negative factors in the work environment that subject workers to undue work pressures and demands (Bhui, Dinos, Galant-Miecznkowska, de Jongh & Stansfeld, 2016) which in turn produce undesirable reactions. Since the 2008-2009 global recession, work-related stress has continued to escalate predominantly due to "job insecurity, work intensity and inter-personal conflict" (Chandola, 2010, p.15). Organizations are beginning to recognize that they have a vested interest in reducing the stressors imposed on their employees. Employees who are subjected to high degrees of work stress are at risk of anxiety, depression, cardiovascular disorders and workplace accidents which contribute to high absenteeism rates (Chandola, 2010). Just as important as the economic benefits that organizations stand to gain by reducing workplace stress, is their legal and ethical duty of care to provide employees with a safe, risk free work environment as far as reasonably practicable. As Generation Z is entering the workforce with a significantly higher incidence of anxiety, stress and depression than previous generations (Twenge, 2017), it is of paramount importance that organizations create a positive and nurturing environment to support them. Eliminating unproductive work stressors and supporting workers' health and emotional wellbeing will enable organizations to sustain their operations in highly competitive market conditions.

CREATING A CAREER-RESILIENT WORKFORCE

Career resilience benefits employees through developing their abilities to manage and navigate their careers, whilst also offering benefits for employers through the development of a resilient and stable workforce. According to Waterman et al. (1994, p.88), a career-resilient workforce is "a group of employees who not only are dedicated to the idea of continuous learning, but also stand ready to reinvent themselves to stay abreast of new skills and keep pace with change; who take responsibility for their own career management and who are committed to the company's success". Career resilient workers are not only dedicated to ensuring that they remain employable through continual skill development for skill portability (Waterman et al., 1994), but are also alert and forward thinking, constantly engaged with their environment to identify and anticipate arising challenges to adapt to new contexts (Kuntz, Connell & Naswall, 2017). Career-resilient workforces possess adaptability and flexibility to sustain positive career trajectories, whilst constructing a repository of coping mechanisms to assist them in future adversities (Luthar et al., 2000; Masten & Reed, 2002; Bonanno, 2004; Caza, 2007).

Whilst career resilience research focuses on the employee's responsibility for self-agency and their intensified role of orchestrating their own career trajectory, employers also have a role in facilitating the development of their workforce's career resilience and ultimately stand to benefit from supporting training interventions (Collard, 1996; Baruch, 2006). Employers often neglect to take an active role in the development of their employees' career resilience due to fear and the misconception that enhancing workers' employability will result in higher turnover to obtain better paying employment with competitor organizations (Baruch, 2001). However, the literature has shown the opposite occurs. Offering development opportunities increases employee satisfaction, retention and organizational commitment (Bartlett, 2001; Tansky & Cohen, 2001; Benson, 2006). Therefore career development initiatives and opportunities to enhance employability, and hence career resilience result in employees' continued engagement in their role and the organization thus contributing to long term business sustainability (Mitchell, Holton, Lee, Sablynski & Erez, 2001). For the sake of operational sustainability, managers must reformulate their workforce strategies and re-conceptualize their role in introducing new human resource management initiatives to bolster their employees' career resilience.

UNDERSTANDING GENERATION Z: NEWEST WORKFORCE ENTRANTS

Generation Z will make up almost one third of the labor market by 2025 (McCrindle, 2019). Understanding how to best sustain the continued engagement and career resilience of this critical young segment of the workforce poses a challenge for management to ensure their business remains sustainable into the future. There are some similarities between this generation and their predecessors, Generation Y. Both age cohorts feel a strong sense of entitlement to good job assignments and rapid career progression, failing to realize the need for sufficient work experience (Parry & Battista, 2019). However there are a number of key differences between the youngest employees and Generation Y. Despite being the most adept users of technology of all generations (Seemiller & Grace, 2017), Generation Z prefer to communicate via text message, often ignoring emails and neglecting to set up voice mail on their mobile phones (Combs & Twachtman, 2019). Despite being digital natives with a strong presence on social media, at work Generation Z prefer interacting face-to-face (Goh & Lee, 2018; Schawbel, 2014). However, through being constantly electronically connected on social media, this generation shows a concerning deficit in face-to-face communication and social skills (Combs & Twachtman, 2019) which can impede their ability to work collaboratively and communicate effectively in co-located teams (Brown, 2017), but equips them well for virtual teamwork. Heavy use of electronic communication tools and social media has also led to a growth of online bullying, sleep deprivation due to too much screen time, and a decline in self-confidence and mental health, with unprecedented levels of anxiety, stress, depression and self-harm (Brown, 2017; Twenge, 2017).

In sharp contrast to the slightly older, highly mobile predecessors, the Generation Y employees (Benson et al., 2015), Generation Z are attracted to job security (Iorgulescu, 2016) due to being raised in the uncertain economic times of the Great Recession era. Hence Generation Z appreciates training initiatives that increase their employability and perceived workplace value (Iorgulescu, 2016). Being born into an era of personalized and highly interactive technologically-enabled solutions (Hernaus & Pološki Vokic, 2014), Generation Z prefer tailor-made and interactive work design solutions and are well-suited to autonomous learning. This youngest generation is attracted to organizations that embrace employee-centered human resource management practices such as attractive compensation, good work-family balance and equity and diversity initiatives (Wayne & Casper, 2012). Opportunity for advancement in their career, a sustainable income, and job security are said to be the top three considerations for Generation Z (Iorgulescu, 2016). They appreciate organizations that demonstrate that they value their employees through the provision of initiatives to help this new generation meet its three key needs. Specifically, organizational practices designed to bolster Generation Z's career resilience will be critical for fostering their sense of job security and long term commitment to their employer.

STRATEGIC HUMAN RESOURCE INITIATIVES TO FOSTER CAREER RESILIENCE IN GENERATION Z

Organizations stand to benefit from career resilience of their Generation Z workforce. "Employers are becoming more dependent on the resourcefulness, commitment, and flexibility of their staff" (Kidd & Smewing, 2001, p.25) and must extend their supervisory roles to support the continuous learning and career development of their employees. To attract and retain talented Generation Z employees, managers must provide them with the opportunity to undertake learning, gain varied work experiences and develop networks to provide career support (Nabi, 2000). By supporting initiatives to bolster the career resilience of their new recruits, organizations can strategically increase the likelihood of retaining a talented pool of employees, whose flexibility and adaptability will be invaluable for ensuring the maintenance of a competitive advantage (Bowen & Ostroff, 2004). Additionally, organizations carry an ethical responsibility (Van Buren, 2003) for assisting their employees to remain relevant by up-dating their skills. In order to reap the benefits of a career resilient workforce, organizations must uphold their responsibility for providing the necessary resources for career management as outlined in the new employer-employee psychological contract.

Theoretical Framework

The new framework presented in Figure 1 draws on the Resource-Based View (RBV) of the firm (Barney 1991) to explain the strategic advantages for organizations through fostering a career resilient workforce. Employees who are adaptable, flexible and thus resilient are inimitable and irreplaceable, as well as necessary for sustaining organizations amidst the uncertainties and complexities associated with the new work environments. A career-resilient workforce that is agile, proactive, flexible and adaptive enables organizations to maintain a strategic competitive advantage (Teece, Pisano & Sheun, 1997) and thrive amid the changes that occur due to their capacity to view these events as opportunities for growth and development instead of fearing change (Maree, 2017). A career-resilient workforce acts as a valuable, and non-substitutable resource which assists in providing and maintaining a sustainable competitive advantage as well as superior performance over competitors (Barney, 1991). Human capital is viewed as a major source of sustainable competitive advantage due to the difficulty for competitors to imitate the career resilience aspect within their own workforces (Wright et al., 1994).

Figure 1. Framework of strategic HRM practices to develop Generation Z's career resilience to maintain business sustainability

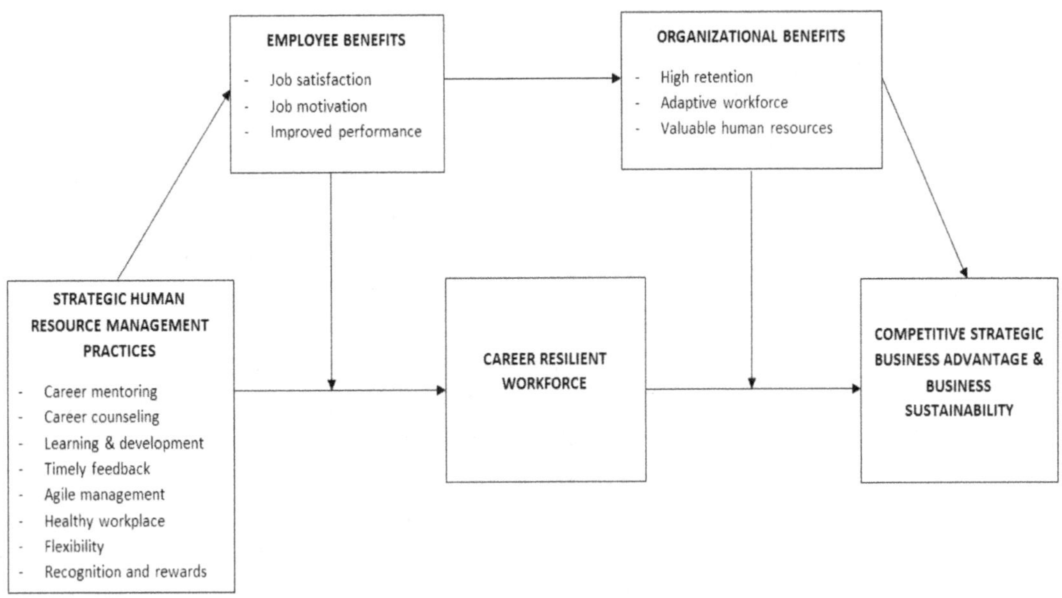

In accordance with the RBV of the firm, for an organization to reap a strategic competitive advantage, its resource (in this case a career-resilient workforce) must be 1. valuable, 2. heterogeneous in nature, and 3. imperfectly mobile (Barney, 1991). First, a resource is considered to be valuable if it works in a manner which reduces the organization's costs and increase its revenue. Since career-resilient employees are adaptable and flexible in responding to changes in their surrounding environment, their performance is less likely to be affected by career shocks and their motivation levels and performance are not so subject to the effects of disruption (Fourie & Van Vuuren, 1998; Tien & Wang, 2017). Due to their enhanced capacity to deal with change, a career-resilient workforce serves as a valuable resource that enables organizations to continue to operate in an efficient and effective manner to maintain their competitive success.

Second, an organization's resource is said to contribute to its competitive advantage if it is heterogeneously distributed; that is, the resource is rare in nature and not readily available. As career resilience must be intentionally fostered and developed, it is not readily available and must be nurtured. The extent to which employees are career resilient is subject to a variety of factors including training and development, experience, workplace culture and individual capacities; hence a career resilient workforce cannot be fully identical. Third, the mobility or imitability of the resource deems its value in obtaining a strategic competitive advantage in that perfectly mobile resources are only regarded as providing temporary competitive advantages to organizations due to the possibility of competitors obtaining these resources for their own benefit (Mata, Fuerst & Barney, 1995). As career-resilient individuals are considered to be highly trained, skilled and flexible, they are also regarded as being highly employable in that skills transferability allows them to seek employment elsewhere (Tien & Wang, 2017). As a career resilient workforce will only provide a temporary strategic advantage if it is not retained, it is in an organizations' best interests to provide effective human resource management practices like learning and development to assist employees in their endeavors to remain skilled and employable as this is likely to result in higher levels of job satisfaction, motivation, and thus retention.

An organization's ability to maintain a strategic competitive advantage rests on developing the career resilience of its workforce. Although research on Generation Z is still is sparse and sometimes contradictory (Zehetner, Lepeyko & Zehetner, 2019), Generation Z displays unique differences from previous generations which mean organizations would be wise to revisit and tailor their existing management practices to meet the needs of young entry-level employees (Cappelli & Tavis, 2018; Chillakur & Mahanandia, 2018). Although the research is scattered across disciplines, studies have identified a number of initiatives to support the development of this generation's career resilience, including career mentoring, career counseling, ongoing learning and development, continuous and timely feedback, agile management, intrapreneurship, healthy workplaces, flexibility, and providing appropriate recognition and rewards. In turn, career resilience can influence important human resource outcomes such as increased employee motivation and job satisfaction (Coetzee & Potgieter, 2014), decreased burnout, increased career success (Salisu, Hashim, Ismail & Isa, 2017) as well as lower staff turnover and higher employee retention (Waterman et al., 1994). Organizations that employ these human resource management practices to foster employee career resilience will reap the benefits of competitive advantage. Each human resource management practice in the framework has been specifically selected for its suitability for Generation Z and will be discussed in more detail in the following sections.

Career Mentoring

Career mentoring activities positively impact employees' level of career resilience (Luthans, Avey, Avolio & Peterson, 2010) through strengthening their overall resilience capacity (Arora & Rangnekar, 2015). Hence, mentoring is an invaluable tool "for talent development, retention and attraction" (Robinson, 2007, p.208) with the potential to assist organizations in encouraging the self-efficacy and career development of employees through facilitating a developmental relationship between a junior Generation Z employee, regarded as the protégé, and an experienced senior acting as the guide or mentor (Shollen, Bland, Canter, Finstad & Taylor, 2014). Such pairings encourage knowledge-sharing and the acquisition of skills and relationships which result in workplace benefits (Noe et al., 2002). Mentors can enable Generation Z protégés to recognize a number of opportunities through the provision of valuable advice which strengthens their resilience (Linberger, 2008). Reverse mentoring which encourages recent graduates to share the latest discipline-specific knowledge and technological advances acquired during their recent education fulfills the dual purpose of building Generation Z's confidence in their own value while up-skilling older, more established employees in the workforce (Roman, 2017).

Mentoring in the workplace can take two main forms: psycho-emotional and career-oriented (Sosik & Godshalk, 2005). Firstly, psycho-emotional mentoring involves establishing interpersonal bonds between the protégé and the mentor via building trust and a focus on enhancing the employee's inner competencies through feedback and acceptance. This supportive form of mentoring is particularly valuable for members of Generation Z who are often unable to deal with adversity and sometimes lack the social skills to develop workplace peer networks for support (Gould, Nalepa & Mignano, 2020). Career-oriented mentoring is the second type of mentoring which is characterized by a less affective, more professional relationship which seeks to provide challenging work assignments to develop the employee's capacities, political protection for the protégée and enhanced visibility of the protégé among senior management to promote opportunities for promotion and career development (Allen, Eby, Poteet, Lentz & Lima, 2004). An organization's ability to provide career mentoring results in benefits to business sustainability. Enhanced employee self-confidence and satisfaction (Tong & Kram, 2013), career advancement opportunities, enhanced skills and psychological support (Eby & Lockwood, 2005) and increased personal learning abilities (Lankau & Scandura, 2002) all lead to the strengthening of employee resilience which in turn enhances organizational performance (Arora & Rangnekar, 2015).

Career Counseling

Easy access to counseling and support services is particularly important for Generation Z who have grown up with often over-protective "helicopter" parents providing high levels of guidance and emotional support to the point of disempowering this new generation (Twenge, 2017). This over-control has led to higher levels of anxiety, stress and depression than were experienced by previous generations (Twenge, 2017). Counseling services are often incorporated in employee assistance programs of individual career counseling, management coaching and change management to support employees through occupational stress (Kirk & Brown, 2003). Such services can nurture career resilience (Johnson, 2008) and hence produce beneficial outcomes for both employers and Generation Z employees alike (Kirk & Brown, 2003). Counseling often focuses on providing employees with training and knowledge about coping strategies to assist workers to prevent, respond to and thrive in the face of both work-related and personal issues (Kirk & Brown, 2003). Such services ensure that Generation Z employees have a support network they can turn to for assistance, guidance, coping mechanisms and support for their ongoing career development.

Learning and Development

The opportunity for career advancement is the number one priority of Generation Z (Iorgulescu, 2016). To further assist Generation Z employees to succeed in uncertain or volatile environments, employers can use smart platforms to collect performance data and analyze each employee's learning needs to provide personalized micro-learning opportunities (Miller, 2019) that enhance their adaptive capacity and employability (Clarke, 2007). Learning and development tailored to Generation Z needs to take into account that they are digital natives, not having known life without the Internet and smart devices (Twenge, 2017; Euromonitor International, 2011) hence they prefer technology-aided self-learning opportunities (Francis & Hoefel, 2018). Although this generation is quick to assimilate information, they also lose interest quickly (Cameron & Pagnattaro, 2017). To cater to their fast information processing skills and their short attention span (Scholz, 2019; Gould, et al., 2020) technologically-enabled, self-paced training is an ideal instructional mode. Being highly visual learners (Hart, 2017) Generation Z enjoy watching short YouTube videos to learn new skills (Combs & Twachtman, 2019). They prefer bite-sized information that they can autonomously access when needed (Seemiller & Grace, 2017) making online modular learning and micro-credentials important training options. Brief learning modules can be designed to provide credentials or badges for successful completion, enabling Generation Z to engage in continuous, self-directed up-skilling, when and where convenient to them.

Kraimer et al. (2011, p. 486) term such programs as 'organizational support for development' (OSD). Their study found that OSD is directly related to "employees' overall perceptions that the organization provides programs and opportunities that help employees develop their functional and managerial skills" which are necessary for the attainment of career resilience. Dedication to providing career support and opportunities for training and ongoing skill development will result in Generation Z employees perceiving that their organization cares for and invests in them (Kraimer et al., 2011). Organizations that offer training and career development opportunities to employees, gain benefits in the form of high degrees of employee commitment, job satisfaction and enhanced performance (Sturges et al., 2005; Barnett & Bradley, 2007; Aguinis & Kraiger, 2009), and create adaptable and flexible employees responsive to change, who contribute to the maintenance of competitive advantage in an increasingly VUCA environment (Clarke, 2007).

Timely Feedback

Compared to earlier generations, Generation Z workers experience greater self-doubt and show lower levels of confidence (Twenge, 2017). To bolster this generation's sense of self-efficacy, organizations can play a key role through the provision of regular feedback that shapes their learning and recognizes good performance, and by creating an environment which accepts failure as an essential element of taking risks, learning and improvement (Quigley & Tymon, 2006). Growing up with video games, Generation Z employees are used to immediate and ongoing feedback (Scholz, 2018) and prefer frequent and concise responses to their actions. Timely and targeted feedback that is both constructive and developmental will allow managers of Generation Z to communicate their expectations about performance and to pinpoint areas which require further improvement and growth (Green, 2002).

Generation Z expect feedback to be a two-way exchange, believing that managers should listen and be responsive to their employees' honest feedback as well (Chicca & Shellenbarger, 2018). This may require further training of managers in the skill of encouraging and receiving constructive feedback. Organizations can also implement technology-enabled practices to ensure that feedback is provided in a "regular, systematic and open" fashion (Clarke, 2007, p.276) and is development-focused as opposed to solely evaluating past performance once a year (Ryan et al., 2000; Atwater, Brett & Charles, 2007). Software like Friday Feedback (fridayfeedback.com) or customized apps can be used collaboratively for weekly progress check-ins to identify and resolve issues quickly and allow employees to track their improvement and learn through iteration by self-correcting in real time (Cappelli & Tavis, 2018). Such ongoing and timely feedback will empower Generation Z employees to successfully manage their career development and in the longer term this will contribute to greater organizational sustainability.

Agile Management

The agile philosophy of management is well-suited to managing complexity (Da Silva, Estácio, Kroll, & Fontana, 2016) in the digital era of Industry 4.0 (Marnewick & Marnewick, 2019). Originating as a more nimble and responsive approach to delivering software projects, the agile philosophy has now been successfully adopted in many other contexts, including general management and human resource management (Rigby, Sutherland & Noble, 2018). Agile is a mindset (not a methodology) that emphasizes people over processes, collaboration over contracts, iterative problem-solving over planning, and usability over documentation (Marnewick & Marnewick, 2019). The responsive, time-limited principles of agile are well-suited to managing the youngest entrants in the workplace. Agile often involves cross-functional, collaborative task forces working intensively on a specific project to achieve rapid results through iterative correction (Cappelli & Tavis, 2018). Agile communication includes the kind of regular feedback (immediate, two-way, brief and authentic) that Generation Z likes and is often delivered in their preferred communication mode of face-to-face daily stand-up meetings (Chicca & Shellenbarger, 2018). Agile managers empower their team members and act as coaches to facilitate rapid behavior change. In addition, they encourage peer-to-peer feedback that allows Generation Z to share with team members any concerns or errors they may be reluctant to discuss with their team leader for fear of a negative performance appraisal (Cappelli & Tavis, 2018).

Intrapreneurial Opportunities

Generation Z are more resourceful and self-motivated than Generation Y and are noted for their entrepreneurial drive and extensive online networking capabilities (Schawbel, 2014). According to one study (Miller, 2019), 58% of Generation Z participants expressed a desire to create a business enterprise of their own. Many of this new generation have studied entrepreneurship subjects at university (Lainier, 2017) and may have even set up their own business while studying (Chillakur & Mahanandia, 2018). Generation Z want to contribute to their organization's success (Roman, 2019), but they prefer to work independently without close supervision (Slavin, 2015). Organizations can foster this generation's entrepreneurial activities within the company (intrapreneurship) by giving them autonomy and a voice in the decision-making process (Slavin, 2015), allowing them ownership of projects to improve products, services and systems, providing access to company big data on customer insights and user experience, and encouraging creativity and innovation with minimal supervision (Schawbel, 2014). Some companies like 3M and Google have successfully created innovative new products by encouraging their employees to spend 20% of their working time on pet projects which allows them to "work within a business in an entrepreneurial capacity [and] flex their leadership and creativity muscles" (Miller, 2019, p.1).

Healthy Workplace

The workplace has the potential to either undermine or enhance the development of Generation Z's career resilience. Healthy workplaces which offer adequate work-life balance combined with good social support can contribute to the development of resilience (Wilson & Ferch, 2005; Bardoel, Pettit, De Cieri & McMillan, 2014) in Generation Z. Positive and caring relationships in the work environment provide a means for employees to make relatable connections and support networks to positively benefit their career development (Wilson & Ferch, 2005). Workplaces that foster a culture that "encourages lifelong learning in an environment that emphasizes and rewards flexibility and resilience over the career lifetime of employees" (Donner & Wheeler, 2005, p.30) bolsters employees' career resilience. Creating a successful and effective healthy work culture requires support and involvement from not just top management, middle managers and supervisors, but also from Generation Z employees themselves (Conger, 2002).

Porath, Spreitzer, Gibson and Garnett (2012) found that instituting positive psychological practices that foster thriving (such as a climate of civility, sharing information, and giving employees a measure of decision-making power) improves both employee mental health and workforce sustainability.

Many workplaces now actively promote positive mental health and wellbeing through their occupational health and safety practices. Since Generation Z's mental health is the most fragile of all generations (Twenge, 2017) they will benefit from training that builds personal resilience through developing the protective behaviors like maintaining a healthy diet and exercise regime, sleeping well, building their social support networks, maintaining perspective, practicing stress management techniques (Winwood, Colon & McKewen, 2013), limiting screen time and social media usage, particularly for Generation Z females (Twenge, 2017), and training employees to avoid on-line bullying and trolling. To help Generation Z regulate their social media usage at work, some managers are encouraging employees to take one-minute social media breaks at regular intervals rather than continually multi-tasking (Twenge, 2017). In a further bid to bolster employee wellbeing and resilience, many organizations are now implementing mindfulness programs to foster employees' concentration, cognitive acuity, self-awareness, relaxation, and emotion-regulation (Knapp, Weber & Moellenkamp, 2017).

Flexibility

With the enhancement of technological advancements and the increased use of technology in workplaces, the adoption of flexible work arrangements has increased (Chess Media Group, 2013). Although Generation Z enjoys the face-to-face contact of a normal office environment, as digital natives, they also expect the convenience and flexibility (Goh & Lee, 2018; Ozkan & Solmaz, 2015) made possible by technological devices such as smartphones, tablets and laptop computers to allow them to remain connected if they choose to work remotely (Holbeche, 2015). Generation Z expresses a greater need to work-life separation than previous generations (Kelliher, Richardson & Boiarintseva, 2019). This newest generation of employees desires to achieve greater work-life balance (Holbeche, 2015) to allow time for personal relationships, relaxation and vacations. This requires "human resource departments to fit work and personal life in a fluid way" (Sánchez-Hernández, González-López, Buenadicha-Mateos & Tato-Jiménez, 2019, p.5123). Although Generation Z expects to work hard during office hours, they dislike working long hours and overtime and do not want to be available 24/7 (Scholz, 2019). By implementing more flexible work arrangements for Generation Z which allow greater choice of when and where to work, employers can expect higher levels of engagement as well as increased productivity and overall organizational performance.

Recognition and Rewards

It is important that employers reward Generation Z's efforts and achievements to encourage their motivation and high performance. Whilst rewards typically elicit better performance, research highlights the importance of individualizing rewards according to each employee's reward preferences (Landry, Schweyer & Whillans, 2017). Although Generation Z value monetary rewards, particularly in the form of a high salary (Scholz & Rennig, 2019), non-monetary rewards are also important. Landry et al. (2017, p.233) argue that "financial incentives are no longer sufficient to motivate workers; particularly those in complex, non-routine, and/or creative careers". Younger generations place a high importance on intangible rewards such as opportunities for training and career development, networking and the creation of meaning and purpose in their careers. This finding highlights that organizations need to re-think their strategies for providing rewards to younger workers and should consider a mix of both financial and non-financial incentives when looking to motivate, retain and satisfy this youngest generation of employees. Some organizations are already responding to these new demands through increasing the non-cash rewards they offer, typically in the form of tangible rewards (such as time-off, gifts and travel rewards) and intangible rewards (e.g., opportunities for flexible work, training and career development opportunities and greater autonomy in decision making) (Morrell, 2011; Srivastava, 2012).

In order to retain talented Generation Z employees and assist in the continual modelling of career resilience in the workforce, organizations must not only reward employees for their efforts and successes, but also ensure there is open recognition of their contributions. Employees value being acknowledged for their efforts by receiving constructive and developmental feedback. In order for recognition and feedback to be effective, managers must ensure it is given in a manner which is timely, meaningful specific, and uniquely tailored to the individual employee's needs and contributions (Landry, Schweyer & Whillans, 2017). To motivate employees and ensure they feel valued, organizations need to combine recognition and rewards in a tailored and authentic manner, or risk losing talented employees to their competition. Such strategies will allow organizations to play an active role in the development and embodiment of career resilience in their workforce, which in turn will see them reaping the benefits of improved motivation, agility, flexibility and positive responses to change, which overall will contribute to better maintenance of ongoing sustainability.

DISCUSSION

This chapter has identified career resilience, especially in the youngest generation in the workforce, as an important feature of a sustainable business environment amidst the complex and rapidly challenging work context of 21st Century. There is a growing need for managers to support their young employees in the face of these changes (Ungar, 2019). Such volatile and uncertain environmental conditions can be particularly distressing to early-career employees, creating high degrees of stress through unexpected shocks such as technological disruptions, high turnover and skills shortages. With the changing nature of careers and employment contracts, to retain a skilled workforce, employers must maintain and fulfill their responsibility for assisting their entry-level employees to develop adaptive capacity. Consistent with the Resource-Based View, oorganizations are now beginning to recognise the strategic importance of developing a career-resilient workforce. Individual employees' career resilience determines their capacity to respond when faced with challenges, allowing them to continue effective functioning, adapt in a flexible manner, and to successfully deliver outcomes. Career resilience enables all employees (and especially vulnerable early-career workers) to adapt and survive the range of shocks and stressors in volatile environments which in turn enables organizations to remain resilient.

Theoretical and Practical Contributions

This chapter presented a new conceptual framework that identifies strategic human resource management practices that may foster career-resilient Generation Z employees. This framework makes a new theoretical contribution to the sporadically studied field of career resilience by adopting the resource-based view to explain the strategic value of career resilience. By applying a generational lens to the management practices that foster career resilience, this chapter provides new knowledge in the field of career resilience and also about the youngest generation in the workforce. By drawing on recommendations scattered across the extant literature and developing these into an integrated conceptual framework, this chapter has identified generationally-tailored human resource management practices for developing Generation Z's career resilience as a strategic resource. Practically, this framework will assist organizations to understand their role in developing employee career resilience and to identify the many potential beneficial outcomes both in their workforce and in enhancing business sustainability. The different management initiatives in the framework can inform human resource management practitioners how to achieve the strategic advantage of creating a career-resilient workforce to ensure their organization has the means to survive and thrive in the new collaborative economy.

FUTURE RESEARCH DIRECTIONS

With the trajectory of changes and disturbances in the work environment expected to continue at a rapid pace, more research is needed on the career resilience of all four generations (Generations Z, Y, X and Baby Boomers) that are currently in the workforce to identify whether levels of career resilience vary according to age, generational cohort, national background, or career and life stage. Through identifying generation-specific attitudes, behaviors and expectations that can impact career resilience, organizations will be able to develop more tailored management initiatives to develop and retain each generational segment of their skilled talent. As studies on Generation Z are still in their infancy, further research on this youngest generation will assist organizations to better understand their particular career expectations and working preferences. This specialized knowledge will assist employers to better attract highly skilled new entrants to counteract high turnover and skills shortages, and to provide companies with a strategic human capital advantage over their competitors. Future research is needed to investigate both the employees' and employers' roles in fostering adaptability and to identify how they can work together in synergy to survive the shocks and shifts in individual careers (Fourie & Van Vuuren, 1998) and in the general work environment. Organizations that do not strategically implement these changes are likely to face major challenges in acquiring and retaining necessary talent. Further research to identify the dynamics and impacts of common career shocks (Akkermans et al., 2018) will assist organizations to better understand and forecast shocks and to develop initiatives to assist their employees to be well-prepared to withstand them.

CONCLUSION

The purpose of this chapter was to understand the defining characteristics of the newest entrants to the workforce, Generation Z, and to identify appropriate strategic human resource management practices to foster their career resilience. If senior managers wish to sustain a resilient workforce, they must empower their human resource managers to strategically plan, develop and deploy these initiatives for fostering employee career resilience. This is one of the first examinations of the career resilience of Generation Z, and one of the few studies that links career resilience with business sustainability. This chapter has developed a new holistic framework of human resource initiatives to support the development of career resilience in young employees. Such practices include career mentoring, career counseling, learning and development, agile management, intrapreneurship, continuous and timely feedback, healthy workplaces, flexible work, and appropriate rewards and recognition. By adopting these initiatives, organizations can play a proactive role in re-designing entry-level work and developing Generation Z's career resilience and thereby increase their job satisfaction, work motivation and intention to remain with their organization. Through strategically planning to build workforce career resilience, organizations can work towards achieving business sustainability to remain competitive in the ever-changing economy. When implemented effectively, these tailored management initiatives will ensure that employers maintain and retain a talented workforce to carry them through the challenges of an uncertain future.

REFERENCES

Aguinis, H., & Kraiger, K. (2009). Benefits of training and development for individuals and teams, organizations, and society. *Annual Review of Psychology*, *60*(1), 451–474. doi:10.1146/annurev.psych.60.110707.163505 PMID:18976113

Akkermans, J., Seibert, S. E., & Mol, S. T. (2018). Tales of the unexpected: Integrating career shocks in the contemporary careers literature. *SA Journal of Industrial Psychology*, *44*(1), 1–10. doi:10.4102ajip.v44i0.1503

Allen, T. D., Eby, L., Poteet, M. L., Lentz, E., & Lima, L. (2004). Career benefits associated with mentoring for proteges: A meta-analysis. *The Journal of Applied Psychology*, *89*(1), 127–136. doi:10.1037/0021-9010.89.1.127 PMID:14769125

Arora, R., & Rangnekar, S. (2015). The joint effects of personality and supervisory career mentoring in predicting occupational commitment. *Career Development International*, *20*(1), 63–80. doi:10.1108/CDI-12-2014-0156

Arthur, W. Jr, Bennett, W. J., Edens, P., & Bell, S. T. (2003). Effectiveness of training in organizations: A meta-analysis of design and evaluation features. *The Journal of Applied Psychology*, *88*(2), 234–245. doi:10.1037/0021-9010.88.2.234 PMID:12731707

Atkinson, C. (2004). Career management and the changing psychological contract. *Career Development International*, *7*(1), 14–23. doi:10.1108/13620430210414838

Atwater, L. E., Brett, J. F., & Charles, A. T. (2007). Multisource feedback: Lessons learned and implications for practice. *Human Resource Management*, *46*(2), 285–307. doi:10.1002/hrm.20161

Bardoel, E. A., Pettit, T. M., De Cieri, H., & McMillan, L. (2014). Employee resilience: An emerging challenge for HRM. *Asia Pacific Journal of Human Resources*, *52*(3), 279–297. doi:10.1111/1744-7941.12033

Barnett, B. R., & Bradley, L. (2007). The impact of organizational support for career development on career satisfaction. *Career Development International*, *12*(7), 617–636. doi:10.1108/13620430710834396

Bartlett, K. (2001). The relationship between training and organizational commitment: A study in the health care field. *Human Resource Development Quarterly*, *12*(4), 335–353. doi:10.1002/hrdq.1001

Baruch, Y. (2001). Employability: A substitute for loyalty? *Human Resource Development International*, *4*(4), 543–566. doi:10.1080/13678860010024518

Benson, G. S. (2006). Employee development, commitment and intention to turnover: A test of employability policies in action. *Human Resource Management Journal*, *16*(2), 173–192. doi:10.1111/j.1748-8583.2006.00011.x

Benson, J., Sandhu, S., Sastrowardoyo, S., & Scott-Young, C. M. (2015). Complexity in multigenerational organizations: A socio-political perspective. In R. J. Burke, C. L. Cooper, & A. S. G. Antoniou (Eds.), *The Multi-Generational and Aging Workforce: Challenges and Opportunities*. Edward Elgar.

Bhui, K., Dinos, S., Galant-Miecznikowska, M., de Jongh, B., & Stansfeld, S. (2016). Perceptions of work stress causes and effective interventions in employees working in public, private and non-governmental organizations: A qualitative study. *British Journal of Psychiatry Bulletin*, *40*(6), 318–325. PMID:28377811

Bigley, G. A., & Roberts, K. H. (2001). The incident command system: High-reliability organizing for complex and volatile task environments. *Academy of Management Journal*, *44*(6), 1281–1299.

Bonanno, G. A. (2004). Loss, trauma, and human resilience: Have we underestimated the human capacity to thrive after extremely aversive events? *The American Psychologist*, *12*(1), 177–192. doi:10.1037/0003-066X.59.1.20 PMID:14736317

Bowen, D. E., & Ostroff, C. (2004). Understanding HRM–firm performance linkages: The role of the 'strength' of the HRM system. *Academy of Management Review*, *29*, 203–221.

Brown, S. (2017). How generations X, Y, and Z may change the academic workplace. *Chronicle of Higher Education*. September. Retrieved from www.ebscohost.com/login.aspx?direct=true&db=eue&AN

Burke, R. J., & Ng, E. (2006). The changing nature of work and organizations: Implications for human resource management. *Human Resource Management Review*, *16*(2), 86–94. doi:10.1016/j.hrmr.2006.03.006

Cameron, E. A., & Pagnattaro, M. A. (2017). Beyond millennials: Engaging generation Z in business law classes. *Journal of Legal Studies Education*, *34*(2), 317–324. doi:10.1111/jlse.12064

Cappelli, P. (1999). Career jobs are dead. *California Management Review*, *42*(1), 146–167. doi:10.2307/41166023

Cappelli, P., & Travis, A. (2018). *HR goes agile*. Retrieved at https://hbr.org/2018/03/the-new-rules-of-talent-managementreferral=03759

Carbery, R., & Garavan, T. N. (2005). Organizational restructuring and downsizing: Issues related to learning, training and employability of survivors. *Journal of European Industrial Training*, *29*(6), 488–508. doi:10.1108/03090590510610272

Chicca, J., & Shellenbarger, T. (2018). Generation Z: Approaches and teaching–learning practices for nursing professional development practitioners. *Journal for Nurses in Professional Development*, *34*(5), 250–256. doi:10.1097/NND.0000000000000478 PMID:30188477

Chillakur, B., & Mahanandia, R. (2018). Generation Z entering the workforce: The need for sustainable strategies in maximizing their talent. *Human Resource Management International Digest*, *26*(4), 34–38. doi:10.1108/HRMID-01-2018-0006

Clarke, M. (2008). Understanding and managing employability in changing career contexts. *Journal of European Industrial Training*, *32*(4), 258–284. doi:10.1108/03090590810871379

Collard, B. (1996). *Career resilience in a changing workplace. Information Series, 366*. ERIC Clearinghouse on Adult, Career, and Vocational Education.

Combs, S., & Twachtman, C. (2019). *Birth of the multi-potentialities: Being undeclared in Generation Z*. Retrieved from apps.nacada.ksu.edu

Conger, S. (2002). Fostering a career development culture: Reflections on the roles of managers, employees and supervisors. *Career Development International*, *7*(6), 371–375. doi:10.1108/13620430210444394

Da Silva, T. S., Estácio, B., Kroll, J., & Fontana, R. M. (2016). *Agile Methods*. Springer.

Dixon, S. (2003). Implications of population ageing for the labour market. *Labour Market Trends*, *111*(2), 67–76.

Donner, G. J., & Wheeler, M. M. (2005). Building and sustaining a career culture. *The Canadian Nurse*, *101*(8), 30. PMID:16295365

Eby, L. T., & Lockwood, A. (2005). Proteges and mentors participating in formal mentoring programs: A qualitative investigation. *Journal of Vocational Behavior*, *67*(3), 441–458. doi:10.1016/j.jvb.2004.08.002

Euromonitor International. (2011). *Make way for generation Z: Marketing for today's teens and tweens*. Retrieved from https://oaltabo2012.files.wordpress.com/2012/03/make-way-for-generation-z1.pdf

Fourie, C., & Van Vuuren, L. J. (1998). Defining and measuring career resilience. *SA Journal of Industrial Psychology*, *24*(3), 52–59. doi:10.4102ajip.v24i3.662

Francis, T., & Hoefel, F. (2018). *'True gen': Generation Z and its implications for companies*. Retrieved at https://www.mckinsey.com

Goh, E., & Lee, C. (2018). A workforce to be reckoned with: The emerging pivotal Generation Z hospitality workforce. *International Journal of Hospitality Management*, *73*, 20–28. doi:10.1016/j.ijhm.2018.01.016

Gould, D., Nalepa, J., & Mignano, M. (2020). Coaching generation Z athletes. *Journal of Applied Sport Psychology*, *32*(1), 104–120. doi:10.1080/10413200.2019.1581856

Green, B. (2002). Listening to leaders: Feedback on 360-degree feedback one year later. *Organization Development Journal*, *20*(1), 8–16.

Hall, D. T. (1996). *The Career is Dead - Long Live the Career: A Relational Approach to Careers*. Jossey-Bass.

Harari, O. (1995). The new job security. *Your Management Review*, *84*(9), 29–31.

Hart, S. (2017). Today's learners and educators: Bridging the generational gaps. *Teaching and Learning in Nursing*, *12*(4), 253–257. doi:10.1016/j.teln.2017.05.003

Hernaus, T., & Pološki Vokic, N. (2014). Work design for different generational cohorts: Determining common and idiosyncratic job characteristics. *Journal of Organizational Change Management*, *27*(4), 615–641. doi:10.1108/JOCM-05-2014-0104

Holtom, B. C., Mitchell, T. R., Lee, T., & Inderrieden, E. J. (2005). Shocks as causes of turnover: What they are and how organizations can manage them. *Human Resource Management*, *44*(3), 337–352. doi:10.1002/hrm.20074

Howe, N., & Strauss, W. (2000). *Millennials Rising: The Next Great Generation*. Vintage Books.

Iorgulescu, M. C. (2016). Generation Z and its perception of work. *Cross-Cultural Management Journal*, *18*(1), 47–54.

Johnson, J. D. (2008). Employee assistance programs: Sources of assistance relations to inputs and outcomes. *Journal of Workplace Behavioral Health*, *23*(3), 263–282. doi:10.1080/15555240802242866

Kelliher, C., Richardson, J., & Boiarintseva, G. (2019). All of work? All of life? Reconceptualising work-life balance for the 21st century. *Human Resource Management Journal*, *29*(2), 97–112. doi:10.1111/1748-8583.12215

Kidd, J. M., & Smewing, C. (2001). The role of the supervisor in career and organizational commitment. *European Journal of Work and Organizational Psychology*, *10*(1), 25–40. doi:10.1080/13594320042000016

Kirk, A. K., & Brown, D. F. (2003). Employee assistance programs: A review of the management of stress and wellbeing through workplace counselling and consulting. *Australian Psychologist*, *38*(2), 138–143. doi:10.1080/00050060310001707137

Knapp, C. A., Weber, C., & Moellenkamp, S. (2017). Challenges and strategies for incorporating Generation Z into the workplace. *Corporate Real Estate Journal*, *7*(2), 137–148.

Kozlowski, S. W., Gully, S. M., Brown, K. G., Salas, E., Smith, E. M., & Nason, E. R. (2001). Effects of training goals and goal orientation traits on multidimensional training outcomes and performance adaptability. *Organizational Behavior and Human Decision Processes*, *85*(1), 1–31. doi:10.1006/obhd.2000.2930 PMID:11341815

KPMG. (2014). *Setting the Course for Growth: CEO Perspectives.* Retrieved at https://assets.kpmg

Kraimer, M. L., Seibert, S. E., Wayne, S. J., Liden, R. C., & Bravo, J. (2011). Antecedents and outcomes of organizational support for development: The critical role of career opportunities. *The Journal of Applied Psychology*, *96*(3), 485–500. doi:10.1037/a0021452 PMID:21114356

Kuijpers, M. A., & Scheerens, J. (2006). Career competencies for the modern career. *Journal of Career Development*, *32*(4), 303–319. doi:10.1177/0894845305283006

Kulik, C. T., Treuren, G., & Bordia, P. (2012). Shocks and final straws: Using exit interview data to examine the unfolding model's decision paths. *Human Resource Management*, *51*(1), 25–46. doi:10.1002/hrm.20466

Kuntz, J., Connell, P., & Naswall, K. (2017). Workplace resources and employee resilience: The role of regulatory profiles. *Career Development International*, *22*(4), 419–435. doi:10.1108/CDI-11-2016-0208

Landry, A. T., Schweyer, A., & Whillans, A. (2017). Winning the war for talent: Modern motivational methods for attracting and retaining employees. *Compensation and Benefits Review*, *49*(4), 230–246. doi:10.1177/0886368718808152

Lanier, K. (2017). Five things HR professionals need to know about generation Z: Thought leaders share their views on the HR profession and its direction for the future. *Strategic Human Resources Review*, *16*(6), 288–290. doi:10.1108/SHR-08-2017-0051

Lee, C., Huang, G. H., & Ashford, S. J. (2018). Job insecurity and the changing workplace: Recent developments and the future trends in job insecurity research. *Annual Review of Organizational Psychology and Organizational Behavior*, *5*(1), 335–359. doi:10.1146/annurev-orgpsych-032117-104651

Lips-Wiersma, M., & Hall, D. T. (2007). Organizational career development is not dead: A case study on managing the new career during organizational change. *Journal of Organizational Behavior*, *28*(6), 771–792. doi:10.1002/job.446

London, M. (1983). Toward a theory of career motivation. *Academy of Management Review*, *8*(4), 620–630. doi:10.5465/amr.1983.4284664

London, M. (1997). Overcoming career barriers: A model of cognitive and emotional processes for realistic appraisal and constructive coping. *Journal of Career Development*, *24*(1), 25–38. doi:10.1023/A:1025082420866

Luthans, F., Avey, J. B., Avolio, B. J., & Peterson, S. (2010). The development and resulting performance impact of positive psychological capital. Management Department Faculty Publications. Lincoln: University of Nebraska. 157. https://digitalcommons.unl.edu/managementfacpub/157

Mack, O., Khare, A., Kramer, A., & Burgartz, T. (Eds.). (2016). *Managing in a VUCA World*. Springer International Publishing. doi:10.1007/978-3-319-16889-0

Mannheim, K. (1928). The problem of generations. *Kölner Vierteljahrshefte für Soziologie, 7,* 157-185, 309-330.

Marnewick, A., & Marnewick, H. B. (2019). The ability of project managers to implement industry 4.0-related projects. *IEEE Access: Practical Innovations, Open Solutions*, *8*. https://ieeexplore.ieee.org/document/8939367

Masten, A. S., & Reed, M. G. J. (2002). Resilience in development. Handbook of Positive Psychology, 74, 88.

McCrindle, M. (2019). *Australia's Population Map and Generational Profile Update*. Retrieved at https://mccrindle.com.au/insights/blogarchive/australias-population-mapand-generational-profile-update

McDonald, P., & Kippen, R. (2001). Labour supply prospects in sixteen developed countries. *Population and Development Review*, *27*(1), 1–32. doi:10.1111/j.1728-4457.2001.00001.x

Mello, J. A. (2011). *Strategic Human Resource Management*. South-Western Cengage Learning.

Miller, J. (2019). *The voice of Generation Z: We want to be intrapreneurs*. Retrieved at https://www.rallyware.com/blog/generation-z-engagement

Mishra, P., & McDonald, K. (2017). Career resilience: An integrated review of the empirical literature. *Human Resource Development Review*, *16*(3), 207–234. doi:10.1177/1534484317719622

Mitchell, T., Holton, B., Lee, T., Sablynski, C., & Erez, M. (2001). Why people stay: Using job embeddedness to predict voluntary turnover. *Academy of Management Journal*, *44*(6), 1102–1122.

Morrell, D. L. (2011). Employee perceptions and the motivation of nonmonetary incentives. *Compensation and Benefits Review*, *43*(5), 318–323. doi:10.1177/0886368711407998

Nabi, G. R. (2000). Motivational attributes and organizational experiences as predictors of career-enhancing strategies. *Career Development International*, *5*(2), 91–98. doi:10.1108/13620430010318963

Nasurdin, A. M., Ramayah, T., & Kumaresan, S. (2005). Organizational stressors and job stress among managers: The moderating role of neuroticism. *Singapore Management Review*, *27*(2), 63–79.

Noe, R. A., Greenberger, D. B., & Wang, S. (2002). Mentoring: What we know and where we might go. *Research in Personnel and Human Resources Management*, *21*, 129–173. doi:10.1016/S0742-7301(02)21003-8

Ozkan, M., & Solmaz, B. (2015). The changing face of the employees – generation Z and their perceptions of work (a study applied to university students). *Procedia Economics and Finance*, *26*, 476–483. doi:10.1016/S2212-5671(15)00876-X

Parry, E., & Battista, V. (2019). The Generation Z in Great Britain- High standards and demands. In C. Scholz & A. Rennig (Eds.), *Generations in Europe: Inputs, Insights and Implications*. Emerald Publishing. doi:10.1108/978-1-78973-491-120191013

Porath, C., Spreitzer, G., Gibson, C., & Garnett, F. G. (2012). Thriving at work: Toward its measurement, construct validation, and theoretical refinement. *Journal of Organizational Behavior*, *33*(2), 250–275. doi:10.1002/job.756

Quigley, N. R., & Tymon, W. G. Jr. (2006). Toward an integrated model of intrinsic motivation and career self-management. *Career Development International*, *11*(6), 522–543. doi:10.1108/13620430610692935

Rigby, D. K., Sutherland, J., & Noble, A. (2018). Agile at scale. *Harvard Business Review*, *96*(3), 88–96.

Rodriguez, M., Boyer, S., Fleming, D., & Cohen, S. (2019). Managing the next generation of sales, Gen Z/Millennial cusp: An exploration of grit, entrepreneurship, and loyalty. *Journal of Business-To-Business Marketing*, *26*(1), 43–55. doi:10.1080/1051712X.2019.1565136

Roman, S. (2017). Engaging Generation Z in the workforce: Technology, intrapreneurship & culture. *Talent is Transforming, 2*(7). Retrieved at https://www.linkedin.com/pulse/engaging-generation-z-workforce-technology-culture-shaara-ives

Rousseau, D. M., Ho, V. T., & Greenberg, J. (2006). I-deals: Idiosyncratic terms in employment relationships. *Academy of Management Review*, *31*(4), 977–994. doi:10.5465/amr.2006.22527470

Ryan, A. M., Brutus, S., Greguras, G. J., & Hakel, M. D. (2000). Receptivity to assessment-based feedback for management development. *Journal of Management Development*, *19*(4), 252–276. doi:10.1108/02621710010322580

Sánchez-Hernández, M. I., González-López, O. R., Buenadicha-Mateos, M., & Tato-Jiménez, J. L. (2019). Work-life balance in great companies and pending issues for engaging new generations at work. *International Journal of Environmental Research and Public Health, 16*(24), 5122–5142. doi:10.3390/ijerph16245122 PMID:31847460

Sandhu, S., Sastrowardoyo, S., Benson, J., & Scott-Young, C. M. (2016). Aging in Asia: Challenges and opportunities in China, India, Japan and South Korea. In A. S. Antoniou, C. L. Cooper, & R. Burke (Eds.), *The Aging Workforce Handbook: Individual, Organizational and Societal Challenges* (pp. 513–536). Emerald Publishing. doi:10.1108/978-1-78635-448-820161021

Schawbel, D. (2014). *Gen Y and Gen Z global workplace expectations study.* Retrieved at http://millennialbranding. com/2014/geny-genz-global-workplaceexpectations-study

Scholz, C., & Rennig, A. (2019). *Generations in Europe: Inputs, insights and implications.* Emerald Publishing. doi:10.1108/9781789734911

Seemiller, C., & Grace, M. (2017). Generation Z: Educating and engaging the next generation of students. *American College Personnel Association, 22*(3), 21–26. doi:10.1002/abc.21293

Seibert, S. E., Kraimer, M. L., & Heslin, P. A. (2016). Developing career resilience and adaptability. *Organizational Dynamics, 45*(3), 245–257. doi:10.1016/j.orgdyn.2016.07.009

Slavin, A. (2015). *Marketers: Forget about Millennials. Gen Z has arrived.* Retrieved at https://women2. com/2015/08/07/engage-gen-z-users

Sosik, J. J., & Godshalk, V. M. (2005). Examining gender similarity and mentor's supervisory status in mentoring relationships. *Mentoring & Tutoring, 13*(1), 39–52. doi:10.1080/13611260500040138

Srivastava, P. (2012). Getting engaged. *Compensation and Benefits Review, 44*(2), 105–109. doi:10.1177/0886368712450982

Sturges, J., Conway, N., Guest, D., & Liefooghe, A. (2005). Managing the career deal: The psychological contract as a framework for understanding career management, organizational commitment and work behavior. *Journal of Organizational Behavior, 26*(7), 821–838. doi:10.1002/job.341

Tansky, J., & Cohen, D. (2001). The relationship between organizational support, employee development, and organizational commitment: An empirical study. *Human Resource Development Quarterly, 12*(3), 285–300. doi:10.1002/hrdq.15

Tapscott, D., & Williams, A. D. (2010). Innovating the 21st-Century university: It's time! *EDUCAUSE Review, 45*(1), 16–29.

Tong, C., & Kathy, E. K. (2013). The efficacy of mentoring – the benefits for mentees, mentors, and organizations. In *The Wiley-Blackwell Handbook of the Psychology of Coaching and Mentoring* (pp. 217–243). John Wiley & Sons.

Twenge, J. (2017). IGen. Atria Books.

Ungar, M. (2019). *Change Your World: What the Science of Resilience Teaches Us about the True Path to Success.* Sutherland House.

Van Buren, H. J. III. (2003). Boundaryless careers and employability obligations. *Business Ethics Quarterly, 13*(2), 131–149. doi:10.5840/beq20031329

Van Vuuren, L., & Fourie, C. (2000). Career anchors and career resilience: Supplementary constructs? *SA Journal of Industrial Psychology, 23*(3), 15–20. doi:10.4102ajip.v26i3.714

Van Wyk, J. (2015). *Generation Z will ruin businesses that fail to adopt new ways of working*. Retrieved at https://www.itweb.co.za/content/XGxwQD71ebV7lPVo

Waterman, R. H., Waterman, J. A., & Betsy, C. A. (1994). Towards a career resilient workforce. *Harvard Business Review*, 87–95.

Wayne, J. H., & Casper, W. J. (2012). Why does firm reputation in human resource policies influence college students? The mechanisms underlying job pursuit intentions. *Human Resource Management, 51*(1), 121–142. doi:10.1002/hrm.21461

Wilson, S. M., & Ferch, S. R. (2005). Enhancing resilience in the workplace through the practice of caring relationships. *Organization Development Journal, 23*(4), 45–60.

Winwood, P., Colon, R., & McKewen, K. (2013). A practical measure of workplace resilience. *Journal of Occupational and Environmental Medicine, 35*(10), 1205–1212. doi:10.1097/JOM.0b013e3182a2a60a PMID:24064782

Zehetner, D., Lepeyko, T., & Zehetner, A. (2019). Formation of the leadership style in the enterprise management in the process of generation transition. *New Economy, 2*, 9–14.

ADDITIONAL READING

Lanier, K. (2017). Five things HR professionals need to know about Generation Z: Thought leaders share their views on the HR profession and its direction for the future. *Strategic Human Resources Review, 16*(6), 288–290. doi:10.1108/SHR-08-2017-0051

Lee, C., Huang, G. H., & Ashford, S. J. (2018). Job insecurity and the changing workplace: Recent developments and the future trends in job insecurity research. *Annual Review of Organizational Psychology and Organizational Behavior, 5*(1), 335–359. doi:10.1146/annurev-orgpsych-032117-104651

O'Boyle, C., Atack, J., & Monahan, K. (2017). Generational and technological challenges in entry-level jobs. Available at: www2.deloitte.com/insights/us/en/focus/technology-and-the-future-of- work.

Seibert, S. E., Kraimer, M. L., & Heslin, P. A. (2016). Developing career resilience and adaptability. *Organizational Dynamics, 45*(3), 245–257. doi:10.1016/j.orgdyn.2016.07.009

KEY TERMS AND DEFINITIONS

Career Mentoring: The relationship between a mentor and protégée, where the mentor provides guidance and advice to assist the protégée in their career.

Career Resilience: The capacity of an individual to adapt to career related challenges and move towards a positive career trajectory.

Career Shocks: Unexpected or expected events which challenge an individual's capacity to conduct their work as planned.

Career Stressors: The pressures and demands from the work environment, which are imposed on the individual and can lead to unfavorable psychological and/or physical outcomes in their career and/or personal life.

Employability: The capacity of an individual to consistently develop and enhance their skills to remain relevant and attractive to the job market.

Resilience: The capacity to respond to, adapt and learn from stressors and changing conditions.

Turnover: The rate at which employees leave an organization and must be replaced.

Chapter 17
3W1H Approach to Understand the Millennial Generation

Sahil Malik
Faculty of Management Studies, Manav Rachna International Institute of Research and Studies, India

Geetika M. Chandra
Gurugram University, India

Anindita Chatterjee Rao
Faculty of Management Studies, Manav Rachna International Institute of Research and Studies, India

Shilpa Arora
Faculty of Management Studies, Manav Rachna International Institute of Research and Studies, India

ABSTRACT

The chapter examines all the facets belonging to the Millennial generation. The utility to understand this generation is to evolve strategies to keep this workforce engaged and retained in their organizations. The chapter under "Who" incorporates all the generations both before and after the Millennials. Millennials, in specific, share birth years from 1980 to 2000 and are 2 billion in number out of 7.4 billion people. Secondly, the chapter includes the "Why" of Millennials asserting the events and situations that have made them "Millennials." It comprises primarily of factors like technology, social media, economy, education, employment, and culture and lifestyle, which are discussed in length in the chapter. Thirdly, the "What" about Millennials informs readers of things required to know about this generation. It consists of work motivations and work values exhibited by Millennials. Finally, the chapter takes account of "How" to engage and retain this generation and gives an account of certain job resources.

INTRODUCTION

With the beginning of the 21st century, the focus on studying and understanding millennial generation has gained manifold importance. The trend to research upon this cohort of generation is yet to remain as the youngest of the lot is still to arrive at their workplaces and the oldest generation Y members have

DOI: 10.4018/978-1-7998-4543-0.ch017

gained work experience for substantial number of years and are geared up for leadership roles in the organization. Therefore a wide scope is available within the millennial generation which could facilitate intra generational comparisons as well. This chapter would focus on understanding millennial generation through 3W1H approach. Although, it is the 5W1H writing technique which is used in an array of professions and universities across the world. Writers adopts this method to gather information (shimazu, Arisawa& Saito, 2006), writing thesis and summary (Regoniel, 2016). In this context, 3W1H means who, why, what & how of the millennial generation. "Who" signifies the definition and birth years that qualify members into millennial generation. "Why" shows the causes in form of defining events which Millennials has faced in their adulthood. It could comprise of events from politics, economy and culture etc. "What" explores the work values and motivations and "How" would explore the engagement and retention strategies adopted by organizations for the millennial generation employees. The underlying research problem that this chapter addresses is to build a holistic understanding of different generations of people with a special focus on Millennials. Chapter also signifies that it is indispensible to understand any generation without knowing the perspectives in which Millennials are born and brought up reflected with life events and incidents. Lastly, chapter attempts to address the universal issue associated with Millennials regarding their engagement and retention by identifying certain ways and means in form of job resources from literature to better engage them.

Who are the Millennials: Defining a Generation

Before discussing about Millennials, it is imperative to study some definitions of a Generation. The term generation typically refers to a group of individuals who share common life experiences such as world events, natural disasters, politics, economic conditions, and pop culture (Smith & Clurman, 1998). The most accepted definition of a generation is given byKupperschmidt (2000, p.66) that it is an "identifiable group that shares birth years, age, location, and significant life events at critical developmental stages". According to Parry and Urwin (2011), generation is defined on the basis of both the birth cohort and a shared experience of historical and political events, collective culture and the competition for resources. It is noticed that contributors to generational studies have used the term 'generation' in sense of 'cohort' however Glenn (1977) is of the view that in technical sense 'generation' is a structural term associated with parent –child relationship used in kinship terminology. A cohort is a group of population who experience same significant event within a given period of time.

Generations Before the Millennials

Researchers have identified three generations of the 20th century before the rise of millennial generation. These are **Silent generation**(1925-1945) also known as Traditionalists, Roaring twenties, Depression babies, World war II; **Baby Boomers** (1946-1964) also addressed by Murphy (2007) as "Woodstock generation" and "Sandwich and Vietnam generation"; **Generation X** or Gen X (1965-1981) addressed by Tolbize (2008) and Yu & Miller (2005) as "Baby busters", "Post boomers", "Slackers", "Shadow Generation".

Consistent birth years among researchers are generally agreed for only the first two generations, Silents' and Boomers' however Dwyer (2009) identified (1922-1946) and (1946-1966) as the birth years respectively. The first birth year for GenX, according to the great majority of researchers cited in literature is either 1964 or 1965, with a generally accepted end date for this generation of 1980 or 1981.

The above classification of generation holds good in the western context as most research is conducted in countries like the US, UK and Canada. However there is a difference of opinion of defining generation in Asian context. Some scholars has categorized Asian generations on the western lines although the events happened in the developed world may not be relevant in Asian context. Due to this fact scholars like Yu and Miller (2005) asserted differences in the Asian context.

- In the context of **China**, Egri and Ralston (2004) have identified four different generations - Republican (born 1930-1950), Consolidation (born 1951-1960), Cultural Revolution (born 1961-1970), and Social Reform (born 1971-1975).Another classification of Chinese generation Post 50s generation (1950-59), Post 60s generation (1960-69), Post 70s generation (1970-79), Post 80s generation (1980-89), Post 90s (1990-99) given by Hole et.al 2010.
- In the context of **Japan**, Hole et. al. (2010) has identified 7 generations from 1946 to 2002. 1st Baby boomer (1946-50), Danso Generation (1951-60), Shinjinrui or bubble generation (1961-70), 2nd Baby boomer or Dankai generation (1971-75), Post Bubble (1976-86), Shinjinrui Junior or Generation Z (1987-1995), Yutori (1996-2002).
- In the context of **South Korea, "**475" generation (1950-59), "386" generation (1960-69), Gen X and Gen Y (1970 - onward).

Unlike the western context, Indian culture is not unitary and homogeneous. It is considered as composite culture (Parekh, 2007) under which groups do have distinct identity but they share their regional, religious and linguistic culture. The social and cultural diversity in India is quite evident as all major religions of the world are being worshipped here along with linguistic diversity with 22 officially recognized languages. The union of India with 29 states is considered as one of the most diverse countries in the world. With such credentials, classification of any generation in Indian context needs to reflect the current diversity. There have been different ways adopted to classify the generations in India.

- Roongrerngsuke (2010) and Erickson (2009) have attempted to categorize generations using the global framework to classify four generations in India. The classification is like from "Traditionalist (1922 – 1943)", "Baby boomers (1943 – 1960)", "Generation X (1960 – 1980)" and "Generation Y (1980 – 2000)".
- Hole, Zhong, & Schwartz (2010) has classified that there are three generations existed in India the "Traditional generation (1948 - 1968)", "the Non-traditional generation (1969 - 1980)" and "Generation Y (1981 onwards)".
- Ghosh &Chaudhari, (2009), identified the three generations existing in India as the "Conservatives (1947 – 1969)", "Integrators (1970 – 1984)" and "Y2K (1985 – 1995)".
- Generations identified in India as per popular literature (Steelcase, 2009) is somewhat replica of US classification especially the recent "Generation X (1965 – 1979)" and "Generation Y (1980 – 2000)". Generation before these were classified as "Freedom Fighters (1900 – 1946)" and "Traditionals (1947 – 1964)".

Figure 1. Generations of the World (Millennials and post Millennials)

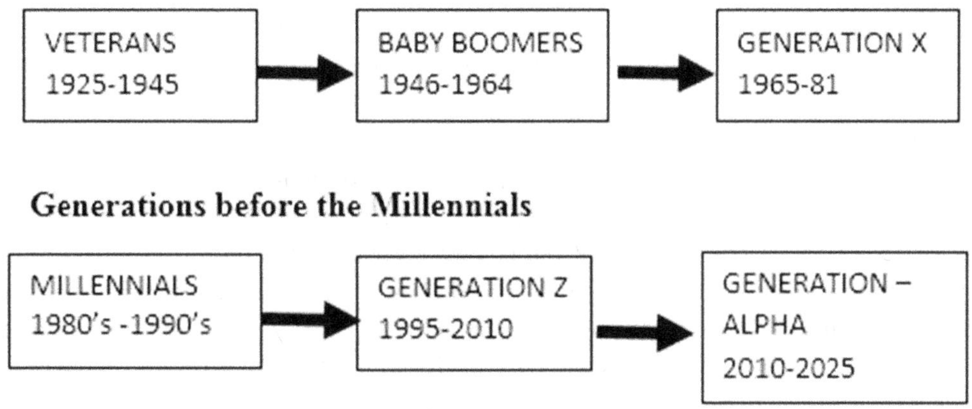

The Millennials

The Millennials term coined in 1987 by William Strauss and Neil Howe and has written about this cohort in their books Generations: The History of America's Future, 1584 to 2069 (1991) and Millennials Rising: The Next Great Generation (2000). The phrase "Generation Y" first introduced in 1993 through an editorial whereas they are also described as "Generation me" by Psychologist Jean Twenge in her 2006 book- "Generation Me: Why Today's Young Americans Are More Confident, Assertive, Entitled – and More Miserable Than Ever Before". Millennials are also known as Net Gen, Gen Y, Generation Me, Gen Net, and Digital Natives.Gen Yers are also known as Millennials, Next generation, Generation me, Echo boomers, Nexters, the Boomlet, Digital generation, Dot com generation, Net Generation, N-Gens, Generation WWW, Digital natives, Ninetendo generation, Sunshine generation (Murphy, 2007), the Do or Die generation, the Wannabes, the Nothing is sacred generation, Cyberkids, the Feel good generation and Non-nuclear family generation.

The date and age range classification is comparatively homogeneous with respect to Millennial generation where most of the research organization like Pew Research, Washington post, Washington times and APA conforms to the age bracket of 1981-1996. However in academic literature, studies conducted in different countries pertaining to Generation Y agree more on bracket of 1981-1999 with slight difference of one or two years at the beginning or the end. One perspective is proposed by Cavagnaro et al. (2018), setting the years from 1980 to the mid-1990s. Similarly, a report by the OECD defines Millennials as those born in the early 1980s to the mid-1990s, and a report by KPMG (2017) marks the years as 1980 to 1995. According to Skinner et al. (2018), while most definitions mark the beginning year of the Millennial era as 1980, some scholars set it as early as 1977.

The generations that are classified in Indian context mentioned above are as per the available literature shows disparity in birth years and the way grouping is done except that of generation Y. Most of the studies assume similar birth years (1980 – 2000) making it a homogeneous cohort of generation and viable for research.

Generations After the Millennials

- **Generation Z** - In the post millennial era, Generation Z is all set to thrive and is considered by Mckinsey& Co. as the first generation of true digital natives. Generation Z members are people born largely between 1995-2010 although different starting and cutoff birth years are also suggested. According to pew research, Gen Z bracket is 1997-2012 similar to APA classification. In Australia, McCrindle research centre defines Generation Z as those born between 1995-2009. In Japan, generations are defined by a ten-year span with "Neo-Digital natives" beginning after 1996. MTV described Generation Z as those born after December 2000. Gen Z is known by names like iGeneration, Gen Tech, Gen Wii, Net Gen, Digital Natives, and Plurals.
- **GenerationAlpha –** It is also known as the Children of Millennial and is the first generation born entirely within the 21st century. This term "Generation Alpha" was coined by Australian researcher Mark McCrindle in 2005. They share their birth years between 2010-2025. Generation Alpha use smartphones and tablets naturally. These children were born along with iPhones, iPads, and applications. They don't know nor can imagine how life was without them.They are logged on and linked up – known as 'digital natives'. They are the most materially endowed and technologically literate generation to ever grace the planet.

Where are the Millennials?

The 2017 survey by Pew Research Center states that Millennials born between 1981 and 1997 account for around 27 percent of the world population i.e. roughly 2 billion population out of 7.4 billion people. The study of the continental spread of the millennial generation points out that Asia is home to 58 percent of the global millennial population. When it comes to spread between the countries, UN world population prospects report 2015 points five countries i.e. India, China, USA, Indonesia and Brazil with largest absolute millennial population. Another important metric in the country analysis according to UN world population prospects, 2015, IMF World Economic outlook and A.T Kearney is the – "The eight millennial majors". These are the selected countries i.e. Bangladesh, Egypt, India, Iran, Pakistan, the Philippines, South Africa, and Vietnam with both large absolute millennial populations and a high share of Millennials in their total population. These countries has the window of demographic dividend of economic growth.

It is a noted fact that India is an important country of analysis when it comes to accounting for millennial generation because of its size. The population of India is 1210 million as per census data 2011. The classification of the population is such that 29.7% of the people fall between the age range of 0-14 years, 64.9% comes between the age range of 15 - 64 years and 5.5% more than 65 years. It is surveyed that by 2020, India would be the youngest country of the world as per the mean age which will be 29 in India and 37 & 48 for countries like China and Japan (Basu, 2007). As per National Youth policy of India 2014, youth belong to age group of 15-29 with 27% population falling in this bracket. Today, one in every three person is counted as youth in an Indian city as claimed by report "State of the Urban Youth, India 2012: Employment, Livelihoods, Skills" published by IRIS Knowledge Foundation in collaboration with UN-HABITAT.

The official records on generation Y count in India is not available but an examination of entire population as done in popular literature demonstrates that generation Y (1980 - 1990) in India makes up a major portion of the population and is the biggest generation-Y populace on the planet. However according to UN report, 2015, India accounts for 19 percent of world millennial population and has largest domestic population of Millennials in the world i.e. 385 million.

Why the Millennials – Developments that led to the Making of Millennial Generation?

The concept of generation was introduced by Mannheim (1952). In his words, generation is a part of wider sociological theory of knowledge as it is firmly located within socio-historical contexts. Here location point means starting and cutoff birth years pertaining to different behavioural modes, feeling and thoughts of generations and their respective formative experiences during the time of youth are highlighted as the key period in which social generations are formed.

According to Strauss et. al, (1991), there are two parameters through which a generation can be defined i.e. years of birth and a particular set of shared social and economic conditions during their formative years. These two aspects give rise to a common generational persona which makes people belonging to a generation similar in their traits, thinking, values and beliefs.

The factors that has influenced millennial generation in their developmental years are classified as follows.

- **Technology and Social Media**–the background of technology is much ancient than the Millennial generation birth years and the era of technology is going to last long donning more influence on the generations of 21st century. In the last couple of decades of the 20th century, the parallel time of millennial generation, technology has already reached an establishment standing on already developed means of mass communication like radio, television and landline phones. This all got invented and spreaded across the world in the pre Millennials time. First IBM PC and apple appeared during the onset of the millennial generation i.e. in the early years of 1980's. Technology that got developed during 1960's and 70's had little impact on the everyday lives as it was seen like a tool used in academics but later in 1980's, it slowly creeped in common man lives and homes deliberating their behaviour. Millennials at this point were still in their early birth years but technology improved the lives of their parents through better communication which helped them make more informed decisions and better choices. Millennials are brought up during the time of rapid changes making them stand out from other generation with unique set of priorities and expectations. They are also called as digital natives as during 1990's technology had made interventions in all domains of work and life enabling people to people connection across the world. Millennials also witnessed the revolution of IT in form of social media which began humbly with 'Six degrees' which is the first social media site launched in 1997 followed by the advent of Linkedin in 2002 and facebook in 2004.

Millennials are considered to be the first generation that has grown up with computers, the internet and easy access to information through google. It has made this generation the most technologically proficient humans on earth to use technology in the best possible manner for making global connections, social networking and entertainment. Technology has created a digital divide between elder and younger generation of employees as the former are less familiar and adept at employing technology than the latter.

Millennials are so much in technology that it has become an essential component of their socio-cultural DNA. Studies point out that technology creates convenience in their life and work and is an essential hygiene factor. Technology also plays a vital role in attracting talented millennial generation by harnessing social media and making communication more effective with relevant content. Millennials can also be tapped for doing reverse mentoring in form of giving hands on session to senior executives on social media and ICT. The 2015 Delloite Millennial survey states that technology is the most sought after sector for Millennials which they wish to enter after leaving university and male preference to work in technology sector is twice that of females. Millennials are so preoccupied with technology that they spend about 7.5 hours per day online and they seek it everywhere – office, car, home as it contributes to their creativity and productivity. Couple of significant happenings that have taken place in the context of Millennials is the outreach of internet and smartphone accessibility (KPMG, 2017). They are the first generation of so-called digital natives and the first "always connected" generation (Skinner et al., 2018; KPMG, 2017). The traits that Millennials have developed due to constant use of technology are such as tech-savvy, hyper –connected etc (CBI, 2019; Skinner et al., 2018; Nielsen, 2017; Visit Scotland, 2017).

- **Economy, Education & Employment –** the economic transformation of the world in the 20th century has been phenomenal in terms of output per capita, structure of production and the financial system. Rapid technological advancement from the onset of industrial revolution in 1750's and widespread use and commercialization of 19th century inventions has played a pivotal role in the increase of per capita output along with level of education and communication infrastructure. Technological progress has led to paradigm shift from home production to mass production giving impetus to state of the art production processes along with the development of new products and services. It has also led to emergence of markets facilitating international trade.

When it comes to studying economy in context of generations, studies point that every generation is exposed to different economic conditions that builds their perception of the present and future of the world. In the times of Millennial generation, economies and business has become more knowledge intensive where Millennials believe that education is key to success and are considered as "education is cool" generation. They favour active kinesthetic learning environment. Zemkeet. al. (2000) states that Millennials are raised in an era where their parents have endeavored to give them improved quality of education and have also provided them constant encouragement, coaching that have inculcated in them traits like ambition, optimism, over confidence and high achievement orientation (Strauss and Howe, 1991; Zemke et al., 2000; Lancaster and Stillman, 2002; Reynolds, 2005).Now it becomes but obvious that recent generations are entering the workforce with an increased demand for higher education (ILO, 2007).

A study confirms that there is a strong urge in Millennials for education and prestigious jobs that they outnumber the actual figure of people attaining these degrees and jobs (Reynolds, Stewart, MacDonald, &Sischo, 2006).It has become a challenge for the managers to provide young generation with opportunities for continuous education to make them stay in the organization. Managers can assure their loyalty if provided them with flexibility to pursue their educational goals.

When it comes to discussing the employment scenario, Arthur (1994) states that traditional career structures has made way for the boundaryless career since the beginning of 1990. Now the employment relationship has become more transactional and short term and employees expect more from their organizations than the other way round. Sensing the reduction in lifetime employment, Millennials are of the opinion that there is a need for constant skill development to remain marketable (Westerman and Yamamura, 2007). Millennials in order to meet their ends have adapted to the temporary work assignments arising out of sharing economy like driving for Uber etc.and complimenting the services offered by shared economy like access to basic facilities without being an owner. In the present job market, Millennials are seen positive about their future but are struggling to find full time employment. The impact of industry 4.0 in form of advanced automation, connectivity, artificial intelligence and robotics have converted full time jobs into tasks and projects. Automation for Millennials is beneficial for productivity and economic growth but are also apprehensive that it could be a reason for massive dislocation of jobs. A win requires educational systems that teach both cognitive and social and emotional skills, businesses that actively support their workforce through retraining and upskilling, individuals who are proactive about lifelong learning, and governments that prepare a supportive environment for these efforts.

- **Culture & Lifestyle –** Culture in this context is studied around millennial workforce which comprise of two aspects –the national culture of the country and the culture within the organization. National culture is the set of customs, values, beliefs, norms shared by the population of a sovereign nation which plays a big role in influencing the behaviour of young generation managers and employees. In terms of respecting hierarchy, research points that countries in Middle East and South Asia fare higher than countries in the western region. This restricts the decision making capability which could frustrate Millennials who aspire to work in an empowered environment. It is also been observed that Millennials around the world carry strong familial support on which they can bank upon which is a hindrance for movement of younger generation. Study done by Gomes and Deuling (2019) on mapping the influence of helicopter parenting in form of career informational support, financial support, family support and family values proves beneficial for affective commitment and job satisfaction of Millennials and negatively related with their turnover intentions. The organizational culture of nurturing creativity, collaboration and flexibility goes well with Millennials. It is because creative culture promotes and recognizes individual achievements and talents. As discussed above, Millennials didn't like to respect conventional hierarchical corporate cultures and wish to assume high responsibility roles sooner than other generations. Millennials also prefers to stay with the organizations where they are encouraged to socialize. A study conducted by Cisco showed that 56% of the 2,800 college students that were interviewed would not accept a job from a company that would ban social media or they would ban the policy (Taylor, 2011).This has made Millennials pro diversity where they feel pleasure to accommodate with people from different cultures and countries.

Millennials are known for their lifestyles that is influenced by global trends which gets reflected through their workplace attires becoming more stylish and individualistic through branded clothes with which they wish to look good 24/7. They are perceived as been raised in good times by extra ordinarily involved parents better known by helicopter parents. It is believed that parents show concern for their millennial children personaand choice in this age of consumerism where for product manufacturers, young generation with high self-esteem is a potential market that can be tapped with devises like smartphones, ipods and other products. The millennial generation carry a say in family decisions and their opinions are seen given due importance. These conditions have created high quotient of expectation and achievement among millennial generation.

Academic literature is convinced that every working generation exhibit different set of needs and expectations which they wish to get fulfilled by their leaders and organizations. Millennials have been labelled as one difficult cohort to understand for managers to accommodate them in present work environment.The Millennials wish to have more balanced lifestyle between their work and non - work roles and they assume work is to finance and compliment their lifestyle. They relish their work but doesn't let it ruin their life. Millennials are willing to contribute over and above their capacity for an honest reason.

Basically studies have portrayed millennial generation as high maintenance seeking workforce. High maintenance means asking for opportunities of professional development to remain worthy in the market because of millennial preference for portable career over lifetime opportunities. Millennials are assertive in expecting workplace flexibility while performing work to meet their ends like professional satisfaction and institutional learning.

What are the Millennials Work Values and Motivations?

Work values are the source of most significant differences among generations and major source of conflict in the workplace. Study conducted by Jassawalla and Sashittal (2017) states that majority of the Millennials involved in a conflict with older coworkers and supervisors in the workplace over the issue of unfairness they experience. Work values are individual centric and reflect one's preferences and expectations in the workplace influencing their attitudes and behaviour. Work values are considered as stable and resistant to change and are highly correlated with motivational factors as it is seen that what one values or considers important gets motivated by it. There are array of work value categories one can identify like intrinsic, extrinsic, social, freedom, altruistic and status related (Cennamo& Gardner, 2008; Twenge et al., 2010).

There has been plethora of studies conducted in measuring the work values of millennial generation in their respective countries. Seminal work on measuring the work values of millennial generation has been done in US particularly by Smola and Sutton in 2002 conducted a longitudinal study and found that work values are more influenced by generational experience than by age or maturity. Since then numerous research has been conducted in measuring the generational differences in work values in countries of Europe, Australia and New Zealand among which few are referred in the following table.

These different studies have explained various types of work values exhibited by Millennials which shows that there is lack of consensus across studies regarding the importance of different motivators and categories. However, studies also suggest that if managed well, those differences can be a source of significant strengths and opportunities (Lancaster and Stillman, 2002).

HOW TO ENGAGE AND RETAIN MILLENNIAL GENERATION EMPLOYEES?

There could be many different ways to engage and retain employees. Job resources refer to the fundamental aspects of the job that are available to employees at task, interpersonal or organizational level that are Instrumental in achieving work goals/Moderates job demands and the associated physiological and psychological costs/Enables capacity building of employees by stimulating personal growth, learning, and development.

Job resources may be located at the level of the organization at large - "pay", "career opportunities", "job security", the interpersonal and social relations – "supervisor and co-worker support", "team climate", the organization of work – "role clarity", "participation in decision making", and at the level of the task - "skill variety", "task identity", "task significance", "autonomy", "performance feedback".

Table 1. Studies on varied work values of Millennial Generation across the globe

Author	Country	Type of study	Results
Twenge, et. al. (2010)	USA	Longitudinal	Leisure and Extrinsic Values Increasing, Social and Intrinsic Values Decreasing
Cennamo and Gardner (2008)	New Zealand	Cross sectional	The youngest groups placed more importance on status and freedom work values than the oldest group
Gursoy et.al (2008)	USA	Qualitative data	The Millennial Generation believes in collective action, with optimism of the future, and trust in centralized authority. They like teamwork, showing a strong will to get things done with a great spirit.
Ching et.al (2012)	Malaysia	Quantitative data, cross sectional	Gen Y Preservice teachers prefer quality supervisory relationships, good workingEnvironment/surroundings, and quality co-workers relationships. Achievement, security, and intrinsic work values are secondary in importance.
Lim (2012)	UAE	Quantitative data, cross sectional	The most important work motivator to Emiratis and expatriates was extrinsic.
Khera& Malik (2017)	India	Quantitative data, cross sectional	Results found that Millennials MBA graduates preferred being materialistic over being altruistic. Gen Y are concerned with their own self who wish to excel in a highly paid profession and want to enjoy the life to the fullest.
Ketter (2019)	Europe	Content analysis, literature review	The technologically obsessed and experiential learning attitude of Millennials are giving way to micro tourism trends like creative tourism, off the beat tourism, alternative tourism and fully digital tourism.

The presence of job resources may lead to satisfaction of basic needs or achievement of work goals leads to engagement, whereas their absence evokes a cynical attitude towards work. It is expected that employees who are engaged have low tendency to leave the organization."

Following are some job resources that could be offered at job to engage and retain employees from millennial generation

- **Meaningful Job Characteristics** - Hackman & Oldham (1980) explained that if the jobs are designed in such a manner to incorporate the essential job characteristics, then the work become worthwhile in the eyes of the employees. Consequently, employees will get high degree of satisfaction in their jobs leading to high-quality work performance. Thus these five core job characteristics qualify to be intrinsically oriented job resources which have the potential to enrich the content factor of the job. Moreover when it comes to subject matter of the study i.e. job characteristics induced engagement, a paper written by Saks (2006) underscore that job characteristics significantly predicts job engagement of employees (R2 = .37) taking SET (social exchange theory) in consideration and concluded that employees who are provided with jobs that are high on the job characteristics are more likely to reciprocate with greater job engagement.

Figure 2. Conceptual framework showing relationship between Job Resources and engagement and retention

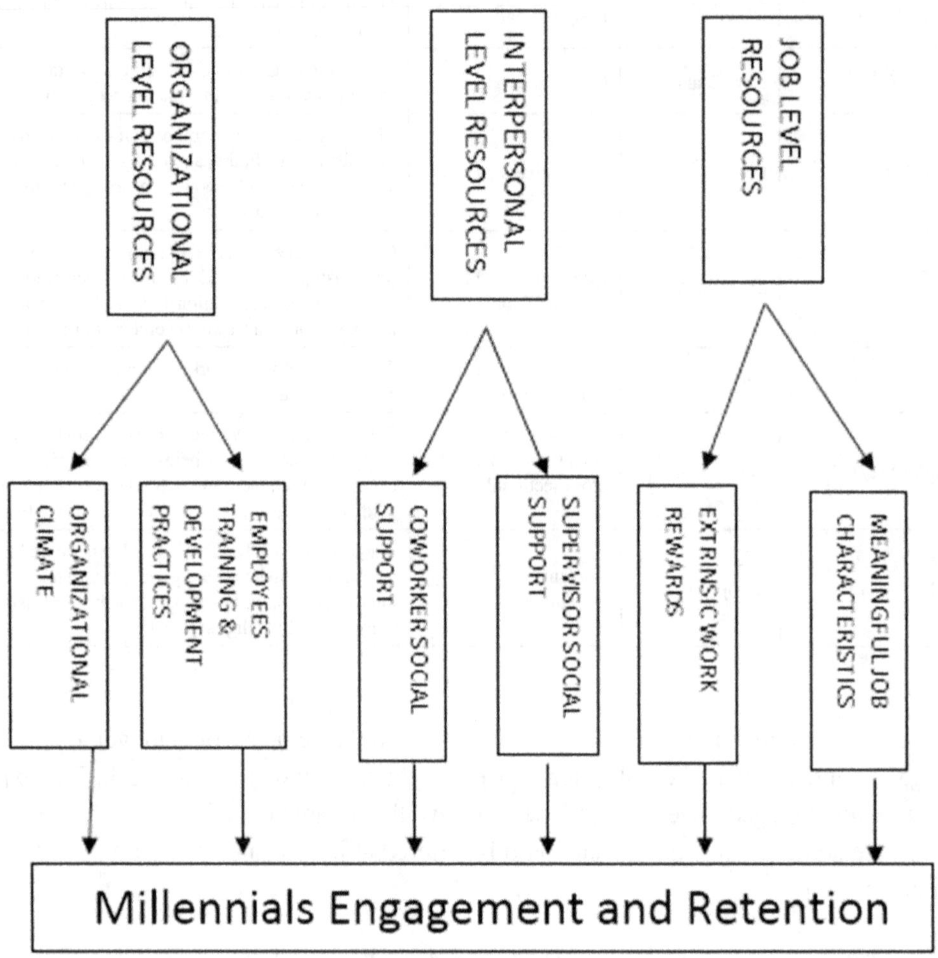

- **Extrinsic Work Rewards -** Extrinsic rewards can be classified into financial and non – financial factors. Financial or monetary rewards consist of pay and benefits and non-financial consist of elements like working conditions, job security, recognition, praise and feedback. Among the classification, monetary factors remains more of a concern for employees as well as employers since it is a vital instrument that will help to attract and retain employees. However employees of young generation do pay lot of attention on non-monetary extrinsic job factors like suitable work environment, recognition and praise for the work done. It is because of possessing high self - esteem and expecting the same from the work or job done. There is a need to further examine the extrinsic benefits into monetary and non-monetary types and its relevance and capacity to engage millennial generation employees.
- **Social Support** - Kim, Kirkman& Chen (2008) defines social support in terms of help through which individuals can enhance emotional well-being and simultaneously reducing psychological

distress. Social support arises at the interpersonal level of organization which is classified in to two sub categories i.e. supervisor support and coworker support.

- **Supervisor Social Support** - General supervisor support focuses on support for personal effectiveness at work. Supervisor support comes in form of understanding employee's needs and wants, giving them genuine responses and confidence to raise their problems and help in resolving work related issues (Deci& Ryan, 1985). When it comes to engaging employees through supervisor support, literature presents Kahn (1990) point of view. He states that to make someone engage, one should provide psychological safety to the subject which according to Kahn is vastly influenced by interpersonal relationships. Studying the requirement of supervisor support in the context of generation Y shows that their productivity rests upon leader behaviour in terms of garnering their respect and getting genuine feedback on job performance (Jones, Brown, Zoltners&Weits, 2005). Similarly Tulgan (2009) states that Managers who "guide, direct, and support them every step of the way" will enable generation Y in delivering quality output. On observing the trends among Indian generation Y, it was found that considerate and sympathetic supervisor is a leading extrinsic motivator for them (IKYA, 2011).
- **Coworker Social Support** - Going by literature, Kahn (1990) states that supportive team and trusting team members facilitates employee engagement. Supportive interpersonal relationship instills a sense of psychological safety among employees in the workplace. With an element of psychological safety employees can try to act with novelty with the faith of not being reprimanded in case of not showing successful results (Kahn, 1990). The more recent studies by Schaufeli& Bakker (2004) and Schaufeli et al. (2009) found significant relationship between co-workers interpersonal support and employee engagement. Co-worker interpersonal support is an important element of work engagement model given by Bakker, van Emmerik&Euwema (2006). According to Andrew & Sofian (2012) the best condition to gain high involvement of employees in work is when they are working in lean organization accompanied with talented and cooperative staff.
- **Organizational Climate** - Organizational climate is described as "the feeling in the air" that one perceives while working in the organization (Schneider, Gunnarson& Niles-Jolly, 1994). Organizational climate is made up of numerous factors that have a bearing on both group as well as individual performance. Halbesleben"s (2010) meta-analysis, consistent with the JD-R (Bakker &Demerouti, 2007) explained the association between organizational climate and engagement or particular facets of engagement. In today"s scenario when workplaces are witnessing a shift in proportion of employees by generation such that more and more young employees are replacing their predecessors, acknowledgement of organizational climate becomes quiet imperative to underline the necessities.
- **Employees T&D Practices** - Human resource development has gained much significance in the recent years in the private sector and is gaining prominence in public sector as well. It is an essential part of human resource management that involves training and career development of employees and organization development. The aim of HRD department is to supplement current workforce with necessary skills and abilities through training to enhance their job performance. This will lead to employees becoming eligible for better work positions being offered in the current organization or elsewhere necessitating their career development. It would be of no surprise to say that the value of HRD practices for today"s generation of employees across the world has increased manifold. Generation Y prefers to work in a setting where there is plethora of opportunities available for advancement and long term career progression. Generation Y show their interest

in organizations that invest in training and development. In Indian scenario, generation Y has started showing preference for portfolio careers which means working with different employers at the same time but not in full time capacity. However still the career advancement remains one of the top factor to motivate this generation (Shrinivasan, 2012).

CONCLUSION

The chapter delves in studying different generations of the world in general and Millennial generation in particular. The chapter opens by discussing the meaning of generation through definitions given by various scholars followed by classification of generations done in a way in which generations before the Millennials and after it are incorporated and discussed adequately. Literature suggest that with respect to generations before the Millennials, there seems no confluence as scholars have recognized different birth years in western countries viz.-a-viz. Asian context. Further in the chapter, Generation Z and Alpha are also introduced to the readers highlighting the present and future trends in generations. Secondly, chapter answers the question of location of Millennial generation around the globe in which India and China spearhead along with US, Indonesia and Brazil. This is important to know the talent hub of the world that would become the future workforce for the organizations. Thirdly, literature review is done to identify the broad themes encompassing technology, social media and economic conditions that has played a significant role in shaping the attitude and behaviour of Millennials. Fourthly, chapter also incorporates the most researched domain in the context of Millennial generation i.e. their work values and motivations and found that generalization cannot be established as it is more contextual and situational. Finally, the last question that has been answered through this chapter is "how to engage and retain this workforce". It comprise of the ways through which organizations can seek active involvement and commitment from millennial generation. A resource based approach is adopted in this chapter in which attempt is to engage millennial talent on resources available at various levels (task, interpersonal and organizational level). It will serve as the resource audit for the organizations that whether the current stock of resources is able to engage and retain the young talent. The framework adopted in this chapter is not exhaustive and many other job resources can be included for millennial engagement and retention.

The chapter advances current body of literature in two ways as it incorporates sufficiently the background conditions that have framed the Millennials of the world and moreover has linked job resources as an essential tool to engage and retain this workforce. Job resources informs the readers about the various aspects of organization like intrinsic and extrinsic rewards, social support, HRD practices and Organizational climate that are available with organization to engage and retain this workforce. Millennials may show some heterogeneity but can be tackled effectively with the above mentioned job resources.

Future scope of study is immense as other set of job resources can be put to test to measure their engagement and retention potential that would enrich the scant body of existing literature. Some proportion of generation Y population or younger generation Y is yet to join their workplaces. Their work motivations, needs and expectations remain largely unexplored. The elder category of generation Y employees would have started assuming leadership roles and responsibilities. Research would be of immense help that explore their leadership behaviour.

REFERENCES

Andrew, O. C., & Sofian, S. (2012). Individual factors and work outcomes of employee engagement. *Procedia: Social and Behavioral Sciences*, *40*, 498–508. doi:10.1016/j.sbspro.2012.03.222

Arthur, M. B. (1994). The boundaryless career: A new perspective for organizational inquiry. *Journal of Organizational Behavior*, *15*(4), 295–306. doi:10.1002/job.4030150402

Bakker, A. B., & Demerouti, E. (2007). The job demands-resources model: State of the art. *Journal of Managerial Psychology*, *22*(3), 309–328. doi:10.1108/02683940710733115

Bakker, A. B., Emmerik, H. V., & Euwema, M. C. (2006). Crossover of burnout and engagement in work teams. *Work and Occupations*, *33*(4), 464–489. doi:10.1177/0730888406291310

Basu, K. (2007). India's demographic dividend. *BBC News*. http://news.bbc.co.uk/2/hi/6911544stm

Cavagnaro, E., Staffieri, S., & Postma, A. (2018). Understanding millennials' tourism experience: values and meaning to travel as a key for identifying target clusters for youth (sustainable) tourism. *Journal of Tourism Futures*.

CBI. (2019). *Which trends offer opportunities or pose threats on the European outbound tourism market?* Available at: www.cbi.eu/market-information/tourism/trends/

Cennamo, L., & Gardner, D. (2008). Generational differences in work values, outcomes and person-organisation values fit. *Journal of Managerial Psychology*, *23*(8), 891–906. doi:10.1108/02683940810904385

Deci, W., & Ryan, R. (1985). *Intrinsic Motivation and Self-Determination in Human Behavior*. Springer US. doi:10.1007/978-1-4899-2271-7

Deloitte. (2015). *Mind the gaps: The 2015 Deloitte millennial survey*. Author.

Dwyer, R. J. (2009). Prepare for the impact of the multi-generational workforce! *Transforming Government: People, Process and Policy*, *3*(2), 101-110.

Egri, C. P., & Ralston, D. A. (2004). Generation cohorts and personal values: A comparison of China and the United States. *Organization Science*, *15*(2), 210–220. doi:10.1287/orsc.1030.0048

Ericksson, T. J. (2009). Generational differences between India and the US. *HBR Blog Network. Harvard Business Review*.

Ghosh, R., & Chaudhuri, S. (2009). Intergenerational differences in individualism/collectivism orientations: Implications for outlook towards HRD/HRM practices in India and the United States. *New Horizons in Adult Education and Human Resource Development*, *23*(4), 5–21. doi:10.1002/nha3.10356

Glenn, N. (1977). *Cohort analysis*. Sage.

Gomes, S. B., & Deuling, J. K. (2019). Family influence mediates the relation between helicopter-parenting and millennial work attitudes. *Journal of Managerial Psychology*, *34*(1), 2–17. doi:10.1108/JMP-12-2017-0450

Gursoy, D., Maier, T. A., & Chi, C. G. (2008). Generational differences: An examination of work values and generational gaps in the hospitality workforce. *International Journal of Hospitality Management, 27*(3), 448–458. doi:10.1016/j.ijhm.2007.11.002

Hackman, J. R., & Oldham, G. R. (1980). *Work redesign*. Addison Wesley.

Halbesleben, J. R. (2010). A Meta-Analysis of Work Engagement: Relationships with Burnout, Demands, Resources, and Consequences. In A. B. Bakker & M. P. Leiter (Eds.), *Work Engagement: A Handbook of Essential Theory and Research* (Vol. 8, pp. 102–117). Psychology Press.

Hole, D., Zhong, L., & Schwartz, J. (2010). Talking about whose generation. *Deloitte Review, 6*, 83–97.

International Labor Organization. (2007). *Key indicators of labor market success* (5th ed.). Retrieved January 1, 2009, from http://www.ilo.org/public/english/employment/strat/kilm/download.htm

Jassawalla, A., & Sashittal, H. (2017). How and why Millennials are initiating conflict in vertical dyads and what they are learning: A two-stage study. *International Journal of Conflict Management, 28*(5), 644–670. doi:10.1108/IJCMA-05-2016-0026

Jones, E., Brown, S. P., Zoltners, A. A., & Weitz, B. A. (2005). The changing environment of selling and sales management. *Journal of Personal Selling & Sales Management, 25*(2), 105–111.

Kahn, W. A. (1990). Psychological conditions of personal engagement and disengagement at work. *Academy of Management Journal, 33*(4), 692–724.

Ketter, E. (2020). Millennial travel: tourism micro-trends of European Generation Y. *Journal of Tourism Futures*.

Khera, S. N., & Malik, S. (2017). Conceptualizing and measuring life priorities of Generation Y: Evidences from Indian context. *Industrial and Commercial Training, 49*(2), 80–86. doi:10.1108/ICT-04-2016-0024

Kim, K., Kirkman, B. L., & Chen, G. (2008). Cultural intelligence and international assignment effectiveness: a conceptual model and preliminary findings. In S. Ang & L. Van Dyne (Eds.), *Handbook of Cultural Intelligence: Theory, Measurement, and Applications* (pp. 71–90). M.E. Sharpe.

KPMG. (2017). *Meet the millennials*. Available at: https://home.kpmg/content/dam/kpmg/uk/pdf/2017/04/Meet-the-Millennials-Secured.pdf

Kupperschmidt, B. R. (2000). Multi-generation employees: Strategies for effective management. *The Health Care Manager, 19*(1), 65–76. doi:10.1097/00126450-200019010-00011 PMID:11183655

Lancaster, L. C., & Stillman, D. (2002). When generations collide: who they are. In *Why They Clash. How to Solve the Generational Puzzle at Work*. Harper Collins.

Lee, C. S., Hung, D. K. M., & Ling, T. C. (2012). Work values of Generation Y preservice teachers in Malaysia. *Procedia: Social and Behavioral Sciences, 65*, 704–710. doi:10.1016/j.sbspro.2012.11.187

Ling Lim, H. (2012). Generation Y workforce expectations: Implications for the UAE. *Education, Business and Society, 5*(4), 281–293. doi:10.1108/17537981211284452

Mannheim, K. (1952). The problem of a sociology of knowledge. *Essays on the Sociology of Knowledge*, 134-190.

Murphy, S. A. (2007). *Leading a multi-generational workforce*. available at: http://assets.aarp.org/www.aarp.org_/articles/money/employers/leading_multi-generational _workforce.pdf

Nielsen. (2017). *Young and ready to travel: a look at millennial travelers*. Available at: www.nielsen.com/wp-content/uploads/sites/3/2019/04/nielsen-millennial-traveler-study-jan-2017.pdf

Parekh, B. (2007). Composite culture and multicultural society. In B. Chandra & S. Mahajan (Eds.), *Composite culture in a multi-cultural society*. National Book Trust.

Parry, E., & Urwin, P. (2011). Generational differences in work values: A review of theory and evidence. *International Journal of Management Reviews*, *13*(1), 79–96. doi:10.1111/j.1468-2370.2010.00285.x

Regoniel, P. A. (2016). *How to write a thesis in the information age*. Academic Press.

Reynolds, J., Stewart, M., MacDonald, R., & Sischo, L. (2006). Have adolescents become too ambitious? High school seniors' educational and occupational plans, 1976 to 2000. *Social Problems*, *53*(2), 186–206. doi:10.1525p.2006.53.2.186

Roongrerngsuke, S. (2010). Attracting and retaining multigenerational workforce in China, India, and Thailand. *SHRM Annual conference*. http://sapphire.shrm.org/annualconferenceondemand/2010-annualconference/6292010-attracting-retaining-multigenerationalworkforce-china-india-thai land.aspx

Saks, A. M. (2006). Antecedents and consequences of employee engagement. *Journal of Managerial Psychology*, *21*(7), 600–619. doi:10.1108/02683940610690169

Schaufeli, W. B., & Bakker, A. B. (2004). Job demands, job resources, and their relationship with burnout and engagement: A multi-sample study. *Journal of Organizational Behavior*, *25*(3), 293–315. doi:10.1002/job.248

Schaufeli, W. B., Bakker, A. B., & Van Rhenen, W. (2009). How changes in job demands and resources predict burnout, work engagement, and sickness absenteeism. *Journal of Organizational Behavior*, *30*(7), 893–917. doi:10.1002/job.595

Schneider, B., Gunnarson, S. K., & Niles-Jolly, K. (1994). Creating the climate and culture of success. *Organizational Dynamics*, *23*(1), 17–29. doi:10.1016/0090-2616(94)90085-X

Shimazu, K., Arisawa, T., & Saito, I. (2006, December). Interdisciplinary contents management using 5W1H interface for metadata. In *2006 IEEE/WIC/ACM International Conference on Web Intelligence (WI 2006 Main Conference Proceedings)(WI'06)* (pp. 909-912). IEEE. 10.1109/WI.2006.104

Skinner, H., Sarpong, D., & White, G. R. (2018). Meeting the needs of the Millennials and Generation Z: Gamification in tourism through geocaching. *Journal of Tourism Futures*, *4*(1), 93–104. doi:10.1108/JTF-12-2017-0060

Smith, J. W., & Clurman, A. (1998). *Rocking the ages, the Yankelovich report on generational marketing*. Harper Collins.

Srinivasan, V. (2012). Multi generations in the workforce: Building collaboration. *IIMB Management Review*, *24*(1), 48–66. doi:10.1016/j.iimb.2012.01.004

Strauss, W., & Howe, N. (1991). *Generations: The history of America's future*. William Morrow.

Taylor, C. (2011). *End of the office? Students want the right to work from home.* Mashable Business. Retrieved fromhttp://mashable.com/2011/11/08/work-from-home-2/?mid=530.

Tolbize, A. (2008). Generational differences in the workplace. *Research and Training Center on Community Living, 5*(2), 1-21.

Twenge, J. M. (2007). *Generation Me: Why Today's Young Americans Are More Con-fident, Assertive, Entitled – and More Miserable Than Ever Before*. Free Press.

Twenge, J. M., Campbell, S. M., Hoffman, B. J., & Lance, C. E. (2010). Generational differences in work values: Leisure and extrinsic values increasing, social and intrinsic values decreasing. *Journal of Management*, *36*(5), 1117–1142. doi:10.1177/0149206309352246

Visit Scotland. (2017). *Millennial travelers*. Available at: www.visitscotland.org/binaries/content/ assets/dot-org/pdf/research-papers/millennial-travellers-topic-paper-jan-2017.pdf

Westerman, J. W., & Yamamura, J. H. (2007). Generational preferences for work environment fit: Effects on employee outcomes. *Career Development International*, *12*(2), 150–161. doi:10.1108/13620430710733631

Yu, H. C., & Miller, P. (2005). Leadership style: The X Generation and Baby Boomers compared in different cultural contexts. *Leadership and Organization Development Journal*, *26*(1), 35–50. doi:10.1108/01437730510575570

Zemke, R., Raines, C., & Filipczak, B. (2000). *Generations at Work: Managing the Class of Veterans, Boomers, X-ers, and Nexters in Your Workplace*. Amacon.

Chapter 18
Talent Management as a Part of Sustainable Human Resources Management

Mária Janošková
https://orcid.org/0000-0002-5975-753X
Department of Management in Poprad, Catholic University of Ružomberok, Poprad, Slovakia

Iveta Ubrežiová
Department of Management in Poprad, Catholic University of Ružomberok, Poprad, Slovakia

Katarína Čulková
Technical University of Košice, Slovakia

ABSTRACT

The development of knowledge society and the conception of human capital stimulated creation of a different view to human resources. The key factors of company success are not just material and financial sources; greater attention is given to talents. Human resources present most important strategic assets of a company. Employees that can be marked as "talents" have the greatest importance. Organizations receive talents differently, which is caused by different environments and conditions. Implementation of talent management in practice is not yet distinct, since there is a lack of process idea. The chapter focuses on an overview of the opinions of experts on talent management in literature, identification and evaluation of career building of employees in an industrial company in Slovakia, with suggestions on the application of a talent management model.

INTRODUCTION

"Talent is the most precious sources, appearing in a present modern world"

DOI: 10.4018/978-1-7998-4543-0.ch018

In spite in present time, there is the opinion that most valuable sources for any company are its employees that can create competitive advantage, experts have various views to the human resources management (HRM) which has undergone several phases of its development yet from the on the turn of 19th to 20th century. In the last time in connection with human resources management there are developing also other managerial accesses and conceptions, for example, *Organizational Development, Organizational Behaviour, Quality Management, Change Management, Learning Organization, Knowledge Management, Talent management,* etc. Mainly people, their motivation, putting and engagement in the work, loyalty, qualification, skills, and ideas in their everyday activity help to achieve the goal of the company. Therefore, managers should orientate attention to the obtaining and development of talented people that are extraordinary in their profession and they can be very successful for the company. Not only in the theory but also in the practice we need to find out the answer to questions: *What is talent? How to obtain talent and how to preserve it? Can talents be managed? What is talent management? What is the importance and task of talent management in the company?*

The chapter is orientated to the review of experts' opinions to talent management with a goal to analyze the process of talent management in a selected industrial company in Slovakia, as well as to evaluate and compare it with presented models and other researches. Authors processed a theoretical base according to the available expert and scientific literature sources from domestic and foreign experts presented their opinions and research results about talent management in monographs, scientific journals, international conferences, as well as internet sources. The primary tool is an analysis of available materials and their comparison. Part of the chapter is also a qualitative analysis of the talent management process in the chosen company in Slovakia, elaborated as a case study. In the chapter there is also realized comparing analysis of chosen results of some researches, evaluating using talent management in the business practice in Slovakia.

BACKGROUND

Idea "Talent" is a hundreds-year-old idea and its importance changed during time running. It can be considered from several points of view, mainly from the general point of view (theoretical) from the view of the individual, as well as from the view of the company. Due to the mentioned it is not simply the idea to define clearly, in expert literature there is the existing various definition, while every definition concludes other characteristics. In general level Becker, Fineman, and Freedman (2004) describes talents as „*individuals that can distinguish their organization from others and at the same time they participate greatly on ability of the company to overcome competition";* Armstrong (2009) defines talent as „*individuals, which have special gift, skills, and abilities, and those have important influence to the improvement of the performance of the company*"; Hartl and Hartlová (2010) characterize talent as "*file of skills, regularly considered as inherited, enabling to achieve over average performances in certain area*"; Kursch (2014) marks talent as „*manifested talent, uncovered by successful performances.*" Other authors (Bláha, 2013; Hroník, 2007) characterize talent as „*anybody that contributes to achievement of organization goals, while there is no favoritism of favorited individuals*" (Lewis & Heckman, 2006); Smilansky, 2005) considers talented individual as „*extraordinary able person that gives high performance and at the same time high potential.*" At the same time talent is not limited by age, but its criteria are high performance and it is characterized by perspective (Horváthová, 2011).

From the beginning of 70-ties in 20th Century various conceptions and models, orientated to the talent, started to rise up. Consequently, multidimensional models were introduced, dealing with talent, as well as the mutual influence of personality factors and factors of the environment. Those are, for example, the Renzull model of talent, which as the first modified Mönks model (Mönks, 1992).

Thorne and Pellant (2007) declare that talent means the individual who fills the following criteria:

- has limited ability to keep his attention;
- is curious and he is easily bored;
- determines high goals for himself;
- produces many ideas on how to realize the goals;
- works long and hard, if he enjoys it;
- needs recognition and incentives;
- has a feeling that without him nothing would work.

The number of experts agrees that in case of talented individuals there is many time rising situation when the talented person is maladjusted, he has adaptation problems and uneven development, therefore it is necessary to regard such factors during work with talents (Hatum, 2010).

Although the origins of talent management can be traced back to 1865 (Simonton, 2011) in the fields of arts, sports, and early education. Interest in "talent management" in the business context started to be spoken at the turn of the 20th and 21st Century, when Michaels, Handfield-Jones, and Axelrod (2001) (from organization McKinsey & Company) published book „The War for Talent", according to results of research from 1997. This study suggested that demand for talented employees exceeded the available supply, thus leading to the problem of talent shortage. Several human resource management practitioners recognized the importance of this trend, and as a result, several studies were done in subsequent years by human resource practitioners and consultants to examine talent shortages (Tarique & Schuler, 2010). As a consequence of this, the phrases "talent acquisition, retention and management" and "attracting, retaining, and developing talent" become popular among human resource management community.

In this way new business reality appeared, based on the thinking, emphasizing the importance of talents for the success of organization and competition during obtaining and preserving of talented employees. A new way of thinking consists according to Michaels et al. (2001) conviction that talented people lead the company to higher performance and talent management should be a basic part of HRM. Talent management is said to be critical to organizational success, being able to give a competitive edge through the identification, development, and redeployment of talented employees (Iles, Xin, & Preece, 2010). Talent management started to be used in the practice as a consequence of a need to provide qualitative employees in the organizations, mainly managers. Companies have addressed this question in a variety of ways, ranging from developing leaders in unlikely emerging markets to investing in new technologies for talent gap assessment (Stahl et al., 2012; Tansley, 2011).

According to Armstrong (2009) "talent management", it presents the process of identification, development, recruitment, preserving and engaging of talented people, which organization needs in the present time and in the future. According to Marants (2012), it belongs in the present time to most actual themes of organization operation and to the priority of managers that are dealing with human resources management. Hroník (2007) warns that the idea of "talent management" is important to be distinguished from expert preparation, as well as from the adaptation process. Expert preparation is orientated to the fact that man would be in a given positionable to effectively done work at his position, at which he is acting, or in close future he would be deployed to this position, and adaptation process is orientated to employees that start to work in the company.

Mostly used definitions agree that the talented individual is the one that disposes certain abilities and characteristics or skills and he has the potential for future growth. At the same time talent is visibly reflecting regularly by the way that given individual is extraordinary good in a certain area and he makes his job better than others. Talent management presents by this way a managed system, consisting of activities, from the identification of actual state and determination of target state in the company, single selection of talent, through their further development, observing and stabilization in the company, to the evaluation of the program (Antošová, 2010). Part of the system is not only exceptional rewarding and benefits, but also motivation, possibilities of further education and career growth, creation of the proper working environment, good access of managers, building of honor, respect, etc. that give employees and company space and possibility to develop and use talents (Antošová, Csikósová, & Mihalčová, 2013).

Finally, and most significantly, studies of HR practices have not explicitly investigated how the choice of practices is tied to strategy. Instead, they have simply measured the extent to which practices have varied by industry. According to Wright et al. (2005), variation in HR practices may reflect differences in competitive climates, geographical regions, and socio-economic variables. We believe this to be a significant flaw in establishing talent management as a strategic and value-added term for if practicing talent management, broadly defined, is simply responding to strategic or environmental demands with high-quality HR practices that produce business results then the term talent management, once again, fails to add incrementally to our current understanding of how a highly functioning HR department operates (Lewis & Heckman, 2006).

Research on Talent Management has been lagging behind businesses in offering vision and leadership in the field. After sketching a comprehensive outline of knowledge about talent management, theoretical as well as practical, Al Ariss, Cascio, and Paauwe (2014) discussed methodological issues in the study of talent management and concludes by identifying several key trends that are now and will continue to influence the practice and study of talent management in the future.

The importance of talent management can be perceived from the view of global competitiveness. The rise of emerging economies in recent years has motivated Calls for research into how multinational enterprises translate their corporate strategies to subsidiaries in these countries. Morris, Snell, and Björkman (2016) describe how different types of human capital development from the individual level to the unit level, and then to the firm level in order to build a talent portfolio for the multinational corporation. Depending on the company's strategy (multi-domestic, mega national, transnational), different configurations of the talent portfolio tend to be emphasized and integrated to achieve competitive advantage (Oakes & Galagan, 2011). Implications for theory and practice are discussed, and a research agenda is introduced. They speak also about the necessity to use the knowledge that drives talent decisions. However, in a post-industrial age, what drives talent decisions is the utilization of knowledge (Kogut & Zander, 1993). Knowledge is embedded in people, and the question of how to globally develop and integrate strategic human capital proves to be of both practical and theoretical significance (Morris et al., 2016). Moreover, according to Beamond, Farndale, and Härtel (2016) corporate talent management is affected by metropolitan and provincial institutional and cultural differences, such as level of corporate decision making, community relations, skills shortages, and diversity. They develop propositions pertaining to corporate-local level decision-making, community relations, skills shortages, and diversity, to inform future research and practice.

If the volume of literature in the popular and practitioner press is any guide, practitioners in the field of human resources are now primarily in the business of talent management. Lewis and Heckman (2006) are address question what is talent management and what basis does it have in scientific principles of human resources and management? They outline research that supports a systems-oriented definition of talent management that focuses on the strategic management of talent.

Global talent management was widely accepted by human resource practitioners, consulting firms and professional associations (e.g. Boston Consulting Group, McKinsey & Company, Hay Group, Watson Wyatt Worldwide, Lominger International, Society for Human Resource Management, World Federation of People Management Associations, Manpower Inc., Economist Intelligence Unit, The Chartered Institute of Personnel and Development, the American Council on International Personnel) and academics recently started to examine the talent management phenomena more closely in the last few years. Several special issues of academic journals such at the *Journal of World Business* (Scullion, Collings, & Caligiuri, 2010) and the *Asia Pacific Journal of Human Resource Management* (McDonnell, 2011) and books such as *Global Talent Management* by Scullion et al. (2010) *Strategy-Driven Talent Management* (Silzer & Dowell, 2010) and *Talent Management of Knowledge Employees* (Vaiman et al., 2012) have been published (Tarique & Schuler, 2010). Universities have also been paying attention to global talent management: The graduate business programs at Pace University (New York, USA) and Reykjavik University (Iceland) are examples of academic programs that specifically focus on global talent management.

Although there is a growing consensus that global talent management is an emerging area, there is no consensus regarding the exact definition or boundaries of global talent management, rather there is considerable debate around the definition of them.

TASK, IMPORTANCE, AND CONTRIBUTION OF TALENT MANAGEMENT

In any company, there can be situations, which can negatively influence the business. Successful is only the company, where employees manage to predict such situations and to react to them in ahead. Every company needs, therefore, talented individuals that in spite of the sophisticated business environment and permanent changes in the business influence serious decisions considerably. According to Cannon and McGee (2011) mainly due to the growth of specialization of various disciplines, growth of knowledge, need of permanent innovations, research, etc., there is necessary to find talented people at job market, but mainly to support and motivate own employees in the company, with aim they would impart their knowledge by the way of value-added.

Human resources are in present time key area for any company, mainly from the view of creation and maintaining competitive advantage, therefore it is proper to work with talents systematically. The personal department can help the company also by this way to solve some situation of strategic importance, for example, problems with occupying important positions, when there is lack of qualified people at the job market and in the company and talents are heavily found, and employees with high potential are heavily identified. There can be also problems with how to preserve talented people, the insufficient motivation of employees, etc. (Silzer & Dowell, 2010; Horváthová, 2010).

The task of talent management is to occupy key position by talented individuals, while there are not only managerial positions but also such positions, which are key for the successful operation of the company, as for example specialists that provide high performance of the company (Phillips & Edwards,

2009).On the other hand, despite the growing attention being paid to talent management in the literature, little empirical research has been conducted on applying talent management in various organizations, particularly in small and medium-sized enterprises. Furthermore, SMEs' strategic approach to talent management is limited, with most adopting an ad hoc approach to talent management practices (Egerová, Lančarič, Eger, & Savov, 2015).

In case the company wants and can in ahead to lead and properly introduce talent management, as main contributions and advantages would be as follows:

- Talented individuals will contribute greatly to the achievement of strategy and economic goals.
- The costs of fluctuation and obtaining of new employees would decrease.
- The company is becoming a demanded and attractive employer.
- Planning of succession of key positions is more effective.
- Talented employees are placed at more proper positions and their potential is better used.
- Losses, connected with not occupied key positions in the company are minimized, etc.

The goal of talent management is also to create the fund, consisting of talented, qualified, engaging and loyal individuals, able to contribute to the achievement of present and future demand, so-called talent–pool (Hatum, 2010).

ACCESSES AND MODEL OF TALENT MANAGEMENT

Talent management is currently addressed by many experts, including academics, human resource management specialists in business practice, and consulting and advisory firms, who present the results of their research in different models. Some of these are listed and compared in the following section of the chapter.

Ø Traditional Linear Model

The model is used in organizations that do not have available a sufficient number of talented employees. Its main task is to obtain formal metrics, while the performance of employees is not monitored. According to Berger and Berger (2011), the model is concentrated on two basic activities; mainly obtaining and preserving talented employees, especially when talent is scarce (see Figure 1). This approach does not have sufficient value-added for the organization, its disadvantage is high financial demand, it does not allow employees flexible growth and it does not make a balance between performance and contribution of the employee for the organization. One of the problems is also orientation only to the obtaining and preserving of talented individuals, while the organization neglects deployment and development of talents (Horváthová, 2011).

Figure 1. The traditional linear model of talent management
Source: Horváthová, 2011

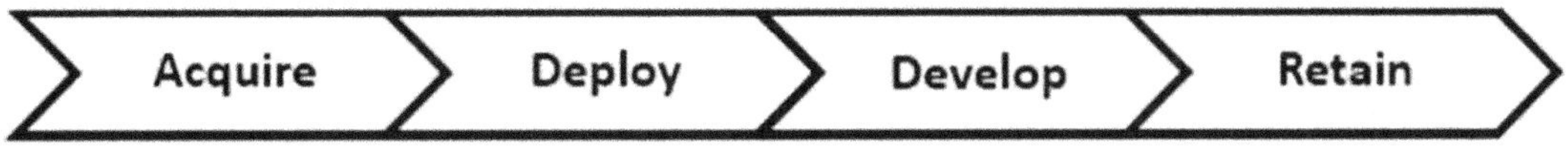

However, the first years of the 21st century show that a fundamental problem for companies is precisely the general lack of talent and skilled labor market professionals, which requires a shift in understanding talent management to the point that if businesses want to maintain their competitiveness in human resources program only for ready talents, but they must seek their talents in the ranks of all their employees and create the conditions for their further development.

Ø Model Develop – Deploy – Connect

Hatum (2010) proposed a model in which the personnel activities are interconnected, in comparison with the traditional model, which uses maximally performance and potential of talented employees (see Figure 2). It mainly considers proper deployment of talents by the way that could develop their skills and potential, their connection with people that enable them to achieve determined goals. This model should be at the core of an organization's talent strategy. By focusing on these three elements, organizations can generate capability, commitment, and alignment in key workforce segments, which in turn improves business performance. When this happens, the attraction and retention of skilled talent largely take care of themselves (Deloitte, 2008).

A study by Deloitte declares also that the model presents a complex approach to talent management. It emphasizes that maximal value can the company achieve in the situation when there are systematic development and motivation of talents in the areas, which contributes to the achievement of strategic goals:

- **Development** means the ability to learn through obtaining skills at working posts or projects (on the job) by the support of the manager, mentor or coach. A talented individual would obtain feedback from others, which enables him to be better identified with the organization.
- **Deployment** means to place the individuals in the organization structure by the way he could have the possibility to work with the best specialists with the aim to identify his knowledge and interests as well as to find the most proper position and to state conditions for filling of the tasks.
- **Connection** means that an employee created a net of relations that would enable him to increase organizational and individual performance and to improve communication and interaction with other employees (Deloitte, 2008).

During the realization of talent management in the practice, companies are many times dealing only with some of the higher mentioned activities, without mutual relations. They invest, for example, a big volume of finances to talents obtaining from external sources, but the care of their future development is already neglected. For effective operation of talent management, all mentioned activities must be in cyclic continuity since they are mutually influencing themselves. Such complexly realized talent management can contribute to the fulfillment of business strategy, but also to the achievement and observing of competitiveness.

Figure 2. Model Develop – Deploy – Connect
Source: Deloitte, 2008

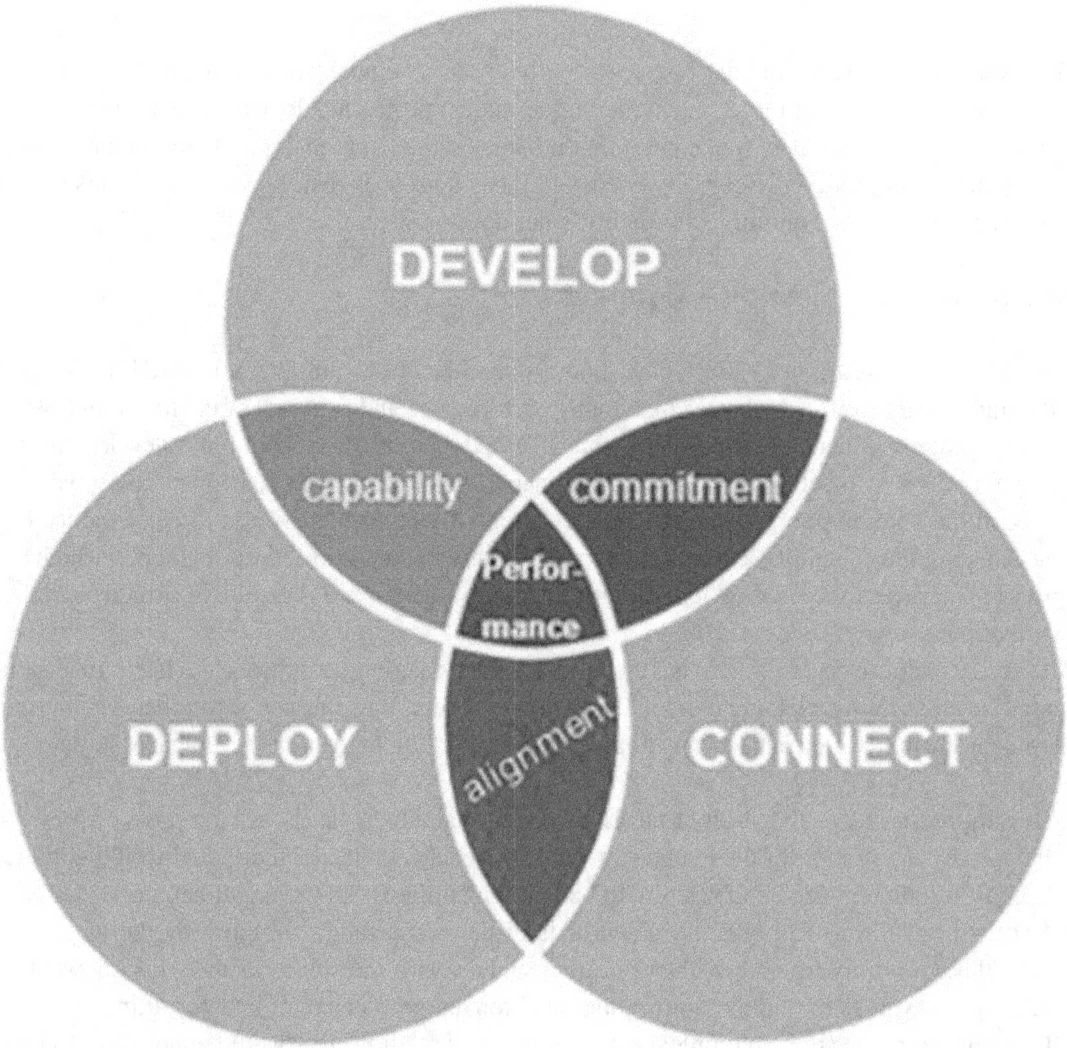

Ø Strategic Human Capital Alignment Model

Part of the model created by The Human Capital Institute (HCI) is the Talent Life Cycle, consisting of a sequence of steps: Plan - Acquire - Engage - Develop - Deploy - Lead - Retain – Evaluate (see Figure 3).

Figure 3. Strategic Aligning & Optimizing Talent Management Practices
Source: American Incite (n.d.)

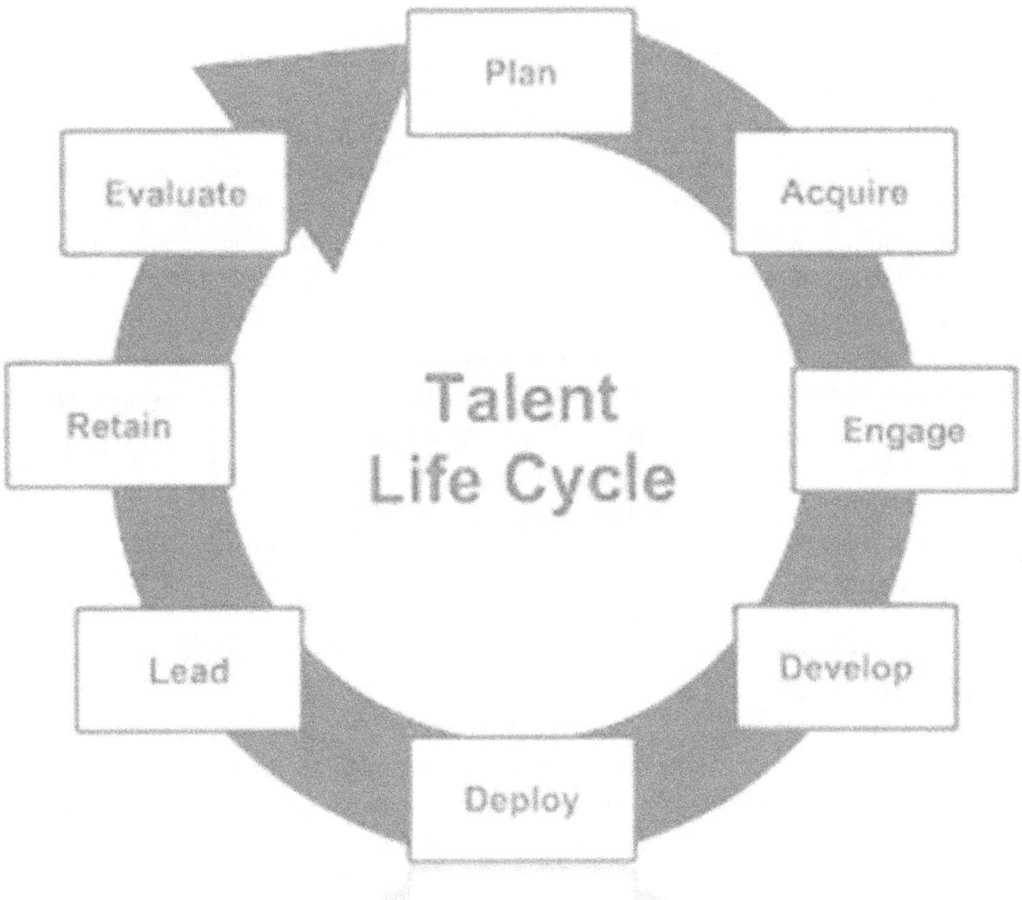

American Incite's (n.d.) use the following process of best practices in Human Capital Management Process coupled with state-of-the-art enabling technology to support measurable talent and business outcomes are achieved.

- **Planning:** start with a comprehensive Human Capital Audit that aligns workforce and that enables the company to build a powerful talent pipeline to Top Performing Teams. Building each department with people engagement with stakeholders at all levels of the enterprise increases job performance, and improves business results.
- **Acquisition:** apply state-of-the-art science and technology; having the ability to attract, select and hire the Right Talent directly impacts ROI and bottom line.
- **Engagement:** according to the Human Capital Institute having and engaging more top performers is a precursor to higher levels of commitment and discretionary effort. It uses the only employment pre-selection instrument that taps the hearts and minds of employees.

- **Development:** Understanding present and future workforce needs are essential to executing a good strategy. American Incite (n.d.) uses a suite of sophisticated pre-employment protocols to align and distribute the Tasks of people and teams. When tasks are distributed properly people more easily achieve higher levels of engagement, performance, and success.
- **Deployment:** the suite of instruments specifically to solve the challenges of deploying the right people into jobs that dovetail with each person's core innate unchanging nature, etc. "The right talent in the right place doing the right things at the right time...all day long."
- **Leadership:** align leadership to the right talent, training, and management skills at all levels. Aligning core capacities to core competencies creates a talent mindset that supports individuals and teams throughout the company. This helps increase performance by creating a talent culture designed to attract, develop, engage, and retain people in jobs they were meant to do and love doing. "Employees join companies... they leave managers."
- **Retention:** aligning core capacities to core competencies makes it much easier to maintain a high rate of renewed attraction. Retention is easier when employees are meaningfully engaged in their work and supported by management. ROI improves and business outcomes increase when a company has tools that enable management to develop organizations staffed with the "right people" doing the "right jobs."
- **Evaluation:** Strategic Talent Alignment drives better business outcomes from high cumulative impacts along the entire talent management chain. More of the right people in the right places inevitably translate into a more productive environment. Investments on the front end of human capital asset management practices result in reduced processing, improved assessment, and the higher-quality selection and a better ROI.

Talents are becoming more and more valuable for companies that want to develop a talent management strategy. They should not only have the knowledge of how to attract and retain the talents that produce the highest value but also according to talents on how to develop an effective strategy for the company. Proactive organizations can use the opportunity by turning their talent management processes into a well-designed talent management strategy. Having the right people, the right team is what differentiates the average from the best competitors.

Ø Integrated talent management

The concept of "Integrated Talent Management" became popular around fifteen years ago, and since then organizations have used this phrase to describe an integrated approach to recruiting, development, performance management, compensation, development planning, and learning (Bersin, 2010). The goal here is not only to make the Human Resources function operates more efficiently, but more importantly to create an "integrated system" for managing people, who let the organization rapidly and effectively respond to business needs (Bersin & Associates, 2010).

Figure 4. Integrated Talent Management
https://joshbersin.com/2010/05/a-new-talent-management-framework/

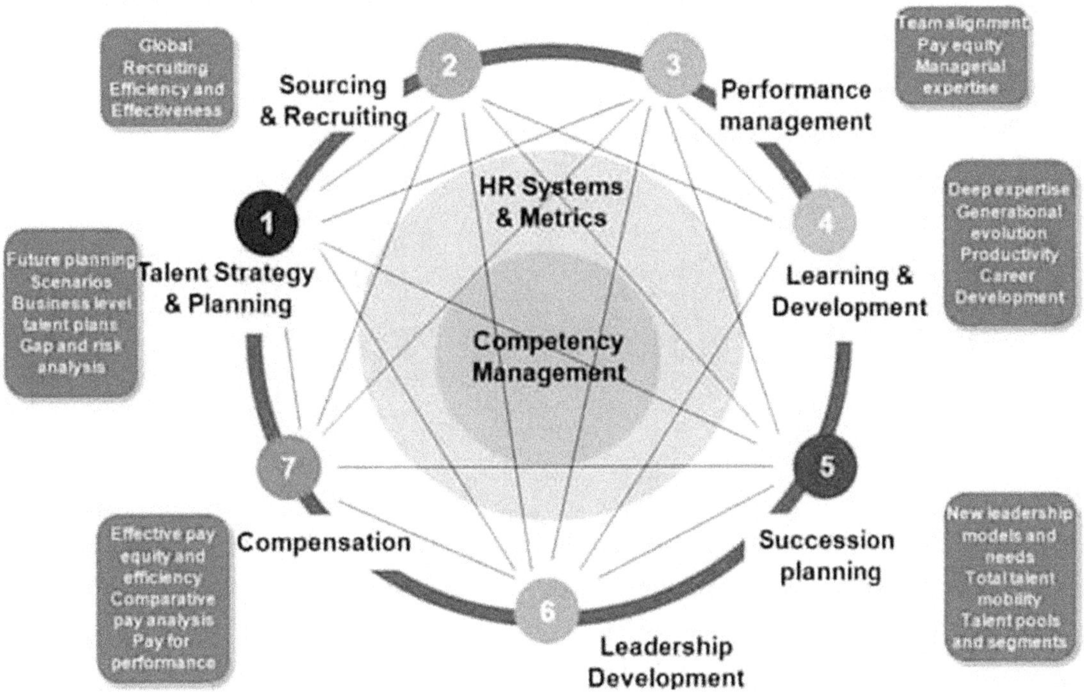

Based on the study of expert resources, available researches, as well as presented models, we incline to believe that in practice it is necessary orientation to talent management not only on finished talent, in the sense that talent development should be concerned only on selected individuals, but real talent development means to develop the strengths of every person and employee. It consists of appreciating diversity and encouraging creativity, originality, and imagination. It is very necessary not only in the discussion of talent development but also in the practice of all organizations (artistic, sports and business) to create the conditions for the development of each individual. Therefore, companies should not pay attention only to a certain part of their human potential.

Process of talent management and its elements

According to Armstrong (2007) process of talent management begins in business strategy, where the goal is to form and maintain qualified, engaging and loyal employees. Elements of talent management are illustrated in Figure 5. The base for proper operation of talent management in the company is a qualitative Human resources strategy, resulting from a business plan. The base is the identification of factors that are key ones for the success of the company and specific needs of talents and their result will be a suggestion of possibilities to satisfy such needs.

Figure 5. Process of talent management and its elements
Source: Armstrong, 2007

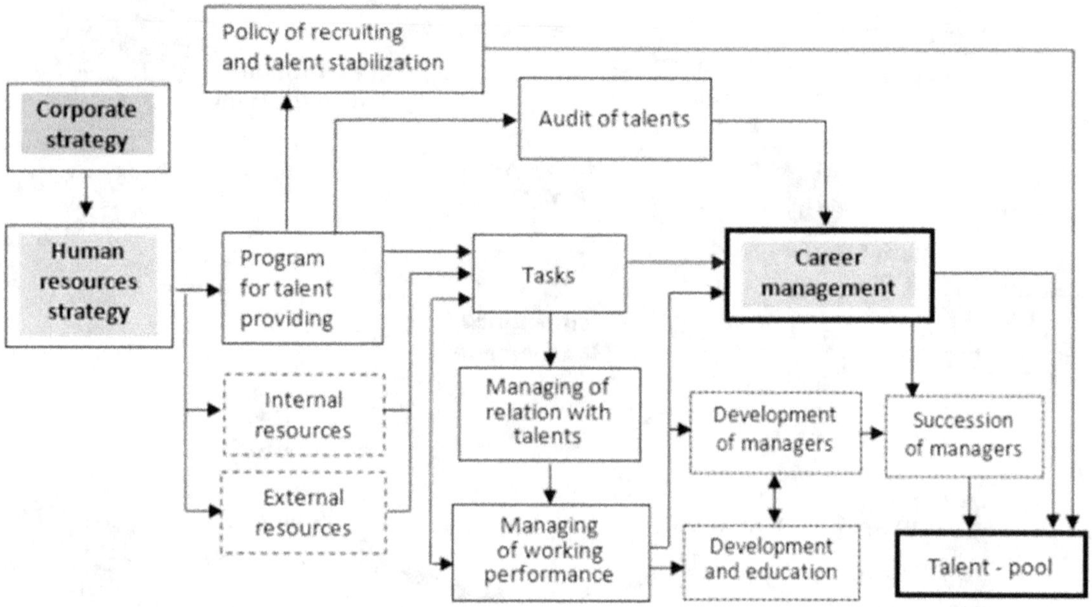

One of the most important tasks of talent management is to stabilize talents, which means to achieve that talented employees would not leave the company, and in this way, it would prevent using obtained knowledge and skill in other companies. Also due to the mentioned company should create a proper motivation environment, which would provide the best conditions for its employees. In the case of the company that would succeed to maintain talented individuals, it will also manage to decrease costs of development and recruitment of new employees. The whole process of talent management is proper to finish by evaluation through an audit, or through evaluation of key indexes. According to the mentioned company can obtain feedback, and evaluate the effectiveness of talent management, or remove shortages.

TALENT MANAGEMENT IN INDUSTRIAL COMPANY - EVIDENCE FROM SLOVAKIA

The following part of the chapter presents an analysis and evaluation of processes for a building of employees´ careers in a big industrial company in Slovakia and consequent suggestion of application of Talent management model.

The selection of the research object results from the fact that it is the largest industrial company in Slovakia, with a significant share of employment and impact on the community. The selected object of our research is an integrated metallurgical enterprise with a tradition of more than 50 years in Slovakia. The metallurgical industry has presented a great influence on the national economy of Slovakia. Since 1998, the parent company has been the world's leading steel producer United States Steel Corporation, a multinational company. The company belongs to important employers, with a number of employees around

9.900, he has in the region good employer´s image, it provides for its employees' financial evaluation and over standard benefits. The company achieved in 2018 net profit of 127 mils. EUR, when the profit of the whole group presented 89 mils. EUR. The rate of industrial production on national productivity is in the last period 20%, while the company presents a significant rate on the industry, together with the automotive and gas industry. The employment in the steel and processing industry presents around 23% when the company participates at the rate the most.

The company pays great attention to the issues of human resources management development, from the preparation of the next generation of employees through the support of pupils at secondary schools and universities and motivation management to the education and development of employees. Particular emphasis is given to the safety and health of employees, which is promoting as a key value. Enhancing the skills of the talented workforce, promoting diversity and an inclusive work environment, and developing a culture of care, are the pillars of the new corporate human resources strategy. In order to maintain the unique knowledge and skills of key employees, the company has implemented a program aimed at sharing knowledge and skills. To develop the potential of talent and prepare the selected employees for the future, the company introduced plans of successions, which begins by identifying employees with high growth potential and continues with the development program.

Through qualitative analysis, we found out that some activities of talent management are realized in cooperation with the Department of HRM and managers in the frame of performance managing. It means that during management or evaluation of working performance individual managers suggest at the same time activities for the development of individuals´ careers.

Planning of talents in the company is perceived as a process, orientated mainly to the emphasizing of fact that development and education are key priorities of every manager. The main task in talent planning is given to direct supervisors, which have the interest to support the development of employees, mainly through providing possibilities for employees with an aim to extend their knowledge and skills that will be necessary for filling their job. The goal of talent planning is to provide development possibilities for talented and ambitious individuals in the company.

The process during the realization of talent management in the company is distributed by a plan to individual months in a calendar year, as it is illustrated in Figure 6:

- At the beginning of a calendar year, the manager announces main priorities for the following year to every member of the team; he finalizes his goals of performance and puts them to the information system Talent management. At the same time, he cascades goals to other members of the team.
- The manager requests employees to formulate their goals of the performance (3-6 goals), and at the same time, he discussed with them, how their goals are connected and contributed to the achievement of the priorities.
- Employees cooperate with their managers with an aim to make goals to be connected with business strategy, with an orientation to the main priorities that could help to achieve sustainable profitability.

Figure 6. Planning of the talent management process in the company

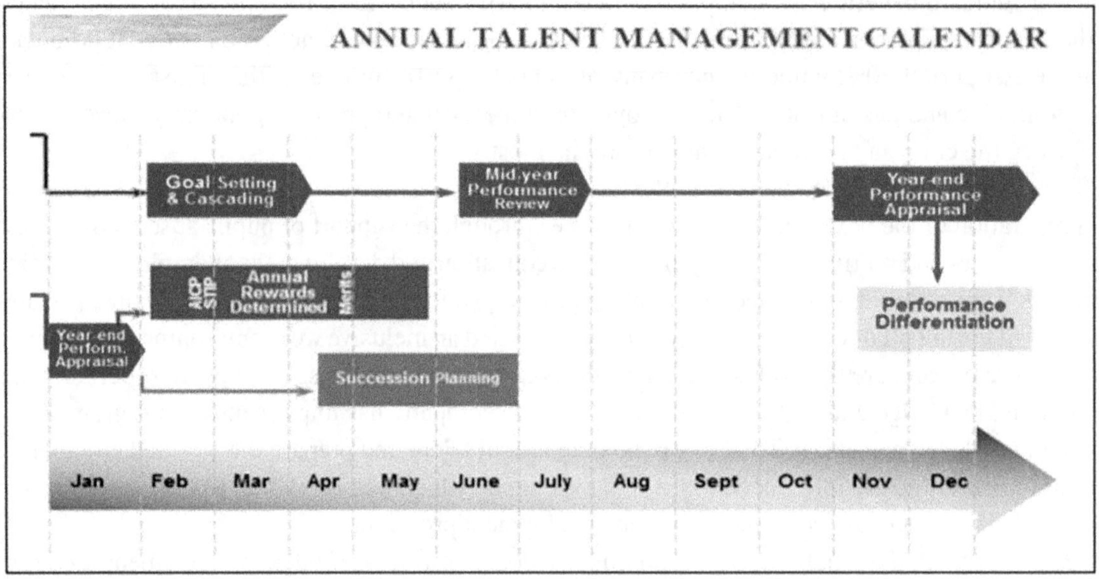

The performance of the employees is measured by filling their annual goals that define main activities. Evaluation is made by managers in a biannual interval in the three following steps:

1. The manager evaluates the goals and competencies of an employee; he prepares formulary and plans discussion with the employee to a biannual evaluation.
2. The manager leads a discussion with an employee after the redefinition of the goals manager writes results to the formulary in the information system and sends them to the employee.
3. The employee adds his commentary, suggestions, and comments to the formulary in the information system; he confirms a document and closes the evaluation.

Year-end evaluation of the performance there is added self-evaluation of the employee that after filling in the information system is sent to the manager. The manager adds to the evaluation formulary his evaluation of all employees with commentary, and he suggests meeting with them. Consequently, the discussion with evaluated employees is executed, after which a manager will send an electronic formulary to the employee. The employee will confirm formulary and finish evaluation in the information system.

Such setting of the system has certain advantages, but also shortages. Among advantages belong fact that the company would obtain talented employees from internal resources, which the company knows already from the view of their engaging in, the work, their working performance, motivation and relation to the employer. Advantages during the regular evaluation of working performance are also regularity of determined goals evaluation and suggestion for educational activities for a further period. To the shortages belong forming of policy for obtaining and stabilization of talents in connection to Human resources strategy and systematic planning of talents, which means mistake in identification or determining of working positions that are the key factors for proper operation of the company, where talented people are supposed to be applied. The shortage is also a regular audit of talents that shows the necessity of talents with potential, and that would be a base for planning and development of the chosen individuals' career. Disadvantages are also finding that in the present time the company is limited by the selection of talents among top managers, and the company is not looking for potential at other levels of management and among experts or specialists. The problem is also that in the present time company is given emphasis only to achieved results of the employees and not regarding their personal assumptions and potential that could present key elements for the future development of the company.

Figure 7. Rate of activities at the Human resources department on processes of staffing, education and talent management

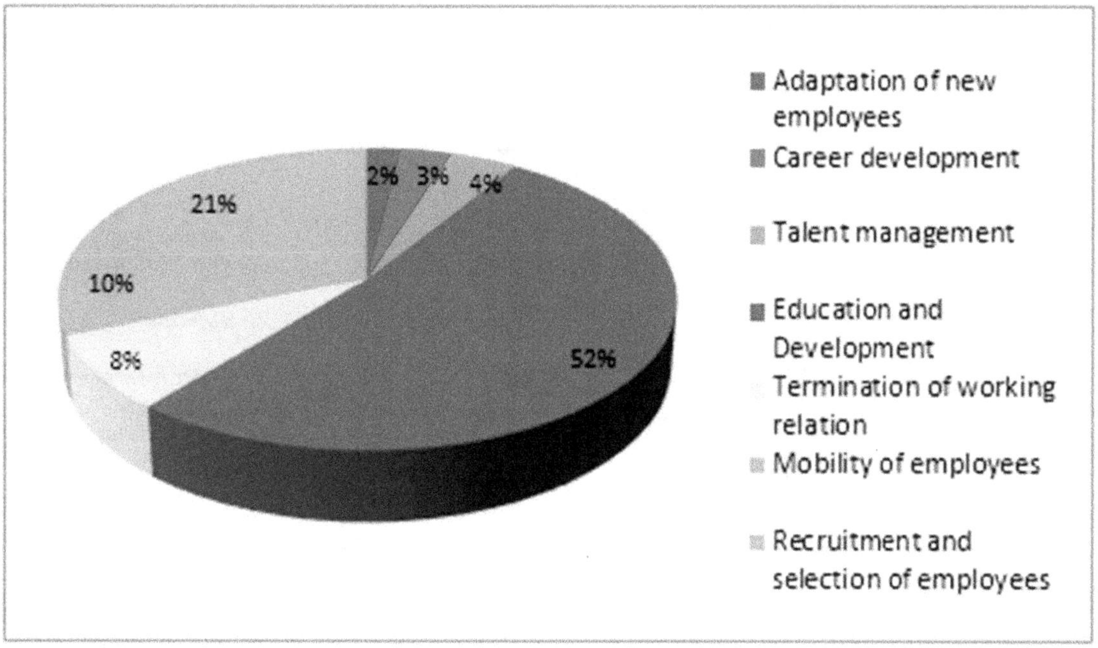

Results and Discussion

Based on the presented literature review, selected talent management models and the above results of the analysis of the talent management process of the selected company, we conclude that the company in Slovakia uses the Develop-Deploy-Connect model. The talent management process is also supported by a corporate strategy that aims to shape and retain qualified and committed employees. However, there is no strategic talent management in the company.

In practice, the company should have defined what is the content of talent management that is part of the business and personal strategy. In this case, there is necessary mainly:

- To determine the goals of talent management;
- To identify or to select talented employees and to orientate to their development;

- To create a structure of talent management, orientated to the development of key abilities and to install rules for talent management process that will be acceptable for all employees;
- To orientate to proper placement of human resources (mainly talents) to working posts and to create an excellent working post;
- To enable connection with the aim, talented employees could create the net of relations that would enable an increase in organizational and individual performance and improve communication and interactivity with others.

Figure 8. Comparing individual processes rate and activities at HR Department

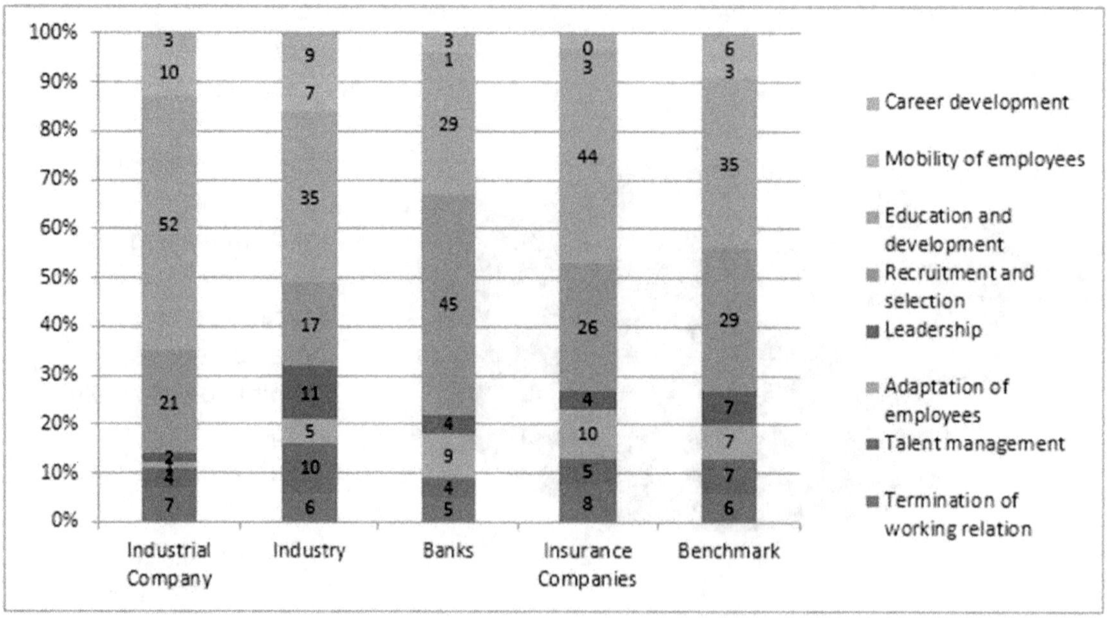

Integrated talent management presents the most suitable model for application in current practice, but especially for sustainability in the future, which means it should be part of an integrated HRM system that enables the company to respond quickly and effectively to business needs.

It is important for the company to be perceived as an attractive employer in the labor market, compared to the competition. Only in this way the company could provide that talented individuals will want to remain its employees, they will want to work for the company. In this way the company will obtain qualified, engaging employees, which would be better stabilized for a longer period.

In addition to the analysis of single talent management processes, we also focused on the analysis of the share of human resources activities in the processes of staffing, education and talent management in the company. Figure 7 illustrates that yet 52% is dealing with education and development, while talent management is given only 4% time, 3% is dealing with career development and 2% means the adaptation of new employees. Workers at the Human resources department deals with other activities of staffing yet 39%, from which 21% means recruitment and selection of employees, 10% is for mobility and 8% for termination of employment.

Mentioned facts had been compared with data from Deloitte Slovakia in 2015, according to which we found out that in analyzed company talent management process is dealt with 6% less than average in the industry, similarly as the process of development of employees´ career. On the other hand, the process of education and development of employees is dealt with yet by 17% more times than average in the industry, as well as in comparison with other sectors (see Figure 8).

Present talent management is not only choosing the best from good, but it finds also mostly hidden potential that is actively formed in accord with the interest of the company. It is concentrating on the recruitment of proper people, with which company further works with an aim to support business strategy. Skillful managers are finding proper ways how to connect internal talent to the goals by the way the process could bring positive results (Kostiviarová & Lutter, 2015). But most important is to provide that talent management would not be underestimated as a contribution to the competition, but be motivated to remain and given a performance for the company that formed the talent. From the point of view in the relation between talent management and practice, higher levels of entrepreneurial intentions are confirmed among males and among students from entrepreneur families (Lančarič, Ubrežiová, Savov, & Kozáková, 2018).

In spite yet in Slovakia there are Professional and advisory agencies that offer the company programs for talent management, tailored to their needs, in business practice, this is a rather exceptional situation. Similarly, it is in area of expert literature some authors present their opinions, supported by research results at the scientific conferences (for example Savov & Lančarič, 2018; Stacho, Stachová, & Gubíniová, 2016; Papula, Volná, Pilková, & Huľvej, 2013), in scientific journals (Horváthová, 2010; Štefko & Sojka, 2014; Stacho, Stachová, & Papula, 2018) and sometimes also in monographs (Horváthová, 2011; Savov, 2019). According to the research of Savov (2019) realized in companies in Slovakia in 2018 at the sample with 381 companies, the biggest influence to the level of talent management has economic results of the company (companies with improving economic results register also a higher level of talent management in their environment), level of talent management of foreign capital (companies with foreign participation have a higher level of implemented talent management) and also existence of human sources department. The least influence on talent management has ownership of the company and its volume. A strong part of talent management in Slovakia can be an understanding of talent management as a prevailing part of human sources strategy. Evaluation of talents is realized systematically, while there are resulting from conclusions, proper for the planning of talented individual's development and during the promotion of employees, there are considered also their over average abilities. On the other hand, the weak side is minimum activities for obtaining talents, planning of carrier growth is not sufficient, and there is a shortage of financial sources for talent development. In this way, there are many times an outflow of talents to other companies.

Results of qualitative analysis of talent management in chosen industrial company in Slovakia had been compared with results of mentioned research according to chosen criteria, which mean volume of the company, participation at the foreign capital, economic results, existence of human sources department, strategy of talent management, process of individual phases of talent management process. From the results of the comparison results that realization of talent management is very similar to in other big companies with foreign participation in Slovakia. One of the reasons are also verified processes, running in parent companies abroad. But as a critical phase can be considered talent development, connected with investment to the human capital, when important factors in this sense present economic results of the company (which means during worsening economic results company decreases sources, determined for employees' development). The same is true of retaining talents for the future; good economic results allow the company to motivate employees and to offer them interesting benefits. Companies must be interested in holding qualitative talented people in the creation of a great working environment for the employees, which could increase the quality of life.

CONCLUSION

Talent management practice within an organization is a human resource strategy that seeks to acquire, develop, deploy and retain talented and high potential employees. Although talent management practices are applied in different companies across the world, they can only contribute optimally to business performance if both top management and employees are aligned on objectives and implementation of talent management in the organization. The objective of talent management implies an organization's capability to create the talent resources and to attract, develop and retain them for executing the organizational business strategy. Organizations can gain success by matching the right talented people to their right roles. Getting the best talent and keeping it are becoming intensely competitive (Dawn & Biswas, 2013).

The area of human resources management is changing from the view of its quality in the time in connection with changes in other areas of organizations´ management. Results of changes are different in individual countries, as well as individual companies, prevailingly according to how high priority this area has for top management. In spite also, in the area of human resources management, there is a number of interesting areas that are many times mutually connected, in the present time there are published few results about the application of talent management in practice in Slovakia. The goal of future research is to find out if in present time talent management presents effective choice in human resources management in industrial companies in Slovakia. The aim will be to find out, if talent management belongs among priorities of human resources management if it is part of personal strategy, which model of talent management has company introduced, etc. The interest is to know how talent management influences other personal activities, but also what is its influence on the employees' fluctuation or total success of the company.

Taking the long term strategic approach to talent management will have a huge impact on the companies in the future. Thus meeting future business challenges primarily requires the adoption of proper practices for talent acquisition, development, deployment, and retention. Savov & Lančarič (2018) state that it is necessary to improve the awareness of the strategic impact of human resources in enterprises, top management must have a clear attitude towards talent management. We propose to develop a clear structure of long-term human resources management objectives based on the company's mission and corporate goals.

We expect that in close future present approach to talent management would change in theory, but and mainly in practice of companies and organizations not only in the world but also in Slovakia (Papula et al., 2013). Except for companies that should deal with the training of their own talents and management of their career can be done by using more new innovative ways of work, for example by work with social media. Innovation technologies, global access and finding of talents, for example through net LinkedIn speak about the flexibility of talented people about possibilities of their applying, mainly in multinational corporations.

Talent management needs to be viewed from a broader perspective; it is more than just achieving the company's goals. Talent management includes a strategy that values the knowledge, skills, attitudes, and skills of the company´s employees to help ensure success. It also means supporting and developing a strategy for better results, building a motivating environment where they have the opportunity to improve their skills and develop their personality, with the assumption of sustainability for the future. In this way, it assumes e.g. reducing the cost, time and effort of finding external candidates that the business may need in the future. Employees are likely to do their maximum, which would lead to higher job satisfaction as well as organizational efficiency and performance.

This could change the traditional role of human resources experts from the supervisory and management functions to the development and maintenance of sufficient talents. Managers are not only expected to work together, but to be able to specify goals and enable their achievement by the creation of a healthy working environment, orientated to the growth when people are willing to actively and enthusiastically accept the challenges of their work.

Effective use of talented workers is seen as the most important factor in achieving business goals. In order to meet the expectations, there is necessary an active role of talent management professionals in understanding the needs, aspirations, and interests of employees, motivating and developing skilled employees, a positive corporate culture and the introduction of programs that reflect and support the basic values of the business. Continuous changes in the globalized business environment affect the management of human resources and hence talent management, for example during an increasing number of employees, the company should pay attention to their requirements, create a qualitative and motivating working environment, in order to retain qualitative employees for the future. The need of managers to meet employees' expectations is a challenge for effective leadership, and participative management, in which employees are involved in the management and decision-making processes because of their talent that the company cannot afford to lose.

ACKNOWLEDGMENT

The publication of this article is supported by the Slovak Agency VEGA project 1/0651/18 *"Research of institutional environment influence to the corporate social responsibility, consumers´satisfaction and performance of the company"*, project 1/0280/21 "*Expansion of research in the area Corporate Social Respoinsibility to sustainable Human Resource Management, with an emphasis on Intellectual capital*", and by Slovak Agency KEGA project 005SPU-4/2019 *"Theory and Practice of the International Management and Entrepreneurship in Multicultural Environment."* Financial support from this Ministry of Education's scheme is also gratefully acknowledged.

REFERENCES

Al Ariss, A., Cascio, W. F., & Paauwe, J. (2014). Talent management: Current theories and future research directions. *Journal of World Business*, *49*(2), 173–179. doi:10.1016/j.jwb.2013.11.001

American Incite. (n.d.). *Strategic Talent Acquisition & Team Alignment.* Retrieved from http://www.americanincite.com/talent-life-cycle/

Antošová, M. (2010). Human resource management and organizational development as a basic for the knowledge management. *Acta Montanistica Slovaca*, *15*(1), 90–95.

Antošová, M., Csikósová, A., & Mihalčová, B. (2013). Application knowledge management in the practice of business subjects in Slovakia. *Procedia: Social and Behavioral Sciences, 83*, 975–979. doi:10.1016/j.sbspro.2013.06.181

Armstrong, M. (2007). *Řízení lidských zdrojů: nejnovější trendy a postupy.* Prague: Grada Publishing.

Armstrong, M. (2009). *Armstrong's handbook of human resource management practice.* Kogan Page.

Beamond, M. T., Farndale, E., & Härtel, Ch. E. J. (2016). MNE translation of corporate talent management strategies to subsidiaries in emerging economies. *Journal of World Business, 51*(4), 499–510. doi:10.1016/j.jwb.2016.01.002

Becker, C. D., Fineman, M. R., & Freedman, R. J. (2004). *Best Practices in Talent Management from a Study of American and European Multinationals.* Retrieved on October 15, 2019, from www.ircounselors.org/irconcepts/ 2004winter.html

Berger, L. A., & Berger, D. R. (2011). *The Talent Management Handbook. Creating a Sustainable Competitive advantage by Selecting, Developing and promoting the best people.* McGraw-Hill.

Bersin, J. (2010). *A new Talent Management Framework.* Retrieved November 17, 2019, from https://joshbersin.com/2010/05/a-new-talent-management-framework/

Bláha, J. (2013). *Pokročilé řízení lidských zdrojů.* Brno: Edika.

Cannon, J. A., & McGee, R. (2011). *Talent Management and Succession Planning.* CIPD.

Dawn, S. K., & Biswas, S. (2013). Talent Management: Designing Strategies. *ASBM Journal of Management, 6*(2), 41–51.

Deloitte. (2004). *It's 2008: Do You Know Where Your Talent Is? Why Acquisition and Retention Strategies Don't Work.* Retrieved on November 15, 2019, from http://www.deloitte.com/assets/

Egerová, D., Lančarič, D., Eger, L., & Savov, R. (2015). Perspectives of talent management: Evidence from Czech and Slovak business organizations. *Economics and Management, 18*(4), 108–120. doi:10.15240/tul/001/2015-4-008

Hartl, P., & Hartlová, H. (2010). Velký psychologický slovník. Prague, CZ. *Portal (Baltimore, Md.).*

Hatum, A. (2010). *Next generation talent management. Talent management to survive turmoil.* Palgrave Macmillan., doi:10.1057/9780230295094

Holt, C. (2010). *Building a Talent Management strategy.* Retrieved on November 13, 2019, from www.slideshare.net/Proesce/proesce-building-a-talent-management-strategy

Horváthová, P. (2010). Talent management a jeho využití při řízení lidských zdrojů v organizaci. *Central European Review of Economic, 13*(2), 77–95.

Horváthová, P. (2011). Talent management. Prague: Wolters Kluwer.

Hroník, F. (2007). *Rozvoj a vzdělávání pracovníků: základy moderní personalistiky.* Grada Publishing.

Iles, P., Xin, C. A., & Preece, D. (2010). Talent Management and HRM in Multinational companies in Beijing: Definitions, differences and drivers. *Journal of World Business*, *45*(2), 179–189. doi:10.1016/j.jwb.2009.09.014

Kostiviarová, Z., & Lutter, J. (2015). *Cesta k efektívnejšiemu fungovaniu HR. Výsledky prieskumu HR Benchmarking 2015*. Deloitte.

Kursch, M. (2014). Management Tool "Talent management". *Promanager*. Retrieved on November 12, 2019, from www.promanager.sk/hr-management/

Lančarič, D., Ubrežiová, I., Savov, R., & Kozáková, J. (2018). Entrepreneurial intentions of students: a case of Slovakia. In E. Horská, Z. Kapsdorferová, & M. Hallová (Eds.), International scientific days 2018. Towards Productive, Sustainable and Resilient Global Agriculture and Food Systems (pp. 1954-1967). Prague: Wolters Kluwer.

Lewis, R. E., & Heckman, R. J. (2006). Talent management: A critical review. *Human Resource Management Review*, *16*(2), 139–154. doi:10.1016/j.hrmr.2006.03.001

Marants, J. (2012). The Evolution of Integrated Talent Management. *Institute for Human Resources*. Retrieved on November 12, 2019, from https://www.hr.com/en?t=/documentManager/sfdoc.file.supply&fileID=1341425076525

McDonnell, A. (2011). Still Fighting the "War for Talent"? Bridging the Science Versus Practice Gap. *Journal of Business and Psychology*, *26*(2), 169–173. doi:10.100710869-011-9220-y

Michaels, E., Hanfield-Jones, H., & Axelrod, B. (2001). *The War for Talent*. Harvard Business Press.

Mönks, F. J. (1992). Development of the gifted child: The issue of identification and programmimg. In F. J. Monks & W. Peters (Eds.), *Talent for the future* (pp. 191–202). Mastricht.

Morris, S., Snell, S., & Björkman, I. (2016). An architectural framework for global talent management. *Journal of International Business Studies*, *47*(6), 723–747. doi:10.1057/jibs.2015.25

Oakes, K., & Galagan, P. (2011). *The executive guide to integrated talent management*. ASTD Press.

Papula, J., Volná, J., Pilková, A., & Huľvej, J. (2013). Analysis of Awareness and Priorities, Focused on Intellectual Capital Among Slovak Companies. In B. Janiūnaitė, A. Pundziene, & M. Petraite (Eds.), *Proceedings of the 14th European conference on knowledge management* (vol. 1-2, pp. 517-526). Reading, UK: ACPI.

Phillips, J., & Edwards, L. (2009). Managing talent retention: an ROI approach. San Francisco, CA: Pfeiffer essential resources for training and HR professionals.

Savov, R. (2019). *Talent manažment v podnikoch na Slovensku*. SPU.

Savov, R., & Lančarič, D. (2018). Factors influencing strategic approach to talent management of companies in Slovakia. In E. Horská, Z. Kapsdorferová, & M. Hallová (Eds.), International scientific days 2018. Towards Productive, Sustainable and Resilient Global Agriculture and Food Systems (pp. 1307-1319). Prague: Wolters Kluwer. doi:10.15414/isd2018.s5.13

Scullion, H., Collings, D. G., & Caligiuri, P. (2010). Global talent management. *Journal of World Business, 45*(2), 105–108. doi:10.1016/j.jwb.2009.09.011

Silzer, R., & Dowell, B. E. (2010). *Strategy-driven Talent Management: A leadership imperative*. Jossey-Bass.

Simonton, D. K. (2011). Exceptional talent and genius. In T. Chamorro-Premuzic, S. von Stumm, & A. Furnham (Eds.), *The Wiley-Blackwell handbook of individual differences* (pp. 635–655). Wiley-Blackwell., doi:10.1002/9781444343120

Smilansky, J. (2005). *The Systematic Management of Executive Talent*. Hydrogen.

Stacho, Z., Stachová, K., & Papula, J. (2018). The changes in the focus of Slovak organisations on talent management. *Verslas teorija ir praktika, 19*(3-4), 255-260. doi:10.3846/btp.2018.25

Stacho, Z., Stachová, Z., & Gubíniová, K. (2016). Implementation of Talent Management as Motivation for High-potential Employees. In M. Blašková, R. Blaško, A. Sokół, & V. Gražulis (Eds.), *13th International Scientific Conference "Human potential development"* (pp. 240-247). Szczecin: University of Szczecin.

Stahl, G. K., Björkman, I., Farndale, E., Morris, S. S., Paauwe, J., Stiles, P., Trevor, J., & Wright, P. (2012). Six Principles of Effective Global Talent Management. *Sloan Management Review, 53*(2), 25–42.

Štefko, R., & Sojka, L. (2014). Position of Talent Management in Context Organizational Functions. *European Scientific Journal, 1*(SI), 346-356.

Tansley, C. (2011). What do we mean by the term „talent" in talent management? *Industrial and Commercial Training, 43*(5), 266–274. doi:10.1108/00197851111145853

Tarique, I., & Schuler, R. S. (2010). Global talent management: Literature review, integrative framework, and suggestions for further research. *Journal of World Business, 45*(2), 122–133. doi:10.1016/j.jwb.2009.09.019

Thorne, K., & Pellant, A. (2007). *Rozvíjíme a motivujeme zaměstnance: výběr, trénink a podpora rozvoje nejlepších*. Computer Press.

Vaiman, V., Scullion, H., & Collings, D. (2012). Talent management decision making. *Management Decision, 50*(5), 925–941. doi:10.1108/00251741211227663

Wright, P. M., & Haggerty, J. J. (2005). Missing variables in theories of strategic human resource management: Time, cause, and individuals. *Management Review, 16*(2), 164–173.

ADDITIONAL READING

Antošová, M. (2012). Managerial perspective of knowledge management in a company. Ostrava, CZ: VŠB-TU Ostrava.

Antošová, M., & Csikosová, A. (2011). Intellectual capital in context of knowledge management. In P. Pachura (Ed.), The Economic Geography of Globalization (pp. 113-142). Rijeka, CR: InTech. doi:10.5772/19186

Čulková, K., Hrehová, D., & Janošková, M. (2017). Business competencies of non-economist's students in conditions of slovakian universities. In P. Madzik (Ed.), *The Poprad Economic and Management Forum 2017* (pp. 150-161). Poprad, SK: VERBUM.

Janošková, M., Bardiovský, G., & Ondrík, B. (2016). Improving the quality of human resources services in the steel company through modern information technologies. *Quality - Access to Success*, *17*(155), 120–124.

Kozáková, J., Savov, R., Lančarič, D., & Ubrežiová, I. (2018). Entrepreneurship education at Slovak University of Agriculture in Nitra: a focus group study. In F. Bylok, A. Albrychiewicz-Słocińska, & L. Cichobłaziński (Eds.), *ICoM 2018 - Leadership, innovativeness and entrepreurship in a sustainable economy* (pp. 378–383). Czestochowa University of Technology.

Ubrežiová, I., Moravíková, K., & Kozáková, J. (2016). Corporate social responsibility as an aspect of business ethics in selected Slovak companies. In *The agri-food value chain: challenges for natural resources management and society* (pp. 296–304). Slovak University of Agriculture.

KEY TERMS AND DEFINITIONS

Career: A developmental sequence of occupations that a person carries out during his or her working life on the basis of deliberate decisions related to his professional interests and business needs, as well as certain coincidences and opportunities.

Human Capital: A certain state of competence, knowledge, creativity, social and personality characteristics that are embedded in the ability to work to produce economic value; it is an economic view of people, employees of the company.

Human Resources Management: The part of management in an organization that deals with the provision and formation of the workforce which includes employment, work performance management, motivation and remuneration, education and development, career management, social policy, etc.

Industrial Company: A legal entity, a socio-economic entity that employs people; it uses its material and financial resources to carry out business activities in the industry of the national economy. Managers and employees of the company share a common purpose, unite the focus of talents and resources on achieving specific accepted goals.

Knowledge: The knowledge acquired through learning, memorized and understood facts or relationships between them; which reflect the knowledge of objective reality in the consciousness of the person who has acquired it.

Talent: The file of skills of the person, regularly considered as inherited, enabling to achieve over average performances in a certain area; a talented individual disposes certain abilities, characteristics or skills and he has the potential for future growth.

Talent Management: A managed process of identifying, developing, recruiting, retaining and deploying talented people that the organization needs in the present and will need in the future to meet its goals.

Compilation of References

Aaker, D. (1991). *Managing brand equity: Capitalizing on the value of a brand name*. Free Press.

Abdollahi, A., Rezaeian, A., & Mohseni, M. (2008). Knowledge strategy: Linking knowledge resources to competitive strategy. *World Applied Sciences Journal*, *4*, 8–11.

Abhari, K., Davidson, E., & Xiao, B. (2019). Collaborative innovation in the sharing economy. *Internet Research*, *29*(5), 1014–1039. doi:10.1108/INTR-03-2018-0129

Abraham, J., & Trimutiasari, M. (2015). Sociopsychotechnological predictors of individual's social loafing in virtual team. *International Journal of Electrical and Computer Engineering*, *5*(6), 1500–1510. doi:10.11591/ijece.v5i6.pp1500-1510

Accenture. (2016). *People first: The primacy of people in a digital age - redictable disruption: Looking to digital ecosystems for the next waves of change*. Retrieved from https://www.accenture.com/_acnmedia/PDF-36/Accenture-Tech-Vision-Malaysian-Perspective.pdf#zoom=50

Acemoglu, D., & Robinson, J. A. (2012). *Why Nations Fail: The Origins of Power, Prosperity, and Poverty*. Crown Publishers.

Acquier, A., Daudigeos, T., & Pinkse, J. (2017). Promises and paradoxes of the sharing economy: An organizing framework. *Technological Forecasting and Social Change*, *125*, 1–10. doi:10.1016/j.techfore.2017.07.006

Adler, N. J. (1991). *International Dimensions of Organizational Behavior* (2nd ed.). PWS-Kent Publishing Co.

Afuah, A., & Tucci, C. L. (2001). *Internet business models and strategies*. McGraw-Hill, Irwin.

Agogué, M., Berthet, E., Fredberg, T., Le Masson, P., Segrestin, B., Stoetzel, M., Wiener, M., & Yström, A. (2017). Explicating the role of innovation intermediaries in the "unknown": A contingency approach. *Journal of Strategy and Management*, *10*(1), 19–39. doi:10.1108/JSMA-01-2015-0005

Aguinis, H., & Kraiger, K. (2009). Benefits of training and development for individuals and teams, organizations, and society. *Annual Review of Psychology*, *60*(1), 451–474. doi:10.1146/annurev.psych.60.110707.163505 PMID:18976113

Aguirre-Urreta, M., & Rönkkö, M. (2018). Statistical inference with PLSc using bootstrap confidence intervals. *Management Information Systems Quarterly*, *42*(3), 1001–1020. doi:10.25300/MISQ/2018/13587

Ahmed, N., & Bassiouny, A. (2018). The Effects of Index Changes on Stock Trading: Evidence from the EGX. *Review of Economics & Finance*, *11*(1), 55–66.

Akerlof, G. A. (1970). The market for "lemons": Qualitative uncertainty and the market mechanism. *The Quarterly Journal of Economics*, *84*(3), 488–500. doi:10.2307/1879431

Akkermans, J., Seibert, S. E., & Mol, S. T. (2018). Tales of the unexpected: Integrating career shocks in the contemporary careers literature. *SA Journal of Industrial Psychology*, *44*(1), 1–10. doi:10.4102ajip.v44i0.1503

Al Ariss, A., Cascio, W. F., & Paauwe, J. (2014). Talent management: Current theories and future research directions. *Journal of World Business*, *49*(2), 173–179. doi:10.1016/j.jwb.2013.11.001

Albinsson, P. A., & Yasanthi Perera, B. (2012). Alternative marketplaces in the 21st century: Building community through sharing events. *Journal of Consumer Behaviour*, *11*(4), 303–315. doi:10.1002/cb.1389

Aleixo, A. M., Leal, S., & Azeiteiro, U. M. (2018). Conceptualization of sustainable higher education institutions, roles, barriers, and challenges for sustainability: An exploratory study in Portugal. *Journal of Cleaner Production*, *172*, 1664–1673. doi:10.1016/j.jclepro.2016.11.010

Ali, F., Rasoolimanesh, S., Sarstedt, M., Ringle, C., & Ryu, K. (2018). An assessment of the use of partial least squares structural equation modeling (PLS-SEM) in hospitality research. *International Journal of Contemporary Hospitality Management*, *30*(1), 514–538. doi:10.1108/IJCHM-10-2016-0568

Allen, T. D., Eby, L., Poteet, M. L., Lentz, E., & Lima, L. (2004). Career benefits associated with mentoring for proteges: A meta-analysis. *The Journal of Applied Psychology*, *89*(1), 127–136. doi:10.1037/0021-9010.89.1.127 PMID:14769125

Alshahrani, A., Dadich, A., & Klikauer, T. (2016). Critical success factors of knowledge management in higher education. *The 30th Australian and New Zealand Academy of Management Conference (ANZAM 2016)*. Retrieved on December 19, 2019, from https://www.anzam.org/wp-content/uploads/pdf-manager/2833_ANZAM-2016-357-FILE001.PDF

Altbach, P. G., Reisberg, L., & Rumbley, L. E. (2019). *Trends in global higher education: Tracking an academic revolution*. Brill.

Alvarez Dominguez, A. (2011). The impact of human resource disclosure on corporate image. *Journal of Human Resource Costing & Accounting*, *15*(4), 279–298. doi:10.1108/14013381111197225

American Incite. (n.d.). *Strategic Talent Acquisition & Team Alignment*. Retrieved from http://www. americanincite. com/talent-life-cycle/

Amit, R., & Zott, C. (2001). Value creation in e-business. *Strategic Management Journal*, *22*(6-7), 493–520. doi:10.1002mj.187

Anantatmula, V., & Shrivastav, B. (2012). Evolution of project teams for generation Y workforce. *International Journal of Managing Projects in Business*, *5*(1), 9–26. doi:10.1108/17538371211192874

Anderson, V. (1991). *Alternative Economic Indicators*. Routledge.

Andrew, O. C., & Sofian, S. (2012). Individual factors and work outcomes of employee engagement. *Procedia: Social and Behavioral Sciences*, *40*, 498–508. doi:10.1016/j.sbspro.2012.03.222

Ang, Z., & Massingham, P. (2007). National culture and the standardization versus adaptation of knowledge management. *Journal of Knowledge Management*, *11*(2), 5–21. doi:10.1108/13673270710738889

Annim, S. K. (2010). *Microfinance efficiency trade-offs and complementarities*. BWPI Working Paper 127. Brooks World Poverty Institute, University of Manchester.

Antošová, M., & Csikósová, A. (2014). Social behavior of companies in Slovakia and their support by European Union. *Procedia Social and Behavioral Sciences, 109,* 307–311. doi:.2013.12.462 doi:10.1016/j.sbspro

Antošová, M. (2010). Human resource management and organizational development as a basic for the knowledge management. *Acta Montanistica Slovaca*, *15*(1), 90–95.

Antošová, M., & Csikósová, A. (2016). Corporate Social Responsibility in small and medium enterprises in Slovakia. *Actual Problems of Economics, 175*, 217–224.

Antošová, M., Csikósová, A., & Mihalčová, B. (2013). Application knowledge management in the practice of business subjects in Slovakia. *Procedia: Social and Behavioral Sciences, 83*, 975–979. doi:10.1016/j.sbspro.2013.06.181

Appelbaum, S., Serena, M., & Shapiro, B. (2005). Generation "X" and the boomers: An analysis of realities and myths. *Management Research News, 28*(1), 1–33. doi:10.1108/01409170510784751

Appleton-Dyer, S., Clinton, J., Carswell, P., & McNeill, R. (2012). Understanding evaluation influence within public sector partnerships: A conceptual model. *The American Journal of Evaluation, 33*(4), 532–546. doi:10.1177/1098214012447672

Apprich, F. (2017). Disruption is the core of everything. *European Scientific Journal, ESJ, 13*(3), 23–36.

Ariansen, P. (1999). Sustainability, morality and future generations. In W. M. Lafferty & O. Langhelle (Eds.), *Towards Sustainable Development and the Conditions of Sustainability* (pp. 84–96). McMillian. doi:10.1057/9780230378797_5

Armstrong, M. (2006). Competition in two-sided markets. *The RAND Journal of Economics, 37*(3), 668–691. doi:10.1111/j.1756-2171.2006.tb00037.x

Armstrong, M. (2007). *Řízení lidských zdrojů: nejnovější trendy a postupy.* Prague: Grada Publishing.

Armstrong, M. (2009). *Armstrong's handbook of human resource management practice*. Kogan Page.

Arora, R., & Rangnekar, S. (2015). The joint effects of personality and supervisory career mentoring in predicting occupational commitment. *Career Development International, 20*(1), 63–80. doi:10.1108/CDI-12-2014-0156

Arsel, Z., & Dobscha, S. (2011). Hybrid pro-social exchange systems: The case of Freecycle. *ACR North American Advances, 39*, 66–67.

Arsenault, J., & Ertz, M. (2019). *Towards a technocratic governance system?* International Journal of Innovation Studies. doi:10.1522/revueot.v27n2.877

Artero, M., & Chiodell, F. (2019). Migration, Religion, and Residential Segregation at the Urban Level: The Case of Muslim Migrants in Rome and Milan. *Sociological Inquiry*, 1–24. doi:10.1111oin.12322

Arthur, M. B. (1994). The boundaryless career: A new perspective for organizational inquiry. *Journal of Organizational Behavior, 15*(4), 295–306. doi:10.1002/job.4030150402

Arthur, W. Jr, Bennett, W. J., Edens, P., & Bell, S. T. (2003). Effectiveness of training in organizations: A meta-analysis of design and evaluation features. *The Journal of Applied Psychology, 88*(2), 234–245. doi:10.1037/0021-9010.88.2.234 PMID:12731707

Ashforth, B. E., Gioia, D. A., Robinson, S. L., & Trevino, L. K. (2008). Re-viewing organizational corruption. *Academy of Management Review, 33*(3), 670–684. doi:10.5465/amr.2008.32465714

Askew, O. A., Beisler, J. M., & Keel, J. (2015). Current Trends Of Unethical Behavior Within Organizations. *International Journal of Management & Information Systems, 19*(3), 107–114. doi:10.19030/ijmis.v19i3.9374

Asrar-ul-Haq, M., Kuchinke, K. P., & Iqbal, A. (2017). The relationship between corporate social responsibility, job satisfaction, and organizational commitment: Case of Pakistani higher education. *Journal of Cleaner Production, 142*(4), 2352–2363. doi:10.1016/j.jclepro.2016.11.040

Assegaff, S., Hussin, A. R. C., & Dahlan, H. M. (2011). Perceived benefit of knowledge sharing: Adapting TAM model. *2011 International Conference on Research and Innovation in Information Systems*, 1–6. 10.1109/ICRIIS.2011.6125744

Aßländer, M. S. (2011). Corporate Social Responsibility as subsidiary co-responsibility: A macroeconomic perspective. *Journal of Business Ethics*, *99*(1), 115–128. doi:10.100710551-011-0744-x

Atack, P. (2019). *Global HE market "hugely competitive" – British Council report*. Retrieved on December 28, 2019, from https://thepienews.com/news/global-he-market-hugely-competitive-british-council-report/

Athena Information Solutions Pvt. Ltd. (2019). All you need to know about Facebook's cryptocurrency announcement. *MediaNama*. Retrieved from https://link.gale.com/apps/doc/A589567097/CDB?u=crepuq_uqac&sid=CDB&xid=61938bb8

Atkinson, C. (2004). Career management and the changing psychological contract. *Career Development International*, *7*(1), 14–23. doi:10.1108/13620430210414838

Atwater, L. E., Brett, J. F., & Charles, A. T. (2007). Multisource feedback: Lessons learned and implications for practice. *Human Resource Management*, *46*(2), 285–307. doi:10.1002/hrm.20161

Aubé, C., Rousseau, V., Mama, C., & Morin, E. M. (2009). Counterproductive behaviors and psychological well-being: The moderating effect of task interdependence. *Journal of Business and Psychology*, *24*(3), 351–361. doi:10.100710869-009-9113-5

Aubé, C., Rousseau, V., & Tremblay, S. (2011). Team size and quality of group experience: The more the merrier? *Group Dynamics*, *15*(4), 357–375. doi:10.1037/a0025400

Autorité des marchés financiers. (2019). *Bitcoin et autres cryptomonnaies*. Retrieved from https://lautorite.qc.ca/grand-public/investissements/bitcoin-et-autres-cryptomonnaies/

Ayuso, S. (2003). *Gestión sostenible en la industria turística. Retórica y práctica en el sector hotelero español* (Unpublished doctoral dissertation). Universidad Autónoma de Barcelona, Spain.

Ayuso, S. (2005). Turismo y desarrollo sostenible. *Revista Cultural. Ejemplar dedicado a Cultura Sostenible, 40*, 101-104.

Ayuso, S., & Argandoña, A. (2009). Responsible Corporate governance: Towards a stakeholder board of directors? *Corporate Ownership and Control*, *6*(4), 9–19. doi:10.22495/cocv6i4p1

Azam, A., Qiang, F., & Sharif, S. M. (2013). Personality based psychological antecedents of consumers' trust in ecommerce. *Journal of WEI Business and Economics*, *2*(1), 31–40.

Azmat, G., Murphy, R., Valero, A., & Wyness, G. (2018). *Universities and industrial strategy in the UK* (No. 539). Retrieved on December 18, 2019, from http://cep.lse.ac.uk/pubs/download/is06.pdf

Azouzi, M., & Jarboui, A. (2013). CEO emotional intelligence and board of directors' efficiency. *Corporate Governance*, *13*(4), 365–383. doi:10.1108/CG-10-2011-0081

Baden-Fuller, C., & Morgan, M. S. (2010). Business models as models. *Long Range Planning*, *43*(2-3), 156–171. doi:10.1016/j.lrp.2010.02.005

Baily, C. (2009). Reverse intergenerational learning: A missed opportunity? *AI & Society*, *23*(1), 111–115. doi:10.100700146-007-0169-3

Baines, P. (2016). Philanthropy vs. Corporate Social Responsibility. *CEO Magazine*. Retrieved on November 17, 2019, from www.theceomagazine.com/business/philanthropy/philanthropy-vs-corporate-social-responsibility/

Baker, M., & Wurgler, J. (2007). Investor Sentiment in the Stock Market. *The Journal of Economic Perspectives*, *21*(2), 129–151. doi:10.1257/jep.21.2.129

Bakici, T., & Almirall, E. (2017). Intervention intermediaries flourish: Matching firms with solutions to complex needs. *The Journal of Business Strategy*, *38*(4), 21–29. doi:10.1108/JBS-04-2016-0039

Bakker, A. B., & Demerouti, E. (2007). The job demands-resources model: State of the art. *Journal of Managerial Psychology*, *22*(3), 309–328. doi:10.1108/02683940710733115

Bakker, A. B., Emmerik, H. V., & Euwema, M. C. (2006). Crossover of burnout and engagement in work teams. *Work and Occupations*, *33*(4), 464–489. doi:10.1177/0730888406291310

Baldi, G., Sadovskis, V., & Šipilova, V. (2014). Economic and Employment Effects of Microloans in a Transition Country. *Folia Pomeranae Universitatis Technologiae Stetinensis, seria Oeconomica, 2014*(4), 5–26.

Baldi, G., & Šipilova, V. (2014). How big are the employment effects of microloans? Evidence from a case study in Latvia. *Theoretical and Practical Research in Economic Field*, *5*(1), 17–31.

Baldonado, A. (2008). *Exploring Workplace Motivational and Managerial Factors associated with Generation Y*. Northcentral University.

Baller, S., Dutta, S., & Lanvin, B. (2016). *Global information technology report 2016*. Ouranos.

Balogh, L., Gál, V., Parádi-Dolgos, A., & Sipiczki, Z. (2013). Kulcs egy alternatív mikrofinanszírozási modell sikeréhez. *Acta Scientiarum Socialium*, *16*(38), 153–161.

Banco Central do Brasil. (2019). *Fintechs*. Retrieved on November 25, 2019, from https://www.bcb.gov.br/estabilidadefinanceira/fintechs

Bansal, P. (2005). Evolving sustainability: A longitudinal study of corporate sustainable development. *Strategic Management Journal*, *26*(3), 197–218. doi:10.1002mj.441

Barakat, S. R., Isabella, G., Boaventura, J. M. G., & Mazzon, J. A. (2016). The Influence of Corporate Social Responsibility on Employee Satisfaction. *Management Decision*, *54*(9), 2325–2339. doi:10.1108/MD-05-2016-0308

Baran, L., & King, T.-H. D. (2012). Cost of Equity and S&P 500 Index Revisions. *Financial Management*, *41*(2), 457–481. doi:10.1111/j.1755-053X.2012.01186.x

Baran, M., & Klos, M. (2014). Managing an intergenerational workforce as a factor of company competitiveness. *Journal of International Studies*, *7*(1), 94–101. doi:10.14254/2071-8330.2014/7-1/8

Bardoel, E. A., Pettit, T. M., De Cieri, H., & McMillan, L. (2014). Employee resilience: An emerging challenge for HRM. *Asia Pacific Journal of Human Resources*, *52*(3), 279–297. doi:10.1111/1744-7941.12033

Barkemeyer, R., Holt, D., Preuss, L., & Tsang, S. (2011). What Happened to the 'Development' in Sustainable Development? Business Guidelines Two Decades after Brundtland. *Sustainable Development*. Retrieved on August 15, 2011 from http://onlinelibrary.wiley.com.ux4ll8xu6v.useaccesscontrol.com/doi /10.1002/sd.521/pdf

Barnea, A., & Rubin, A. (2010). Corporate Social Responsibility as a Conflict Between Shareholders. *Journal of Business Ethics*, *97*(1), 71–86. doi:10.100710551-010-0496-z

Barnett, M. (2017). *4 trends disrupting events – CEIR Blog*. Retrieved May 1, 2019, from https://ceirblog.wordpress.com/2017/05/07/4-trends-disrupting-events/

Barnett, B. R., & Bradley, L. (2007). The impact of organizational support for career development on career satisfaction. *Career Development International*, *12*(7), 617–636. doi:10.1108/13620430710834396

Bartlett, K. (2001). The relationship between training and organizational commitment: A study in the health care field. *Human Resource Development Quarterly*, *12*(4), 335–353. doi:10.1002/hrdq.1001

Baruch, Y. (2001). Employability: A substitute for loyalty? *Human Resource Development International*, *4*(4), 543–566. doi:10.1080/13678860010024518

Basu, K. (2007). India's demographic dividend. *BBC News*. http://news.bbc.co.uk/2/hi/6911544stm

Baucus, M., & Near, J. P. (1991). Can Illegal Corporate Behavior Be Predicted? An Event History Analysis. *Academy of Management Journal, 34*(1), 9-36. doi: doi:10.2307/256300

Bauman, C. W., & Skitka, L. J. (2012). Corporate Social Responsibility as a Source of Employee Satisfaction. *Research in Organizational Behavior*, *32*, 63–86. doi:10.1016/j.riob.2012.11.002

Beal, G. (2016). 8 Key Differences between Gen Z and Millennials. *HuffPost*. Retrieved on August 13, 2019 from https://www.huffingtonpost.com/george-beall/8-key-differences-between_b_12814200.html

Beamond, M. T., Farndale, E., & Härtel, Ch. E. J. (2016). MNE translation of corporate talent management strategies to subsidiaries in emerging economies. *Journal of World Business*, *51*(4), 499–510. doi:10.1016/j.jwb.2016.01.002

Becchetti, L., Di Giacomo, S., & Pinnacchio, D. (2008). Corporate Social Responsibility and Corporate Performance: Evidence from a Panel of US Listed Companies. *Applied Economics*, *40*(5), 541–567. doi:10.1080/00036840500428112

Beck, R., Czepluch, J. S., Lollike, N., & Malone, S. O. (2016). Blockchain—the gateway to trust-free cryptographic transactions. *Proceedings of the 24th European conference on information systems, (ECIS)*. Retrieved from https://pdfs.semanticscholar.org/ee1e/fd77e8b6287438d312b244177bb143f7a072.pdf

Becker, C. D., Fineman, M. R., & Freedman, R. J. (2004). *Best Practices in Talent Management from a Study of American and European Multinationals*. Retrieved on October 15, 2019, from www.ircounselors.org/irconcepts/ 2004winter.html

Becker, G. S. (1962). Investment in Human Capital: A Theoretical Analysis. *Journal of Political Economy*, *70*(5), 9–49. doi:10.1086/258724

Becker, G. S. (1964). *Human Capital: A Theoretical and Empirical Analysis*. Columbia University Press.

Becker, J. M., Klein, K., & Wetzels, M. (2012). Hierarchical latent variable models in PLS-SEM: Guidelines for using reflective–formative type models. *Long Range Planning*, *45*(5), 359–394. doi:10.1016/j.lrp.2012.10.001

Beckett, A. J., Wainwright, C. E. R., & Bance, D. (2000). Knowledge management: Strategy or software? *Management Decision*, *38*(9), 601–606. doi:10.1108/00251740010357221

Beck, R., Müller-Bloch, C., & King, J. L. (2018). Governance in the blockchain economy: A framework and research agenda. *Journal of the Association for Information Systems*, *19*(10), 1020–1034. doi:10.17705/1jais.00518

Belk, R. (2014). You are what you can access: Sharing and collaborative consumption online. *Journal of Business Research*, *67*(8), 1595–1600. doi:10.1016/j.jbusres.2013.10.001

Bell, R., & Buchner, A. (2018). Positive effects of disruptive advertising on consumer preferences. *Journal of Interactive Marketing*, *41*, 1–13. doi:10.1016/j.intmar.2017.09.002

Bell, S. (2018). The ugly gaze. In S. Rodrigues & E. Przybylo (Eds.), *On the politics of ugliness* (pp. 411–426). Palgrave Macmillan. doi:10.1007/978-3-319-76783-3_19

Benson, G. S. (2006). Employee development, commitment and intention to turnover: A test of employability policies in action. *Human Resource Management Journal*, *16*(2), 173–192. doi:10.1111/j.1748-8583.2006.00011.x

Benson, J., Sandhu, S., Sastrowardoyo, S., & Scott-Young, C. M. (2015). Complexity in multigenerational organizations: A socio-political perspective. In R. J. Burke, C. L. Cooper, & A. S. G. Antoniou (Eds.), *The Multi-Generational and Aging Workforce: Challenges and Opportunities*. Edward Elgar.

Berger, L. A., & Berger, D. R. (2011). *The Talent Management Handbook. Creating a Sustainable Competitive advantage by Selecting, Developing and promoting the best people*. McGraw-Hill.

Bersin, J. (2010). *A new Talent Management Framework*. Retrieved November 17, 2019, from https://joshbersin.com/2010/05/a-new-talent-management-framework/

Bertoncel, T., Erenda, I., Pejić Bach, M., Roblek, V., & Meško, M. (2018). A Managerial Early Warning System at a Smart Factory: An Intuitive Decision-making Perspective. *Systems Research and Behavioral Science*, *35*(4), 406–416. doi:10.1002res.2542

Bhattacharya, C. B., Sen, S., & Korschun, D. (2006). Using corporate social responsibility to win the war for talent. *MIT Sloan Management Review*, *49*(2), 37–44.

Bhui, K., Dinos, S., Galant-Miecznikowska, M., de Jongh, B., & Stansfeld, S. (2016). Perceptions of work stress causes and effective interventions in employees working in public, private and non-governmental organizations: A qualitative study. *British Journal of Psychiatry Bulletin*, *40*(6), 318–325. PMID:28377811

Bigley, G. A., & Roberts, K. H. (2001). The incident command system: High-reliability organizing for complex and volatile task environments. *Academy of Management Journal*, *44*(6), 1281–1299.

Bird, A., & Fang, T. (2009). Cross cultural management in the age of globalization. *International Journal of Cross Cultural Management*, *9*(2), 139–143. doi:10.1177/1470595809335713

Bisson, C., & Diner, O. Y. (2017). Strategic Early Warning System for the French milk market: A graph theoretical approach to foresee volatility. *Futures*, *87*, 10–23. doi:10.1016/j.futures.2017.01.004

Black, A. (2004). *The quest for sustainable, healthy communities*. Paper presented at the Effective Sustainability Education Conference, NSW Council on Environmental Education, UNSW, Sydney.

Bláha, J. (2013). *Pokročilé řízení lidských zdrojů*. Brno: Edika.

Blome, M. W., Borell, J., Hakansson, C., & Nilsson, K. (2020). Attitudes toward elderly workers and perceptions of integrated age management practices. *International Journal of Occupational Safety and Ergonomics*, *26*(1), 112–120. doi:10.1080/10803548.2018.1514135 PMID:30130462

Blumberg, P. (2020, February 8). *Facebook vows to improve security after hack of 29 million users*. Retrieved from https://www.bloomberg.com/news/articles/2020-02-08/facebook-vows-to-improve-security-after-hack-of-29-million-users

Blum-Kusterer, M., & Husain, S. S. (2001). Innovation and corporate sustainability: An investigation into the process of change in the pharmaceutical industry. *Business Strategy and the Environment*, *10*(5), 300–316. doi:10.1002/bse.300

Bocken, N. M. P., Short, S. W., Rana, P., & Evans, S. (2014). A literature and practice review to develop sustainable business model archetypes. *Journal of Cleaner Production*, *65*, 42–56. doi:10.1016/j.jclepro.2013.11.039

Böcker, L., & Meelen, T. (2017). Sharing for people, planet or profit? Analysing motivations for intended sharing economy participation. *Environmental Innovation and Societal Transitions*, *23*, 28–39. doi:10.1016/j.eist.2016.09.004

Bocquet, R., Le Bas, C., Mothe, C., & Poussing, N. (2013). Are Firms with Different CSR Profiles Equally Innovative? Empirical Analysis with Survey Data. *European Management Journal*, *31*(6), 642–654. doi:10.1016/j.emj.2012.07.001

Bocquet, R., & Mothe, C. (2011). Exploring the relationship between CSR and innovation: A comparison between small and largesized French companies. *Revue Sciences de Gestion. Institut de Socio-Economie des Entreprises et des Organisations*, *2011*, 101–119.

Bogan, C. E., & English, M. J. (1994). *Benchmarking for Best Practices: Winning Through Innovative Adaptation*. McGraw-Hill.

Boj Viudez, J. J., Rodríguez-Rodríguez, R., & Alfaro-Saiz, J. J. (2014). An ANP-multicriteria-based methodology to link intangible assets and organizational performance in a Balanced Scorecard context. *Decision Support Systems*, *68*, 98–110. doi:10.1016/j.dss.2014.10.002

Bolisani, E., & Bratianu, C. (2018). Knowledge strategies. In E. Bolisani & C. Bratianu (Eds.), *Emergent knowledge strategies: Strategic thinking in knowledge management* (pp. 97–116). Springer International Publishing. doi:10.1007/978-3-319-60657-6_5

Bolzan, L., Bitencourt, C., & Volkmer Martins, B. (2019). Exploring the scalability process of social innovation. *Innovation & Management Review*, *16*(3), 218–234. doi:10.1108/INMR-05-2018-0029

Bonanno, G. A. (2004). Loss, trauma, and human resilience: Have we underestimated the human capacity to thrive after extremely aversive events? *The American Psychologist*, *12*(1), 177–192. doi:10.1037/0003-066X.59.1.20 PMID:14736317

Bonilla, S. H., Silva, H. R. O., da Silva, M. T., Gonçalves, R. F., & Sacomano, J. B. (2018). Industry 4.0 and sustainability implications: A scenario-based analysis of the impacts and challenges. *Sustainability*, *10*(10), 3740. doi:10.3390u10103740

Bonvoisin, J., Stark, R., & Seliger, G. (2017). Field of Research in Sustainable Manufacturing. In R. Stark, G. Seliger, & J. Bonvoisin (Eds.), *Sustainable Manufacturing: Challenges, Solutions and Implementation* (pp. 3–20). Springer. doi:10.1007/978-3-319-48514-0_1

Boonnnan, T. M., Jacobs, J. P. A. M., Kuper, G. H., & Romero, A. (2019). Early Warning Systems for Currency Crises with Real-Time Data. *Open Economies Review*, *30*(4), 813–835. doi:10.100711079-019-09530-0

Boons, F., & Lüdeke-Freund, F. (2013). Business models for sustainable innovation: State-of-the-art and steps towards a research agenda. *Journal of Cleaner Production*, *45*, 9–19. doi:10.1016/j.jclepro.2012.07.007

Borman, W. C., & Motowidlo, S. J. (1993). Expanding the criterion domain to include elements of contextual performance. In N. Schmitt & W. C. Borman (Eds.), *Personnel Selection in Organizations* (pp. 71–98). Jossey-Bass.

Bos-Brouwers, H. E. J. (2010). Corporate Sustainability and Innovation in SMEs: Evidence of Themes and Activities in Practice. *Business Strategy and the Environment*, *19*(7), 417–435. doi:10.1002/bse.652

Bothwell, E. (2017). *Universities 'generate £95 billion for UK economy*. Retrieved on January 02, 2020, from https://www.timeshighereducation.com/news/universities-generate-ps95-billion-uk-economy

Botsford Morgan, W., Nelson, J., King, E., & Mancini, V. (2018). Reactions to men's and women's counterproductive work behavior. *Equality, Diversity and Inclusion*, *37*(6), 582–599. doi:10.1108/EDI-08-2017-0161

Botsman, R. (2013). The Sharing Economy Lacks A Shared Definition. *Fast Company*. Retrieved from https://www.fastcoexist.com/3022028/the-sharing-economy-lacksa-shared-definition

Botsman, R. (2015). *Defining the sharing economy: what is collaborative consumption-and what isn't*. Repéré à https://www.fastcompany.com/3046119/defining-the-sharing-economy-what-is-collaborative-consumption-and-what-isnt

Botsman, R., & Rogers, R. (2010). *What's mine is yours*. Penguin Press.

Botsman, R., & Rogers, R. (2011). *What's mine is yours: how collaborative consumption is changing the way we live* (Vol. 5). Collins.

Botsman, R., & Rogers, R. (2011). *What's mine is yours: How collaborative consumption is changing the way we live.* Collins.

Bouncken, R. B., & Kraus, S. (2013). Innovation in knowledge-intensive industries: The double-edged sword of coopetition. *Journal of Business Research*, *66*(10), 2060–2070. doi:10.1016/j.jbusres.2013.02.032

Bowen, D. E., & Ostroff, C. (2004). Understanding HRM–firm performance linkages: The role of the 'strength' of the HRM system. *Academy of Management Review*, *29*, 203–221.

Boxwell, R. J. (1994). *Benchmarking for Competitive Advantage*. McGraw-Hill.

Braat, L. (1991). The Predictive Meaning of Sustainability Indicators. In O. Kuik & H. Verbruggen (Eds.), *Search of Indicators of Sustainable Development* (pp. 57–70). Kluwer Academic Publishers. doi:10.1007/978-94-011-3246-6_6

Brabham, D. C. (2010). Moving the crowd at Threadless: Motivations for participation in a crowdsourcing application. *Information Communication and Society*, *13*(8), 1122–1145. doi:10.1080/13691181003624090

Bradley, P., Parry, G., & O'Regan, N. (2020). A framework to explore the functioning and sustainability of business models. *Sustainable Production and Consumption*, *21*, 57–77. doi:10.1016/j.spc.2019.10.007

Brammer, S. J., & Pavelin, S. (2006). Corporate Reputation and Social Performance: The Importance of Fit. *Journal of Management Studies*, *43*(3), 435–455. doi:10.1111/j.1467-6486.2006.00597.x

Bratianu, C., & Orzea, I. (2013). Knowledge strategies in using social networks. *Management Dynamics in the Knowledge Economy*, *1*(1), 25–38.

Breen, M. (2000). The Good the Bad and the Ugly: The Media and the Scandals. *An Irish Quarterly Review*, *89*(356), 332–338.

Brettel, M., Friederichsen, N., Keller, M., & Rosenberg, M. (2014). How virtualization, decentralization and network building change the manufacturing landscape: An Industry 4.0 perspective. *International Journal of Mechanical, Aerospace, Industrial. Mechatronic and Manufacturing Engineering*, *8*(1), 37–44.

Bridges, E. (2018). Executive ethical decisions initiating organizational culture and values. *Journal of Service Theory and Practice*, *28*(5), 576–608. doi:10.1108/JSTP-07-2017-0106

British Council. (2012). *The shape of things to come: higher education global trends and emerging opportunities to 2020.* Retrieved on January 02, 2020, from https://www.britishcouncil.org/sites/default/files/the_shape_of_things_to_come_-_higher_education_global_trends_and_emerging_opportunities_to_2020.pdf

Broek, F. V. D. (2010). *Green Supply Chain Management, Marketing Tool or Revolution?* Retrieved on December 10, 2019, from http://www.yieldopedia.com/paneladmin/reports/f744f7e72bd9617b57e09809a21042e8.pdf

Brown, S. (2017). How generations X, Y, and Z may change the academic workplace. *Chronicle of Higher Education.* September. Retrieved from www.ebscohost.com/login.aspx?direct=true&db=eue&AN

Bruck, C. (2006). Millions for millions. *The New Yorker*. Retrieved June 12, 2016, from https://www.newyorker.com/magazine/2006/10/30/millions-for-millions

Buller, M. (2014). *Attraction, aesthetics and advertising: An interdisciplinary look at the presentation of "Ugly Models"*. Department of Arts and Cultural Sciences, Lund University. Retrieved from https://lup.lub.lu.se/student-papers/search/publication/4450299

Burke, R. J., & Ng, E. (2006). The changing nature of work and organizations: Implications for human resource management. *Human Resource Management Review*, *16*(2), 86–94. doi:10.1016/j.hrmr.2006.03.006

Bylok, F. (2016). The Concept of Corporate Social Responsibility in Strategies of SMEs. *Club of Economics in Miskolc TMP*, *1*(12), 19–26. doi:10.18096/TMP.2016.01.03

Cachin, C. (2016). Architecture of the hyperledger blockchain fabric. In *Workshop on distributed cryptocurrencies and consensus ledgers* (*Vol. 310*, p. 4). Academic Press.

Cadez, S., & Guilding, C. (2008). An exploratory investigation of an integrated contingency model of strategic management accounting. *Accounting, Organizations and Society*, *33*(7-8), 836–863. doi:10.1016/j.aos.2008.01.003

Cadmus, E. (2002). Defining generations in succession planning: There are four. *Seminars for Nurse Managers*, *10*(4), 246–253. PMID:12526620

Cai, J. (2007). What's in the News? Information Content of S&P 500 Additions. *Financial Management*, *36*(3), 113–124. doi:10.1111/j.1755-053X.2007.tb00083.x

Cameron, E. A., & Pagnattaro, M. A. (2017). Beyond millennials: Engaging generation Z in business law classes. *Journal of Legal Studies Education*, *34*(2), 317–324. doi:10.1111/jlse.12064

Cammock, P., Nilakant, V., & Dakin, S. (1995). Developing a lay model of managerial effectiveness: A social constructionist perspective. *Journal of Management Studies*, *32*(4), 443–474. doi:10.1111/j.1467-6486.1995.tb00784.x

Campbell-Verduyn, M. (Ed.). (2018). Bitcoin and beyond: Cryptocurrencies block chains, and global governance. Abingdon, UK: Routledge.

Cândea, D. (2006). De la dezvoltarea durabilă la întreprinderea sustenabilă. *Întreprinderea sustenabilă*, *1*, iii-vi.

Cannon, J. A., & McGee, R. (2011). *Talent Management and Succession Planning*. CIPD.

Cao, Y., Chen, X., Wu, D. D., & Mao, M. (2011). Early warning of enterprise decline in a life cycle using neural networks and rough set theory. *Expert Systems with Applications*, *38*(6), 6424–6429. doi:10.1016/j.eswa.2010.09.138

Cappelli, P., & Travis, A. (2018). *HR goes agile*. Retrieved at https://hbr.org/2018/03/the-new-rules-of-talent-managementreferral=03759

Cappelli, P. (1999). Career jobs are dead. *California Management Review*, *42*(1), 146–167. doi:10.2307/41166023

Carbery, R., & Garavan, T. N. (2005). Organizational restructuring and downsizing: Issues related to learning, training and employability of survivors. *Journal of European Industrial Training*, *29*(6), 488–508. doi:10.1108/03090590510610272

Carlos, V. S., & Rodrigues, R. G. (2016). Development and validation of a self-reported measure of job performance. *Social Indicators Research*, *126*(1), 279–307. doi:10.100711205-015-0883-z

Carlucci, F. M., Nardi, L., Iocchi, L., & Nardi, D. (2015). Explicit representation of social norms for social robots. *2015 IEEE/RSJ International Conference on Intelligent Robots and Systems (IROS)*, 4191–4196. 10.1109/IROS.2015.7353970

Carson, T. L. (2003). Self-Interest and Business Ethics: Some Lessons of the Recent Corporate Scandals. *Journal of Business Ethics*, *43*(4), 389–394. doi:10.1023/A:1023013128621

Carver, B. T., Cline, B. N., & Hoag, M. L. (2013). Underperformance of founder-led firms: An examination of compensation contracting theories during the executive stock options backdating scandal. *Journal of Corporate Finance, 23*, 294-310. doı: doi:10.1016/j.jcorpfin.2013.09.002

Casadesus-Masanell, R., & Ricart, J. (2010). From strategy to business models and to tactics. *Long Range Planning*, *43*(2-3), 195–215. doi:10.1016/j.lrp.2010.01.004

Casadesus-Masanell, R., & Zhu, F. (2013). Business model innovation and competitive imitation: The case of sponsor-based business models. *Strategic Management Journal*, *34*(4), 464–482. doi:10.1002mj.2022

Castka, P., Bamber, C., & Sharp, J. M. (2004). *Implementing effective corporate social responsibility and corporate governance*. British Standards Institution.

Cavagnaro, E., Staffieri, S., & Postma, A. (2018). Understanding millennials' tourism experience: values and meaning to travel as a key for identifying target clusters for youth (sustainable) tourism. *Journal of Tourism Futures*.

CBI. (2019). *Which trends offer opportunities or pose threats on the European outbound tourism market?* Available at: www.cbi.eu/market-information/tourism/trends/

Cennamo, L., & Gardner, D. (2008). Generational differences in work values, outcomes and person-organisation values fit. *Journal of Managerial Psychology*, *23*(8), 891–906. doi:10.1108/02683940810904385

Chala, Y. V. (2014). Sotsial'na vidpovidal'nist' pidpryyemstv yak osnova innovatsiynoho rozvytku suchasnoyi ekonomiky. In *Zbirnyk naukovykh prats, „Problemy i perspektyvy rozvytku bankivs'koyi systemy Ukrayiny* (pp. 275–285). Kirovohrad National Technical University.

Chamber of Deputies. (2018). *Ley Project no. nº5.587-A/2016* [Projeto de Lei nº5.587-A de 2016]. Retrieved on November 13, 2019, from http://www.camara.gov.br/proposicoesWeb/fichadetramitacao?idProposicao=2088280

Chamorro-Premuzic, T. (2017). *A psychologist finally explains why you hate teamwork so much*. Retrieved from https://www.fastcompany.com/3068194/a-psychologist-finally-explains-why-you-hate-teamwork-so-much

Chang, L. (2007). The NHS performance assessment framework as a balanced scorecard approach limitations and implications. *International Journal of Public Sector Management*, *2*(20), 101–117. doi:10.1108/09513550710731472

Chang, Y. W., Hsu, P. Y., & Yang, Q. M. (2018). Integration of online and offline channels: A view of O2O commerce. *Internet Research*, *28*(4), 926–945. doi:10.1108/IntR-01-2017-0023

Chang, Y., Hsu, P., Li, M., & Chang, C. (2011). Performance evaluation of knowledge management among hospital employees. *International Journal of Health Care Quality Assurance*, *24*(5), 348–365. doi:10.1108/09526861111139188 PMID:21916089

Chan, Y. (2009). How strategy map works for Ontario's health system. *International Journal of Public Sector Management*, *22*(4), 349–363. doi:10.1108/09513550910961628

Charlo, M. J., Moya, I., & Muñoz, A. M. (2015). Sustainable Development and Corporate Financial Performance: A Study Based on the FTSE4Good IBEX Index. *Business Strategy and the Environment*, *24*(4), 277–288. doi:10.1002/bse.1824

Chassin, M. R., & Loeb, J. M. (2011). The on going quality improvement journey: Next stop, high reliability. *Health Affairs*, *30*(4), 559–568. doi:10.1377/hlthaff.2011.0076 PMID:21471473

Chatlani, S. (2018). 8 global trends impacting higher education. *EducationDive*. Retrieved on January 09, 2020, from https://www.educationdive.com/news/8-global-trends-impacting-higher-ed/515272/

Cheah, J. H., Ting, H., Cham, T. H., & Memon, M. A. (2019). The effect of selfie promotion and celebrity endorsed advertisement on decision-making processes: A model comparison. *Internet Research*, *29*(3), 552–577. doi:10.1108/IntR-12-2017-0530

Chebeň, J., Lančarič, D., Savov, R., Tóth, M., & Tluhoř, J. (2015). Towards Sustainable Marketing: Strategy in Slovak Companies. *Amfiteatru Economic*, *17*(40), 855–871.

Cheng, S. F., De Franco, G., Jiang, H. B., & Lin, P. K. (2019). Riding the Blockchain Mania: Public Firms' Speculative 8-K Disclosures. *Management Science*, *65*(12), 5901–5913. doi:10.1287/mnsc.2019.3357

Cheng, S. Y. Y., White, T. B., & Chaplin, L. N. (2012). The effects of self-brand connections on responses to brand failure: A new look at the consumer–brand relationship. *Journal of Consumer Psychology*, *22*(2), 280–288. doi:10.1016/j.jcps.2011.05.005

Chen, H., Noronha, G., & Singal, V. (2004). The Price Response to S&P 500 Index Additions and Deletions: Evidence of Asymmetry and a New Explanation. *The Journal of Finance*, *59*(4), 1901–1929. doi:10.1111/j.1540-6261.2004.00683.x

Chen, H., & Wang, X. (2011). Corporate Social Responsibility and Corporate Financial Performance in China: An Empirical Research from Chinese Firms. *Corporate Governance*, *11*(4), 361–370. doi:10.1108/14720701111159217

Chenhall, R. H., Hall, M., & Smith, D. (2017). The expressive role of performance measurement systems: A field study of a mental health development project. *Accounting, Organizations and Society*, *63*(C), 60–75. doi:10.1016/j.aos.2014.11.002

Chesbrough, H. (2017). The Future of Open Innovation. *Research Technology Management*, *60*(1), 35–38. doi:10.1080/08956308.2017.1255054

Chesbrough, H., & Rosenbloom, R. S. (2002). The role of the business model in capturing value from innovation: Evidence from Xerox Corporation's technology spin-off companies. *Industrial and Corporate Change*, *11*(3), 529–555. doi:10.1093/icc/11.3.529

Cheung, A. W. K. (2011). Do Stock Investors Value Corporate Sustainability? Evidence from an Event Study. *Journal of Business Ethics*, *99*(2), 145–165. doi:10.100710551-010-0646-3

Chevrier, S. (2009). Is national culture still relevant to management in a global context? The case of Switzerland. *International Journal of Cross Cultural Management*, *9*(2), 169–184. doi:10.1177/1470595809335723

Chicca, J., & Shellenbarger, T. (2018). Generation Z: Approaches and teaching–learning practices for nursing professional development practitioners. *Journal for Nurses in Professional Development*, *34*(5), 250–256. doi:10.1097/NND.0000000000000478 PMID:30188477

Chillakur, B., & Mahanandia, R. (2018). Generation Z entering the workforce: The need for sustainable strategies in maximizing their talent. *Human Resource Management International Digest*, *26*(4), 34–38. doi:10.1108/HRMID-01-2018-0006

Chira, I. (2014). Bad news and bank performance during the 2008 financial crisis. *Applied Financial Economics*, *24*(18), 1187–1198. doi:10.1080/09603107.2014.925048

Chládková, H., & Formánková, S. (2016). Strategy for SMEs in the area of primary agricultural production. *Agricultural Economics, 9*(62), 395-406. doi:/2015-AGRICECON doi:10.17221/260

Cho, D. W., Lee, Y. H., Ahn, S. H., & Hwang, M. K. (2012). A framework for measuring the performance of the service supply chain management. *Computers & Industrial Engineering*, *62*(3), 801–818. doi:10.1016/j.cie.2011.11.014

Choi, B., Poon, S. K., & Davis, J. G. (2008). Effects of knowledge management strategy on organizational performance: A complementarity theory-based approach. *Omega: The International Journal of Management Science*, *36*(2), 235–251. doi:10.1016/j.omega.2006.06.007

Cho, S. H., Ali, F., & Manhas, P. S. (2019). Examining the impact of risk perceptions on intentions to travel by air: A comparison of full-service carriers and low-cost carriers. *Journal of Air Transport Management*, *71*, 20–27. doi:10.1016/j.jairtraman.2018.05.005

Christen, R., & Drake, D. (2002). Commercialization. The new reality of microfinance. In D. Drake, & E. Rhyne (Eds.), The commercialization of microfinance balancing business and development (pp. 2-22). Bloomfield: Kumarian Press.

Christensen, C. M., Raynor, M., & McDonald, R. (2015). What is disruptive innovation? *Harvard Business Review*. Retrieved on May 1, 2019, from https://hbr.org/2015/12/what-is-disruptive-innovation

Christodoulou, P., Christodoulou, K., & Andreou, A. (2018). A decentralized application for logistics: Using blockchain in real-world applications. *The Cyprus Review*, *30*(2), 181–18. http://cyprusreview.org/index.php/cr/article/view/577

Chukhray, N. I., & Lisovs'ka, L. S. (2015). *Upravlinnya innovatsiyamy. Navchal'nyy posibnyk.* L′viv: Vydavatelsvo L′viv. politekhniky.

Chuwiruch, N., Jhundra-Indra, P., & Boonlua, S. (2015). Marketing Innovation Strategy and Marketing Performance: A Conceptual Framework. *Allied Academies International Conference. Academy of Marketing Studies. Proceedings*, *20*(2), 82–93. http://sbiproxy.uqac.ca/login?url=https://search.proquest.com/docview/1764885744?accountid=14722

Çıtak, L., & Ersoy, E. (2016). Firmaların BIST Sürdürülebilirlik Endeksine Alınmasına Yatırımcı Tepkisi: Olay Çalışması ve Ortalama Testleri ile Bir Analiz. *International Journal of Alanya Faculty of Business*, *8*(1), 43–57.

City Council of João Pessoa. (2015). *Ordinary Law no. 13.105 of November 30, 2015* [Lei ordinária nº 13.105, de 30 de novembro de 2015]. Retrieved on November 13, 2019, from http://177.200.32.195:9673/sapl/sapl_documentos/norma_juridica/16865_texto_integral

Clacher, I., & Hagendorff, J. (2012). Do Announcements About Corporate Social Responsibility Create or Destroy Shareholder Wealth? Evidence from the UK. *Journal of Business Ethics*, *106*(3), 253–266. doi:10.100710551-011-1004-9

Clarke, M. (2008). Understanding and managing employability in changing career contexts. *Journal of European Industrial Training*, *32*(4), 258–284. doi:10.1108/03090590810871379

Clark, L., & Çallı, L. (2014). Personality types and Facebook advertising: An exploratory study. *Journal of Direct, Data and Digital Marketing Practice*, *15*(4), 327–336. doi:10.1057/dddmp.2014.25

CNBC Indonesia. (2019, December 6). *Cara menghilangkan iklan di Chrome pada HP Android*. Retrieved from https://www.cnbcindonesia.com/tech/20191206193838-37-121109/cara-menghilangkan-iklan-di-chrome-pada-hp-android

Coldwell, D., Joosub, T., & Papageorgiou, E. (2012). Responsible leadership in organizational crises: an analysis of the effects of public perceptions of selected SA business organizations. *Journal of Business Ethics, 109*(2), 133-144. doı: doi:10.100710551-011-1110-8

Collard, B. (1996). *Career resilience in a changing workplace. Information Series, 366*. ERIC Clearinghouse on Adult, Career, and Vocational Education.

Combs, S., & Twachtman, C. (2019). *Birth of the multi-potentialities: Being undeclared in Generation Z.* Retrieved from apps.nacada.ksu.edu

Conger, S. (2002). Fostering a career development culture: Reflections on the roles of managers, employees and supervisors. *Career Development International*, *7*(6), 371–375. doi:10.1108/13620430210444394

Consolandi, C., Jaiswal-Dale, A., Poggiani, E., & Vercelli, A. (2009). Global Standards and Ethical Stock Indexes: The Case of the Dow Jones Sustainability Stoxx Index. *Journal of Business Ethics*, *87*(1), 185–197. doi:10.100710551-008-9793-1

Conway, J. M. (1999). Distinguishing contextual performance from task performance for managerial jobs. *The Journal of Applied Psychology*, *84*(1), 3–13. doi:10.1037/0021-9010.84.1.3

Correa, J. C., Garzón, W., Brooker, P., Sakarkar, G., Carranza, S. A., Yunado, L., & Rincón, A. (2019). Evaluation of collaborative consumption of food delivery services through web mining techniques. *Journal of Retailing and Consumer Services*, *46*, 45–50. doi:10.1016/j.jretconser.2018.05.002

Cortez, N. (2014). Regulating Disruptive Innovation. *Berkeley Technology Law Journal*, *29*(1), 177–179. doi:10.15779/Z38NM5G

Cortland, M. (2017). 2017 Adblock report. *PageFair*. Retrieved from https://pagefair.com/blog/2017/adblockreport/

Cosgrove, D. M., Fisher, M., Gabow, P., Gottlieb, G., Halvorson, G. C., James, B. C., Toussaint, J. S., & … . (2013). Ten strategies to lower costs, improve quality, and engage patients: The view from leading health system CEOs. *Health Affairs*, *32*(2), 321–327. doi:10.1377/hlthaff.2012.1074 PMID:23381525

Cox, L. (2016). *Disrupting the advertising industry*. Retrieved from https://disruptionhub.com/technology-disrupting-ad-industry/

Csikszentmihalyi, M. (1990). *Flow: The psychology of optimal experience*. Harper & Row.

Cui, J., Jo, H., & Na, H. (2018). Does Corporate Social Responsibility Affect Information Asymmetry? *Journal of Business Ethics*, *148*(3), 549–572. doi:10.100710551-015-3003-8

Currie, W. (2012). Tempest: An integrative model for health technology assessment. *Health Policy and Technology*, *1*(1), 35–49. doi:10.1016/j.hlpt.2012.01.004

Curşeu, P. L., Schruijer, S. G. L., & Fodor, O. C. (2016). The influences of knowledge loss and knowledge retention mechanisms on the absorptive capacity and performance of a MIS department. *Management Decision*, *54*(7), 1757–1787. doi:10.1108/MD-02-2016-0117

Custance, P., Walley, K., & Jiang, D. (2012). Crisis brand management in emerging markets. *Marketing Intelligence & Planning*, *30*(1), 18–32. doi:10.1108/02634501211193895

Czaika, E., & Valerdi, R. (2009). *The culture of innovation styles: Are our corporate cultures tuned for innovation? Motivation for study and study context*. Retrieved from https://dspace.mit.edu/bitstream/handle/1721.1/84551/cp_090719_czaika,valerdi_incose.pdf;sequence=1

D'Anselmi, P. (2011). *Values and Stakeholders in an Era of Social Responsibility*. New York: Free Press.

D'Espallier, B., Guérin, I., & Mersland, R. (2011). Women and Repayment in Microfinance: A Global Analysis. *World Development*, *39*(5), 758–772. doi:10.1016/j.worlddev.2010.10.008

Da Silva, T. S., Estácio, B., Kroll, J., & Fontana, R. M. (2016). *Agile Methods*. Springer.

Daboub, A. J., Rasheed, A. M., Priem, R. L., & Gray, A. D. (1995). Top Management team Characteristics and Corporate İllegal Activity. *Academy of Management Review*, *20*(1), 138-170. doı: doi:10.2307/258890

Daily, G. C., & Walker, B. H. (2000). Seeking the great transition. *Nature*, *403*(6767), 243–245. doi:10.1038/35002194 PMID:10659827

Dameyasani, A. W., & Abraham, J. (2013). Impulsive buying, cultural values dimensions, and symbolic meaning of money: A study on college students in Indonesia's capital city and its surrounding. *International Journal of Research Studies in Psychology*, *2*(4), 35–52. doi:10.5861/ijrsp.2013.374

Daunorienė, A., Drakšaitė, A., Snieška, V., & Valodkienė, G. (2015). Evaluating Sustainability of Sharing Economy Business Models. *Procedia: Social and Behavioral Sciences*, *213*, 836–841. doi:10.1016/j.sbspro.2015.11.486

Davenport, T. H., & Prusak, L. (1998). *Working Knowledge: How Organizations Manage What They Know*. Harvard Business School Press.

Davis, F. D. (1989). Perceived usefulness, perceived ease of use, and user acceptance of information technology. *Management Information Systems Quarterly*, *13*(3), 319. doi:10.2307/249008

Davlembayeva, D., Papagiannidis, S., & Alamanos, E. (2019). Mapping the economics, social and technological attributes of the sharing economy. *Information Technology & People*, ITP-02-2018-0085. Advance online publication. doi:10.1108/ITP-02-2018-0085

Dawar, N., & Pillutla, M. M. (2000). Impact of product-harm crises on brand equity: The moderating role of consumer expectations. *JMR, Journal of Marketing Research*, *37*(2), 215–226. doi:10.1509/jmkr.37.2.215.18729

Dawn, S. K., & Biswas, S. (2013). Talent Management: Designing Strategies. *ASBM Journal of Management*, *6*(2), 41–51.

Day, G. S., & Schoemaker, P. J. H. (2005). Scanning the Periphery. *Harvard Business Review*, *83*(11), 135–150. PMID:16299966

De Bondt, W. F., & Thaler, R. (1985). Does the Stock Market Overreact? *Journal of Finance*, *40*(3), 793-805. doı: doi:10.2307/2327804

De Man, J. C., & Strandhagen, J. O. (2017). An Industry 4.0 Research Agenda for Sustainable Business Models. *Procedia CIRP*, *63*, 721–726. doi:10.1016/j.procir.2017.03.315

De Reuver, M., Sørensen, C., & Basole, R. C. (2018). The digital platform: A research agenda. *Journal of Information Technology*, *33*(2), 124–135. doi:10.105741265-016-0033-3

De Toni, A. F., Nonino, F., & Pivetta, M. (2011). A model for assessing the coherence of companies' knowledge strategy. *Knowledge Management Research and Practice*, *9*(4), 327–341. doi:10.1057/kmrp.2011.36

De Wit, H. (2017). Global: Internationalization of Higher Education: Nine Misconceptions: International Higher Education, Summer 2011, Number 64. In *Understanding higher education internationalization* (pp. 9–12). Brill Sense. doi:10.1007/978-94-6351-161-2_2

Debrah, Y., & Smith, I. (2000). Globalization, employment and the workplace: responses for the millennium. *Management Research News, 23*(2/3/4), 1-16. doi:10.1108/01409170010782019

Deci, W., & Ryan, R. (1985). *Intrinsic Motivation and Self-Determination in Human Behavior*. Springer US. doi:10.1007/978-1-4899-2271-7

Deep Focus. (2015). *Deep Focus Cassandra Report: Gen Z Uncovers Massive Attitude Shifts Toward Money, Work and Communication Preferences*. Retrieved on August 29, 2019 from http://www.marketwired.com/press-release/deep-focus-cassandra-report-gen-z-uncovers-massive-attitude-shifts-toward-money-work-2004889.html

Dekker, M. M., Panja, D., Dijkstra, H. A., & Dekker, S. C. (2019). Predicting transitions across macroscopic states for railway systems. *PLoS One*, *14*(6), e0217710. doi:10.1371/journal.pone.0217710 PMID:31170230

Deloitte Development LLC. (2017). *La technologie de la chaîne de blocs et son incidence potentielle sur la profession d'auditeur et de certificateur*. Retrieved from URL://01529-RG-chaine-de-blocs-profession-auditeur-certificateur.pdf

Deloitte. (2004). *It's 2008: Do You Know Where Your Talent Is? Why Acquisition and Retention Strategies Don't Work*. Retrieved on November 15, 2019, from http://www.deloitte.com/assets/

Deloitte. (2014). *Industry 4.0: Challenges and solutions for the digital transformation and use of exponential technologies*. Deloitte.

Deloitte. (2015). *Mind the gaps: The 2015 Deloitte millennial survey*. Author.

Demailly, D., & Novel, A.-S. (2014). *The sharing economy: make it sustainable, Studies N03/14*. IDDRI.

Denford, J. S., & Chan, Y. E. (2011). Knowledge strategy typologies: Defining dimensions and relationships. *Knowledge Management Research and Practice*, *9*(2), 102–119. doi:10.1057/kmrp.2011.7

Denning, S. (2014). An economy of access is opening for business: Five strategies for success. *Strategy and Leadership*, *42*(4), 14–21. doi:10.1108/SL-05-2014-0037

Dervojeda, K. (2013). The sharing economy. Accessibility based business models for Peer to Peer markets. *European Union*.

Desouza, K., & Evaristo, R. (2003). Global Knowledge Management Strategies. *European Management Journal*, *21*(1), 62–67. doi:10.1016/S0263-2373(02)00152-4

Deswal, S. (2015). *How fear, uncertainty, doubt are used positively for more readership*. Retrieved from https://www.adpushup.com/blog/increase-readership-using-fud-psychology/

Di Gregorio, R., & Nustad, S. S. (2017). *Blockchain Adoption in the Shipping Industry* (Master's Thesis). Copenhagen Business School, Copenhagen, Denmark.

Diačiková, A., & Daňková, A. (2019). Green Marketing Communication. In P. Madzík (Ed.), *Conference Proceedings „Current trends and challenges in businesses management"* (pp. 241-249). Ružomberok, Slovakia: VERBUM.

Dikmen, I., Talat Birgonul, M., Ozorhon, B., & Egilmezer Sapci, N. (2010). Using analytic network process to assess business failure risks of construction firms. *Engineering, Construction, and Architectural Management*, *17*(4), 369–386. doi:10.1108/09699981011056574

Ding, H., Wang, L., & Zheng, L. (2018). Collaborative mechanism on profit allotment and public health for a sustainable supply chain. *European Journal of Operational Research*, *2017*(1), 478–495. doi:10.1016/j.ejor.2017.11.057

Dissanaike, G. (1997). Do Stock Market Investors Overreact? *Journal of Business Finance & Accounting*, *24*(1), 27–49. doi:10.1111/1468-5957.00093

Dixon, S. (2003). Implications of population ageing for the labour market. *Labour Market Trends*, *111*(2), 67–76.

Dobrovnik, M., Herold, D. M., Fürst, E., & Kummer, S. (2018). Blockchain for and in logistics: What to adopt and where to start. *Logistics*, *2*(3), 1-18. Retrieved from https://www.mdpi.com/2305-6290/2/3/18

Dodd, E. M. Jr. (1932). For whom are corporate managers trustees? *Harvard Law Review*, *45*(7), 1145–1163. doi:10.2307/1331697

Dois, J., Landrum, P., & Wirck, K. L. (2010). Leading and managing an intergenerational workforce. *Creative Nursing*, *16*(2), 68–74. doi:10.1891/1078-4535.16.2.68 PMID:20486642

Donate, M. J., & Canales, J. I. (2012). A new approach to the concept of knowledge strategy. *Journal of Knowledge Management*, *16*(1), 22–44. doi:10.1108/13673271211198927

Donner, G. J., & Wheeler, M. M. (2005). Building and sustaining a career culture. *The Canadian Nurse*, *101*(8), 30. PMID:16295365

Dooley, K., Rossetti, C., & Handfield, R. (2011). Forces, trends, and decisions in pharmaceutical supply chain management. *International Journal of Physical Distribution & Logistics Management*, *6*(41), 601–622.

Duarte, S., & Cruz-Machado, V. (2017). Green and Lean Model for Business Sustainability. In J. Xu, A. Hajiyev, S. Nickel, & M. Gen (Eds.). *Proceedings of the Tenth International Conference on Management Science and Engineering Management. Advances in Intelligent Systems and Computing* (pp. 1281-1292). Singapore: Springer. 10.1007/978-981-10-1837-4_105

Dunn, A., & Westbrook, J. (2011). Interpreting social network metrics in healthcare organisations: A review and guide to validating small networks. *Social Science & Medicine*, *72*(7), 1064–1068. doi:10.1016/j.socscimed.2011.01.029 PMID:21371798

Dunphy, D., Griffiths, A., & Benn, S. (2003). *Organizational Change for Corporate Sustainability*. Routledge.

Durand, R., Paugam, L., & Stolowy, H. (2019). Do Investors Actually Value Sustainability Indices? Replication, Development, and New Evidence on CSR Visibility. *Strategic Management Journal*, *40*(9), 1471–1490. doi:10.1002mj.3035

Durnin, M. (2019). *Global student recruitment outlook: June 2019 update*. Retrieved on December 28, 2019, from https://education-services.britishcouncil.org/insights-blog/global-student-recruitment-outlook-june-2019-update

Dutta, U. P., Gupta, H., & Sengupta, P. P. (2019). ICT and health outcome nexus in 30 selected Asian countries: Fresh evidence from panel data analysis. *Technology in Society*, *59*, 101184. doi:10.1016/j.techsoc.2019.101184

Dwyer, R. J. (2009). Prepare for the impact of the multi-generational workforce! *Transforming Government: People, Process and Policy*, *3*(2), 101-110.

Dwyer, R. J., & Azevedo, A. (2016). Preparing leaders for the multi-generational workforce. *Journal of Enterprising Communities: People and Places in the Global Economy*, *10*(3), 281–305. doi:10.1108/JEC-08-2013-0025

Dyllick, T. (2015). Responsible management education for a sustainable world: The challenges for business schools. *Journal of Management Development*, *34*(1), 16–33. doi:10.1108/JMD-02-2013-0022

Dyllick, T., & Hockerts, K. (2002). Beyond the business case for corporate sustainability. *Business Strategy and the Environment*, *11*(2), 130–141. doi:10.1002/bse.323

Dyllick, T., & Muff, K. (2015). Clarifying the Meaning of Sustainable Business: Introducing a Typology from Business-as-Usual to True Business Sustainability. *Organization & Environment*, *29*(2), 156–174. doi:10.1177/1086026615575176

Eby, L. T., & Lockwood, A. (2005). Proteges and mentors participating in formal mentoring programs: A qualitative investigation. *Journal of Vocational Behavior*, *67*(3), 441–458. doi:10.1016/j.jvb.2004.08.002

Edmans, A. (2011). Does the Stock Market Fully Value Intangibles? Employee Satisfaction and Equity Prices. *Journal of Financial Economics*, *101*(3), 621–640. doi:10.1016/j.jfineco.2011.03.021

Egerová, D., Lančarič, D., Eger, L., & Savov, R. (2015). Perspectives of talent management: Evidence from Czech and Slovak business organizations. *Economics and Management*, *18*(4), 108–120. doi:10.15240/tul/001/2015-4-008

Egri, C. P., & Ralston, D. A. (2004). Generation cohorts and personal values: A comparison of China and the United States. *Organization Science*, *15*(2), 210–220. doi:10.1287/orsc.1030.0048

Ehrenhard, M. L., & Fiorito, T. L. (2018). Corporate values of the 25 largest European banks: Exploring the ambiguous link with corporate scandals. *Journal of Public Affairs*, *18*(1), 1–9. doi:10.1002/pa.1700

Eisenbart, B., Garbuio, M., Mascia, D., & Morandi, F. (2016). Does scheduling matter? When unscheduled decision making results in more effective meetings. *Journal of Strategy and Management*, *9*(1), 15–38. doi:10.1108/JSMA-03-2014-0017

Eisenhardt, K. M., & Zbaracki, M. J. (1992). Strategic decision making. *Strategic Management Journal*, *13*(S2), 17–37. doi:10.1002mj.4250130904

Eisenmann, T., Parker, G., & van Alstyne, M. W. (2006). Strategies for two-sided markets. *Harvard Business Review*, *84*(10), 92–101.

Elezi, E., & Bamber, C. (2018a). Knowledge management factors affecting educational partnerships within the British HE/FE sector. *International Journal of Knowledge Management Studies*, *9*(3), 243–259. doi:10.1504/IJKMS.2018.094213

Elezi, E., & Bamber, C. (2018b). Understanding the Role of Knowledge Management in Higher Education Partnerships through Experts. In E. Bolisani, E. Di Maria, & E. Scarso (Eds.). *19th European Conference on Knowledge Management* (pp. 225-234). Reading, UK: ACPI.

Elliott, G. (2017). Challenging assumptions about values, interests and power in further and higher education partnerships. *Journal of Further and Higher Education*, *41*(2), 143–154. doi:10.1080/0309877X.2015.1070397

Encyclopedia. (2019). *CPU cycle*. Available at: https://www.encyclopedia.com/computing/dictionaries-thesauruses-pictures-and-press-releases/cpu-cycle

Ericksson, T. J. (2009). Generational differences between India and the US. *HBR Blog Network. Harvard Business Review*.

Ernst & Young. (2016). *From Innovation to Expectation – How M & E Leaders are Responding to Gen Z.* Retrieved on August 30, 2019 from https://www.ey.com/Publication/vwLUAssets/ey-media-entertainment-leaders-respond-to-gen-z/$FILE/ey-media-entertainment-leaders-respond-to-gen-z.pdf

Ertz, M., Durif, F., & Arcand, M. (2016). Collaborative Consumption: Conceptual Snapshot at a Buzzword. *Journal of Entrepreneurship Education*, *19*(2), 1–23. doi:10.2139srn.2799884

Ertz, M., Durif, F., & Arcand, M. (2018a). Towards Multilife Marketing: How Goods Multiple Lives Practices Create Value for Consumers. *Journal of Promotion Management*, *24*(6), 863–894. doi:10.1080/10496491.2017.1408527

Ertz, M., Durif, F., & Arcand, M. (2019b). A conceptual perspective on collaborative consumption. *Academy of Marketing Science Review*, *9*, 27–41. doi:10.100713162-018-0121-3

Ertz, M., Hallegatte, D., & Bousquet, J. (2019a). *La reconfiguration de l'échange marchand. Tour d'horizon, enjeux et perspectives*. Les Presses de l'Université du Québec.

Ertz, M., Lecompte, A., & Durif, F. (2018b). "It's not my fault, I am in the right!" Exploration of neutralization in the justification of the support and use of a controversial technological collaborative consumption service. *Technological Forecasting and Social Change*, *134*, 254–264. doi:10.1016/j.techfore.2018.06.032

Ervits, I. (2018). Geography of corporate innovation: Internationalization of innovative activities by MNEs from developed and emerging markets. *Multinational Business Review*, *26*(1), 25–49. doi:10.1108/MBR-07-2017-0052

Eslami, M., Krishna Kumaran, S. R., Sandvig, C., & Karahalios, K. (2018). Communicating Algorithmic Process in Online Behavioral Advertising. In *Proceedings of the 2018 CHI Conference on Human Factors in Computing Systems - CHI '18* (pp. 1–13). New York, NY: Association for Computing Machinery. 10.1145/3173574.3174006

Estadão. (2020). *Scooter giant, Lime closes operation in Brazil after six months* [Gigante dos patinetes, Lime encerra operação no Brasil após seis meses]. Retrieved on January 15, 2020, from https://link.estadao.com.br/noticias/inovacao,lime-encerra-operacao-no-brasil-apos-seis-meses,70003150714

Euchner, J., & Ganguly, A. (2014). Business model innovation in practice. *Research Technology Management*, *57*(6), 33–39. doi:10.5437/08956308X5706013

Euromonitor International. (2011). *Make way for generation Z: Marketing for today's teens and tweens.* Retrieved from https://oaltabo2012.files.wordpress.com/2012/03/make-way-for-generation-z1.pdf

European Commission. (2001). *Green Paper: Promoting a European framework for Corporate Social Responsibility. COM(2001)366*. European Commission.

European Commission. (2002). *Corporate Social Responsibility: A business contribution to Sustainable Development. COM(2002)347*. European Commission.

European Commission. (2003). Opinion of the Committee of the Regions on the 'Communication from the Commission to the Council, the European Parliament, the European Economic and Social Committee and the Committee of the Regions — Basic orientations for the sustainability of European tourism'. COM(2003) 716 final. Brussels: European Commission.

European Union. (2016). *Public Health –Policy*. Retrieved on November 29, 2019 from https://ec.europa.eu/health/ehealth/policy/index_en.htm

Evans, S., Vladimirova, D., Holgado, M., Fossen, K. V., Yang, M., Silva, E. A., & Barlow, C. Y. (2017). Business Model Innovation for Sustainability: Towards a Unified Perspective for Creation of Sustainable Business Models. *Business Strategy and the Environment*, *26*(5), 597–608. doi:10.1002/bse.1939

Everstring. (2020). *What is intent data and how can i use it?* Retrieved from https://www.everstring.com/what-is-intent-data/

Exame. (2019). *99 gives up bikes and scooters in Brazil* [99 desiste de empreitada de bikes e patinetes no Brasil]. Retrieved on January 15, 2020, from https://exame.abril.com.br/blog/primeiro-lugar/99-desiste-de-empreitada-de-bikes-e-patinetes-no-brasil/

Falasca, M., & Kros, J. F. (2018). Success factors and performance outcomes of healthcare industrial vending systems: An empirical analysis. *Technological Forecasting and Social Change*, *126*, 41–52. doi:10.1016/j.techfore.2016.06.024

Fang, T. (2003). A critique of Hofstede's fifth national culture dimension. *International Journal of Cross Cultural Management*, *3*(3), 347–368. doi:10.1177/1470595803003003006

Fang, T. (2005). From 'onion' to 'ocean': Paradox and change in national cultures. *International Studies of Management & Organization*, *35*(4), 71–90. doi:10.1080/00208825.2005.11043743

Fang, T. (2006). Negotiation: The Chinese style. *Journal of Business and Industrial Marketing*, *21*(1), 50–60. doi:10.1108/08858620610643175

Fang, T. (2012). Yin Yang: A new perspective on culture. *Management and Organization Review*, *8*(1), 1–26. doi:10.1111/j.1740-8784.2011.00221.x

Fan, Y., Xia, M., Zhang, Y., & Chen, Y. (2019). The influence of social embeddedness on organizational legitimacy and the sustainability of the globalization of the sharing economic platform: Evidence from Uber China. *Resources, Conservation and Recycling*, *151*, 104490. doi:10.1016/j.resconrec.2019.104490

Farashah, A. D., & Blomquist, T. (2019). *Exploring employer attitude towards migrant workers. Evidence from managers across Europe*. Evidence-based HRM. doi:10.1108/EBHRM-04-2019-0040

Fassin, Y., & Buelens, M. (2011). The hypocrisy-sincerity continuum in corporate communication and decision making: A model of corporate social responsibility and business ethics practices. *Management Decision*, *49*(4), 586–600. doi:10.1108/00251741111126503

Fathollahi-Fard, A. M., Govindan, K., Hajiaghaei-Keshteli, M., & Ahmadi, A. (2019). A green home health care supply chain: New modified simulated annealing algorithms. *Journal of Cleaner Production*, *240*, 118200. doi:10.1016/j.jclepro.2019.118200

Fatma, M., Rahman, Z., & Khan, I. (2015). Building Company Reputation and Brand Equity Through CSR: The Mediating Role of Trust. *International Journal of Bank Marketing*, *33*(6), 840–856. doi:10.1108/IJBM-11-2014-0166

Faychuk, O. M. (2013). Innovatsiynyy protses yak rushiyna syla ekonomichnoho zrostannya. *Bìznes Ìnform*, *10*, 66–70.

Feil, A. A., Quevedo, A. M., & Schreiber, D. (2015). Selection and identification of the indicators for quickly measuring sustainability in micro and small furniture industries. *Sustainable Production and Consumption*, *3*, 34–44. doi:10.1016/j.spc.2015.08.006

Feiz, D., Dehghani Soltani, M., & Farsizadeh, H. (2019). The effect of knowledge sharing on the psychological empowerment in higher education mediated by organizational memory. *Studies in Higher Education*, *44*(1), 3–19. doi:10.1080/03075079.2017.1328595

Feng, Z.-Y., Wang, M.-L., & Huang, H.-W. (2015). Equity Financing and Social Responsibility: Further International Evidence. *The International Journal of Accounting*, *50*(3), 247–280. doi:10.1016/j.intacc.2015.07.005

Fielt, E. (2013). Conceptualising Business Models: Definitions, Frameworks and classifications. *Journal of Business Models*, *1*(1), 85–105. doi:10.5278/ojs.jbm.v1i1.706

Fiksel, J. (2006). Sustainability and resilience: toward a system approach. *Sustainability: Science. Practice & Police*, *2*, 14–21.

Fiksel, J. (2006). Sustainability and resilience: toward a system approach. *Sustainability: Science. Practice & Policy*, *2*(2), 14–21. doi:10.1080/15487733.2006.11907980

Fiori, G., di Donato, F., & Izzo, M. F. (2015). Corporate Social Responsibility and Stock Prices: A Study on the Italian Market. *Corporate Ownership & Control*, *12*(2), 608–617. doi:10.22495/cocv12i2c6p3

Flavell, J. H. (1979). Metacognition and cognitive monitoring: A new area of cognitive–developmental inquiry. *The American Psychologist*, *34*(10), 906–911. doi:10.1037/0003-066X.34.10.906

Fliegner, W. (2017). Analysis of the business model elements and their relationships. *Research Papers of the Wroclaw University of Economics*, *474*(474), 54–64. doi:10.15611/pn.2017.474.05

Fombrun, C., & Shanley, M. (1990). What's in a name? Reputation building and corporate strategy. *Academy of Management Journal, 33*(2), 233-258. doı: doi:10.2307/256324

Forbes Insights. (2017). *Data-driven marketing: Push forward or fall behind.* Retrieved from http://www.oracle.com/us/products/applications/wp-forbes-data-driven-marketing-3847636.pdf

Ford, M. (2009). *The lights in the tunnel.* Acculant Publishing.

Formánková, S., Kučerová, R., & Prísažná, M. (2016). ISO 26 000: Concept of Social Responsibility at Czech University. In *International Conference on Management "Trends of Management in the Contemporary Society"* (pp. 97-101). Brno, Czech Republic: Mendel University.

Fourie, C., & Van Vuuren, L. J. (1998). Defining and measuring career resilience. *SA Journal of Industrial Psychology*, *24*(3), 52–59. doi:10.4102ajip.v24i3.662

Francis, T., & Hoefel, F. (2018). *'True gen': Generation Z and its implications for companies.* Retrieved at https://www.mckinsey.com

Frankenfield, J. (2018, Jun 24). *Collaborative Economy.* Retrieved from https://www.investopedia.com/terms/c/collaborative-economy.asp

Freedman, S., Kearney, M., & Lederman, M. (2012). Product Recalls, Imperfect Information, and Spillover Effects: Lessons from the Consumer Response to the 2007 Toy Recalls. *The Review of Economics and Statistics*, *94*(2), 499–516. doi:10.1162/REST_a_00162

Freeman, R. E. (1994). The politics of stakeholder theory: Some future directions. *Business Ethics Quarterly*, *4*(4), 409-421. doi: doi:10.2307/3857340

Frenken, K., & Schor, J. (2017). Putting the sharing economy into perspective. *Environmental Innovation and Societal Transitions*, *23*, 3–10. doi:10.1016/j.eist.2017.01.003

Frenken, K., & Schor, J. (2019). Putting the sharing economy into perspective. In O. Mont (Ed.), *A Research Agenda for Sustainable Consumption Governance* (pp. 121–136). Edward Elgar Publishing. doi:10.4337/9781788117814.00017

Friedman, M. (1970). The Social Responsibility of Business is to Increase its Profits. *The New York Times Magazine*, 1-6.

Friedman, M. (1970, Sept. 13). The responsibility of business is to increase its profits. *The New York Times Magazines*, 32-33.

Fundação Getúlio Vargas. (2016). *Sharing and intensive use of urban roads in São Paulo. Follow-up report of the seminar held jointly with the São Paulo City Council* [Compartilhamento e uso intensivo do viário urbano em São Paulo. Relatório de acompanhamento do seminário realizado em conjunto com a Câmara Municipal de São Paulo]. São Paulo: Centro de Estudos de Política e Economia do Setor Público da Fundação Getúlio Vargas. Retrieved on November 23, 2019, from https://bibliotecadigital.fgv.br/dspace/handle/10438/19431

Gaál, Z., Szabó, L., Kovács, Z., Obermayer-Kovács, N., & Csepregi, A. (2009). Consequence of Cultural Capital in Connection with Competitiveness. *International Journal of Knowledge. Culture and Change Management*, *8*(10), 79–90.

Galbreath, J. (2006). Corporate Social Responsibility Strategy: Strategic Options, Global Considerations. *Corporate Governance*, *6*(2), 175–187. doi:10.1108/14720700610655178

Galo, A. M. (2011). Beyond the Classroom. Using Technology to Meet the Educational Needs of Multigenerational Perinatal Nurses. *The Journal of Perinatal & Neonatal Nursing*, *25*(2), 195–199. doi:10.1097/JPN.0b013e3182163993 PMID:21540699

Garcia Martin, M. A. (2014). *La responsabilidad social corporativa en las entidades públicas y el proceso de reforma de las Administraciones Públicas*. Retrieved November 15, 2016 from http://www.pap.minhap.gob.es/sitios/140aniversario/Documents/DEBATEMiguelAngelGarciaMartin.pdf

García Martín, J. C., & Herrero, B. (2018). Boards of directors: Composition and effects on the performance of the firm. *Economic Research-Ekonomska Istraživanja*, *31*(1), 1015–1041. doi:10.1080/1331677X.2018.1436454

Gatautis, R., Vaiciukynaite, E., & Tarute, A. (2019). Impact of business model innovations on SME's innovativeness and performance. *Baltic Journal of Management*, *14*(4), 521–539. doi:10.1108/BJM-01-2018-0035

Gauthier, C., & Gilomen, B. (2016). Business models for sustainability: Energy efficiency in urban districts. *Organization & Environment*, *29*(1), 124–144. doi:10.1177/1086026615592931

Gberevbie, D., Joshua, S., Excellence-Oluye, N., & Oyeyemi, A. (2017). Accountability for sustainable development and the challenges of leadership in Nigeria, 1999-2015. *SAGE Open*, *7*(4), 1–10. doi:10.1177/2158244017742951

Geissdoerfer, M., Vladimirova, D., & Evans, S. (2018). Sustainable business model innovation: A review. *Journal of Cleaner Production*, *198*, 401–416. doi:10.1016/j.jclepro.2018.06.240

Genc, E., Duffie, N., & Reinhart, G. (2014). Event-based supply chain early warning system for an adaptive production control. *Procedia CIRP*, *19*, 39–44. doi:10.1016/j.procir.2014.04.076

Gerpott, F. H., Lehmann-Willenbrock, N., & Voelpel, S. C. (2016). A phase model of intergenerational learning in organizations. *Academy of Management Learning & Education*, *16*(2), 193–216. doi:10.5465/amle.2015.0185

Ghazawneh, A., & Henfridsson, O. (2015). A Paradigmatic Analysis of Digital Application Marketplaces. *Journal of Information Technology*, *30*(3), 198–208. doi:10.1057/jit.2015.16

Ghilal, A., & Nach, H. (2019). La technologie de la chaîne de blocs: fondements et applications. In *La reconfiguration de l'échange marchand. Tour d'horizon, enjeux et perspectives* (pp. 113–131). Les Presses de l'Université du Québec. doi:10.2307/j.ctv10qqx4s.12

Ghosh, R., & Chaudhuri, S. (2009). Intergenerational differences in individualism/collectivism orientations: Implications for outlook towards HRD/HRM practices in India and the United States. *New Horizons in Adult Education and Human Resource Development*, *23*(4), 5–21. doi:10.1002/nha3.10356

Gibbons, R. (1992). *Game Theory for Applied Economists*. Princeton University Press.

Gioia, D. A., & Pitre, E. (1990). Multiparadigm perspectives on theory building. *Academy of Management Review*, *15*(4), 584–602. doi:10.5465/amr.1990.4310758

Gironda, J. T., & Korgaonkar, P. K. (2018). iSpy? Tailored versus invasive ads and consumers' perceptions of personalized advertising. *Electronic Commerce Research and Applications*, *29*, 64–77. doi:10.1016/j.elerap.2018.03.007

Glaser, F. (2017). Pervasive Decentralisation of Digital Infrastructures : A Framework for Blockchain enabled System and Use Case Analysis. *Proceedings of the 50th Hawaii International Conference on System Sciences (HICSS-50)*. Retrieved from https://ssrn.com/abstract=3052165

Glaser, P., Liu, J. H., Hakim, M. A., Vilar, R., & Zhang, R. (2018). Is social media use for networking positive or negative? Offline social capital and internet addiction as mediators for the relationship between social media use and mental health. *New Zealand Journal of Psychology*, *47*(3), 11–17.

Glenn, N. (1977). *Cohort analysis*. Sage.

Godebarge, F., & Rossat, R. (2016). Principes clés d'une application Blockchain. *EMLyon Business School*. Retrieved from https://www.coursehero.com/file/29197828/GODEBARGE-ROSSAT-Blockchain-version-finalepdf/

Goh, E., & Lee, C. (2018). A workforce to be reckoned with: The emerging pivotal Generation Z hospitality workforce. *International Journal of Hospitality Management*, *73*, 20–28. doi:10.1016/j.ijhm.2018.01.016

Gok, I. Y., Duranay, S., & Uzunoglu Unlu, H. (2019b). Co-movement Dynamics of Sustainability Indices: Investigating the Diversification Opportunities Through FTSE4Good Index Family and Borsa Istanbul Sustainability Index. *Social Responsibility Journal*, *ahead-of-print*(ahead-of-print). Advance online publication. doi:10.1108/SRJ-02-2019-0073

Gök, İ. Y., & Gökşen, H. (2020). *Bankaların Sürdürülebilirlik Endeksine Dahil Edilmelerinin Getiri Üzerindeki Etkisinin Araştırılması*. Süleyman Demirel Üniversitesi Vizyoner Dergisi.

Gök, İ. Y., & Özdemír, O. (2017). Borsa İstanbul Sürdürülebilirlik Endeksinin Performans Karakteristiği. *Sosyoekonomi*, *25*(34), 87–105.

Gok, I. Y., Ozdemir, O., & Unlu, B. (2019a). The Effect of Corporate Sustainability Practices on Financial Performance: Evidence From Turkey. In A. Antonaras & P. Dekoulou (Eds.), *Cases on Corporate Social Responsibility and Contemporary Issues in Organizations* (pp. 52–70). IGI Global. doi:10.4018/978-1-5225-7715-7.ch004

Gomes, S. B., & Deuling, J. K. (2019). Family influence mediates the relation between helicopter-parenting and millennial work attitudes. *Journal of Managerial Psychology, 34*(1), 2–17. doi:10.1108/JMP-12-2017-0450

Gould, D., Nalepa, J., & Mignano, M. (2020). Coaching generation Z athletes. *Journal of Applied Sport Psychology, 32*(1), 104–120. doi:10.1080/10413200.2019.1581856

Goyal, R., Kakabadse, N., & Kakabadse, A. (2019). Improving corporate governance with functional diversity on FTSE 350 boards: Directors' perspective. *Journal of Capital Markets Studies, 3*(2), 113–136. doi:10.1108/JCMS-09-2019-0044

Grebe, S. K. (2012). The importance of being genuinely sorry when organizations apologize: How the Australian Wheat Board (AWB Limited) was damaged even further by its response to a corporate scandal. *Journal of Public Affairs, 13*(1), 100–110. doi:10.1002/pa.1450

Green, B. (2002). Listening to leaders: Feedback on 360-degree feedback one year later. *Organization Development Journal, 20*(1), 8–16.

Greenslade, J. H., & Jimmieson, N. L. (2007). Distinguishing between task and contextual performance for nurses: Development of a job performance scale. *Journal of Advanced Nursing, 58*(6), 602–611. doi:10.1111/j.1365-2648.2007.04256.x PMID:17442026

Gregoriou, A. (2011). The Liquidity Effects of Revisions to the CAC40 Stock Index. *Applied Financial Economics, 21*(5), 333–341. doi:10.1080/09603107.2010.530216

Greyser, S. A. (2009). Corporate brand reputation and brand crisis management. *Management Decision, 47*(4), 590–602. doi:10.1108/00251740910959431

Groome, L., & Mayeaux, E. Jr. (2010). Decreasing extremes in patient waiting time. *Quality Management in Health Care, 19*(2), 117–128. doi:10.1097/QMH.0b013e3181dafeac PMID:20351538

Grunwald, G., & Hempelmann, B. (2010). Impacts of Reputation for Quality on Perceptions of Company Responsibility and Product-related Dangers in times of Product-recall and Public Complaints Crises: Results from an Empirical Investigation. *Corporate Reputation Review, 13*(4), 264–283. doi:10.1057/crr.2010.23

Grybaitė, V., & Stankeviciene, J. (2018). An empirical analysis of factors affecting sharing economy growth. *Oeconomia Copernicana, 9*(4), 635–654. doi:10.24136/oc.2018.031

Grydzhuk, I. (2008). Innovatsiyna skladova stiykoho rozvytku ekonomiky rehioniv. In Teoriyi mikromakroekonomiky, Zbirnyk naukovykh prats, Akademiya munitsypal'noho upravlinnya (pp. 239-240). Academic Press.

Guedes da Luz Neto, L. (2017a). The Shared Economy and its Challenges in Brazil [A Economia Compartilhada e seus Desafios no Brasil]. In M. R. Gonçalves, F. S. Veiga, & M. M. Magalhães (Eds.), *Derecho, gobernanza e innnovación: Dilemas jurídicos de la contemporaneidad em perspectiva transdisciplinar* (pp. 420–427). Universidade Portucalense.

Guedes da Luz Neto, L. (2017b). Shared Economy: Regulatory Approaches between Brazil and Portugal [Economia Compartilhada: Aproximações Regulatórias entre Brasil e Portugal]. In M. R. Gonçalves & F. S. Veiga (Eds.), *O Direito Actual e as Novas Fronteiras Jurídicas no Limiar de uma Nova Era* (pp. 972–978). Universidade Católica Editora.

Gündüz, Ç. (2018). Sürdürülebilirlik Endeksi Kapsamına Alınmanın Hisse Senedi Değerine Etkisi: BIST Uygulaması. *Bankacılar Dergisi, 106*, 37–58.

Guo, F. (2017). The spirit and characteristic of the general provisions of civil law. *Law and Economics, 3*, 5–16.

Gursoy, D., Maier, T. A., & Chi, C. G. (2008). Generational differences: An examination of work values and generational gaps in the hospitality workforce. *International Journal of Hospitality Management*, *27*(3), 448–458. doi:10.1016/j.ijhm.2007.11.002

Gutierrez-Neito, B., Serrano-Cinca, C., & Mar Molinero, C. (2007). Microfinance institutions and efficiency. *International Journal of Management Sciences*, *35*(2), 131–142.

Guzmán Raja, M., & Martínez Franco, C. M. (2016). Un nuevo paradigma de negocio: La empresa social. *Revista AECA*, *102*, 5–8.

György, B. (2017). To What Extend is Hungary a Knowledge Based Economy? *Club of Economics in Miskolc TMP*, *1*(13), 69–84. doi:10.18096/TMP.2017.01.06

Haanaes, K., Reeves, M., von Streng Velken, I., Audretsch, M., Kiron, D., & Kruschwitz, N. (2012). *Sustainability nears a tipping point*. Boston Consulting Group.

Habibi, M. R., Davidson, A., & Laroche, M. (2017). What managers should know about the sharing economy? *Business Horizons*, *60*(1), 113–121. doi:10.1016/j.bushor.2016.09.007

Hackman, J. R., & Oldham, G. R. (1980). *Work redesign*. Addison Wesley.

Hahn, J. (2009). Effectively manage a multigenerational staff. *Nursing Management*, *40*(9), 8–10. doi:10.1097/01.NUMA.0000360765.52105.ed PMID:19734749

Hahn, J., & Andor, L. (2013). *Guide to Social Innovation*. European Commission.

Hahn, T., Figge, F., Pinkse, J., & Preuss, L. (2010). Trade-Offs in Corporate Sustainability: You can't Have Your Cake and Eat It. *Business Strategy and the Environment*, *19*(4), 217–229. doi:10.1002/bse.674

Hair, J. F., Hult, G. T. M., Ringle, C. M., & Sarstedt, M. (2014). *A primer on partial least squares structural equation modeling (PLS-SEM)*. SAGE Publications.

Hair, J. F., Hult, G. T. M., Ringle, C. M., Sarstedt, M., & Thiele, K. (2017). Mirror, mirror on the wall: A comparative evaluation of composite-based structural equation modeling methods. *Journal of the Academy of Marketing Science*, *45*(5), 616–632. doi:10.100711747-017-0517-x

Hair, J. F. Jr, Black, W. C., & Babin, B. J. (2012). *Multivariate data analysis*. Prentice Hall.

Hair, J. F., Ringle, C. M., & Sarstedt, M. (2011). PLS-SEM: Indeed a silver bullet. *Journal of Marketing Theory and Practice*, *19*(2), 139–152. doi:10.2753/MTP1069-6679190202

Hair, J. F., Risher, J. J., Sarstedt, M., & Ringle, C. M. (2019). When to use and how to report the results of PLS-SEM. *European Business Review*, *31*(1), 2–24. doi:10.1108/EBR-11-2018-0203

Haji-Kazemi, S., & Andersen, B. (2013). Application of performance measurement as an early warning system. *International Journal of Managing Projects in Business*, *6*(4), 714–738. doi:10.1108/IJMPB-04-2012-0015

Halasi, D., Schwarcz, P., Mura, L., & Roháčiková, O. (2019). The impact of EU support resources on business success of family-owned businesses. *Potravinarstvo Slovak Journal of Food Sciences*, *13*(1), 846–853. doi:10.5219/1167

Halbesleben, J. R. (2010). A Meta-Analysis of Work Engagement: Relationships with Burnout, Demands, Resources, and Consequences. In A. B. Bakker & M. P. Leiter (Eds.), *Work Engagement: A Handbook of Essential Theory and Research* (Vol. 8, pp. 102–117). Psychology Press.

Hall, D. T. (1996). *The Career is Dead - Long Live the Career: A Relational Approach to Careers*. Jossey-Bass.

Hall, E. T. (1977). *Beyond Culture*. Doubleday. Anchor Press.

Hall, E. T. (1981). *The Silent Language*. Anchor Press.

Hallowell, M. R., & Yugar-Arias, I. F. (2016). Exploring fundamental causes of safety challenges faced by Hispanic construction workers in the US using photovoice. *Safety Science*, *82*, 199–211. doi:10.1016/j.ssci.2015.09.010

Hamari, J., Sjöklint, M., & Ukkonen, A. (2016). The sharing economy: Why people participate in collaborative consumption. *Journal of the Association for Information Science and Technology*, *67*(9), 2047–2059. doi:10.1002/asi.23552

Hanaeda, H., & Serita, T. (2003). Price and Volume Effects Associated with a Change in the Nikkei 225 Index List: New Evidence from the Big Change on April 2000. In J. J. Choi, & T. Hiraki (Eds.), International Finance Review Vol. 4- The Japanese Finance: Corporate Finance and Capital Markets in Changing Japan (pp. 199-225). Bingley: Emerald Group Publishing Limited.

Hansen, M. T., Nohria, N., & Tierney, T. (1999). What's your strategy for managing knowledge? *Harvard Business Review*, *77*(2), 106–116. PMID:10387767

Haq, M., Skully, M., & Pathan, S. (2010). Efficiency of microfinance institutions: A data envelopment analysis. *Asia-Pacific Financial Markets*, *17*(1), 63–97. doi:10.100710690-009-9103-7

Harari, O. (1995). The new job security. *Your Management Review*, *84*(9), 29–31.

Harris, L., & Gurel, E. (1986). Price and Volume Effects Associated with Changes in the S&P 500 List: New Evidence for the Existence of Price Pressures. *The Journal of Finance*, *41*(4), 815–829. doi:10.1111/j.1540-6261.1986.tb04550.x

Hartl, P., & Hartlová, H. (2010). Velký psychologický slovník. Prague, CZ. *Portal (Baltimore, Md.)*.

Hart, S. (2017). Today's learners and educators: Bridging the generational gaps. *Teaching and Learning in Nursing*, *12*(4), 253–257. doi:10.1016/j.teln.2017.05.003

Hassini, E., Surti, C., & Searcy, C. (2012). A literature review and a case study of sustainable supply chains with a focus on metrics. *International Journal of Production Economics*, *140*(1), 69–82. doi:10.1016/j.ijpe.2012.01.042

Hatfield, S. L. (2002). Understanding the four generations to enhance workplace management. *AFP Exchange*, *22*(4), 72–74.

Hatum, A. (2010). *Next generation talent management. Talent management to survive turmoil*. Palgrave Macmillan., doi:10.1057/9780230295094

Hautala, J. (2011). Cognitive proximity in international research groups. *Journal of Knowledge Management*, *15*(4), 601–624. doi:10.1108/13673271111151983

Have, R. P., & Rubalcaba, L. (2016). Social innovation research: An emerging area of innovation studies? *Research Policy*, *45*(9), 1923–1935. doi:10.1016/j.respol.2016.06.010

Hawlitschek, F., Teubner, T., & Gimpel, H. (2016). Understanding the Sharing Economy—Drivers and Impediments for Participation in Peer-to-Peer Rental. *Conference: Hawaii International Conference on System Sciences*. doi: 10.1109/HICSS.2016.593

Hawlitschek, F., Notheisen, B., & Teubner, T. (2018). The limits of trust-free systems: A literature review on blockchain technology and trust in the sharing economy. *Electronic Commerce Research and Applications*, *29*, 50–63. doi:10.1016/j.elerap.2018.03.005

Hegde, S. P., & McDermott, J. B. (2003). The Liquidity Effects of Revisions to the S&P 500 Index: An Empirical Analysis. *Journal of Financial Markets*, *6*(3), 413–459. doi:10.1016/S1386-4181(02)00046-0

Heidrich, B. (2002). Business as Unusual the Role of National Cultural Back-ground in Corporate Life. *European Integration Studies*, *1*(2), 25–36.

Henderson, J. C. (2007). Corporate social responsibility and tourism: Hotel companies in Phuket, Thailand, after the Indian Ocean tsunami. *International Journal of Hospitality Management*, *26*(1), 228–239. doi:10.1016/j.ijhm.2006.02.001

Henseler, J., Ringle, C. M., & Sarstedt, M. (2012). Using partial least squares path modeling in advertising research: Basic concepts and recent issues. In S. Okazaki (Ed.), *Handbook of research on international advertising* (pp. 252–276). Edward Elgar. doi:10.4337/9781781001042.00023

Henseler, J., Ringle, C. M., & Sarstedt, M. (2015). A New Criterion for Assessing Discriminant Validity in Variance-based Structural Equation Modeling. *Journal of the Academy of Marketing Science*, *43*(1), 115–135. doi:10.100711747-014-0403-8

Henseler, J., Ringle, C. M., & Sarstedt, M. (2016). Testing measurement invariance of composites using partial least squares. *International Marketing Review*, *33*(3), 405–431. doi:10.1108/IMR-09-2014-0304

Henseler, J., Ringle, C. M., & Sinkovics, R. R. (2009). The use of partial least squares path modeling in international marketing. *Advances in International Marketing*, *20*(1), 277–319. doi:10.1108/S1474-7979(2009)0000020014

Hermes, N., & Lensink, R. (2011). Microfinance: Its Impact, Outreach, and Sustainability. *World Development*, *39*(6), 875–881. doi:10.1016/j.worlddev.2009.10.021

Hermes, N., Lensink, R., & Meesters, A. (2011). Outreach and Efficiency of Microfinance Institutions. *World Development*, *39*(6), 938–948. doi:10.1016/j.worlddev.2009.10.018

Hernandez Ticono, M., Holmes, P., & Wilson, N. (2018). Polytomous response financial distress models: The role of accounting, market and macroeconomic variables. *International Review of Financial Analysis*, *59*, 276–289. doi:10.1016/j.irfa.2018.03.017

Hernaus, T., & Pološki Vokic, N. (2014). Work design for different generational cohorts: Determining common and idiosyncratic job characteristics. *Journal of Organizational Change Management*, *27*(4), 615–641. doi:10.1108/JOCM-05-2014-0104

Highman, K. (2018). *The Brexit White Paper: what does it mean for higher education and research.* Retrieved on January 02, 2020, https://www.researchcghe.org/perch/resources/publications/pb9.pdf

Hockerts, K., & Morsing, M. (2008). *A literature review on corporate social responsibility in the innovation process.* Center for Corporate Social Responsibility.

Hofstede, G. (1980). *Cultures's consequences: International differences in work-related values.* Sage.

Hofstede, G. H., & Hofstede, G. (2001). *Culture's Consequences: Comparing Values, Behaviors, Institutions, and Organizations Across Nations* (2nd ed.). Sage Publications.

Hofstede, G., Hosfstede, G. J., & Minkov, M. (2010). *Cultures and Organizations: Software of the Mind.* McGraw-Hill.

Hofstetter, R., Zhang, J. Z., & Herrmann, A. (2018). Successive Open Innovation Contests and Incentives: Winner-Take-All or Multiple Prizes? *Journal of Product Innovation Management*, *35*(4), 492–517. doi:10.1111/jpim.12424

Høgevold, N. M., Svensson, G., Padin, C., & Dos Santos, M. (2016). A comparison of sustainable business models between goods and service industries: Similarities and differences. *International Journal of Business Excellence*, *10*(1), 20–36. doi:10.1504/IJBEX.2016.077616

Hoi, C. K., Wu, Q., & Zhang, H. (2013). Is Corporate Social Responsibility (CSR) Associated Tax Avoidance? Evidence from Irresponsible CSR Activities. *The Accounting Review*, *88*(6), 2025–2059. doi:10.2308/accr-50544

Holcomb, J. L., Upchurch, R. S., & Okumus, F. (2007). Corporate social responsibility: What are top hotel companies reporting? *International Journal of Contemporary Hospitality Management*, *19*(6), 461–475. doi:10.1108/09596110710775129

Holden, N. J. (2002). *Cross-cultural management: a knowledge management perspective*. Harlow, UK: Financial Times/ Prentice Hall.

Hole, D., Zhong, L., & Schwartz, J. (2010). Talking about whose generation. *Deloitte Review*, *6*, 83–97.

Hollenbeck, J. R., Beersma, B., & Schouten, M. E. (2012). Beyond team types and taxonomies: A dimensional scaling conceptualization for team description. *Academy of Management Review*, *37*(1), 82–106. doi:10.5465/amr.2010.0181

Holliday, C. O. J., Schmidheiny, S., & Watts, S. P. (2002). *Walking the Talk: The Business Case for Sustainable Development*. World Business Council for Sustainable Development.

Holt, C. (2010). *Building a Talent Management strategy*. Retrieved on November 13, 2019, from www.slideshare.net/ Proesce/proesce-building-a-talent-management-strategy

Holtom, B. C., Mitchell, T. R., Lee, T., & Inderrieden, E. J. (2005). Shocks as causes of turnover: What they are and how organizations can manage them. *Human Resource Management*, *44*(3), 337–352. doi:10.1002/hrm.20074

Hong, J. H., Kim, B. C., & Park, K. S. (2019). Optimal risk management for the sharing economy with stranger danger and service quality. *European Journal of Operational Research*, *279*(3), 1024–1035. doi:10.1016/j.ejor.2019.06.020

Hope, A. (2018). Sustainable business model design: A review of tools for developing responsible business models. In L. Moratis, F. Melissen, & S. O. Idowu (Eds.), *Sustainable Business Models: Principle, Promise and Practice* (pp. 377–394). Springer. doi:10.1007/978-3-319-73503-0_17

Horváthová, P. (2011). Talent management. Prague: Wolters Kluwer.

Horváthová, P. (2010). Talent management a jeho využití při řízení lidských zdrojů v organizaci. *Central European Review of Economic*, *13*(2), 77–95.

Hosie, P., & Nankervis, A. (2016). A multidimensional measure of managers' contextual and task performance. *Personnel Review*, *45*(2), 419–447. doi:10.1108/PR-02-2014-0038

Hossain, M. (2018). Motivations, challenges, and opportunities of successful solvers on an innovation intermediary platform. *Technological Forecasting and Social Change*, *128*, 67–73. doi:10.1016/j.techfore.2017.10.018

Houben, R., & Snyers, A. (2018). *Cryptocurrencies and blockchain: legal context and implications for financial crime, money laundering and tax evasion*. European Parliament study: PE 619.024. Repéré à https://publications.europa.eu/en/ publication-detail/-/publication/631f847c-b4aa-11e8-99ee-01aa75ed71a1

Hou, M., Liu, H., Fan, P., & Wei, Z. (2016). Does CSR Practice Pay Off in East Asian Firms? A Meta-Analytic Investigation. *Asia Pacific Journal of Management*, *33*(1), 195–228. doi:10.100710490-015-9431-2

Howe, N., & Strauss, W. (2000). *Millennials Rising: The Next Great Generation*. Vintage Books.

Howe, N., & Strauss, W. (2007). The next 20 years: How customer and workforce attitudes will evolve. *Harvard Business Review*, *85*(7/8), 41–52. PMID:17642125

Hroník, F. (2007). *Rozvoj a vzdělávání pracovníků: základy moderní personalistiky*. Grada Publishing.

Huang, J., Su, S., Zhou, L., & Liu, X. (2013). Attitude toward the viral ad: Expanding traditional advertising models to interactive advertising. *Journal of Interactive Marketing*, *27*(1), 36–46. doi:10.1016/j.intmar.2012.06.001

Huang, J., Wang, H., & Kochenberger, G. (2017). Distressed Chinese firm prediction with discretized data. *Management Decision*, *55*(5), 786–807. doi:10.1108/MD-08-2016-0546

Huang, M. C., & Chiu, Y. P. (2018). Relationship governance mechanisms and collaborative performance: A relational life-cycle perspective. *Journal of Purchasing and Supply Management*, *24*(3), 260–273. doi:10.1016/j.pursup.2017.12.002

Huckle, S., & White, M. (2016). Socialism and the Blockchain. *Future Internet, 8*(4), 49. Retrieved from https://www.mdpi.com/1999-5903/8/4/49

Huckle, S., Bhattacharya, R., White, M., & Beloff, N. (2016). Internet of Things, Blockchain and Shared Economy Applications. *Procedia Computer Science*, *98*, 461–466. doi:10.1016/j.procs.2016.09.074

Hudson, R. (2005). Ethical Investing: Ethical Investors and Managers. *Business Ethics Quarterly*, *15*(4), 641–657. doi:10.5840/beq200515445

Hunt, S., & Boliver, V. (2019). *Private providers of higher education in the UK: mapping the terrain.* Retrieved on January 01, 2020, from https://www.researchcghe.org/perch/resources/publications/to-publishwp47.pdf

Hurtado-Jaramillo, C. H., Chiu, M.-C., Arimany-Serrat, N., Ferràs, X., & Meijide, D. (2018). Identifying Sustainability-Value Creation Drivers for a Company in the Water Industry Sector: An Empirical Study. *Water Resources Management*, *32*(3), 3961–3978. doi:10.100711269-018-2030-5

Hur, W.-M., Kim, H., & Woo, J. (2014). How CSR Leads to Corporate Brand Equity: Mediating Mechanisms of Corporate Brand Credibility and Reputation. *Journal of Business Ethics*, *125*(1), 75–86. doi:10.100710551-013-1910-0

Husted, B. W., & Allen, D. B. (2007). Strategic Corporate Social Responsibility and Value Creation among Large Firms: Lessons from the Spanish Experience. *Long Range Planning*, *40*(6), 594–610. doi:10.1016/j.lrp.2007.07.001

Hu, X., & Liu, D. (2019). The research into screening crisis early warning indicators of supply chain quality based on fuzzy inference system. *Journal of Intelligent & Fuzzy Systems*, *36*(2), 935–942. doi:10.3233/JIFS-169870

Iacobucci, D., & Nordhielm, C. (2000). Creative Benchmarking. *Harvard Business Review*, (November-December), 24–25.

Ibarra, D., Ganzarain, J., & Igartua, J. I. (2018). Business model innovation through Industry 4.0: A review. *Procedia Manufacturing*, *22*, 4–10. doi:10.1016/j.promfg.2018.03.002

Ibidunni, A. S., Ogunnaike, O. O., & Abiodun, A. J. (2017). Extending the knowledge strategy concept: Linking organizational knowledge with strategic orientations. *Academy of Strategic Management Journal, 16*(3), 1-11.

Iles, P., Xin, C. A., & Preece, D. (2010). Talent Management and HRM in Multinational companies in Beijing: Definitions, differences and drivers. *Journal of World Business*, *45*(2), 179–189. doi:10.1016/j.jwb.2009.09.014

Ilieva, J., Killingley, P., Tsiligiris, V., & Usher, A. (2019). *The shape of global higher education: international comparisons with Europe, British Council, UK.* Retrieved on January 08, 2020, from https://www.britishcouncil.org/sites/default/files/k006_02_the_shape_of_global_higher_education_in_europe_final_v5_web.pdf

Imai, K. S., Arun, T., & Annim, S. K. (2010). Microfinance and Household Poverty Reduction: New Evidence from India. *World Development*, *38*(12), 1760–1774. doi:10.1016/j.worlddev.2010.04.006

Information Resources Management Association. (2019). *Human Performance Technology: Concepts, Methodologies, Tools, and Applications*. IGI Global.

Innocent, M., Gabriel, P., & Divard, R. (2017). Understanding the participation experience of the top contributors in a crowdsourcing of inventive activities context. *Recherche et Applications en Marketing*, *32*(1), 2–20. doi:10.1177/2051570716676257

Inoue, Y., Kent, A., & Lee, S. (2011). CSR and the Bottom Line: Analyzing the Link Between CSR and Financial Performance for Professional Teams. *Journal of Sport Management*, *25*(6), 531–549. doi:10.1123/jsm.25.6.531

International Labor Organization. (2007). *Key indicators of labor market success* (5th ed.). Retrieved January 1, 2009, from http://www.ilo.org/public/english/employment/strat/kilm/download.htm

Iorgulescu, M. C. (2016). Generation Z and its perception of work. *Cross-Cultural Management Journal*, *18*(1), 47–54.

Iqbal, A., Latif, F., Marimon, F., Sahibzada, U. F., & Hussain, S. (2019). From knowledge management to organizational performance: Modelling the mediating role of innovation and intellectual capital in higher education. *Journal of Enterprise Information Management*, *32*(1), 36–59. doi:10.1108/JEIM-04-2018-0083

Ismail, A. (2015, January 18). *How the sharing economy will impact marketing*. Retrieved from https://techcrunch.com/2015/01/17/how-the-sharing-economy-will-impact-marketing/

Jackson, A., Boswell, K., & Davis, D. (2011). Sustainability and Triple Bottom Line Reporting – What is it all about? *International Journal of Business. Human Technology*, *1*(3), 55–59.

Jacquemet, M. (2015). Asylum and superdiversity: The search for denotational accuracy during asylum hearings. *Language & Communication*, *44*, 72–81. doi:10.1016/j.langcom.2014.10.016

Jafari, S. M., Jandaghi, G., & Taghavi, H. (2016). Factors influencing the intention to accept advertising in mobile social networks. *Marketing and Management of Innovations*, *1*, 57–72.

Janney, J. J., & Gove, S. (2011). Reputation and corporate social responsibility aberrations, trends, and hypocrisy reactions to firm choices in the stock option backdating scandal. *Journal of Management Studies*, *48*(7), 1562–1585. doi:10.1111/j.1467-6486.2010.00984.x

Janošková, M., & Palaščáková, D. (2018). Corporate social responsibility as a strategic goal in business: A case study. In C. R. Baker (Ed.), Corporate Social Responsibility (CSR): Practices, Issues and Global Perspectives (pp. 109-144). New York, NY: Nova Science Publishers.

Jassawalla, A., & Sashittal, H. (2017). How and why Millennials are initiating conflict in vertical dyads and what they are learning: A two-stage study. *International Journal of Conflict Management*, *28*(5), 644–670. doi:10.1108/IJCMA-05-2016-0026

Javeed, S. A., & Lefen, L. (2019). An Analysis of Corporate Social Responsibility and Firm Performance with Moderating Effects of CEO Power and Ownership Structure: A Case Study of the Manufacturing Sector of Pakistan. *Sustainability*, *11*(1), 248. doi:10.3390u11010248

Jelenic, D. (2011). The importance of knowledge management in Organizations - With emphasis on the balanced scorecard learning and growth Perspective. *Proceedings of the Management, Knowledge and Learning International Conference, 2011*, 33–43.

Jenkins, H. (2006). Small Business Champions for Corporate Social Responsibility. *Journal of Business Ethics*, *67*(3), 241–256. doi:10.100710551-006-9182-6

Jennings, P. D., & Zandbergen, P. A. (1995). Ecologically sustainable organizations: An institutional approach. *Academy of Management Review*, *20*(4), 1015–1052. doi:10.5465/amr.1995.9512280034

Jensen, A. B. (2013). Do we need one business model definition? *Journal of Business Models, 1*(1), 61–84. doi:10.5278/ojs.jbm.v1i1.705

Jerrima, J., Chmielewskib, A. K., & Parker, Ph. (2015). Socioeconomic inequality in access to high-status colleges: A cross-country comparison. *Research in Social Stratification and Mobility, 42*, 20–32. doi:10.1016/j.rssm.2015.06.003

Jhunjhunwala, S. (2014). Intertwining CSR with Strategy – The Way Ahead. *Corporate Governance, 14*(2), 211–219. doi:10.1108/CG-03-2011-0021

John, L. K., Kim, T., & Barasz, K. (2018). *Ads that don't overstep.* Retrieved from https://hbr.org/2018/01/ads-that-dont-overstep

Johnes, J. (2016). Why UK universities are returning to the public debt markets. *The Conversation.* Retrieved on December 18, 2019, from http://eprints.hud.ac.uk/id/eprint/27831/1/Why%20UK%20universities%20are%20returning%20to%20the%20public%20debt%20markets.pdf

Johnson, W. (2016). *Disrupt yourself: Putting the power of disruptive innovation to work.* Retrieved from http://www.thegoblegroup.com/wp-content/uploads/2016/01/Disrupt_Yourself.pdf

Johnson, J. D. (2008). Employee assistance programs: Sources of assistance relations to inputs and outcomes. *Journal of Workplace Behavioral Health, 23*(3), 263–282. doi:10.1080/15555240802242866

Jones, T. M. (1991). Ethical decision making by individuals in organizations: An issue-contingent model. *Academy of Management Review, 16*(2), 366-395. doı: doi:10.2307/258867

Jones, E., Brown, S. P., Zoltners, A. A., & Weitz, B. A. (2005). The changing environment of selling and sales management. *Journal of Personal Selling & Sales Management, 25*(2), 105–111.

Jory, S., Ngo, T. N., Wang, D., & Saha, A. (2015). The market response to corporate scandals involving CEOs. *Applied Economics, 47*(17), 1723–1738. doi:10.1080/00036846.2014.995361

Judge, T. A., Scott, B. A., & & Ilies, R. (2006). Hostility, job attitudes, and workpace deviance: Test of a multilevel model. *Journal of Applied Psychology, 91*(1), 126-138. doı: doi:10.1037/0021-9010.91.1.126

Junglas, I. A., Johnson, N. A., & Spitzmüller, C. (2008). Personality traits and concern for privacy: An empirical study in the context of location-based services. *European Journal of Information Systems, 17*(4), 387–402. doi:10.1057/ejis.2008.29

Junglas, I., & Spitzmüller, C. (2006). Personality traits and privacy perceptions: An empirical study in the context of location-based services. In S. Ceballos (Ed.), *Proceedings of the International Conference on Mobile Business* (pp. 36–46). Los Alamitos, CA: IEEE Computer Society. 10.1109/ICMB.2006.40

Jung, S.-Y., Lee, S., & Dalbor, M. (2016). The Negative Synergistic Effect of Internationalization and Corporate Social Responsibility on US Restaurant Firms' Value Performance. *International Journal of Contemporary Hospitality Management, 28*(8), 1759–1777. doi:10.1108/IJCHM-07-2014-0361

Kagermann, H., Wahlster, W., & Helbig, J. (2013). *Securing the future of German manufacturing industry: Recommendations for implementing the strategic initiative INDUSTRIE 4.0: Final report of the Industrie 4.0 Working Group.* National Academy of Science and Engineering.

Kahn, W. A. (1990). Psychological conditions of personal engagement and disengagement at work. *Academy of Management Journal, 33*(4), 692–724.

Kalyango, D. L. (2009, December). *Uganda's experience with tiered banking regulation.* Paper presented at the Tiered Banking Workshop, Kampala, Uganda. Retrieved June 12, 2016, from http://www.finmark.org.za/sites//wp-content/uploads/pubs/Paper_Kalyango_tiered_04.pdf

Kamalul Ariffin, S., Ismail, I., & Mohammad Shah, K. A. (2016). Religiosity moderates the relationship between ego-defensive function and attitude towards advertising. *Journal of Islamic Marketing*, *7*(1), 15–36. doi:10.1108/JIMA-11-2014-0074

Kamble, S. S., Gunasekaran, A., & Gawankar, S. A. (2018). Sustainable Industry 4.0 framework: A systematic literature review identifying the current trends and future perspectives. *Process Safety and Environmental Protection*, *117*, 408–425. doi:10.1016/j.psep.2018.05.009

Kaminska, R., & Borzillo, S. (2017). Challenges to the learning organization in the context of generational diversity and social networks. *The Learning Organization*, *25*(2), 92–101. doi:10.1108/TLO-03-2017-0033

Kantar. (2017). *DIMENSION: Communication planning in a disrupted world | Kantar Media.* Retrieved from https://www.kantarmedia.com/us/thinking-and-resources/reports/dimension-communication-planning-in-a-disrupted-world

Kaplan, R. S., & Norton, D. P. (1992). The balanced scorecard – Measures that drive performance. *Harvard Business Review*, *70*(1), 71–79. PMID:10119714

Kappou, K., & Oikonomou, I. (2016). Is There a Gold Social Seal? The Financial Effects of Additions to and Deletions from Social Stock Indices. *Journal of Business Ethics*, *133*(3), 533–552. doi:10.100710551-014-2409-z

Karpoff, J., Lee, D., & Martin, G. (2008). The cost to firms of cooking the books. *Journal of Financial and Quantitative Analysis*, *43*(3), 581–611. doi:10.1017/S0022109000004221

Katz, V. (2015). Regulation the sharing economy. *Berkeley Technology Law Journal*, *30*(4), 1067–1126. doi:10.15779/Z38HG45

Keepnews, D., Brewer, C., Kovner, C., & Shin, J. (2010). Generational difference among newly licensed registered nurses. *Nursing Outlook*, *58*(3), 155–163. doi:10.1016/j.outlook.2009.11.001 PMID:20494691

Keller, A. (2015). *Social norms in commercial ads – welcome to the National Social Norms Center.* Retrieved from http://socialnorms.org/social-norms-in-commercial-ads/

Kelliher, C., Richardson, J., & Boiarintseva, G. (2019). All of work? All of life? Reconceptualising work-life balance for the 21st century. *Human Resource Management Journal*, *29*(2), 97–112. doi:10.1111/1748-8583.12215

Ketelaar, P. E., Van Gisbergen, M. S., Bosman, J. A. M., & Beentjes, J. (2010). The effects of openness on attitude toward the ad, attitude toward the brand, and brand beliefs in Dutch Magazine Ads. *Journal of Current Issues and Research in Advertising*, *32*(2), 71–85. doi:10.1080/10641734.2010.10505286

Ketelaar, P. E., van't Riet, J., Thorbjornsen, H., & Buijzen, M. (2018). Positive uncertainty: The benefit of the doubt in advertising. *International Journal of Advertising*, *37*(2), 256–269. doi:10.1080/02650487.2016.1231163

Ketola, T. (2010). Five Leaps to Corporate Sustainability through a Corporate Responsibility Portfolio Matrix. *Corporate Social Responsibility and Environmental Management*, *17*(6), 320–336. doi:10.1002/csr.219

Ketter, E. (2020). Millennial travel: tourism micro-trends of European Generation Y. *Journal of Tourism Futures.*

Khan, M. M., Mahmood, N., & Jalees, T. (2017). Perceived usefulness of mobile and mobile advertising: Understanding relationship through structural approach. *Global Management Journal for Academic & Corporate Studies*, *7*(2), 111–120.

Khera, S. N., & Malik, S. (2017). Conceptualizing and measuring life priorities of Generation Y: Evidences from Indian context. *Industrial and Commercial Training*, *49*(2), 80–86. doi:10.1108/ICT-04-2016-0024

Khrushch, O. V. (2016). Innovatsiyni pidkhody u formuvanni stratehiyi korporatyvnoyi sotsial'noyi vidpovidal'nosti pidpryyemstva. *Visnyk Khmel'nyts'koho natsional'noho universytetu. Ekonomichni nauky, 4*(2), 261-265.

Khun, T. S. (1997). *The Structure of Scientific Revolutions* [A estrutura das revoluções científicas] (5th ed.). Editora Perspectiva S.A.

Kidd, J. M., & Smewing, C. (2001). The role of the supervisor in career and organizational commitment. *European Journal of Work and Organizational Psychology*, *10*(1), 25–40. doi:10.1080/13594320042000016

Kilkki, K., Mäntylä, M., Karhu, K., Hämmäinen, H., & Ailisto, H. (2018). A disruption framework. *Technological Forecasting and Social Change*, *129*, 275–284. doi:10.1016/j.techfore.2017.09.034

Kim, K., Kirkman, B. L., & Chen, G. (2008). Cultural intelligence and international assignment effectiveness: a conceptual model and preliminary findings. In S. Ang & L. Van Dyne (Eds.), *Handbook of Cultural Intelligence: Theory, Measurement, and Applications* (pp. 71–90). M.E. Sharpe.

Kinapti, T. T. (2019, January 28). *Cara menghilangkan iklan di HP Android tanpa root, aman dan cepat.* Retrieved from https://www.liputan6.com/tekno/read/3881293/cara-menghilangkan-iklan-di-hp-android-tanpa-root-aman-dan-cepat

Kipkirong Tarus, D., & Aime, F. (2014). Board demographic diversity, firm performance and strategic change: A test of moderation. *Management Research Review*, *37*(12), 1110–1136. doi:10.1108/MRR-03-2013-0056

Kira, M., & van Eijnatten, F. M. (2008). Socially Sustainable Work Organizations: A Chaordic System Approach. *Systems Research and Behavioral Science*, *25*(6), 743–756. doi:10.1002res.896

Kirk, A. K., & Brown, D. F. (2003). Employee assistance programs: A review of the management of stress and wellbeing through workplace counselling and consulting. *Australian Psychologist*, *38*(2), 138–143. doi:10.1080/0005006031 0001707137

Kish-Gephart, J. J., Harrison, D. A., & Trevino, L. K. (2010). Bad Apples, Bad Cases, and Bad Barrels: Meta-Analytic Evidence About Sources of Unethical Decisions at Work. *The Journal of Applied Psychology*, *95*(1), 1–31. doi:10.1037/a0017103 PMID:20085404

Kivisto, P., & La Vecchia-Mikkola, V. (2015). The integration of Iraqis in two European cities: Emotions and identity work. *Emotion, Space and Society*, *16*, 90–98. doi:10.1016/j.emospa.2015.01.002

Kiyani, A. A., Ayupp, K., & Rasool, S. (2018). Exploring the construct of task performance of academicians in an Asian context: teaching is different from research. *Evidence-based HRM: A Global Forum for Empirical Scholarship, 6*(1), 25-38. doi:10.1108/EBHRM-03-2016-0008

Klein, J., & Dawar, N. (2004). Corporate social responsibility and consumers' attributions and brand evaluations in a product–harm crisis. *International Journal of Research in Marketing*, *21*(3), 203–217. doi:10.1016/j.ijresmar.2003.12.003

Kluckhohn, C. K. (1951). Values and Value Orientations in the Theory of Action. In T. Parsons & E. A. Shils (Eds.), *Toward a General Theory of Action* (pp. 388–433). Harvard University Press. doi:10.4159/harvard.9780674863507.c8

Kluckhohn, F. R., & Strodtbeck, F. L. (1961). *Variations in Value Orientations*. HarperCollins.

Knapp, C. A., Weber, C., & Moellenkamp, S. (2017). Challenges and strategies for incorporating Generation Z into the workplace. *Corporate Real Estate Journal*, *7*(2), 137–148.

Knouse, S. B. (2011). Managing generational diversity in the 21st century. *Competition Forum, 9*(2), 255-260.

Kochan, T. (2002). Addressing the crisis in confidence in corporations: Root causes, victims, and strategies for reform. *The Academy of Management Executive*, *16*(3), 139–141. doi:10.5465/ame.2002.8540394

Kodjamanis, A., & Angelopoulos, S. (2013). Consumer perception and attitude towards advertising on social networking sites: The case of Facebook. In *Proceedings of International Conference on Communication* (pp. 53–58). Media, Technology and Design. Retrieved from http://www.cmdconf.net/2013/makale/PDF/11.pdf

Kogan, M. (2001). Bridging the gap. *Government Executive, 33*(12). Retrieved on August 15, 2019 from https://www.govexec.com/magazine/magazine-human-resources-management/2001/09/bridging-the-gap/9752/

Kollmann, T., Stoeckmann, C., Kensbock, J. M., & Peschl, A. (2020). What satisfies younger versus older employees, and why? An aging perspective on equity theory to explain interactive effects of employee age, monetary rewards, and task contributions on job satisfaction. *Human Resource Management*, *59*(1), 101–115. doi:10.1002/hrm.21981

Kollmus, A., & Agyeman, J. (2002). Mind the gap: Why do people act environmentally and what are the barriers to pro-environmental behavior. *Environmental Education Research*, *8*(3), 239–260. doi:10.1080/13504620220145401

Koopmans, L., Bernaards, C., Hildebrandt, V., van Buuren, S., van der Beek, A., & de Vet, H. (2013). Development of an individual work performance questionnaire. *International Journal of Productivity and Performance Management*, *62*(1), 6–28. doi:10.1108/17410401311285273

Kosba, A., Miller, A., Shi, E., Wen, Z., & Papamanthou, C. (2016, May). Hawk: The blockchain model of cryptography and privacy-preserving smart contracts. In *2016 IEEE symposium on security and privacy (SP)* (pp. 839-858). IEEE.

Kostiviarová, Z., & Lutter, J. (2015). *Cesta k efektívnejšiemu fungovaniu HR. Výsledky prieskumu HR Benchmarking 2015*. Deloitte.

Kotler, P., & Caslione, J. A. (2009). *Chaotics: The Business of Managing and Marketing in the Age of Turbulence*. AMACOM.

Kourti, I. (2017). Effective performance management of inter-organisational collaborations through the construction of multiple identities. *International Journal of Business Performance Management*, *18*(2), 236–251. doi:10.1504/IJBPM.2017.083077

Kovalenko, O. V. (2015). Problemni aspekty stanovlennya innovatsiynoyi systemy Ukrayiny v konteksti teoriyi tekhnolohichnoho rozvytku. *Efektyvna ekonomika, 3*, 31-33.

Koyuda, P. M., & Sheyko, I. A. (2013). *Efektyvnist' ekonomichnoyi diyal'nosti pidpryyemstv: teoriya ta praktyka*. Kompaniya SMIT.

Kozlowski, S. W., Gully, S. M., Brown, K. G., Salas, E., Smith, E. M., & Nason, E. R. (2001). Effects of training goals and goal orientation traits on multidimensional training outcomes and performance adaptability. *Organizational Behavior and Human Decision Processes*, *85*(1), 1–31. doi:10.1006/obhd.2000.2930 PMID:11341815

KPMG. (2014). *Setting the Course for Growth: CEO Perspectives*. Retrieved at https://assets.kpmg

KPMG. (2017). *Meet the millennials*. Available at: https://home.kpmg/content/dam/kpmg/uk/pdf/2017/04/Meet-the-Millennials-Secured.pdf

Kraimer, M. L., Seibert, S. E., Wayne, S. J., Liden, R. C., & Bravo, J. (2011). Antecedents and outcomes of organizational support for development: The critical role of career opportunities. *The Journal of Applied Psychology*, *96*(3), 485–500. doi:10.1037/a0021452 PMID:21114356

Kramer, L. (2010). Generational diversity. *Dimensions of Critical Care Nursing*, *29*(3), 125–128. doi:10.1097/DCC.0b013e3181d24ba9 PMID:20395729

Krosnick, J. A., Boninger, D. S., Chuang, Y. C., Berent, M. K., & Carnot, C. G. (1993). Attitude strength: One construct or many related constructs? *Journal of Personality and Social Psychology*, *65*(6), 1132–1151. doi:10.1037/0022-3514.65.6.1132

Kuhn, T., & Ashcraft, K. L. (2003). Corporate Scandal and the Theory of the Firm: Formulating the Contributions of Organizational Communication Studies. *Management Communication Quarterly*, *17*(1), 20–57. doi:10.1177/0893318903253421

Kuijpers, M. A., & Scheerens, J. (2006). Career competencies for the modern career. *Journal of Career Development*, *32*(4), 303–319. doi:10.1177/0894845305283006

Kulik, C. T., Treuren, G., & Bordia, P. (2012). Shocks and final straws: Using exit interview data to examine the unfolding model's decision paths. *Human Resource Management*, *51*(1), 25–46. doi:10.1002/hrm.20466

Kuntz, J., Connell, P., & Naswall, K. (2017). Workplace resources and employee resilience: The role of regulatory profiles. *Career Development International*, *22*(4), 419–435. doi:10.1108/CDI-11-2016-0208

Kunz, V., Ferencová, M., Hronová, Š., & Singer, M. (2015). Researching of socially responsible behaviour in selected companies and organizations through their corporate websites. *Polish Journal of Management Studies*, *12*(2), 91–102.

Kupperschmidt, B. R. (2000). Multi-generation employees: Strategies for effective management. *The Health Care Manager*, *19*(1), 65–76. doi:10.1097/00126450-200019010-00011 PMID:11183655

Kursch, M. (2014). Management Tool "Talent management". *Promanager*. Retrieved on November 12, 2019, from www.promanager.sk/hr-management/

Kwon, I. - W. G., Kim, S-H., & Martin, D. G. (2016). Healthcare supply chain management; strategic areas for quality and financial improvement. *Technological Forecast and Social Change, 113*(B), 422-428. doi:10.1016/j.techfore.2016.07.014

Lacina, M. J., & Karim, K. E. (2004). Tests of Market Reaction and Analysts' Forecast Revisions to the Disclosure of Improved Management Earnings Expectations: A Case of Concurrent Bad News Management Earnings Forecasts. *Review of Quantitative Finance and Accounting*, *23*(2), 123–148. doi:10.1023/B:REQU.0000039508.11607.9d

Lackmann, J., Ernstberger, J., & Stich, M. (2012). Market Reactions to Increased Reliability of Sustainability Information. *Journal of Business Ethics, 107*(2), 111-128. doi: 1-1026-3 doi:10.100710551-01

Laitinen, E. K., & Chong, H. G. (1999). Early warning system for crisis in SMEs: Preliminary evidence from Finland and the UK. *Journal of Small Business and Enterprise Development*, *6*(1), 89–102. doi:10.1108/EUM0000000006665

Lamberti, L., & Noci, G. (2012). The Relationship Between CSR and Corporate Strategy in Medium-Sized Companies: Evidence from Italy. *Business Ethics (Oxford, England)*, *21*(4), 402–416. doi:10.1111/beer.12002

Lambert, S. C., & Davidson, R. A. (2013). Applications of the business model in studies of enterprise success, innovation and classification: An analysis of empirical research from 1996 to 2010. *European Management Journal*, *31*(6), 668–681. doi:10.1016/j.emj.2012.07.007

Lančarič, D., Ubrežiová, I., Savov, R., & Kozáková, J. (2018). Entrepreneurial intentions of students: a case of Slovakia. In E. Horská, Z. Kapsdorferová, & M. Hallová (Eds.), International scientific days 2018. Towards Productive, Sustainable and Resilient Global Agriculture and Food Systems (pp. 1954-1967). Prague: Wolters Kluwer.

Lancaster, L. C., & Stillman, D. (2002). When generations collide: who they are. In *Why They Clash. How to Solve the Generational Puzzle at Work.* Harper Collins.

Landrum, N. E., & Ohsowski, B. (2018). Identifying Worldviews on Corporate Sustainability: A Content Analysis of Corporate Sustainability Reports. *Business Strategy and the Environment*, *27*(1), 128–151. doi:10.1002/bse.1989

Landry, A. T., Schweyer, A., & Whillans, A. (2017). Winning the war for talent: Modern motivational methods for attracting and retaining employees. *Compensation and Benefits Review*, *49*(4), 230–246. doi:10.1177/0886368718808152

Lanier, K. (2017). 5 things HR professionals need to know about Generation Z: Thought leaders share their views on the HR profession and its direction for the future. *Strategic HR Review*, *16*(6), 288–290. doi:10.1108/SHR-08-2017-0051

Laukkanen, T. (2015). How Uncertainty avoidance affects innovation resistance in mobile banking: The moderating role of age and gender. In *Proceedings of the 48th Hawaii International Conference on System Sciences* (pp. 3601–3610). Washington, DC: IEEE Computer Society. 10.1109/HICSS.2015.433

Lave, J., & Wenger, E. (1991). *Situated learning: legitimate peripheral participation.* Cambridge University Press. doi:10.1017/CBO9780511815355

Lee, S., Lee, D., & Schniederjans, M. (2011). Supply chain innovation and organizational performance in the healthcare industry. *International Journal of Operations & Production Management, 11*(31), 1193 1214. doi:10.1108/01443571111178493

Lee, C. S., Hung, D. K. M., & Ling, T. C. (2012). Work values of Generation Y preservice teachers in Malaysia. *Procedia: Social and Behavioral Sciences*, *65*, 704–710. doi:10.1016/j.sbspro.2012.11.187

Lee, C., Huang, G. H., & Ashford, S. J. (2018). Job insecurity and the changing workplace: Recent developments and the future trends in job insecurity research. *Annual Review of Organizational Psychology and Organizational Behavior*, *5*(1), 335–359. doi:10.1146/annurev-orgpsych-032117-104651

Lee, D. (2015). *Handbook of Digital Currency*. Elsevier.

Lee, D. K. C., Guo, L., & Wang, Y. (2018). Cryptocurrency: A new investment opportunity? *Journal of Alternative Investments*, *20*(3), 16–40. doi:10.3905/jai.2018.20.3.016

Lee, J. K., Lee, S.-Y., & Hansen, S. S. (2017). Source credibility in consumer-generated advertising in youtube: The moderating role of personality. *Current Psychology (New Brunswick, N.J.)*, *36*(4), 849–860. doi:10.100712144-016-9474-7

Lee, J. Y. (2019). A decentralized token economy: How blockchain and cryptocurrency can revolutionize business. *Business Horizons*, *62*(6), 773–784. doi:10.1016/j.bushor.2019.08.003

Lee, J.-H., & Fan, W.-M. (2014). Investors' perception of corporate governance: A spillover effect of Taiwan corporate scandals. *Review of Quantitative Finance and Accounting*, *43*(1), 97–119. doi:10.100711156-013-0366-8

Lee, J., Kim, S., & Ham, C.-D. (2016). A double-edged sword? Predicting consumers' attitudes toward and sharing intention of native advertising on social media. *The American Behavioral Scientist*, *60*(12), 1425–1441. doi:10.1177/0002764216660137

Lee, K.-H., & Kim, D. (2019). A peer-to-peer (P2P) platform business model: The case of Airbnb. *Service Business*, *13*(4), 647–669. doi:10.100711628-019-00399-0

Lee, K.-H., & Shin, D. (2010). Consumers' Responses to CSR Activities: The Linkage Between Increased Awareness and Purchase Intention. *Public Relations Review*, *36*(2), 193–195. doi:10.1016/j.pubrev.2009.10.014

Lee, M. D. P. (2008). A review of the theories of corporate social responsibility: Its evolutionary path and the road ahead. *International Journal of Management Reviews*, *10*(1), 53–73. doi:10.1111/j.1468-2370.2007.00226.x

Legisweb. (2017). *Law no. 1866 / 09.03.2017* [Lei nº 1866 de 09/03/2017]. Retrieved on November 13, 2019, from https://www.legisweb.com.br/legislacao/?id=350888

Lei, J., Dawar, N., & Gürhan-Canlı, Z. (2012). Base-Rate Information in Consumer Attributions of Product-Harm Crises. *JMR, Journal of Marketing Research*, *49*(3), 336–348. doi:10.1509/jmr.10.0197

Leinonen, T., Chandola, T., Laaksonen, M., & Martikainen, P. (2020). Socio-economic differences in retirement timing and participation in post-retirement employment in a context of a flexible pension age. *Ageing and Society*, *40*(2), 348–368. doi:10.1017/S0144686X18000958

Lennihan, M. (2018). *Google's Chrome browser starts blocking 'disruptive' ads*. Retrieved from https://www.cbc.ca/news/technology/ad-blocking-chrome-1.3713568

Leonard, K. L., & Masatu, M. C. (2017). Changing health care provider performance through measurement. *Social Science & Medicine*, *181*, 54–65. doi:10.1016/j.socscimed.2017.03.041 PMID:28371629

Leon, R. D. (2013a). Sustainable knowledge based organization from an international perspective. *International Journal of Management Science and Information Technology*, *10*, 166–181.

Leon, R. D. (2013b). A managerial early warning system for the sustainable knowledge based organization. *Ovidius University Annals. Economic Sciences Series*, *13*(1), 842–847.

Leon, R. D. (2018a). The sustainable knowledge based organizations – definitions and characteristics. *Environmental Engineering and Management Journal*, *17*(6), 1425–1437. doi:10.30638/eemj.2018.141

Leon, R. D. (2018b). A Managerial Early Warning System: From an Abstract to a Subjective Approach. In R. D. Leon (Ed.), *Managerial Strategies for Business Sustainability during Turbulent Times* (pp. 100–121). Information Science Publishing., doi:10.4018/978-1-5225-2716-9.ch006

Leon, R. D., Rodriguez-Rodriguez, R., Gomez-Gasquet, P., & Mula, J. (2017). Social network analysis: A tool for evaluating and predicting future knowledge flows from an insurance organization. *Technological Forecasting and Social Change*, *114*, 103–118. doi:10.1016/j.techfore.2016.07.032

Le, T. D., & Vo, H. (2017). Consumer attitude towards website advertising formats: A comparative study of banner, pop-up and in-line display advertisements. *International Journal of Internet Marketing and Advertising*, *11*(3), 202–217. doi:10.1504/IJIMA.2017.085654

Letmathe, P., & Rossler, M. (2019). Tacit knowledge transfer and spillover learning in ramp-ups. *International Journal of Operations & Production Management*, *39*(9/10), 1099–1121. doi:10.1108/IJOPM-08-2018-0508

Lévy, P. (1999). *Collective intelligence: Mankind's emerging world in cyberspace*. Perseus Books.

Lewis, R. E., & Heckman, R. J. (2006). Talent management: A critical review. *Human Resource Management Review*, *16*(2), 139–154. doi:10.1016/j.hrmr.2006.03.001

Li, C. P., Qin, J. X., Li, J. J., & Hou, Q. (2016). The accident early warning system for iron and steel enterprises based on combination weighting and Grey Prediction Model GM (1,1). *Safety Science*, *89*, 19–27. doi:10.1016/j.ssci.2016.05.015

Lichtenthaler, U. (2007). Hierarchical strategy and strategic fit in the keep-or-sell decision. *Management Decision*, *45*(3), 340–359. doi:10.1108/00251740710744990

Lieu, P. T., Lin, C. W., & Yu, H. F. (2008). Financial early-warning models on cross-holding groups. *Industrial Management & Data Systems*, *108*(8), 1060–1080. doi:10.1108/02635570810904613

Lievens, F., Conway, J. M., & De Corte, W. (2008). The relative importance of task, citizenship and counterproductive performance to job performance ratings: Do rater source and team-based culture matter? *Journal of Occupational and Organizational Psychology*, *81*(1), 11–27. doi:10.1348/096317907X182971

Lii, Y.-S., & Lee, M. (2012). Doing right leads to doing well: when the type of CSR and reputation interact to affect consumer evaluations of the firm. *Journal of Business Ethics, 105*(1), 69-81. doi:s10551-011-0948-0

Li, J. (2020). Examining the Literature on Comprehensive Global Competence for Individual in Contemporary China. In J. Li (Ed.), *Comprehensive Global Competence for World-Class Universities in China* (pp. 89–100). Springer. doi:10.1007/978-981-15-1640-5_6

Lima Crisóstomo, V., de Souza Freire, F., & Cortes de Vasconcellos, F. (2011). Corporate Social Responsibility, Firm Value and Financial Performance in Brazil. *Social Responsibility Journal*, *7*(2), 295–309. doi:10.1108/17471111111141549

Lin, C. H., Yang, H. L., & Liou, D. Y. (2009). The Impact of Corporate Social Responsibility on Financial Performance: Evidence from Business in Taiwan. *Technology in Society*, *31*(1), 56–63. doi:10.1016/j.techsoc.2008.10.004

Lin, C.-S., Chang, R.-Y., & Dang, V. T. (2015). An Integrated Model to Explain How Corporate Social Responsibility Affects Corporate Financial Performance. *Sustainability*, *7*(7), 8292–8311. doi:10.3390u7078292

Ling Lim, H. (2012). Generation Y workforce expectations: Implications for the UAE. *Education, Business and Society*, *5*(4), 281–293. doi:10.1108/17537981211284452

Lin-Hi, N., & Blumberg, I. (2018). The Link Between (Not) Practicing CSR and Corporate Reputation: Psychological Foundations and Managerial Implications. *Journal of Business Ethics*, *150*(1), 185–198. doi:10.100710551-016-3164-0

Lin, L., Hung, P.-H., Chou, D.-W., & Lai, C. W. (2019). Financial Performance and Corporate Social Responsibility: Empirical Evidence from Taiwan. *Asia Pacific Management Review*, *24*(1), 61–71. doi:10.1016/j.apmrv.2018.07.001

Lin, Z., Yu, Z., & Zhang, L. (2014). Performance outcomes of balanced scorecard application in hospital administration in China. *China Economic Review*, *30*, 1–15. doi:10.1016/j.chieco.2014.05.003

Lips-Wiersma, M., & Hall, D. T. (2007). Organizational career development is not dead: A case study on managing the new career during organizational change. *Journal of Organizational Behavior*, *28*(6), 771–792. doi:10.1002/job.446

Li, Q., Wei, F., & Zhou, S. (2017). Early warning systems for multi-variety and small batch manufacturing based on active learning. *Journal of Intelligent & Fuzzy Systems*, *33*(5), 2945–2952. doi:10.3233/JIFS-169345

Li, S., & Davies, B. J. (2001). GloStra – a hybrid system for developing global strategy and associated Internet strategy. *Industrial Management & Data Systems*, *101*(3), 132–140. doi:10.1108/02635570110386643

Littlefield, E., Morduch, J., & Hashemi, S. (2003). Is microfinance an effective strategy to reach the millennium development goals? *Focus Note*. Retrieved June 12, 2016, from https://www.cgap.org/sites/default/files/CGAP-Focus-Note-Is-Microfinance-an-Effective-Strategy-to-Reach-the-Millennium-Development-Goals-Jan-2003.pdf

Liu, M. T., Wong, I. A., Shi, G., Chu, R., & Brock, J. L. (2014). The Impact of Corporate Social Responsibility (CSR) Performance and Perceived Brand Quality on Customer-Based Brand Preference. *Journal of Services Marketing*, *28*(3), 181–194. doi:10.1108/JSM-09-2012-0171

Liu, S. (2006). The Impacts of Index Rebalancing and Their Implications: Some New Evidence from Japan. *Journal of International Financial Markets, Institutions and Money*, *16*(3), 246–269. doi:10.1016/j.intfin.2005.02.006

Li, Y. Z., Xia, J. B., Li, C. G., & Zheng, M. Y. (2015). Construction of an Early-Warning System for Vegetable Prices Based on Index Contribution Analysis. *Sustainability*, *7*(4), 3823–3837. doi:10.3390u7043823

Li, Y., Ding, R., Cui, L., Lei, Z., & Mou, J. (2019). The impact of sharing economy practices on sustainability performance in the Chinese construction industry. *Resources, Conservation and Recycling*, *150*, 104409. doi:10.1016/j.resconrec.2019.104409

Llull, A. (2003). *Contabilidad medioambiental y desarrollo sostenible en el sector turístico* (Unpublished doctoral dissertation). Palma de Mallorca: Govern de les Illes Balears/Conselleria d'Economia, Comerç i Industria.

London, M. (1983). Toward a theory of career motivation. *Academy of Management Review*, *8*(4), 620–630. doi:10.5465/amr.1983.4284664

London, M. (1997). Overcoming career barriers: A model of cognitive and emotional processes for realistic appraisal and constructive coping. *Journal of Career Development*, *24*(1), 25–38. doi:10.1023/A:1025082420866

Long, D. M., & Rao, S. (1995). The Wealth Effects of Unethical Business Behavior. *Journal of Economics and Finance*, *19*(2), 65–73. doi:10.1007/BF02920510

Lovett, C. M. (2013). The global contexts of higher education. *Change: The Magazine of Higher Learning*, *45*(1), 73–78. doi:10.1080/00091383.2013.749169

Lozano, R. (2008). Developing collaborative and sustainable organizations. *Journal of Cleaner Production*, *16*(4), 499–509. doi:10.1016/j.jclepro.2007.01.002

Lu, D. (2019). Facebook launches a digital currency. *New Scientist*, *242*(3236), 11. doi:10.1016/S0262-4079(19)31157-1

Luo, X., & Bhattacharya, C. B. (2006). Corporate Social Responsibility, Customer Satisfaction, and Market Value. *Journal of Marketing*, *70*(4), 1–18. doi:10.1509/jmkg.70.4.001

Luo, X., & Du, S. (2012). "Good" Companies Launch More New Products. *Harvard Business Review*, *90*(4), 28.

Luo, X., & Du, S. (2015). Exploring the Relationship Between Corporate Social Responsibility and Firm Innovation. *Marketing Letters*, *26*(4), 703–714. doi:10.100711002-014-9302-5

Luthans, F., Avey, J. B., Avolio, B. J., & Peterson, S. (2010). The development and resulting performance impact of positive psychological capital. Management Department Faculty Publications. Lincoln: University of Nebraska. 157. https://digitalcommons.unl.edu/managementfacpub/157

Ma, B., Zhang, L., Li, F., & Wang, G. (2010). The effects of product-harm crisis on brand performance. *International Journal of Market Research*, *52*(4), 443–458. doi:10.2501/S1470785309201399

MacGregor, S. P., & Fontrodona, J. (2008). Exploring the fit between CSR and Innovation. *IESE Business School – University of Navarra*. Retrieved on November 17, 2019, from https://pdfs.semanticscholar.org/ 619d/e1d0acce38bdd-8568159939661555bf6bf0f.pdf

Machado, C. G., Winroth, M. P., & Silva, E. H. D. (2019). Sustainable manufacturing in Industry 4.0: An emerging research agenda. *International Journal of Production Research*. Advance online publication. doi:10.1080/00207543.2019.1652777

Mack, O., Khare, A., Kramer, A., & Burgartz, T. (Eds.). (2016). *Managing in a VUCA World*. Springer International Publishing. doi:10.1007/978-3-319-16889-0

Maddox, J. (2000). Positioning the goalposts. *Nature*, *403*(6766), 139–140. doi:10.1038/35003065 PMID:10646578

Maese, V. A., Avery, A. W., Naftalis, B. A., Wink, S. P., & Valdez, Y. D. (2016). Cryptocurrency: A primer. *The Banking Law Journal, 133*(8), 468-471. Retrieved from https://www.lw.com/thoughtLeadership/cryptocurrency-a-primer

Magretta, J. (2002). Why business models matter. *Harvard Business Review*, *80*(5), 86–92. PMID:12024761

Mahajan, R., & Bose, M. (2018). Business sustainability: Exploring the meaning and significance. *IMI Konnect*, *7*(2), 8–13.

Malik, N. (2018). Authentic leadership – an antecedent for contextual performance of Indian nurses. *Personnel Review*, *47*(6), 1244–1260. doi:10.1108/PR-07-2016-0168

Malone, T. W. (2018). *Superminds: The Surprising Power of People and Computers Thinking Together*. Little, Brown and Company.

Mangano, R. (2018). Blockchain Securities, Insolvency Law and the Sandbox Approach. *European Business Organization Law Review*, *19*(4), 715–735. Advance online publication. doi:10.100740804-018-0123-5

Mannheim, K. (1928). The problem of generations. *Kölner Vierteljahrshefte für Soziologie, 7,* 157-185, 309-330.

Mannheim, K. (1952). The problem of a sociology of knowledge. *Essays on the Sociology of Knowledge*, 134-190.

Mantymaki, M., Baiyere, A., & Islam, A. K. M. N. (2019). Digital platforms and the changing nature of physical work: Insights from ride-hailing. *International Journal of Information Management*, *49*, 452–460. doi:10.1016/j.ijinfomgt.2019.08.007

Marants, J. (2012). The Evolution of Integrated Talent Management. *Institute for Human Resources.* Retrieved on November 12, 2019, from https://www.hr.com/en?t=/documentManager/sfdoc.file.supply&fileID=1341425076525

March, J. G. (1991). Exploration and exploitation in organizational learning. *Organization Science*, *2*(1), 71–87. doi:10.1287/orsc.2.1.71

Maringe, F., & de Wit, H. (2016). Global higher education partnerships: Equity and epistemic concerns with distribution and flows of intellectual capital. In J. E. Cote & A. Furlong (Eds.), *Routledge handbook of the sociology of higher education* (pp. 299–314). Routledge. doi:10.4324/9781315772233-27

Marini, G., Locke, W., & Whitchurch, C. (2019). *The future higher education workforce in locally and globally engaged higher education institutions: a review of literature on the topic of 'the academic workforce'.* Retrieved on January 02, 2020, from https://www.researchcghe.org/perch/resources/publications/wp43.pdf

Marin, L., Martín, P. J., & Rubio, A. (2017). Doing Good and Different! The Mediation Effect of Innovation and Investment on the Influence of CSR on Competitiveness. *Corporate Social Responsibility and Environmental Management*, *24*(2), 159–171. doi:10.1002/csr.1412

Mariotto, F. L., Zanni, P. P., & Marcondes de Moraes, G. H. S. (2014). What is the use of a single-case study in management research? *Revista de Administração de Empresas*, *54*(4), 358–369. doi:10.1590/S0034-759020140402

Marnewick, A., & Marnewick, H. B. (2019). The ability of project managers to implement industry 4.0-related projects. *IEEE Access: Practical Innovations, Open Solutions*, *8*. https://ieeexplore.ieee.org/document/8939367

Marshall, C., & Rossman, G. B. (2011). *Designing qualitative research* (5th ed.). Sage.

Martin, C. J. (2016). The sharing economy: A pathway to sustainability or a nightmarish form of neoliberal capitalism? *Ecological Economics*, *121*, 149–159. doi:10.1016/j.ecolecon.2015.11.027

Martin, K. D., & Cullen, J. B. (2006). Continuities and extensions of ethical climate theory: A meta analytic review. *Journal of Business Ethics*, *69*(2), 175–194. doi:10.100710551-006-9084-7

Maslow, A. H. (1981). *Motivation and personality*. Prabhat Prakashan.

Maslow, A. H. (2013). *Toward a psychology of being*. John Wiley & Sons.

Mason, C. H., & Perreault, W. D. Jr. (1991). Collinearity, power, and interpretation of multiple regression analysis. *JMR, Journal of Marketing Research*, *28*(3), 268–280. doi:10.1177/002224379102800302

Massa, L., & Tucci, C. (2014). Business model innovation. In M. Dodgson, D. M. Gann, & N. Phillips (Eds.), *The Oxford handbook of innovation management* (pp. 420–441). Oxford University Press.

Masten, A. S., & Reed, M. G. J. (2002). Resilience in development. Handbook of Positive Psychology, 74, 88.

McCrindle, M. (2019). *Australia's Population Map and Generational Profile Update*. Retrieved at https://mccrindle.com.au/insights/blogarchive/australias-population-mapand-generational-profile-update

McDonald, K. M., Schultz, E., Albin, L., Pineda, N., Lonhart, J., Sundaram, V., & Davies, S. (2014). *Care coordination measures atlas update* (AHRQ Publication No. 14–0037-EF). Retrieved on November 23, 2019 from https://www.ahrq.gov/professionals/prevention-chronic-care/improve/coordination/atlas2014/index.html

McDonald, P., & Kippen, R. (2001). Labour supply prospects in sixteen developed countries. *Population and Development Review*, *27*(1), 1–32. doi:10.1111/j.1728-4457.2001.00001.x

McDonnell, A. (2011). Still Fighting the "War for Talent"? Bridging the Science Versus Practice Gap. *Journal of Business and Psychology*, *26*(2), 169–173. doi:10.100710869-011-9220-y

McKenzie, J., & Van Winkelen, C. (2004). *Understanding the knowledgeable organization: Nurturing knowledge competence*. Thomson.

McNeil, K., Johnson, O., & Johnson, A. (2001). "Did you hear what Tommy Hilfiger said?" Urban legend, urban fashion and African-American generation Xers. *Journal of Fashion Marketing and Management*, *5*(3), 234–240. doi:10.1108/EUM0000000007289

McSweeney, B. (2015). Hall, Hofstede, Huntington, Trompenaars, GLOBE: Common foundations, common flaws. In Y. Sánchez & C. F. Brühwiler (Eds.), *Transculturalism and Business in the BRIC States: A Handbook* (pp. 13–58). Gower Punlishing.

Mello, J. A. (2011). *Strategic Human Resource Management*. South-Western Cengage Learning.

Memon, A. H., & Rahman, I. A. (2014). SEM-PLS analysis of inhibiting factors of cost performance for large construction projects in Malaysia: Perspective of clients and consultants. *TheScientificWorldJournal*, *165158*, 1–9. Advance online publication. doi:10.1155/2014/165158 PMID:24693227

Mendenhall, R. R., & Nichols, W. D. (1988). Bad News and Differential Market Reactions to Announcements of Earlier-Quarters Versus Fourth-Quarter Earnings. *Journal of Accounting Research, 26*, 63-86. doı: doi:10.2307/2491180

Mensah, J., & Ricart Casadevall, S. (2019). Sustainable development: Meaning, history, principles, pillars, and implications for human action: Literature review. *Cogent Social Sciences*, *5*(1). Advance online publication. doi:10.1080/23311886.2019.1653531

Mercer, M. (2004). How Do Investors Assess the Credibility of Management Disclosures? *Accounting Horizons*, *18*(3), 185–196. doi:10.2308/acch.2004.18.3.185

Merkaš, Z., Perkov, D., & Bonin, V. (2020). The Significance of Blockchain Technology in Digital Transformation of Logistics and Transportation. *International Journal of E-Services and Mobile Applications*, *12*(1), 1–20. doi:10.4018/IJESMA.2020010101

Merriman, M. (2015). What if the Next Big Disruptor Isn't a What but a Who? *Ernst & Young*. Retrieved on August 28, 2019 from https://www.ey.com/Publication/vwLUAssets/EY-rise-of-gen-znew-challenge-for-retailers/$FILE/EY-rise-of-gen-znew-challenge-for-retailers.pdf

Merriman, M., & Valerio, D. (2016). One Tough Customer: How Gen Z is Challenging the Competitive Landscape and Redefining Omnichannel. *Ernst & Young*. Retrieved on August 29, 2019. https://www.ey.com/Publication/vwLUAssets/EY-one-tough-customer/$FILE/EY-one-tough-customer.pdf

Mersland, R., & Storm, R. O. (2010). Microfinance Mission Drift? *World Development, 38*(1), 28–36. doi:10.1016/j.worlddev.2009.05.006

Metaxiotis, K., & Ergazakis, K. (2008). Exploring stakeholder knowledge partnerships in a knowledge city: A conceptual model. *Journal of Knowledge Management, 12*(5), 137–150. doi:10.1108/13673270810902993

Mettler, T., & Rohner, P. (2009). Performance management in health care: the past, the present, and the future. In *Proceedings of 9th International Conference on Business Informatics* (pp. 699-708). Vienna, Austria: AIS Electronic Library.

Michaels, E., Hanfield-Jones, H., & Axelrod, B. (2001). *The War for Talent*. Harvard Business Press.

Middleton, V. (1998). *Sustainable Tourism. A Marketing Perspective*. Butterworth-Heinemann.

Milagres, R., & Burcharth, A. (2019). Knowledge transfer in interorganizational partnerships: What do we know? *Business Process Management Journal, 25*(1), 27–68. doi:10.1108/BPMJ-06-2017-0175

Miller, J. (2019). *The voice of Generation Z: We want to be intrapreneurs*. Retrieved at https://www.rallyware.com/blog/generation-z-engagement

Ministry of Industry, Tourism and Trade. (2006). Plan Nacional de Adaptación al Cambio Climático. Madrid: Oficina Española de Cambio Climático, Ministry of Industry, Tourism and Trade.

Mishra, J., Chiwenga, K., & Ali, K. (2019). Collaboration as an enabler for circular economy: A case study of a developing country. *Management Decision*, MD-10-2018-1111. Advance online publication. doi:10.1108/MD-10-2018-1111

Mishra, P., & McDonald, K. (2017). Career resilience: An integrated review of the empirical literature. *Human Resource Development Review, 16*(3), 207–234. doi:10.1177/1534484317719622

Mitchell, T., Holton, B., Lee, T., Sablynski, C., & Erez, M. (2001). Why people stay: Using job embeddedness to predict voluntary turnover. *Academy of Management Journal, 44*(6), 1102–1122.

MIX. (2019). *Countries & Regions Database*. Retrieved November 05, 2019 from https://www.themix.org/mixmarket/countries-regions

Mizrahi, A. (2019). *Total surveillance coin will be a dystopia if controlled by Facebook or government*. Available at: https://news.bitcoin.com/total-surveillance-coin-will-be-a-dystopia-if-controlled-by-facebook-or-government/

MobileAds Com. (2018). *Best mobile ad formats for display advertising campaigns*. Retrieved from https://www.mobileads.com/blog/best-mobile-ad-formats-sizes-display-ad-campaigns

Model, S. (2005). Triangulation between case study and survey methods in management accounting research: An assessment of validity implications. *Management Accounting Research, 16*(2), 231–254. doi:10.1016/j.mar.2005.03.001

Mojzisch, A., Grouneva, L., & Schultz-Hardt, S. (2010). Biased evaluation of information during discussion: Disentangling the effects of preference consistency, social validation, and ownership of information. *European Journal of Social Psychology, 40*(6), 946–956. doi:10.1002/ejsp.660

Mönks, F. J. (1992). Development of the gifted child: The issue of identification and programmimg. In F. J. Monks & W. Peters (Eds.), *Talent for the future* (pp. 191–202). Mastricht.

Montecchia, A., Giordano, F., & Grieco, C. (2016). Communicating CSR: Integrated approach or selfie? evidence from the milan stock exchange. *Journal of Cleaner Production*, *136*, 42–52. doi:10.1016/j.jclepro.2016.01.099

Moon, J. (2007). The contribution of corporate social responsibility to sustainable development. *Sustainable Development*, *15*(5), 296–306. doi:10.1002d.346

Morden, T. (1999). Models of national culture: A management review. *Cross Cultural Management*, *6*(1), 19–44. doi:10.1108/13527609910796915

Moreira, J., Silva, M., Simoes, J., & Sousa, G. (2012). Marketing Innovation: Study of Determinants of Innovation in the Design and Packaging of Goods and Services—Application to Portuguese Firms. *Contemporary Management Research*, *8*(2). Advance online publication. doi:10.7903/cmr.11047

Morgan, G., & Smircich, L. (1980). The case of qualitative research. *Academy of Management Review*, *5*(4), 491–500. doi:10.5465/amr.1980.4288947

Morioka, S. N., Evans, S., & Carvalho, M. M. (2016). Sustainable business model innovation: Exploring evidences in sustainability reporting. *Procedia CIRP*, *40*, 659–667. doi:10.1016/j.procir.2016.01.151

Morrar, R., Arman, H., & Mousa, S. (2017). The Fourth Industrial Revolution (Industry 4.0): A social innovation perspective. *Technology Innovation. Management Review*, *7*(11), 12–20. doi:10.22215/timreview/1117

Morrell, D. L. (2011). Employee perceptions and the motivation of nonmonetary incentives. *Compensation and Benefits Review*, *43*(5), 318–323. doi:10.1177/0886368711407998

Morris, C. (1956). *Varieties of Human Value*. University of Chicago Press. doi:10.1037/10819-000

Morris, M., Schindehutte, M., & Allen, J. (2005). The entrepreneur's business model: Toward a unified perspective. *Journal of Business Research*, *58*(6), 726–735. doi:10.1016/j.jbusres.2003.11.001

Morris, S., Snell, S., & Björkman, I. (2016). An architectural framework for global talent management. *Journal of International Business Studies*, *47*(6), 723–747. doi:10.1057/jibs.2015.25

Motowidlo, S. J., Borman, W. C., & Schmit, M. J. (1997). A theory of individual differences in task and contextual performance. *Human Performance*, *10*(2), 71–83. doi:10.120715327043hup1002_1

Motowidlo, S. J., & Schmit, M. J. (1999). Performance assessment in unique jobs. In D. R. Llgen & E. D. Pulakos (Eds.), *The Changing Nature of Performance* (pp. 56–86). Jossey-Bass.

Mowers, S. (2019). *#CryptoCorner: Brexit could benefit bitcoin according to recent research, facebook (NASDAQ: $FB) hiring more blockchain positions*. Retrieved from https://www.spreaker.com/show/crypto-corner-podcast

Muñoz, R. M., de Pablo, J. D. S., & Peña, I. (2015). Linking Corporate Social Responsibility and Financial Performance in Spanish Firms. *European Journal of International Management*, *9*(3), 368–383. doi:10.1504/EJIM.2015.069133

Murillo, D., Buckland, H., & Val, E. (2017). When the sharing economy becomes neoliberalism on steroids: Unravelling the controversies. *Technological Forecasting and Social Change*, *125*, 66–76. doi:10.1016/j.techfore.2017.05.024

Murillo, D., & Lozano, J. M. (2006). SMEs and CSR: An Approach to CSR in their Own Words. *Journal of Business Ethics*, *67*(3), 227–240. doi:10.100710551-006-9181-7

Murphy, S. A. (2007). *Leading a multi-generational workforce*. available at: http://assets.aarp.org/www.aarp.org_/articles/money/employers/leading_multi-generational _workforce.pdf

Myers, S. D., Sen, S., & Alexandrov, A. (2010). The moderating effect of personality traits on attitudes toward advertisements: A contingency framework. *Management & Marketing*, *5*(3), 3–20.

Nabi, G. R. (2000). Motivational attributes and organizational experiences as predictors of career-enhancing strategies. *Career Development International*, *5*(2), 91–98. doi:10.1108/13620430010318963

Nærland, K., Müller-Bloch, C., Beck, R., & Palmund, S. (2017). *Blockchain to Rule the Waves – Nascent Design Principles for Reducing Risk and Uncertainty in Decentralized Environments*. Retrieved from https://www.researchgate.net/publication/319990622_Blockchain_to_Rule_the_Waves_-_Nascent_Design_Principles_for_Reducing_Risk_and_Uncertainty_in_Decentralized_Environments

Nakamoto, S. (2008). *Bitcoin: A Peer-to-Peer Electronic Cash System*. Retrieved from https://bitcoin.org/bitcoin.pdf

Nasurdin, A. M., Ramayah, T., & Kumaresan, S. (2005). Organizational stressors and job stress among managers: The moderating role of neuroticism. *Singapore Management Review*, *27*(2), 63–79.

Ndofor, H. A., & Levitas, E. (2004). Signaling the Strategic Value of Knowledge. *Journal of Management*, *30*(5), 685–702. doi:10.1016/j.jm.2004.04.002

Newberry, C. (2017). *The Facebook pixel: What it is and how to use it*. Retrieved from https://blog.hootsuite.com/facebook-pixel/

Ng, E. S., & Burke, R. J. (2010). Predictor of Business Student's Attitudes toward Sustainable Business Practices. *Journal of Business Ethics*, *95*(4), 603–615. doi:10.100710551-010-0442-0

Nghiem, H., Coelli, T., & Rao, D. S. P. (2006). The efficiency of microfinance in Vietnam: Evidence from NGO schemes in the north and the central regions. *International Journal of Environmental, Cultural, Economic and Social Sustainability*, *2*(5), 71–78. doi:10.18848/1832-2077/CGP/v02i05/54258

Nguyen, V. H., Agbola, F. W., & Choi, B. (2019). Does Corporate Social Responsibility Reduce Information Asymmetry? Empirical Evidence from Australia. *Australian Journal of Management*, *44*(2), 188–211. doi:10.1177/0312896218797163

Nicolau, J. L. (2008). Corporate Social Responsibility: Worth-Creating activities. *Annals of Tourism Research*, *35*(4), 990–1006. doi:10.1016/j.annals.2008.09.003

Nielsen. (2017). *Young and ready to travel: a look at millennial travelers*. Available at: www.nielsen. com/wp-content/uploads/sites/3/2019/04/nielsen-millennial-traveler-study-jan-2017.pdf

Niemimaa, M., Järveläinen, J., Heikkilä, M., & Heikkilä, J. (2019). Business continuity of business models: Evaluating the resilience of business models for contingencies. *International Journal of Information Management*, *49*, 208–216. doi:10.1016/j.ijinfomgt.2019.04.010

Noe, R. A., Greenberger, D. B., & Wang, S. (2002). Mentoring: What we know and where we might go. *Research in Personnel and Human Resources Management*, *21*, 129–173. doi:10.1016/S0742-7301(02)21003-8

Nourayi, M. M. (1994). Stock Price Responses to the SEC's Enforcement Actions. *Journal of Accounting and Public Policy*, *13*(4), 333–347. doi:10.1016/0278-4254(94)90003-5

Nowiński, W., & Kozma, M. (2017). How Can Blockchain Technology Disrupt the Existing Business Models? *Entrepreneurial Business and Economics Review*, *5*(3), 173–188. Advance online publication. doi:10.15678/EBER.2017.050309

Nunkoo, R., Teeroovengadum, V., Ringle, C. M., & Sunnassee, V. (2019). Service quality and customer satisfaction: The moderating effects of hotel star rating. *International Journal of Hospitality Management*, 102414. Advance online publication. doi:10.1016/j.ijhm.2019.102414

O'Reilly, N. M., Robbins, P., & Scanlan, J. (2019). Dynamic capabilities and the entrepreneurial university: A perspective on the knowledge transfer capabilities of universities. *Journal of Small Business and Entrepreneurship*, *31*(3), 243–263. doi:10.1080/08276331.2018.1490510

O'Riordan, T. (1976). *Environmentalism*. Pion Limited.

Oakes, K., & Galagan, P. (2011). *The executive guide to integrated talent management*. ASTD Press.

OC&C Strategy Consultants. (2019). *A generation without borders. Embracing Generation Z*. Retrieved on June 21, 2019 from https://www.occstrategy.com/media/1806/a-generation-without-borders.pdf

Ogan, M., & Yigitbasioglu, O. V. (2012). A review of dashboard in performance management: Implications for design and research. *International Journal of Accounting Information Systems*, *13*(1), 41–59. doi:10.1016/j.accinf.2011.08.002

Ogbeide, G., & Harrington, R. (2011). The relationship among participative management style, strategy implementation success, and financial performance in the foodservice industry. *International Journal of Contemporary Hospitality Management*, *23*(6), 719–738. doi:10.1108/09596111111153448

Oginni, O. S., & Omojowo, A. D. (2016). Sustainable development and corporate social responsibility in sub-Saharan Africa: Evidence from industries in Cameroon. *Economies*, *4*(2), 1–15. doi:10.3390/economies4020010

Oh, W., & Park, S. (2015). The Relationship Between Corporate Social Responsibility and Corporate Financial Performance in Korea. *Emerging Markets Finance and Trade, 51*(sup3), 85-94. doi:10.1080/1540496X.2015.1039903

Ohatka, F., & Fukazawa, Y. (2009). Managing risks symptom: A method to identify major risks of serious problem projects in SI environment using cyclic causal model. *Project Management Journal*, *41*(1), 51–60. doi:10.1002/pmj.20144

Olmedilla, D. (2016). Applying machine learning to ads integrity at Facebook. In *Proceedings of the 8th ACM Conference on Web Science - WebSci '16* (pp. 4–4). New York, NY: Association for Computing Machinery. 10.1145/2908131.2908134

Olsson, O., Aronsson, H., & Sandberg, E. (2017). Middle management involvement in handling variable patient flows. *Management Research Review*, *40*(9), 1007–1024. doi:10.1108/MRR-05-2016-0114

Orcutt, M. (2019). Once hailed as unhackable, blockchains are now getting hacked. *Technology Review*. Available at: https://www.technologyreview.com/s/612974/once-hailed-as-unhackable-blockchains-are-now-getting-hacked/

Organ, D. W., & Paine, J. (1999). A new kind of performance for industrial and organizational psychology: recent contributions to the study of organizational citizenship behavior. In C. L. Cooper & I. T. Robertson (Eds.), *International Review of Industrial and Organizational Psychology* (pp. 338–368). Wiley.

Osland, J. S., & Bird, A. (2000). Beyond sophisticated stereotyping: Cross-cultural sensemaking in context. *The Academy of Management Executive*, *14*(1), 1–12. doi:10.5465/ame.2000.2909840

Osterwalder, A. (2004). *The business model ontology – a proposition in a design science approach* (PhD. Thesis). University of Lausanne: Ecole des Hautes Etudes Commerciales HEC. Retrieved on December 15, 2019, from http://www.hec.unil.ch/aosterwa/Phd/Osterwalder_PhD _BM_Ontology.pdf

Osterwalder, A., & Pigneur, Y. (2010). *Business model generation*. Wiley.

Ozkan, M., & Solmaz, B. (2015). The changing face of the employees – generation Z and their perceptions of work (a study applied to university students). *Procedia Economics and Finance*, *26*, 476–483. doi:10.1016/S2212-5671(15)00876-X

Pace, S., Balboni, B., & Gistri, G. (2014). The effects of social media on brand attitude and WOM during a brand crisis: Evidences from the Barilla case. *Journal of Marketing Communications*, *23*(2), 135–148. doi:10.1080/13527266.2014.966478

Palos-Sanchez, P. R., & Correia, M. B. (2018). The collaborative economy based analysis of demand: Study of airbnb case in Spain and Portugal. *Journal of Theoretical and Applied Electronic Commerce Research, 13*(3), 85–98. doi:10.4067/S0718-18762018000300105

Papadakis, V. (2006). Do CEOs shape the process of making strategic decisions? Evidence from Greece. *Management Decision, 44*(3), 367–394. doi:10.1108/00251740610656269

Papadakis, V., & Barwise, P. (1998). *Strategic Decisions*. Kluwer Academic Publishers. doi:10.1007/978-1-4615-6195-8

Papula, J., Volná, J., Pilková, A., & Huľvej, J. (2013). Analysis of Awareness and Priorities, Focused on Intellectual Capital Among Slovak Companies. In B. Janiūnaitė, A. Pundziene, & M. Petraite (Eds.), *Proceedings of the 14th European conference on knowledge management* (vol. 1-2, pp. 517-526). Reading, UK: ACPI.

Parayitam, S., & Papenhausen, C. (2016). Agreement-seeking behavior, trust, and cognitive diversity in strategic decision making teams: Process conflict as a moderator. *Journal of Advances in Management Research, 13*(3), 292–315. doi:10.1108/JAMR-10-2015-0072

Parekh, B. (2007). Composite culture and multicultural society. In B. Chandra & S. Mahajan (Eds.), *Composite culture in a multi-cultural society*. National Book Trust.

Parida, V., Sjödin, D., & Reim, W. (2019). Reviewing Literature on Digitalization, Business Model Innovation, and Sustainable Industry: Past Achievements and Future Promises. *Sustainability, 11*(2), 391. doi:10.3390u11020391

Parker, G., & van Alstyne, M. W. (2005). Two-sided network effects: A theory of information product design. *Management Science, 51*(10), 1494–1504. doi:10.1287/mnsc.1050.0400

Parry, E., & Battista, V. (2019). The Generation Z in Great Britain- High standards and demands. In C. Scholz & A. Rennig (Eds.), *Generations in Europe: Inputs, Insights and Implications*. Emerald Publishing. doi:10.1108/978-1-78973-491-120191013

Parry, E., & Urwin, P. (2011). Generational differences in work values: A review of theory and evidence. *International Journal of Management Reviews, 13*(1), 79–96. doi:10.1111/j.1468-2370.2010.00285.x

Pasqualini Blass, A., Gouvêa da Costa, S. E., de Lima, E. P., & Borges, L. A. (2016). Measuring environmental performance in hospitals: A practical approach. *Journal of Cleaner Production, 141*(1), 279–289. doi:10.1016/j.jclepro.2016.07.213

Patel, N. (2018). *Your ads are getting ignored: 5 smart strategies to overcome banner blindness*. Retrieved from https://neilpatel.com/blog/your-ads-are-getting-ignored-5-smart-strategies-to-overcome-banner-blindness/

Patton, M. Q. (2002). *Qualitative research and evaluation methods*. Sage.

Pauluzzo, R., & Cagnina, M. R. (2016). Cultural dynamics and their impact on knowledge and organizational strategies of multinational corporations. In *Proceedings 11th International Forum on Knowledge Asset Dynamics - Towards a New Architecture of Knowledge: Big Data, Culture and Creativity*. (pp. 1297-1309). Dresden University of Technology.

Pazaitis, A., De Filippi, P., & Kostakis, V. (2017). Blockchain and value systems in the sharing economy: The illustrative case of backfeed. *Technological Forecasting and Social Change, 125*, 105–115. doi:10.1016/j.techfore.2017.05.025

Pearce, D., Markandya, A., & Barbier, E. B. (1989). *Blueprint for a Green Economy*. Earthscan.

Pérez, K. M., & Salgado, M. M. (2019). Mobility and the mobile: A study of adolescent migrants and their use of the mobile phone. *Mobile Media & Communication, 8*(1), 104–123. doi:10.1177/2050157918824626

Peri, G., Romiti, A., & Rossi, M. (2015). Immigrants, Domestic Labor and Women's Retirement decisions. *Labour Economics, 36*, 18–34. doi:10.1016/j.labeco.2015.07.004

Pes, A. (2016, December). *La economía será digital o no será sostenible*. Paper presented at the meeting El Protagonismo de las empresas ante la Agenda 2030, Madrid, Spain.

Peters, R., & Mullen, M. R. (2009). Some Evidence of the Cumulative Effects of Corporate Social Responsibility on Financial Performance. *Journal of Global Business Issues*, *3*(1), 1–14.

Philip, T., & Schwabe, G. (2018). Understanding early warning signs of failure in offshore-outsourced software projects at team level. *Journal of Global Operations and Strategic Sourcing*, *11*(3), 337–356. doi:10.1108/JGOSS-12-2017-0057

Phillips, J., & Edwards, L. (2009). Managing talent retention: an ROI approach. San Francisco, CA: Pfeiffer essential resources for training and HR professionals.

Pin-Chao, L., Jing-Qiu, L., Guangdong, W., Chun-Lin, W., Xiao-Ling, Z., & Meng-Chen, M. (2018). Comparing international contractors' CSR communication patterns: A semantic analysis. *Journal of Cleaner Production*, *203*, 353–366. doi:10.1016/j.jclepro.2018.08.218

Pin-Chao, L., Ni-Ni, X., Chun-Lin, W., Xiao-Ling, Z., & Jui-Lin, Y. (2017). Communicating the corporate social responsibility (CSR) of international contractors: Content analysis of CSR reporting. *Journal of Cleaner Production*, *156*, 327–336. doi:10.1016/j.jclepro.2017.04.027

Pinto, J., Leana, C. R., & Pil, F. K. (2008). Corrupt Organizations or Organizations of Corrupt Indiviudlas? Two Types of Organization-Level Corruption. *Academy of Management Review*, *33*(3), 685–709. doi:10.5465/amr.2008.32465726

Pojasek, R. B. (2007). A framework for business sustainability. *Environmental Quality Management*, *17*(2), 81–88. doi:10.1002/tqem.20168

Porath, C., Spreitzer, G., Gibson, C., & Garnett, F. G. (2012). Thriving at work: Toward its measurement, construct validation, and theoretical refinement. *Journal of Organizational Behavior*, *33*(2), 250–275. doi:10.1002/job.756

Porter, J. (2018). *Google accused of GDPR privacy violations by seven countries*. Retrieved from https://www.theverge.com/2018/11/27/18114111/google-location-tracking-gdpr-challenge-european-deceptive

Porter, M. E., & Van der Linde, C. (1995). Green and Competitive: Ending the Stalemate. *Harvard Business Review*, *73*(5), 120–134.

Prayoga, T., & Abraham, J. (2016). Behavioral intention to use IoT health device: The role of perceived usefulness, facilitated appropriation, big five personality traits, and cultural value orientations. *International Journal of Electrical and Computer Engineering*, *6*(4), 1751–1765. doi:10.11591/ijece.v6i4.pp1751-1765

Privett, N., & Gonsalvez, D. (2014). The top ten global health supply chain issues: Perspectives from the Field. *Operations Research for Health Care*, *3*(4), 226–230. doi:10.1016/j.orhc.2014.09.002

Prokopenko, J., & Bureau international du travail. (1990). *Gérer la productivité. Bureau International du Travail*. Genève, Suisse: Bureau international du travail.

Putri, V. M. (2019, July 17). *3 cara menghilangkan iklan di smartphone Android*. Retrieved from https://inet.detik.com/tips-dan-trik/d-4627910/3-cara-menghilangkan-iklan-di-smartphone-android

Pzytuła, S., Formánková, S., Ubrežiová, I., & Dunay, A. (2019). Corporate Social responsibility in Visegrad countries (Poland, Czech Republic, Slovakia, Hungary). In A. Dlugopolska-Mikonowicz, S. Przytula, & C. Stehr (Eds.), *Corporate Social Responsibility in Poland. Strategies, Opportunies and Challenges* (pp. 325–353). Springer. doi:10.1007/978-3-030-00440-8_20

QAA. (2019). *Review for Educational Oversight: OLC (Europe) Ltd trading as Organisational Learning Centre, monitoring visit report, July 2019*. Retrieved on January 02, 2020, from https://www.qaa.ac.uk/reviewing-higher-education/quality-assurance-reports/provider?UKPRN=10021609#

Quéré, B. P., Nouyrigat, G., & Baker, C. R. (2018). A Bi-Directional Examination of the Relationship Between Corporate Social Responsibility Ratings and Company Financial Performance in the European Context. *Journal of Business Ethics*, *148*(3), 527–544. doi:10.100710551-015-2998-1

Quigley, N. R., & Tymon, W. G. Jr. (2006). Toward an integrated model of intrinsic motivation and career self-management. *Career Development International*, *11*(6), 522–543. doi:10.1108/13620430610692935

Raes, A. M. L., Heijltjes, M. G., Glunk, U., & Roe, R. A. (2011). The interface of the top management team and middle managers: A process model. *Academy of Management Review*, *36*(1), 192–126. doi:10.5465/amr.2009.0088

Rahman, A. A., Castka, P., & Love, T. (2019). Corporate social responsibility in higher education. *Corporate Social Responsibility and Environmental Management*, *26*(4), 916–928. doi:10.1002/csr.1731

Ramdhani, N. (2012). Adaptasi bahasa dan budaya dari skala kepribadian Big Five. *Jurnal Psikologi*, *39*(2), 189–205. doi:10.22146/JPSI.6986

Ramirez, M. D., Liebig, Th., Thoreau, C., & Veneri, P. (2018). *The Integration of Migrants in OECD Regions: A First Assessment.* OECD Regional Development Working Papers 2018/01. doi:10.1787/fb089d9a-en

Rashid, A. (2018). Board independence and firm performance: Evidence from Bangladesh. *Future Business Journal*, *4*(1), 34–49. doi:10.1016/j.fbj.2017.11.003

Rea, B., Wang, Y. J., & Stoner, J. (2014). When a brand caught fire: The role of brand equity in product-harm crisis. *Journal of Product and Brand Management*, *23*(7), 532–542. doi:10.1108/JPBM-01-2014-0477

Rego, A. (2002). *Comportamentos de Cidadania nas Organizações*. McGraw Hill.

Regoniel, P. A. (2016). *How to write a thesis in the information age*. Academic Press.

Reid, D., Bussiere, D., & Greenaway, K. (2001). Alliance formation issues for knowledge-based enterprises. *International Journal of Management Reviews*, *3*(1), 79–100. doi:10.1111/1468-2370.00055

Reinlie, M. B. (2017). *Corporate Social Responsibility (CSR) and Innovation* (Master thesis). University of Oslo. Retrieved on November 21, 2019, from https://www.duo.uio.no/bitstream/handle/10852/57995/CSR-and-Innovation--ESST-Master-thesis--Maria-Borgeraas-Reinlie.pdf?sequence=1&isAllowed=y

Rexhepi, G., Kurtishi, S., & Bexheti, G. (2013). Corporate Social Responsibility (CSR) and Innovation–The Drivers of Business Growth? *Procedia: Social and Behavioral Sciences*, *75*, 532–541. doi:10.1016/j.sbspro.2013.04.058

Reynolds, J., Stewart, M., MacDonald, R., & Sischo, L. (2006). Have adolescents become too ambitious? High school seniors' educational and occupational plans, 1976 to 2000. *Social Problems*, *53*(2), 186–206. doi:10.1525p.2006.53.2.186

Rezvani, J. (2017). *3 ways technology will continue to disrupt digital marketing in 2018*. Retrieved from https://medium.com/the-mission/3-ways-technology-will-continue-to-disrupt-digital-marketing-in-2018-60a3ee0a1fa7

Rhyne, E. (1998). The Yin and Yang of microfinance. Reaching the poor and sustainability. *MicroBanking Bulletin*, *2*(1), 6–9.

Richardson, B. J. (2009). Keeping Ethical Investment Ethical: Regulatory Issues for Investing for Sustainability. *Journal of Business Ethics*, *87*(4), 555–572. doi:10.100710551-008-9958-y

Richter, N. F., Cepeda, G., Roldán, J. L., & Ringle, C. M. (2015). European management research using partial least squares structural equation modeling (PLS-SEM). *European Management Journal, 33*(1), 1–3. doi:10.1016/j.emj.2014.12.001

Rigby, D. K., Sutherland, J., & Noble, A. (2018). Agile at scale. *Harvard Business Review, 96*(3), 88–96.

Rigdon, E. E. (2012). Rethinking partial least squares path modeling: In praise of simple methods. *Long Range Planning, 45*(5–6), 341–358. doi:10.1016/j.lrp.2012.09.010

Ringland, G. (2010). The role of scenarios in strategic foresight. *Technological Forecasting and Social Change, 77*(9), 1493–1498. doi:10.1016/j.techfore.2010.06.010

Ringle, C. M., Wende, S., & Becker, J. M. (2015). *SmartPLS 3*. Retrieved November, 15, 2019, from http://www.smartpls.com

Robinson, H., Carrillo, P., Anumba, C. J., & Patel, M. (2009). *Governance and knowledge management for public-private partnerships*. John Wiley & Sons.

Robinson, M. S. (2001). *The Microfinance Revolution. Sustainable Finance for the Poor*. World Bank., doi:10.1596/0-8213-4524-9

Rockcontent. (2018). *Digital platforms: what they are and how do the big companies in the world use them?* [Plataformas digitais: o que é e como as grandes empresas do mundo utilizam?]. Retrieved on November 23, 2019, from https://inteligencia.rockcontent.com/plataformas-digitais/

Rodriguez, M., Boyer, S., Fleming, D., & Cohen, S. (2019). Managing the next generation of sales, Gen Z/Millennial cusp: An exploration of grit, entrepreneurship, and loyalty. *Journal of Business-To-Business Marketing, 26*(1), 43–55. doi:10.1080/1051712X.2019.1565136

Roehm, M., & Tybout, A. M. (2006). When Will a Brand Scandal Spill Over, and How Should Competitors Respond? *JMR, Journal of Marketing Research, 43*(3), 366–373. doi:10.1509/jmkr.43.3.366

Rogers, P., Ojha, D., & White, R. (2011). Conceptualizing complementarities in manufacturing flexibility: A comprehensive view. *International Journal of Production Research, 49*(12), 3767–3793. doi:10.1080/00207543.2010.499116

Roldán, J. L., & Sánchez-Franco, M. J. (2012). Variance-based structural equation modeling: Guidelines for using partial least squares. In M. Mora, G. Ovsei, A. Steenkamp, & M. S. Raisinghani (Eds.), *Research methodologies, innovations and philosophies in software systems engineering and information systems* (pp. 193–221). Information Science Reference. doi:10.4018/978-1-4666-0179-6.ch010

Roman, S. (2017). Engaging Generation Z in the workforce: Technology, intrapreneurship & culture. *Talent is Transforming, 2*(7). Retrieved at https://www.linkedin.com/pulse/engaging-generation-z-workforce-technology-culture-shaara-ives

Roome, N., & Louche, C. (2016). Journeying toward business models for sustainability: A conceptual model found inside the black box of organizational transformation. *Organization & Environment, 29*(1), 11–35. doi:10.1177/1086026615595084

Roongrerngsuke, S. (2010). Attracting and retaining multigenerational workforce in China, India, and Thailand. *SHRM Annual conference*. http://sapphire.shrm.org/annualconferenceondemand/2010-annualconference/6292010-attracting-retaining-multigenerationalworkforce-china-india-thai land.aspx

Roos, D., & Hahn, R. (2019). Understanding Collaborative Consumption: An Extension of the Theory of Planned Behavior with Value-Based Personal Norms. *Journal of Business Ethics, 158*(3), 679–697. Advance online publication. doi:10.100710551-017-3675-3

Rosati, F., Costa, R., Calabrese, A., & Pedersen, E. R. G. (2018). Employee attitudes towards corporate social responsibility: A study on gender, age and educational level differences. *Corporate Social Responsibility and Environmental Management, 25*(6), 1306–1319. doi:10.1002/csr.1640

Rousseau, D. M., Ho, V. T., & Greenberg, J. (2006). I-deals: Idiosyncratic terms in employment relationships. *Academy of Management Review, 31*(4), 977–994. doi:10.5465/amr.2006.22527470

Rudolph, R. L., Klemz, B. R., & Asquith, J. A. (2013). Young female users of social media and Internet addiction. *Journal of Mass Communication & Journalism, 4*(2), 1–4. doi:10.4172/2165-7912.1000177

Rupčic, N. (2018). Intergenerational learning and knowledge transfer – challenges and opportunities. *The Learning Organization, 25*(2), 135–142. doi:10.1108/TLO-11-2017-0117

Rutledge, R. W., Karim, K. E., Aleksanyan, M., & Wu, C. (2014). An Examination of the Relationship Between Corporate Social Responsibility and Financial Performance: The Case of Chinese State-Owned Enterprises. In *Accounting for the Environment: More Talk and Little Progress* (pp. 1–22). Emerald Group Publishing Limited. doi:10.1108/S1479-359820140000005001

Ryan, A. M., Brutus, S., Greguras, G. J., & Hakel, M. D. (2000). Receptivity to assessment-based feedback for management development. *Journal of Management Development, 19*(4), 252–276. doi:10.1108/02621710010322580

S&P DJI. (2019). *S&P U.S. Indices Methodology*. Author.

Saaty, T. L. (1996). *The Analytic Network Process: Decision Making with Dependence and Feedback*. RWS Publications.

Sackett, P. R., & DeVore, C. J. (2001). Counterproductive behaviors at work. In N. Anderson, D. S. Ones, H. K. Sinangil, & C. Viswesvaran (Eds.), *Handbook of Industrial, Work and Organizational Psychology: Personnel Psychology* (Vol. 1, pp. 145–164). Sage Publications. doi:10.4135/9781848608320.n9

Saddy, A. (2014). *Regulation of Direct Delivery of Public Services: Divergences Arising from the Regulatory Framework for Basic Sanitation* [Regulação da Prestação Direta de Serviços Públicos: Divergências Decorrentes do Marco Regulatório para o Saneamento Básico]. Retrieved on November 25, 2019, from http://www.cedipre.fd.uc.pt

Saks, A. M. (2006). Antecedents and consequences of employee engagement. *Journal of Managerial Psychology, 21*(7), 600–619. doi:10.1108/02683940610690169

Salzano, E., Garcia Agreda, A., Di Carluccio, A., & Fabbrocino, G. (2009). Risk assessment and early warning systems for industrial facilities in seismic zones. *Reliability Engineering & System Safety, 94*(10), 1577–1584. doi:10.1016/j.ress.2009.02.023

Sánchez-Hernández, M. I., González-López, O. R., Buenadicha-Mateos, M., & Tato-Jiménez, J. L. (2019). Work-life balance in great companies and pending issues for engaging new generations at work. *International Journal of Environmental Research and Public Health, 16*(24), 5122–5142. doi:10.3390/ijerph16245122 PMID:31847460

Sandhu, S., Sastrowardoyo, S., Benson, J., & Scott-Young, C. M. (2016). Aging in Asia: Challenges and opportunities in China, India, Japan and South Korea. In A. S. Antoniou, C. L. Cooper, & R. Burke (Eds.), *The Aging Workforce Handbook: Individual, Organizational and Societal Challenges* (pp. 513–536). Emerald Publishing. doi:10.1108/978-1-78635-448-820161021

Sarstedt, M., Hair, J. F., Ringle, C. M., Thiele, K. O., & Gudergan, S. P. (2016). Estimation issues with PLS and CBSEM: Where the Bias Lies! *Journal of Business Research, 69*(10), 3998–4010. doi:10.1016/j.jbusres.2016.06.007

Sarstedt, M., Henseler, J., & Ringle, C. (2011). Multigroup Analysis in Partial Least Squares (PLS) Path Modeling: Alternative Methods and Empirical Results. In M. Sarstedt, M. Schwaiger, & C. Taylor (Eds.), *Measurement and Research Methods in International Marketing* (Vol. 22, pp. 195–218). Emerald Group Publishing Limited., doi:10.1108/S1474-7979(2011)0000022012

Sarstedt, M., Ringle, C. M., & Hair, J. F. (2017). Partial least squares structural equation modeling. In C. Homburg, M. Klarmann, & A. Vomberg (Eds.), *Handbook of Market Research* (pp. 1–40). Springer. doi:10.1007/978-3-319-05542-8_15-1

Saunila, M., Nasiri, M., Ukko, J., & Rantala, T. (2019). Smart technologies and corporate sustainability: The mediation effect of corporate sustainability strategy. *Computers in Industry*, *108*, 178–185. doi:10.1016/j.compind.2019.03.003

Savov, R., & Lančarič, D. (2018). Factors influencing strategic approach to talent management of companies in Slovakia. In E. Horská, Z. Kapsdorferová, & M. Hallová (Eds.), International scientific days 2018. Towards Productive, Sustainable and Resilient Global Agriculture and Food Systems (pp. 1307-1319). Prague: Wolters Kluwer. doi:10.15414/isd2018.s5.13

Savov, R. (2019). *Talent manažment v podnikoch na Slovensku*. SPU.

Saxena, M., & Mishra, D. K. (2017). CSR perception: A global opportunity in management education. *Industrial and Commercial Training*, *49*(5), 231–244. doi:10.1108/ICT-12-2016-0085

Schaltegger, S., Ludeke-Freund, F., & Hansen, E. G. (2012). Business cases for sustainability: The role of business model innovation for corporate sustainability. *International Journal of Innovation and Sustainable Development*, *6*(2), 95–119. doi:10.1504/IJISD.2012.046944

Schaufeli, W. B., & Bakker, A. B. (2004). Job demands, job resources, and their relationship with burnout and engagement: A multi-sample study. *Journal of Organizational Behavior*, *25*(3), 293–315. doi:10.1002/job.248

Schaufeli, W. B., Bakker, A. B., & Van Rhenen, W. (2009). How changes in job demands and resources predict burnout, work engagement, and sickness absenteeism. *Journal of Organizational Behavior*, *30*(7), 893–917. doi:10.1002/job.595

Schawbel, D. (2014). *Gen Y and Gen Z global workplace expectations study*. Retrieved at http://millennialbranding.com/2014/geny-genz-global-workplaceexpectations-study

Schnall, R., Higgins, T., Brown, W., Carballo-Dieguez, A., & Bakken, S. (2015). Trust, perceived risk, perceived ease of use and perceived usefulness as factors related to mHealth technology use. *Studies in Health Technology and Informatics*, *216*, 467–471. PMID:26262094

Schneider, B., Gunnarson, S. K., & Niles-Jolly, K. (1994). Creating the climate and culture of success. *Organizational Dynamics*, *23*(1), 17–29. doi:10.1016/0090-2616(94)90085-X

Scholz, C., & Rennig, A. (2019). *Generations in Europe: Inputs, insights and implications*. Emerald Publishing. doi:10.1108/9781789734911

Schullery, N. M. (2013). Workplace engagement and generational differences in values. *Business Communication Quarterly*, *76*(2), 252–265. doi:10.1177/1080569913476543

Schwartz, M. S., & Carroll, A. B. (2008). Integrating and Unifying Competing and Complementary Frameworks: The Search for a Common core in the Business and Society Field. *Business & Society*, *47*(2), 148–186. doi:10.1177/0007650306297942

Schwarz, J. O. (2005). Pitfalls in implementing a strategic early warning system. *Foresight*, *7*(4), 22–30. doi:10.1108/14636680510611813

Schwieger, D., & Ladwig, C. (2018). Reaching and Retaining the Next Generation: Adapting to the Expectations of Gen Z in the Classroom. *Information Systems Education Journal*, *16*(3), 45–53.

Scott, B. (2016). *How Can Cryptocurrency and Blockchain Technology Play a Role in Building Social and Solidarity Finance*. United Nations Research Institute for Social Development.

Scullion, H., Collings, D. G., & Caligiuri, P. (2010). Global talent management. *Journal of World Business*, *45*(2), 105–108. doi:10.1016/j.jwb.2009.09.011

Secchi, D. (2007). Utilitarian, managerial and relational theories of corporate social responsibility. *International Journal of Management Reviews*, *9*(4), 347–373. doi:10.1111/j.1468-2370.2007.00215.x

Seemiller, C., & Grace, M. (2016). *Generation Z Goes to College*. Jossey-Bass.

Seemiller, C., & Grace, M. (2017). Generation Z: Educating and engaging the next generation of students. *American College Personnel Association*, *22*(3), 21–26. doi:10.1002/abc.21293

Seibert, S. E., Kraimer, M. L., & Heslin, P. A. (2016). Developing career resilience and adaptability. *Organizational Dynamics*, *45*(3), 245–257. doi:10.1016/j.orgdyn.2016.07.009

Selloni, D. (2017). *New Forms of Economies: Sharing Economy*. Collaborative Consumption, Peer-to-Peer Economy. doi:10.1007/978-3-319-53243-1_2

Sengupta, M. (2016). Impact of CSR on Education Sector. In N. Mitra & R. Schmidpeter (Eds.), *Corporate Social Responsibility in India: Cases and Developments After the Legal Mandate* (pp. 33–50). Springer.

Shafer, S. M., Smith, H. J., & Linder, J. (2005). The power of business models. *Business Horizons*, *48*(3), 199–207. doi:10.1016/j.bushor.2004.10.014

Shafiei Gol, E., Stein, M.-K., & Avital, M. (2018). *Why take the risk? motivations of highly skilled workers to participate in crowdworking platforms*. Paper presented at the 39th International Conference on Information Systems. ICIS 2018 International Conference on Information Systems, San Francisco, CA.

Shandu, R., Gill, H. K., & Sood, S. K. (2016). Smart monitoring and controlling of Pandemic Influenza A (H1N1) using Social Network Analysis and cloud computing. *Journal of Computational Science*, *12*, 11–22. doi:10.1016/j.jocs.2015.11.001 PMID:32362959

Shatto, B., & Erwin, K. (2017). Teaching Millennials and Generation Z: Bridging the generational divide. *Creative Nursing*, *23*(1), 24–28. doi:10.1891/1078-4535.23.1.24 PMID:28196564

Shattock, M. (2019). *University governance and academic work: the 'business model' and its impact on innovation and creativity*. Retrieved on January 05, 2020, from https://www.researchcghe.org/perch/resources/publications/to-publish-wp48.pdf

Sheel, A., & Nath, V. (2019). Effect of blockchain technology adoption on supply chain adaptability, agility, alignment and performance. *Management Research Review*, *42*(12), 1353–1374. doi:10.1108/MRR-12-2018-0490

Shimazu, K., Arisawa, T., & Saito, I. (2006, December). Interdisciplinary contents management using 5W1H interface for metadata. In *2006 IEEE/WIC/ACM International Conference on Web Intelligence (WI 2006 Main Conference Proceedings)(WI'06)* (pp. 909-912). IEEE. 10.1109/WI.2006.104

Shi, Y. (2018). The impact of consumer innovativeness on the intention of clicking on SNS advertising. *Modern Economy*, *9*(2), 278–285. doi:10.4236/me.2018.92018

Shmueli, G., Ray, S., Velasquez Estrada, J. M., & Chatla, S. B. (2016). The elephant in the room: Evaluating the predictive performance of PLS models. *Journal of Business Research*, *69*(10), 4552–4564. doi:10.1016/j.jbusres.2016.03.049

Shmueli, G., Sarstedt, M., Hair, J. F., Cheah, J. H., Ting, H., Vaithilingam, S., & Ringle, C. M. (2019). Predictive model assessment in PLS-SEM: Guidelines for using PLSpredict. *European Journal of Marketing*, *53*(11), 2322–2347. doi:10.1108/EJM-02-2019-0189

Silzer, R., & Dowell, B. E. (2010). *Strategy-driven Talent Management: A leadership imperative*. Jossey-Bass.

Simonton, D. K. (2011). Exceptional talent and genius. In T. Chamorro-Premuzic, S. von Stumm, & A. Furnham (Eds.), *The Wiley-Blackwell handbook of individual differences* (pp. 635–655). Wiley-Blackwell., doi:10.1002/9781444343120

Siomkos, G., & Kurzbard, G. (1994). The hidden crisis in product-harm crisis management. *European Journal of Marketing*, *28*(2), 30–41. doi:10.1108/03090569410055265

Sivakumar, N. (2011). Management of financial market scandals – regulatory and values based approaches. *Humanomics*, *27*(3), 153–165. doi:10.1108/08288661111165204

Skinner, D. J. (1994). Why Firms Voluntarily Disclose Bad News. *Journal of Accounting Research, 32*(1), 38-60. doı: doi:10.2307/2491386

Skinner, H., Sarpong, D., & White, G. R. (2018). Meeting the needs of the Millennials and Generation Z: Gamification in tourism through geocaching. *Journal of Tourism Futures*, *4*(1), 93–104. doi:10.1108/JTF-12-2017-0060

Skoludova, J., & Horakova, L. (2016). *The impact of motivating and stimulating generation Y employees on company performance.* Paper presented at the 17th International Scientific Conference on Economic and Social Development, Warsaw, Poland.

Skudiene, V., & Auruskeviciene, V. (2012). The Contribution of Corporate Social Responsibility to Internal Employee Motivation. *Baltic Journal of Management*, *7*(1), 49–67. doi:10.1108/17465261211197421

Slavin, A. (2015). *Marketers: Forget about Millennials. Gen Z has arrived.* Retrieved at https://women2.com/2015/08/07/engage-gen-z-users

Slawinski, N., Pinkse, J., Busch, T., & Banerjee, S. B. (2017). The role of short-termism and uncertainty avoidance in organizational inaction on climate change. *Business & Society*, *56*(2), 253–282. doi:10.1177/0007650315576136

Smilansky, J. (2005). *The Systematic Management of Executive Talent*. Hydrogen.

Smith, J. W., & Clurman, A. (1998). *Rocking the ages, the Yankelovich report on generational marketing*. Harper Collins.

Sölvell, I. (2018). Managers' silent whisper innovation involvement and role-modeling in service firms. *European Journal of Innovation Management*, *21*(1), 2–19. doi:10.1108/EJIM-02-2017-0020

Song, W., Ren, S., & Yu, J. (2018). Bridging the gap between corporate social responsibility and new green product success: The role of green organizational identity. *Business Strategy and the Environment*, *28*(1), 88–97. doi:10.1002/bse.2205

Sosik, J. J., & Godshalk, V. M. (2005). Examining gender similarity and mentor's supervisory status in mentoring relationships. *Mentoring & Tutoring*, *13*(1), 39–52. doi:10.1080/13611260500040138

Soto, C. J., & John, O. P. (2017). The next Big Five Inventory (BFI-2): Developing and assessing a hierarchical model with 15 facets to enhance bandwidth, fidelity, and predictive power. *Journal of Personality and Social Psychology*, *113*(1), 117–143. doi:10.1037/pspp0000096 PMID:27055049

Spence, M. (1973). Job Market Signaling. *The Quarterly Journal of Economics*, *87*(3), 355–374. doi:10.2307/1882010

Spence, M. (2002). Signaling in Retrospect and the Informational Structure of Markets. *The American Economic Review*, *92*(3), 434–459. doi:10.1257/00028280260136200

Srinivasan, V. (2012). Multi generations in the workforce: Building collaboration. *IIMB Management Review*, *24*(1), 48–66. doi:10.1016/j.iimb.2012.01.004

Srivastava, N., Srivastava, S., & Rai, A. K. (2014). Attitude and perception towards online advertising among students and young professionals: A study. *International Journal of Management*, *5*(5), 33–39.

Srivastava, P. (2012). Getting engaged. *Compensation and Benefits Review*, *44*(2), 105–109. doi:10.1177/0886368712450982

Stacho, Z., Stachová, K., & Papula, J. (2018). The changes in the focus of Slovak organisations on talent management. *Verslas teorija ir praktika, 19*(3-4), 255-260. doi:10.3846/btp.2018.25

Stacho, Z., Stachová, Z., & Gubíniová, K. (2016). Implementation of Talent Management as Motivation for High-potential Employees. In M. Blašková, R. Blaško, A. Sokół, & V. Gražulis (Eds.), *13th International Scientific Conference "Human potential development"* (pp. 240-247). Szczecin: University of Szczecin.

Stahl, G. K., Björkman, I., Farndale, E., Morris, S. S., Paauwe, J., Stiles, P., Trevor, J., & Wright, P. (2012). Six Principles of Effective Global Talent Management. *Sloan Management Review*, *53*(2), 25–42.

Stajkovic, A. D., Bandura, A., Locke, E. A., Lee, D., & Sergent, K. (2018). Test of three conceptual models of influence of the big five personality traits and self-efficacy on academic performance: A meta-analytic path-analysis. *Personality and Individual Differences*, *120*, 238–245. doi:10.1016/j.paid.2017.08.014

Štefko, R., & Sojka, L. (2014). Position of Talent Management in Context Organizational Functions. *European Scientific Journal, 1*(SI), 346-356.

Steinke, C., Webster, L., & Fontaine, M. (2010). Evaluating building performance in healthcare facilities: An organizational perspective. *Journal Citation Reports*, *2*(3), 63–83. doi:10.1177/193758671000300207 PMID:21165871

Stern, E. (2004). Evaluating partnerships. In O. N. Feinstein (Ed.), *Evaluation & Development: The Partnership Dimension* (pp. 29–41). Routledge.

Stewart, D. (2018). *Are consumers 'adlergic'? A look at ad-blocking habits*. Retrieved from https://deloitte.wsj.com/cmo/2018/04/03/are-consumers-adlergic-a-look-at-ad-blocking-habits/

Stewart, S. C., Witte, J. E., & Witte, M. M. (2019). Workforce Development and Higher Education Partnerships: Transdisciplinarity in Practice. In V. X. Wang (Ed.), *Handbook of Research on Transdisciplinary Knowledge Generation* (pp. 369–382). IGI Global. doi:10.4018/978-1-5225-9531-1.ch025

Sthapit, E. (2019). My bad for wanting to try something unique: Sources of value co-destruction in the Airbnb context. *Current Issues in Tourism*, *22*(20), 2462–2465. doi:10.1080/13683500.2018.1525340

Stillman, D., & Stillman, J. (2017). *Gen Z @ Work: How the Next Generation Is Transforming the Workplace*. Harper Collins Publishers.

Stock, T., & Seliger, G. (2016). Opportunities of Sustainable Manufacturing in Industry 4.0. *Procedia CIRP*, *40*, 536–541. doi:10.1016/j.procir.2016.01.129

Stofberg, N., & Bridoux, F. (2019). Consumers' choice among peer-to-peer sharing platforms: The other side of the coin. *Psychology and Marketing*, *36*(12), 1176–1195. doi:10.1002/mar.21265

Strauss, W., & Howe, N. (1991). *Generations: The history of America's future*. William Morrow.

Sturges, J., Conway, N., Guest, D., & Liefooghe, A. (2005). Managing the career deal: The psychological contract as a framework for understanding career management, organizational commitment and work behavior. *Journal of Organizational Behavior*, *26*(7), 821–838. doi:10.1002/job.341

Sujit, K. S., & Rajesh, B. K. (2016). Determinants of Discretionary Investments: Evidence from Indian Food Industry. *SAGE Open*, *6*(1). Advance online publication. doi:10.1177/2158244016636429

Sumner, A. (2012). Where do the poor live? *World Development*, *40*(5), 865–877. doi:10.1016/j.worlddev.2011.09.007

Sumpter, D. J. T. (2018). *Outnumbered: From Facebook and Google to fake news and filter-bubbles -- The algorithms that control our lives*. Retrieved from https://www.bloomsbury.com/us/outnumbered-9781472947420/

Sun, J., Yan, J., & Zhang, K. Z. K. (2016). Blockchain-based sharing services: What blockchain technology can contribute to smart cities. *Financial Innovation, 2*(1), 26. Retrieved from https://jfin-swufe.springeropen.com/track/pdf/10.1186/s40854-016-0040-y

Sundararajan, A. (2018). Crowd-based capitalism, digital automation, and the future of work. *University of Chicago Legal Forum.* Retrieved from https://chicagounbound.uchicago.edu/cgi/viewcontent.cgi?article=1606&context=uclf

Sundararajan, A. (2016). *The sharing economy: The end of employment and the rise of crowd-based capitalism*. MIT Press.

Supeekit, T., Somboonwiwat, T., & Kritchanchai, D. (2016). DEMATEL-modified ANP to evaluate internal hospital supply chain performance. *Computers & Industrial Engineering*, *102*, 318–330. doi:10.1016/j.cie.2016.07.019

Su, S., Su, S. I., Gammelgaard, B., & Yang, S. (2011). Logistics innovation process revisited: Insights from a hospital case study. *International Journal of Physical Distribution & Logistics Management*, *6*(41), 577–600.

Sutherland, E. (2016). Corporate social responsibility: the case of the telecommunications sector. *Info, 18*(5), 24-44. doi:10.1108/info-05-2016-0022

Su, W., Peng, M. W., Tan, W., & Cheung, Y.-L. (2016). The Signaling Effect of Corporate Social Responsibility in Emerging Economies. *Journal of Business Ethics*, *134*(3), 479–491. doi:10.100710551-014-2404-4

Svensson, G., Høgevold, N., Ferro, C., Varela, J. C. S., Padin, C., & Wagner, B. (2016). A Triple Bottom Line Dominant Logic for Business Sustainability: Framework and Empirical Findings. *Journal of Business-To-Business Marketing*, *23*(2), 153–188. doi:10.1080/1051712X.2016.1169119

Svensson, G., & Wagner, B. (2015). Implementing and managing economic, social and environmental efforts of business sustainability: Propositions for measurement and structural models. *Management of Environmental Quality*, *26*(2), 195–213. doi:10.1108/MEQ-09-2013-0099

Swan, M. (2015). *Blockchain: Blueprint for a New Economy*. O'Reilly Media.

Swanson, T. (2005). *Consensus-as-a-service: A brief report on the emergence of permissioned, distributed ledger systems*. Report. Available at: https://www.ofnumbers.com/

Swant, M. (2016, March 22). *Adobe is creating a data co-op to compete with Google and Facebook*. Retrieved from https://www.adweek.com/digital/adobe-creating-data-co-op-compete-google-and-facebook-170347/

Syahrir, I., Suparno, I. V., & Vanany, I. (2015). Healthcare and disaster supply chain: Literature review and future research. *Procedia Manufacturing*, *4*, 2–9. doi:10.1016/j.promfg.2015.11.007

Szabó, L., & Csepregi, A. (2016). Strategic management tools and techniques: the cultural influence. In *Proceedings 11th International Forum on Knowledge Asset Dynamics - Towards a New Architecture of Knowledge: Big Data, Culture and Creativity*. (pp. 178-193) Dresden University of Technology.

Tan, C., & Dihardjo, H. (2001). A study of using artificial neural networks to develop an early warning predictor for credit union financial distress with comparison to the probit model. *Managerial Finance*, *27*(4), 56–77. doi:10.1108/03074350110767141

Tanimura, J. K., & Okamoto, M. G. (2013). Reputational Penalties in Japan: Evidence from Corporate Scandals. *Asian Economic Journal*, *27*(1), 39–57. doi:10.1111/asej.12004

Tansky, J., & Cohen, D. (2001). The relationship between organizational support, employee development, and organizational commitment: An empirical study. *Human Resource Development Quarterly*, *12*(3), 285–300. doi:10.1002/hrdq.15

Tansley, C. (2011). What do we mean by the term „talent" in talent management? *Industrial and Commercial Training*, *43*(5), 266–274. doi:10.1108/00197851111145853

Tapscott, D., & Williams, A. D. (2010). Innovating the 21st-Century university: It's time! *EDUCAUSE Review*, *45*(1), 16–29.

Tarasova, O. V. (2012). Teoretyko-metodolohichni osnovy innovatsiynoyi diyal′nosti pidpryyemstv. *Ekonomika kharchovoyi promyslovosti, 1*, 37-41.

Tarique, I., & Schuler, R. S. (2010). Global talent management: Literature review, integrative framework, and suggestions for further research. *Journal of World Business*, *45*(2), 122–133. doi:10.1016/j.jwb.2009.09.019

Tavares, A. I. (2018). eHealth, ICT and its relationship with self-reported health outcomes in the EU countries. *International Journal of Medical Informatics*, *112*, 104–113. doi:10.1016/j.ijmedinf.2018.01.014 PMID:29500007

Taylor, C. (2011). *End of the office? Students want the right to work from home.* Mashable Business. Retrieved fromhttp://mashable.com/2011/11/08/work-from-home-2/?mid=530.

Teece, D. J. (2010). Business Models, Business Strategy and Innovation. *Long Range Planning*, *43*(2-3), 172–194. doi:10.1016/j.lrp.2009.07.003

Temiz, H., & Acar, M. (2018). Sürdürülebilirlik Endeksinde İşlem Gören Firmaların Finansal Performansı: Olay Çalışması Örneği. *Hitit Üniversitesi Sosyal Bilimler Enstitüsü Dergisi*, *11*(3), 1971–1987.

Terwiesch, C., & Xu, Y. (2008). Innovation contests, open innovation, and multiagent problem solving. *Management Science*, *54*(9), 1529–1543. doi:10.1287/mnsc.1080.0884

Thorne, K., & Pellant, A. (2007). *Rozvíjíme a motivujeme zaměstnance: výběr, trénink a podpora rozvoje nejlepších.* Computer Press.

Thrasher, E., Craighead, C., & Byrd, T. (2010). An empirical investigation of integration in healthcare alliance networks. *Decision Support Systems*, *1*(50), 116–127. doi:10.1016/j.dss.2010.07.007

Tidd, J., & Bessant, J. (2013). *Managing Innovation. Integrating Technological, Market and Organizational Change.* University of London.

Timmers, P. (1998). Business models for electronic markets. *Electronic Markets*, *8*(2), 3–8. doi:10.1080/10196789800000016

Ting, H., Run, E. C., & Thurasamy, R. (2015). Young adults' attitude towards advertising: A multi-group analysis by ethnicity. *Review of Business Management*, *17*(54), 769–787. doi:10.7819/rbgn.v17i54.1777

Tiwana, A., Konsynski, B., & Bush, A. (2010). Research commentary — Platform evolution: Coevolution of platform architecture, governance, and environmental dynamics. *Information Systems Research*, *21*(4), 675–687. doi:10.1287/isre.1100.0323

Tolbize, A. (2008). Generational differences in the workplace. *Research and Training Center on Community Living*, *5*(2), 1-21.

Tong, C., & Kathy, E. K. (2013). The efficacy of mentoring – the benefits for mentees, mentors, and organizations. In *The Wiley-Blackwell Handbook of the Psychology of Coaching and Mentoring* (pp. 217–243). John Wiley & Sons.

Torjman, S. (2000). *The social dimension of sustainable development*. Caledon Institute of Social Policy.

Torugsa, N. A., O'Donohue, W., & Hecker, R. (2012). Capabilities, Proactive CSR and Financial Performance in SMEs: Empirical Evidence from an Australian Manufacturing Industry Sector. *Journal of Business Ethics*, *109*(4), 483–500. doi:10.100710551-011-1141-1

Trompenaars, F., & Hampden-Turner, C. (2002). *Riding the waves of culture: Understanding diversity in global business*. Nicholas Brealey Publishing.

Tsai, B. H. (2013). An Early Warning System of Financial Distress Using Multinomial Logit Models and a Bootstrapping Approach. *Emerging Markets Finance & Trade*, *49*(2), 43–69. doi:10.2753/REE1540-496X4902S203

Tung, R. L., & Verbeke, A. (2010). Beyond Hofstede and GLOBE: Improving the quality of cross-national research. *Journal of International Business Studies*, *41*(8), 1259–1274. doi:10.1057/jibs.2010.41

Turner, A. (2015). Generation Z: Technology and Social Interest. *Journal of Individual Psychology*, *71*(2), 103–113. doi:10.1353/jip.2015.0021

Tuwey, J., & Tarus, D. (2016). Does CEO power moderate the relationship between board leadership and strategy involvement in private firms? Evidence from Kenya. *Corporate Governance*, *16*(5), 906–922. doi:10.1108/CG-01-2016-0010

Twenge, J. (2017). IGen. Atria Books.

Twenge, J. M. (2007). *Generation Me: Why Today's Young Americans Are More Con-fident, Assertive, Entitled – and More Miserable Than Ever Before*. Free Press.

Twenge, J. M. (2017). *IGen: Why Today's Super-Connected Kids Are Growing Up Less Rebellious, More Tolerant, Less Happy - Completely Unprepared for Adulthood*. Atria Books.

Twenge, J. M., Campbell, S. M., Hoffman, B. J., & Lance, C. E. (2010). Generational differences in work values: Leisure and extrinsic values increasing, social and intrinsic values decreasing. *Journal of Management*, *36*(5), 1117–1142. doi:10.1177/0149206309352246

Twenge, J. M., Freeman, E. C., & Campbell, W. (2012). Generational differences in young adults' life goals, concern for others, and civic orientation, 1966-2009. *Journal of Personality and Social Psychology*, *102*(5), 1045–1062. doi:10.1037/a0027408 PMID:22390226

Uadiale, O. M., & Fagbemi, T. O. (2012). Corporate Social Responsibility and Financial Performance in Developing Economies: The Nigerian Experience. *Journal of Economics and Sustainable Development*, *3*(4), 44–54.

Ubrežiová, A., & Horská, E. (2011). *Perception and Approach towards Corporate Social Responsibility in SMEs: Case Study of Slovak and Czech Republic*. Paper presented at the PEFnet 2011 "European Scientific Conference of Ph.D. Students.

Ubrežiová, I., & Gurská, S. (2012). *International Management and Entrepreneurship*. Wolters Kluwer ČR.

Ubrežiová, I., & Sokil, O. (2018). The evaluation of three pillars of corporate social responsibility in practise. In E. Horská, Z. Kapsdorferová, & M. Hallová (Eds.), *International scientific days 2018. Towards productive, sustainable and resilient global agriculture and food systems* (pp. 1331–1343). Wolters Kluwer ČR.

Ulutaş, D. D., Giritli, H., & Mcdermott, P. (2016). Corporate social responsibility in construction industry: A comparative study between UK and Turkey. *Built Environment Project and Asset Management*, *6*(2), 218–231. doi:10.1108/BEPAM-08-2014-0039

Ungar, M. (2019). *Change Your World: What the Science of Resilience Teaches Us about the True Path to Success.* Sutherland House.

United Nations Global Compact. (2013). The UN Global Compact-Accenture CEO Study on Sustainability 2013. *Architects of a Better World.* Retrieved on December 3, 2019, from https://www.unglobalcompact.org/library/451

United Nations. (2015). *Transforming our world: the 2030 Agenda for Sustainable Development.* United Nations.

UNWTO. (1995). *Charter for sustainable tourism.* Retrieved November 7, 2016 from http://www.e-unwto.org/doi/pdf/10.18111/unwtodeclarations.1995.21.13.1

Upadhyay, P., & Kundu, A. (2019). Linkage between business sustainability and tacit knowledge management in MSMEs A case-based study. *VINE Journal of Information and Knowledge Management Systems, ahead-of-print*(ahead-of-print). Advance online publication. doi:10.1108/VJIKMS-08-2019-0133

Urzelai, B., & Puig, F. (2019). Developing international social capital: The role of communities of practice and clustering. *International Business Review, 28*(2), 209–221. doi:10.1016/j.ibusrev.2018.08.008

Usha, N., & Devakumar, G. (2019). Modelling Business Sustainability in Agri Engineering Manufacturing Companies: Effect of Innovation, Technology and Business Model. *International Journal of Recent Technology and Engineering, 8*(1C), 341–345.

Uslu, B., Calikoglu, A., Seggie, F. N., & Seggie, S. H. (2019). The entrepreneurial university and academic discourses: The meta-synthesis of Higher Education articles. *Higher Education Quarterly, 73*(3), 285–311. doi:10.1111/hequ.12198

Usman, A. B., & Amran, N. A. B. (2015). Corporate Social Responsibility Practice and Corporate Financial Performance: Evidence from Nigeria Companies. *Social Responsibility Journal, 11*(4), 749–763. doi:10.1108/SRJ-04-2014-0050

UUK. (2016). *Working in partnership: enabling social mobility in higher education. The final report of the Social Mobility Advisory Group, London.* Retrieved on January 10, 2020, from https://dera.ioe.ac.uk/27586/1/working-in-partnership-final.pdf

UUK. (2018a). *Patterns and trends in UK higher education 2018, London.* Retrieved on January 01, 2020, from https://www.universitiesuk.ac.uk/facts-and-stats/data-and-analysis/Documents/patterns-and-trends-in-uk-higher-education-2018.pdf

UUK. (2018b). *Solving future skills challenges, London.* Retrieved on December 23, 2019 from https://www.universitiesuk.ac.uk/policy-and-analysis/reports/Documents/2018/solving-future-skills-challenges.pdf

UUK. (2019). *Higher education in Facts and figures, London.* Retrieved on January 03, 2020, from https://www.universitiesuk.ac.uk/facts-and-stats/data-and-analysis/Documents/higher-education-facts-and-figures-2019.pdf

Vafaei, N., Ribeiro, R. A., & Camarinha-Matos, L. M. (2019). Fuzzy Early Warning Systems for Condition Based Maintenance. *Computers & Industrial Engineering, 128*, 736–746. doi:10.1016/j.cie.2018.12.056

Vaida, A., & Cândea, D. (2010). Model pentru internalizarea sustenabilităţii în organizaţii. *Întreprinderea sustenabilă, 5*, 1-62.

Vaiman, V., Scullion, H., & Collings, D. (2012). Talent management decision making. *Management Decision, 50*(5), 925–941. doi:10.1108/00251741211227663

Van Buren, H. J. III. (2003). Boundaryless careers and employability obligations. *Business Ethics Quarterly, 13*(2), 131–149. doi:10.5840/beq20031329

Van der Walt, N., Ingley, C., Shergill, G., & Townsend, A. (2006). Board configuration: Are diverse boards better boards? *Corporate Governance, 6*(2), 129–147. doi:10.1108/14720700610655141

Van Dyne, L., & Le Pine, J. A. (1998). Helping and voice extra-role behaviors: Evidence of construct and predictive validity. *Academy of Management Journal*, *41*(1), 108–119. doi:10.2307/256902

van Marrewijk, M. (2003). Concepts and Definitions of CSR and Corporate Sustainability: Between Agency and Communion. *Journal of Business Ethics*, *44*(2–3), 95–105. doi:10.1023/A:1023331212247

Van Scotter, J. R., & Motowidlo, S. J. (1996). Interpersonal facilitation and job dedication as separate facets of contextual performance. *The Journal of Applied Psychology*, *81*(5), 525–531. doi:10.1037/0021-9010.81.5.525

Van Valkenburgh, P., Dietz, J., De Filippi, P., Shadab, H., Xethalise, G., & Bollier, D. (2015). *Distributed collaborative organisations: Distributed networks and regulator frameworks*. Harvard Working Paper.

Van Vuuren, L., & Fourie, C. (2000). Career anchors and career resilience: Supplementary constructs? *SA Journal of Industrial Psychology*, *23*(3), 15–20. doi:10.4102ajip.v26i3.714

Van Wyk, J. (2015). *Generation Z will ruin businesses that fail to adopt new ways of working*. Retrieved at https://www.itweb.co.za/content/XGxwQD71ebV7lPVo

Vansteenkiste, M., Niemiec, C. P., & Soenens, B. (2010). The development of the five mini-theories of self-determination theory: an historical overview, emerging trends, and future directions. In T. C. Urdan & S. A. Karabenick (Eds.), *The decade ahead: theoretical perspectives on motivation and achievement* (Vol. 16, pp. 105–165). Emerald Group Publishing., doi:10.1108/S0749-7423(2010)000016A007

Varela, L., Araújo, A., Ávila, P., Castro, H., & Putnik, G. (2019). Evaluation of the relation between lean manufacturing, industry 4.0, and sustainability. *Sustainability*, *11*(5), 1439. doi:10.3390u11051439

Veiga Ávila, L., Beuron, T., Brandli, L., Damke, L., Pereira, R., & Klein, L. (2019). Barriers to innovation and sustainability in universities: An international comparison. *International Journal of Sustainability in Higher Education*, *20*(5), 805–821. doi:10.1108/IJSHE-02-2019-0067

Verdecho, M. J., Alfaro, J. J., & Rodriguez-Rodriguez, R. (2009). Foundations for collaborative performance measurement. *Production Planning and Control*, *20*(3), 193–205. doi:10.1080/09537280902721001

Verdin, J. (2020). Emerging technologies in the health-care supply chain. In A. Pagano & M. Liotine (Eds.), *Technology in Supply Chain Management and Logistics: Current Practice and Future Applications* (pp. 111–126). Elsevier. doi:10.1016/B978-0-12-815956-9.00006-5

Visit Scotland. (2017). *Millennial travelers*. Available at: www.visitscotland.org/binaries/content/ assets/dot-org/pdf/research-papers/millennial-travellers-topic-paper-jan-2017.pdf

Vitale, M. R., & Mavrinac, S. C. (1995). How effective is your performance measurement system? *Management Accounting*, *77*(2), 43–47.

Vladimirova, D. (2016). The Cambridge Value Mapping Tool. *IfM Review*. Retrieved on December 18, 2019, from https://www.ifm.eng.cam.ac.uk/news/the-cambridge-value-mapping-tool/

Vladimirova, D. (2019). Building sustainable value propositions for multiple stakeholders: A practical tool. *Journal of Business Models*, *7*(1), 1–8. doi:10.5278/ojs.jbm.v7i1.2103

Voloskovets, N. Y. (2010). Korporatyvna sotsial′na vidpovidal′nist′ pidpryyemstv yak osnova innovatsiynoho rozvytku suchasnoyi ekonomiky. *Naukovi pratsi Kirovohrads'koho natsional'noho tekhnichnoho universytetu. Ekonomichni nauky*, *17*, 125-130.

Von Krogh, G., Nonaka, I., & Aben, M. (2001). Making the most of your company's knowledge: A strategic framework. *Long Range Planning*, *4*(4), 421–439. doi:10.1016/S0024-6301(01)00059-0

Voorveld, H. A. M., van Noort, G., Muntinga, D. G., & Bronner, F. (2018). Engagement with social media and social media advertising: The differentiating role of platform type. *Journal of Advertising*, *47*(1), 38–54. doi:10.1080/00913367.2017.1405754

Waelbroeck, P. (2017). Les enjeux économiques de la blockchain. *Annales des Mines - Réalités industrielles, 2017*(3), 10-19. Retrieved from https://www.cairn.info/revue-realites-industrielles-2017-3-page-10.htm

Wang, Q., Dou, J., & Jia, S. (2016). A Meta-Analytic Review of Corporate Social Responsibility and Corporate Financial Performance: The Moderating Effect of Contextual Factors. *Business & Society*, *55*(8), 1083–1121. doi:10.1177/0007650315584317

Wang, S., Wan, J., Li, D., & Zhang, C. (2016). Implementing smart factory of Industrie 4.0: An outlook. *International Journal of Distributed Sensor Networks*, *12*(1), 3159805. Advance online publication. doi:10.1155/2016/3159805

Watanabe, E. H., Silva, R. M., Junqueira, F., Santos, D. J., & Miyagi, P. E. (2016). An Emerging Industrial Business Model considering Sustainability Evaluation and using Cyber Physical System Technology and Modelling Techniques. *IFAC-PapersOnLine*, *49*(32), 135–140. doi:10.1016/j.ifacol.2016.12.203

Waterman, R. H., Waterman, J. A., & Betsy, C. A. (1994). Towards a career resilient workforce. *Harvard Business Review*, 87–95.

Wayne, J. H., & Casper, W. J. (2012). Why does firm reputation in human resource policies influence college students? The mechanisms underlying job pursuit intentions. *Human Resource Management*, *51*(1), 121–142. doi:10.1002/hrm.21461

Weill, P., Malone, T. W., D'Urso, V. T., Herman, G., & Woerner, S. (2005). *Do some business models perform better than others? A study of the 1000 largest US firms*. Working Paper 226. Sloan School of Management Massachusetts Institute of Technology. Retrieved on January 12, 2020 from https://mpra.ub.uni-muenchen.de/4752/1/MPRA_paper_4752.pdf

West, H. (2018). *The attention economy to the addiction economy*. Retrieved from https://blog.mozilla.org/internetcitizen/2018/07/27/attention-addiction/

Westerman, J. W., & Yamamura, J. H. (2007). Generational preferences for work environment fit: Effects on employee outcomes. *Career Development International*, *12*(2), 150–161. doi:10.1108/13620430710733631

White, G. R. T. (2017). Future applications of blockchain in business and management: A Delphi study. *Strategic Change*, *26*(5), 439–451. doi:10.1002/jsc.2144

Wigfield, A., & Eccles, J. S. (2000). Expectancy–value theory of achievement motivation. *Contemporary Educational Psychology*, *25*(1), 68–81. doi:10.1006/ceps.1999.1015 PMID:10620382

Williams, K. C., Page, R. A., Petrosky, A. R., & Hernandez, E. H. (2010). Multi-generational Marketing: Descriptions, Characteristics, Lifestyles, and Attitudes. *The Journal of Applied Business and Economics*, *11*(2), 21–36.

Williams, T., Klakegg, O. J., Walker, D. H. T., Andersen, B., & Magnussen, O. M. (2012). Identifying and acting on early warning signs in complex projects. *Project Management Journal*, *43*(2), 37–53. doi:10.1002/pmj.21259

Willians, R. J., & Barrett, J. D. (2000). Corporate Philanthropy, Criminal Activity, and Firm Reputation: Is There a Link? *Journal of Business Ethics*, *26*(4), 341–350. doi:10.1023/A:1006282312238

Wilson, S. M., & Ferch, S. R. (2005). Enhancing resilience in the workplace through the practice of caring relationships. *Organization Development Journal*, *23*(4), 45–60.

Winch, G., & Schneider, E. (1993). Managing the knowledge-based organization: The case of architectural practice. *Journal of Management Studies*, *30*(6), 923–937. doi:10.1111/j.1467-6486.1993.tb00472.x

Winwood, P., Colon, R., & McKewen, K. (2013). A practical measure of workplace resilience. *Journal of Occupational and Environmental Medicine*, *35*(10), 1205–1212. doi:10.1097/JOM.0b013e3182a2a60a PMID:24064782

Wisse, B., van Eijbergen, R., Rietzschel, E. F., & Scheibe, S. (2018). Catering to the Needs of an Aging Workforce: The Role of Employee Age in the Relationship Between Corporate Social Responsibility and Employee Satisfaction. *Journal of Business Ethics*, *147*(4), 875–888. doi:10.100710551-015-2983-8

Wissman, B. (2018). *Micro-influencers: The marketing force of the future?* Retrieved from http://www.forbes.com/sites/barrettwissman/2018/03/02/micro-influencers-the-marketing-force-of-the-future/#3ab3827f6707

Wong, K. K.-K. (2013). Partial Least Squares Structural Equation Modeling (PLS-SEM) Techniques Using SmartPLS. *Marketing Bulletin*, *24*, 1–32.

World Bank. (2019). *Poverty and Equity Database*. Retrieved November 05, 2019, from http://databank.worldbank.org/data/reports.aspx?source=poverty-and-equity-database#

Wright, A., & De Filippi, P. (2015). *Decentralized blockchain technology and the rise of lex cryptographia, SSRN Scholarly Paper, no 2580664*. Social Science Research Network Rochester., doi:10.2139srn.2580664

Wright, P. M., & Haggerty, J. J. (2005). Missing variables in theories of strategic human resource management: Time, cause, and individuals. *Management Review*, *16*(2), 164–173.

Wydick, B., Karp, H., & Hilliker, S. (2011). Social networks, neighborhood effects and credit access. *World Development*, *39*(6), 974–982. doi:10.1016/j.worlddev.2009.10.015

Xu, X., Zeng, S., & Chen, H. (2018). Signaling Good by Doing Good: How Does Environmental Corporate Social Responsibility Affect International Expansion? *Business Strategy and the Environment*, *27*(7), 946–959. doi:10.1002/bse.2044

Yadav, M., Choudhary, S., & Jain, S. (2019). Transformational leadership and knowledge sharing behavior in freelancers: A moderated mediation model with employee engagement and social support. *Journal of Global Operations and Strategic Sourcing*, *12*(2), 202–224. doi:10.1108/JGOSS-08-2017-0030

Yang, C. (2012). Research on internet public opinion detection system based on domain ontology. In F. L. Wang, J. Lei, Z. Gong, & X. Luo (Eds.), *WISM'12 Proceedings of the 2012 international conference on Web Information Systems and Mining* (pp. 105-110). Berlin: Springer-Verlag. 10.1007/978-3-642-33469-6_15

Yang, L. (2019). From general principles of civil law to general provisions of civil law: A historical leap in contemporary Chinese civil law. *Social Sciences in China*, *2*, 85–91.

Yang, M., Vladimirova, D., & Evans, S. (2017). Creating and capturing value through sustainability: The Sustainable Value Analysis Tool. *Research Technology Management*, *60*(3), 30–39. doi:10.1080/08956308.2017.1301001

Yang, Q., & Wei, H. (2017). Ethical leadership and employee task performance: Examining moderated mediation process. *Management Decision*, *55*(7), 1506–1520. doi:10.1108/MD-09-2016-0627

Yang, Y., Bi, G. B., & Liu, L. D. (2020). Profit allocation in investment-based crowdfunding with investors of dynamic entry times. *European Journal of Operational Research*, *280*(1), 323–337. doi:10.1016/j.ejor.2019.07.016

Ye, K., & Zhang, R. (2011). Do Lenders Value Corporate Social Responsibility? Evidence from China. *Journal of Business Ethics*, *104*(2), 197–206. doi:10.100710551-011-0898-6

Yeo, V. C. S., Goh, S.-K., & Rezaei, S. (2017). Consumer experiences, attitude and behavioral intention toward online food delivery (OFD) services. *Journal of Retailing and Consumer Services*, *35*, 150–162. doi:10.1016/j.jretconser.2016.12.013

Yin, R. K. (2009). *Case study research: design and methods* (4th ed.). Sage.

Yin, R. K. (2014). *Case Study Research Design and Methods*. Sage.

Yoo, B., Donthu, N., & Lenartowicz, T. (2011). Measuring Hofstede's five dimensions of cultural values at the individual level.pdf. *International Consumer Marketing*, *23*(3–4), 193–210. doi:10.1080/08961530.2011.578059

Yu, H. C., & Miller, P. (2005). Leadership style: The X Generation and Baby Boomers compared in different cultural contexts. *Leadership and Organization Development Journal*, *26*(1), 35–50. doi:10.1108/01437730510575570

Zaal, R. O., Jeurissen, R. J., & Groenland, E. A. (2019). Organizational architecture, ethical culture, and perceived unethical behavior towards customers: Evidence from wholesale banking. *Journal of Business Ethics*, *158*(3), 825–848. doi:10.100710551-017-3752-7

Zack, M. H. (1999). Developing a knowledge strategy. *California Management Review*, *41*(3), 125–145. doi:10.2307/41166000

Zahra, S. A., Priem, R. L., & Rasheed, A. A. (2005). The Antecedents and Consequences of Top Management Fraud. *Journal of Management*, *31*(6), 803–828. doi:10.1177/0149206305279598

Zehetner, D., Lepeyko, T., & Zehetner, A. (2019). Formation of the leadership style in the enterprise management in the process of generation transition. *New Economy*, *2*, 9–14.

Zemke, R., Raines, C., & Filipczak, B. (2000). *Generations at Work: Managing the Class of Veterans, Boomers, X-ers, and Nexters in Your Workplace*. Amacon.

Zervas, G., Proserpio, D., & Byers, J. W. (2017). The rise of the sharing economy: Estimating the impact of Airbnb on the hotel industry. *JMR, Journal of Marketing Research*, *54*(5), 687–705. doi:10.1509/jmr.15.0204

Zhai, T., & Chang, Y. C. (2019). Standing of environmental public-interest litigants in China: Evolution, obstacles and solutions. *Journal of Environmental Law*, *30*(3), 369–397. doi:10.1093/jel/eqy011

Zhang, X., & Zhou, J. (2014). Empowering leadership, uncertainty avoidance, trust, and employee creativity: Interaction effects and a mediating mechanism. *Organizational Behavior and Human Decision Processes*, *124*(2), 150–164. doi:10.1016/j.obhdp.2014.02.002

Zha, W., & Wu, H. D. (2014). The impact of online disruptive ads on users' comprehension, evaluation of site credibility, and sentiment of intrusiveness. *American Communication Journal*, *16*(2), 15–28.

Zheng, Z., Xie, S., Dai, H., Chen, X., & Wang, H. (2017, June). An overview of blockchain technology: Architecture, consensus, and future trends. In *2017 IEEE International Congress on Big Data (BigData Congress)* (pp. 557-564). IEEE.

Zheng, G., Zhu, N., Tim, Z., Chen, Y., & Sun, B. (2012). Application of a trapezoidal fuzzy AHP method for work safety evaluation and early warning rating of hot and humid environments. *Safety Science*, *50*(2), 228–239. doi:10.1016/j.ssci.2011.08.042

Zhou, S., Oginhara, A., Nishimura, S., & Jin, Q. (2019). Analysis of health changes and the association of health indicators in the elderly using TCM pulse diagnosis assisted with ICT devices: A time series study. *European Journal of Integrative Medicine*, *27*, 105–113. doi:10.1016/j.eujim.2019.02.010

Zinchenko, A., & Saprykina, M. (2017). *Rozvytok KSV v Ukrayini: 2010–2018*. Kyiv, Ukraine: Yuston.

Zmigrod, L., Rentfrow, P. J., & Robbins, T. W. (2019). Cognitive Inflexibility Predicts Extremist Attitudes. *Frontiers in Psychology*, *10*, 989. doi:10.3389/fpsyg.2019.00989 PMID:31133930

Zmigrod, L., Rentfrow, P. J., & Robbins, T. W. (2020). The Partisan Mind: Is Extreme Political Partisanship Related to Cognitive Inflexibility? *Journal of Experimental Psychology. General*, *149*(3), 407–418. doi:10.1037/xge0000661 PMID:31380695

Zona, F., Minoja, M., & Vittorio, C. (2013). Antecedents of Corporate Scandals: CEOs' Personal Traits, Stakeholders' Cohesion, Managerial Fraud, and Imbalanced Corporate Strategy. *Journal of Business Ethics*, *113*(2), 265–283. doi:10.100710551-012-1294-6

Zott, C., & Amit, R. (2010). Business model design: An activity system perspective. *Long Range Planning*, *43*(2-3), 216–226. doi:10.1016/j.lrp.2009.07.004

Zott, C., Amit, R., & Massa, L. (2011). The business model: Recent developments and future research. *Journal of Management*, *37*(4), 1019–1042. doi:10.1177/0149206311406265

About the Contributors

Ramona-Diana Leon worked in several projects about strategic knowledge management and quality management. In the last five years, Ramona published several books, book chapters and articles in the field of knowledge management, strategic management, and emotional intelligence. Besides, she is a full member of the International Association for Knowledge Management and she has a wide experience in Europe, collaborating with academics and managers from Romania, Spain, and the UK.

* * *

Juneman Abraham is a social psychologist from Bina Nusantara University in Indonesia who puts interest in Psychoinformatics and general human issues. His research record could be accessed via ORCiD - http://orcid.org/0000-0003-0232-2735. He serves as a reviewer on various scientific journals and conference proceedings - https://publons.com/author/1219841/juneman-abraham.

Juan-Jose Alfaro-Saiz is an associate professor in Operations Management and Operations Research at the Polytechnic University of Valencia). He received his doctoral degree in Industrial Engineering from Universidad Politécnica de Valencia in 2003. He is a member of the CIGIP (Research Centre on Production Management and Engineering). His research interests include performance measurement systems, integration enterprise and modelling process business. He has published several papers in books, journals and conferences in these fields. He is member of the Association for the Organization Engineering (ADINGOR). He works as researcher in several Spanish Government Projects (CICYT, GV, etc.) and European Projects.

Rolf K. Baltzersen received his PhD in educational science from the University of Oslo in 2017. He has been working at the Faculty of Education at Østfold University College in Halden, Norway, since 2004, and is currently working as a coordinator of the teacher training programme. His research interests cover a range of different topics within learning and education, but with a special interest in new digital technologies and the development of the Internet. At present he is finishing a book about collective intelligence which is to be published in 2020.

Chris Bamber has been Managing Director and Dean of the Organisational Learning Centre (OLC) for 21 years. Prior to that worked as Operations Manager for a multi-national manufacturing company for 8 years and prior to this worked as Quality Manager for a leading UK manufacturing organisation. Chris now draws upon over 38 years industry and academic experience to provide OLC with strong leadership and direction. He is Director of Studies at the University of Bolton for PhD candidates in the Business School and research interests include analysing the roles of Entrepreneurs, Intrapreneurs and Lean Thinkers in the Modern Enterprise.

Zsuzsanna Banász is an associate professor at the Department of Quantitative Methods, Faculty of Business and Economics, University of Pannonia, Hungary. She was an assistant research fellow in MTA-PE Networked Research Group on Regional Innovation and Development Studies, Hungary between 2013 and 2016. From 2017 she is a research fellow in MTA-PE Budapest Ranking Research Group. Her research interests include macro- and micro-level effects of renewable energies and the economics of poverty. Since 2004 she has been teaching a variety of bachelor and master courses including Statistics, Microeconomics, and Econometrics.

Émilie Boily is a graduate student in Organization Management at Université du Québec à Chicoutimi and member of the LaboNFC. Her research interests focus on the collaborative economy and technology. Her research has already appeared in the *International Journal of Innovation Studies* and in the journal *Organisations & Territoires*.

Naomi Borg is currently studying for a PhD at RMIT University. She also works as a Project Manager at Montlaur Project Services in Melbourne, Australia.

Maria do Rosário Cabrita holds a Ph.D. in Business Administration (Institute of Economics and Business Administration, Lisbon Technical University). She is Assistant Professor and researcher at the Universidade Nova de Lisboa. She is also Assistant Professor at the Portuguese Banking Management School in Lisbon and in ISCTE-Business School. She teaches several disciplines in graduate and post-graduate courses (strategic management, intellectual capital, knowledge management, innovation, measurement of intangibles and entrepreneurship programmes). She has more than 50 published articles in conferences, book chapters and scientific specialized journals. She is co-author, with Prof. José Maria Viedma, of the book entitled Entrepreneurial Excellence in the Knowledge Economy: ICBS: Intellectual Capital Benchmarking System. Involved in international projects (in Africa and Europe) she also works as consultant in private and public sectors. She has several years of experience in various management positions in international banks. She is member of Editorial Board of some scientific journals. Research areas of interest are: intellectual capital, knowledge management and measuring intangibles. She has received some papers-award in Portugal and abroad. In January 2005, Maria do Rosário received the Edvinsson-Saint Onge's best paper award at the 26th McMaster World Congress.

Betül Çal owns a PhD in the field of Business Management with a specialty in Marketing. Dr. Çal's fields of interest include financial service marketing, consumer behavior especially in a financial services context and strategic branding. Having academic publications in a number of international journals, Dr. Çal is currently working as an assistant professor at Alanya Alaaddin Keykubat University, Turkey.

Anikó Csepregi is an associate professor at University of Pannonia, Hungary. She obtained her Ph.D. in 2011 at University of Pannonia. She has been teaching a variety of bachelor and master courses including Management, Competence and Incentive Management, Project Management, and Project Planning and Controlling. Since 2006 she has worked as a researcher: "International Mapping of Knowledge

Sharing Excellence" (2006-2009), "Middle Managers' Knowledge Sharing and Knowledge Sharing Competences" (2009-2013), "Project Management in the XXI. Century" (2014-present) research. She has been an editorial board member of Management&Marketing and a reviewer of Knowledge Management Research & Practice and for other international management journals. She was also a conference committee member of international conferences: European Conference on Knowledge Management since 2012, and International Conference on Knowledge Management in 2015. Her main fields of interest are organizational and national culture, knowledge, competence, and project management. She has published numerous papers and has presented her research results at national and international conferences.

Katarína Čulková works at Institute of Earth Sources, Faculty BERG of Technical university of Košice, Slovakia. Her pedagogical and science activity is concentrated to financial analysis and financial management of industrial companies, as well as financial investment of organizations. In her scientific and research activity she deals with sustainable development from the view of financial management, resource policy of the state, and preparation of post-gradual students for the business in practice and at the job market. She published several scientific monographs, chapters of monographs, more than 50 articles in international journals, participated in several international scientific conferences.

Susana Duarte holds a Ph.D. in Industrial Engineering. She is Assistant Professor in the Department of Mechanical and Industrial Engineering at Universidade Nova de Lisboa, Portugal. She is a research member of the UNIDEMI Research Center where develops their investigation in lean and green management and sustainability. She participates in the project "Lean, Agile, Resilient and Green Supply Chain Management" and she has published scientific papers in international journals and conferences proceedings. She was awarded with Excellence Award from Emerald Group Publishing and three awards from International Conferences. She is a member of the board of the Portuguese Institute of Industrial Engineering.

Enis Elezi has a degree in International Agribusiness Management and has completed a PhD by research at University of Bolton focused on Knowledge Management and Knowledge Transfer practices among British educational partnerships. Currently, Enis is Lecturer in Business and Management at Teesside University, UK. His areas of research interests include Knowledge Transfer, Partnership Development in Higher Education and Organisational Learning.

Myriam Ertz is assistant professor in marketing, and head of the LaboNFC at Université du Québec à Chicoutimi. Her research interests include consumer choice modeling, sustainability, technology and the reconfiguration of commercial exchanges. Her research has already appeared in many top-tier journal articles (e.g., *Resources, Conservation & Recycling; Journal of Cleaner Production; Business Strategy & The Environment; Journal of Business Research; Technological Forecasting & Social Change; Environment & Behavior; International Marketing Review*). She also published several book chapters, a book, and contributed to professional reports. She regularly presents her research in conferences as an invited or regular speaker, has recently co-edited a collective book on the reconfigurations of commercial exchanges, and serves as Guest Editor for the Special Issue "Better Product Lifetimes" of the Sustainability journal.

Ibrahim Yasar Gok has a PhD degree and has been working as an assistant professor of finance in the Banking and Finance Department of the Süleyman Demirel University since November, 2013. He was a visiting scholar in the University of Oklahoma's Michael F. Price College of Business in 2011-2012. He lectures in Financial Markets and Institutions and Portfolio Management. His current interests are focused on Corporate Sustainability Practices and Financial Literacy Curriculum Design for High School Students. His articles were published in academic journals, which are indexed in SCI, ESCI, Scopus or EconLit.

Mária Janošková works at Institute of Business and Management of Technical university of Košice, and at Department of Management in Poprad, Slovakia. She is a candidate of management sciences, assoc. professor of university. Her pedagogical activity is concentrated to Management of company, Strategic management, Human resources management, Corporate Social Responsibility and Business. Her scientific and research activity she deals with Human resources management with emphasize to Knowledge management, problems of Corporate Social Responsibility in practice, as well as transfer of managerial knowledge to the business practice. She is author or co–author of some scientific monographs, chapters of monographs, more than 80 articles in the scientific international journals, she participated in more than 50 International scientific conferences. She was a main coordinator and co-coordinator of the scientific VEGA projects, and other KEGA educational projects.

Olga Martinez Moure is a professor at the Open University of Madrid, in the Degrees of Labor Sciences, Labor Relations and Human Resources, and Business and Tourism Activities. She is Dr. Cum Laude from the University of Zaragoza. She has combined her teaching work with the participation in numerous congresses and conferences. She is the author of several books and university manuals. She has participated in numerous research projects, linked to both public and private entities.

Nader Naderpajouh is an educator, researcher, and consultant with expertise in resilience, systems theory, institutional theory, innovation sciences, and infrastructure management. Nader gained his PhD in Civil Engineering at Purdue University. He lectures across three programs in the School of Property, Construction, and Project Management at RMIT University in Melbourne, Australia.

Luiz Luz Neto is a lawyer, lecturer and researcher in law. Master in Economic Law from UFPB and PhD (in progress) in Development from UFPB. As a Lawyer, has experience in the Brazilian higher courts working in administrative, tax and real estate law.

Tommy Prayoga is an alumnus of Psychology Department, Bina Nusantara University and Atma Jaya Catholic University, Jakarta, Indonesia; Business Development Executive at Content Collision, a media agency and technology firm in Southeast Asia. Site: https://tommyyoung.c2live.com.

Raquel Garcia Revilla has a PhD in Tourism from the University of Malaga. It also has the Official Master in Management and Tourism Planning from the University of Malaga, the Official Master's Degree in Education and New Technologies at the Open University of Madrid and the II Course in Knowledge and Innovation applied to management strategic Sustainable Tourism Destination. She currently teaches in the area of hotels and Quality Programs and Graduate of the Open University of Madrid (UDIMA); and assumes the role of coordinator of the Masters in Business and Hotel Management in Tourism Planning and Management of the same university, which teaches several subjects of Hotel Management and Quality. Since inception, she has given priority to quality studies and management, as evidenced by their training and throughout her career, as a teacher in tourism and participation in various courses, seminars, conferences and master. She has participated in several R + D + i both nationally and internationally and has published several studies related, inter alia, Tourism, Quality, Sustainability, Accessibility and Hotels, Technology and Educational Innovation, etc. where a priority focus their invstigación lines.

Raul Rodriguez-Rodriguez (Industrial Management Engineer, MBA, PhD) is an associate professor in Operations Management and Research at the Polytechnic University of Valencia (UPVL). He has worked in several projects about performance management, operations management, supply chain management and information systems in different activity sectors such as automotive, retail, consumer goods, ceramic or textile. Additionally, he is a full member of the CIGIP (Research Centre on Production Management and Engineering) at the UPVL, having participated on several research projects at European level (ECOSELL, GPM-SME) as well as on national research projects (INPREX, SP7). He lectures in both graduate and undergraduate courses and his research preferences are on performance measurement and management, operations management and information system management. He is Certified Quality Engineer and a full member of the American Society for Quality. He has published several papers in books, journals and conferences in these fields.

Yustinus Suhardi Ruman is a sociologist; Faculty Member-Subject Content Coordinator (FM-SCC) on Character Building and Development Center, as well as affiliated with Communication Science Department, Bina Nusantara University, Jakarta, Indonesia.

Christina M. Scott-Young is a clinical psychologist and educator who researches in the fields of resilience, project teamwork, leadership, work-readiness, well-being, and diversity. Christina is currently an Associate Professor at RMIT University, having previously held academic positions at Pennsylvania State University, the University of South Australia, and at the University of Melbourne, where she was awarded her PhD in Management in 2008. Her research has been published in the Journal of Operations Management, International Journal of Operations and Production Management, International Journal of Project Management, Project Management Journal, Construction Management and Economics, Studies in Higher Education, and Higher Education Research & Development.

Dean Lauda Septian is an alumnus of Psychology Department, Bina Nusantara University, Jakarta, Indonesia.

Oksana Sokil is an engineer and at this time is a doctoral student in third year at the Department of Management, Slovak University of Agriculture, Faculty of Economics and Management, Nitra, Slovakia. She is interested in the sphere of corporate social responsibility development among small and medium-sized enterprises. She is the author and co-author of many scientific publications. She has participated in many international conferences. She is the winner of DAAD Programme (Germany). She is the participant of the Erasmus+ internship programme in Portugal and Poland. She took the participation in CEEPUS project in The Cracow University of Economics.

Carmen-Elena Tănăsescu has a master degree in Entrepreneurship and Strategic Management and in the last five years, she increased her experience in the banking system and marketing research. The results of her research activity are presented in several international journals and approach topics like performance appraisal, employee satisfaction, and reward management.

Ramona-Ioana Tănăsescu has a master degree in Entrepreneurship and Strategic Management and in the last five years, she concentrated on developing her career in the banking system. She published several articles in international journals and her research interests include subjects like emotional intelligence, organizational stress, and job performance.

Iveta Ubrežiová works at Department of Management in Poprad, Catholic University, Faculty of Education in Ružomberok, Slovakia. She is a candidate of economic sciences, university professor in economics and management of business. She is interested in International Management and Entrepreneurship, Corporate Social Responsibility. She has a rich activity of publication; she is author or co–author of more than 200 publications. Her research activity is expressed in the several national and international books, monographs, the scientific articles cited in Web of Sciences and SCOPUS and more than 200 articles from domestic and international conferences. She was a main coordinator and co–coordinator of the scientific VEGA projects and a member of research team of national or international both scientific and educational projects. She attended the universities like Erasmus+ teacher in Finland, Spain, Latvia, Lithuania, Hungary, Ukraine, Poland and Russian Federation. She took the participation in CEEPUS project as a teacher in Albania, Poland and Serbia.

Maria Jose Verdecho is an Associate Professor in Operations Management and Operations Research at Universitat Politècnica de Valencia (UPV) (Spain). She is a member of CIGIP (Research Centre on Production Management and Engineering) at UPV. She has led and participated in several research projects about supply chain management, operations management, performance measurement systems and enterprise interoperability. Her main research interests include performance measurement systems, operations management, sustainability, supply chain management and multi-criteria decision analysis. She has published several papers in journals, books and conferences in these fields.

Index

F

G

H

I

K

L

M

N

O

P

Q

R

S

T

U

W

www.ingramcontent.com/pod-product-compliance
Lightning Source LLC
LaVergne TN
LVHW080120011026
849160LV00013B/1138